PAUL J. OLSCAMP, Ph.D., University of Rochester, is Professor of Philosophy and Dean of Faculties at Roosevelt University. He formerly taught at The Ohio State University where he also served as Associate Dean of the College of Humanities. He is a member of the American Philosophical Association and the author of books on Descartes and Berkeley and of numerous scholarly articles in professional journals.

AN INTRODUCTION TO
PHILOSOPHY

PAUL J. OLSCAMP

ROOSEVELT UNIVERSITY

THE RONALD PRESS COMPANY · NEW YORK

Library of Congress Catalog Card Number: 77–144104
PRINTED IN THE UNITED STATES OF AMERICA

100
OL8

Dedication

This book is for my mother and my father, in fulfillment of their honest desire to know more about what it is that professional philosophers do. As such, it is an expression of my respect and love for them.

Preface

This is a textbook for undergraduate philosophy students which tries to do three things: first, to study philosophy through the analysis of skilled argumentation; second, in its organization to move progressively from simpler to more difficult material; and third, to make the coverage of both individual thinkers and types of theories as broad as possible.

The first aim is especially reflected in Part One of the three-part book, where the basic structure of arguments is explored. Elementary symbolic techniques up to the level of quantification, the concepts of soundness and validity, and the use of some technical terminology are presented, and definitions, theories of meaning and truth, and several informal fallacies are also studied. After this there are sections on induction, argument by analogy, the counter-example technique, and means for evaluating competing theories. It is hoped that this first part will provide the student with a framework he can use to evaluate the arguments in the rest of the book.

All of the parts of the book are organized so that the topics of each chapter move from lesser to greater degrees of difficulty. This enforces the normal learning process and also permits the instructor to begin or end the study of a particular problem or type of theory at various levels of undergraduate competence.

Many of the theories of major philosophers and many of the major problems in philosophy are presented and analyzed in the book. Among the theories developed by major philosophers which are discussed are those of the following: Aristotle, Aquinas, Berkeley, Hume, Kant, Locke, Russell, Wittgenstein, Austin, Ducasse, Taylor, Ryle, Mill, Schlick, Descartes, Marx, Ayer, Anselm, Paley, Hobbes, Hare, Plato, Leibniz, Hartshorne, Shaftesbury, Collingwood, Wheelwright, Beardsley, Nagel, Ockham, James, and Santayana. The areas and types of philosophy considered are also extensive, as a glance at the contents will illustrate. In each case, the aim has been to formulate the issues and theories in the form of arguments and then to evaluate these in the light of the procedures developed in Part One.

Many have helped me in the preparation of this book, and I should like to thank the following in particular: Professors Wallace Anderson,

Richard Garner, Alan Hausman, Charles Keilkopf, Bernard Rosen, and Robert Turnbull of the Department of Philosophy, The Ohio State University; Professor Jack Bertsch, Mr. James Blue, Mr. James McFarland, and my wife Joyce, who read the proofs; and a special word of thanks to Charles L. Babcock, who encouraged me in several ways, tangibly and personally. I am, of course, responsible for any errors in the text.

PAUL J. OLSCAMP

Chicago, Illinois
March, 1971

Contents

Arguments and Evaluation

1

The Method of
Critical Thinking

THE NATURE OF ARGUMENTS

Because my mother, bless her heart, is very fond of avoiding arguments, discussions of politics and religion are *verboten* in her home. In her view, which is often justified around her house, it is impossible to have a discussion without having an argument. By "argument" she means "heated discussion," and by "discussion," she means "argument without heat." This, of course, is not the sort of thing that philosophers think about when they think of arguments. If we leave the "heat" out of it for the moment, my mother is closer to the philosopher's thinking when she speaks of a discussion, provided it is a discussion designed to prove something and provided again that the discussion takes certain forms. Discussions, after all, except for those casual cocktail conversations whose purpose is to agree with everything everyone else says in an engaging way, are normally for the purpose of supporting some point, or discovering another's views, or some such thing. But even a discussion intended to prove something is not a very accurate characterization of what philosophers mean when they speak of argument, because "discussion intended to prove a point" is much too general. Philosophers would normally take this to include *several* arguments, presumably those presented by you, and those presented by your opposition, whether the opposition be one or many persons. In addition, the discussion might include at least two different *kinds* of arguments, and if we agree that any means whatsoever that succeeds in obtaining someone's assent to some claim may be called an argument, then an indefinitely large number of tactics might be included in our discussion.

Deductive and Inductive Arguments

For the moment, then, let us confine our attention to the sort of thing that one person might say in order to support some one particular claim. Furthermore, let us restrict the discussion to two kinds of argument, that in which the person intends to prove what he says conclusively, and that in which he intends to prove it probably. The first sort of argument is called a "deductive" argument, and the second a "probable," or "inductive" argument. Finally, for the moment, let us stipulate that whatever is said in the argument must be such that it is either true or false. The reasons for this requirement and the problems that arise in connection with it, will be examined at some length later in the book.

Keeping these three things in mind, let us see what an argument might look like. The following is a case of an argument which is designed to prove one particular point and to prove it conclusively, using only sentences which may be either true or false:

1. If Hannibal was the son of Hamilcar, then he was the son of a Carthaginian.
2. Hannibal was the son of Hamilcar.
3. Therefore, he was the son of a Carthaginian.

Because this argument is designed to prove that the last sentence is conclusively true, and because it does in fact do this if the first two sentences are true (and they are), it is a *sound, valid, deductive argument.*

An example of a probable or inductive argument might be the following:

1. All *Glotzmobiles* tested over the last two years have had defective clutches.
2. This car is a *Glotzmobile,* made within the last two years.
3. Therefore it is likely that this car has a defective clutch.

It is clear that the car under consideration might be an exception, even if every other *Glotzmobile* ever known had a defective clutch. So the most we can claim for the conclusion is that it is probably true, rather than certainly true, even if the first two sentences of the argument are true.

It was observed that the first example above of a deductive argument is a sound and valid deductive argument. "Sound" and "valid" are terms which are predicated of all deductive arguments that succeed in proving their conclusions. Because of this, they must have uniform meanings in all such cases if they are to provide a *precise* way of classifying arguments. When an argument is sound, it is valid, and all the statements in it are true. This is simple enough, but defining validity is much more difficult. The best way to approach the matter is to consider a number of arguments that have something in common:

A

1. If (sugar is placed in water of a temperature between 35 and 200 degrees Fahrenheit,) then [some or all of it will dissolve.]
2. (Sugar is placed in water of a temperature between 35 and 200 degrees Fahrenheit.)
3. Therefore, [some or all of it will dissolve.]

B

1. If (the *Morning Blurt* endorses Rosenkrantz,) then [I'll eat your hat.]
2. (The *Morning Blurt* endorses Rosenkrantz.)
3. Gulp! [I'll eat your hat.]

C

1. If (Henry is a widower,) then [he was once married and his former wife is dead.]
2. (Henry is a widower.)
3. Therefore, [Henry was once married and his former wife is dead.]

It is clear that the type of connection between the antecedents and the consequents in the first sentence of all three arguments is different in each case. In A, we might call it a *causal* connection. In B, the consequence occurs because of a decision of mine, and so we might call it a *voluntary* connection. In C the connection is *analytic*, which is to say that "widower" *means* that whoever is the widower was once married but that his former spouse is now dead. But A, B, and C also have something in *common*, which we shall call their *form*. Parts of each argument have been enclosed, some with parentheses and others with brackets. If you place the capital letter "Q" where you find brackets, and the capital letter "P" where you find parentheses, you will discover that all three arguments have this form:

1. If (P), then [Q].
2. (P).
3. Therefore, [Q].

Valid and Invalid Arguments

Validity is a property of any argument having a form which meets certain specifications. The specifications can be stated simply in terms of the form of A, B, and C. These three arguments are valid if, and only if, it is impossible, when sentences are substituted for 1, 2, and 3, for 1 and 2 to be true and 3 to be false. To state the same thing another way, a valid argument is one such that if the reasons offered to prove the conclusion or conclusions are true, then the conclusion or conclusions *must* be true. A little reflection will confirm that this is a justified definition of validity, for if 1 and 2 were true and 3 were false in any of A, B, or C, then obviously 3 would *not* have been proven by 1 and 2. But, is not proving 3 the very point of saying 1 and 2 in these arguments? An invalid argument, then, is one such that the reasons offered to prove the conclusion or conclusions do *not* prove it or them; that is, the reasons (which will henceforth be called "premises") may be true, but the conclusion or conclusions are false. Naturally, in the case of the argument form of A, B, and C, and in all valid argument forms, whatever is substituted for P and Q in the first premise must also be substituted for them in whatever follows. Otherwise, the argument would not be valid. Consider the following example:

1. If anything exists, it must be perceived.
2. Some things exist, but are not always perceived by some human mind.
3. Therefore, there must be some non-human mind perceiving them.

This is an argument we shall examine in connection with a set of problems in the philosophy of Bishop George Berkeley. Here, you should notice that there is some question as to whether "perceives" means the same thing in the conclusion as it does in the premises. When we speak of human perception, at least part of what we normally mean is *sense-perception*. The non-human mind of which Berkeley was speaking was God, and this argument was intended by him to be part of a proof that God exists. But God presumably has no senses, and hence no sense-perception. A question about the validity of this argument thus arises, for if the "perception" of the conclusion is not the same as that of the premises, then the premises might be true, and the conclusion false. In effect what such an invalid argument is doing is asserting something like this, though of course the example above does not have this form:

1. If A, then B.
2. A.
3. Therefore, C.

Now clearly "if A, then B" may be true, and "A" may be true, but "C" false, in which case the argument is invalid. This fairly common mistake, in which the same word is used with different meanings in the same argument, is called the fallacy of *equivocation*.

Although a valid argument whose premises are true will always have a true conclusion, it is important to notice that an argument may be valid but have all false premises; or all the statements in it may be false including the conclusion; or some of the premises and the conclusion may be false; or some of the premises may be false. This may seem paradoxical, but if you consider the definition of a valid argument again, you will see that it is not. A valid argument is one such that, *if* the statements substituted in its form for the premises are true, then the conclusion must be true. The definition says nothing about what happens if the premises are *false*. Given that good arguments are both sound and valid, it follows from this that there may be bad but valid arguments, namely those whose form is such that there is no substitution instance of the form where the premises may be true but the conclusion false. Such arguments may be unsound because they may contain false statements. However, since soundness indicates validity *plus* the property of containing nothing but true statements, there are no bad arguments which are sound.

So far, then, we have discovered what a good deductive argument is: an argument whose form is such that there is no substitution instance of it where the premises may be true but the conclusion false and which contains nothing but true statements. But how is one to discover whether or not there *is* a substitution instance where the premises are true but the conclusion false, since for any argument form there are an infinite number of possible substitution instances? After all, life is short—certainly too short to do anything an infinite number of times! Fortunately, there is a way, though it takes a little work to understand it.

TRUTH-FUNCTIONALITY AND TRUTH-TABLES

Arguments, which are the substitution instances of argument forms, are composed of sentences. Some sentences are simple, and others are complex. Hence, the sentence "John is tall" is simple, whereas the sentence "If John is tall, then he will make a good basketball player" is complex. The truth of complex sentences depends upon the truth of their parts, or to put it technically, the *truth-value* of a complex sentence is a *function* of the truth-values of its parts. The study of truth-functionality is the study of the *ways* in which complex sentences have their truth-values (their truth or their falsity) determined by the truth-values of their parts. The question of what determines the truth of the parts is another matter which will arise later on when we discuss what it means to say that a sentence is true or false. For the moment, we shall consider only one kind of simple sentence: the kind which is true if, and only if, there is a set of facts corresponding to what is said by the sentence. Hence, "John is tall" will be true if, and only if, John is in fact tall, and it will be false if John is short.

8 ARGUMENTS AND EVALUATION

Conjunctions

Consider, then, a conjunction such as "John is tall and Mary is short." This sentence is complex, because it has two parts, namely, the component sentences "John is tall" and "Mary is short." Each of these two sentences, which when joined together form the complex sentence, is either true or false on its own merits. There may of course be conjunctions of more than two parts, but none of less than two. For convenience' sake, let the letters "P" and "Q" stand for the two component sentences, and let the dot symbol "·" stand for "and." It is also customary to use parentheses rather than quotation marks to set off a symbolic sentence, so the form of our conjunction will be $(P·Q)$. The truth of complex sentences of this form will now depend upon the truth-values of the component parts substituted for P and Q. What the conjunction asserts is that it is true that $(P·Q)$, that is, it is true that P is true and that Q is true. When will this be false? Clearly, when either P is false, or Q is false, or both P and Q are false. Or to put it another way, $(P·Q)$ will be true if and only if both P and Q are true. There is a way we can *define* the conditions under which any conjunction is true which involves the use of a mechanism called a "truth-table." The truth-table that defines "·" or the conditions *under* which complex sentences which are conjunctions are true, looks like this:

P	Q	$(P · Q)$
T	T	T
T	F	F
F	T	F
F	F	F

If you will examine the table, you will see that the only case in which $(P·Q)$ is true is the case in which P is true and Q is true. This is true for all possible conjunctions, no matter how long they are. The techniques for making truth-tables are simple and standard. You will never make a mistake if you follow these three rules:

1. *Number of rows across.* There should be one for each statement to be given a truth-value, whether the statement is simple or complex.
2. *Number of rows down.* This is determined by the simple formula "2^n," where "n" stands for the number of *simple* statements to be given truth-values. The *simple* statements in the table above are P and Q, so the number of rows down is therefore 2^2, which is 4.
3. *Construction.* Begin with the *innermost simple statement.* Write *alternating* "T's" and "F's" under it, to the number determined by

the second rule. When the appropriate number is reached, move to the next column to the *left* and write alternating *pairs* of "T's" and "F's" under it. Then move to the next column, where you will write alternating sets of *four* "T's" and "F's," and then to the next where there will be sets of eight, then sixteen, then thirty-two, and so on. Do *not* fill in the truth-values for the *complex* statements until *after* you have completed all the columns for simple statements. The reason for this will be clear when you consider the purpose of the truth-table, which is to say under what conditions the complex sentence or sentences are true, and these depend upon the values of the simple statements.

Consider a longer truth-table, which tells us under what conditions a more complex conjunction is true:

P	Q	R	$(P \cdot Q \cdot R)$
T	T	T	T
T	T	F	F
T	F	T	F
T	F	F	F
F	T	T	F
F	T	F	F
F	F	T	F
F	F	F	F

This table tells us that only when all of the component sentences of the conjunction are true is the entire conjunction true. It has four rows across the top, because that is the number of statements to which we wish to assign truth-values. It has eight rows down, because there are three *simple* statements in the top row, and 2^3 is 8. Starting with the inner-most simple statements, we have alternating "T's" and "F's," then pairs of them, then fours, and the final result is an exhaustive listing of all the possible combinations of truth-values of which this combination is capable.

Conjunctions are, of course, only one kind of complex statement. There are in fact an infinite number of kinds of complex statement, but they may all be constructed out of a very few basic kinds, using but a very few connectives in addition to the dot symbol. It is necessary to examine the other fundamental kinds of complex sentences before we can discuss the role of truth-tables in the evaluation of valid argument forms, and the reason should by now be obvious—arguments are composed of sentences, some simple, some complex. If we know the conditions under which the complex sentences of arguments are correct and if we have the truth-value of any simple sentences involved, then we are well on the way to being able to tell whether the form of any given deductive argument is valid by using truth-tables.

Disjunctions

Another kind of complex statement is the "disjunction." Disjunctions are composed of simple statements joined by the logical connective "or." Just as we could define in a truth-table the conditions under which conjunctions are true, so we can do the same for disjunctions. The logical symbol used to symbolize "or" is the *vel*, which is written simply as "v." A disjunction of two simple statements would therefore appear, using the letters "*P*" and "*Q*" again, like this: $(P \vee Q)$. In ordinary languages, there are two senses of "or," which are customarily called the "inclusive" and the "exclusive" senses. The inclusive sense of "or" may be stated, using our symbols, as "$(P \vee Q)$, or *both* *P* and *Q*." We also sometimes express this sense of "or" by saying "*P* and/or *Q*," which simply means that *P* may be true, or *Q* may be true, or both *P* and *Q* may be true. The exclusive sense of "or" excludes the possibility of both *P* and *Q* being true. We sometimes express it by saying "*P* or *Q*, but not both." The exclusive "or" therefore tells us that one of *P* or *Q* is true, but not both of them. Now it follows from this that a disjunction in the exclusive sense of "or" will be false if *neither* of the component parts *P* and *Q* is true, or if *both* of them are true. We can state the conditions under which this disjunction is true by this truth-table:

P	Q	$(P \vee Q)$
T	T	F
T	F	T
F	T	T
F	F	F

The first row of truth-values tells us that if both the components are true, then the whole statement is false; for we intend to say that either one or the other is true, but not both. The last row tells us that if both parts are false, the whole thing is false, because one part or the other must be true. The two middle rows, therefore, tell us under what conditions an exclusive disjunction is true.

The inclusive sense of "or" is expressed by changing the first "F" under $(P \vee Q)$ to a "T," which indicates that both parts, as well as either, may be true. Inclusive disjunctions are therefore only false when all components are false. Whenever disjunctions are mentioned hereafter, we shall be referring to this kind of disjunction.

Denials

The third kind of sentence we need to define is not complex in the sense that the first two are, since it involves the simple denial of other sentences. If a sentence *P* is true, then its denial is false, and vice versa.

The sign "−" indicates denial. This may be easily indicated by this table:

P	$-P$
T	F
F	T

Conditionals

The last sort of complex sentence with which we shall be concerned is the sort with which this section began, conditional sentences. In the conditional sentence "*If* John is tall, then he will make a good basketball player," call the component part "John is tall" by the letter "*P*," and the component part "He (John) will make a good basketball player" by the name "*Q*." The complex conditional sentence will therefore be statable as "If *P* then *Q*," or, more carefully, "If *P* is true, then *Q* is true." This says that the truth of *Q* is contingent upon that of *P*, or to state it another way, if *Q* is not true, then *P* is not true. Hence, (if *P* then *Q*) would be *false*, if the conjunction (*P·−Q*) were *true*, for what this asserts is that *P* is true and *Q* is not true. Conversely, (if *P* then *Q*) would be true if the *denial* of this conjunction were *true*, that is, if −(*P·−Q*) is true. In short, (if *P* then *Q*) and −(*P·−Q*) have the same truth-values, and since this is so, a truth-table for one of these is also a truth-table for the other.

It is customary to use a special symbol in order to connect an antecedent and a consequent in the conditional relation. It is the "horseshoe" symbol which, as you might expect, looks like a horseshoe, "⊃." This is the reason that the last column to the right in the following truth-table is said to define the horseshoe. It tells us that (*P⊃Q*) has the same truth-values as −(*P·−Q*), and that hence they are logical synonyms.

P	Q	$-Q$	$(P \cdot -Q)$	$-(P \cdot -Q)$	$(P \supset Q)$
T	T	F	F	T	T
T	F	T	T	F	F
F	T	F	F	T	T
F	F	T	F	T	T

If you examine the table, you will notice that there is only one condition under which a conditional statement is false, namely, when the antecedent is true, and the consequent false, which is consistent with what has been said above.

Further Considerations

We now have four kinds of truth-functional complex statements, together with the tables which tell us under what conditions they are true and false:

Conjunctions: True only when all component statements are true.
Disjunctions:
  Inclusive—False only when all components are false.
  Exclusive—False only when either all components are false, or all
    are true.
Denials: True only when the statement denied is false, and vice versa.
Conditionals: False only when the antecedent is true, but the conse-
  quent is false.

Now all of this may seem fairly simple. But a moment's thought will
convince you that things may get pretty sticky. For example, consider
the following sentence: "Either your mother stays home or I'll leave and
you can find another husband." Let "*M*" stand for "your mother stays
home," "*L*" stand for "I'll leave" and "*H*" stand for "you can find another
husband." Let us suppose that M is true, L is true, and H is false. Our
sentence in symbols is now presumably as follows:

$$M \text{ v } L \cdot H$$

But this will not do, for even when we know the truth-values of the
component parts, as we do in this case, we cannot tell whether the above
complex sentence is true or false, because as it stands we are free to
interpret it in at least two ways:

$$M \text{ v } (L \cdot H)$$

or

$$(M \text{ v } L) \cdot H$$

Which of these two ways we choose makes an immense difference, for
one of them, given the truth values of the parts, is false, and the other is
true. You may see this by writing in the truth-values of the parts over
the respective letters as follows:

$$\text{T v } (\text{T} \cdot \text{F})$$
$$M \text{ v } (L \cdot H)$$

and

$$(\text{T v T}) \cdot \text{F}$$
$$(M \text{ v } L) \cdot H$$

Assume that the sentence when interpreted in the second sense is using
the exclusive sense of "or," that is, the sense in which we mean "either
P is true or Q is true, but not both P and Q are true." When we do this,
the first of the two sentences is true, but the second is false. In the case
of the first sentence, M is true; but, because H is false and because a
conjunction, to be true, must have all of its parts true, the second com-

ponent of the total disjunction, $(L \cdot H)$, is false. In the case of the second sentence, which is a conjunction rather than a disjunction, the first half of the conjunct, $(M \text{ v } L)$, is false if we are using the exclusive sense of "or," because only *one* of the parts of the disjunct may be true and in this case both of them are true. Since H is also false, both parts of the conjunction are false and hence the whole thing is false. In fact, even if we were using the inclusive sense of "or," the second sentence would be false while the first sentence would be true; since even if $(M \text{ v } L)$ were true, H is still false, and *all* of the parts of a conjunction must be true if the entire conjunction is to be true. So no matter what sense of "or" we use, given the truth-values we have, the first sentence will be true and the second false.

The same result may be obtained by various modes of bracketing in mathematics. Hence $(3 \times 9) + 4$ gives a sum of 31, while $3 \times (9 + 4)$ gives a product of 39. Bracketing, which is the logical and mathematical equivalent of punctuation in verbal languages, is therefore very important. Sadly, however, there is no absolutely precise way to bracket correctly; or perhaps more accurately, there is no exact way to tell you how to bracket in every case. You simply have to practice it until you are able almost every time to say in symbols what you *mean* in English. But this ought not to be too discouraging, since it is no more difficult than proper punctuation. You would not, for example, normally write "If Joyce is my, wife and she has, children then I am, their father." Nor would you *say* this in the way it is written, that is, you would not pause where the commas are in the sentence. So why should you symbolize it that way? With some practice, symbolic bracketing will become quite easy.

Constants and Variables

You have probably noticed by now that complex *sentences*, as well as arguments, have forms. For example, all conditional sentences have the same form, namely $(P \supset Q)$. At this point another logical convention should be introduced, namely the distinction between "constants" and "variables." The *capital* letters of the alphabet are used to stand for simple sentences or phrases, and the *small* letters from "p" through "z" as place-markers, or as they are called, variables. The small letters from "a" through "o" will be used later on as names of entities—people, places, things—and we shall call them "name constants" to differentiate them from the capital letters that stand for simple sentences. The latter we shall call "sentence-constants." Hence, there are two types of constants, one type for sentences, the other type for all other things. A variable, as has been noted, is nothing but a place-marker. To illustrate, consider the sentence "If we keep murdering our politicians, and no new ones come along, we'll soon have no government." Let "*A*" stand for "we keep murdering our politicians," "*B*" stand for "no new ones come along," and "*C*" stand for "we'll soon have no government." This sentence can then be translated symbolically as $(A \cdot B) \supset C$. Clearly, this is a conditional, or "if, then" sentence. The complete antecedent is $(A \cdot B)$, the complete consequent, *C*. Using blanks to mark the place of the antecedent and consequent, the *form* of the sentence is, (if _____ then _____), or, using the horseshoe symbol, (_____ ⊃ _____). $(A.B)$ is simply one of an infinite number of antecedents which can be put in the first slot or place; *C* is also one of an infinite number of consequents substitutable in the second place. But we can't very well go around just using blanks to indicate the places where the sentence constants should be put. If we did, there would be chaos when we tried to decide where to put what constants in a sentence of a form such as {[(_____) ⊃ (_____ · _____)] v [_____ · (_____ v _____)]}. Instead of blanks, variables are used. Hence, $(p \supset q)$ is the form of all sentences such as $[(A \cdot B) \supset C]$, $(A \supset B)$, $(A \supset C)$, $(B \supset C)$, *ad infininitum*. The only thing some students occasionally find difficult about this notion is the fact that *complex* antecedents and consequents can fit into the places marked by a single variable such as "*p*" or "*q*." The reason for this confusion is that when logicians wish to show the form of a *particular* sentence such as $[(A \cdot B) \supset C]$, rather than the form of, for example, *all* sentences which are conditionals, they normally use one variable for each sentence-constant in the sentence. Hence, $[(p \cdot q) \supset r]$ would be written to show the particular form of $[(A \cdot B) \supset C]$, rather than $(p \supset q)$. To avoid this confusion, we shall always use the variables to give the form of *classes* of sentences and arguments, rather than particular sentences or arguments, which latter shall always be written using sentence-constants and name-constants.

Modus Ponens and the Hypothetical Syllogism

What is the relevance of all this to the fact that sentences as well as arguments have forms? You may recall (if you don't at this stage, you're doomed!) the three arguments with which we began this chapter. They all had the form:

1. If (P) then $[Q]$.
2. (P).
3. Therefore, $[Q]$.

We would now write this form, using the conventions developed to date as:

1. $(p \supset q)$

2. p

3. Therefore, q

This argument form, which is the most common one, is called *modus ponens*. It has an infinite number of substitution instances such that, if 1 is true, and 2 is true, then 3 is true. Consider that again: "If 1 is true, and 2 is true, then 3 is true." But is *this* not a conditional sentence? Let "D" stand for "1 is true," "E" stand for "2 is true," and "F" stand for "3 is true." May we not now symbolize the sentence as $[(D{\cdot}E) \supset F]$? Or, using variables to symbolize the infinitely large class of substitution instances for *modus ponens*, is there not a conditional sentence corresponding to this argument form which has the form $\{[(p \supset q){\cdot}p] \supset q\}$? This is important because we know that the conditions under which conditional sentences are false are simply these: if the antecedent is true, but the consequent false, then the conditional sentence is false. Hence, if *modus ponens* is an *invalid* argument form, then the conditional sentence corresponding to the given argument in question is false. Moreover, this holds true for *any* argument. Consider this one, which is of a type known as the *hypothetical syllogism:*

1. $A \supset B$
2. $B \supset C$
3. Therefore, $A \supset C$

The conditional sentence corresponding to this argument is:

$$[(A \supset B) \cdot (B \supset C)] \supset (A \supset C)$$

Now if the form hypothetical syllogism is invalid, then some substitution instance of it, such as the one above, must be invalid. If so, then the corresponding conditional sentence must be false. Because of this, there is a short way of testing for the invalidity of any argument form. It should be noted that although argument forms are valid, they are not sound or unsound, because to be so they would have to be composed of sentences which are either true or false. But variables, being simply place-markers, are neither true nor false. Thus, to test for invalidity, we must test a substitution instance of some argument form. This is no obstacle to the test, however; that is, it is no obstacle to the universal applicability of the test, nor to the universal acceptability of its conclusions, because we may adopt the mathematician's technique of letting some particular argument stand for all arguments of the same type, as when the geometrician asks us to allow ABC to stand for or be "any triangle," and draws conclusions about what all triangles have in common. Let us then consider first *modus ponens* and then the Hypothetical Syllogism. Suppose the argument of the form *modus ponens* we are considering is:

1. $(A \supset B)$
2. A
3. Therefore, B

The conditional sentence corresponding to this argument is:

$$[(A \supset B) \cdot A] \supset B$$

We know that for this conditional sentence to be false, the antecedent must be true, and the consequent false. So, let "B" be false. If it is false in the consequent, of course, it has to be false in the antecedent. Since there are only two sentence-constants in the conditional sentence, "A" and "B," we should now be able to give "A" a truth-value which will make the antecedent true if the sentence is to be false. But we cannot. If we make "A" true, the first part of the conjunct in the antecedent of the conditional sentence is false, which makes the whole thing false. If we make "A" false, the first part of the conjunct which is the antecedent is true; but the second part is false, which again makes the whole thing false. And if the antecedent of a conditional sentence is false, then the whole conditional is true. The same thing happens in the case of *any* deductive argument which has a valid argument form. A moment ago we considered the conditional sentence which would correspond to a hypothetical syllogism using the sentence-constants "A," "B," and "C." If that sentence is to be false, then the consequent of it, $(A \supset C)$, must be false, which means that A must be true, and C false. If these two sentence-constants are to stand for sentences which are respectively true and false in the conclusion, then they must have the same truth-value in the premises of the argument, or, using the conditional sentence which corresponds to the argument, if they have a given value in the consequent, then they must have the same value in the antecedent. And what happens when we assign these truth-values? This is the result:

$$
\begin{array}{ccccccc}
 & & & 1 & 2 & 3 \\
A & B & C & (A \supset B) & (B \supset C) & (A \supset C) \\
\hline
T & F & F & T \quad F & F \quad F & T \quad F \\
 & & & F & T & F \\
\end{array}
$$

$$
\left[\overset{4}{\underset{\underset{F}{F}}{(A \supset B)} \cdot \underset{T}{(B \supset C)}} \right] \quad \left[\underset{F}{(A \supset B) \cdot (B \supset C)} \right] \overset{5}{\underset{T}{\supset}} \underset{F}{(A \supset C)}
$$

The conclusion of the argument, and hence the consequent of the conditional sentence, is 3. To be false, which it must be if the argument is invalid or the sentence false, A must be true and C must be false. If they are true and false in the conclusion or consequent, they must have these values in the premises or the antecedent. Hence, 2 is true, for the consequent of 2, namely C, must be false, which means that in order for 2 to be true, B, the antecedent, must also be false. Remember that what we are trying to do is to make 1 and 2 true, and 3 false. Now from 3 and 2, we know the truth-values of 1: A is true and B is false. Thus, 1, the first conjunct of the antecedent of the conditional sentence $[(A \supset B) \cdot (B \supset C)] \supset (A \supset C)$, must be false. It therefore appears that we cannot make the sentence false, and therefore the argument is not invalid.

What we have in effect been doing here is a short truth-table—short because we have been exhausting the truth-value possibilities only for that row of the truth-table which would show the argument to be invalid, if it were. You may wonder how truth-tables for *arguments* slipped in here, and the answer is simple. If you look at the line of the table above, you will notice that the statements across the top constitute what would be the top of a truth-table which, when completed in full, would define the conditions under which the statement numbered 5 above would be true and false. If you care to prove this, you may do so simply by completing the table in full, using the rules previously developed. In effect then, truth-tables for the conditional sentences corresponding to arguments are actually tables for those arguments themselves. To prove that the statement may be false is to prove that the argument is invalid. If the sentence or statement may be false, and the argument, hence, invalid, then of course the argument *form* is invalid, since by definition an argument form is invalid if it has at least one (and there need be *only* one) substitution instance (argument) where the premises are true and the conclusion false.

LONGER ARGUMENTS, QUANTIFICATION, AND PROVING VALIDITY

Thus far, the arguments and argument-forms have been fairly simple. There are, of course, arguments with many more premises composed of many more parts than the ones we have been considering. But no matter how long the argument, its premises still constitute a conjunction which either implies or does not imply its conclusion or conclusions, and our basic method of proving invalidity, with some additions in certain more complex kinds of arguments, will always work. As it happens, the kinds of argument used thus far are all *syllogisms*. A syllogism is a deductive argument with two premises and a conclusion, and three "terms" which, in a valid syllogism, are related in certain ways which need not concern us here, since our method of determining invalidity covers all kinds of deductive arguments and not just syllogisms. *Modus ponens* is one kind of syllogism, and the hypothetical syllogism is another. A third sort is the *disjunctive syllogism*. Its form is:

1.$(p \text{ v } q)$
2. $-p$
3. Therefore, q

This argument form is valid no matter which sense of "or" you employ, as you may see for yourself if you do a shorter truth-table and try to prove it invalid. It is easy to see that you can build long arguments by adding arguments of these various kinds together. Consider the following:

1. $(A \supset B)$
2. $(B \supset C)$
3. $(A \supset C)$

4. $(C \text{ v } D)$
5. $-C$
6. D

7. $(D \supset E)$
8. D
9. Therefore, E

Statements 1 to 3 constitute by themselves a hypothetical syllogism; statements 4 to 6 are an argument of the form disjunctive syllogism; and, or course, the last three statements are an instance of *modus ponens.*

If you look at the argument above again, you may notice some interesting features. Remember that we know from our previous efforts that all three argument forms used in this argument—hypothetical syllogism, disjunctive syllogism, and *modus ponens*—are valid argument forms, and hence, the three arguments in this long argument are all valid. If we were asked, then, why $(A \supset C)$ follows from 1 and 2, we could say that it did because 1, 2, and 3 constitute a valid argument since they together have the form hypothetical syllogism. We could make the same sort of reply if asked why D follows from 4 and 5, why E follows from 6 and 7. To indicate this in writing we might add the following to our arguments:

1. $(A \supset B)$
2. $(B \supset C)$
3. $(A \supset C)$ 1 follows from 2 by hypothetical syllogism

4. $(C \text{ v } D)$
5. $-C$
6. D follows from 4 and 5 by disjunctive syllogism

7. $(D \supset E)$
8. D
9. E follows from 7 and 8 by *modus ponens.*

Here again, we are answering the questions about why 3, 6, and 9 follow from the statements before them. Instead of writing out the names of the valid argument forms which provide the explanation in full every time, it is customary to abbreviate them. Hence, hypothetical syllogism becomes simply "H.S.," disjunctive syllogism is "D.S.," and *modus ponens* is "M.P."

Still looking at the same argument, you might notice that D occurs alone in two premises—8 and 6. Although this does not affect the validity of the argument, it is redundant, because the conclusion E follows just as well from 7 and 6 and it does from 7 and 8. A person speaking the sentences of this argument in an attempt to prove the conclusion would simply be repeating himself if he said the sentence D twice. For the sake of economy, which mathematicians and logicians prize highly for some reason, it is customary to leave unnecessary repetitions out. Hence our argument now becomes:

1. $(A \supset B)$
2. $(B \supset C)$
3. $(A \supset C)$ 1, 2, H.S.

4. $(C \lor D)$
5. $-C$
6. D 4, 5, D.S.

7. $(D \supset E)$
8. E 7, 6, M.P.

It is also customary to write the numbers of the statements from which a conclusion follows in the order in which they would normally be in an argument of the valid form to which one is referring for justification. This is why step 8 reads "7, 6, M.P." rather than "6, 7, M.P."

What we have just done is to prove that the argument we are considering is a *valid* argument. This, of course, is different than a proof for *invalidity*; if you are ignorant of the invalidity of an argument, that does not mean that the argument is valid, just as, if you are ignorant of its validity, it does not follow that the argument is invalid. Logic is largely composed of performing these two operations—proving validity and invalidity. The reason we have just done a *proof* will be evident upon a moment's reflection. We saw that this argument was composed of three kinds of other argument forms which we already know to be valid forms. If each of the arguments it contains is valid, then the whole thing is valid. Hence, this argument is proven valid by showing that all of its parts are valid.

There are, of course, an infinite number of valid argument forms, and each new argument form which we proved valid could be used as a justification for claiming that any new argument of this form was valid. Instead of doing this forever, logicians usually stick to about nine or ten argument forms which they have proven valid. They then use these as rules of inference to prove that arguments which have other arguments of these forms in them are valid. H.S., D.S., and M.P. are three of these argument forms. Another, which has not been mentioned yet, is called *modus tollens*. The form of *modus tollens* is:

1. $(p \supset q)$
2. $-q$
3. Therefore, $-p$

If we use *modus tollens* (M.T.) in the argument we have been considering, we can obtain several other conclusions which follow from the same premises, in addition to E:

1. $(A \supset B)$
2. $(B \supset C)$
3. $(A \supset C)$ 1,2, H.S.
4. $(C \text{ v } D)$
5. $-C$
6. D, 4, 5, D.S.
7. $(D \supset E)$
8. E, 7, 6, M.P.
9. $-A$, 3, 5, M.T.
10. $-B$, 2, 5, M.T.

Since this it not a textbook in logic, we shall not go through the other argument forms which are used as rules of inference in proving validity. Rather, they will be introduced if and when they are needed in the chapters that follow.

Logical Equivalencies

In addition to using valid argument forms as rules of inference in proving validity, logicians normally use certain common, logically equivalent, sentence forms. The reason for this is that it is often impossible to prove validity unless you can retranslate some sentence in a given argument into such a form that it combines with other sentences in it to form an argument with a valid form. For example, if we have this argument:

1. $(A \cdot B) \supset C$
2. A
3. Therefore, $(B \supset C)$

the argument form *modus ponens* cannot presently be used to justify the conclusion. But it so happens, as a truth-table will show should you care to prove it, that sentences of the form $[(p \cdot q) \supset r]$ are logically equivalent, that is, logically synonymous with, statements of the form $[p \supset (q \supset r)]$, provided of course, that the terms in the two statements are the same. Thus, for $[(A \cdot B) \supset C]$, we may write $[A \supset (B \supset C)]$ without changing either the truth-value or the meaning of the statements. If we do this with the argument above, we get:

1. $[A \supset (B \supset C)]$
2. A
3. Therefore, $(B \supset C)$ 1, 2, M.P.

On a truth-table, you can always tell whether two statements are logically equivalent by the fact that the column which states their equivalence contains nothing but "T's," that is, this statement is always true. Statements of logical equivalence are expressed by the sign "$\equiv$." The following table tells us that for any sentence p, the denial of *its* denial is logically equivalent to p:

p	$-p$	$-(-p)$	$p \equiv -(-p)$
T	F	T	T
F	T	F	T

For purposes of proving validity, some logical equivalencies are more important than others, just as certain argument forms, such as *modus ponens* and the others which have been used, are more important than just any argument form. The reason for this is again a matter of economy and elegance, which together make up that criterion for argumentation which logicians call "simplicity." The ideal symbolic language will contain the fewest possible rules of inference, and they will be as brief as possible individually. As mentioned, nine or ten argument forms are normally used in proofs of validity, and there are about ten logical equivalencies which are also used. In what follows, these equivalencies will not be of great importance, but it might be well for the student to consult an introductory logic text in order to familiarize himself with the principle of logical equivalency, and to see how these statement forms are used to justify steps in arguments.

Other Argument Forms

At this point, it is necessary to discuss another kind of argument and supplement the outline of the theory of proofs for validity and invalidity which we have studied. The reason is that the methods given thus far cover only one kind of argument, which for our purposes is best defined by saying that it covers only those arguments which do not contain the words "all" and/or "some." So far "statement-constants" have been used to stand for entire sentences or simple sentences which are parts of complex ones used in arguments. The kinds of sentences which have been used are, as was noted, "truth-functional" sentences, and "simple" sentences. But there are sentences which are simple in the sense that they are not composed of more than one sentence, but which cannot be symbolized by the use of sentence-constants. A classic argument used since the time of Aristotle will illustrate why this is so:

1. All humans are mortal.
2. Socrates is human.
3. Therefore, Socrates is mortal.

Now clearly this is a valid argument. But if we were to use the techniques developed up until now to symbolize it, we might well come up with an argument of the following nature:

1. *M*
2. *S*
3. Therefore, *H*

This argument, according to what has been said so far, might be invalid, for the truth of the conclusion does not depend in any way upon the truth of the premises, and hence may be false while the premises are true. In order to handle such arguments, then, an expansion of our techniques is necessary. This expansion will involve among other things the use of those symbols earlier called "name-constants"—these are the small letters of the alphabet, usually but not always those from "a" through "o." The expansion will also involve a new use for the capital letters of the alphabet. In any argument where the sentences contain the words "all" or "some" or both, the capital letters will be used as names for *predicates.* The name of the entity which has the predicate, symbolized by a small letter, will always be written to the *right* of the capital letter naming the predicate which the entity has. In the sentence "Socrates is human," the entity is Socrates and the predicate which he presumably has is humanity in the generic sense. Let the small letter "*s*" be the name-constant for Socrates, and let the letter "*H*" be the name of the predicate "humanity." The sentence will now be symbolized as "*Hs*." Similarly, the sentence "Thomas Aquinas was a monk" would be symbolized, using "*M*" as the name of the predicate "being a monk" and "*t*" for Thomas Aquinas, as "*Mt*." And so on for any sentence of this kind.

Just as we saw that all sentences which we have discussed up until now have forms, so this is true of the new kind of sentence. The letter "*H*," probably because it has been used since antiquity for the purpose, is customarily used as the place-marker for the predicate, and the letter "*x*" as the place-marker for the name of the entity. Thus, the *form* of sentences of the "Socrates is human" type, which are called *singular* sentences, is "*Hx*," or, as it is often written, $H(x)$. Just as $(p \supset q)$ is neither true nor false because p and q are variables or place-markers, so the same is true of $H(x)$, since H and x are also variables, H being a *predicate variable* and x being a *name variable*. And just as $(A \supset B)$ *is* either true or false, so *Hs* is either true or false, and for the same reason. $H(x)$ is sometimes called a "propositional function," because when particular predicate names and name-constants are substituted for the variables, we get a particular proposition, for example, *Hs*, which is either true or false. To put it another way, true or false propositions of the type *Hs* are functions of the propositional form $H(x)$.

Quantification

Although we now have a way to symbolize singular sentences or propositions, we still have not handled *general* sentences such as "All humans are mortal," and "Some humans are mortal."[1] We cannot symbolize such sentences in the way we did singular sentences, because no names of individual entities are included in them and they do not refer to specific individuals. The words "all" and "some" refer to *quantities* of entities, and the process whereby we handle such general statements is therefore known as "quantification." Consider the general sentence "All humans are mortal." There are a number of ways in which we can say the same thing: "Nothing is human and not mortal"; "If anything is human, then it is mortal"; "All things which are human are mortal"; and so on. The second of these versions comes closest to the literal translation of what will eventually be our symbolic sentence: "If anything in the universe is human, then it is mortal." The symbol "(x)," called the "Universal Quantifier," is used to signify the phrase "for anything in the universe," or "all." The symbolic version of our sentence begins with this. Then we want to say, "if it is human . . ." which we can symbolize simply by *Hx*. Finally we want to say ". . . then it is mortal," which may be stated in symbols as "$\supset Mx$." Putting the pieces together, and using the bracketing procedure we have adopted, the complete sentence "If anything in the universe is human, then it is mortal" becomes $(x)(Hx \supset Mx)$.

"Some" has the same logical meaning as "something," "at least one x exists," "there is at least one x," "there is at least one thing," and so on. The symbol used to state this is "$(\exists x)$." It is called the "existential quantifier." A sentence such as "Some men are bald," using "*Mx*" for "x is a man" and "*Bx*" for "x is bald," would be translated into the sym-

---

[1] For our purposes it is not necessary to distinguish between a sentence and a proposition.

bolic language as (∃ x) (Mx·Bx). A precise English retranslation would then be "There is at least one x such that x is a man and x is bald." It is possible, though we shall not find occasion to do it, to state all other English quantifiers, such as "a few," in terms of the universal quantifier, the existential quantifier or a combination of both.

The foregoing mechanism now allows us to express our simple argument without much difficulty. The argument again is:

1. All humans are mortal.
2. Socrates is human.
3. Therefore, Socrates is mortal.

This now becomes, using Hx for "x is human," Mx for "x is mortal," and s for "Socrates":

1. (x) $(Hx \supset Mx)$
2. Hs
3. Therefore, Ms

As yet, however, we cannot do a proof of the validity of the argument, because the first statement in it is not in a form appropriate to the use of *modus ponens*, the valid argument form that we would use in this instance to justify the conclusion's being drawn from those two premises. The appropriate form would be:

1. $Hs \supset Ms$
2. Hs
3. Therefore, Ms

Universal Instantiation

We can in fact put the argument into this form, but in order to do so we require yet another mechanism, and to enable us to handle such moves with existentially as well as universally quantified arguments, we need four rules. The first of these, which enables us to move from a sentence of the form (x) $(Hx \supset Mx)$ to one such as $(Hs \supset Ms)$, is called the rule of "universal instantiation," "universal" because it is used only with sentences quantified by the universal quantifier, and "instantiation" because the rule enables us to move from the general sentence to a particular sentence which must be true if the general sentence is true. That the move is justified will be easily understood if we consider just what a general sentence of this kind *says*. General sentences are either about all the things there are, or about all the things there are in a particular species or sort or class. Suppose, for the sake of argument, that there are only three men in the universe, whose names are "s," "t," and "u." Suppose also that (x) $(Hx \supset Mx)$, that is, "All humans are mortal," is true. If this is so, then if s is a man, he is mortal; if t is a man, he is mortal too, and so is *u*. In symbols, if (x) $(Hx \supset Mx)$ is true, then $(Hs \supset Ms)$, $(Ht \supset Mt)$, and $(Hu \supset Mu)$ must all also be true, for they constitute all the men that exist. To say the same thing another way: if it is true of *any* man that he is mortal, then we may select *arbitrarily* any individual man and truly say that he is mortal. We are in effect picking an *instance* of the general truth and saying that it is therefore true also. The rule universal instantiation is normally expressed by using the Greek letter ϕ to stand for the predicate variable, and the Greek letter α stand for the name-variable, and expressing the rule as follows:

(x) ϕ X, (where alpha is any arbitrarily selected individual)
therefore, ϕ α

The abbreviation of universal instantiation is "U.I." We may now handle the argument we are discussing in this way:

1. (x) $(Hx \supset Mx)$
2. Hs / Ms
3. $Hs \supset Ms$, 1, U.I.
4. Ms, 3, 2, M.P.

The "/ Ms" next to the second premise is simply a more convenient way of writing "Therefore, Ms."

Universal Generalization

Now we must move to a slightly different kind of argument, one whose conclusion is a universally quantified sentence. If you glance at the rules we have thus far, you will see that we have no way to move from an instantiated premise, that is, a sentence such as statement 3 above, to the corresponding universally generalized statement. But it is often necessary to do just this, as for example in the argument:

1. All men are mortal.
2. All mortals are human.
3. Therefore, all men are human.

This is a valid, though unsound argument, and would be symbolized as:

1. (x) $(Mx \supset Nx)$
2. (x) $(Nx \supset Hx)$
3. / (x) $(Mx \supset Hx)$

where "Nx" is the symbol for "*x* is mortal," and the others are self-explanatory. Since we must instantiate the premises in order to do our proof of validity, we must have a way of getting the conclusion back into the generalized form. The rule for doing this is called "universal generalization," or simply "U.G." It works this way: if a general truth such as (x) $(Mx \supset Nx)$ is true for all members of the class of men, then it is true for any arbitrarily selected man. If so, it is true for all men, because to say that it is true for *any arbitrarily* selected man is to say that you cannot pick a man of whom this statement is false. The letter "y" is normally used to stand for any arbitrarily selected entity, and the only way this letter can be put into a proof is through the use of Universal Instantiation. Hence, if we use y and instantiate the above argument, we get:

1. (x) $(Mx \supset Nx)$
2. (x) $(Nx \supset Hx)$ / (x) $(Mx \supset Hx)$
3. $My \supset Ny$, 1, U.I.
4. $Ny \supset Hy$, 2, U.I.
5. $My \supset Hy$, 3, 4, H.S.

Since y, as opposed to any other name-constant, stands for any arbitrarily selected individual, just as the geometer's ABC stands for any arbitrarily selected triangle, we may now move from step 5 to the conclusion by universal generalization:

6. (x) $(Mx \supset Hx)$, 5, U.G.

The formal statement of U.G., using the Greek letter ϕ again, is:

$$\phi \, y$$
$$\therefore (x) \, \phi \, x$$

The most important point about this rule, and the one most often forgotten, is that U.G. is only good from an instantiation using y.

Existential Generalization

So far, we have been talking exclusively about *universally* general sentences. But we must also consider *existentially* general ones; and, as there were two rules enabling us to instantiate and generalize from and to universally general sentences, so the same is true of existentially general ones. Let us use as an example of an argument involving both existential instantiation and existential generalization the following:

1. All criminals are vicious.
2. Some humans are criminals.
3. Therefore, some humans are vicious.

This is another valid, but unsound argument. It is unsound because the first premise is false. In symbols, using "Cx" for "x is criminal" or "x is a criminal," "Hx" for "x is human," and "Vx" for "x is vicious," this argument would appear as follows:

1. (x) $(Cx \supset Vx)$
2. $(\exists x)$ $(Hx{\cdot}Cx)$
3. / $(\exists x)(Hx{\cdot}Vx)$

Now statement 2 and the conclusion assert that there is at least one entity such that, if 2 is true, it is human and criminal, and if 3 is true, it is human and vicious. If there were several existentially general statements in the premises of this argument, instead of just one, we would have no way of knowing that the individual referred to in one of these statements was the same individual as that referred to in the others. For this reason, the name-constant which we use to instantiate an existentially general statement cannot have been used before in the same proof. Also, in existentially general statements we are speaking about a *specific* individual, not any arbitrarily selected one; and, therefore, we may not use the letter y to instantiate such sentences, given that it has been set aside for use as a term referring to any arbitrarily selected entity. Given these two restrictions, however, the inference from the second premise $(\exists x)$ $(Hx{\cdot}Cx)$ to $(Ha{\cdot}Ca)$ is justified. The formal statement of this rule, which is abbreviated as "E.I.," is this:

$(\exists x)\, \phi\, x,$
/ $\phi\, a$, (where "a" is any individual name-constant other than "y," having no previous occurrence in the proof)

You should also notice here that whenever E.I. is involved in a proof, you will want to do this step *before* any other, such as U.I. This is because of the restriction prohibiting use of name-constants used previously in the proof. Although the universally general sentence could be instantiated with the constant a, for example (provided you did not later want to use U.G. on the instantiation, which may only be done if y is used), this would prohibit the use of the same constant in the step of E.I. That this is crucially important may be seen by considering our argument when we do U.I. first, and then when we do E.I. first:

1. (x) $(Cx \supset Vx)$
2. $(\exists x)$ $(Hx{\cdot}Cx)$
3. $Cy \supset Vy$ 1, U.I.
4. $Ha{\cdot}Ca$ 2, E.I. (a different name-constant because "y" may only be used with U.I., and though another *could* have been used in this step of U.I. since we are not going to do U.G., we still must use a different constant for every step of E.I.)

Now the obvious question is, where do we go from here? And the answer, if we make this mistake, is nowhere! But when we do E.I. *first,* we get the following:

1. (x) $(Cx \supset Vx)$

2. $(\exists x) \, (Hx \cdot Cx)$
3. $Ha \cdot Ca$ 2, E.I.
4. $Ca \supset Va$, 1, U.I. (nothing prohibits the use of a constant already in the proof with a step of U.I.)
5. $Ca \cdot Ha$ 3, by Commutation (a logical equivalence which we did not discuss, but which is obvious)
6. Ca 5, Simplification (another valid argument form—obviously if $(p \cdot q)$ is true, then p is true)
7. Va, 6, 4, M.P.
8. Ha, 3, Simplification
9. $Ha \cdot Va$, 8, 7, Conjunction (yet another valid argument form, namely, if p is true, q is true, therefore $(p \cdot q)$ is true)

A glance at step 9 will show you that we have there the instantiation which, if we could generalize it, would be identical to the conclusion we want. And we can generalize it with the last of the four rules we need, namely, existential generalization, or E.G. as it is called, which seems intuitively justified, because if the statement "a is human and a is vicious" is true (statement 9), then obviously the statement "at least one thing is human and vicious" is true, which is what the conclusion says. The formal statement of E.G. is:

$$\phi \, a,$$
$$/ \; (\exists x) \, \phi \, x$$

Using E.G. then, we derive from step 9 the conclusion $(\exists x) \; (Hx \cdot Vx)$, and we have proven the argument valid. Clearly, using E.I. first does make a considerable difference!

In case you have not figured out why it is not permissible to use the same name-constant in more than one step of E.I. per proof, the following argument will explain the issue:

1. $(\exists x) \, (Mx \cdot Hx)$ = Some men are handsome.
2. $(\exists x) \, (Wx \cdot Hx)$ = Some women are handsome.
Therefore,
$(\exists x) (Mx \cdot Wx)$ = Some men are women.

Proof:

3. $Ma \cdot Ha$, 1, E.I.
4. $Wa \cdot Ha$, 2, (E.I., using the same name-constant)
5. Ma, 3, Simplification
6. Wa, 4, Simplification
7. $Ma \cdot Wa$, 5, 6, Conjunction
8. $(\exists x) \, (Mx \cdot Wx)$. 7, E.G.

That is why you should never use the same name-constant in a step of E.I. more than once in the same argument!

THE EXPANDED PROOF OF INVALIDITY

Except for one or two expansions and certain other modification which need not concern us here, the apparatus we now have will enable us to prove the validity or invalidity of most deductive arguments. The first expansion or addition pertains to proofs for invalidity. As matters stand, we cannot use the shorter truth-table method to prove any argument invalid if it contains quantified statements. The technique is not applicable to such arguments as it presently stands for two reasons. First, there were no existential assumptions involved in our earlier, non-quantified logic, and, secondly, in the earlier logic we were discussing only those argument forms which contained truth-functional or complex statements. But now in addition to the truth-functional statements used in the original arguments, we have singular statements and quantified statements; and some of the latter, namely the existentially general ones, assume the existence of the entities of which they speak. But if we assume that a valid argument form is valid no matter how many entities or individuals there are in the universe in which the argument of this form applies, we can still use our technique. Now this requires some explanation.

It is clearly the case that at least *one* individual must exist in any universe in which arguments are to be formulated, for if not, then there would be nothing to formulate any argument about. In addition, if you and I knew exactly how many individuals there were in the universe to which our arguments applied, we could also set up a series of logical equivalencies between the universally general sentence about that universe and the truth-functional compound or complex sentences, or the sentences, which made the corresponding assertion or assertions about each of the individuals in that universe. That is to say, if there were only one entity in the universe, then $(x)\ \phi\ x$ would be true if and only if $\phi\ a$ was true, if and only if $(\exists x)\ \phi\ x$ was also true. Or to put it in English, in a universe of only one thing, call it "a":

if "all x's are ϕ," then "a is ϕ" must be true, and
if "a is ϕ" is true, then it is clearly the case that "there is at least one x which is ϕ" is also true.

Suppose there are two, and only two, entities in our universe, and call them "a" and "b." In such a universe:

$(x)\ \phi\ x$ will be true if and only if $(\phi\ a \cdot \phi\ b)$ is true, and
$(\exists x)\ \phi\ x$ will be true if and only if $(\phi\ a \lor \phi\ b)$ is true.

Notice that for the universally general statement, the equivalent statement, which must be true if the general statement is true, is a *conjunction,* since the universally general statement, of course, asserts something to be true of *all* things or all members of some class. The statement which must be true if the existentially general statement is true is a *disjunction,* because to be true, there need be only *one* entity of which the existentially general statement holds. If there were three rather than two entities in the universe, the statements which must be true if the general statements are true would simply be expanded by one more conjunct and one more disjunct respectively. This may be done indefinitely, so let us generalize the process and say that if there are just a number of entities in some universe, then:

(x) ϕ x is true if and only if $(\phi\ a \cdot \phi\ b \cdot\ \ldots\ \phi\ n)$ is true, and
$(\exists x)$ ϕ x is true if and only if $(\phi\ a$ v $\phi\ b$ v $\ldots$ v $\phi\ n)$ is true.

The purpose for introducing all of this is to enable you to understand the theory behind the concept of invalidity. For now you may see that when we prove an argument invalid, we are finding at least one individual in that universe such that the premises of the argument are true of that individual, while the conclusion is not. Suppose we consider this argument:

1. All legislators are bribable.
2. No professors are legislators.
3. Therefore, no professors are bribable.

Using the first letters of the important terms, we have in symbols:

1. (x) $(Lx \supset Bx)$
2. (x) $(Px \supset -Lx)$
3. / (x) $Px \supset -Bx)$

Assume that there is only one indivdual in the universe of whom we are speaking, and call that individual "a." If this argument is invalid, then the following must be invalid:

1. $La \supset Ba$
2. $Pa \supset -La$
3. / $Pa \supset -Ba$

The question is, then, can we assign truth-values to the parts of this argument such that 1 and 2 are true, and 3 false? Yes we can: if the conclusion is to be false, then Pa is true and $-Ba$ is false, which makes Ba in the first statement true, and Pa in the second premise also true. Now if we make $-La$ true, then the second premise is true, and if $-La$ is true, then La is false, which makes the first premise true. So we can make the premises true and the conclusion false, and the argument is invalid. Hence, the original argument is also invalid.

Sometimes it really matters how many individuals there are in the universe we are considering. Consider the following argument, which has been used before:

1. Some men are handsome.
2. Some women are handsome.
3. Therefore, some men are women.

Suppose we are talking about a universe in which there is only one individual which we will again name "*a*." If this argument is valid, then the following must be valid:

1. *Ma·Ha*.
2. *Wa·Ha*.
3. / *Ma·Wa*.

And indeed, this argument *is* valid, in a universe of only one entity. This would be a strange universe, but you can see why it is valid if you remember that the argument says that there is at least one entity which is a man and handsome, and there is at least one entity which is a woman and handsome, and if there is only *one* thing in the universe, then the man and the woman must be the same being. However, this is really a misuse of the term "validity," for to be truly valid, an argument must hold for any universe of whatever size. When this argument is tested for universes of more than one member, it is invalid. Suppose for example that there are *two* entities in our universe. Then, if the argument is valid, the following argument must be valid:

1. (*Ma·Ha*) v (*Mb·Hb*)
2. (*Wa·Ha*) v (*Wb·Hb*)
3. / (*Ma·Wa*) v (*Mb·Wb*)

The statements are disjunctions because in our original argument all the statements are existentially general, and you will recall that the corresponding statements for the particular universe which must be true in such cases are disjunctions. Now this argument is invalid, as you will see if you make *Ma*, *Mb*, *Wa* true, and *Ha*, *Wb*, and *Hb* false. With this expansion of our technique, we can now prove all invalid arguments to be just that.

Relational Statements

There is one kind of statement that is very important which we do not yet know how to symbolize. This is a *relational* statement. For example:

Paul is taller than Joyce.
Toronto is between Windsor and Montreal.
John sold his car to Peter for ten cents.

All of these express relations holding between different numbers of entities. In the first sentence, there are two entities, Paul and Joyce, and it is customary to call this kind of relation a *dyadic* relation. In the second sentence there are three entities that are related, and this is therefore called a *triadic* relation. The third sentence, expressing a *tetradic* relation, asserts a relation among four entities. The kind of relation expressed, therefore, depends partly upon the *number* of entities related, and also upon certain properties which the relation itself possesses. Three properties which relations may have are *symmetry, transitivity,* and *reflexiveness.* Consider symmetry first.

A relation is symmetrical if one of two related entities has a given relation to the other, and that other has the same relation to the first entity. For example, I stand in the relation of "being married to" my wife, and she also stands in that relation to me.

On the other hand, some relations are such that if one of the entities has the relation to a second, then that second entity cannot have the same relation to the first. There is a certain cottage many hundreds of miles to the north of Columbus, Ohio. This cottage stands in the relation "to the north of" Columbus, and Columbus therefore cannot stand in that same relation to the cottage. This is an example of an asymmetrical relation.

Some relations are neither symmetrical nor asymmetrical, and are therefore non-symmetrical. From the fact that a man loves his wife, it does not follow that she loves him, nor does it follow that she does not love him.

Relations may also be transitive, intransitive, or non-transitive. If my cottage is to the north of Columbus, and Columbus is to the north of Louisville, Kentucky, then my cottage is to the north of Louisville. This is a transitive relation. On the other hand, if I am the father of Adam, and Adam is the father of Peter, then I cannot be the father of Peter, and this is an intransitive relation.

Still other relations are non-transitive. For example, if I love Joyce and Joyce loves Sid, it neither follows nor does it not follow that I love or do not love Sid.

A reflexive relation is difficult to define, but for our simplified purposes we may say that a relation is reflexive if it is such that if two or more entities stand in that relation to one another, then each of them stands in that relation to itself. If I am exactly the same height as you, then I am exactly the same height as myself. But if I am to the right of you, it does not follow that I am to the right of myself, because the first relation is reflexive and the second irreflexive. Finally, the relation of loving is non-reflexive, because if Sally loves you it may or not be the case that she loves herself.

You may have noticed that some relations have more than one of these properties, and that in some cases if they have one property, then they must have another. All asymmetrical relations are irreflexive, for example, and "being taller than" is transitive, irreflexive and asymmetrical. Which properties relations have is often crucially important. Suppose that an action of mine for which I am responsible is the cause of an action of yours, which is in turn the cause of an immoral action by a third person. Am I responsible for the action of the third party? Did I cause his action in causing yours? If "being the cause of" and "being morally responsible for" are relations which are transitive, then the answers are both "yes." Yet there are obvious cases in which we would have to say what is absurd in order to hold that these relations are transitive.

Relational statements are not very difficult to translate into symbols at the elementary level. Consider "Tom is taller than Paul." Let "T" be the constant standing for "taller than," "t" be "Tom," and "p" be "Paul." The sentence in symbols would be written "Ttp." The order of the letters is most important, because, for example, "Tpt" means "Paul is taller than Tom." Using such simple non-quantified relation statements, consider this argument:

1. Tom is taller than Paul.
2. Paul is taller than Adam.
Therefore, Tom is taller than Adam.

In symbols this would be written:

1. Ttp
2. Tpa
/ Tta

This is simple enough when no quantified premises are in the argument. With them, things are a bit harder. Suppose we have:

1. Tom is taller than Paul.
2. If anyone is taller than Paul, then he is taller than John.

Therefore, Tom is taller than John.

The symbolic equivalent:

1. Ttp
2. $(x) \ (Txp \supset Txj)$
/ Ttj

In this case, we must use U.I. to instantiate the second premise using "t" as the constant, and then the conclusion follows from the instantiation and the first premise by *modus ponens.*

More complex arguments containing relational statements of this type are obviously harder to do, but they raise no new principles nor do they involve addition theoretical difficulties.

SOME TERMINOLOGY AND A TRANSITION

The more formal part of our examination of logic is now over. We have barely scratched the surface, of course, but the aim here is not to create mathematical logicians, but rather to provide some theoretical understanding of what philosophers mean when they speak about arguments. There are still some common terms, "logical" in the broad sense, which have not been carefully outlined and which will occur in what follows. It is now time to discuss them briefly.

Some Logical Terms

Earlier it was noted that for every valid deductive argument there is a corresponding conditional sentence which is always true. Sentences that are always true—that have nothing but "T's" occurring under them in a truth-table—are called *tautologies*. Sentences that are always false— that have nothing but "F's" under their column in the truth-table—are called *contradictions*. The sentence "Either it is raining or it is not raining" is an example of a tautology, while "It is raining and it is not raining" is a contradiction, assuming that we are speaking of the same place at the same time. Sentences which are sometimes true and at other times false are called *contingent* statements, because whether they are true or false depends not upon their logical form, as in the case of tautologies and contradictions, but rather upon the circumstances surrounding their use and utterance. They will have both "T's" and "F's" in the columns of any truth-table in which they are found.

It is clear that there is a distinction between tautologies and contingent statements. There is a parallel distinction between statements that are called *a priori* and those that are called *a posteriori*. A statement is *a priori* if its truth can be known independently of any confirming or disconfirming experience. A statement is *a posteriori* if, on the contrary, it requires confirmation or disconfirmation before its truth-value can be known. A tautology does not require the verification of experience in order to ascertain its truth. You do not have to look out the window to discover that it is either raining or not raining. Tautologies are therefore *a priori* truths. It is sometimes customary to use another term to refer to *a priori* truths, or tautologies. This term is *analytic*. Tautologies are, therefore, *analytic a priori* truths.

Contingent statements are the obvious partner for *a posteriori* truths. These statements are sometimes true and sometimes false, and which they are will depend upon the facts of the case. You cannot tell whether the sentence "It is raining" is true until you do check the facts.

Some philosophers believe that there is a third sort of sentence in addition to the *analytic a priori* (tautology) and *a posteriori* (contingent) types. This kind of sentence, named *synthetic a priori* by Immanuel Kant, is one which is not a tautology, which is informative and ampliative, but which is nonetheless universally and necessarily true in all times and places and which can be known to be such independently of confirming experience. An example of such a sentence is "All events have causes." It is not analytic because its predicate may not be obtained by an analysis of its subject; that is, it is not contained in the subject. It is therefore synthetic, because our knowledge is amplified by the addition of the awareness of this truth. On the other hand, people like Kant thought that you did not have to check your experience in order to know that it was true, always and everywhere—that is, necessarily. We shall soon study why Kant thought that this was so. But it should be noted here that not all philosophers agree that there is this third kind of sentence or proposition. Many would argue, for example, that the concept of an event *does* include the concept of a cause, and hence they would say that the sentence "All events have causes" is *analytic a priori,* or a tautology, much like "All red hats are red."

A term which is often used to characterize good deductive arguments, or at least those which are valid, is *consistent.* The word refers to more than just an argument. It is predicated of the entire logic system or calculus of which the argument is a part, and it means that the system is such that no contradiction may be derived within it. In short, given the axioms and postulates of the system, you cannot get a proposition which is a contradiction. It should be clear to you by now that if the system did permit the derivation of contradictions, it would be a valid system, but a useless one, given that from a contradiction anything else is deducible. A contradiction can occur in any argument within a consistent system, but it must be introduced from the outside, as it were. A consistent system does not contain in its principles any axiom which enables a derivation of a contradiction from the principles alone.

Three Common Kinds of Arguments

There are three kinds of arguments that often occur in philosophical discourse of which you should be aware, although we shall not have occasion to use them in this book. The first of these is the indirect proof, also called the *reductio ad absurdum* argument. The *reductio* proceeds to prove the conclusion of an argument, call it *C,* by showing that the *denial* of *C,* together with the other premises in the argument, entails a contradiction. C itself with the same premises does not entail a contradiction. Now the fact that the denial of C plus these other premises entails a contradiction does not strictly speaking prove that C is true, because it is always possible that the other premises with which the denial of C is used themselves contain one or more false premises. To be effective, the premises with which the denial of C is used should therefore be known to be true so that this criticism can be overcome, that is, so that C will be accepted.

The second argument is called the conditional proof. The proof is exactly what the name implies—conditional. It begins by assuming certain premises, call them P, P_1, P_2, . . . P_n, and then deduces the conclusion C from them. The set of premises contains not only the assumed premises but also the premises given with the argument, and the assumed premises are added to these. The additions are justified in this way: if the conclusion is derived from the additions, the hypothetical statement of which the assumed premises are the antecedent and the conclusion, the consequent is true. We know that if any statement is true, and, hence, if the conclusion C is true, then it is implied by any other statement, whether true or false. If C follows from the assumed premises, then the assumption of the additions is justified.

Finally, there is a sort of argument called a dilemma. You are familiar with the phrase "on the horns of a dilemma." There are two kinds of dilemmas, constructive and destructive. Both have logically the same form. The first premise is always a conjunction whose two parts are conditional or hypothetical statements. The second premise is always a disjunction. If the dilemma is constructive, then the disjunctive premise affirms the antecedents of the two hypothetical statements in the first statement. Its form is therefore as follows:

1. $[(p \supset q) \cdot (r \supset s)]$
2. p v r
3. / q v s

A destructive dilemma is one such that the disjunctive statement denies the consequents of the conditional statements which make up the first premise. So its form is:

1. $[(p \supset q) \cdot (r \supset s)]$
2. $-q$ v $-s$
3. / $-p$ v $-q$

The dilemma is an extremely forceful kind of argument if it is used well. Some famous examples may be found throughout *Hansard*, the record of British parliamentary debates. An example of some contemporary influence might be something such as the following:

If autos produce smog, they harm the ecological balance; if they cause traffic congestion, new taxes for highways will be needed. Autos produce either smog or congestion. Therefore, they either harm the ecological balance, or necessitate new taxes.

The dilemma can be even more effective if the antecedents of the two conditional statements are logical opposites, for then the second premise can be tautologically true and leave that much less for the opponent to contest. For example:

If autos produce smog, they harm the ecological balance; if they do not produce smog, they lead to a planned-obsolescence economy. They either produce smog or they don't. So they either harm the ecological balance or they lead to a planned-obsolescence economy.

Criticisms of the dilemma obviously must involve the denial of the truth of one or more of the parts of the premises.

A Transition

Although we have not investigated the subject of logic with sufficient depth to enable us to use it in even a significant number of its possible applications, we cannot in a general textbook devote more time to the subject. So far, we have only studied deductive logic, but our examination of inductive logic will be even shorter, and less formal. Yet, even with this short study, several things should be evident. For one thing, we now know what the concept of the *form* of an argument is. We also understand the notions of validity and invalidity, the role of valid inference forms in proving arguments to be valid, and what it means for an argument to be both sound and valid, i.e., good. This knowledge alone, with the mechanisms of proof that have been given, enables us to reject any argument and any theory of which it might be a part, if it fails to meet the tests. If it does meet the tests, this does not of itself entail that the theory is totally acceptable, for reasons which will become apparent. Even these short steps forward give us an immense power, a systematic method for accepting and rejecting arguments used to support what may be exceedingly important beliefs affecting the lives of millions.

At the same time, the limits of logic by itself are evident. It is a *formal* science and does not tell us how to decide the truth or falsity of the premises and conclusions which its arguments contain. It always operates upon the assumption that these premises and conclusions have one of the two truth-values or that they are demonstrably tautologies or contradictions. Clearly, we must be able to make decisions about just these matters or we cannot begin to formulate theories and criticisms of other views. Before we can decide whether a statement is true rather than false, we must be able to understand it—that is, we must know what the words in it mean and what their various roles are. These necessities bring us naturally to a set of topics that are primitive in the sense that some solutions to the problems they raise must be obtained before serious philosophical solutions can be found for the problems of the field. Even now, as we shall see, many of the "solutions" are really only rejections of traditional theories because of the discovery of mistakes in expression that render premises meaningless or misdirected.

EXERCISES

1. What are the two major kinds of arguments? What is the difference between them, logically speaking?

2. If an argument is sound, is it therefore also valid? Why or why not? If it is valid, is it therefore also sound? Why or why not?

3. Define the concept of deductive validity.

4. What is a good deductive argument?

5. Write a paragraph discussing the notion of the *form* of a deductive argument.

6. Why must a term used in a deductive argument have the same meaning in all of its instances in the argument?

7. Compose an argument which is valid and sound, and which has the form of the first argument given as an example in the section.

8. Why do inductive arguments not prove their conclusions conclusively?

9. Three different arguments illustrating three different kinds of connections between premises and conclusion were used as examples on page 5. Consider argument B, which concerns the *Morning Blurt*, Rosenkrantz, and your hat. Suppose that after saying that I will eat your hat, I later change my mind. Is the validity of the argument affected by my change of heart? Defend your answer.

10. We know that the argument form "If P, then Q; P; therefore, Q" is valid. What about the argument form "If P, then Q; but Q is not true; so P is not true"? After defending your answer, read the material on truth-functionality and truth-tables.

11. What does it mean to say that the truth-value of a sentence is a function of the truth-values of its parts?

12. Make up a truth-table defining the horseshoe symbol.

13. Make up a truth-table for the sentence $\{[(A \supset B) \cdot A] \cdot \supset B\}$. To what argument form does this sentence correspond?

14. Make up a truth-table for the argument form, hypothetical syllogism.

15. Is the sentence form $(p \supset q)$ either true or false? Why or why not?

16. Make up a shorter truth-table for the sentence $\{[(A \supset B) \cdot A] \supset B\}$. Is the argument form to which this sentence corresponds valid or invalid? Why?

17. Under what condition are conditional or hypothetical statements true?

18. State the justification which supports the claim that if one substitution instance of an argument form is invalid, then the argument form is invalid.

19. Using an example from ordinary English and one from mathematics, illustrate the importance of the bracketing convention in logic.

20. Suppose that the two sentences $-(A \cdot -B)$ and $(A \supset B)$ are logically equivalent, which in fact they are. What is the relation between their truth-values under all possible circumstances? Explain your answer.

21. Name four standard valid argument forms and write our examples of arguments of these forms.

22. Compose an argument which embodies all three forms in the same argument.

23. Why is it legitimate to use a valid elementary argument form as a justification for an inference drawn within an argument?

24. Make up a truth-table proving that two complex statements of your choice are logically equivalent.

25. Give two examples of deductive arguments (not the ones used in the text) which illustrate the need for the mechanism of quantification. Why do they show this need?

26. Prove that the examples you need in your answer to question (25) are valid or invalid.

27. What is the justification for the universal instantiation rule? For universal generalization?

28. Why must we instantiate general quantified statements in an argument before we can use elementary argument forms to prove that the argument is valid?

29. Explain why it is not permissible to use the same name constant in more than one step of existential instantiation in the same proof.

30. Why is the use of "y" restricted to universal instantiation?

31. Why is the expanded version of the proof for invalidity necessary?

32. $(x) \phi x$ is true if and only if $(\phi a \cdot \phi b \ldots \ldots \phi n)$ is true, and $(\exists x) \phi x$ is true if and only if $(\phi a \vee b \vee \ldots \ldots \phi n)$ is true. Why is a conjunction used as the connective in the one case, and the disjunction in the other?

33. Compose three examples of dyadic relational sentences.

34. What are (a) symmetry, (b) transitivity, and (c) reflexiveness? Use examples to illustrate your answer.

35. Symbolize your examples in the previous answer.

36. Compose a valid deductive argument containing nothing but relational statements. What kind of relational statement is each one? Are they all symmetrical? Transitive? Reflective? Why or why not?

37. Symbolize your argument in the previous answer, and do a proof of validity for it.

38. Compose a simple argument using nothing but quantified statements and then prove it to be *invalid*.

39. Find two arguments on the editorial page of your newspaper tonight which can be evaluated by the methods we have developed so far.

40. What determines whether a relational statement is dyadic, triadic, tetradic, etc.? If there were just four entities in the universe, now many kinds of relations (and therefore, relational statements) could there be?

41. Is the conditional sentence corresponding to *modus ponens* a tautology, a contingent truth, or a contradiction? Prove your answer by a truth-table.

42. Discuss the relations between *a priori* sentences and analytic truths, *a posteriori* sentences and contingent truths.

43. What are the characteristics of synthetic *a priori* truths? Do you think there are such sentences? Why or why not?

44. From an inconsistent set of premises in an argument, anything can be

derived. The sentence $(A \cdot -A)$ is a contradiction. Assume that it is a premise in an argument. Using the logical rules: simplification, commutation, addition (if p is true, then $(p \vee q)$ is true), and disjunctive syllogism, show that you can imply any proposition you wish from this contradiction.

45. If inconsistent premises imply *anything*, then they imply what you want to prove. Why then is an inconsistent argument not a good one?

46. Why does logic not enable us to decide *whether* a given simple sentence is true rather than false, or vice versa?

47. Suppose that you are given an argument such that you personally understand none of the statements in it, but you *do* know which of the parts of the argument are statements, and you *do* know what truth-values these statements have. Can you decide whether the argument is valid or not? Why or why not?

48. Explain the justification for the indirect proof.

49. Compose an example of a destructive dilemma and prove that it is a valid argument by the truth-table method.

50. Write a five-page essay that summarizes what you have learned in the first chapter.

2

Issues of Content and the Informal Fallacies

DEFINITION

In the course of a conversation, one sometimes hears a remark such as "Well, it's all a matter of how you define your terms, isn't it?" Very often it is, especially in philosophy. Hence, it is very important to understand the differences among various kinds of definitions and to know something about related issues. Many of the difficulties with definitions center upon the question of what properties, characteristics, or attributes are *essential* to a thing as opposed to those which are *accidental*, fortuitous, or unnecessary. For example, being a certain height or having some precise color are not essential attributes for something's being a man. But, if something had no capacity for speech, no ability to laugh, and could not make inferences, and if we knew that all this was not due to some specific defect in it but rather that things of that sort never had these capacities, we would not be likely to call it a man. At the same time, suppose that something was intelligent, risible, spoke exquisite English, and understood physics, but was blue all over and exactly one millimeter tall. Would we call it a man?

Such questions do not specify the problem of an adequate definition very well, but they do give us one hint about what one sort of definition would do if it was a good definition. It would list all of the essential characteristics of a given kind of thing, or of an individual thing, which would be sufficient to claim that it was a class, or a member of a class. This kind of definition is a *definition by abstraction*. Where the thing being defined by abstraction (the definition) is a class, it has to be a member of a still larger class.

Kinds of Definitions

Although a definition by abstraction proceeds by identifying the properties or characteristics which something must have to be a member of some class or other, the problems of deciding what these particular characteristics are and deciding what a good definition should do are not the same except for one particular sort of definition called a *stipulative* definition. Stipulative definitions do just what their name indicates: they stipulate that such and such a term shall be used in such and such a way. Hence, if the term is "x" and if it is stipulated that x is always to be used to refer to property p of some entity e, that is the end of the matter. Stipulative definitions are most common in technical disciplines. One important feature of stipulative definitions is that you cannot disagree with the person who uses them by arguing against his definition unless you are simply proposing that he use another one which is, for example, less cumbersome.

A *lexical* definition, sometimes also called a *reportive* definition, does not stipulate the meaning of a term, but rather states a meaning or use which the term already has in the language. When one disagrees with a lexical definition, one is saying that the definition is in fact not the correct report of the use that the term has in the language. If you define the word "bachelor" as "any unmarried male," and you intend this to be a lexical definition, it should be said that, in fact, the word is more severely limited than this, because males under the age of fourteen are not called bachelors. If you intend the definition to be stipulative, however, it might do perfectly well.

A fourth kind of definition is called a *dictionary* definition, because it follows the method of defining most common in those books, namely, giving synonyms. This technique, of course, assumes that you already know the meaning of the synonym, and that what you require is the knowledge that *this* term has the same meaning as that one. If you do not know the meaning of the synonym, then still others must be given until one is found with which you are familiar. In all languages, this process must come to an end at some point or another, and at that point the basic terms of a language are defined ostensively. *Ostensive* definition is an activity, a method of showing you the meanings of words by pointing out that which they are used to name. If someone says "rose" to you, and at the same time directs your attention to a flower named by that word, that person is ostensively defining "rose" for you. Not all words in a language require such definition in the last analysis, but some do in any language. Words such as "and," "or," and so forth are not ostensively defined. An ostensive definition, like all other kinds, presupposes linguistic ability, but it does not explicitly involve reference to a context in which the word is used, though it may implicitly assume this. *Contextual* definitions do make such a reference; and in fact, it is *only* within some context that they define terms. As such, contextual definitions are pragmatic or instrumental in the broad sense; that is, contextual definitions give us information of the form "when in circumstances *a, b, c,* word *x* is to be used (or not to be used) in the following ways . . ."

Finally, there is one of the oldest theories of definition, that of Aristotle. This great thinker set up a system which has come to be known as the method of defining *per genus et differentiam,* organized according to how and what properties and characteristics are predicated of things or subjects. He began by giving the *essential* definition of a word, which consists in listing, as was indicated at the beginning of this section, the properties which are the essence of the thing the word names or denotes. These will be the properties without which the thing will not be what it is. The essence of a thing is composed of characteristics of two kinds, those which are predicable not just of that particular thing but also of others, and those which are unique to that particular thing. The first kind is called properties of the *genus,* and the second, properties of the *differentia,* i.e., that which differentiates the thing from all others. The genus properties are those which define not only the essence of the particular thing, but also of the class of which it is a member. The definitions which result are applicable to an individual or to a class of things. For example, in the definition "The man named Paul Olscamp is rational, an animal, and the eldest son of James Olscamp and Luella Brush," the genus properties are animality and rationality; and the differentiating ones, the ones that make him different from all other men, are that his parents are who they are, and that he is their eldest male offspring. In the more general definition "Man is a rational animal," the genus property, that which can be predicated of more than man, is animality, and the differentiating property is rationality, for it presumably makes man a distinct species of animal.

Denoting and Designating Functions

It is customary to distinguish between the *denoting* functions of definitions and words, and their *designating* functions. The definition "A triangle is a three-sided plane figure whose interior angles add up to 180 degrees," denotes the particular triangles named A, B, C . . . N; but the characteristics of having three sides, being a plane figure, and having interior angles whose sum is 180 degrees are designated and not denoted. The same distinction is often made by calling the designating function the term's *connotation.*

We should note that the logical status of a definition depends upon the sort that it is. A stipulative definition will always be analytic, while a lexical or reportive definition will be contingently true or false because it purports to state a truth, namely that such and such a term is used in such and such ways in a language. Moreover, there is a certain systematic vagueness about all except stipulative definitions, for they depend upon the state of the language at any given time. What is a synonym today may not be five years or decades hence, and what were once thought to be the essential features of some kinds of things are no longer thought to be so. Even the doctrine of natural kinds itself, which was an underpinning of the *genus et differentiam* theory, has been largely rejected. At the most we seem able to claim that the stability of a definition is only as good as the stability of the meanings of a language. This brings us to the extraordinarily complex issues of meaning.

MEANING

The heading above might more appropriately be the same as that of a famous book by Professors Ogden and Richards, *The Meaning of Meaning,* because we are not going to speak about the meanings of particular words, but of what it means to say that a word means. Although one would think that this kind of issue should have been met before one could begin thinking about such matters as the nature of argumentation —after all, how can you say that something is either true or false unless you know what it means?—it is in fact the case that very few of the problems associated with the topic have been solved. Part of the explanation consists in the deceiving nature of the problems themselves.

When you say "typewriter," do you not mean the kind of machine with which we are all familiar? Where is the problem then? The issues and problems only begin to show themselves when we consider the vast range of uses that the term "mean" has. When you say "The sentence 'Jones never finished his book' is true," are you referring to the sentence of which you are speaking or to Jones and his unfinished book? When the detective warns his client "He means to kill you," is the detective referring to the intention of the putative killer, or past actions which the detective has found to be followed by murder, or to some statement the agent has made, or what? When the senator says "This bill means the relief of suffering for millions," is he referring to the provisions of the bill as stated, the anticipated consequences of it, or is he asking for the votes of his constituents? What does "Hurrah!" at the football game mean? It does not seem to refer to anything, so are there kinds of meaning which do not involve reference? If so, how are these other kinds of meaning to be explained? And if you do say that the meaning of sentences consists in that to which they refer, then how about *false* sentences? To what do they refer? What about rules and directions? Can different sentences have the same meanings? It would seem so, for the same meaning must be expressible in different sentences if translation from one language to another is to be possible, as it certainly is. If the sentence is the carrier of the meaning, what is it that it carries?

These questions begin to indicate the complexity of the problems involved. Here, we will solve none of these problems, but some suggestions will be made about directions in which it seems we must move if we are to solve them.

There have been many theories of meaning developed, some of which purport to deal with all kinds of meaning and others with only some kinds. The basic theories are the *ideational*, the *denotative* or *referential*, the *behavioral*, the *emotive*, the *pragmatic* or *instrumental*, and the *contextualist*. In addition, a theory which is related to both the instrumental and the contextualist views is the *verifiability* theory of meaning. The emotive theory is discussed at some length in Chapter 6 and the Verifiability theory in Chapter 5, so it will not be necessary to examine them here.

The Ideational Theory

The ideational theory of meaning is one of the oldest theories of meaning, though not *the* oldest, and its most famous proponent was John Locke. It stemmed from the conviction that the chief and only use of language was the communication of ideas. When one speaks, one has ideas; and, indeed, the very nature of thought itself is a succession of ideas passing in the mind. Successful communication consists of arousing in the mind of the person hearing the words the same ideas which the speaker has when he speaks them. Words are names of ideas, and it is only because of this fact that communication is possible in the first place. Every meaningful word must therefore have some idea that is constantly associated with it, for otherwise the hearing of the word would not call up the requisite idea on repeated occasions.

On the face of it, this theory has much to recommend it. It provides a coherent explanation of how it is possible for us to understand one another. It notes the fact that we do have, at least for very many words, images which occur to us upon the hearing of the words. It does not exclude the possibility that words have other functions as well, such as naming objects; indeed, it requires this. It recognizes the causative function of words and signs, and it provides for changes in meanings as the associations between words and ideas change. But it is much too simple a theory, and it is quite inadequate.

The first criticism of the theory—and the most obvious one—is that language has an indefinitely large number of uses aside from the communication of ideas. Locke's most famous critic, George Berkeley, was the first of his near-contemporaries to recognize this, and many of his arguments against the position are detailed in Chapter 5. This first criticism was his major one. Among the uses of language which Berkeley saw in addition to the communication of ideas was the causing and inhibiting of passion and action. Secondly, there are very many words for which there simply are no corresponding ideas. Among them are connective words, or *syncategorematic* terms, as they are often called, such as "and," "to," and so forth, and wholly emotive terms such as the cheer at the home game. Certainly when we hear a complex sentence, there is not one idea associated with every word in the sentence as we hear it. Furthermore, different images are often associated with the same words, so that the ideational theorist must be able to explain why one of the associated ideas rather than the other is to be counted as *the* meaning of the word. The words "northern lake" are associated with the image of a lake with which I am familiar. But they also are associated with images of woods, boats, and fond childhood memories of various sorts. Why is the image of the lake the meaning rather than some or all of the others? One problem with a theory resting upon the principle of association is that almost anything can become associated with almost anything else.

There is also some difficulty with the notion of "idea" itself. Surely it is excessively narrow, indeed simply false, to say that all ideas are images. It is not suggested here that Locke made such a claim, though Berkeley thought that he had; but if ideas and images are not coextensive, then what else does the concept include? The theory is uncomfortably close to some "picture-in-my-head" analogy, requiring what Gilbert Ryle calls a "ghost in the machine" to "have" the pictures, and "cause" a bodily reaction. We shall see later on that this sort of analysis of human thought and action is untenable, because it involves a fallacy which Ryle called a "category-mistake."

For all of these reasons, and many more, the ideational theory, or as it is sometimes called elsewhere in this book, the *idea-correspondence* theory, is inadequate to account for the nature of meaning.

The Denotative or Referential Theory

The next theory is the *denotative* or *referential* view. According to this explanation, the meaning of a word consists in that to which it refers, or, in some versions, in the relation between the word and that to which it refers. The paradigm for meaning for this theory is the proper name, for it seems incontestable that the significance of these words is their reference. The move from the particular case of proper names to the general view that the meaning of *all* words is their reference is but a giant step made possible by the fallacy of *hasty generalization,* which we shall discover near the end of this chapter.

Fatal criticisms of this view are easy to come by. The most common, and the simplest, is that, if the theory is correct, then words which are different cannot have different meanings and the same referents. However, it is easy to discover different words with the same referent but different meanings. So the theory is mistaken. Examples of different words with the same referents but different meanings are these: "The first Roman Catholic ever elected to the presidency of the United States," and "The author of 'Profiles in Courage' "; "The morning star," and "The evening star"; "The moon," and "Diana's silvr'y orb." If these pairs of phrases with the same referent also had the same meaning, then, by understanding the meaning of one of the terms in each pair, one would automatically know the meaning of the second term. But this is not the case, as you can see from examining the pairs for yourself.

The referential theory is also prey to the criticism that it cannot account for the meaning of false sentences. If the sentence "The cat is on the mat" is false, then to what do the words in the sentence refer? This problem led some philosophers who were overly addicted to the theory, and therefore could not recognize a counter-example when they saw one, into saying that there must be a realm of "negative facts" to which false sentences referred, for otherwise one could not account for their meaning. The more appropriate conclusions seem to be that, since the theory cannot account for these cases, the theory is either good only for true sentences or mistaken at the outset.

That version of the theory which identifies meaning with the relation between the word and what it refers to does not work either. For one thing (and this applies to the first version as well), there are very many words which do not seem to refer to anything. Fictional words of various kinds, syncategorematic terms, numerals and so forth seem to have no reference, for example, or at least certainly not the same logical sort of reference as object-words have. Furthermore, what is the nature of the relation between words which do name, and what they name? If it is simply a relation of reference *per se,* then, given that there are many other functions of words, and that referring is but one of them, what is the justification for assuming that the referring function is the one which gives the word its meaning? And is it the case that words have functions all by themselves? Or is it rather the case that words are simply arbitrary signs, invented by men for their own convenience, and that *we use them* for certain purposes; that is, the functions like reference are not functions of words, but of the people who use them? If this is true, then the referential theorist who identified the meaning of a word with the relation between it and that to which it referred would have to bring in a third element—the user of the sign—and claim that all meaning relations are triadic. This in itself is not a criticism, for in the case of some words it is defensible, but what it does point out is the necessity for broadening the theory to account for the meanings of all those words whose function, that is, whose use, is *not* to refer but to do some other job. The referential or denotative theory is simply not broad enough to do this. Its narrowness, and the factually mistaken assumptions upon which it rests (such as that every word has a referent) are sufficient to reject it.

Behavioral Theories

It is misleading to call *behavioral* theories of meaning *one* theory, for there are very many theories which would fall under this general heading. Among them are the emotive, some versions of the verifiability theory, some kinds of pragmatic, operationalist and instrumentalist theories, most dispositional theories, and so forth. Here, we shall be concerned with a general statement of the principles involved in almost all of these other views.

All behavioral theories of meaning concentrate upon the *activity* of using language. Furthermore, they are all aware of the epistemological problems in theories in meaning, especially those concerned with the nature of a public object of knowledge. Because of this, they are all prone to look to the context of an utterance, including its effect upon the hearer, for the analysis of meaning. In many cases, they were strongly influenced by discoveries in applied psychology in this century, especially those concerned with the determination of behavior by stimulus and reward, and publicized in the writings of such researchers as Watson and Skinner. The writings of these and other psychological behaviorists are replete with dispositional analysis; that is, the significance of a stimulus is explained in terms of either the overt response to it, or the disposition of an organism to respond in predictable ways to it, even if the organism does not actually manifest the response upon every occasion of the stimulus. The language theorists saw in this a way to explain meanings without becoming entangled in the major difficulties of the theories which we have already considered. The dispositional view allowed the theorists to identify any utterance, object, or event as a sign, to make a distinction between artificial signs (those made by man) and natural ones, and to explain the significance of signs in terms of the patterns of customary response—dispositional response—to them. It had other advantages as well. The *kinds* of meanings of signs become identified with the kinds of responses and dispositions to respond, and therefore they are not committed to identifying one or two functions of language as the central ones so far as meaning is concerned. Dispositional meaning theory is comprehensive enough to embrace both theories of cognitive meaning, and those of emotive meaning. Charles Stevenson is a dispositional theorist as are Charles Morris, Gilbert Ryle, and the pragmatists such as John Dewey and William James. Furthermore, the view is wide enough to permit changes in meanings, and the development of totally new signs, for all that is required is the establishment of a dispositional response to an object, event, or utterance. In short, it is a view which recognizes the complexity of language and the diversity of functions which we perform with both natural and artificial objects in our communication with one another. As such, it is a more adequate theory than the others which have been mentioned.

Dispositional meaning theory is not totally adequate, however, and its very breadth renders it relatively ineffective in the sort of detailed analysis required to explain the complex meanings of many signs. The central problem is that for any sign, artificial or natural, there are an indefinitely large number of possible dispositional reactions, and once again we are confronted with the difficulty of specifying *the* meaning of meanings of such signs. The principle of association, which is after all a psychological principle, makes possible the association of almost anything with almost anything else, and if the resulting dispositions to respond result in a similarly large range of meanings, then all terms become systematically vague. Not only are there an indefinitely large number of *possible* dispositional responses, but there are also a very large range of *actual* ones to any sign. Even to such a simple command as "Close the door," depending upon the context, the dispositions might include anger at the abruptness of the order, an impulse to get up and close the door, an impulse to slam it, to open it wider, to tell the commander to shut it himself, to ask why he wanted it shut, to reply that you would prefer that it remain open, to agree that it would be better shut, to ask someone else to shut it, and so forth. There are also difficulties with the notion of being a "sign" which are implicit in some versions of the theory, especially those similar to the version of Morris. Sign of what? Of the disposition? That would be begging the question, for it would entail our saying that the analysis of the meaning of a sign was the disposition to respond to it, and the definition of a sign was any object, event, or utterance that had a meaning, that is, a dispositional response to it. But the sign cannot be a sign of some particular state of affairs either, if the explanation of how it comes to be so is the principle of association, without getting into the difficulties already mentioned: why a sign of this state of affairs rather than that? Furthermore, the theory runs into difficulties when we speak about signs which are sentences about the remote past. It is not easy to see how the meaning of sentences about the Jurassic Age can be a disposition to respond in the present. And the same will be true of certain kinds of predictions about the remote future.

As has been mentioned, a very broad range of theories is included under the general heading "behavioral." One kind of theory generally included is the *pragmatic* theory, as developed by Charles Peirce, William James, and John Dewey, and a few remarks might be appropriate about that theory here because it illustrates another important fact about behavioral theories as a whole—that they tend to obliterate the distinction between theories of truth and theories of meaning. Pragmatism was developed first of all as a theory of meaning by Peirce, but with James's changes and additions it became as much a theory of truth. Pragmatism was originally a theory about the nature and uses of signs; and in the origin, signs were conceived as ways in which objects, events, marks, gestures, and so forth were used conventionally. The meanings of signs were identified with their "practical consequences" or effects. If an utterance made no practical difference in our lives, then the utterance was meaningless, and if two utterances had the same effects, then they had the same meanings. One effect which this view had was to make metaphysics suspect in the eyes of the pragmatists. Peirce also attempted to give an analysis of the meaning of certain concepts by specifying certain operations about them that would produce predictable results. The form this took was a conditional statement in which the concept to be clarified and the operation by which it could be clarified were both stated. Sentences such as (to use an example of Ryle's) "Glass is brittle" might be analyzed by saying that " 'Glass is brittle' means that if in given contexts glass is struck with objects such as rocks, etc., then it will shatter." The concept of brittleness has the same meaning as the conditional sentence asserted here. Peirce himself looked upon this analysis as more of a *method* for the clarification of concepts than an analysis of meaning, but in the words of James and Dewey the two became indistinguishable. For James especially, it became impossible to distinguish between meaning and truth. The usefulness or practicality of ideas *was* their meaning and truth, and for Dewey to say that a sentence was "true" meant that it was "warranted" by the context in which it was used. In science, the "truth" of laws was interpreted in terms of their effectiveness as rules or directions for scientific procedures. Hence, evaluation of laws and rules becomes a function of their contribution to clarity and practical fruitfulness, not a matter of correspondence or reference.

There are many things which recommend pragmatism, especially in the interpretation of scientific laws, which are clearly not true or false in the manner of descriptions and which are obviously related to the direction of practices of a technical variety. But as with some other varieties of behavioral theories, pragmatism must confront the difficulty of accounting for statements about the past. The sort of analysis which is proposed may do at least in part for the laws of science, but it is difficult to see how a statement such as "The battle of Hastings was fought in 1066" can be explained in pragmatic terms. It is also open to the charge that meanings can vary over a wide range if the theory is correct, a range far too wide for any sort of precise analysis, because the practical effects of any proposition may change from moment to moment. Furthermore, truth becomes a function of success; and, although this may be satisfactory in some contexts, it is not in others. Whenever the distinction between truth and meaning becomes blurred, we are no longer able to make claims such as that the property of being either true or false presupposes meaningfulness. Our inability to make such claims is of course not a criticism unless it can be shown that the distinction is essential, but for some classes of propositions it does seem to be both sensible and required.

Contextualist Theories

The continued emphasis in the development of theories of meaning upon the *activity* of speech, and the coordinate wide variety of the *uses* of language, has led in more recent times to a set of views which are grouped here under the title of *contextualist* theories of meaning. The distinction between these values and such other positions as pragmatism in some of its varieties is not always clear, but in general there is a shift from an emphasis on either *both* the speaker's activities *and* the hearer's response, or from an analysis of the effects of an utterance, toward a concentration upon what it is that a speaker *does* when he speaks. The two thinkers who have exerted the most influence here are Ludwig Wittgenstein and J. L. Austin.

Wittgenstein's later work, especially his *Philosophical Investigations,* emphasized that the search for the meanings of words was really a search for their various uses. A speaker does much more than produce a set of sounds. His gestures, his behavior of various sorts, all are a part of his speaking activity. These activities can vary so widely from culture to culture and from place to place that there is really nothing common to all languages. There is a resemblance among them, and even among segments or parts of a given language, but it is not a resemblance such that true general statements about it can be made which will enable us to make accurate predictions about the future of the language, relate any possible language to any other, and so forth. There is an analogy which can be drawn between languages and *games*. A game has certain procedures—rules if you like—moves that must be made in order to play the game, contexts within which the moves must be made, etc. These might all be very different in different games, or they might be very similar. One can conceive of two different games, one game being baseball and the other exactly like it except there is no catcher; instead, the pitcher runs and gets the ball every time he throws it and his skill at this activity counts in the score. The second game would not be baseball. Nor could we say that some one feature of it, or of baseball, is what makes the two of them *games*, for no matter which feature you pick out, there will be some other game which does not have that property. So the analysis of their resemblance is exceedingly difficult and will not provide us with the necessary and sufficient conditions for classifying these form of activity as games. Instead, their resemblance is more like that of a family, extended over generations, wherein no feature is necessary for being a member of the family, but in which there are sometimes shared resemblances even though no individual feature is distributed throughout the people who belong to the family. Nonetheless, it is still one family.

Because of all of this, we are not going to discover a paradigm for meaning that is common to all languages, nor even to the various "language games" that are "played" within the same language. So we should cease to look for common features, and concentrate upon the uses of words. What these are will be dictated by the rules of the game as it were, and they will vary from context to context because the requirements of the game will differ, depending upon its purposes. The total set of uses of some expression is identical to the language game of that expression; it is a set of practices. To discover the meaning is to discover this set of practices.

J. L. Austin concentrated more than anyone else upon the analysis of the speech act itself. A major consequence of his views was that philosophers moved away from the conception that words have meaning in and of themselves. Nor is it correct, if Austin is right, to say that we "give" meanings to words by using them in certain ways and intend to do so. In support of such claims he asks what happens when we utter sentences, for he does not think that people really say anything with single words in most contexts, and that therefore we ought to look for the smallest "bit" of language in which they *do* say things. Austin thinks that three distinct kinds of "acts" occur when we speak to someone. He calls these the *locutionary* act, the *illocutionary* act, and the *perlocutionary* act. A locutionary act consists simply in saying something; an illocutionary act is what we do *in* the saying of something, for example, questioning, advising, commanding, and so forth; a perlocutionary act is the effect or set of effects that the locution and the illocution has. Suppose for example that I say to you "Close the door." The locution is "Close the door"; the illocution is my ordering, asking, commanding, pleading, or whatever it was that I did when I said this; the perlocutionary act (we shall assume) is your closing the door. In Austin's view, meaning is but one component of the total speech situation. It is the reference and the sense, the denotation and the connotation, of the locutionary act. As such, it is not *prima facie* the most important thing there is to know about communication, and the uses to which we can put our knowledge of meanings need have little to do with illocutionary and perlocutionary acts.

In one sense, Austin and Wittgenstein seem to move us backward rather than forward in the attempt to solve the problems of meaning, because their analyses introduce more unanalyzed components than do the other theories. And in Austin's case, the function of reference seems to be placed at the heart of the meaning of "meaning" once again. But there is a significant difference. The original objections to the referential theory were largely based upon the fact that the theory could not handle functions of language. Most, if not all of these functions are explained by Austin in terms of the other aspects of the speech act which he has outlined, and are hence removed from the sphere of meaning in the first place. In addition, Austin's analysis includes certain classifications of kinds of speech acts which explain these utterances in terms of context, success and failure in the performance of the act, and convention, in such a way that it is not necessary to refer to meaning in these cases. For example, utterances such as "I christen thee 'Queen Elizabeth,'" "I apologize," "I swear to tell the truth, the whole truth . . . ," etc., are called *"performative utterances"* by Austin. They are neither true nor false; they are *actions* and the doing of christening, apologizing, swearing an oath, and so on *consists* in the utterance and nothing else. To work, these acts require an established convention and they must be performed in the appropriate circumstances, or they will "misfire." The point here is that the meaning of such statements as these is not what is relevant for an understanding of them; what *is* relevant is an awareness of what you are *doing*, or what someone else is doing when they use performative utterances.

Obviously, all the criticisms that have been raised against the other theories have not been answered in these last few pages. It is premature, however, to say that the type of procedure used by Austin and Wittgenstein and their students will not succeed in answering these questions.

At the least, this new approach has given us more knowledge about what an adequate theory of meaning would have to be in order to be satisfactory. Among other things, at least these criteria must be met:

1. No adequate theory can be tied to a single function or use of language.
2. Any use of "ideas" or their analogue in a theory of meaning will have to be given in terms that render the "idea" an object or a possible object of public knowledge.
3. The principle of association alone will not be a sufficient principle for a theory of meaning.
4. Not only the intention of the speaker, but also the effects on the hearer must be explained.
5. The reification of meanings, as in the case of false propositions and the referential theory, is not permissible.
6. The *activity* of speech and other modes of communication and ceremonial language must be related to any adequate analysis of meaning.
7. The concept of a "language," that is, the set of signs which will be carriers of meaning in any sense, must be delimited, while at the same time provisions for relating such signs to the contexts in which they are used must be made.

This is only a partial and therefore inadequate listing of the tests that must be met. It is clear that some of the solutions to problems of meaning will in turn have an effect upon concepts such as validity and soundness. The latter concepts depend in their turn upon the concepts of truth and falsity, among others, and these will be affected by, for example, the exclusion of certain kinds of utterances as candidates for truth-values, or conversely, the inclusion of other kinds normally not thought to be usable within arguments. The moral of the story is fairly clear—philosophy is not yet in sight of the answers to its most basic questions.

The connections between theories of meaning and theories of truth are many, and some of them have just been mentioned. More will become evident in the discussion of truth which follows.

TRUTH

Theories of truth purport to explain what it means to say that propositions or judgments are true or false. As such, they are a species of theory of meaning, for they are explicating the meanings of the words "true," "false," and "truth-value." There is this much truth at least in the pragmatist's refusal to separate the two kinds of theories. Something has been said earlier about the pragmatic view, and a little more will be added here. In addition, three other views will be considered. The first is the *coherence* theory of truth, the second is the *correspondence* theory, including some remarks about its relation to the idea-correspondence or ideational theory of meaning, and the third is the *performative* theory.

The Coherence Theory

The coherence theory of truth is based largely upon the model of the deductive mathematical system. It holds that to say that a proposition or a judgment is true is to say that it coheres with a body of other propositions or judgments which together with it constitute a system. The relations between these propositions or judgments are those of logical implication. The analogy with mathematics is easy to see here. In a deductive system which is consistent, as we know, it is not possible to derive a contradiction, that is, a proposition which is necessarily false. In mathematics, when a proposition is said to cohere with the set of which it is a member, it is meant that this proposition can be inferred from the others, that is, deduced from them. In the strictest versions of the coherence theory, any proposition in the system implies all of the other judgments in it. Coherence not only becomes a theory about the meaning of "truth," but also becomes the only test for the presence of truth. The theory has even wider implications.

Before coherence can be fully defined, the nature of the cohering propositions must be specified. It would be impossible for *meaningless* propositions to be either true or false given this theory of truth, because by definition, no relations of implication hold among such utterances. This is one reason that in traditional thinking theories of meaning, or at least meaningfulness itself, is presupposed by theories of truth. Which propositions are said to be the set within which judgments cohere depends in part upon the view one has of meaningfulness. For example, as we shall see, the adherents of the principle of verifiability, who were known as logical positivists, thought that metaphysical propositions were meaningless and that the only meaningful utterances were either tautologies or observation statements. Tautologies are uninformative except perhaps as directions for the formation of equations, mathematical or otherwise. A positivist who held the coherence theory of truth would therefore say that a judgment is true if and only if it coheres with the set of observation statements of which it is a member, or, if the statement is a tautology, with the set of other analytic truths of which it is a member. But not everyone is a positivist of course, and those thinkers who held a theory of meaning which permitted metaphysical statements to be sensible argued that the set of cohering statements must include these. Since metaphysical statements are usually a part of what purports to be a cosmology, then any true statement would have to be consistent with the account of reality which the cosmology reflects.

A theory known as the *doctrine of internal relations* is a frequent concomitant of the coherence theory of truth, though not always. This theory holds that the nature of any entity includes its relations to all other entities, so that complete knowledge of any one thing implies complete knowledge of everything else. Such knowledge is of course impossible to attain, perhaps even in principle, if the relations are to include all *possible* as well as actual ones, and in versions of the coherence theory that include the doctrine of internal relations it seems to follow that certain knowledge of truth is not possible. This of course does not falsify the theory, because it may *be* impossible to attain certain knowledge of the truth of a judgment.

Finally, a further consequence of coherence theories of truth which accept the doctrine of internal relations is that strictly speaking, truth is one judgment in the set. A given judgment in the set will therefore be true only *to the extent* that it participates in the truth-value of the set Another way of saying this is that any given proposition is true only to some *degree,* and this has been said to have the consequence that if it is true only in degree, then it seems false in some degree as well. The latter consequence is intended by critics of the coherence theory as an attack, of course, but it is not well founded because from the claim that a proposition is true only to a degree it does not follow that it is false to some degree as well. Nonetheless, the difficulty does remain of making some sense out of the concept of "true in degree," because the normal concept of truth-values seems to require that a proposition have one value or the other value or neither value, and does not include the possibility of having *part* of one value or the other.

The coherence theory of truth has some obviously attractive features. It is certainly the case that we reject a proposition as false in limited contexts if it is inconsistent with other judgments about the subject matter of that context which we accept as true. Furthermore, it seems obvious that we could not judge of the truth or falsity of statements about the past except in the context of other statements that are about that same period. If we did not possess a body of claims about William the Conqueror and his invasion of England, how could we make sense out of the statement "The battle of Hastings was fought in 1066, and Harold lost"? But immediately some difficulties become evident. The first is that in any context, consistency does not in fact tell us which statements are true and which are false. Consider a court of law where the defendant insists that he did not commit the crime while all of the witnesses swear that he did. Their claims are therefore inconsistent. But the believability of one set of claims rather than the other is not due to the consistency or inconsistency of the set. It may be that all the witnesses are lying, that no evidence short of their admission could be brought forth which would prove this, and that the poor defendant is telling the truth. Or it may be that they are not lying, but that their statements have resulted from a misinterpretation of the facts, and so forth. In short, the claims of the defendant are rejected as false only because the statements of the witnesses are believed to be true, and the grounds for believing one set of claims rather than the other are not consistency. It will not do to appeal to mathematics as a case where consistency *is* the test of truth, because even if this is so, mathematical truths are not informative; they are tautologies, and to be a workable theory of truth the theory must account for synthetic truths as well. Even if, as some philosophers of mathematics have wanted to argue, the statements of mathematics are not analytic, the analogy is insufficient. This is because the acceptability of the truth of mathematical claims now comes to rest on a footing other than consistency alone, as with other non-analytic judgments. In fact, the more one examines coherence, the more it seems that coherence is something quite different from truth, or at least, it seems that we *mean* something quite different by the two words "coherence" and "truth." When I say that "the picture in my office is predominantly blue" and then add that this sentence is both consistent with the set of other claims about my office, and is true, am I uttering a redundancy? It does not seem so. Rather, I seem to be saying two distinct things, which might have different truth-values. This cannot be the case if the coherence theory is correct.

Finally, there are serious, perhaps fatal criticisms of the doctrine of internal relations; and, in so far as the coherence theory of truth depends upon this doctrine, it will be mistaken. We cannot investigate the doctrine of internal relations here; however, we mention in passing that if it is true that a total knowledge of everything requires a total knowledge of every entity's relations to every other entity, this does not necessarily imply that no complete knowledge of some particular given entity is possible. Nor does it follow that truths about this given entity are in any way logically dependent upon truths about other entities and its relation to them. The doctrine of internal relations makes sense only from a vantage point where one considers the universe "from outside," as it were, as a limited and finite whole. Viewed from the "inside," where the observer is an entity in the universe himself, relations are not seen as internal but as external.

The Correspondence Theory

Probably the most common philosophical theory of truth is the *correspondence* theory. It has a great many forms, some of them very complex indeed, and it is one of the oldest, if not the oldest, theory about the nature of truth and what it means to say that a statement is true. Its basic principle can be stated simply thus: a proposition is true if and only if there is a correspondence between that proposition and a fact or set of facts, or between some belief and a fact or set of facts. As with many philosophical theories, this turned out to be much too simple an explanation. The first problem which confronted the adherents of this view was that of false sentences. To what set of facts do they correspond? How can we think about that which does not exist, which is nothing? Philosophers were aware of these issues by the time of Plato, and indeed that great thinker discussed this problem, but there are those who believe that the problem is not yet solved.

One of the clearest arguments in support of the correspondence theory is Bertrand Russell's, in a small masterpiece called *The Problems of Philosophy*.[1] Russell has changed his view of the nature of truth many times, but at no time did he give up all forms of the correspondence theory. In the twelfth chapter of his book, Russell sets out to answer the question "What do we *mean* by truth and falsehood?" Whatever theory is our answer, it must in his view meet three criteria: (1) it must admit the opposite of truth, that is, falsehood; (2) it must take cognizance of the fact that without "beliefs and statements," there would be no truth of falsehood, and that therefore a world that contains truth values contains more than "mere matter"; (3) it must realize that since truth and falsehood must depend upon something outside of the belief or statement that has the truth-value (otherwise the analysis would be circular), then truth and falsehood must be "dependent upon the relations of the beliefs to other things," and not upon any intrinsic property of the belief or statement itself. Notice that the coherence theory also attempts to account for these three points.

The correspondence theory seems to answer the question concerning the nature of the relation between the belief or statement and whatever it is to which it is related. It also attempts to tell us about what that *relata* is. Russell notes that the coherence theory of truth, as has just been stated, is also an attempt to take account of three criteria, but he rejects it on two major grounds, both of which are similar to the ones offered here. His first ground for rejecting the theory is that more than one coherent body of truths is possible. Secondly, he argues that the theory assumes that the meaning of "coherence" is known, whereas, in fact, it presupposes the truth of the laws of logic, which of course begs the question about the meaning of "truth." He does say, however, that coherence is a valuable *test* for truth.

Russell thinks that belief has a relation with fact, in virtue of which the belief is either true or false. A statement is that in which a belief

[1] Bertrand Russell, *The Problems of Philosophy* (London: Oxford University Press, 1912), chapter 12.

is given or expressed, so it too has this relation. He then sets out to analyze the nature of fact, and his analysis is fairly complex. Russell thinks that fact cannot be a single or simple object, for it would then not permit the fulfilling of the first criterion. If, to use his example, Othello believes falsely that Desdemona loves Cassio, then this belief cannot be directed to the single object 'Desdemona's love for Cassio,' because if there were such an object, then of course the belief would be true, not false. So the object, whatever it is, must be more than one, or complex, and the relation will therefore be more than dyadic. In fact, in the case of the example just mentioned, Russell thinks the relation is one of four terms, the terms related being Desdemona, Cassio, loving, and Othello. A mind which believes (the subject), in the present case Othello, puts the other three terms in a certain order when he believes. If the belief is true, then there is a complex fact associated with the elements of his judgment in the order he puts them. If it is false, then there is no such complex fact. The relation between the belief and the facts is that of believing. Hence, Othello judges that the relation of loving exists between Desdemona and Cassio, and in the light of this judgment he believes that 'Desdemona loves Cassio' is true. If this is true, then there is a complex object 'Desdemona loving Cassio,' which corresponds to the belief; if it does not, the belief is false, and some *other* set of facts is the case; for example, 'Cassio loving Desdemona,' but not vice versa, would not have bothered Othello nearly as much.

This theory will not work for several reasons, and Russell, who was never afraid to give up a position in the face of sound criticism, came to realize that they were fatal. For one thing, Russell hoped that the relation in virtue of which a belief was true, namely the relation of believing, would be the same in each and every case of a true belief; indeed, his theory required this. But it turned out that if the judgment that was believed was general, or complex, the number of terms in the relation altered dramatically, making the theory not only cumbersome but also destroying the uniformity of the relation of believing in different cases.

Furthermore, although Russell wanted at this time to reject the notion that there were such things as propositions (the meaning of two different sentences cannot be identical with either of them) and wanted to assert that only beliefs and facts were necessary for the theory, his facts seemed to turn out to be nothing more than the propositions he wanted to reject. If I believe something falsely, it is not the sentence which expresses this belief that I believe, but the belief itself. Therefore, the belief is not identical to the sentences in which it can be expressed, for these are different. Besides, if the belief is false, to what does it correspond? If the related objects are not as my belief posits them, then there is just *no* correspondence. But the theory would have to say that there is a correspondence of a different kind from that present when my belief is true, which is unconvincing. In the case of false beliefs at least, we seem to have a case of a "negative fact." The alternative seems to be to reject both facts and propositions, which Russell's theory will not permit.

Another way in which the problem of negative facts raises its head for correspondence theorists is in cases of disjunctions. Suppose I say "Either it is raining or it is not raining." This is a tautology, and hence necessarily true. But it also presumably corresponds with some set of facts, for one or the other of the disjuncts must be true. Suppose that it is raining. To what does the *other* half of the disjunction correspond?

Earlier in this chapter, we studied the idea-correspondence theory of meaning, or, to use the more general name for this sort of view, the ideational theory. As we shall see in Chapter 5, Locke among others thought that a sentence was true if the ideas denoted by its terms corresponded in certain ways. "Man is an animal" is true if the ideas denoted by "man" and "animal" are such that the one is included in the other. We saw that the ideational theory of meaning was inadequate, in part because there are not ideas corresponding to every meaningful word. It follows that as a general theory of truth, the idea-correspondence theory would likewise be inadequate; and to show it was, we would only have to come up with a meaningful sentence in which no distinct idea was denoted by one of the terms in the supposedly true sentence. The parallel with the correspondence theory is clear. To disprove this theory, we only require a sentence, or a part of one, such that no facts correspond to it. The difference in the two theories consists not in the mechanism of the theory for the most part, but in the nature of that which is the counterpart to the sentence. In the one it is an idea; in the other, a fact.

There are many other versions of the correspondence theory, some more adequate than others; and with some modern versions, such as Alfred Tarski's, the verdict is not yet in. But more and more, philosophers are coming to the view that there is no *one* theory of truth. An instance of this tendency is to be found in the last theory we shall consider here, the *performative* theory of truth.

The Performative Theory

We have already examined part of J. L. Austin's theory about performative utterances. Peter Strawson believes that in spite of Austin's contribution, and his avoidance of the major faults in a correspondence theory, which in Strawson's eyes are the assumption that "truth" names a property of sentences and the belief that the relation of correspondence is anything more than a purely conventional one, Austin still has a correspondence theory of truth. He believes this because Austin's analysis still posits a relation between speech acts and the world, a relation which is conventional, but nonetheless a relation in virtue of which truth is predicated of utterances. Strawson does not think the correspondence theory needs such revision—he thinks it ought to be rejected altogether.

Strawson does not deny that when we say that something is true, we are talking about something we can call "statements" in general. A statement is what I say when I say something. But when we say that a statement is true, we are not asserting that such and such conditions hold between the statement and something else, a fact or set of facts, nor is it the case that the word "true" in general is a descriptive word. It is rather a *performative* word with many uses; it is used to assert things in certain *ways* which require that certain conditions have been fulfilled. We may, for example, when we say that a statement is true, be granting a point, or confirming it, or supporting its denial, and so on.

In the sentence that begins the last paragraph, the phrase "talking about" must be clarified. What Strawson means is that when we say a statement is true, we are performing certain acts which are (not "which express," or "which indicate") our agreeing to, granting, confirming, supporting, the statement. As such we are not strictly speaking making a claim *about* the statement. We are not saying something like "The sentence 'Snow is white' is true," except in an elliptical way. We are supporting or endorsing the statement. In fact, phrases such as "I endorse," "I grant," "I confirm," may be substituted, in some contexts, for the phrase "It is true that," or ". . . (e.g., 'What John said') is (was) true." What has misled many theorists is the fact that the word "true" functions very often as a grammatical predicate in English. But to function as a grammatical predicate is not of necessity actually to predicate some property of something else.

It must also be said that often when we use phrases such as "That's true," we are supporting the *way* in which someone said something else as well as *what* he said. Here the distinction between a statement (what is said) and the utterance (the act in which the statement is said) becomes a bit blurred. But the role of "true" is still performative. "I promise" is a favorite case that Strawson uses to illustrate what a performative utterance is. If I promise you to do something, I am not saying *that* I will promise to do something; I *am* promising. Similarly, when I say "It's true that *p*," I am not saying something *about* *p* as I would be in the sentence "*p* has six distinct words in it," I *am* endorsing *p*, confirming it, and so forth.

The uses of "true" are quite diverse and very complex. We cannot go through them all here. The major point however is simple: the function of "true" and its associated phrases is not to assert the existence of a relation between a statement and something else, nor is it to ascribe a property such as coherence to a proposition, nor to say that a statement in an object language has a certain property relative to a meta-language. Rather the term functions in kinds of speech acts such as confirming and so forth. As such, the meaning of "truth" is as wide as the uses of the term, and so there is no one single theory of truth. What "truth" means will depend upon an empirical investigation of the ways in which it is used, the contexts in which it is used, and the acts which are performed with it.

Two criticisms are commonly offered (among others of course) against Strawson's position. One of them is that, in fact, the word "true" and its associated speech acts ("that's true," etc.) do *not* always function in ways similar to phrases or speech acts such as "I confirm," "I support," "I agree," and so on. There is about the uses of "true" when applied to statements the connotation of *adequate reason* for what is said to be true, and this is not always the case with these other acts. Furthermore, in cases such as "Caesar crossed the Rubicon" and other claims about fairly remote history, it sounds strange to say that one supports this claim, or confirms it, or agrees with it, though it does not sound strange to say that such claims are true. Certainly, contexts are imaginable in which such historical claims could be confirmed, supported, and so forth in the ways Strawson suggests. But the point is that if we are doing performative utterances when we say that claims of history or science are true, then the notion of a performative utterance is wider than Strawson knew. Later on, Strawson came to modify his position in the light of things like historical claims, and cases in which agreement was being expressed with someone's position when the exact position itself was not known. In these latter cases, if Strawson were correct when he claimed that the word "true" is unnecessary and indeed redundant so far as the assertive meaning of a statement is concerned, then it ought to be the case that when I endorse or confirm your position when I do not know what that position is, I ought to be asserting your position. It is clearly the case, however, that I cannot be doing this if I do not know your position. The use of "true" in this way is called its "blind" use.

Strawson's replies to these criticisms have involved his admission that when we say that some statement is true, we are at least in part saying something about the statement, and not merely performing an act such as endorsing, confirming, and so forth. In short, he is admitting that phrases such as "That's true" have an assertive role as well as the other roles which have been discussed. For other reasons which cannot concern us here, his replies have not been completely adequate. The important point for our purposes is that the diversity of the functions of "true" and the various phrases in which it occurs is again recognized in Strawson's replies to his critics. This is so because in agreeing with them that this term and its associated context do function to make assertions about statements, he does not withdraw, nor need he do so, the claim that they are also used to make performative utterances. The affinities between Strawson's theory and that of Austin should be obvious, though they disagree upon the nature of a theory of truth. Both would agree that there are uses of "true" which are themselves neither true nor false, and which are incorrectly analyzed as instances of making assertions about anything. If they are correct, then theories of truth on the correspondence and coherence models are relevant to a much smaller class of sentences and the propositions they express than at least the early adherents to the theories believed. To the extent that the class of sentences to which they apply is smaller, their philosophical significance is also diminished, though, of course, the class of sentences may be a significant one. But clearly the emphasis of people such as Wittgenstein, Strawson, and Austin is on the *uses* of sentences and utterances, and upon their contexts and the diversity of functions which linguistic devices have, rather than upon the search for a single theory of truth which can handle all cases of true and false statements. In later chapters, we will come upon this conviction again, the conviction that no one theory of truth is adequate for the analysis of the many uses of language. We will see it in our discussion of Ayer, Stevenson, Hare, and Berkeley, and it will be reflected in criticisms of certain positions contained in this text.

Whether we would be justified in moving from the position that no one theory of truth is adequate, to the view that there are no theories of truth adequate for the analysis of *any* kind of statements, is another question. In this author's view, we would not be justified in making this move. For defined sets of mathematical statements which are not instantiated, for example, it would seem that some version of the coherence theory would be sufficient for the purpose for which we would require a theory of truth in such contexts. When we are speaking of the more complex contexts of the laws of science and grammatical rules, a pragmatic or instrumental approach would seem to serve our purposes better. For some classes of utterances, such as the ceremonial uses of language noted by Austin and Margaret MacDonald among others, theories of truth are inappropriate analytic devices and should be discarded accordingly. The problem of identifying an utterance as mathematical, scientific, ceremonial or performative and so forth are exceedingly complex, as Wittgenstein's analysis of the language game shows us, and perhaps we can never do better than approximate completeness and accuracy. The same may be true of theories of truth themselves. But this very realization of the complexity of the issues involved, and of the inadequacy of the attempts made to solve them until now, is after all an advance in knowledge and a challenge to those who find puzzles the occasion for greater efforts rather than resignation.

The close affinity among several of the problems concerned with truth and theories of truth, and those associated with meaning and theories of meaning, should be evident. The most obvious evidence of this fact might be the pragmatic theory of meaning, which as we know makes no separation between theory of meaning and theory of truth, at least in many of its versions. Generally, however, it may be said that questions of meaning have a logical priority over those of truth, since it is generally accepted that a sentence must be meaningful before it may be said to have a truth-value. Whether "meaningful" means more than "under-standable" here depends upon the theory of meaning and the theory of truth with which one is dealing. Many sentences are understandable, but do not have definite empirical references, whether direct or indirect; and as we shall see in a later chapter, this is enough to disqualify them as candidates for meaning and hence for truth according to the views of the Logical Positivists. But there are also many sentences which are so vague that we cannot decide which of the possible meanings they might have is the one they do in fact have. Given the notions of validity which we have already discussed, it is clear that this vagueness can often lead to invalid arguments. Moreover, it is not enough that a sentence have a specifiable meaning, and that it be true, in order for it to be a premise in a valid argument. It must also stand in a relation of implication to the conclusion of that argument, for if it does not, it is irrelevant for the purposes of the argument.

Finally, there are some confusions rooted in these questions of vague-ness or ambiguity and relevance that are fairly common and have come to have distinct names. At this point it is appropriate to discuss these kinds of errors.

INFORMAL AND PHILOSOPHICAL FALLACIES

The kinds of mistakes just mentioned are usually divided into two broad categories. They are called fallacies of *relevance* and fallacies of *ambiguity*. Together, they are usually called *informal* fallacies, but this name is not very accurate. Fallacies of relevance are just what the name indicates: there is a question, in arguments making this mistake, about the relevance of the premises to their conclusion or conclusions. Be-cause it is possible for such mistakes to lead to invalid arguments (clearly, if the premises are irrelevant to the conclusion, then the conclusion does not follow from them), it is misleading to call them "informal" fallacies. A fallacy is presumably informal when no question about the correctness of the *form* of an argument is involved, and such questions do become central in the cases of several fallacies of relevance. The same is true of fallacies of ambiguity. As with fallacies of relevance, the name indicates the difficulty. Ambiguous statements in an argument often enable us to draw more than one conclusion, or an improper conclusion from them, and in some cases the nature of the ambiguity may involve or entail the invalidity of the argument in question. In such cases, it is also misleading to say that the fallacy is "informal," and for the same reasons. Some question may arise about why the name was used in the first place, and the answer is fairly clear. Formal fallacies are those which may be defined without reference to the *content* of an argument. As we saw in the first chapter, it is possible to define the conditions under which an argument is valid or invalid strictly by referring to its formal structure. An invalid argument is one whose form is such that there is at least one possible substitution instance of it where the premises can be true and the conclusion false. Such a definition presupposes the clarity of the meaning of the statements in the argument of course, and purely logical evaluations of arguments therefore make no reference to content, meaning, and truth conditions. By far the greater percentage of problems in philosophy, however, rests upon misunderstandings of meaning, definition, and conceptual clarity than upon confusions over logical form. Attempts to solve such problems usually begin with an effort to clarify the content of statements. It is because of this that these fallacies are called "informal."

Fallacies of Relevance

Among the most common examples of fallacies of relevance are *petitio principii* or *begging the question,* the *ad hominem argument,* and the fallacy of *hasty generalization.* Strictly speaking, only the last two are fallacies of relevance, that is, fallacies where the relevance of the premises to the conclusion or conclusions is questioned. In the case of the first fallacy, there is no doubt of the relevance of the premises to the conclusion because the premises *contain* the conclusion. Suppose for example that someone was to argue, as people often do, that God exists because the Bible tells us so, and that we can trust the authenticity of the Bible because the men who wrote it were divinely inspired. Presumably the very *purpose* of this argument is to prove that "God exists" is true, on the grounds of certain evidence, namely that the statement is enunciated in the Bible. Of course, the Bible must be correct, and the grounds given for its authority are that it is divinely inspired, that is, that God inspired its writers. Now to inspire these writers, presumably God has to exist—or *had* to exist, a possibility the argument does not consider—and hence the question is begged. Not all instances of begging the question are so blatant, and it often takes a considerable amount of work to uncover the unjust assumption.

Ad hominem arguments are more common in everyday life than they are in technical philosophy, but since what you learn here ought to be applicable in many other areas, we shall discuss them briefly. In essence, they consist in attacking a person rather than what he says, or in appealing to someone to accept the truth of a proposition not on the basis of the evidence for it, but on the basis of your own beliefs, even if ill-founded. If someone were to argue against the proposition that fluoridation is good for the teeth on the grounds that the Russians advocate it, he would be committing this mistake, as you would be if you were to argue that alcohol should be outlawed because some group of which you are a member says so. It may be true that fluoridation is bad for the teeth or that alcohol should be outlawed, but, if these propositions *are* true, they are not true either because the Russians advocate the one or your group the other.

Hasty generalization means exactly what it says. If you argue that a general statement is true on the basis of an insufficient number of particular instances which seem to verify it, you are committing this mistake. A generalization such as this may be disproven by offering a counter-example to it. If, for example, one were to argue that all mongrel dogs are stupid, untrustworthy, and ugly on the grounds that the mongrels in the local pound meet these criteria, you could show that this was a mistake simply by coming up with a smart, faithful and attractive pet. Hasty generalization often seems to occur in the polling occupation as well as in the profession of politics.

Although these three fallacies seem to be more common than any others, there are still many more which should be mentioned here. The argument from *ignorance* or *argumentum ad ignoratiam* claims that because no one has proven a statement to be true, it must be false. The argument from *authority* or *argumentum ad verecundiam* involves an appeal either directly to some person claiming to be an authority, or whom others think to be an authority, in order to support the claim that a statement is true. There is always the possibility, of course, that he is wrong. The argument from *appeal to the people* or *argumentum ad populum* is an attempt to attain assent to something by playing upon the feelings and/or convictions of large numbers of the population. Almost all modern advertising illustrates this fallacy. Modern advertising, or its results, also illustrates how *effective* such mistaken justifications can be. The *appeal to force* or *argumentum ad baculum* involves the mistaken assumption that might makes right. Those who claim that justice is identical with the law, or that moral right and legal right are identical often commit this fallacy. The fallacy of *False Cause* or *post hoc ergo propter hoc* is very common. This fallacy consists in concluding that one thing is the cause of another on the grounds that the one thing came before the other. A common counter-example points out that if this were so, pain must be the cause of childbirth, since it comes before childbirth. The fallacy of *accident* is also common. It consists in applying a general rule to a specific case when particular circumstances have rendered the rule inapplicable. One ought to repay one's debts, but if you have borrowed a gun from a friend who has since gone mad, and the particular form of his insanity is manifested in a peculiar compulsion to kill you, it would be unwise to follow this rule in this case.

Fallacies of Ambiguity

Fallacies of *ambiguity* are just what the name implies. They arise when a word or a sentence is ambiguous, that is, may be interpreted in more than one way in an argument. One kind of ambiguity is *equivocation*, which was mentioned briefly in the first chapter in the context of an example from George Berkeley which involved an ambiguity over the word "perceived." A special sort of equivocation, which may be exhibited in Berkeley's argument, concerns the use of relative terms. If I were to say that my friend Al is large, and the planet Pluto is also large, the word "large" would not mean the same thing in both cases.

When the ambiguity arises within the framework of whole sentences rather than with individual terms, the fallacy is called *amphiboly*. Amphiboly comes about as the result of the structure of a sentence rather than because of the meanings of the terms used. A frivolous example from the world of sly wits is "Bachelors have no children to speak of," though the grammar is not exactly Churchillian.

Two other fallacies—not, strictly speaking, informal ones because they are often the cause of invalid arguments—are the fallacies of *composition* and *division*. Each of these fallacies has two species. The first species of the fallacy of composition consists in arguing that because something is true of the parts of a whole, it is therefore true of the whole itself. If I were to argue that because none of the blocks in the Empire State building is particularly heavy, it follows that the whole building is not very heavy, I would be making this mistake. The second sort of fallacy of composition argues that because a given statement or set of statements is true of a group *distributively*, it is also true of them *collectively*. When one says that a class of things has a given property or properties distributively, he means that each and every member of the class has the property or properties. When a sort of object has a property or properties collectively, however, this does not preclude the possibility that several members of the class do *not* have the property or properties. For example, if I claim that the faculty at Harvard is brainy, this does not preclude the presence of a tenured blockhead, or even two of them.

The difference between the two sorts of fallacy of composition is this: in the first case, the whole of which we are speaking (in this case the Empire State building) is an organized planned whole. But in the second sort of fallacy of composition, we are speaking of a mere collection of entities, such as the human race, or the faculty of Harvard.

If you know what the two sorts of fallacy of composition are, then the two sorts of the fallacy of *division* are easily explained. The two fallacies of division are the converse of the two fallacies of composition: the first fallacy argues from the properties of an organized, planned whole to the conclusion that the parts have the same properties, and the second fallacy argues that what is true of a group of entities collectively is also true of them distributively.

The fallacy of *accent* is a fallacy of ambiguity arising from the way in which a key word is accented in the writing or pronunciation of a sentence. If your professor tells you "This is a *good* paper!" when you have received a "D," you may have cause to suspect that the word "good" has something other than its normal connotation; and if a conservative political figure says in a speech that students who are pressing for voting participation in faculty committees ". . . are working toward a *revolution*" there may be some question in your mind about what he means by "revolution." The fallacy of *complex question* arises when a question cannot be answered by a simple "yes" or "no" without implying one or the other of these answers to still another question. If the police ask the suspect "Where did you hide the body of your victim?" and the suspect says "By the river bank," he implies not only that he knows where the body is but also that he killed the person, which he may not wish to be known. When the inquisitive neighbor asks if your divorce proceedings have begun yet, you tell him more than you know if you say either "yes" or "no."

Three fallacies, which appear to be formal ones though often grouped with the informal fallacies, are the fallacy of *four terms,* the fallacy of *affirming the consequent,* and the fallacy of *denying the antecedent.* The fallacy of four terms is associated with arguments of the syllogistic form and occurs when four or more terms are used in that sort of argument. The example of equivocation from George Berkeley which involved two meanings of the word "perceives" is also an example of this fallacy. Affirming the consequent occurs when one argues in this way: "If John is a putative father, then Mary is having a baby. Mary is having a baby, so John is a putative father." Poor John—George may be the cause, you know. Denying the antecedent is similar to affirming the consequent: "If John is a putative father, then Mary is having a baby. John is not a putative father, so Mary is not having a baby." Again, no one seems to have noticed George.

Philosophical Fallacies

Three fallacies often called "philosophical" fallacies, because they depend upon an adherence to a given position or positions in various areas of philosophy, are the *naturalistic* or *factualistic* fallacy (the two names mean approximately the same thing), the *category-mistake*, and the *pathetic* fallacy. G. E. Moore is generally given the credit for inventing the name "naturalistic fallacy," which presumably consists in arguing from factual premises to normative conclusions. For example, "This act contributes to the greatest happiness of the greatest number, therefore this act is right" presumably commits this fallacy, since whether an act contributes to the general happiness or not is a factual question, whereas whether an act is right or not is presumably a normative judgment. I say "presumably" because there are those, such as W. K. Frankena and John Searles, who would argue that the naturalistic fallacy is not a mistake at all.

Gilbert Ryle is the inventor of the category-mistake, which consists in a certain sort of equivocation. When one argues about one set of events in terms which are only appropriately used in conjunction with another sort of event, one *may* commit this mistake. The actual commission of the fallacy depends upon whether one's *beliefs* are trapped by the misuse of language in this way. Hence, we often say that physical events are causally related to other physical events, and in the same breath, that minds are also causally related to physical events, or at least that mental events are so related. It seems clear that if there are mental events, they are of a different sort of entity than physical events, and that if they are related to physical events, they do not stand in the same sort of relation to them as other physical events do. Hence, the word "cause" does not have the same sort of purport or connotation in the one case as in the other, and if our notion of causality is derived mainly from one rather than the other type of event, we are technically misusing the concept if we apply it without discriminating between the senses to both kinds of events. If this indiscriminate use of the term leads to the mistaken belief that there is really only one sense of "cause" involved, a category-mistake has been made.

Ruskin is the man who gave the name to the *pathetic* fallacy, and his example of it was "finding sadness in the eyes of the ruminating cow."

There is, of course, no *prima facie* reason to think that cows suffer the human emotion of sadness, though future evidence might show that in fact they do. This unthinking attribution of human emotions, thoughts, feelings, and other characteristics to non-human things is the essence of the pathetic fallacy. Anti-vivisectionists, English women, and the writers of children's books seem especially prone to this mistake.

Finally, there are four common mistakes which result from an ignorance of what constitutes formal deductive validity, and which are really themselves invalid arguments about other arguments, whether valid or invalid. They have no traditional names, and we shall give them none, since you now understand the notion of formal validity and will see them for the simple mistakes that they are. The first consists in arguing that because the conclusion of an argument is true, the premises must be true. The second involves the claim that because some or all of the premises of an argument are false, the conclusion must be false as well. The third is the converse of the second, that because the conclusion is false, the premises must be false. The fourth says that because a given argument is invalid, the conclusion must be false. These four mistakes are the foundation of successful propaganda.

The importance of the informal fallacies is difficult to overemphasize. Time and again philosophers have discovered that some traditional philosophical problem turns out not to be a problem at all, and that the only reason it was thought to be one is that confusions over the meanings of words in the premises of arguments have been perpetuated or overlooked. Some versions of the mind-body problem, and some versions of determinism are but two examples. Speaking more broadly, we shall see that a standard approach in the opening efforts to solve a philosophical problem is the attempt to make the meanings of terms in sentences and arguments so precise that there is little if any question of a misunderstanding. The effort at conceptual analysis and clarification is a *sine qua non* for the doing of adequate philosophy. Very often the result is the discovery that previous efforts directed at the same problem have committed informal fallacies, category-mistakes, hasty generalizations, begged the question in hidden ways, and so forth. In fact, the lack of precision in meaning, which conceptual analysis is designed to overcome, is at the foundation of almost all of the mistaken theories which we shall consider.

So far, we have been concerned primarily with deductive rather than inductive arguments, when we have been talking about arguments. Before proceeding to the study of some actual theories and an attempt to criticize them, it is necessary to consider induction, analogy, and the manner in which one ought to compare two or more competing theories about the same subject-matter. These are the topics of the next chapter.

EXERCISES

1. Why are definitions important in arguments?

2. Find three stipulative definitions from science.

3. Are all dictionary definitions such that they give synonyms for the listed words? What other sorts of definition do you find in your dictionary?

4. Are some dictionary definitions *both* reportive or lexical, and dictionary definitions? Are both reportive and dictionary definitions either true or false?

5. Might the meaning of a stipulative definition be conveyed by ostensive definition? Why or why not?

6. Describe the denoting and designating functions of two definitions not used in the text. Why is it important to distinguish between these two functions?

7. Are stipulative definitions true? What is the difference between the kind of truth a stipulative definition has, if it is true, and a reportive or lexical definition's truth?

8. According to the *per genus et differentiam* theory of definition, what are the essential characteristics of a dog? How would you define a dachshund according to this theory?

9. Compose a valid deductive argument containing nothing but definitions.

10. If an argument was composed of nothing but stipulative definitions, and one of them was false, would the argument be consistent or inconsistent? Why?

11. By examples, illustrate five different senses of the word "mean."

12. Think of five different sentences whose meaning may be plausibly analyzed according to the ideational theory of meaning.

13. Think of five uses of language which are not amenable to treatment by the ideational theory.

14. Give five examples of words with more than one image associated with them.

15. Give five examples of sentences which are clearly meaningful, but which do not refer to anything.

16. Why is it not possible for the referential theory of meaning to account for the meanings of false sentences?

17. Analyze the meaning of the sentence "Patriotic Americans are the only true Americans" as you think a behavioral theorist would. Does it have one meaning? Many? An indefinitely large number of meanings? Different meanings at one and the same time? Defend your answers.

18. William James once got involved in an argument concerning the following incident: He was in a hunting party, and during the talk the case was brought up of a squirrel on a tree and a man on the opposite tree trunk. The man moves around the tree, but he never gets to see the squirrel because it always keeps the tree between it and the man. The question is: Does the man move around the squirrel or the squirrel around the man? James was asked to settle the quarrel. Given the pragmatic theory of truth and meaning, what do you think the answer was?

19. Is there a single contextualist theory of meaning? Why or why not?

20. Give five examples of utterances which are analyzable into locutionary, illocutionary and perlocutionary acts.

21. Suppose the coherence theory of truth is adequate. Could anyone, practically speaking, ever know that any sentence was true? Why or why not?

22. Why is any given statement only *partially* true if the coherence theory and the doctrine of internal relations are true?

23. Do you think that it is possible for a set of sentences to cohere with one another if all of them are false? Why or why not?

24. How would you argue that coherence is not a test for truth? Use examples in your answer.

25. Outline Russell's version of the correspondence theory of truth in your own words.

26. Think of three examples of sentences that are not analytic but true, yet correspond to nothing.

27. If Strawson is correct, is it incompatible with his theory to say that, even though we might be supporting or confirming when we say that a sentence is true, there is *in addition* a relation between a belief and fact or set of facts by virtue of which at least some sentences are true? That is, might some version of the correspondence theory be good for at least some sentences, even if, at the same time, the performative theory is also true of them? Defend your answer.

28. Give some examples (at least three) of grammatical predicates in sentences which do not predicate properties of anything.

29. How, if at all, is Wittgenstein's theory of "language games" related to Strawson's analysis?

30. Discuss the affinities between Strawson's and Austin's views.

31. What is a fallacy of relevance? Of ambiguity?

32. What is the difference between a formal and an informal fallacy? Are some fallacies of relevance also formal fallacies? Why or why not?

33. Define begging the question, hasty generalization, and the ad hominem argument.

34. Why are arguments that beg the question always valid? Need they also be sound?

35. Give examples taken from the news media of the fallacies of authority, ignorance, appeal to the people, and accident.

36. Though it was not named in the text, there is a fallacy called "converse accident." Look again at the fallacy of accident, and then say what you think the fallacy of converse accident is. Is it given in the text under another name?

37. Compose an argument in which at least two fallacies of equivocation occur.

38. Compose two arguments in which the fallacies of composition and division are illustrated.

39. Have you made a category-mistake if you use a word out of its appropriate context but are perfectly aware that you have done this?

40. The section includes a specification of four fallacies which have no names and which are really arguments about other arguments. Compose four arguments which illustrate these mistakes.

3

Induction and
Counter-Examples

But for minor details, almost all philosophers and logicians are agreed upon the essential structure and significance of deductive logic. The state of inductive logic in its philosophical sense is indicated by the fact that very many philosophers do not think that there is any such thing! That is, they do not think that induction provides any justification for conclusions supposedly drawn from such foundations. At the outset, we should note three things. First, we are *not* here concerned with mathematical induction, or, as it is sometimes called, proof by recursion; rather we are concerned with philosophical induction—what it is, and how it presumably justifies its own conclusions. Secondly, we shall not discuss the arguments against the viability of inductive argumentation, except insofar as certain criticisms of John Stuart Mill's Methods of Agreement and Difference are concerned. Third, the question of the role or roles that probability in its mathematical sense plays in inductive reasoning will not be examined, both because of the complexity of the issues involved, and because the theory of mathematical probability presupposes in its application the general soundness of the sorts of inductive argument with which we are here concerned.

Inductive Argument

There are two fundamental sorts of inductive argument which we shall study, both of which have at least this much in common: neither kind is such that its premises entail its conclusion; that is, in both sorts of argument, it is always logically possible that the premises are true but the conclusion false, and therefore the denial of such arguments is never a contradiction. The first sort of argument we shall call *induction proper,* and it is illustrated by John Stuart Mill's celebrated methods.[1] Then we shall discuss arguments from *analogy.* Hence, induction proper and arguments from analogy are two species or kinds belonging to the genus or class "inductive arguments."

Suppose that John Jones seems to have the remarkable ability to cause lightning to strike simply by lighting his cigarette. This would certainly seem almost counter-intuitive, not to say in opposition to most of our scientific beliefs, but a set of circumstances is certainly possible in which people would *believe* that Jones had this ability. These circumstances are remarkably easy to describe. If, every time Jones lit a cigarette, lightning struck immediately thereafter in his proximity, it would be very unlikely that anyone who was aware of these facts would stand close to Jones when he was about to light up. The conclusion "Jones can make lightning strike by lighting his cigarette" would be warranted, justified, indicated, etc. by the evidence for it, namely, that at times T, T^1, T^2, T^3, . . . T^n, when Jones lit up, lightning struck. Now it is possible, though not likely, that some cynical soul would want to maintain, no matter how many times this happened, that it was a coincidence, his justification being that events such as Jones's lighting his cigarette are not the kinds of events that are causally related to bolts of lightning. If Jones then lit his cigarette, and nothing happened, our cynic would be proven correct.

The kind of induction we are here discussing is known as induction by simple enumeration, and the fanciful example illustrates two things traditionally thought to be wrong with it. The first is that this sort of enumeration does not enable us to distinguish between events which are causally related to another event or events, and those which merely accompany one another. The second fault is that simple enumeration does not allow for the *possibility* of any disconfirming instance, because such an instance is one in which either the cause occurs but not the effect, or vice versa, whereas in the sort of argument we are considering, the evidence for the conclusion is always a report of events in which both cause and effect always occur. Hence, for the conclusion "Jones causes lightning to strike by lighting his cigarette," the evidence is always "At time T Jones lit up and lightning struck," "At time T^1, Jones lit up . . . ," and so on. Now if this is true, there is no way in which simple enumeration as a method of inductive argumentation can be tested, or, perhaps more accurately, there is no way by which we can,

---

[1] John Stuart Mill, *A System of Logic* (London: Longmans, Green and Co., 1875).

within its framework, test the causal law or laws which are suggested by its conclusions.

Mill's Methods of Inductive Argumentation

Sir Francis Bacon, English scientist, philosopher and stateman, saw these difficulties, and he proposed a different sort of method for inductive argumentation, which embodied the comparison of various instances of the event in question, a study of variations occurring in the test cases, and a method for excluding or including counter-examples according to their relevance, among other things. John Stuart Mill developed and expanded Bacon's theses, and Mill's methods are the result. There are five methods: the Method of Agreement, the Method of Difference, the Joint Method of Agreement and Difference, the Method of Residues, and the Method of Concomitant Variation.

The Method of Agreement. The supposition of this method is that in any group of instances of events having an identical effect, the cause may be isolated from among the antecedents of the effect by ascertaining which of the antecedents occurs in all of the instances. For example, if we have five auto accidents, each of them occurring in circumstances that resemble each other in some respects, but such that only in *one* respect do they *all* resemble one another, Mill would conclude that this one respect was the cause, or the effect, or the clue to the cause, or to the effect of all the accidents. It might, for example again, be the fact that all five drivers had been drinking before the accident, given that in all cases only one car was involved.

The Method of Difference. The first method does not always work, because of course there may be *more* than one common antecedent in all of the cases. The Method of Difference attempts to account for this. Suppose that in our five accidents, both drinking and a very recent rotation of the tires were common to all five. It might be that we then could not determine without further examination which of the two antecedents was the cause, or a necessary condition for the occurrence of the accident. But imagine that we now find a sixth person who was driving that day, such that all of the factors in the other accidents were also true of him, except that he was not drinking and did *not* have an accident. From this we could conclude, Mill would say, that the rotation of the tires was *not* the cause of the accident.

The Joint Method of Agreement and Difference. This method is simply the combined use of the first two methods. Doing both, we would conclude that the rotation of the tires was not the cause of the accidents, and that the drinking was. Since in any *future* cases of this sort we could presumably assign some quantitative probability-value both to the prediction that tire-rotation will not be the cause of the accident, and to the prediction that drinking will be, the combined methods should yield a conclusion with a probability still higher than the individual conclusions of the two methods taken separately.

The Method of Residues. The difference between this method and the first two rests upon the fact that it presumes a knowledge of the causal relations among some of the antecedent factors or circumstances and their effects. Knowing this, we may isolate the cause of the effect we are considering by a process of elimination. Suppose that the antecedents are composed of A, B, and C, and the consequents are a, b, and c. If we know that A is the cause of a, and B the cause of b, then by the Method of Residues, we conclude that C is the cause of c. Some have held that the Method of Residues is deductive rather than inductive, but this seems to be a mistake, because the position assumes two premises not stated in the method: (1) that all causes and effects have been exhaustively enumerated, and (2) that one of the antecedents *must* be the cause of the relevant effect.

The Method of Concomitant Variation. The first four methods depend upon our ability to eliminate various factors as causally relevant. Clearly, there are cases in which it is not possible to eliminate all of the antecedent circumstances which are not causes, and in such cases the first four methods will not do the job. This is where the Method of Concomitant Variation comes in. Essentially, like the other four methods, it is very simple. Suppose that we use Mill's own example, which concerns the attempt to discover the causal relation between the tides and the moon. The fixed stars are of course also present as antecedent circumstances, and cannot be eliminated. How then to decide whether the stars or the moon are the relevant factor? Mill tells us that if we notice that the tides vary with the position of the moon in a uniform manner, then even though we cannot eliminate the stars, nor remove the moon for purposes of experimentation, we will have the answer, for the corresponding variations are not present in the other antecedent phenomena. This method is perhaps more widely used than any other. It is present in almost all "trial and error" experiments, and inherent in our very learning processes. If, for example, your car begins to chug whenever it gets both hot and humid, but chugs still more if the humidity gets higher while the temperature remains the same, and less if the humidity lowers while the temperature still remains the same, you would be wise to assume that the chugging has something to do with the humidity.

These, then, are Mill's methods. There are a few things we should note about them. First, they never prove their conclusions certainly— only probably. And the attempt to specify just *how* probable they are is the problem of probability theory. Secondly, the methods do not specify a procedure by which we can separate *relevant* from non-relevant circumstances, and their fruitful use requires that we already have this knowledge. Hence, the methods do not seem to be very good tools of discovery, if by that we mean discovery of relevant connections. The usual example that demonstrates this involves the Method of Agreement, and concerns the reform-minded drunkard who, interested in discovering the cause of his debility in order to conquer it, consumed on successive days to the point of utter intoxication bourbon and water, scotch and water, rye and water, brandy and water, and gin and water. After applying the Method of Agreement, he swore off water.

We may safely say then, that using Mill's methods presupposes some knowledge of causal connections, which raises many problems of a peculiar sort. But the methods *do* have value, provided they are used in conjunction with the assumption that the circumstances being considered *are* the (causally) relevant ones. In fact, an excellent case may be made for the thesis that when they are so used, they constitute a large part of the method of experimental science. For do we not, in a controlled experiment, attempt to isolate the circumstances we think relevant, and then alter the environmental conditions of these circumstances in order to cause isolation or elimination of some factors, and concomitant variations in others? And do we not conclude that those factors are causative which are isolated, eliminated, or varied, in just the way that Mill enjoins? True, we never achieve *proof* of the deductively certain sort even here, but we *do* achieve workable hypotheses, which through further confirmation attain a probability approaching one. The important point to remember is that Mill's methods are not by themselves *sufficient* for the discovery of causal laws, though they are an invaluable tool for investigation, and an admirable methodology for testing hypotheses.

LOGICAL ANALOGY AND
THE COUNTER-EXAMPLE TECHNIQUE

In the discussion of Mill's methods, it was mentioned that their fruitful application depends upon our ability to distinguish relevant from non-relevant circumstances. This is also true, and even more important, in the case of arguments from analogy. But arguments from analogy are not the only sort of argument to be discussed here: the term *"logical analogy"* is actually the name for a *method* of arguing, rather than a name for a sort of argument. So we shall first talk about arguments from analogy and then about the technique of arguing by the method of logical analogy as it applies in the giving of counter-examples.

The Nature of Arguments from Analogy

Arguments from analogy depend, at bottom, upon the notions of comparison and proportion. As with the case of the kind of inductive procedure Mill was discussing, so in the case of analogy as well, there are many who doubt the viability of the justification. Mill was predominantly concerned with discovering the *causes* of events, or the effects, for his methods are also amenable to this purpose. Arguments from analogy are often used for these purposes, but they also have a much broader application, because they may be used to establish *any* similarity between two or more cases that resemble each other in relevant respects. Essentially, all such arguments have a form which might be presented schematically as follows:

1. A, B, C, D all have properties a, b.
2. A, B, C all have the property c.
3. Therefore, D has the property c.

This is the sort of reasoning you use when you conclude that since Monday, Tuesday, and Wednesday were characterized by the surliness of your professor and a test, Thursday will be no exception so far as the test is concerned, because he's surly again. If the last n number of times you mixed your drinks at night, you experienced excruciating pain the next morning, and you are mixing your drinks tonight, you may well conclude by analogy that you are in for it in the morning. If I have purchased four cars of type X from dealer Y, all of which were lemons, I would be wise to shop elsewhere. Of course, your professor may have a good day, you may be bright-eyed and bushy-tailed in the morning, and my new car of type X from dealer Y may be the greatest thing on wheels—but these things are not very likely.

Now in all these examples of analogy, certain factors become obvious upon a little examination. They all concern just *how* probable the conclusion should be taken to be and the reasons for this. Suppose, for example, that you have mixed your drinks very many times but that your hangover the following morning has been noteworthy only a few times; suppose that the times you did have a miserable headache after mixing your drinks only occurred after mixing vodka and brandy but not after mixing any two other kinds of spirits; suppose that, of the times you have mixed these two kinds of liquor and had the resultant discomfort, only one or two times have been *really* agonizing; suppose that on the previous occasions of relevant mixing, you imbibed at least six drinks, whereas this time, because of the brilliant conversation and the excellent cuisine, you only took two; or suppose that all other nights preceding these infamous mornings-after were *dis*similar in all respects save that you mixed these two drinks and were quite ill the next day. All of these factors, the number of resembling instances, the number of ways in which they resemble one another, the strength of the conclusion based upon what is given in the premises, the relevant dissimilarities and their role *vis à vis* the conclusion, the significance of a *single* resemblance or similarity happening again and again in differing circumstances—all of these factors together determine whether an analogy is good or bad, strong or weak. For example, as we shall see later on, there is an argument for the existence of God known as the *teleological* argument or the argument from design. It rests upon the comparison between the evident design of human products plus the consequent conclusion that they have designers and the supposed presence of design in the entire universe together with the desired conclusion that *it* must have a Designer. But if there are more *dis*similarities between, say, a watch and the universe, than similarities, if there are no repeated instances to consider (there is, after all, only one universe of which we are aware), and so on, we would question the strength of this analogy.

Much of the difficulty with some analogical arguments results from the expansion of the mode of argumentation since it was originally conceived. Euclid conceived analogy to consist in a similarity of proportions; for example, $(2:6) :: (3:9)$ is an analogy. In this view, analogy is a purely quantitative notion. But later on, especially in the age of the scholastics, the idea was extended to include qualitative similarities. Heads of states were analogically styled "pilots" because of the comparison with the captain of a ship; as sight stands to the eyes, so insight was thought to stand to the intellect (the very word "insight" is revealing); as one physical cause stands to its effect, so God is thought to stand to the first material cause; and so on. Furthermore, in addition to the confusion that these factors raise, we are still left with the problem of how it is that we discover the causal connections and the similarities upon which both analogy and Mill's methods are founded in the first place. The analysis of what a cause is, and the analysis of the relation of similarity, are perhaps the two oldest problems in philosophy.

Counter-Examples

Logical analogy also involves comparison. Suppose one were to argue as follows:

1. If it rains, then the streets get wet.
2. The streets are wet.
3. So, it must have rained.

To such an argument one might reply that if the proponent wants to hold this argument, then he must hold this one too, because they both have the same form:

1. If Sam shoots at George, then George will be dead.
2. George is dead.
3. So, Sam shot him.

Now clearly, Sam might object to this on the grounds that George died of a heart attack while Sam was a thousand miles away. The point is of course that both of these arguments have the same *form*, so if one of them is invalid, the other must be. The second argument is invalid, so the first one is too. By drawing an *analogy* between the two arguments, based upon the common form they have, one is able to point out the original argument is not a good one. This type of logical analogy is one way to give *counter-example*. It is not the only way, nor, strictly speaking, does this procedure accord with the ordinary meaning of "counter-example." Normally, "counter-example" connotes the presentation of an exception to a rule, or the giving of an instance which ought to be explicable by some law of science but is not, or the discovery of something which does not have a property attributed to it by some supposedly true general statement. Nonetheless, because it *is* a method of countering an argument by presenting an example which would not be acceptable to one's opponent but which is such that he must hold it if he retains his original position, we shall consider it as part of the counter-example technique.

Another method of presenting counter-examples consists in giving an interpretation of some argument such that the interpretation renders it invalid, that is, such that its premises are true but its conclusion false. Like the method of logical analogy, the aim of this method is to show that the argument in question is invalid. For example:

1. All Christians are forbidden entry to the Kabba in Mecca.
2. Albert is forbidden entry to the Kabba in Mecca.
3. Therefore, Albert is a Christian.

In this argument, the conclusion does not follow from the premises. To demonstrate this, you could of course simply do a truth table after rendering the argument in symbols. But it is sometimes just as easy, and even more illustrative, to point out that in this case, Albert is an atheist, that atheists are also forbidden entry to the Kabba, and hence that premises one and two might be true, while the conclusion does not follow. It will do no good for your opponent to insist that this counter-example is unacceptable on grounds that Albert *is*, in fact, a Christian and not an atheist, because the nice thing about this kind of counter-example is that it need only be *possible*. This is due to the nature of the definition of an invalid argument, which, you will recall, stipulates that an argument is invalid if there is at least one substitution instance of its form such that the premises are true but the conclusion false. So long as the substitution instance contains nothing but sentences which may be true or false (and of course there is a possible universe in which Albert is an atheist), this is all that is required. You may therefore, as it were, "think up" counter-examples.

You may be puzzled over the inclusion of this discussion in a chapter that deals chiefly with induction, for the last few arguments have been deductive in form. The reason it has been placed here is that the technique of logical analogy and counter-example can be used in connection with *both* deductive and inductive arguments. In the case of deductive arguments, the counter-example proves the argument invalid, or sometimes merely unsound. It shows it to be unsound if it points out the falsity of one of the premises, or more than one, or the falsity of one or more premise and the conclusion. In the case of inductive arguments, the technique points out the *weakness* of the proposed analogy, or inductive argument. In both cases, the central point is the *comparison* of one argument *thought* to be valid, sound, and/or strong, and another *known* to be invalid, unsound, or weak. What determines the acceptability of the counter-example is, in the case of deductive arguments, whether the counter-example fits the form of the proposed argument, and whether it is a possible counter-example. In inductive arguments, analogical or otherwise, what counts is the strength of the counter-example relative to the proposed argument, as measured by the factors set out in the discussions of analogical argument and Mill's methods. If the strength of the counter-example is at least equal to that of the proposed argument, what you have done in effect is to demonstrate that the proposed argument is no stronger than the counter-example.

In the ordinary connotation of the word "counter-example," the sense is rather that of "exception to the rule" than what we have been discussing here. This "ordinary" sense is, as has been mentioned, quite important. Suppose, for example, that as of midnight tonight it happened that whenever bricks made of red clay were thrown out of windows, they "fell" *up* rather than down. It is difficult for us even to imagine such a situation, but there is nothing logically impossible about it. First, we should no doubt want to examine the bricks minutely; but, if they proved upon careful study to be perfectly normal bricks and if a considerable period of time passed in which they still fell up rather than down, then we should have to revise the laws of gravity, because they would not account for such a phenomenon. Such examples are far-fetched, but they do illustrate the point of counter-examples of the "exception-to-the-rule" type. A less unlikely example might be this: suppose that a scientist suggested that cigarette smoking is the cause of lung cancer. There seems no doubt that it is *a* cause, but the question is whether it is *the* cause. To disprove this general claim, it would be sufficient to discover one unfortunate who suffered from this awful malady and was a non-smoker. Sadly, such examples are easy to come by.

THE EXTERNAL CRITERIA

As of now, we have several methods for evaluating arguments when considered by themselves. We know how to tell whether they are valid or invalid, sound or unsound, strong or weak, good or bad. Naturally, there are arguments about different kinds of subjects and issues and arguments which contain different kinds of propositions. Some of these propositions are *empirical*, that is, they are either true or false, and which of these they are depends upon a relation or relations in which they stand to physical fact or sensible experience. They may accordingly be confirmed or disconfirmed by appeal to such fact or experience. Other propositions are *analytic* or *a priori*. *Analytic* propositions are tautologies, which are always true by virtue of the relation of their terms alone. *A priori* propositions are those which may be known to be true independently of any confirming experience, and hence they include all analytic propositions. Some philosophers have held that there are, in addition, other kinds of *a priori* propositions called *synthetic a priori* propositions, which are not tautologies but which are nonetheless necessarily true. At the moment, however, we may concentrate on the other two kinds, plus certain others to be introduced in a moment.

Now a *theory* is a series of arguments, deductive, inductive, or both; and if arguments can be evaluated, then so can theories. Theories must meet all of the criteria we have discussed to date. But even if they do this, we may still not be able to judge them comparatively; that is, we may not be able to decide which of two theories is the better one, without additional criteria. Making such evaluations is the goal of the use of the *external criteria*. Before discussing these we must spend some moments looking again at the subjects of truth and meaning. Not all theories are testable by all of the external criteria, since some theories are empirical while others are not. Those theories which are empirical we shall call "scientific" theories; those theories which are not empirical, and are not intended to be so, will be called "metaphysical," including for the moment in this category all moral systems.

It was mentioned before that propositions must be meaningful to be either true or false but that the converse did not seem to be the case, or at least, many philosophers do not think that the converse is the case. There are, as we know, a number of different meanings of "meaning." If you ask someone "What do you mean?" you could be asking for an explanation of his purpose or intention, that is, you could be asking what he intends to *do*. But the same question might be a request for him to identify an object, person or state of affairs to which he intends to refer. He might, for example, say "chien," and when you ask your question, he might point to a dog and say "That's what I mean." Again, you might be asking him for a definition, or you might be asking for an explanation of something, in causal or other terms. You might even receive in reply some expression of anger, love, chagrin, worry, and so on; or his reply, not itself an expression of his emotions, might arouse these or other emotions in you. It is clearly not easy to keep all these different possibilities separate from each other; and therefore, it is equally clear that the kinds of meaning are not easily, or, in some cases, even possibly classifiable. They often merge, as when the description of a loved one arouses great emotion, or when the intention of someone *is* to refer to a given thing. In spite of this obvious fact, attempts have been made to define different kinds of meaning, and the two broadest categories are usually given as *cognitive* and *emotive* meaning.

Cognitive and Emotive Meaning

Cognitive meaning is closely associated with the *content* of certain kinds of propositions, whereas emotive meaning is more closely concerned with certain of their *functions*. Cognitive propositions are either true or false, that is, they assert something about some fact or state of affairs, and, if true, they are often said to be true by virtue of a "correspondence" between the proposition and the relevant fact or state of affairs. If there is no such correspondence, cognitive propositions are false. The truth or falsity of cognitive propositions should be distinguished from *logical* truth or falsity, because the latter has nothing to do with the content of propositions: a proposition is logically true if it is a tautology, false if it is a contradiction.

Propositions with emotive meaning *may* also have cognitive meaning; that is, they may be true or false in the same way as are cognitively meaningful propositions. For example, "Your wife was out with your boss last night" may be such a proposition. On the other hand, such utterances as "Long live the Queen!" are neither true nor false in the way that cognitive sentences are. Emotive propositions may be primarily expressive of the speaker's mental states, or they may attain emotive meaning primarily by arousing in the hearer a range of emotions; or, of course, both elements may be involved. Those propositions which have no cognitive meaning and which do have emotive meaning we shall call "merely emotive" propositions.

Metaphysical propositions are not notably emotive; but, on the other hand, they do not refer to physical events or states of affairs in their normal employment, though they may be explanatory of them. They are nevertheless thought by those who propose them to be either true or false. The concept of *primary substance* in Greek philosophy, or propositions concerning it, provides a good example. The concept of such a substance was used (indeed, still is) to explain the continuity of the real world, and of individuals in it, while at the same time allowing for the changes that take place in that world. A man is said to be the "same" man at 70 as he was at 20, but none of the particles composing his body are the same, he may have lost his hair, and so on. What remains the same then is presumably his "substance." Now this substance is not a possible object of perception, nor is it in principle subject to any sort of direct or indirect testing or investigation. It is an "explanatory entity," invented, if you will, for the purpose of "hanging the world together."

It is difficult to see how such propositions as those concerning substance can be either true or false by any sort of relation of correspondence, if a necessary condition of knowing that such sentences are true is being able in some way to verify the correspondence. On the other hand, these sentences seem to have no emotive significance, except perhaps in the cases of those philosophers whose livelihood depends upon convincing others to believe in such entities. This issue is raised to point out once more the perilous difficulties associated with questions of meaning and truth and also to emphasize three important facts about theories: (1) not all theories contain only propositions that are either true or false on some correspondence model; (2) the most likely theoretical candidates for testing, confirmation, or verification by empirical or scientific means are those which *do* contain propositions true or false on such a model; (3) theories not containing such propositions, and not intended to do so, may still be evaluated by reference to other criteria. We shall be dealing with both kinds of theory in the discussion that follows, and one of the matters that we shall have to decide is whether the theories at issue *ought* to be testable by all or only some of the external criteria.

Criteria for Evaluating Theories

A theory is an explanation. To be a good one, it must meet the conditions so far explicated, plus certain others. Some of these "others" are related to criteria we already know. For example, the description of the phenomenon that is being explained must be logically deducible from the statements which purport to be the explanation. In this way the explanation is shown to be *relevant* to what is explained. The explanatory premises must also be *true;* though, as we have seen, this raises many problems depending upon the sort of theory with which we are dealing. The explanation must have *predictive* value, that is, we must be must be able to explain other events besides the event we are actually explaining. The more events explicable by the theory, the greater its *scope* and *fruitfulness* are said to be. This is especially important in science. If I say that men love women because of their amatory tendencies or that bricks fall down because they have invisible spirits inside them with the tendency to jump toward the center of the earth at a uniform speed, the scope and fruitfulness of these explanations are open to some doubt. But Newton's work was an advance over that of Kepler, Galileo, and Brahe because it did not merely explain *either* earthly or heavenly events such as falling apples and planetary movements, as did the theories of these other men, but *both* sets of events by the *same* laws, and in a non-vacuous or non-tautologous manner.

Although the criterion of predictive power, and the accompanying standards of scope and fruitfulness are most often used to evaluate scientific theories, they are also important in other areas. For example, some philosophers have found it necessary to posit the existence of what are called "universals" and "individuating particulars" in order to explain how two or more things can be the same, but different. The universal *redness*, for example, is that in which two red things share and in virtue of which they are similar in this respect. Now if such theories are to be good ones, they must explain all possible cases of similarity and difference, not just the one under consideration. The more the theory explains, the better it is.

If the theory is a scientific explanation, then it must be directly or indirectly *testable* by reference to empirical fact. As has been mentioned, this condition does not apply to non-scientific theories which do not purport to be so explicable, though it is not always clear which theories have a just claim to exemption from this test. Theories must also be *consistent with* other theories to which they are logically related; and in the case of scientific theories, they should be consistent with other well-established or confirmed scientific theories.

If two competing theories meet all of these criteria, or all of them which are applicable, then the final test is *simplicity.* The classical example is the conflict between the theories of Ptolemy and Copernicus, both of which purported to explain the motion of the planetary bodies, one with the earth as the center of the universe, the other with the sun as the center. At the same time, both theories seemed to meet all the criteria we have enumerated (whether internal or external) equally well. Both theories involved the use of epicycles in their explanations, but that of Copernicus required *fewer* of them. On this ground, it was held to be the better explanation.

In metaphysics the explanation of such problems as the nature of the permanent which underlies change, and similarity and difference, often involve the positing of what have been called hypothetical explanatory entities—substance, universals, individuating particulars, and so forth. It has long been thought (at least since the time of William of Ockham, who died in 1349) that the better theory was the one with the fewer of these entities.

These, then, are the external criteria. With them we now have techniques for evaluating deductive arguments and inductive arguments, and for comparing two or more theories made from these kinds of arguments.

A LOOK BACK

In the first three chapters a great amount of material has been presented in very compact form. Yet in spite of this, each of the treatments of the various topics is incomplete and must be counted as a mere sketch of some standard kinds of approaches to the analysis of philosophical problems. Some of this material will be used in the chapters that follow to evaluate the arguments presented there. Before this, however, it might be of value to review what has been discussed so as to assure an understanding of the items one by one before going on. After the list, we shall consider in what order and in what circumstances the various parts of these methodological procedures can be used most effectively. In what follows every attempt will be made to remain consistent with this outline.

In the first chapter, we discussed:

What an argument is, and specifically what a deductive argument is;
What a good deductive argument is; that is, what a sound, valid deductive argument is;
What the notion of truth-functionality is and how to define the various conditions under which various kinds of sentences (conjunctions, disjunctions, implications, negations) are true and false;
How to simplify, and render into symbols, simple deductive arguments;
How to do elementary proofs for validity and invalidity for deductive arguments;
What the roles of elementary valid argument forms are in proofs for validity;
What logical equivalencies are, and what their roles are in proofs for validity;

What the names are of several elementary valid argument forms that are used as rules of inference;

Quantification, and elementary generalization and instantiation procedures;

What the nature of simple relational statements is;

What tautologies, contradictions, analytic statements, *a priori* statements, synthetic statements, *synthetic a priori* statements, *a posteriori* statements, and consistency are;

What the indirect proof, *reductio ad absurdum*, conditional proof, and dilemma are.

The purpose of the first chapter was threefold: (1) to make you familiar with what professional philosophers mean when they speak about deductive arguments, and to enable you to understand the nature of such arguments; (2) to familiarize you with some of the terminology which will be used in other parts of the book; (3) to familiarize you with the basis of some of the criticisms which will be used elsewhere in the text.

In the second chapter, we examined:

The nature of definition, and some of the kinds of definitions used in philosophy;

The difference between the denoting and the designating functions of definitions and terms:

The nature of some problems associated with meaning;

Several theories of meaning, and criticisms of them;

The criteria which an adequate theory of meaning would have to meet;

Some of the relations between problems of meaning and problems of truth;

Three theories of truth, and some criticisms of them;

Some reasons for thinking that no single theory of truth can be adequate for the analysis of all the functions of language;

The relations between meaning, truth, and the two major kinds of informal fallacies;

The explanation of informal fallacies;

Descriptions of the more common fallacies of relevance and ambiguity;

Descriptions of some common but important logical and philosophical fallacies.

The purpose of the second chapter was to accomplish the following things: (1) to familiarize you with certain philosophical problems associated with the content rather than the form of arguments; (2) to make you aware of some common errors concerning content and the effects they may have upon validity and soundness; (3) to help you understand the types of definition and the extreme complexity of the problems of meaning and truth.

The third chapter deals with:

The difference between inductive and deductive arguments;
The nature of inductive arguments and some problems with inductive arguments based upon enumeration;
Mill's methods of inductive argumentation or justification;
Some criticisms of Mill's methods;
The nature of arguments from analogy;
The grounds for strong analogies;
Various kinds of techniques for giving counter-examples;
Means for evaluating competing theories by using the external criteria, together with a specification of two different kinds of theory, according to the sorts of propositions which they contain.

The purposes of the third chapter were: (1) to introduce you to two kinds of inductive argument often used in philosophy; (2) to familiarize you with means for the evaluation of these arguments; (3) to outline the counter-example technique of criticism; (4) to consider means for the evaluation of competing theories composed of one or both of the major sorts of arguments, deductive and inductive, which we have examined.

How to use this knowledge is the major question. First, when confronted with any argument in philosophy, or with any theory, you must first ascertain what kind of argument it is, or, if you are considering a theory, what kinds of arguments are involved. If the argument is deductive and questions of validity are raised, then, at more advanced levels of philosophy, the next step would be to symbolize the argument and test it for validity. In this text, if a question of validity arises, the solution to the problem will be given and explained. If the argument is deductive and valid, then the next step is to ascertain that the premises are not ambiguous, and that they are all true. This, of course, will involve using or at least referring to some theory of truth and some theory of meaning in order to justify your claims about the status of the claims in the argument. If it is an empirical statement, then some theory that relates the statement to a set of facts will constitute a part of your justification, whereas other means must be used if it is a metaphysical claim or a purely emotive utterance. If the statements are all true, then you know the argument is sound as well as valid. If any statement or all the statements are false in whole or in part, then the argument may be rejected. If the statements or some of them which are essential to the proof are neither true nor false, then the argument must either be rejected because it is not an argument or a new conception of validity is required—an alternative which is mentioned in the sixth chapter. If the topic of examination is a theory composed of exclusively deductive arguments, all of which meet the tests given, then the theory as a whole is sound and valid.

Many of the claims in deductive arguments, or indeed in any kind, will be general claims based upon evidence. If it is possible to give exceptions to the general claims, this will render the argument unsound. If the argument is invalid, the counter-example technique which involves logical analogy will enable you to illustrate this fact. The argument may be sound and valid, but may be guilty of one of the informal fallacies, such as begging the question, or the fallacy of accent. All of these tests must be met.

If the argument is inductive and if it is also an argument from analogy, the tests for the strength of the analogy must be passed. These were detailed in this present chapter. Even if the analogy is strong, no claim for certainty of a conclusion may be made upon the basis of analogy.

Throughout the examination of the claims made in arguments, whether they are inductive or deductive, a consistent effort to achieve conceptual and written clarity must be made. In addition to the formal and informal fallacies, the philosophical fallacies must be considered, and we must make sure that the premises of our arguments are relevant to the conclusions. Finally, if we have two arguments or theories which meet all of our tests and they concern the same subject and purport to be explanations of that subject, then the better one will be the one that meets the external criteria most adequately.

This method may seem to be so detailed that following it would inevitably take too long, and be too cumbersome, to be of practical use. This is not the case, and part of the reason is that it is very rare for the entire method to be required in the case of any one theory. But even if, in some rare instance, it should be necessary to use it all, you will find that practice makes it easy and that you develop an "eye" for the more obvious kinds of errors. In no case in this book will you have to apply all of the criteria, and in the one or two cases where advanced techniques are required, they will be explained step by step.

EXERCISES

1. What is the difference between an inductive and a deductive argument?
2. What is wrong with the inductive method of simple enumeration?
3. Compose arguments illustrating each of Mill's methods.
4. Is the criticism that Mill's methods are not really very good tools for discovery justified? Why or why not? In your answer, use the methods to illustrate the discovery of some inductive truths.
5. List the criteria for evaluating an argument from analogy. Compose two *weak* arguments from analogy and explain why they are weak.
6. Logical analogy is the technique of comparing arguments, one of which is known to be either good or bad and the other not. Need the *compared* arguments be inductive in form? Why or why not?
7. Compose a valid argument which is not *obviously* valid and which illus-

trates its validity by comparison with another argument which *is* obviously valid.

8. Name two common general claims used to justify racism which are easily disproven by ordinary counter-examples.

9. Compose an inductive argument in which you show that it is highly probable that dropouts will be less successful than graduates. Defend your claim that your argument is strong by reference to the criteria developed in the section.

10. Pick an inductive argument from your newspaper editorial page, and evaluate it using our criteria.

11. Before we can use the external criteria to evaluate a theory, what must be known about the arguments which compose the theory?

12. Would a theory in pure mathematics require empirical testing? Would a purely metaphysical theory? Why or why not?

13. Why is one scientific theory better than another if it enables us to make more predictions, other things being equal? Is it possible that a theory which enabled us to make fewer predictions, but with greater accuracy, could be a better one than a theory which enables us to make many predictions with dubious accuracy? Do the external criteria enable us to account for your answer to this question? How?

14. Why do you think that *simplicity* is counted among the external criteria?

15. From one of your science courses, pick out two theories purporting to account for the same phenomena and evaluate them according to the external criteria.

16. From your present knowledge of foreign affairs, compose two theories purporting to explain the decline in U.S. foreign aid programs in the last ten years. Evaluate your theories and defend your choice of one of them as better than the other. Remember that not only the external criteria must be used.

17. Is it possible that two arguments or theories might meet the external criteria equally well, but that neither of them satisfies the other methods for evaluation which we have studied? Why or why not?

18. Not all theories need to meet *all* of the criteria discussed in this section. Name a kind of theory that would not need to meet the predictability test.

19. Does it seem to you that there is a constant conjunction between theories which meet the test of fruitfulness and predictability well, and those which are the simplest? Why do you think there is, or is not, such a conjunction?

20. Review the first three chapters before going on.

II

Metaphysics
and
Epistemology

4

Metaphysics

THE SCOPE OF METAPHYSICS

It is fairly simple to define the scope of logic; and the fields of ethics, political philosophy, philosophy of religion, philosophy of science, and aesthetics, though more difficult to define, present no insuperable problems. With metaphysics and epistemology the difficulty is much greater. Many philosophers doing what they call metaphyhics or ontology are said by others to be doing epistemology and *vice versa*, and the snarl may be aptly illustrated by a phrase currently in use, "the ontology of the knowing situation." For this reason, it is appropriate to say what "metaphysics" will mean here, and the same procedure will be followed at the start of the next chapter for the subject called "epistemology."

The word "metaphysics" supposedly was invented by Andronicus of Rhodes to characterize what was then called the "science of being as such." It was intended that this should distinguish the subject from the study of any particular aspect of being, such as the study of the biological nature of plants, the specific nature of man, and so on. Because metaphysics was supposed to be the study of being in general, it has often been thought to be a sort of super science, including within itself all other sciences, or at least their principles. If this were so, then it would obviously be impossible for anyone to be a competent metaphysician for simple practical reasons: no one would live long enough to master even a part of the field! Accordingly, its scope has become modified with the development of the specific sciences. Probably the first modification consisted in restricting metaphysics to the study of the most *general* of first principles, in the belief that the particular principles of the various sciences were deductively related to these. This belief held sway at least until the time of Descartes, who died in 1650. Even after that time, people whom we would now call scientists, such as Newton, called them-

93

selves "natural philosophers" in order to distinguish themselves from philosophers concerned with more general matters.

Other trends in the evolution of the subject matter of metaphysics are discernible from a very early date. With the realization in pre-Socratic times that what appeared to be to the senses was not always identical with what really is, the problem of trying to say what "reality" is, as opposed to "appearance," became one of the focal interests of metaphysics and has remained so until the present. Is there but one element which makes up the real world? Material substance perhaps? Or are there also minds? If we grant that resembling things are a part of reality, need we posit the existence of a third sort of thing, universals, in order to account for this resemblance? If there are universals, is there a distinction in status between them and particular things, so far as what we mean when we say that both sorts of entity "exists"? If reality is composed, say, of minds, bodies, universals, and particulars, then what is the nature of the relations between them? Are these relations still another type of entity which must exist? If we do claim that all these kinds of things exist, is our reason that if they did not, we could not provide a proper conceptual analysis of the way things "hang together," as it were? And is this a satisfactory reason for claiming that some sort of thing exists, even if it is in principle not perceivable? Plato thought that the answer to the last question was yes; George Berkeley thought it was no. This trend led to the development of metaphysics as the attempt to provide a coherent explanation of the structure of reality with the fewest possible components. This view of the subject remains today the most prominent.

There have been thinkers, however, who denied that metaphysics so conceived is even possible. A. J. Ayer in his earlier days was one such thinker, as were the other Logical Positivists. We shall discuss them later.

Another trend in metaphysics, which has found its way into very many other branches of philosophy as widely separate from metaphysics as aesthetics, is conceptual analysis. This trend has taken metaphysics away from the analysis of the components of the real to the study of the conditions for the meaningfulness of metaphysical propositions. Ayer could be included in the group of men who take this view, but so can Immanuel Kant. Ayer's early conclusions caused him to say that meta-physical propositions were meaningless, but Kant's led him to say that at least some of them were a special sort of proposition, which he called "synthetic a priori." Kant thought that such propositions as that expressed in "Every event has a cause" were not tautologies but none-theless could be known to be true independently of any sort of confirm-ing or disconfirming experience. At this point, as we shall see in the next chapter, the distinction between metaphysics and epistemology starts to blur.

These two trends, the attempt to analyze reality and explain it, and the turning to the consideration of the conditions of meaningfulness in metaphysical utterances, both have very many problems which fall within their province of study. The total of these two sets of problems today constitutes most of the subject matter of metaphysics. It would be impossible here to discuss even a fraction of them. In this chapter and in the next we shall study sample problems from each trend. Those from the tradition of conceptual analysis will be left to the chapter on epistemology, for reasons which will be explained at the beginning of that chapter.

ON AN ARGUMENT FROM ZENO OF ELEA

One of the first problems which entertained the earliest western philosophers was the problem of change. Specifically, the problem was how to account for the permanence of the world in the face of its continually changing appearance. In ancient times (and this has not changed appreciably today), the effort concentrated upon the identification of elements which did *not* change. Philosophers attempted to account for change in terms of the various combinations of these elements at different times. But at various periods some thinkers became convinced that nothing at all was permanent, that the very essence of reality was change or flux, and at other times they denied change and asserted that the real was unchanging and permanent. To do the latter consistently, they had to argue that sense-perception was illusory and that motion was impossible.

One man who became famous for a series of arguments that seemed to prove conclusions contrary to our normal interpretations of sense-experience was Zeno of Elea. He was born around 490 B.C. and he knew Parmenides, who was the major early Greek exponent of the view that change is an illusion. Zeno apparently also adhered to this theory. We shall consider one of Zeno's two most famous arguments, which attempts to prove this conclusion. A motion over a finite space, taking place through finite time, once begun can never be completed. Some of Zeno's other arguments try to prove that motion can never begin in the first place. If motion either can never begin, or never end, it is not motion. The heroes of the argument we shall examine are Achilles and a tortoise. The context of the argument is a race between Achilles and the tortoise in which the tortoise starts with a lead. To win the race, Achilles must obviously first catch, and then pass, the tortoise. To do this, he must first reach the line where the tortoise started, because the tortoise began with a lead. By this time, the tortoise will have covered more ground, no matter how little, so Achilles will now have to cover this lead. By then, the tortoise will have covered a little more ground, and Achilles will have to make up this lead too before he can catch the tortoise. The point is, of course, that no matter how many leads Achilles makes up, there will still be another one to overcome, so he can never catch the tortoise, let alone pass him. To state the same thing in a slightly different way, there is no possible number of leads that Achilles can make up such that the total of these leads adds up to a number equal to the number of leads or spaces in the total race; because, by hypothesis, there is always another lead that Achilles has not covered.

Two additional points should be mentioned here. The first is that the lead of the tortoise, no matter how small, is always finite in length. The second is that this argument works, if it does work, for leads of time as well as those of space. The reason for the second of these two points is that on the one hand, if Achilles takes any time at all to make up a lead (and if he did not, he would not have moved), he has enabled the tortoise in that time to make up another lead. On the other hand, no matter how small the interval of time Achilles takes to cover the space of one lead, there is always a still smaller time in which the tortoise can cover still another smaller space. No matter whether you are talking in terms of time or space, there is never a point at which the total of the leads overcomes, or the total of the times taken to do it, adds up to either the total of the spaces in the race, or the total of the times taken to cover them if your name is Achilles!

Ryle's Interpretation

There are a great many interpretations of this argument, and an astonishingly vast literature covering it. Here we shall adopt the interpretation of Professor Gilbert Ryle. [1]

First, the argument seems to fly in the face of the ancient and surely true maxim that wholes are the sum of their parts. Recall that no matter how many leads poor Achilles makes up, whether 1, 100, or 1,000,000, they never add up to the total spaces in the race, because there is always at least one more lead to be covered. But as we shall see, the argument only *seems* to question this maxim; it does not *really* do so. Zeno is forcing us to concentrate upon a *method* of dividing up the race track, rather than upon the nature of the sum of the total number of components of the race. His argument proves that if you follow this method of division, the units of the division never add up to the total number of

[1] Gilbert Ryle, *Dilemmas* (New York: Cambridge University Press, 1960), chapter 3.

units in the track. When the argument is viewed in the light of this conclusion, it is valid, and it is sound. But what the argument does *not* prove is that in a race between Achilles and the tortoise, where Achilles is running twice as fast as the tortoise, he can never catch the reptile. And hence the argument does *not* prove that a motion over a series of finite spaces and times, once begun, can never be completed. If *this* be taken as the conclusion which follows from Zeno's premises, then the argument is invalid and hence unsound. In order to prove this, it is necessary to formulate the argument in precise terminology, and then to use an analogy to illustrate the deceptive character of it.

Let a "run" be a portion of the race course for either or both Achilles and the tortoise. By hypothesis, the tortoise begins with a lead of one run, and his successive leads are never less than one run, though the length of the run progressively diminishes.

1. Achilles and the tortoise begin their runs, and continue to cover them at the same instant, and through the same time intervals.
2. Achilles will catch the tortoise if and only if a run covered by Achilles and a run covered by the tortoise reach the same point at the same instant.
3. But since the tortoise has a lead of one run, then at any point in the race reached by Achilles which is composed on n number of runs, the tortoise at that instant will be at the point composed of $(n + 1)$ number of runs.
4. Since n is never equal to $(n + 1)$, no matter how small a portion of the total race is denoted by 1, it follows that Achilles can never catch the tortoise.

Gilbert Ryle uses an analogy between Zeno's argument and a mother who gives an uncut cake to her children with the instruction that each child may take as much as he wants of the cake but that no child may take the last piece of cake on the plate. That is, they may in any case take only a part of what is left on the plate. Assuming that they do what she tells them, there is always a bit of cake left, no matter how small it is. It follows that at no time do the pieces of cake that the children have eaten add up to the total number of pieces of the cake. The whole cake will be the addition of all the pieces eaten by the children, *plus* the bit left on the plate. If this is so, then in principle the cake can never give out.

Now suppose that an addition is made to mother's instructions. Suppose that each child is to take exactly half of what is on the plate when it comes his turn. The first child eats half the cake, the second child a quarter, the third child an eighth, and so on. On this hypothesis, any slice that any child takes is a measurable part of the whole cake. That is, any piece eaten is an exact fraction of the whole cake. If some child were to argue that because all the cake the children eat never can add up to the entire cake, then there never was a cake of some finite size to eat, he could be asked what it was that the last piece of cake he ate was a fraction *of*. After all, the concept of "being a finite fraction of" makes sense only if the concept "finite whole divisible into finite fractions" makes sense. Ryle is saying that Zeno is in this child's position. He is claiming that because the fractions of the race which Achilles takes never add up to the whole race, then there never was a finite race to run, and, hence, Achilles could never have started such a race. And the refutation is indicated by the answer to the question "What are Achilles' runs fractions *of*?" to which the only possible answer is "A *finite* race." There is a suppressed premise in Zeno's argument, and this suppressed premise is a principle of division. Only if this principle is followed, or only if the descriptive statement corresponding to it is true, is the argument valid. The principle is something like this: "Always consider the race that Achilles runs as comprised of all the segments which may be cut *off* the total distance that the tortoise has run." The sum total of these segments will always be one less than the tortoise has run. If the principle were, however: "Always consider the race that Achilles runs as comprised of all the segments which the total distance the tortoise runs may be cut *into*," then the distance that Achilles and the tortoise run over the whole course of the race would be the same, and the question would be: "Can Achilles cover this distance at a speed sufficient to overcome the lead of the tortoise?" The answer may still be no of course—Achilles may have cut his tendon or something—but what prevents him from winning will not be logical necessity!

Consider the two following statements, the first corresponding to one principle of division, the second to the other principle:

> The length of the race course is equal to the runs of Achilles plus one. The length of the race is equal to the total number of runs into which it is fractionally divisible, when the length of the course is finite.

Which of these two statements one puts into the argument depends upon which principle of division one adopts. If one puts the first statement in, then what the argument proves, if valid, is that if you follow the corresponding principle of division, the total of Achilles' runs is never more than one less than those of the tortoise. But this is not to say that Achilles either can never catch the tortoise, or that he cannot start the race. It says just what it says—that if you use the method of "cutting off" rather than "cutting into," there is always something left to cut. And this conclusion is built into the premises (in the third premise, to be exact). In short, the argument begs the question. This renders it valid, although to decide that it was sound (valid, and all statements true), we still have to decide the truth of the first premise on a contingent basis. Because the argument begs the question, it fails in its purpose *as an argument*, for the reasons mentioned in the third chapter.

If Zeno were to insist that his use of the principle "Always consider the race that Achilles runs as comprised of all the segments which may be cut *off* the total distance that the tortoise has run" is perfectly justified, and that *we*, his critics, are the ones who are begging the question, we still have a rejoinder. It is that Zeno has committed what Professor Ryle in another place calls a "category-mistake"; he has, in remaining committed to this principle, attributed to his race track a property which is really not appropriately predicated of race tracks at all, but rather is only appropriately predicated of a given kind or method of division. This property is that of "non-finality," which the method of division characterized here as the "cutting-off" method, exhibits.

MENTAL CAUSATION AND THE CATEGORY-MISTAKE

Gilbert Ryle is one of the most important of living philosophers. One of his major contributions is the concept of the category-mistake, to which you were introduced in a brief way in the third chapter, and earlier in this chapter. Now we are going to consider an application of the category-mistake to a theory in philosophy which, if Ryle is correct, fails just because of this error. The theory which is to be criticized is the Cartesian view of the relation between mind and body, and it also includes a view about the ontological status of minds. Ryle calls this the "official doctrine" about minds in his famous book *The Concept of Mind*.[2]

The Mind–Body Problems: Cartesian View

René Descartes believed that there were two sorts of substances, minds and bodies, that they were fundamentally different, but that nonetheless they interacted with one another. Bodies are the objects of our perceptions. They exist in space and time, and to say that they exist in space is naturally to say that they are extended. They have weight and mass, color, a surface of some texture or other, and they interact causally with one another in a way that is specifiable by the laws of science. In particular, Descartes thought that the laws of motion, plus the laws of mechanics, were sufficient to enable us to predict the behavior of any body. Indeed, bodies are for him the objects of solid geometry in motion. Bodies are observable by more than one observer.

[2] Gilbert Ryle, *The Concept of Mind* (London: Hutchinson University Library, 1960).

Minds are quite different from bodies. Although they exist in time, they do not have a spatial location. If you cut up a body, you would never find a mind in it. Because they have no spatial location, they are not extended, and if a thing is not extended, then it has none of the properties which presuppose the possession of extension, such as color, weight, mass, and so on. Further, where bodies are public objects in the sense that they are preceivable by more than one person, minds are knowable only to the person as such; knowledge of minds is private. Even in principle, it is not possible for you to observe the workings of my mind, nor for me to observe yours, whereas it is possible for us both to observe the workings of our respective brains, given the appropriate conditions. Yet we assume that minds act causally upon bodies. When you think that I am doing some mental job such as working out a problem with figures, you are making an inference based upon what you see my body doing. I am sitting with my head cupped in my palm, holding a pencil, muttering equations aloud, looking puzzled, etc. The official doctrine would hold that the same sort of situation obtains in the case of my being in pain, and your deciding that I am. The person who is in pain, or who is working out the problem, does not have to make any inferences in order to know that he is in these states. It is not necessary for him to observe his body and conclude "I am working out a problem." He is immediately and directly familiar with his own mental states. This mode of private knowledge is usually called "introspection," and Ryle expresses this fact by saying that minds are insulated fields. Further, we cannot be mistaken about the workings of our own minds. When we think that we are in pain, we are, period. When you know that you are working out a problem in mathematics, that is what you are doing, and not some other sort of thing.

The "Para-Mechanical Relationship"

There *is*, however, one way in which minds and bodies *are* similar according to the official doctrine. They both exert causal force. This is not to say that minds are mechanical as bodily processes are, but the effects of mental activity are similar to the effects of bodily processes upon the body. The effect of the bodily processes called "arm muscles contracting" is that (we shall say) the arm rises into the air. Similarly, the effect of my deciding to raise my arm, which decision is a mental act, is that my arm rises into the air. Hence, it seems that the relation between mental acts and their bodily effects, and physical processes and their effects, are very much alike. The relation between bodily processes and their effects was for Descartes, and hence for the official doctrine, a mechanical one. The relation between minds and bodies or bodily effects, being similar, is therefore a *para*-mechanical relationship, and this is the name which Ryle uses to characterize the nature of the mind-body relationship according to the official doctrine.

It is easy to see that the para-mechanical theory is a tempting one, for it seems to permit or enable us to do many things that we want to do. We want to explain the behavior of men in a scientifically acceptable way, and the paradigm case of scientific explanation is mechanical explanation. Galileo had invented a theory which for the first time, when extended to its logical limit, would explain the actions and reactions of every possible occupant of space mechanically. All that was needed were the laws of mechanics and the laws of motion. Descartes found himself in a very strange position. He realized that Galileo was largely correct, and that mechanical explanation would indeed, given controlled conditions, explain all bodily behavior. Yet at the same time, he realized that if this were true of man, then man was nothing more than a very complex machine. This, to a man of Descarte's religious convictions and of his historical setting, was very nearly incomprehensible and, in any event, obviously heretical. Still, the realization of the dilemma shows up time and again in his writings.

Given that words characterizing mental acts could not in Descartes's eyes refer to mechanical processes except at the cost of admitting that man is a machine, he thought that they must refer to *non*-mechanical processes, which were, nonetheless, processes. Given that mechanical laws explain the movements of bodies in space as effects of yet other movements of yet other bodies in space, it seemed clear to Descartes that there must be another set of laws which explain mental acts in terms of other non-spatial mental acts. The difference between intelligent and non-intelligent behavior, whether in humans or other beings, is therefore a difference in their causation. Intelligent action is caused by minds, the rest by mechanical action. The effects might be the same, but the causes were different, and the relations between minds and bodies were thought to be similar, though not the same as, those between bodies and other bodies. Minds are not bodies, but they are *like* bodies in that they exert causal force.

But even with this theory, Descartes and the other holders of the view could never explain the exact nature of the relation between minds and bodies. As the official theory became more developed, it became clear that the mind was not a ghost harnessed to the bodily machine, but was itself a ghostly machine that caused effects, namely mental acts, just as the body and its processes together with the external world caused bodily action.

The privacy of minds and mental acts as opposed to bodies and bodily events is even reflected in our languages. We think it is humorous to speak of mental events as though they had spatial location. For example, General de Gaulle and general contentment may be present at the same party, but they do not hold the same rank. One may go home in both a sedan chair and a flood of tears, but "go" does not have the same force in both cases. The man who witnesses a foreign sport, having all the roles of the various players explained to him, and then asks who the player is who provides the *esprit de corps* has made a mistake, unless he understands that the force of his question is to ask for the *outstanding* man of *panache* and heart on the team. The mental power of a man is not measurable in units of volts or watts, and his strength of character is not tensile. It does not make much sense to ask where a man's honesty is, if we expect an answer naming a place, and although a sword may be in a man's hand, his intent to kill cannot be two inches beneath the center of his skull. When someone says that he is "feeling blue," he is not referring to the color of his mind or mental state, for we cannot see mental states. If anyone was in fact guilty of such confusions, we might surmise that he was not familiar with our language. If we discovered that he was familiar with it and he still persisted in this sort of usage, we might take him for a bad poet or a punster. But if we learned that he was neither, and was not insane, we would certainly accuse him of mistakes in his use of our tongue. Yet not all mistakes of this same type are so easily discoverable, and certain sorts of linguistic confusions, not realized as such by the speakers of the language, are quite common. They are nonetheless mistakes, and may be seen to be such upon careful consideration. The failure to realize that they *are* mistakes has led to mistaken inferences, because the unrecognized mistake has been enshrined in one of the premises from which the mistaken conclusion has been drawn. Ryle thinks that this kind of mistake has been made by the proponents of the official theory. It is now time to turn to some of the criticisms of the official theory, and see whether or not Ryle is right.

Criticisms of the Cartesian View

It has been noted that knowledge of minds is private, that we have privileged access to knowledge of our mental acts only through introspection. It follows that we can never know, if we take as the standard of knowing the sort of awareness we have of our own mental acts, that other minds exist, if the official theory is correct. We can *infer* that there are other minds, but it is an indirect analogical inference. We consider *bodily* behavior, and infer from it that the individual has a mind. The form of such an inference is this:

1. In my own experience, mental events of the sort X are the cause of physical events of the sort Y.

2. I observe that S's behavior is comprised in this case by the class of physical events Y.
3. Hence, mental events of the sort X are "going on" in S's mind.

This is a very weak sort of argument. It can never be disconfirmed or confirmed, if by confirmation or disconfirmation we count only those things that are observable as evidence, because all we can observe is S's behavior, and never his mental actions. This is true no matter how many instances of this argument we apply to S's different sorts of visible behavior. It is also weak in another way. We are in effect arguing here from only one case of association of a mind with presumably intelligent behavior to a very large number of cases. This mistake, as you know, is called hasty generalization. Because the argument *is* weak, we can never know that there are other minds if the official doctrine is correct. We can never discover whether anyone is in one rather than another mental state, such as worrying, guessing, feeling angry, feeling sad, and so forth. Since this is so, we can never accurately apply mental conduct terms in any regular and effective way. If I say to you that I am feeling sad, this can have little or no significance to you, because you have no very good reason to suppose that I have a mind, and even if you do suppose this, you cannot know that I am in one mental state rather than another, nor even what it would be like for me to be in a given mental state.

But this is absurd of course, because in fact you *do* understand perfectly well what one means when he says that he is feeling sad, and you are perfectly capable of using mental conduct words in a regular and effective way. What are we to make of this? If you consider the last four sentences, you will see that they constitute a *modus tollens* argument (actually, two of them) from which the conclusion that the official doctrine is a mistake clearly follows. In fact, this is one of the arguments that Ryle uses against the theory. The claim that if the official theory is correct, we cannot know when someone is in a given mental state can be carried to even farther extremes. It will be possible, given the Cartesian view, for the seemingly intelligent behavior of an intelligent man to be the result of physiological processes and not of his mind at all; while, on the other hand, it will make sense to say of an idiot that he is really very clever—it's just that his mind and body are not very well connected. And clearly all of this simply flies in the face of what we do know and how we do make up our minds about another person's mental states. When we decide that someone is angry, for example, do we ponder about the hidden causes of his state, meaning by this, of course, do we wonder about whether his anger does or does not result from mental action? Clearly we do not. We make up our minds on the basis of what we see. We operate upon the assumption that in fact, having a mind is *just being able* to do the things which we observe. This is one reason that we distrust, and quite reasonably, people who claim that they understand something but simply cannot write it down nor explain it to anyone.

Another fact which would seem to be true if the official doctrine were correct is that psychoanalysts ought not to be able to discover and explain our subconscious mental desires. This is simply because the only basis that they would have would be the weak argument from analogy which has just been given. Yet the whole history of psychoanalysis gives us good evidence for believing that psychoanalysts can in fact make such discoveries, explain them, and, in many cases, treat problems arising from the desires. Therefore, again by *modus tollens*, it follows that the official doctrine is mistaken.

Moreover, if the Cartesians were correct, it would be theoretically impossible to tell a man from a robot, because there is no objection in principle which prohibits us from constructing a robot which looks, talks and "behaves" exactly like a man. Such a robot would differ from a man in just one respect—it would not have a mind to cause its behavior. But the point is, one could never tell this, one could never know whether or *not* it had a mind, because mental events are totally private. Here again however, the claims which follow from the official doctrine fly directly in the face of experience which disconfirms them, for quite clearly we *can* tell a man from a robot. Even if someone constructed a terribly clever one that did fool us for a time, when we discovered that the thing was not a man, it would not be because we discovered that it did not have a mind, but because we found out that its body was full of springs, cogwheels, and batteries.

Later in this chapter we shall discuss determinism. One sort of determinist is called a *mechanist;* and he believes (rather obviously, given the word "mechanist"), that all so-called "mental" events can be explained mechanically, that is, in terms of the laws of physics, which most mechanists view as laws concerning the motion of elemental particles. Given that macroscopic bodies are made from little ones, their behavior is also totally explicable in mechanical terms. No mental "force" is required in order to provide a complete explanation of human behavior.

A *vitalist* on the other hand holds just the opposite position. He believes that purely mechanical explanations will never be completely adequate, because such explanations can never fully account for animal organisms and their behavior. In addition to mechanical explanation, we must posit spiritual or mental force, which is analyzable only in terms of goal-directed or teleological frameworks.

It might seem that the arguments against the official doctrine given thus far support the mechanist's cause, but in fact this is not so unless further specifications are added to the mechanist position. A mechanist could of course accept all of the arguments we have used so far. On the other hand, he could (and some do) also *hold* the official doctrine but maintain that, since there is no scientific evidence for the operation of minds, assertions and arguments about the causal relations between minds and bodies are not acceptable in behavioral explanations. The point is that a mechanist of this latter type finds nothing *conceptually* odd about the notion of minds exerting causal force upon bodies; he simply thinks that the Cartesians and neo-Cartesians are *factually* mistaken when they assume that there *is* such evidence, but that right now, we do not have it. As we shall now see, Ryle's arguments will hold against this kind of mechanist and his vitalistic opponent alike, so it is clear that the denial of the official doctrine does not entail the soundness of mechanism.

The Category-Mistake

We have so far considered three arguments which Ryle offers against the Cartesians. Now it is time to consider the final and central one. Its point is beautifully simple: when you say that bodies cause other bodies to move, and when you say that minds cause bodies to move, you are not using the word "cause" in such a way that it means the same thing in both cases. You are making a mistake if you fail to realize this; *just* the sort of mistake you would be making if you thought General de Gaulle and general contentment were both generals, or both slept in the same bed. The world of scientific explanation is concerned just with causes in the physical world. Minds are not a part of the physical world, and hence they are not subject to scientific explanation. In the scientific sense of "cause," they do not cause anything; they are in a logically different category than bodies are. When we give a mental explanation of a man's behavior, we are not giving the causes of his behavior. This can be discovered by considering two kinds of explanation for the same piece of behavior. Suppose I go to the post office because I want to pick up mail. This is a mental explanation because it explains my action in terms of a purpose that I have. I might also explain the same action by saying that I went to the post office because my nerves and muscles contracted in specified ways. This is a physical or causal explanation. Now the point is that these are not *alternative* ways of explaining the same event, and they are perfectly compatible with one another because they could never *possibly* conflict. They are completely different sorts of explanation, and simple though this seems, people have failed to see it. They have persisted in believing that *either* we must explain mental behavior in terms of our reasons, intentions, or purposes in acting, and in terms of our minds somehow "causing" our bodies to act, *or* we must explain our actions in terms of mechanical connections and physical causes.

How does this help us to understand what mind is and what "mind" means? If we consider it carefully, we will see that we already know what the meaning of this word is. In the knowing that under certain conditions, we use mental words such as "thinking," "reasoning," "choosing," and so forth, we know what the conditions are for something's having a mind. For example, we know when someone is "making sense," when he is speaking "intelligently," when he is "in pain." Knowing how to use such terms *is* understanding them, and there is nothing more to say. If someone were to tell you that you always had either no grounds or very weak ones for saying these things about other people because you have no grounds for inferring that they have minds, you simply would not understand what he was saying. As we shall see, this position of Ryle's is very similar to one of Wittgenstein's, which we shall consider later on.

The error involved in thinking that the two sorts of explanations are alternatives is fairly easy to explain. It stems from the fact that often when we speak about the behavior of men we seem to be using language that refers to events and things that we do not see directly, such as willing, thinking, and minds. Explanations of why we do certain things are often offered in terms of mental acts. Originally, this was a sort of metaphor, because we were speaking *as if* there were occult powers, forces, or the like, acting in some mysterious way upon our bodies and our environment. We are all familiar with expressions such as "mental powers," "the influence of his will," his "force of mind and personality," etc. There is no mistake in this sort of speech, as long as we *realize* that we are speaking metaphorically. When we forget that we are speaking "as if" language however, and come to take words such as "force," "willing," "thinking," and so on *literally*, then we do make a mistake, which Ryle calls a "category-mistake." It is this mistake that has led many thinkers into believing that we have each of us *two* personal and parallel histories, the one of the observable changes associated with our bodies, the other occult and unobservable, the histories of our minds and their mental events.

The Effect of the Category-Mistake

In Ryle's eyes the effect of a category-mistake is not to make a theory false, but technically *meaningless*. A proposition, to be either true or false, must first be meaningful. Category-mistakes render a claim meaningless, and hence neither true or false. One of Ryle's examples will illustrate this. Suppose that you are a military man and that you are showing a visitor the division which you command by having him take the salute. The division parades by, and as it does you name and identify the various units which compose it. At the end of the parade, your guest says "That was wonderful, but I wonder where the division is? You gave me the names of all those units, but I missed the division." If he had asked for information about a *unit* that did or did not come by, you could reply that he had indeed missed it because it had passed by, or you could say that the particular unit was undergoing field exercises today and would not be coming. But neither of these answers, nor any other resembling them, is appropriate when he asks the question about the division, because the division is not something like another unit! When you have seen the units, you have seen the division. Therefore, all you can do in this case is to explain to him that he has misunderstood the meaning of the word "division." When we take a mind to be a thing, and when we take mental action words to denote or name something like a physical event, we make this kind of mistake if Ryle is right. Descartes and his heirs are viewing the mind as some sort of thing, a substance, which has qualities that are manifested in bodily events. But if Ryle is right, most if not all psychological terms are *dispositional* and we commit category-mistakes when we use them as terms which refer to entities or properties as "brick" and "red" do. What then *is* a dispositional property, and how does it differ from ordinary sense qualities, and from objects?

A good example is a lump of sugar. The lump itself is the object. Descartes would have agreed with this and then added that the total connotation of the word "sugar" also includes a list of the properties which the lump has. It has a number of different kinds of properties. For example, it is (we shall say) shaped like a cube, sweet, white in color, fairly hard, and when crushed it has a fairly rough texture and looks like powder. Now sugar is also soluble. But if I say that I perceive the whiteness and the solubility of the sugar, I have made a category-mistake, because solubility is not a property of the same sort as whiteness. This is not to say that solubilty is not a property of sugar; it is. But it is a special *sort* of property, namely, a dispositional one. One does not hear, taste, see, or feel dispositional properties. What does it mean to say that sugar is dispositional then? What it means is this: sugar is soluble if it dissolves when it is dropped into certain sorts of liquids under certain conditions. This process involves a series of events. Dropping the sugar into the liquid is an event, and so is the subsequent dissolution of the sugar. All events are entities which are caused by something and are in turn causes of things or events themselves. Events have temporal and spatial locations, though they are not always perceivable. But in the case of dispositional claims about dispositional properties, given the occurrence of one event, it is always possible to test for the other. If I drop the sugar, it is possible to test for its dissolution. And this is true even though I cannot perceive solubility. The state of being dissolved is not the same as solubility, for the lump of sugar we are considering is not in the state of being dissolved, yet it is soluble. It will remain soluble even if it is never dropped into a liquid under the requisite conditions.

To say then that sugar is soluble implies that it will dissolve if it is dropped into liquid under these conditions. Dispositional claims almost always imply conditional statements similar to this. To say that glass is brittle implies that it will break if you hit it with a stone under certain conditions; to say that a man is quick-tempered implies that he will get angry under situations of certain sorts of stress; to say that some girl is promiscuous implies a set of corresponding conditional claims, as does the claim that she is virtuous.

Assume that I come home tonight and find that the plate-glass window of my living room is broken and that I wish to find out what happened. My wife tells me that the window smashed because it has the dispositional property of being brittle. My daughter tells me that my son Adam threw a brick at it. Both statements together form a fairly complete explanation of the event. The fact of the window's being brittle is not alone a sufficient explanation, because it was brittle before it was smashed, and from its being brittle, it does not follow that it will break whenever anything hits it. The weight of the object might not be sufficient, or the window might cease to exist for other reasons, such as being melted. Neither is the fact that Adam hit the window with a brick sufficient to explain (in the technical sense) why the window is broken, because there are many things at which he could throw the brick without their breaking and because the window *need* not break every time it is hit. But together, the two statements do give us an explanation which is formulable as follows:

1. The window is brittle.
2. Therefore, if it is hit with a hard object of at least weight X, it will break.
3. Adam hit the window with a brick of at least weight X.
4. Therefore, the window broke.

I am assuming that certain other variables have been taken care of, such as the velocity of the brick and so on. With this assumption, the explanation is complete.

Now if Ryle is right, whenever we give an explanation of an intelligent action, the only mental concept involved is a dispositional property which can be interpreted in terms of one or more conditional or hypothetical statements which relate *physical* events. Suppose, for example, that you say that Jones prevented a bully from beating his friend's child. Someone asks why Jones did this. You reply that he did it out of sympathy. He asks what "sympathy" means. If you were an adherent of the official doctrine, you would now begin to talk of hidden or occult mental states occurring in Jones's mind which "cause" him to act in certain ways upon given occasions. You would have to assume that he could not fully understand what you meant when you said that Jones was sympathetic, because that would require that he be familiar with Jones's mental states, and this he can never be. You would therefore have to conclude that whenever anyone made a claim like this, the degree of certainty for that claim was very much less than that for normal empirical claims, and that the very grounds for arguing that some man was in some mental state are suspect from the beginning. Ryle tells you that you need in fact, however, never be in any of these awkward positions. He suggests that all you need reply when asked what "sympathy" means, is to say that it is a dispositional property. If you are required to give further explanation, you can say that "Jones is sympathetic" is a statement which implies a set of conditional statements such as "Whenever Jones sees children being beaten by bullies, he tries to stop it," "Whenever Jones observes someone who is bereaved, he does his best to distract their attention from their sufferings," "Whenever Jones sees a weak person trying to do something requiring physical exertion of a considerable degree, he helps him," and so on.

This set of dispositional, or as Ryle often calls them, "law-like" statements, is in a sense the definition of the dispositional term in question. When you understand the term, you understand the set of statements, and vice versa. They are law-like because they have a logical form similar to that of physical laws, and they enable you to predict the sort of reactions the object or person will have given the conditions in the antecedents of the conditionals, and that is all there is to it. Nothing more need be added, and the skepticism which the official doctrine seems to justify is unjustified. Being sympathetic is simply a disposition, and not some mental event which occurs in my head, forever unobservable. Since the dispositional claims implied by the statement that some entity has a dispositional property express connections only among physical events, there is no need to posit the existence of another sort of substance, mind, in order to complete our explanations of mental events. This kind of explanation does not imply materialism, that is, it does not imply the truth of the denial that there is mental substance. Rather, it points out that whenever we offer explanations of our behavior in terms which are only appropriately used within physical contexts, that is, within the context of possibly perceivable things, we must not interpret the words we use as though they refer to occult, unperceivable events unless we are intentionally speaking in metaphors. If we do, the result will be a meaningless utterance, involving a category-mistake. The category-mistake which the official doctrine made was the taking of dispositional terms as terms which referred to such occult events.

DETERMINISM AND FREE WILL

Determinism is a theory about the logic of the causal relation, and there is more than one sort of deterministic position. One kind is called *"hard"* determinism, and another, *"soft."* Proponents of the latter sort of view argue that it permits two seemingly incompatible claims to be true. The two claims are that everything has a cause, and that if the cause occurs, the effect will surely follow, and at the same time, the decisions of at least human beings are free in a meaningful sense of "free." Hard determinists do not see how human decision-making can justifiably be made an exception to the causal necessity which governs the rest of the universe. They therefore deny that the will is free.

Libertarians deny that determinism is true of human behavior and affirm instead that our choices are spontaneous and uncaused in any sense of the term "cause" which is viable in explanations of the physical world.

There is an entire set of related problems which run the gamut of the divisions and types of philosophy. There have been and still are philosophers who affirm the existence of two distinct sorts of entities, minds and bodies, and wish to hold that the causal relation as that is understood in physics holds only within the realm of bodies. At the same time, they are then confronted with explaining the nature of the connection between minds and bodies, which seems to necessitate either the postulation of a second sort of causality, the denial of what they wish to affirm concerning the restriction of causality to the physical world, or the acceptance of a very implausible theory of coincidence in the occurence of mental and physical events. On the other hand, if one wishes to deny the existence of minds, one then has the problem of explicating what are normally called mental events in physical terms, a feat that has not as yet been accomplished in spite of tremendous effort and persistence.

The ramifications are not only ontological. The obvious relevance of the matter is in the field of moral philosophy. What can it possibly mean to say that a man is morally responsible if he is not free to choose among alternative courses of action for reasons which he thinks good? What is the significance of blame and praise, whether morally relevant or not, if a man cannot help but do what he does? What becomes of scientific attempts to predict and control the natural world in order that man may have wider choices for action in the future? This is *so* obviously the import of the question that one may wonder why the topic is being discussed here rather than in the chapter on moral philosophy. The answer is that although the solution to the problem matters greatly for moral philosophy, the problem itself is not at all a problem in either ethics or meta-ethics. It involves no normative evaluations, and no justifications for value judgments. No ultimate principles of conduct are involved, and modern meta-ethical questions, such as the nature of the logic of moral reasoning, the relevance of certain theories of truth and meaning for ethical statements, and the role of speech acts and emotion in normative thought are irrelevant to it. This is stressed here only because discussions of the problem are so often found in texts on moral philosophy or in the ethics section of general texts. Any viable moral philosophy must presuppose an affirmative answer to the question "May men make free choices?" at the outset. This is one way to express the opinion that ontology is in at least some respects logically prior to moral philosophy.

Truth Values and Determinism

Determinism in its various guises is a very old problem in the history of philosophy. In antiquity, it was reflected in literature, especially tragedy, in the doctrine that Fate governs the crucial actions of men. But as soon as the problem came to be conceived in terms of the truth-values of sentences, it became much less general, and at the same time much more technical. Without drawing the customary distinctions between logical, physical, and psychological determinism (which is justified because the "truth-value" question cuts across all three), the problem is this: a proposition or the sentence in which it is expressed must be either true or false, or neither. If we know that a given event, whether physical, psychological, supernatural, or whatever took place at a given moment, then we know that the sentence "X (the event) took place at time t" is true rather than false. The same sentence in the present tense is true while X is taking place. Now, was the sentence true *before* X took place? If it was, then may we not conclude that for every event which will take place, there is a true sentence asserting that it will, and that this sentence is true before the event happens? Similarly, may we not say that for every event which does not and will not take place, there is a sentence asserting that it will take place which is false before the time at which the event is predicted to occur? The most famous example used to illustrate this controversy is the sea fight in Aristotle's *de Inter-pretatione*. If the sea fight happened yesterday, then a sentence such as "A sea fight will take place at time *t*," referring to this particular battle, must have been true no matter how long before *t* it was said, and in fact, it must have been true even if it was not said. But, if it was true that the battle was going to occur thousands of years before it did happen, then what role can the naval commander's decision, when *t* arrives, play in the battle? After all, presumably his decision to order the battle is presupposed by the thousand-year-old truth. The problem is not changed significantly if the prediction is that the naval battle will *not* take place at *t*, for if that prediction is true, the point now is that since it *is* true, no possible decision by anyone including the commander could falsify it at a later date.

There are a number of ways in which one can disagree with the argument illustrated in the case of the sea fight. One of them involves a distinction between the truth conditions for predictions as opposed to other sorts of utterance. Another entails a distinction among what logicians call "modal concepts," and a limitation among the kinds of inferences permissible between sentences in different logical modes. A third consists in various arguments based upon the distinction between causal and logical necessity and sufficiency. In what follows the first of these ways of disagreement will receive some discussion, as will the third. The discussion of modal logic is too complex for this book, though the subject must be studied for a complete knowledge of the topic.

Although the role that truth-values play in the theory of determinism cuts across the various sorts or kinds of this view, the problems to be faced in each kind are not identical. In particular, the rise of modern science raised new issues for determinists, though in the early days of the new science the evidence was thought to support determinism in general. The sort of science which is relevant here is generally physical science. The fairly recent advent and development of psychology, particularly behavioral psychology, is also relevant; but it raises unique issues, and we shall leave it aside for the moment.

The Rise of Mechanics

In the seventeenth and eighteenth centuries, the most remarkable accomplishment of the new science was the rise of mechanics, typified by Newton, Laplace, Descartes, and many others. The discoveries of Galileo, Kepler, Huygens, Brahe and their contemporaries had focused the attention of the learned world on the search for "laws" which governed the physical motion of the universe. Even this was not wholly new. The primitive atomic theories of men like Democritus and Leucippus, who lived 400 years before Christ, contained the principle, and it was disseminated by the Epicureans. But what was conceptually enticing about the determinism which seemed to be supported by mechanics in the seventeenth and eighteenth centuries was its success in explaining *qualitative* changes in terms of *quantitative* ones, and the degree of precision which the developing technology of science revealed. As both of these advanced, the credence given to "feeling," "intuition," and "immediate awareness" as sources of evidence for viable explanations and defenses of freedom of the will declined. It became the "reasonable" thing to do to look upon man as merely another type of entity in the firmament, subject to the same sort of laws as applied to everything else. The onus fell upon those who wished to make him an exception, and there it has remained. Much depended, however, on the mechanist's ability to explain *all* events in terms of mechanics, and this soon proved to be impossible. The question then became, in terms of what particular science, if any, is determinism to be defined? Or is determinism not a scientific claim at all, but rather solely a philosophical claim? It has also been argued that determinism is a scientific theory, but the most general one, and that it is a general theory *about* scientific theories rather than a member of such a class of theories itself.

Two facts mitigate against the claim that determinism is a scientific theory. The first of these is that there seems to be no conceivable counter-example which can prove determinism false, or disconfirm it. This is because the determinist can always claim of any proposed counter-example that it only *seems* to be evidence against this theory, whereas if we had the required knowledge, the counter-example would be explicable in terms of causal law. Hence, any counter-example is dismissed on the grounds of ignorance. This is of course not an acceptable scientific procedure. The second fact is that any attempt at confirmation for determinism is always viciously circular, since testing presupposes the theses of being law-governed and predictable, which constitute the principles of this theory. A further claim against the "science" theory of determinism, which is of current interest in the literature of the philosophy of science, is that the concept of causation which the determinist uses is in fact not the one that is used in science. It is argued that the ordinary language meanings of "cause" do not entail that the cause of an effect is *sufficient* of itself for the effect, which is a claim that determinists seem obliged to hold, and hence determinism is not a theory about beliefs reflected in our language. On the other hand, statistical correlation, which is the basis of many if not all scientific "causal" claims, is again not sufficient for the claim that causes necessitate their effects. So determinism does not seem to use "cause" as science does.

If determinism is a theory about neither of these things, then what is it about? Many modern determinists believe that this argument and many other criticisms of determinism which are based upon analyses of "cause" have missed the central concern of determinists, which is the place of the concept of *law,* not causation. Such philosophers would argue that the relevant concept of causation may vary from discipline to discipline, but at least in scientific determinism, the concept of what a law is must be the same in all cases. Furthermore, the concept of law that is used in such fields as moral philosophy and in discussions of free will is *not* the same as that used in science. Hence, they have argued, the supposed conflict between scientific determinism and moral responsibility is not really a conflict at all. This theory, together with a theory which argues that free will is a fact but that the distinction among kinds of laws just mentioned is irrelevant to the issue, will be the second of the studies to follow. The first, as you may recall, is an examination of determinism as characterized in Aristotle's "sea-fight" example and various discussions of it.

Richard Taylor's Defense of Fatalism

We shall here be considering not just Aristotle's argument, but more particularly an argument about fatalism which is also an argument about determinism and which is defended today by Professor Richard Taylor.[3] Though it is very ingenious, Taylor's argument does not seem to prove its point, and we shall examine it critically here.

Taylor argues that a fatalist, (and, we presume, a determinist), regards the future as we normally regard the past, that is, as something which is settled once and for all, and which we cannot change because it is impossible for things to be other than they are. In any argument designed to support fatalism, (and again this will be true of determinism as well), there are certain presuppositions which must be accepted. It is easy to state what these are, and not very easy to define them:

1. The law of excluded middle.
2. The principle of sufficiency.
3. The principle of necessity.
4. The mutual implication holding between sufficient and necessary conditions.
5. The principle that no event (and hence no action) may occur unless there occurs at some time a set of conditions or states of affairs that are necessary for the event to occur.
6. The principle that time is not efficacious.

Taylor believes that he can give two arguments resting upon these principles which are such that, if you accept one, you must accept the other.

---

[3] Richard Taylor, "Fatalism," *Philosophical Review,* 71 (January, 1962), pp. 56–66; 72, pp. 497–99. Also see Bruce Aune, "Fatalism and Professor Taylor," *Philosophical Review,* 71 (October, 1962), pp. 512–19 and Razel Abelson, "Taylor's Fatal Fallacy," *Philosophical Review,* 72 (January, 1963), pp. 93–96.

The first of these makes use of the sea-fight example. Imagine that you are about to read your morning paper. Assume that it is true that only if there was in fact a naval battle yesterday will your paper carry a headline about it, so that if it has any other headline, that is sufficient to show that there was no such battle. Call the act of seeing the head-line which refers to the battle S, and call the act of seeing a certain different kind of headline S'. Further, call the two sentences "A naval battle occurred yesterday" and "No naval battle occurred yesterday" by the names P and P', respectively. Taylor thinks that if S happens, this ensures that there was a battle yesterday and hence that P is true, whereas if S' occurs, then there was no battle and P' is true. Now if what has been said so far is true, then Taylor thinks that we will have to reject as false the claim that it is within our power at the same time to do S and to do S', and if that is so, then he believes that this establishes fatalism (and, we could say, determinism) as true. His argument for this conclusion is very simple:

1. If P is true, then it is not now within my power to do S'.
2. But if P' is true, then it is not now within my power to do S.
3. Either P is true or P' is true.
4. Therefore, either it is not now within my power to do S, or it is not now within my power to do S'.

Before giving the second argument, a point about the phrase "is not now within my power" should be noted. It is a commonplace truth that, in most cases, we are not the cause of what it is that we see when we open our eyes. It is in this sense that it is no subject for controversy to say that we have no power to see one thing rather than another. But it is quite another thing, and a very much stronger assertion, to claim that we *never* cause what it is that we see to happen, and the two claims ought not to be confused.

Secondly, one should keep in mind that Taylor is talking about a particular identifiable headline and a particular naval battle identifiable as the one which occurred yesterday. This will become important in a little while.

The second argument differs from the first only in that it refers to a future naval battle rather than a past one, with the stipulation that instead of being a newspaper reader, you are now a naval commander. As commander, you are about to issue your order of the day to the fleet. You know that if you order one thing, other conditions being what they are at the time, at battle will occur the next day, and if you give another order, that will be enough to ensure that the battle does not happen. Call these two acts of ordering O *and* O', respectively, and call the sentences "A naval battle will occur tomorrow" and "No naval battle will occur tomorrow" Q and Q', respectively. Hence, according to Taylor, if you do O, there will be a battle and Q will be true, and *is* true now, and if you do O', no battle will happen and Q' is true. The question now is, as it was in the first argument, whether you can at one and the same time do O and O', or more precisely, the question is whether the statement "It is now within my power to do O, and it is also now within my power to do O'" is true or false. Taylor thinks that it is false, and here is his second argument, designed to proved that it is:

1. If Q is true, then it is not now within my power to do O'.
2. But if Q' is true, then it is not now within my power to do O.
3. Either Q is true or Q' is true.
4. Therefore, either it is not now within my power to do O, or it is not now within my power to do O'.

Criticisms of Taylor's Position

Taylor's contention is that in order to avoid both of his conclusions, we must deny one of his presuppositions. We can question whether this is wholly true, although we must certainly agree that at the very least, one or more of the presuppositions must be confined in the scope of its application, or restricted in other ways.

It might be well to state one of the possible restrictions which does not involve complete rejection here. It concerns certain problems in modal logic which, as mentioned before, are too difficult for treatment in detail here. The law of excluded middle may be stated as $(p \text{ v} -p)$, or, "A is either B or it is not B." It is possible to reject this law, as mathematical intuitionists do, for example. But in the case of Taylor's arguments, that rejection is probably not necessary. Rather, a revision in certain kinds of theories about the nature of truth is necessary, and a corresponding restriction of the law of excluded middle may be possible. The revision is this: it is usually held that truth is a timeless property, which is to say that propositions are either meaningless, or if they are meaningful, they are either true or false regardless of the time of their assertion.

Taylor's argument depends upon propositions about the future having a truth value which does not change. But suppose that it was possible to formulate and defend a theory of truth and a theory of meaning such that propositions *change* their truth-values, and that they are neither true nor false prior to the occurrence of the event or events which validate or invalidate them. Such a theory would hold that a prediction such as "A sea fight will occur in the year 2000," if uttered in 1968, is neither true nor false at that time. But neither is it meaningless. It may, for example, have pragmatic or instrumental significance, serving as a guide for the actions of certain people, and so on. If the year 2000 ends without a naval battle having occurred, the proposition will become false. It will become true if such an event comes to pass during that time. There are many problems with such a theory, but one of them is *not* the necessity for rejecting the law of excluded middle. The law may still apply to all propositions with truth-values, *when they have those values*. If such a theory is defensible (and at least it has the evidence of common sense on its side, a sort of evidence that Taylor and others often use for their positions), then it seems incumbent upon the supporters of fatalism and determinism to show why their views should be accepted in spite of this. If it is not defensible, then these philosophers must show why it is not, which they apparently have not done.

To proceed with further criticisms involves a closer examination of the arguments in question. It is to be noted that in the case of the naval battle, one of the statements, P, refers to a specific, identifiable, particular event, namely a battle at sea which took place at a given time on a given date while the other, P', does not refer to any such event. There are no descriptions of non-battles in newspapers, nor are there lists of prevented casualties, ships not sunk, names of non-commanders, and so on. To say that the absence of the headline P about the battle, or the consequent act of seeing a different sort of headline, ensures that there was no battle, that is, that P' is true, is merely to say that there was a period of time in which none of the identifiable events was a naval battle. The point in this is to emphasize the misleading feature of the phrase "a naval battle" as it is used in both P and P'. The point might be clarified by noting that only in the case of P can "the" be substituted for "a": in short, no definite description of the naval battle which did not take place ("the naval battle which did not take place" is not a definite description!) is possible. The reason is that it is not possible to specify any of the properties of an event which has not yet occurred. It *is* possible to predict *that* it will have such and such properties when and if it occurs, but that is not quite the same thing. Until it *does* occur, it does not actually have the properties, and predictions are not the same as descriptions. Were this not so, I could reasonably expect you to tell me all about the finer points of the battle you predict for 100 years hence. Some determinists indeed would want to say that this is quite feasible and that the only reason it cannot yet be done is that we do not know enough about the antecedent details. But reasons have already been given for suspecting this reply (it rules out all *possible* counter-examples) and the progress of science, and everything else for that matter, gives us no evidence to expect that such predictions are possible. Indeed, what *could* count as evidence for such a claim? But back to the original point, which is that no definite description of a future event is possible, and no description of such an event can render a naming identification of it. But if Taylor and his supporters are correct, it seems that this is just the sort of information we must have in order for the headline to ensure the occurrence of the event; for it is not just any old battle that it ensures but *this* battle with *these* casualties and *those* ships sunk.

These criticisms of course bear upon the second of the two arguments rather than the first. In the first argument, if *P* is true, then the battle has taken place and the headline ensures that it has. Since it has happened, then the law of excluded middle tells us that *P'* is indeed false. But, of course, the two arguments, contrary to Taylor's claim, are not identical. The propositions in the first one concern, on the one hand, a describable, nameable event and, on the other, a closed span of time in which all events have already occurred and are therefore in principle completely describable; while in the second argument neither the predicted naval battle nor the series of events which will be included in the relevant time span meet these conditions. The first argument proves that it is impossible to alter the past through any of our acts, and this is, indeed, perfectly in accordance with common sense, as Taylor says. It is not very informative, however. The second argument does not seem to be in accordance with common sense, since the average man certainly thinks that he can have some influence upon what events do and do not occur. But of more importance philosophically is the point made above, namely that acceptance of the one argument does not entail acceptance of the other because they are two quite different arguments, albeit of the same *basic* form though not in the same modality. *Q* and *Q'* remain predictions, while *P* and *P'* are descriptions, and the two are fundamentally different. What ensures the truth of a prediction is the subsequent occurrence of what is predicted. When that *happens*, the prediction is no longer a prediction of the *future*. When we remark that after all, prediction *A* was true, we do not say much of philosophical interest.

The Different Kinds of Necessity

A common philosophical mistake which occurs in many arguments about determinism and fatalism is the confusing of different kinds of necessity. One kind of necessity is the sort we normally attribute to propositions. Historically, this necessity is of two sorts, logical and *a priori*. There is little controversy about the nature of at least the basic definition of logical necessity. Logically necessary propositions are those which are tautologies, and whose denials are therefore contradictions. Logical necessity is often equated with mathematical necessity, for both are properties accruing to a proposition in virtue of its form alone. A *priori* necessity is the subject of heated controversy, and has been ever since the time of Immanuel Kant and even before this. There are two main prongs to the discussion. One is the question of whether there are any *synthetic a priori* propositions, and the other question concerns the meaning of "*a priori*," and such related questions as the problem of innate ideas. Still, in spite of these difficulties it is at least not impossible to understand something about what we mean when we speak of propositional necessity.

A second sort of necessity is physical necessity or as it is sometimes called, causal necessity. The concept is best understood in terms of physical law. An event is said to be physically necessary when the assertion of its non-occurrence violates the descriptions or prescriptions stated in or implied by a physical law or set of laws. For example, a rate of acceleration in excess of 32 feet per second per second for falling bodies in a vacuum is physically impossible because such an event would violate the laws of gravity. Or if something were thrown out a window and did not fall down, other things being equal, this too would violate gravitational laws, and hence be physically impossible. It should be clear that what is physically impossible may well be, logically possible. There is no contradiction involved in asserting that the feather in the vacuum tube falls faster than the piece of steel, nor is it a conceptual mistake to assert that it is logically possible for objects thrown out windows to fall up rather than down. Moreover, the concept of *degrees* of necessity is sensible in terms of physical necessity, and senseless in logic. A proposition either violates a law of logic or it does not; its denial is either a contradiction or it is not. But a physical event is necessitated only to the degree that the law with which it conforms is confirmed. Since the degree of confirmation of a physical law never reaches 1, it is always possible that future events will violate the law, that is to say, disconfirm it. But the concept of disconfirmation, or for that matter, confirmation, has no application to logical necessity.

The question now becomes, what sort of necessity is reflected in the concept of "ensuring" used in both of Taylor's arguments? At times in his writings on this subject, he seems to be saying that the truth or falsity of some proposition or other has implications for actions and events rather than for propositions about those actions or events, which would certainly be a sort-crossing, a category mistake, involving the two sorts of necessity just described. Taylor often makes disclaiming statements about the role of causation and hence of physical necessity in his arguments; but if he is right, then, once an order sufficient for the occurrence of a naval battle tomorrow is given, the battle could not fail to take place, no matter what else happened. It is certainly true that if a proposition P is sufficient for the truth of another proposition P', if P is true, then P' is true also. This is a logical truth. But it is another matter to speak as though this logical truth necessitated the occurrence of physical events, as Taylor seems to hold. A naval battle tomorrow is not, after all, a proposition. In order to hold the thesis that the one sort of necessity, or necessary truth, necessitates another kind of occurrence which is not logically necessary, one would have to posit still a *third* sort of necessity, namely, that in virtue of which logical truths can necessitate physical events! But this thesis, the "third necessity" thesis, is not one defended by determinists, nor do determinists appear to realize that this is entailed by Taylor's sort of argument.

The nature of "ensurance" in the arguments we are examining is misleading in yet another way which concerns the nature and extent of the circumstances and conditions which surround the future event. We have already noticed that there is a problem about being able to specify and describe the future naval battle, and that this leads to some basic differences between the two arguments Taylor compares. If this is true of the future event, it is also true of the circumstances and conditions which surround it at the time it takes place, and in the intervening time between the prediction that the battle will happen, and its happening. Now Taylor speaks of conditions and circumstances as though they are already determined, and that is precisely the problem—the way he puts the issue does not enable him to *prove* fatalism or determinism, because the mode of presentation already assumes a determined state of affairs. In other words, there is some reason to believe that the argument begs the question of fatalism. A metaphor suggested by James Blue might help to illustrate the point. Taylor's view of the relation between the naval battle and the conditions and circumstances surrounding and preceding it is much like that between a jigsaw puzzle with one piece removed and that removed piece. From one point of view we might well say that the missing piece ensures what the picture of the puzzle shows; but, on the other hand, it might be said with equal justice that the picture shown ensures what the missing piece is like. Now the problem is this: the analogy, and what it illustrates, shows us nothing about fatalism or about determinism at all, because both of these have already been assumed by stipulation in the premises concerning the conditions. Some of the circumstances are of course part of the future themselves, but Taylor treats them as if we already knew them, as if they were a part of the past. This presumes that they are describable and specifiable in the manner already discussed. But it was shown that this is in fact not true of future events, and that this is one reason to doubt this sort of fatalism. To assume the opposite is therefore to beg the question.

The Libertarians and Their Critics

So far, our examination of determinism has been concerned with a set of arguments designed to show, roughly, the logical necessity of fatalism and determinism. Reference to the laws of science is not an essential part of these arguments. The next discussion which we shall undertake depends precisely upon the relation between the differences among kinds of law. On the one hand, philosophers who are called *libertarians*, represented here primarily by arguments such as those of Professor C. A. Campbell,[4] hold that if moral responsibility is possible, then choice must involve a breach of causal continuity. This is so because, if there is no such breach in the causal chain, no one could have acted otherwise than he did. If such a claim is correct, then of course determinism is false. Moreover, it is not necessary to restrict the claim to moral choice, and hence moral responsibility. Whenever we speak of responsibility it should therefore be taken to include moral responsibility, but not to be restricted to it.

The opponents to the libertarian view are of two types, both of them determinists. We shall be considering only one type of opponent, normally called *soft determinists,* and the primary source of the arguments in support of this position is the work of Professor Moritz Schlick.[5]

The libertarian claim rests on the following assumptions, which together constitute an argument:

1. If there is no breach in causal continuity, then no one is able to act other than he did.
2. If no one is able to act other than he did, then no one is responsible for any act he performs.
3. Thus, if there is no breach in causal continuity, then no one is responsible for any act.

In opposition to this position, the soft determinists hold the following statements to be true, and offer a series of arguments in support of them:

1. Determinism is true.
2. To say that an act is caused is not to say that this act is compelled.
3. The sort of freedom required for responsibility is not freedom from causality, but freedom from compulsion.
4. Causality and responsibility are therefore compatible.
5. Indeed, without causality responsibility is impossible.

[4] C. A. Campbell, "Is 'Free-Will' a Pseudo-Problem?" *Mind,* 60, no. 3 (1951); pp. 441–65.
[5] Moritz Schlick, *Problems of Ethics* (Englewood Cliffs, N.J.: Prentice-Hall, Inc., 1939).

Let us begin with the soft determinists' defense of the claim that to say that an act is caused is not to say that it is compelled, and see what relevance it has to the question of responsibility. A compelling cause, they say, is one which prevents us from doing what we want to do. If I want to get to my office on time, but cannot because the traffic this morning is particularly heavy, then I have been compelled to be late despite my desire not to be late. But when I eat avocado pears rather than anchovies as my hors d'oeuvre, it is not because I was forced to do so, but because I wanted to do so. It is only when our actions are contrary to or in conflict with our desires that the question of freedom and responsibility arises at all. When the bandit tells you at gunpoint to raise your hands or he will shoot you, you are indeed being compelled in one sense of the term "compelled" to raise your arms, but it is *not* that sense we mean or would mean if your arms were tied to a derrick which then pulled them up. Let's face it: in a holdup you raise your arms because you *want* to since the alternative seems distasteful.

Now this defense of the claim that causality and compulsion are not the same bears directly upon the first of the assumptions which form the libertarian argument, namely, "If there is no breach in causal continuity, then no one is able to act other than he did." The position of the soft determinist here can also be formulated in another way, which we shall mention before we go back to the libertarian's first assumption. Briefly, the soft determinist is saying that since compulsion and causality are not the same thing, then the laws governing physical events which *are* compelled are not the same as laws which concern behavior which is not compelled. Schlick draws this distinction by saying that there are *descriptive* laws, such as those of physics, and *prescriptive* laws, such as those of morality and manners. The latter sort assume lack of compulsion, the former sort the opposite.

Some libertarians, especially C. A. Campbell, are willing to accept the distinction between sort of laws which philosophers such as Schlick defend, but argue that this distinction is irrelevant to the truth or falsity of the first assumption we are now considering. The soft determinists think it is very relevant indeed. They would argue that the first assumption is only defensible if we interpret the consequent "No one is able to act other than he did" as meaning "Everyone is compelled to act as he did act." But to do this, we must deny what the soft determinsts affirm, namely, that to say that an act is caused and to say that it is compelled are two different things. Since the distinction between descriptive and prescriptive laws is based precisely on this distinction between causality and compulsion, then surely the libertarians are wrong when they say that it has no bearing upon the truth of the first assumption. It has just this bearing: if the grounds for the distinction are true, then the first assumption is false, and the libertarians' argument is unsound!

The determinist is in effect arguing that if the libertarian wishes to support the first assumption and the argument of which it is a part, he must also support a second argument, namely this one:

1. If there is no breach in causal continuity, then all acts are caused.
2. If all acts are caused, then all acts are compelled.
3. If all acts are compelled, then no one can act other than he did.
4. Thus, if there is no breach in causal continuity, then no one can act other than he did.

It is the second premise of *this* argument that the determinist says is false, rendering the argument unsound. If the acceptance of the first argument is contingent upon the acceptance of this second one, then the first one is unsound too. That it is so contingent is shown (in the determinist's eyes) by the fact that to be defensible the consequent of the first assumption (premise) of the first argument must be interpreted in the manner we have considered.

In Campbell's famous article "Is 'Free Will' a Pseudo-Problem?" he claims that he does not need this second premise of the second argument, but if this is true, then he cannot be using *this* argument to justify the first premise in the first argument. That first premise, again, is "If there is no breach of causal continuity, then no one is able to act other than he did." Unfortunately, no *other* justification is forthcoming, but we might try to supply one here.

Later on in this same paper, Campbell agrees that freedom from compulsion is essential for moral responsibility, but that something else is needed too. It may be the case that I am free to do what I want and that hence I am not compelled to do what I in fact do. But now the question is whether I am free to want what I want, that is, am I really free to want anything but what I in fact do want? He is really arguing here that choice is an illusion, because what we call choice, if determinism is correct and our wants are caused, cannot result in any other act than it does result in. He is therefore saying that what determinism says is that if everything that happens is caused, then there is nothing that can be other than it is, and this must, if determinism is true, include human wants as well. Indeed, he might well say, though he does not, that if he is right about determinism here, then the first premise of the the first argument must be true, given that our acts are caused by our wants.

But although this is a defense of the first premise of the first argument that is consistent with Campbell's position, it implies some claims that make it suspect. It implies among other things that all events are absolutely predictable given a sufficient knowledge of environment and history. If we knew enough about the past, nothing in the future could surprise us. If some universal or ideal observer did have such knowledge, and did predict that I would perform X on January 15, 2000, then that is what I would do, if determinism is true.

Two points may be made here. One is that the version of determinism which is implied by the defense suggested for Campbell's position here is not soft but *hard* determinism. We have already considered some criticisms of this theory, since it is the theory implied by the Taylor arguments already examined. In order to make this defense viable, Campbell would have to show that if you are a determinist, you are either a hard determinist or not a determinist at all. Some case might be made for this against people like Schlick, but certainly Campbell has not accomplished this.

Secondly, it is difficult to see how one could reject only *part* of hard determinism, for example, the claim that mental events such as choices are determined, while retaining the claim that physical events are caused. It seems to be all or nothing. If it is, then what is to become of science, for surely if events have no causes, then science becomes senseless. But the soft determinist, with his analysis of compulsion *versus* causality, can defend himself against such a criticism. Indeed, the soft determinist not only maintains that responsibility and causality are compatible, but that they are very closely tied together by the fact that without causality, responsibility makes no sense. Let us now consider his justification for the latter claim, plus some arguments about it.

The Issue of Responsibility

Moritz Schlick argued that when we say that someone is responsible, and in particular, morally responsible, at least a part of what we mean is that by rewarding or punishing that person, we can change his behavior in the future, or, through example, change the behavior of others by our treatment of him. Responsible action is that which involves choice, so if it is true that by reward and punishment, praise and blame, we can change his actions, then it must be because we believe that our praising and blaming him has an effect upon his choosing. We discipline people because we believe that *they* will change their ways. It must be then that we believe that choice, and the consequent action, is causally determined, i.e., caused. If we do not believe this, then what possible reason could we have for punishing and rewarding, praising and blaming? If a man's choices are uncaused, then our doing these things is completely gratuitous and irrational. True, we might still punish for other motives, such as revenge, but that is beside the point since here we are not saying that praising or blaming in order to change someone's actions or cause them to stay the same is the *only* reason we do it, but that it is surely one of the reasons. And Schlick together with many other soft determinists believes that this is all they need to make their case. The argument, however, when formulated carefully is more complex than it seems at first sight. It would appear something like this:

1. If "X is responsible" means at least that if X is praised or blamed, etc., then his behavior and/or the behavior of others will be changed; then if X is responsible, we reward or punish him etc., in order to change his future choices and/or those of others.
2. If we reward or punish X in order to change X's future choices or those of others, then it is possible to effect such changes.
3. If it is possible to effect such changes, then X's future choices, and those of others, are caused.
4. If "X is responsible" means what the first premise says it means, then if X is responsible his future choices and/or those of others are caused.
5. "X is responsible" does mean what the first premise says it does.
6. Therefore, if X is responsible, then X's future choices and/or those of others are caused.

In the particular case of Schlick's own argument, he is speaking of *moral* responsibility, but there is no reason that the argument cannot be broadened to include all sorts of responsibility.

The Libertarian Reply

The libertarians, in order to defend themselves against this argument, must deny that at least part of the meaning of the sentence "X is responsible" is that X is liable to praise and blame, etc., such that it will result in a change in his behavior and/or that of others. (His conduct's remaining the same will count as a change here, if that is the purpose of the praise.) It is understood that we are not talking about marginal or doubtful cases, such as those where a person is responsible because of negligence or omission, but only of straightforward instances of responsible decision-making. The libertarians could refute the argument if they could give examples of cases in which we said that some agent X was responsible, but denied that we mean at least what the soft determinist says we mean in all such cases. It would follow such a counter-example by *modus tollens* that we do not mean by "X is responsible" at least that if X is praised or blamed, etc., then his behavior and/or that of others will be changed. But that this is what we *do* mean is what is asserted in the fifth premise of the argument, and if this statement is false, then the argument is unsound.

Another method of refutation might consist in showing that if we accept the soft determinists' claims, then we have to make other claims which in fact we believe to be false. If such a tactic were successful, it would not only show that the argument under attack was unsound because it contained a false statement or perhaps more than one, but, if the premises are assumed to be true, it would show the argument to be invalid. This latter method is one which Campbell adopts in his early criticisms of the Schlick position.

Campbell thinks that if Schlick is correct (and this would be true of our slightly changed and expanded version if it were true of Schlick), we must say that animals are responsible. The argument is:

1. If we reward or punish X in order to change his behavior, then X is responsible.
2. But we reward and punish animals in order to change their behavior.
3. Therefore, animals are responsible.

We do not want to say that (3) is true, so either the argument is invalid if the premises are true or by "X is responsible" we do not mean what the soft determinist says we mean.

But what appears on first sight to be a good criticism is not. No soft determinist, Schlick included, says that all cases where we reward and punish are cases where the agent is responsible. He only claims that all cases where we say that the agent is responsible are cases where we believe that the agent's behavior and/or that of others can be changed by praise or blame, reward or punishment. The two claims are quite different. One is the converse of the other, and converse propositions do not imply each other. Soft determinists hold the converse of the first premise in this argument, but this does not force them to hold the premise.

Two Other Replies by Campbell

A second criticism which Campbell uses consists in arguing that if Schlick is correct, then we cannot hold dead agents to be responsible. But we do, so Schlick must be wrong. The argument:

1. If X is responsible, then X is the person whom we intend to punish or reward.
2. Some dead agents are responsible.
3. Therefore, some dead agents are persons whom we intend to punish or reward.

The last statement is obviously absurd, and if it follows from the soft determinists' premises, then they must be wrong.

But again, this is not a good criticism, and the mistake is blatant. It is simply a case of bad grammar. All three statements in the argument should be changed into the past tense, and when this is done, there is no objection to agreeing with what is said from the soft determinists' viewpoint. This is the alternative for Campbell unless he simply wishes to face the fact that no one says dead agents are responsible, and that hence the second premise in the criticism, as it now stands, is false. Dead agents do not do anything, now or in the future, and hence are not responsible, and thus would not be punishable agents for the determinist.

The third criticism Campbell raises is the most interesting from the scientific point of view. It begins with the truth that whenever we assess the degree of responsibility for an action, we normally consider such factors as heredity, environment in the present, childhood upbringing, and so on. But, in Campbell's opinion, if Schlick is correct we should not do this. The argument is as follows:

1. If "X is responsible" means "X is the person liable for reward or punishment in order to change X's behavior or the behavior of others" (at least in part), then in assessing the degree of X's responsibility we need only consider those factors which bear upon X's ability to change his actions.
2. If the consequent of the last statement is true, then, in assessing the degree of X's responsibility, we need not consider environmental and hereditary elements.
3. Therefore, if the meaning of "X is responsible" is that given in the first premise, we need not consider environment and heredity in assessing the degree of X's responsibility.

The difficulty with this criticism is that the second statement is false; hence the argument is unsound. It is false because the antecedent of (2) is true, and the consequent false, making the entire conditional false. We need only consider the reasons for the falsity of the consequent of (2) here, given that the determinist grants the antecedent as true. This evidence is scientific, and massive. We know from sociology, biology, microbiology, psychology and many other related disciplines that certain types of inherited characteristics as well as environmental ones *do effect* an agent's ability to change and respond to correction. The very latest evidence indicates that the presence of the double-Y chromosome has a very high statistical correlation with criminality, especially of the more aggressive varieties, though there is some question about the significance of this. But there is *no* evidence contrary to the environmental and hereditary influence thesis. Statement (2) is therefore false.

A Sound Criticism of Schlick's View

Interestingly enough, a good criticism of Schlick's view *does* arise in connection with this last point. It concerns the fact that when we include an evaluation of the effects of heredity and environment in our judgments of responsibility, the normal result, if the effects of these factors are significant, is to *lessen* the degree of responsibility. This is not always the case, of course. Often we say that some agent, by reason of his training, upbringing, and breeding, ought not to have done some act, or that he could have been expected to do something that he did not do, or that we expect things of him that we would not expect of a person with a more conventional background. But a more normal sort of situation is that in which it is shown that some agent comes from a deprived home, has had little opportunity, has never been exposed to attitudes of respect for the law, and so on. When this is discovered, the force of it usually is, or ought to be, to lessen the severity of the judgment passed upon him.

Paradoxically, however, a serious consideration of Schlick's analysis, coupled with the findings of science, indicates that he must hold a person to be *more* responsible as the effects of heredity and environment are greater. For Schlick, degree of responsibility is measured mostly in terms of the severity of reward or punishment that is imposed. Science tells us that the more severe and intense environmental circumstances are upon an individual, the greater the difficulty in changing his behavioral patterns. We can suppose that the same is true of inherited factors. It therefore seems that Schlick is placed in the odd position of having to claim that the greater the influence of environmental and inherited factors, the greater the degree of reward and punishment required. But normally, when we accept evidence of lessened degree of responsibility in those cases where punishment is required, we lessen the punishment rather than increase it. The only other way out of this dilemma for Schlick seems to be the thesis that degree of responsibility and amount and intensity of punishment are not essentially connected in any way; but his "out" seems unacceptable for many reasons. Surely, for example, we cannot accept the thesis that a man might justly or appropriately receive a sentence of life imprisonment for a consistent tendency to jay-walk!

It may well be that a revision of the definition of "punishment" might enable Schlick and other soft determinists to avoid this difficulty. Such efforts in the direction of rehabilitation and reform as therapeutic treatments would count as punishment if we consider Schlick's position without revision. But there seems no reason to believe that such a classification is either fair or necessary. It might well be true that the greater the influence of environment and heredity, the more therapy is required to change behavior, but this does not mean that physical beating, imprisonment, or threat need be a part of the therapy. Once this distinction among kinds of "punishment" is made, the soft determinists avoid the criticism. They might then well agree that, as the influence of circumstance is shown to be stronger, it is fitting that the amount of corporal and penal and social punishment be lessened, thereby recognizing the lessened degree of responsibility for the act while at the same time strengthening the argument for increased therapeutic and other rehabilitative measures. If the determinists argue in this way, they seem to vitiate the major point of their opponents, which is the determinists' presumed inability to account for the proper ratios between responsibility and punishment.

The Libertarian vs. the Determinist

At this point, it is possible to give a restatement of the major issue dividing the determinist from the libertarian by emphasizing the respective replies one might make to the other over this issue of environmental and genetic factors and the effect they have upon conduct. The determinist might well say (indeed, most determinists do) that in his very recognizing of the fact that such factors do have an influence upon conduct, the libertarian agrees that human conduct is caused and that it may be altered by influencing its causes. How, the determinist asks, can the libertarian criticize the determinist on the ground that his conception of punishment does not fit our ordinary conduct (when we make judgments of lessened responsibility in the light of knowledge about an agent's background), without at the same time acknowledging that, by this very criticism, he implies that determinism is true? Does not the judgment of lessened responsibility prove that we do, in fact, not only admit that our behavior is caused but that, depending upon the nature of the operative cause, praise and blame, etc., are to be bestowed?

The libertarian replies that indeed it is true that, as we become aware of causal factors operating upon our behavior, we tend to blame and praise less because we attribute less responsibility. But, he says, this is *just* the point: either we have to abandon the notion of responsibility altogether in the face of an ever more complete causal explanation of all kinds of human action, or, if we are to claim that responsibility is a fact, we must make human decisions an exception to the causal laws of nature. You cannot have it both ways, he argues. Either you are responsible because *you* are the cause of your actions, or your actions are caused independently of your choice; or what is the same thing, your choice is caused, and responsibility is an empty notion. What it means for *you* to be the cause of your action now becomes the crucial issue, to which we must now turn.

The libertarians argue that to say that someone is responsible for an act is to imply that this agent could have acted otherwise than he did. We have already mentioned this, and we have noted that one of the determinists' replies is that all the claim requires so far as responsibility is concerned is for the agent not to be *compelled* to do what he does where compulsion and causation are carefully distinguished. But we have not given full credit to, nor a careful examination of, the libertarian's own exfoliation of what "could have acted otherwise" means and the soft determinist's criticisms of the libertarian views.

One of the first attempts Campbell makes involves the use of the term "ought" and depends upon our acceptance of the maxim "ought implies can." We must grant Campbell the acceptance of this maxim if we are to make any sense out of ascriptions of responsibility at all, but just exactly what implications it has remains a moot point, because the determinist can accept the maxim with equanimity as well as the libertarian. The argument runs like this:

1. If X is morally blameworthy for not doing some act, then he ought to have acted otherwise than he did. (That is, he ought to have done the act.)
2. If X ought to have acted otherwise than he did, then he could have acted differently than he did (because "ought" implies "can").
3. Therefore, if X is morally blameworthy for not doing some act, then X could have acted otherwise than he did.

The determinist replies to this argument that he agrees with the second premise and hence with the "ought implies can" maxim, but that the phrase "could have acted otherwise" is ambiguous. Some of the meanings of this phrase imply no breach with causal continuity. For example, if we mean merely that X was not *compelled* to do what he did, then we might still agree that he was caused to do what he did, if causality and compulsion are different. The determinist, of course, holds just this position. The soft determinist would say that we never *merely* say that "X could have acted otherwise"; what we mean is that "X could have acted otherwise *if* . . . ," where the "if" clause is filled in with claims about circumstances being other than they were at the time, and so on. In short, when we say that X could have acted otherwise than he did, we do not mean that he could have done so given exactly the same circumstances at the time, and presupposing that he had exactly the same character. This is a criticism of libertarians tendered by P. H. Nowell-Smith.[6] Campbell assumes from this criticism that Nowell-Smith and indeed all soft determinists must hold that to say that X could have acted otherwise is to say that he could, provided he was not in fact the being that he was at the time and/or that he was in circumstances other than those in which he was in fact at the time. The center of Campbell's attack on this view amounts to the claim that Nowell-Smith's position is a violation of the law of identity. Either X is X, or some other being, not-X. If he is not-X, then in determining what we mean when we say that X could have acted otherwise, we need not consider not-X. But if we are going to talk about X and not someone else, we cannot very well be talking about someone who, at the time when they made the choice and performed the act of which we are speaking, did not have the character of *and* was not in X's circumstances, for such a being would *be* not-X.

Certain difficulties arise even in the case of this justified criticism so far as libertarianism is concerned. If X's decisions are consistent with his character, as the criticism of Nowell-Smith would seem to imply, and if we knew what his character was, then we ought to be able to predict his decisions. This, of course, would be to admit determinism of some variety, and libertarians certainly do not want that. To avoid the dilemma, most libertarians do two things: they offer an analysis of what someone's character is which is based upon a dispositional description of his decisions, and they define "out of character" choices, actions, and decisions in terms of the lack of consistency which such occurrences have with the dispositional characterization of the agent. Both such explanations seem to be justified, though many problems remain in connection with the structure of dispositional analyses.

Essentially, the explanation of "X could have acted otherwise" which Campbell and most other libertarians find acceptable is this: "X would have acted otherwise if he had willed, or chosen, otherwise." When we say that someone could have done something other than he did, we very often mean simply that he would have done something else if he had chosen differently.

The Role of Choice

To the careful student a none too subtle shift will have been apparent in all of this. It is the move from talking about the relations between causes and actions to that between causes and *choices or decisions*. In effect, the libertarians are all saying, though they differ in

[6] P. H. Nowell-Smith, "Free-Will and Moral Responsibility," *Mind*, 57, (1948), pp. 45–61. Also see his *Ethics* (London: Penguin Books, 1954), chapters 9 and 10.

details, that the cause of a man's actions *is* his choice or decision. They seem to believe that this overcomes the problem about causal continuity by making the cause the choice. But the obvious question is, are the *choices* caused; or, in other words, if we speak of volitions rather than choices, is the will free? And this seems to raise the entire range of problems which we had with actions over again, this time in the context of choices or volitions. The soft determinists immediately reply that the thesis that a man's choices are not a part of the causal sequence entails a breach of continuity between one's character and one's conduct which is a violation of our personal experience, our common beliefs about others, and science, especially psychology. It is the very consistency of conduct and character that is the ground of predictability in psychology, and indeed seems to be verified in our everyday convictions about how the people we know will react in given types of situations. To deny this consistency, they say, is in effect to say that choices are accidents because they do not follow causally from the character of the chooser. But if choices are accidents, then what sense does it make to attribute responsibility to the person who makes them?

In Campbell's particular case, he reacts to this criticism by agreeing that there are choices which are inconsistent with a man's character but denying that such choices are always accidents. Indeed, the hypothesis that the choice was made by an agent automatically rules out the truth of the claim that it was an accident. And, Campbell might have said, were it not possible for some choices to be inconsistent with character, a man could *never* "act out of character." But surely this is not a senseless phrase: the problem is to give it the correct meaning. What a man's character is, from the third-person viewpoint, is the set of actions he typically performs in similar sets of circumstances. The observer can observe his actions, but Campbell argues that the agent's *choices* are not observable by anyone. This is *very* important, not new with Campbell, and not pursued adequately and fully by him or anyone else in its application to the determinism–free will issue. Campbell goes on to give an analysis of choice-making which is understandable only through self-inspection.

His first move in this argument is the assertion that free will only operates in cases where there is a conflict in the mind between what the agent believes to be his duty and what he feels to be his strongest desire. In the normal course of events, there is no reason that the agent should not act in accordance with his strongest desire, and his strongest desire is nothing other than the after-the-fact expression of the matrix of emotive and connative dispositions which we normally call his "character." This, of course, is in accordance with the dispositional analysis of character which has already been mentioned. In so far as a man's strongest desire is reflected in his character, it follows that his choice, that is, his will, is determined by his character, and this largest part of his character is therefore not free. To the extent that this is true of any agent, his behavior can be predicted, and the predictions can be expected to be accurate in proportion to the data we have about the agent's character. *Free* will however is a different matter. It is operative only in that area where there is a conflict between his strongest desires as expressed in his character and those instances where these desires conflict with his sense of duty. It is this claim that allows Campbell to argue that some choices are incompatible or inconsistent with a man's character. And more importantly, it is, in his view, this claim which provides the *major* defense against the soft determinist's thesis. In line with what was said just a moment ago, it should be noted again here that neither Campbell nor any other libertarian need rest upon this fragile basis.

The case for the indeterminist or libertarian continues with an accusation against the determinist which is related to the remarks just made. The first criticism is that the determinists do not understand that it is quite intelligible to hold that some act may be a result of the choice of an agent, but at the same time not a result of the *character* of the agent in the sense that it may not be consistent with the behavior of that agent as it is observed before the fact. The reason that the determinists do not see the possibility of this is that they think that behavior is to be analyzed *solely* in terms of observable behavior. But in fact, much of the relevant information pertaining to behavior which results from choice is *not* observable, even in principle.

Two Kinds of Evidence

At this point, we come to the most convincing of the arguments for the inability of the determinists to refute libertarianism as the two positions are stated here. Until this point, but for expansions of the arguments of Schlick and Campbell, we have stayed reasonably within the scope of the applications of their competing theories. Now we shall begin from the premises which Campbell suggests, add some others, and introduce conclusions not to be found in his theory. It will be necessary first of all to provide some examples of events relevant to agent behavior which in Campbell's view are not in principle observable. One such "event" is what he calls "creative activity." Another is the exercise of free will itself, and a third is the unique experience, knowable only by introspection, of the conflict between a "rise to duty" and our strongest desires. Campbell argues that (1) since behavior of character is from the observer's viewpoint simply that which is consistent with what has gone before, and (2) since there are events that are knowable intro-spectively and that in no other way affect overt behavior, then (3) it is compatible with this to assert that some behavior may be agent-be-havior which is not knowable in the way that behavior of character is knowable. If this is true, then it may be the case that events which are knowable only in an introspective manner affect behavior which is not predictable on the basis of past observed behavior alone. And this is all that the libertarian needs in order to support his thesis that there may be agent-behavior, that is, behavior caused by an agent who is respon-sible for it, which is inconsistent with the character of that agent as it is defined dispositionally. It is important to remember that "disposition-ally" here is to be defined in third-person observational terms.

Campbell himself is not satisfied with this argument, for he goes on to say that even in those cases where the course of action chosen *is* in con-formity with the agent's strongest desires as these are known by observa-tion, we (the agents themselves) are still introspectively aware that we could have chosen otherwise. That is to say, he would argue that intro-spective awareness is sufficient of itself to gainsay any claim that the observer might make on the basis of his evidence.

In all of this, Campbell has an excellent point, but it is not clearly stated, nor are all of its implications traced out. It is not, as he seems to think, that introspective evidence is sufficient to *outweigh* what the observer concludes on the basis of his "second-hand" evidence, as it were, but rather that two different *kinds* of "evidence" are involved and only one of them is even relevant to dispositional character analysis of the sort which supports the determinist's position.

To put it more strongly, the sort of evidence which the determinist offers in support of his position is really scientific evidence. There is ab-solutely nothing wrong with scientific evidence. But the true scientist would be the first to admit that if this sort of evidence cannot in principle bear upon an issue, then that sort of issue cannot be settled by an appeal to such evidence. One might even claim without stretching a point that this is ordinary common sense. A husband and wife do not solve their problems by discussing the laws of physics, nor by examining the ways in which they have acted, and nothing else. Ultimately, if they succeed in solving their problems it is because they have become aware of facts about *themselves*, facts which a psychoanalyst may have helped them to realize but which, because of the essentially private and personal nature of these facts, are only knowable *by* themselves. This is not an argument against behavioral psychology. It is quite compatible with the ability of a behavioral psychologist to change the behavior patterns of a man through various external stimuli without at the same time changing the man's personal and private feelings and convictions about what he does.

The main point here is this: "mental events" are in principle not observable. If this is true, then mental events are not even *in principle* a possible part of what counts as scientific evidence. If that is so, then expressions of an agent which purport to be descriptions of his mental events are in fact not descriptions. If anything, they are of the nature of reports or expressions and the criteria for deciding what truth-value they have are not the same as those on the basis of which we accept or reject scientific evidence, because the latter criteria are *publicly* applicable. In short, mental and physical events are different, and evidence supporting a thesis about the one is not even possible evidence about the other.

As you will see in Chapter 5, this claim does not entail any thesis at all about the ontological status of minds as opposed to bodies. It is an epistemological claim and nothing more. But, if we are correct, this is all that we need in this case, because the criteria for what will count as scientific evidence are also in a crucial way epistemological. No scientist would accept as evidence any data that were observable in principle only by him. But this is precisely the sort of experience to which we must appeal here. Ultimately the libertarian must rest upon an appeal to the individual agent: do you, or do you not, have an "immediate awareness" of facts about your "self" or your "ego," for lack of better terms, which others cannot have, and which are only expressible to other individuals in reports which you make? Is there any evidence in support of these reports other than merely your report itself? It will not do to claim support for a report on the grounds that its content is consistent with your overt behavior, for *ex hypothesis*, you beg the question in making such a claim.

It seems that we all do have such experiences and indeed that it is in terms of precisely these experiences that we define and discover what terms such as "self-identity" and "self" mean. If the existentialist literature of this century has any philosophical significance, this is surely a part of its message: our private isolation and responsibility rests upon the inaccessability of our mental life to the public purview. This has its advantages and its drawbacks, but surely it is a fact—not the sort of fact which science will eventually enable us to study together, but the sort of fact for which there can never be any principle of evidence.

Whether the particular examples of mental events which Campbell reports are the type of which we are all privately aware is beside the point. If there is but *one* such event and if we are aware of its bearing upon our overt behavior, then it seems that the libertarian has a case which the determinist cannot refute. The reason? The determinist's evidence is public and scientific; the libertarian's is of a different logical sort.

EXERCISES

1. Write a paragraph stating in your own words just exactly what a category-mistake is.

2. Compose an argument which contains a category-mistake.

3. Symbolize your answer to question (2) using the methods of the first chapter. Do a proof of invalidity for the argument as symbolized.

4. Restate Zeno's argument in simple deductive form as illustrated in the first chapter.

5. If a category-mistake is a type of equivocation, what is the *difference* between it and other types of equivocations?

6. Even without the category-mistake as a part of your analysis, you should be able to show that Zeno's argument is unsound. Use the techniques developed to date to show that it is.

7. What mistake, in addition to a category-mistake, and in addition to being unsound, does the argument make?

8. Compose an argument analogous to Zeno's and, making the same mistakes, designed to show that an arrow can never get to a point B once shot from a point A.

9. Zeno had another argument in which he argued that a bushel of grain will make no noise when dropped, because a single grain does not, and after all, a bushel is only a lot of grains. What mistakes does this argument make?

10. Zeno and Parmenides believed that change was an illusion. Change is the process of becoming. They argued that everything either comes from something, or from nothing. Nothing comes from nothing. But if something comes from something, it already exists, so nothing begins to exist, i.e., nothing becomes, or changes. Evaluate this argument.

11. What are the properties of minds for Descartes? Of bodies?

12. What are bodies, in the terminology of mathematics, for Descartes? Can we know anything about the future behavior of bodies in his view? Would modern science agree with him or not? Why or why not?

13. Are the workings of *your* mind possible objects of knowledge for *me* if Descartes is right? Why or why not?

14. Are both minds and bodies causes for Descartes? Are the ways in which they cause things, if they are causes, the same or different? Explain your answers.

15. If a man's behavior was purely explicable in terms of the laws of motion and mechanics, what would we have to conclude if Descartes is correct? Do you agree that these premises imply this conclusion? Defend your answer.

16. Describe an occurrence of the fallacy called "hasty generalization" which may be used against Descartes and which is discussed in the section.

17. One argument used against Descartes in the section is that if he is right, we could never in principle tell a man from a robot, given that minds are of the nature he describes. But we *can* tell the difference between the two. So he is wrong. Do you think that this is a good argument? Why or why not?

18. Descartes is a mechanist so far as his theory about the causal relations between bodies is concerned. Mechanists are also determinists. Explain the two terms "mechanist" and "determinist."

19. What is the category mistake which Descartes makes in his theory about the causal relations between minds and bodies? Formulate the argument in

simple deductive form. What effect does the category-mistake have upon the argument?

20. Discuss Ryle's dispositional analysis of human behavior.

21. What is the definition of determinism?

22. Does the truth of hard determinism entail that there are no minds? That is, does determinism entail that matter is the only substance? Why or why not?

23. If determinism is true, what are some of the implications for moral philosophy?

24. If men make free choices, does this mean that *no* events are determined? Why or why not?

25. State briefly the difficulties surrounding "necessity" and "ensurance" in Taylor's arguments for fatalism.

26. What is the difference between hard determinism, soft determinism, and libertarianism?

27. Evaluate two of Campbell's arguments against the determinists, using the criteria which have been developed already.

28. Evaluate Schlick's argument that determinism is required *for* moral responsibility, because it is the only thing that ensures that we can change a person's behavior through reward and punishment.

29. Use the *external* criteria to evaluate Campbell's and Schlick's positions, assuming for the discussion that both of them meet the others.

30. Evaluate the argument given in the section that mental and physical events are two quite different things, and that a thesis about the one cannot provide evidence for claims about the other.

5

Causality

Once in a very great while a thinker creates an idea of such novelty and with such widespread application in his field that it can truly be called a watershed in the history of that discipline. Immanuel Kant's works, especially his *Critique of Pure Reason*,[1] embody just such an idea, and subsequent philosophy, both in epistemology and in metaphysics, has never been the same. Kant did not settle the question of the nature of causality, for even today there are many proponents of the view held by his theoretical opponent, David Hume. However, he did suggest an entirely new way of looking at the problem, which was based upon his claim that Hume and all previous philosophers had failed to see that we have knowledge of three kinds of propositions and not just two. The three kinds of propositions are analytic, synthetic, and *synthetic a priori* propositions. The last of these was the invention of Kant—or perhaps discovery is a better term—and he himself thought that this discovery was of such importance that he referred to his own analysis of causality and the knowing situation as a "Copernican Revolution" in the history of ideas. We shall discuss Hume's theory first, for it was that theory which, in Kant's words, woke him from his "dogmatic slumber." Then we shall discuss Kant's view. Criticisms of both views will be included in the discussion. Finally, we shall examine the causal theory of a contemporary philosopher, C. J. Ducasse.

DAVID HUME

David Hume lived from 1711 until 1776. He was the last of three great British empiricists, the first two of whom were John Locke and George Berkeley. In Hume's work the principles ennunciated by Locke

[1] Immanuel Kant, *The Critique of Pure Reason*, translated and edited by Norman Kemp-Smith (New York: St. Martin's Press, 1961).

and developed by Berkeley are carried to their logical conclusions, conclusions which had such an effect upon Kant. The latter was convinced that if Hume was correct, then science, indeed all knowledge, was impossible. Hume's most famous work is *An Enquiry Concerning Human Understanding.* In it, Hume argued that there is an experimental method through which we can develop a science of man, which would include as its subjects the nature of our ideas and their origins, the nature of our reasoning processes, and ethics, aesthetics and politics, among other matters. For our purposes here, the most important part of the science of man concerns the nature of the world of our perception, and our relations to it. The method which he uses to analyze these matters is the method of science as he saw it, which is inductive. This method of science was the method followed by the scientists of Hume's time. Hume did not think that human nature and the subjects of physics were identical, of course, for he, together with Locke and Berkeley, also was aware of introspection as as mode of self-knowledge. It was clear to him that this mode of knowledge was not amenable to the public observation that is essential to purely empirical science. His insistence upon scientific method in the broad sense meant rather that whether the mode of knowledge must be built upon a base of data gathered from both sources, from which we infer general truths inductively. In Hume's eyes this was the essence of Newtonian science.

Hume's first efforts were directed at exactly the same questions that puzzled Locke and Berkeley, namely, the nature of the basic elements which are the foundation of all our knowledge, and the nature of the knowing mind which has this knowledge. This was his primary interest, and it is because of this that the study of Hume is predominantly concerned with his epistemological writings. All of his other studies, of which there are many, ranging from his criticisms of the teleological argument for the existence of God to his analysis of aesthetic perception, are founded in his basic conclusions about the origins, extent, and limits of human understanding. As Berkeley and Locke found all of the possible elements of our knowledge in our perceptions and the data of introspection, so did Hume. He uses the word "perceptions" generally, so that it covers both the data of sense, which he calls "impressions," and the images of these impressions used in our reasoning, which he calls "ideas." When comparing these three British empiricists, it is essential to notice their different uses of such terms. Notice, for example, that for Berkeley "ideas" refers to the same data that "impressions" refers to for Hume but that there are no "ideas" of the mind for Berkeley.

For Hume, ideas and impressions stand in a relation of correspondence, since our ideas resemble the impressions from which they are derived. But this is only true on the simplest or most basic level. Like the other empiricists, Hume knew that we have complex as well as simple ideas. He thought that complex ideas were composed from simple ones. Each and every one of the simple ideas does correspond to a simple impression, and so the relation of resemblance holds on this level. But it is clear that we may make complex images in our minds to which there is no correspondent entity in the real world. We may create the mental image of a gold mountain, but there are no such things outside our minds. Nonetheless, the simple ideas out of which we compose this complex image, our idea of the color gold, our ideas of immensity, solidity, and so on, each do resemble some impression we must have had.

But how do we distinguish between impressions and ideas? That is, how do we know what is an impression and what is an idea? The first criterion for distinguishing the two is vividness and strength. Impressions are more vivid, and they strike the senses and the mind with more force than do ideas. The second criterion is temporal priority. Impressions always occur before ideas. Among other things, this seems to entail that there are no simple ideas we have which are not preceded in their origination by a simple impression. Hume mentioned only one case in which he thought that this might not be true, which we shall discuss later in the text.

Again like his predecessors, Hume quickly found that he had to proliferate the sources of our knowledge in order to account for its variety and scope. He also says that we have what he calls "secondary ideas," which are, as the name implies, ideas of ideas we already have rather than copies of impressions.

Hume draws an important distinction between impressions of sensation and impressions of reflection. Impressions of sensation, he says, "arise(s) in the soul originally from unknown causes." We might take this to mean that so far as our *knowledge* of impressions of sensation are concerned, the most we can say is that they are given, in the philosophical sense of that term. That is, we simply find ourselves having sensations and impressions of them, and we can say no more in the way of a knowledge claim about the matter. The same sort of point comes out in Kant when he acknowledges that the given in sensation must have a cause, which he calls the *noumenal* world, but that we remain ignorant of this because of the limitations of our understandings and perceptions.

Impressions of reflection are more difficult to explain. The easiest way is to use an impression which occurs, then ceases, but is remembered. What remains after the impression ceases to exist is clearly an idea of that impression, which is remembered. Let us assume that the original impression was one that gave us pleasure. The contemplation of the idea of that impression, after the impression is gone, will give rise to yet another impression, that of pleasure. This latter impression is an impression of reflection. Impressions of reflection play an important role in Hume's analysis of the aesthetic experience, but this need not detain us here except in so far as the roles of memory and imagination which are involved bear upon the analysis of causation. The remembering of an idea, in Hume's eyes, is characterized by the degree of vividness of the idea that is remembered. Remembering is then the *mode* of recalling impressions in this way, that is, calling them into our minds with this particular sort of vividness. But we can also remember impressions with only that degree of vividness which is possessed by faint or weak copies of the original impression. This mode of recalling images is the imagination.

Hume also notes that remembering includes the order in which the impressions occurred, while this is not so with imagination. In one sense, this frees the imagination for its work in our aesthetic experiences, which memory alone cannot serve. We must be able to break up our complex ideas and recombine their simple elements into fantasies in some sorts of aesthetic experiences, and this the imagination could not do if it were confined by the order requirement. This is not to say that the imagination combines and recombines ideas and impressions in a completely random way. Hume thought that it did its work according to a "gentle force" or principle of association which he did not try to explain, because he thought it was basic to human nature and hence could only be identified. But Hume *did* think that he could point out the occasions upon which the gentle force manifested itself through our tendencies to associate certain impressions and ideas in certain ways. He thought that the imagination tended to associate ideas on the basis of: (1) their resemblance to one another, (2) their contiguity in time or place, (3) their relationship to one another as cause to effect. Even if all of these conditions are present, it is not *necessary* that the imagination combine the ideas so related together. That is, if A and B stand in a causal relationship, resemble one another, and are contiguous in time or place, it does not logically *follow* that the imagination would identify A as the cause of B, or associate A and B in any other way.

The Theory of Relations

It may be well to pause at this point and move ahead to the beginning of the next chapter. There you will notice that John Locke's primary reason for positing the existence of material substance was that, without it, he could not explain the origin of our primary and secondary ideas, nor could he account for the coherence of the world in terms of the subject which possesses primary and secondary qualities. The general topic of the next chapter is epistemology, and the general topic of this one is metaphysics. In both chapters it is observed at the outset that it is often difficult to distinguish between the two fields, and the case in point provides an excellent example. Locke is arguing that material substance must exist in order to explain what is; Hume will say that we have no idea of material substance, because we have no impressions from which it could be derived. Neither does this idea derive from our impressions of reflection. So we do not have such an idea. How then are we to account for the coherence of what it is that we perceive? Hume argues that it is to be explained in terms of the association of ideas on the basis of their contiguity, resemblance, and causal relations, and nothing else. It will be noted that all three of these are relations. Hume argues that there are two kinds of relations, which he calls *natural* and *philosophical* relations. Natural relations include contiguity, resemblance, and causality, which are the qualities in virtue of which the imagination "naturally" associates ideas having these qualities.

The second sort of relations are "philosophical," and there are seven of them. They are: (1) resemblance, (2) proportion in quantity of number, (3) degrees in quality, (4) identity, (5) relations of time and place, (6) contrariety, and (7) causation. Now it is immediately apparent that resemblance and causality occur in both lists, and since contiguity is a relation of time and place, it too is both a natural and a philosophical relation. This is explicable according to Hume because some natural relations must exist in order for there to be philosophical ones. For example, given that the philosophical relations all involve comparison, which includes resemblance, there must be some sort of natural resemblance before there can be any philosophical relations based upon it. Moreover, some philosophical relations are reducible to natural ones, and causation in the philosophical sense is one of these. We will return to this point in a moment.

From this beginning of a discussion of Hume's theory of relations, it is now necessary to turn momentarily to a discussion of the kinds of propositions which express relations. Hume believes that all the possible objects of human understanding and reason are divisible into either relations of ideas or matters of fact. Relations of ideas are expressed in certain kinds of propositions, and these propositions are the content of the mathematical disciplines, that is, algebra, arithmetic, and geometry. The propositions of the mathematical disciplines do not exhaust all the propositions which express relations of ideas, but all the rest have this much in common with mathematical statements: they are all "intuitively or demonstratively certain." Intuitive certainty is exemplified both in the propositions of mathematics and in the perception of the truth or falsity of statements asserting resemblance among things, a relation of contrariety between them, and differences expressible as variations in degrees of quality. Demonstrative certainty is more properly confined to the area of mathematics, for mathematical propositions express relations among ideas and nothing else, and their truth or falsity is not dependent upon the existence of objects corresponding to the ideas. The denial of a true mathematical proposition is for Hume a contradiction, and therefore he believes that such statements are analytically true. He had some reservations about this claim in connection with the sorts of propositions which are expressed in geometry, but we need not consider this intricate matter here.

Propositions concerning matters of fact are not analytic for Hume. They are synthetic because their truth or falsity depends upon the relation of correspondence between them and the facts they characterize. The denial of such a proposition, even if the proposition is true, is not a contradiction. Furthermore, no amount of evidence for a proposition about matters of fact will ever give it the degree of certainty that mathematical truths have. In Hume's eyes, there are no other sorts of propositions in addition to analytic and synthetic ones. This was to be the center of the Kantian attack upon his doctrine. Now it is time to return to his discussion of relations.

In addition to the distinction between natural and philosophical relations, Hume further divides the latter into what he calls variable and invariable relations. Invariable relations only change if there is a corresponding change in the objects or ideas which are to be related. This is the sort of relation which is expressed in a mathematical proposition, for the relations expressed therein depend upon the constant meaning of the symbols employed. For example, $(2 + 2 = 4)$ will forever express the same relation, *unless* the meaning of one or more of the symbols change, which presupposes a change in the objects or ideas named by the symbols. Variable relations, obviously, may change without a prior change in the ideas or the objects. The relation of contiguity may change without any change in the objects which are contiguous, nor in our ideas or impressions of them. Propositions which express such relations are therefore not such that the relations expressed in them depend upon the constant meaning of the symbols employed. This is the reason that such propositions are synthetic and not analytic. Earlier it was mentioned that in Hume's eyes the philosophical relation of causation is reducible. Let us now turn to the examination of causation.

Causes and Effects

All inference in mathematics is demonstrative for Hume. But when we are confronted with a proposition about our perceptions, we cannot make any further inferences from it without introducing causation. The connection of cause and effect is in his eyes the basis for any conclusions which we draw from observation statements. All reasoning about matters of fact involves sentences concerning our perceptions and therefore such reasoning rests upon the causal relation. It is only this relation that enables us to go beyond what is immediately presented to the senses and draw conclusions about the origin and the consequences of whatever we perceive.

Where do we derive our idea of this relation? All ideas, as we know, are derived from impressions, either directly or indirectly. But we have no impression of anything which is a quality or property of each and every one of the things which we denominate by the word "cause." From this it follows that our idea of causation must be derived not from some properties of things, but from relations which hold between them. The problem is therefore to examine the relations which we find among things in order to see which of them are the source of our idea of the causal relation. Hume goes about this by considering those things called "causes" and those things called "effects" together, in an effort to discover whether such complexes have common properties. He believes that two fundamental properties are found in such situations. These properties are contiguity of cause and effect, and temporal priority of the cause. It need not be the case that the cause and effect are *immediately* contiguous, but if they are not, the intervening events must be contiguous with one another and with the cause and the effect. Hence, if A is the cause of D, then B and C may occur between A and D, but B and C will be contiguous with one another, and with A and D. Furthermore, it is essential for a proper understanding of Hume to realize that this contiguity need not be *spatial* contiguity, because he understood that this would make it impossible to explain the ordinary belief that feelings and decisions, which have no spatial location, are causally related to our actions.

The requirement of temporal priority is important, for Hume thought that there were no instances of the causal relation in which the cause was not prior to the effect, and that experience confirmed this.

These two properties alone are nonetheless not sufficient to explain the relation, because one thing may be contiguous with and prior to another without being its cause. That is, it may be *necessary* that to be the cause of B, A must occur before B and be contiguous with B, but having these two properties alone is not *sufficient* to make A the cause of B. This is sometimes expressed in ordinary discourse by our saying, when presented with the fact that A has these properties relative to B, "But that doesn't mean that A *must* be the cause of B." In short, we normally speak as though there was something *necessary* about the causal relation, something which makes the thought that something could exist but not have been caused repugnant to us. Furthermore, we also seem to be convinced that certain particular *kinds* of things have certain particular *kinds* of effects. We would find it absurd if John Smith insisted that he had no parents, and we would find it equally silly if he insisted that he did have parents, and that they were both non-human. The belief that nothing exists uncaused, certain though we find it, is not necessarily true in the technical sense in Hume's eyes, because he thinks that the concept of an entity existing at some time does not contain within it the idea of a cause of that entity. Hence, the proposition, "Every event has a cause," is not *implied* by sentences asserting the existence of particulars, and is therefore not demonstrable. He is less clear about whether the claim is intuitively certain, or at least about the reasons for his denying that it is so certain, but nonetheless denies that it is. Furthermore, he finds that arguments which attempt to prove the proposition *a priori* usually beg the question by assuming that, for example, the maxim "Nothing comes from nothing" is true, which is to assume that everything has a cause.

Not only is it conceptually possible to have the idea of an object without having the idea of its cause, but our daily experience, if we examine it carefully, gives us no grounds for making the inference to cause or effect. We *learn* that fire causes pain, but in the simple perception of fire as such, the idea of pain is not seen to be included in it nor to follow from it. Yet clearly we do believe that fire causes pain, and if we believe this because we have learned it, then *experience* must in some way be the foundation of our belief. What is it that we have experienced? The *constant conjunction* of things like putting our hand in fire and feeling pain: with repetition of the constant conjunction, and memory of its past occurrence, we come to call the one "cause" and the other "effect." A cause is therefore an object or event which is always followed by another object or event and which is repeatedly conjoined with these particular objects or events in our experience. With the experience, a habit or custom is established by virtue of which we come to expect that when an instance of the first event occurs, an instance of the second will follow upon it. This is why we expect that the future will resemble the past, even though in fact it may not. It is not a contradiction to say that the sun will not rise tomorrow as it did yesterday, but we nonetheless believe that it will because of the habit and custom supporting this belief based on our past experience of the fact that morning follows evening.

The contiguity and succession of similar events which constitute causal sequences therefore do not contain the idea of necessity within them. But we seem to have this feeling about the necessity of causal relations;

and, if it does not originate with our experience of objects and events, then there is only one other possible source for it if Hume's philosophy is correct. That source is that the feeling of necessity is founded upon some impression or impressions of reflection. The impression of reflection from which Hume thinks it originates is that which our perception of the repetition of constant conjunction produces. Once this impression is established, Hume thinks that the mind has an almost irresistible impulse to associate a particular cause with the effect we expect to follow upon it. Repetition is, of course, a fact which happens independently of our perception of it. The impression of reflection we have of repetition comes from our consideration of the ideas caused by the sequence of impressions in our experience. Causal "necessity" is therefore in Hume's eyes a *psychological* phenomenon. It is not that objects are in fact necessarily connected in the real world; it is rather that the experience of the constant conjunction of objects determines us to *feel* that if one object of a given sort occurs, then a second of a given sort *must* follow. It is not for Hume a matter of explaining something about the nature of objects in the real world; it is rather a matter of explaining the foundation for our association of different ideas, and a matter of explaining what he thinks we *mean* when we say that something is the cause of something else.

Causality Defined

It was stated earlier that for Hume causality is both a philosophical and a natural relation. Which classification one uses depends upon whether one includes in the explanation or definition of a cause its connection with the principle of the association of ideas. Considered independently of this principle, the causal relation is a philosophical one. Hume's definition of a cause considered as a philosophical relation is that a cause is "an object precedent and contiguous to another, and where all the objects resembling the former are placed in like relations of precedency and contiguity to those objects that resemble the latter." When we consider causality as a natural relation, he defines a cause as "an object precedent and contiguous to another, and so united with it that the idea of the one determines the mind to form the idea of the other, and the impression of the one to form a more lively idea of the other." This definition clearly includes reference to perceivers and to the principle of association. The original concern with causation for Hume arose from his pondering over the grounds for the inferences we draw from our perceptions, and it is the causal relation considered as a natural one which in his eyes explains this. It should also be clear that no "proof" for this explanation is forthcoming in the way of evidence, because evidence itself rests upon the causal relations it has to what is being proved. Nor, as we have seen, is the principle that everything has a cause *demonstrable* on the basis of Hume's notion of natural causality. Our belief in this principle, and hence in the uniformity of nature, rests only upon habit or custom established through the principle of the association of ideas, and nothing more.

Given this explanation of the causal relation, there is no way to escape the conclusion that skepticism in science is at least logically justifiable, and Hume realized this. He did not think that it was *pragmatically* justifiable, and no doubt he is correct in this opinion. But it remains possible to doubt the possibility of science if he is right. Furthermore, metaphysics seems to lose all point if Hume is right, because the propositions of metaphysics are then either all analytic, and hence uninformative, or they are synthetic, and hence of no greater validity than the claims of science. When Kant read Hume, he realized that both of these positions followed upon the Humean position. But that did not prove that Hume was wrong. So, to defend science and metaphysicas, Kant created an entire new philosophy, which he called "critical philosophy," in which he attempted to show how it was possible on the one hand to agree with Hume that necessity in causal relations is not given with our sense experience of the real world, yet still maintain in opposition to Hume that such relations *are* necessary. It is now time to turn to an examination of what Kant said.

IMMANUEL KANT

Immanuel Kant was born in Königsberg, East Prussia, on April 22, 1724. He is famous for having led a life of frugality and regularity. He never traveled more than a few miles from Königsberg in his life, we are told, and apparently his daily regimen was so rigorous that a rumor sprang up to the effect that the clocks of Königsberg were set by his afternoon walks. For the larger part of his life, he had a local renown, due to his excellence as a lecturer and as a kindly man who enjoyed meeting people of different walks of life. Two other unsubstantiated reports about Kant have it that he invented the garter and that he played skillfully at billiards. We also know that he was reared in the Pietist tradition and that he reacted against his early upbringing. He was well read in Newtonian science and had read Hume closely. Kant was 57 years of age before his first really major work, the *Critique of Pure Reason,* was *published.* When one considers the ages at which other scholars, then and now, publish their major works, this is surprising enough. In Kant's case, however, it was merely the beginning, though the first *Critique,* as it is called, published in 1781, remains his most famous piece. In rapid succession, books appeared thereafter from 1783 to 1798. He died on February 12, 1804, and some Kantian scholars of considerable influence have been heard to express the unqualified opinion that, for the sake of their careers, it was a good thing that he did.

Kant was not overly modest, a failing not widely known among German philosophers; and although he did say of the first *Critique* that it was "dry, obscure, opposed to all ordinary notions and moreover long-winded" (which is certainly true), he also referred to his discoveries as a "Copernican Revolution" and said of his major thesis: "All metaphysicians are therefore solemnly and legally suspended from their occupations till they shall have adequately answered the question 'How are synthetic cognitions *a priori* possible?'" The only thing which usually troubles philosophers about his remarks is the fact that he was right when he claimed that he had wrought a revolution of Copernican magnitude in philosophy; in fact it is now certainly true that every metaphysician must answer the questions which he poses.

Kant's philosophical style is mind-boggling; and, even when stated in simpler language, his thinking is exceedingly difficult to follow. For that reason, we shall need some explanatory background before beginning a critique of Kant and Hume.

Metaphysics Before Kant and Hume

Prior to the times of Kant and Hume, with the exception of a very few philosophers who were predominantly natural philosophers or scientists, such as Descartes, Kepler, Newton, and the early British empiricists, most philosophers had been preoccupied with the so called "School Metaphysics." There were exceptions, of course, in addition to the ones named, but the generalization is true. One mark of this school of thought, as ancient as the Greeks, was that a knowledge of reality with a capital "R," the stuff of the universe and men's minds, could be achieved through the discovery of an adequate metaphysical system. It was thought that although our sensations might vary, it was still possible to know what was truly real because the truly real was not supposed to be the subject of sensation in any event. Rather, the nature of the truly real was thought to be derivable from some set of metaphysical principles known through reason alone as true and consistent with the laws of logic. Experience therefore played a subsidiary role. Since the time of Aristotle, most thinkers had been convinced that such claims as "Every event has a cause" were necessarily true statements, discoverable through reason alone, and without which we could not understand the universe. Moreover, given that this is a claim about the real world, then if it is certain, we have certain knowledge about the real world.

But David Hume changed all this, though he was not the first to raise questions about it. As we know, Hume tried to show that statements such as "Every event has a cause" were not necessarily true, and that if they were true at all, they were not discoverable from an examination of reason alone. It is not contradiction to deny this sentence, and others like it, if the Scotsman is correct. This was why the whole foundation of science and metaphysics was brought into question in the issues between Hume and Kant. What is science if it is not the study of causal relations, and how can science help our future choices if we cannot know that the future will resemble the past? These were the questions that philosophers asked after they had read Hume.

Kant took the results of Hume's studies even more generally than Hume did. How, Kant asked, can we know anything at all if Hume is right? And if we do know, what is it that we can know? These are the fundamental questions of epistemology, and they still are today. This is why Kant is considered the father of modern epistemology: he not only formulated the justification for the questions clearly, but provided an answer to them which is still influential. Before Kant, relations such as causality were thought to be real properties of objects independent of our perceptions of them. Kant proposed a radically different approach. He argued that understanding *minds* are the source of such relations as causality, not what is given in sensation. Causality, and other "categories" like it (as Kant calls them) are categories of our understanding, modes in which we must think and perceive, given the sort of beings we are; they are not given in sensation. The world of knowledge is for Kant the result of a *combination* involving what is given in sensation and the mind's contribution to this. Since we are only *able* to perceive in certain ways, among which is the mode of perceiving which determines that we perceive the given in sensation as causally connected, it follows that the world of knowledge is *necessarily* causally ordered. That is, it follows that if it is not causally ordered, then it is not a possible object of our understanding. But it is such a possible object, thought Kant, so it is so ordered.

It is of the utmost importance for the undrstanding of Kant to note at the outset that when he speaks of Nature, or the world in which causal laws apply, he is speaking about the world of appearances. This world is known as the "phenomenal" world. Although the phenomenal world is a combination, or as Kant calls it, a *synthesis* of the given as combined in the understanding, even the given must have a cause. We do not know this cause of the given, however, and Kant calls it the "noumenal" world. This is an important point because, as we shall see, it leads to a skepticism as critically important for Kant as that which he attributes to Hume.

Kant calls the modes of our sense perception "forms of sensible intuition." There are two such modes or forms, space and time. That is to say, we perceive what is given to the senses *in* space and *through* time. There are, therefore, three elements which together are required for the existence of an object of knowledge: the given in sensation, the forms of sensibility (space and time), and the categories of the understanding. Because this is so, the answer to the question "Is metaphysics possible?" is a resounding NO, if by metaphysics we understand what was meant before Kant, which presumed that the real was discoverable and knowable, in essence independently of the knowing mind. Nonetheless, as we shall see there is a sense of "metaphysics" which is viable.

Kant's Terminology

In order to understand Kant, it is first necessary to master his technical terminology. The first important technical term is "analytical proposition," which is roughly what Hume was referring to when he spoke of a proposition expressing relations of ideas. Analytical propositions are necessarily and logically true, that is, their denials are contradictions. The explanation of this is simple. The predicates of all analytic propositions are contained in the concept of their subjects, as, for example, the concept of being unmarried is contained in the concept of a bachelor in the analytic sentence "All bachelors are unmarried." The meaning of the predicate may, therefore, be found through an analysis of the meaning of the subject term in such sentences. Hume thought, and it is the most widely held view today, that all mathematical propositions are analytic. Some of the continental rationalists, such as Leibniz, also thought that sentences such as "All events have causes" were analytically true, that is, that an analysis of the concept of an event would disclose that it included the concept of a cause. Were this true, it would be a logical contradiction to deny that all events have causes.

Contrasted to analytic propositions are "synthetical" or "synthetic" ones, which are concerned with what the empiricists called "matters of fact," and what rationalists sometimes called "truths of fact." Synthetic propositions are not necessarily true, that is, their denials are not contradictions, and in order to know that they are true we therefore require more than just the law of non-contradiction. Indeed, we require the confirmation of experience, and we learn the meaning of sentences of this sort through experience. At best therefore, it was thought that synthetic propositions are only probably true, and as we can now know, Hume thought that causal laws expressed this sort of proposition. For Hume, however, it turns out in the end that causal claims are not even probably true sentences. In no synthetic proposition can the predicate be found by an analysis of the subject term or its concept. It is because of this that the predicate term in such sentences adds to our knowledge of the subject when predicated of it. Hence, synthetic propositions are not only explicative but ampliative, because we learn something about the subject which we did not know before. Analytic propositions do not provide us with any new knowledge in this way. At the most, they teach us something about words, namely, that the same subject has two names.

Up until the time of Kant, it was largely thought that these were the only two kinds of propositions. Hence, all sentences, if they were either true or false, had to be either analytic or synthetic. They were either true because their predicates were contained in their subjects, or they were true contingently, in virtue of some sort of correspondence with the proposition and a set of facts independent of the proposition. Kant, however, thought that there was a *third* sort of proposition, which was true not because the predicate was contained in the subject, but because we could show that it is impossible for things to be other than as these propositions state them to be. These propositions do not require confirmation by experience, that is, in Kant's words, they are "*a priori.*" One such proposition, he thought, was "Every event has a cause," and he tried to show that this proposition must be true of all possible events, without appealing to experience in order to do this. At the same time, such propositions were in Kant's view ampliative or informative, because they gave us information which we did not have before. They are, therefore, "*synthetic a priori*"; synthetic because they are ampliative and not analytic, and *a priori* because they can be known to be true independently of confirming experience, as opposed to "*a posteriori*" or "after experience" propositions, which do require such confirmation. All other synthetic propositions will be *a posteriori*. We therefore have, if Kant is right, analytic propositions, synthetic *a posteriori* propositions, and synthetic *a priori* propositions.

Kant thought that mathematics, natural science, and metaphysics contained such synthetic *a priori* judgments. His problem was therefore to find out how such judgments are *possible*, given that they must be because they are actual. That is, given that statements such as "Every event has a cause" occur in science and metaphysics, and that such sentences are universally and necessarily true, then his problem is to explain the foundations of their necessity and universality. Clearly, he cannot do this by claiming that their denials are contradictions, because this is the definition of an analytic proposition, and these sentences are not analytic. Specifically, he wants to find out how such judgments are possible in mathematics and science, and whether or not they are possible in metaphysics, or at least in what he calls "speculative" metaphysics.

Kant thought that there were such propositions in mathematics, and especially geometry, because he believed that mathematics does not describe things as they are in themselves but rather things as they appear to us. If he is correct about the forms of intuition under which we perceive what is given to us in sensation, and if he is right when he claims that how we see the given is determined by the "categories" of the understanding as well as the two forms of sensible intuition, then the world is a composite or synthesis of what is given independently of us, plus the organization, if you will, given to it by the forms of intuition and the categories. If applied mathematics gives us knowledge, and if the objects of all knowledge are synthetic, that is, products of this synthesis of the understanding and the given in sensation, then mathematics indeed must contain synthetic *a priori* propositions. Kant looked upon mathematics as the formal expression or formalized elucidation of these forms of sensible intuition, space and time, and insofar as these are necessary conditions for the existence of the world *qua* object of knowledge, mathematics too must be true of that world.

"Representations" is the word Kant used to mean what "ideas" meant for Locke and Berkeley, and what "impressions" meant for Hume. Representations are given to us in sensation; they are lights and colors, tangible sensations, and so forth. When we "associate" these representations, we are making what Kant calls "judgments of perception." Kant argues that judgments of perception have only a subjective validity because they depend upon our individual sets of senses. But when we associate the given in sensation, representations, through the *understanding*, the result is a "judgment of experience," and this is valid not just subjectively but objectively, or for everyone. In Kant's terms, judgments of experiences are valid for "consciousness in general."

Kant later gave up the distinction between judgments of perception and judgments of experience, because it turned out to be impossible to distinguish the two. He came to concentrate upon judgments of experience as the foundation of all our knowledge of the world. What makes our experience be a knowledge of *objects* as opposed to an awareness of mere disconnected data is that the judgments we make of our experience are made under the categories of the understanding and the *a priori* forms of the sensible intuition, space and time. The reason it proved impossible to distinguish judgments of perception from those of experience was that both are made under these categories and forms.

The Critique of Pure Reason

The result of organizing our sensations under the categories and the forms of sensible intuition is what Kant called "Nature," which he also defined as "phenomena under laws." These laws are not found *in* nature, or at least they are not discovered as possible objects in nature, but are rather the necessary conditions for the existence of nature at all. That is, if we did not think and perceive in the way that we do, we would clearly not know what we do in the way we do. Thus, the attempt to derive these laws which make nature as an object of knowledge possible cannot begin with any attempt to verify them by reference to the empirical world, since this would beg the question. Kant rather proceeded to an investigation of the nature and structure of the understanding, in an attempt to show that it is the structure of the understanding, the ways in which it judges, which makes the phenomenal world what it is. More accurately, the modes of judgment of the understanding are necessary conditions for the existence of the phenomenal world, and hence for the possibility of knowledge of objects. This investigation is the central topic of the *Critique of Pure Reason*. It proceeds in three steps. The first of these concerns the categories of the understanding. These categories are the forms in which the understanding judges or thinks, and the only ways in which it does. If we could discover without remainder all the ways or forms in which the understanding thinks, we would thereby have discovered the only ways in which it can form concepts.

Secondly, the categories or forms of judgment of the understanding must actually be applied to something if they are to result in actual judgments about the phenomenal world. What they are applied to are the data given in sensation. But before they can be applied to this data the categories must be shown to be applicable to it under the forms in which we perceive the data. These forms, as we have seen, are space and time. The second step therefore consists in showing that the categories are applicable to data as perceived in space and through time. Before being applied to the data, the categories are applied to these forms. There is a distinction between space and time which is very important for detailed Kantian scholarship, namely that time is an "internal" form of intuition and space an "external" one. Time is not properly speaking due to the structure of the senses, as is space. But for our purposes here, we may say that the central point of importance is that the categories must be applicable in space and through time if they are to be applicable to the data of sensation, since the given in sensation only occurs under these forms. The application of the categories to the forms of sensible intuition gives rise to what Kant calls the "transcendental schema," a most difficult concept. The transcendental schema enables us to formulate rules according to which we can apply the categories to the data of sense.

The third step in the investigation is the derivation of the synthetic *a priori* principles which are universally and necessarily true for all human beings, and which apply for all of us to nature or the world of our experience. These principles are the laws of nature which are necessary conditions for the existence of the phenomenal world as a possible object of our knowledge. They are in effect "legislated" (Kant's term) for nature by the understanding. The central and most important of these laws of nature is the causal law, which is based under the hypothetical form of judgment, $(p \supset q)$. When we apply this form of judgment to the *a priori* forms of intuition, space and time, we discover that events which occur in space which fit this judgment always precede other events, their effects, in time. Once we know this, we can arrive at the conclusions that *all* changes in nature occur according to the law of necessary connection between cause and effect, that is, that we have no other way in which to understand nature *except* to interpret the phenomenal world as a series of necessary connections between causes and effects, in the sense that a cause is necessary for an effect and the effect is sufficient for the occurrence of the cause. This does not mean that we can now tell what the specific causes and effects are, but it does mean that independently of experience, we can know that if anything is a cause, then it must be necessarily connected with its effect, no matter what that effect might be.

These laws are not analytic statements, because their predicates are not contained in the concepts of their subjects. But neither are they completely synthetic, as Hume thought, for their truth is a necessary condition of any experience of nature whatsoever, if by "nature" or the "phenomenal world" we understand a possible object of knowledge, and they may be discovered and known to be true independently of any confirming experience. Propositions that have these properties are synthetic *a priori* propositions, *universally* and *necessarily* true.

In the sense that "metaphysics" was used prior to the time of Kant, it did not contain synthetic *a priori* propositions and therefore did not constitute synthetic *a priori* knowledge, because knowledge is nothing but the sum total of the body of true propositions which are known to be true. Indeed, Kant thought that all previous metaphysics had fallen into one of several kinds of errors: either it involved the logical fallacy of "parallogism," or it entailed "antinomies," which are logical contradictions, or it committed one among certain other sorts of mistakes. You already know that logical contradictions render any theory unsound and enable us to imply anything we might wish.

It is important to understand the difference in the problems posed by natural science and mathematics on the one hand, and metaphysics on the other. The principles of science and mathematics were in Kant's eyes such that the understanding applies the categories and, through the transcendental schema, the laws of nature, to our immediate experience, and both natural science and mathematics are applicable to the result. Their principles are "immanently" applied in experience. But in speculative metaphysics the understanding attempts to go *beyond* what is immanently or immediately experienced, and to apply the categories to the noumenal world. It then tries to explain, through this unjustified application of the categories or forms of judgment, the causes of all our phenomenal experience and of the world of nature itself. Metaphysical judgments are still judgments; but because we do not have any forms of intuition under which we can apply the categories outside of the realm of sensible experience, we have no rules (no transcendental schema) for applying the categories to the noumenal world. Hence, we can never know whether our metaphysical judgments, which are the result of just such an unjustified attempt, are either true or false. When the understanding is used in this way, Kant refers to it as "Reason," and in this context he calls the categories "Ideas." Reason applying the Ideas "transcendently" is unjustified speculative metaphysics. The word "transcendent" for Kant means outside or above the limits of experience. "Transcenden*tal*," on the other hand, means just the opposite: it means foundational to experience. Natural science and mathematics are for Kant transcendental, because the former deals with a subject matter which is the synthesis wrought by the understanding upon the given in sense, and the latter is the formalized expression of space and time, the forms of sense. Mathematics is indeed the formal structure of the rules, the transcendental schema, for the application of the categories.

Yet in all of this it is easy to see that the very investigation into the structure of the understanding and the rules according to which it operates upon what is given *is* metaphysical in a sense, because it is in the most accurate sense *prior to* and *before* scientific knowledge. In the literal sense of the term "metaphysics," it follows that Kant was performing a metaphysical investigation, the difference being, in his opinion, that his metaphysics was founded in fact, transcendental rather than transcendent, whereas what had gone before was speculative.

Although we cannot, strictly speaking, have knowledge of anything beyond the world of experience, we suffer from a fatal inability to avoid trying to extend our knowledge into these illegitimate areas. We are therefore psychologically incapable, from all the evidence, of refraining from metaphysics of the speculative sort in our attempts to prove the existence of God, immortality, and so on. But just because of the impossibility of having any knowledge in these areas, Kant thinks that there is room for what he calls "rational faith," which is the application of Reason and the Ideas in realms of which we have no knowledge for "regulative" rather than "constitutive" purposes. This has been a common notion in the history of philosophy, raised by the Pre-Socratics, resurrected by

Descartes and Kant, formulated carefully by Berkeley, William James, and Dewey. The idea that utterances about God, the hereafter, etc., can be used to regulate our conduct is true, for we do it all the time. Whether it is justified is quite another matter, and one which will raise some questions later on.

The Categories of the Understanding

At this point, having considered the general outline of the Kantian system of metaphysics, we ought to look with greater attention to detail at the categories of the understanding. The categories are the ways in which the understanding thinks. As such, they are the laws of logic. Kant does not mean that the categories are the laws of formal logic; formal logic is rather included in what he means, but logic includes in addition the content of the experience to which the laws are applied. He calls it "transcendental logic." In formal logic, we consider only the abstract form of our judgments, but in transcendental logic we consider the ways in which we connect the objects of our experience through the use of these forms. Transcendental logic is therefore concerned with those concepts and principles of the understanding which are necessary conditions for our thinking objects, that is, connecting the data of sense into objects and making judgments about them. Kant thinks that to judge means to take different representations and unite them through the use of concepts applied to them so that they form a single thought, as it were, or a single cognition or apprehension. This process of putting together our representations of sense into a single cognition is called "synthesizing," and although the number of possible syntheses is infinite, the number of methods for doing synthesis is not. The reason is that there is only a finite number of logical types of judgment because there are only so many forms of logical synthesis. Previous philosophers had failed to realize that these forms of judgment are the clue to understanding the nature and structure of reasoning. In fact, these forms upon examination turn out to be the ways in which the understanding can unite different representations in *one* consciousness (the consciousness of the "judger"). A unified consciousness is of course necessary for judgment; and the unity of it, that is, the feeling of personal identity, is given as a datum of personal experience.

What then are the forms of judgment which are determined by the categories of the understanding? They are listed below on the left, and the corresponding categories, or as Kant often calls them, "pure concepts of the Understanding," are given on the right: [2]

[2] For a complete listing of the forms of judgment and the corresponding categories of the understanding, plus a discussion of their relations, see F. C. Copleston, *A History of Philosophy* (Westminster, Md.: Newman Press, 1965), volume VI.

A. Quantity
  1. Universal
  2. Particular
  3. Singular

B. Quality
  4. Affirmative
  5. Negative
  6. Infinite

C. Relation
  7. Categorical
  8. Hypothetical
  9. Disjunctive

D. Modality
  10. Problematic
  11. Assertoric
  12. Apodictic

A. Quantity
  1. Unity
  2. Plurality
  3. Totality

B. Quality
  4. Reality
  5. Negation
  6. Limitation

C. Relation
  7. Inherence and Subsistence (substances and accident)
  8. Causality and Dependence (cause and effect)
  9. Community (reciprocity between agent and patient)

D. Modality
  10. Possibility–Impossibility
  11. Existence–Non-Existence
  12. Necessity–Contingency

Perhaps one of the most difficult parts of the *Critique*, and certainly one about which an astonishing amount has been written, is called the "transcendental deduction of the categories." The name of this part is misleading, because in fact it is an attempt to justify the need for the 12 categories rather than an attempt to deduce them from the facts of experience. Indeed, since this justification is *a priori*, the very attempt to derive or deduce them from experience would be wrong-headed for Kant. He thinks that the justification is necessary because without some proof that the categories are essential for the very *formation* of objects of judgment, it could be argued that objects are given in experience, i.e., sensation, and that hence there is no need for categories in order to explain the world of knowledge. More precisely, Kant wants to show that we cannot *think* objects without the categories. The forms of judgment are valid for particular, thinking, unified, conscious minds, he argues in the *Prolegomena to Any Future Metaphysics,* and, hence, judgments made by individual minds using these forms have subjective validity. But in the *Critique* he argues that the categories enable us to make judgments of objects for *all minds*, or as he puts it, for "consciousness in general." So the justification of the categories is the justification for Kant's claim that universally and necessarily true judgments of objects of knowledge are possible.

As has been mentioned, the transcendental deduction of the categories is very difficult. Here, we can do no more than sketch its outlines; and, since there are two versions of it in two different editions of the *Critique,* we shall concentrate on the one most frequently used, which is the version in the second edition.

The key to any understanding of Kant, and especially of the deduction, is his definition of an object of knowledge. For Kant, a possible object of knowledge is the *result* of a combination of that which is presented to the senses, together with the categories of the understanding as applied to this given material through the transcendental schema. But there is one other factor which is essential if such a combination is to be possible. This third element, without which there are no objects of knowledge, is the "unity" of the thinking subject as related to the given as synthesized by the application of the categories through the schema. In simpler language, there must be an "I" to which the synthesis, or more accurately the results of the synthesis, can be related. If there were not, then we would be confronted with the strange fact of an object of *knowledge* without a relation to any *knower*, and the concept of "object of knowledge" would then be senseless. For every thinker, there is a given in sensation, under the forms of space and time. This alone is not sufficient for the existence of objects. Objects are *unities* of data. A "red" is not an object, nor is some odor, tactile sensation, sound, or the like. An object is a synthesis of these—something with a smell, a feel, a color, and so on.

But how does this thing happen? What are the necessary occurrences for its advent? Or to put it Kant's way, how does this become an object of *thought*? The answer is that the given in sensation and the modes of thinking must be relatable in one consciousness. To put it another way, it must be possible, although it does not actually happen every time I think of an object, that I be able to be aware of what I perceive as *mine*, that is, as a thing of knowledge to *me*, a thinking being. Objects of knowledge are always known to somebody, so this must be possible for all thinking minds, for everybody who is a human perceiver. This assumes of course that all human perceivers have the same thinking structure, that they must receive the given in sensation in the same forms (in space and through time), that they have the same logical forms of judgment, and that they perceive or synthesize what is given in sensation in the same way, that is, that they have the same categories or modes of understanding corresponding to their forms of logical judgment. It also assumes that they are possessed of the same unity of person, the same sense of "I" as it were. But what *justifies* these assumptions? The answer is deceptively simple: one component of our experience is given —the empirical in sensation. One component is original in us—the modes in which we think what is given. Without the assumption that we are unified thinking beings, there is no way we can relate these two components, and without both the components, there are no objects of knowledge. In short, objects of knowledge are the result, the effect, of a combination, connection, or synthesis. In order to explain this combination, connection, or synthesis, we *must* presuppose these things. If we do not, we have no explanation for it; we cannot account even for its possibility. What are these things? (1) That something is given to the senses. (2) That this material is organized in a certain way. (3) That the organization is a synthesis *for some thinking mind*, for otherwise it is nothing.

The human understanding performs syntheses by the categories which correspond to its logical forms of judgment. It is possible to confirm this by introspection, and when this is done we will see that indeed, we think in those ways about whatever is presented to us, and something that is presented to us is what is given in our sensations. But it is only *as* organized by our understandings that we think of what is given as an *object,* that is, without such organization, there would only be a disconnected, uncoordinated mass of sensations. Hence, objects of knowledge depend for their existence upon the application of the categories of the understanding to what is presented in sense. And this in turn presupposes an appl*ier* of those categories, the unified mind or "I." If there are objects of knowledge, it therefore follows that the conditions which Kant lays down must be satisfied, for without them, no objects are possible.

Now if Kant is right, this is true for every human mind, and hence for all human minds. The possibility of thinking an object, and hence of making judgments about objects for all and any human minds therefore presupposes the *a priori* conditions which have been discovered and justified. Since these must hold universally (for all minds) and necessarily (thinking objects is impossible unless they hold) and since science is the study of objects, we have justified the possibility of science and have defeated skepticism about it. It is important to note that Kant is speaking of what he calls the *"pure* science of Nature," rather than any of the particular sciences which one studies in class. Pure science includes all those synthetic *a priori* propositions which must be true if there are to be any objects for the particular sciences to study. They are the laws governing the synthesis wrought by the understanding, so they are laws of Nature because Nature is composed of the body of possible objects of our experience. The major peg in the skeptical structure built by Hume was the impossibility of proving that the future will resemble the past, or as it is sometimes stated, the impossibility of proving that nature is uniform by appeal to experience, without begging the question. Kant thinks that he has proven nature to be necessarily uniform without appealing to experience, and, hence, without begging the question.

Kant's View of Causality

The topic under discussion is the nature of a cause. For Hume, causality was both a natural and a philosophical relation. Considered as a natural relation, its definition includes the specification that a cause and effect are so united that the idea of the one "determines the mind to form the idea of the other, and the impression of the one to form a more lively idea of the other." Kant, too, thought that causality was a relation, as you can see from the list of categories given earlier in the chapter. But the principle of association of ideas would be relevant to Kant only in one way: it would help to explain the psychological processes of given individuals, but it would not help to explain causality as a necessary condition for the very existence of a world of objects.

In the list of categories you will note that the category of cause and effect corresponds to the hypothetical form of logical judgment (p implies q) The category or pure concept yields no knowledge unless and until it is applied, that is, it give us no knowledge about the empirical world unless applied. Here again, the place of the schema becomes important, for it provides the connection between the categories and the representations given in intuition without which we cannot decide which of the categories ought to be applied in any given case. Whatever this connection is going to be, it must have something in common with both the categories and our intuitions in order for us to be able to subsume given intuition under certain categories rather than others. Here the imagination plays the important role for Kant that it did for Hume, although the two roles are quite different. For Kant, the imagination is a faculty or power of the mind standing between understanding and sensibility which produces schemata. A schema we have defined as a rule according to which the categories are applied to representations. But that is too general. In more detail, what happens is this: a schema is a rule according to which the imagination produces *images*. These images provide us with the boundaries for the application of the categories to representations. Notice that the schema itself is not the image, but the rule for producing it. Rules of course are general, and so are the categories, so the schema and the categories have this in common. But images are always particular, so they have something in common with the representations given in intuition, which are also particular. Because of these shared characteristics with both the manifold of intuition and the categories, the imagination provides a middle ground, as it were, between them. The schema of the imagination allows us to apply the categories of the understanding to the phenomenal world by giving us an image in accordance with which we "form" an object in representation. The recognition of this representation as similar to the image allows us to apply the categories to it, identify it as a certain sort of thing, and relate it to other objects.

The most important function of the schema is to determine the temporal conditions under which the categories can be applied to representations; because when we consider all representations whatsoever, we discover that the only feature common to them all is that they have a location in time. The connection of the representations in different ways by the use of the categories also occurs in time. What Kant calls the "transcendental determination of time" is the general rule of all schemata (particular schema for applying particular categories) according to which we apply categories in general to all and any events in time. This rule of rules, and the particular schema, have in common with the categories the property of universality and the property of assuming time as a necessary condition *a priori* for their validity. That is, both the categories and all of the schema or rules for their application have in common the fact that both are universal and both can only be applicable in time. But experience of what is given to sensation can also only take place in time. Now in the case of the category of causality, or cause and effect, the rule or schema through which the category is applied is this: ". . . the real upon which, whenever posited, something else always follows. It consists, therefore, in the succession of the manifold, in so far as that succession is suject to a rule" (B 183, A144). We read this to mean that, in applying the category of causality, Kant would have to say that the following things happen, or must be able to happen: (1) my imagination makes an image according to a rule which posits that the image must be made through time; (2) my understanding perceives that the "events" of the image are such that when one of them occurs, the other follows, i.e., that their succession through time is necessary for the image to be what it is; (3) a set of representations is given to sense under the forms of space and time; (4) my intellect recognizes the similarity between the image and the representations, and notes that the temporal determination of the representations, their succession, is identical to that of the components of the image; (5) in this process, the category of causality is applied and an object of a causal judgment is formulated.

It is not meant that these five events occur chronologically in the order given; it is meant that they seem for Kant to be logical components of applying the categories. Nor is it pretended that this is a complete analysis, or one which takes account of the technical differences between, for example, the schema and the transcendental determination of time. For our purposes here, however, enough has been said to elucidate the central points which Kant has in mind. The schema and the image-making role of the imagination are the enabling conditions for the application of the categories to given representations. The transcendental determination of time, with the universality and necessity of time, space, the logical forms of judgment, and the categories, together with the unity of apperception or, as we have called it, the unified "I," are necessary conditions for experience of the phenomenal world as we know it.

For Kant then, in the final analysis, a cause in the real world is this: it is an object or event such that when it occurs, another object or event necessarily follows upon it. What has gone before this page is an explication of the concepts "object," "necessarily," and the pure concept or category of causality which make this definition intelligible for Kant.

CRITICISMS OF KANT

It is now time to consider some criticisms of Kant. Unlike the exposition of his theory, it is possible to give several criticisms which are not extraordinarily difficult to understand. The first of these concerns Kant's view of mathematics, especially geometry, and the relation of his position here to his defense of science, by which he primarily meant Newtonian physics.

If Kant is right, we know that empirical reality must conform to geometry. This is so because geometry is a series of propositions presenting the formal properties of space and space is a necessary condition for any experience of the physical world at all—hence, geometry must be true *a priori*. By "geometry," Kant meant Euclidian geometry, because that was the only kind with which he was familiar. Euclidian geometry is, as we all know, a straightline geometry. Now if Kant was right, if this geometry is the expression of the formal properties of space, then no other geometry should be applicable to space. Moreover, other geometries may not even be conceivable, if a condition of their conceivability is acquaintance with the spaces they characterize. But not only are they conceivable, they may also be fruitfully applied, as the development of curvedline geometries has proven. Kant therefore was wrong. It is not clear just how serious this mistake is. If, as some scholars think, he excluded the very possibility of other kinds of systems, it is a serious criticism. It would be even more serious if the consequence of the application of other non-Euclidian geometries was that our concept of space is contingent upon the view we give to it and is hence no more necessary than the purposes to which we put it.

A criticism of serious consequence concerns the so-called "noumenal" world which Kant found it necessary to posit as an explanation for the source of the given in sensation. Some have argued that in claiming that it exists, he violated his own precept which says that it is not possible to have knowledge of this world. But it seems he could escape this by drawing a distinction between knowing *that* something is the case and knowing it directly. More important, however, is the consequence of having this unknowable realm at all. It seems to justify a skepticism as profound as that which Kant attributes to Hume. We will later see how George Berkeley criticized John Locke's theory of material substance. Part of that criticism concerns what the possible relations between material substance and what is given in sensation, or our ideas of it, *could* be. Had the same question been asked of Kant, he could not have answered it; but not being able to answer would be as serious as giving the wrong answer.

This sort of response leaves us free to speculate about the possibilities. It will do no good for Kant to reply that such speculation is unjustified, because at least the *attitude* of skepticism will nonetheless prevail. The point is this: if we cannot account for the origin of a major component in what we count as an object of knowledge, then how are we to know that we are not in fact being deceived? René Descartes postulated the hypothesis of an evil deceiver whose hypothetical function was to make us believe that we perceived certain things to be the case when in fact they were not. We might ask of Kant, "What prevents the evil deceiver from working his will upon us?" He can give us no answer except that we are not justified in speculating about the question. Somehow, this does not seem to satisfy the questioner. Part of the reason that it does not satisfy is that the question does not seem to be senseless, at least when put in more modern terms. As so stated, we might ask Kant, "How do you justify the assumption that what is given to our senses is veridical?" But again, he does not seem to have an answer. He *could* say, with Berkeley, that what is given is final, and to ask for anything more is to ask a meaningless question. But he closes that door by insisting that although we do not know the noumenal world, and cannot, we must posit it in order to indicate that our given-to-sense has an origin. This very procedure contains the seeds of skepticism, for it says that although we know that the given has an origin, we cannot know what it is, nor anything about it. Hence, the skeptic might say, it may be that what we *think* is given, even though we interpret it and make objects of knowledge from it, is not in *fact* veridical, that is, does not represent, resemble, or correspond to its cause. It is not incumbent upon the skeptic, given Kant's premises, to say why this doubt is justified. It is only necessary that he point out that such doubt is possible, given what Kant says. It seems that the skeptic is right here, for there is no doubt that Kant posits the noumenal world as a necessary condition for the existence of objects in so far as objects are a synthesis of what is given in sensation under the forms of space and time.

There is another "level" of the same problem. Suppose we agree with Kant about the nature of the given. What is it? The data of the different senses. And what are these? Light and colors, tangible sensations (hardness, softness, maleability, etc.), odors, tastes, sounds, and that is about it. They are, in the technical sense, gross data. We do not perceive microscopic phenomena, and there is some reason to believe that we cannot perceive such phenomena even in principle, unless we redefine what we mean by "perceive." Indirectly, we can perceive at least in principle a great number of microscopic phenomena. No one has ever seen a magnetic field, nor an electron. But we can test for these facts through the use of sophisticated apparatus. The same is true of macroscopic events. Yet, even if we grant Kant these truths, of which he was unaware, problems still remain. How do we synthesize what is known only indirectly into a possible object of knowledge? To be synthesized, after all, it must be given in sensibility, and it is clear that what is indirectly known is not so given. Moreover, a great deal of our so-called scientific knowledge is based upon hypotheses which are not as yet called laws because they do not have sufficient confirmation. The fact that we need this confirmation indicates that such future laws are not synthetic *a priori* propositions. Upon what synthetic *a priori* propositions are they based? It is not an adequate answer to say that they are based upon such truths as "Every event has a cause." One reason that this is inadequate is that if you examine the literature of modern science, you will almost never find the word "cause." Science today determines what used to be called causal relations in terms of statistical correlations, non-empty intersections between classes, and so forth.

This does not mean that, without further discussion, modern science is right and Kant is wrong—in spite of the obvious pragmatically justifiable evidence which modern science would have in its favor in such an argument. After all, it is not inconsistent with Kant's theory to say, on the one hand, that such and such an X is the cause of such and such a Y because X has correlation of (a) with Y and, on the other hand, that X is the cause of Y because X and Y meet the conditions of perception, synthesis, and coordination that Kant lays down. They may turn out to be the same thing. Nor does Kant say that from his premises one can determine all of the actual specific causes and the specific effects which will occur in the real world. The question is whether evidence gathered empirically is *sufficient*, at least in principle, for determining what a cause is and what an effect is. On a broader scope: if empirical evidence is sufficient in this case and that case and other cases, then why is it not sufficient in all cases? It is this latter question that Kant must answer. For if we can decide what the particular causes are in any given case by empirical means, then it follows that we can do so, at least in principle, in all cases. But if we can do so in all cases, then what is the status of Kant's position? He cannot reply that if we discover in some case that X, the supposed cause of Y, is in fact not the cause of Y, then we have contradicted ourselves, because synthetic *a priori* propositions are not analytic. Nor can he impune our empirical evidence, because if he is right, it is irrelevant to begin with. In the last analysis, what he must say is that what we mean in practice by "science" and what he means by the "possibility of science" are two different things. He would most assuredly agree; but he would argue that his "science," or the presuppositions of it, are necessary conditions for our science, because, without what he has discovered, we could not justify knowledge claims on our level. This will not do, however, because science claims that things are, in fact, *not* as we see them sensibly in reality, but quite different. Tables are buzzing, blooming masses of confusion; what appears flat is not; matter and energy do not stand in an unvarying relationship; energy does simply dissipate; and so forth. In short, science tells us that the perceptively real is *not* the Real. Operating upon these assumptions, we have made great strides. But Kantian science must be consistent with what we perceive, for that is the world of knowledge for him.

Questioning Kant's Basic Theory

We might also raise questions about the very foundation of Kant's theory, the assumption that there are synthetic *a priori* propositions. His favorite case is the proposition "All events have causes." If he is right, the denial of this sentence is not a contradiction, and the concept of a cause is not obtainable from an analysis of the concept of an event. But is this in fact the case? If you had never studied Kant nor any other philosopher and if someone asked you to consider in full the concept of an event, would a part of your answer be that it was caused by another event or thing, and/or that it was the cause of something else? Consider this carefully, and let us perform an experiment, admitting beforehand that the experiment has been at least partly colored by what has gone before this. Suppose that you are asked to tell everything you can about the following event: a rock falling. You are told nothing more than this. What would your analysis contain? Surely, whatever else you said, it would mention the following: the rock would fall from somewhere; it would fall at a certain speed, given the frictional properties of the atmosphere through which it passed; it would stop falling somewhere; when it stopped falling, certain other things would take place, such as an impression in what it hit, or the dissipation of energy, or the diminishing of the mass of the rock, etc.; other things being equal, some change must have taken place in the rock's environment in order for it to fall. Now none of this information has been elicited from anything but the description of the event, given the conditions of our experiment. True, you no doubt have much experience of various kinds of causes, but this does not help Kant's case. He, after all, cannot appeal to experience except to ask if you understand the question in the first place.

Someone may wish to assert that Kant's analysis is incorrect, suggesting an answer consistent with suggestions made here—that we are somehow born with an awareness of what an event is, which includes the notion of an event as a cause. Some thinkers have indeed wanted to hold just this position, but evidence from the behavioral studies of infants seems to suggest that it is incorrect. If we refuse to accept this suggestion (the theory of innate ideas), the only other answer is that some empirical solution, or the Kantian one, is the right view. Since, assuming ignorance of what Kant has said, it does not seem to be true in the analysis of such a situation that we call into our explanations any of the factors which he claims to be the true explanation, some empirical approach appears to be the correct one. But are we being fair if we argue that, since the Kantian explanation is not the sort of explanation that is normally called upon to explain such events, it is therefore wrong?

It is not intended to suggest that any correct answer to the question "Is there synthetic *a priori* knowledge?" must be based upon what might be called "ordinary experience"; nor will it be argued that necessary connections in the real world are impossible unless they can be justified empirically. Certainly there is a good case for arguing on *a priori* grounds that there is no coherence to the real world unless there are such connections, and many philosophers wish to posit the existence of such connections as essential explanatory entities. But it does seem that if we opt for the position which asserts the existence of explanatory entities called necessary connections, we must make a distinction between the world of *being* and the world of *knowledge* and admit that, although explanatory entities may be necessary as postulates of a world of being, they are not components of the world of our knowledge. Knowledge can only be of our own minds, what is given in sensation, and what may be inferred certainly or probably from these. Kant, of course, recognized this difficulty when he spoke about the noumenal world. He does not actually assert the existence of such a world, but his premises imply that it must exist. Furthermore, the reason that it must exist seems to be that, without it, we cannot account for the origin of what is given in sensation. But to say this is surely to posit the noumenal world as the *cause* of the given, and this would involve an illicit application of the category of causality to the transcendental world on Kantian grounds. So far as the world of *knowledge* is concerned then, it would seem that if Kant is right, we cannot account for the origin of one of its components, the given, although we know that it must have *some* origin. But to assume that it must have *some* origin is to assume that nothing exists without a cause, although we cannot say what it is. This seems to beg the question at issue, which is just what Hume pointed out.

Kant, of course, would reply that the given is *not* part of the world of knowledge, since the world of knowledge is composed of objects of possible judgments, which are the result of synthesis. But it is not clear what this position rules out as an object of knowledge. Consider the sensation of red, simply as such. Is it or is it not an object of knowledge for Kant? It seems that it *is* an object of knowledge, at least in the sense that it is directly apprehended, and that this sort of direct contemplation is a mode of knowing, quite common in aesthetic experiences. But red *qua* object of knowledge seems not to be the result of any synthesis of the understanding, and whether it could be an object of knowledge for Kant is at least moot. Moreover, his claim that there are universally and necessarily valid conditions for the existence of knowledge rests upon certain undefended assumptions, such as that the nature of human understanding is constant, as are its modes of sensibility. But to assume this is again to beg the question about the uniformity of nature. It may be simply inconceivable that we here and now could understand what it would be like to perceive in a manner in which entities were not in space nor lasting through time, or in a manner in which the concepts of substance, quality and relation did not apply; but that does not mean that it is impossible. Kant may want to *stipulate* that a human understanding has the properties which he enumerates, but the cost of such stipulation might be in some future eon that his theory of knowledge, if true, is true of only certain retarded beings in an otherwise far advanced species.

Finally, there is the problem of Kantian idealism. Briefly, it can be stated like this: the world of knowledge is a synthesis, or the result of syntheses. These are performed by individual understandings. There are therefore as many worlds of knowledge as there are individual understandings. How, then, are we to justify the claim that these worlds of knowledge are one and the same? Moreover, given that without the synthesis of the understanding there are no objects of knowledge, does this not make what is knowable totally mind dependent? It will not do to reply that what is given exists independently of the knowing mind, because this is to make assumptions about the noumenal world. Nor, it seems, can we claim that there is but one world of knowledge on the grounds that the categories and modes of sensibility are the same for all perceivers; for, as we have seen, this begs the question of uniformity. If Kant is forced into the position where he must hold that (a) the world of knowledge is mind-dependent, and (b) we can make no claims about the origins of any of its components in the noumenal world, then he is an idealist. Secondly, if in addition to this he cannot defend the universal similarities of understandings, then he is a *solipsist*, one whose knowledge is confined to the world of his own immediate perceptions. It is not certain that he is forced into the latter position, though he may be. But it does seem that he is indeed in the idealist tradition and subject to all of the criticisms which can be brought against it.

CRITICISMS OF HUME

On the other hand, Hume has his problems too. The most important of these is that in effect, he does not face the problem of causality at all. He denies that there is real causality in the world, while affirming that all those things called causes are contiguous with and prior to their effects. If Hume is right, when we speak of a "cause" we mean an event that occurs before and is contiguous with another event called its "effect"; but this does not tell us that there is an existing relation, the causal relation, in the real world. This he denies on the grounds that the analysis of our impressions of objects discloses no such relation, and that is that. At the same time, he allows that men speak *as if* causal relations were necessary; and he sets out to explain this feeling of necessity, which explanation is couched in terms of the principle of the association of ideas. But such an explanation does not tell us *anything* about whether there actually is, or is not, some subsistent causal relation which necessitates causal connections. In short, the psychological part of Hume's theory, the principle of the association of ideas, is irrelevant to the question "What is the nature of a cause?" if that question is one, not about how we *feel* about causes, but about what they *are*. Now here again the concept of an explanatory entity becomes important. It may be that Hume is correct when he argues that we are not directly acquainted with real causality; but, at the same time, it may be that there must *exist* real causality if the world that we do perceive is to have any coherence. An argument which moves from the premise that X is not directly known by human minds to the conclusion that X does not exist is invalid; and if the conclusion is from that same premise to "X cannot exist," then it seems invalid too. It therefore appears that if Hume's arguments culminating in the conclusion that real causality is not a fact are considered carefully, one must conclude that he did not succeed in establishing this claim.

Hume does not draw the distinction between the world of knowledge and the world of being which seems essential in the consideration of this topic. As with Kant, he misses the simple truth that the objects of our acquaintance are not in all cases the objects that exist. Like Kant he fails to see that it may be sufficient to know *that* what we perceive has a cause in order to defeat skepticism, and that it is not necessary to be directly acquainted with the actual cause itself. Instead, he analyzes the beliefs we have about the necessity of the causal relation in psychological terms, giving no ground to the principle of the association of ideas.

Hume is also subject to the possibility of solipsism, as is Kant. The world of knowledge for Hume is the world of impressions and the ideas caused by them. But impressions are always someone's impressions, and mine are never yours. So how are we to know the objective ground of these impressions? Hume has no answer to this vexing question.

DUCASSE'S VIEW OF HUME

Of all the critical examinations of Hume's theory of causality, perhaps none is more clearly stated than that of C. J. Ducasse in his book *Nature, Mind and Death*. Ducasse sees Hume as simply following a set of principles which he accepts to their logical conclusions, (sometimes regretfully). The chief of these principles is that nothing can be known to us, and nothing can exist, unless it is a "perception." He summarizes Hume's view in these words: "To be is to be perceived. No connection is ever perceived between a cause and its effect. Therefore there is none."[3]

Hume avows that the connection between a cause and its effect is never "necessary." Ducasse understands this in the standard way, namely, that if "necessary," as in logic, means "the contradictory of which is self-contradictory," then no self-contradiction is involved in asserting that something we call a "cause" occurs without that thing we have been accustomed to call its "effect" following. For Hume necessity becomes merely "an internal impression of the mind," a relation among ideas which does not exist in the world of objects because it is not perceived there.

Hume's Theory and Some Counter-Examples

Hume, of course, thought that his analysis was a study of the ordinary, common notion which we all have of the causal relation. Ducasse disagrees with his contention. That is to say, Ducasse thinks that our everyday use of the term "cause" is not always consistent with the meanings which Hume gives to the word. Ducasse thinks that in order to show that Hume is mistaken, the counter-example technique may be used. If we could show that there are situations where Hume's definition of cause and effect applies, but which are such that we do not think that the parts of the situation are related as cause and effect, and if, secondly, we could show that there are cases where we do judge the objects and

[3] C. J. Ducasse, *Nature, Mind and Death* (Lasalle, Ill.: Open Court Publishing Co., 1951), p. 92.

events to be related as cause to effect but where Hume's definition does not apply, then we would have shown that Hume was wrong when he thought that he had defined the ordinary notion of the causal relation. In Ducasse's eyes, this would do more than show merely that Hume had not understood ordinary language as well as he thought he had (for of course, the correct notion of the causal relation may not be the common one). Ducasse has a particular view of the task of philosophy. He believes that, in essence, the common sense view of causality is the correct one and that a correct philosophical theory about causality is therefore an exfoliation of this ordinary view. If Hume has mistaken that view (if Ducasse is right), it follows that Hume has an incorrect theory of causality.

Ducasse asks us first to consider the case of a man who has always heard two striking clocks, such that one of these clocks has always struck just before the other. If Hume were right, the man should say that the cause of the second clock's striking was the striking of the first clock, which of course we know to be false. We know in fact that the cause of both clocks' striking is a third cause, namely their respective mechanisms. The point here is that Hume's definition fits a case where in fact it should not; that is, the case is one where the causal relation is not between the first clock and the second clock, but between both of them and something else. But, following Hume's definition, we must claim that the relation of causality holds between the two clocks. There are many similar examples. Among others Ducasse mentions Thomas Reid's case of the succession of day and night, the fact that in infants the appearance of teeth regularly happens after the growth of hair, and that the birth of human beings always happens after the tenth return of the moon following conception.

Ducasse argues that in fact we do not conclude from the constant association of two things that the one is the cause of the other, but rather this regular succession causes us to raise the question of *whether* one is the cause of the other. But raising a question and answering it are two quite different things. If A is the cause of B, then B surely does follow upon the occurrence of A; but B's following always upon A does not imply that A is the cause of B.

This first set of counter-examples shows that there are cases where Hume's definition applies that we do not acknowledge as cases of causation. The second sort of counter-example shows that there are cases where it does not apply that are such that we do think the causal connection is involved.

Ducasse has performed an experiment in his classes for years which he takes as a model for this second sort of example. He brings a paper-wrapped parcel into his class and places it on the desk. Then, he slowly puts his hand on the parcel, and when he does, the end of the parcel lights up. He then asks the students what caused the parcel to glow. The answer, he says, almost always is that what he did to the parcel just before it began glowing was the cause, i.e., his placing his hand on it. It must be noted here that this is their response even though this is the *first time* they have seen the experiment. Hence, Ducasse argues, by "cause" in this case they cannot mean "some event having repeatedly preceded" the effect, which is what "cause" should mean if Hume is right. Rather, he thinks, they must mean "the only change introduced into the situation immediately before the glowing occurred." The students, of course, might be quite mistaken in their judgment, but that is not the point. The point is the analysis of the concept of causation which they gave. That analysis seems to indicate, contrary to Hume, that by "cause" they do not mean something which has repeatedly been observed to occur before that which they take to be the effect. In fact, only a single instance was required before they made their judgment, and what they indicated as the cause was either identical to or closely related to the only change in the circumstances prior to the occurrence of the effect.

Hume's Own Views of Such Cases

As Ducasse notes, Hume agrees that we could discover some particular cause by a single experiment, under carefully controlled circumstances. Yet there is a grave question as to how this view can be consistent with the rest of his theory. He is saying that in effect, if B follows upon A just once, we may ascertain from this single instance that all instances of A are followed by instances of B. But given Hume's definition of "cause" as simply constant conjunction, Ducasse notes that it is difficult to see how one could discover a cause in any other way than by observing *constant* conjunction, i.e., *many* instances of A and B. Hume is aware of this problem, and he tries to solve it by what might be called the "likeness" principle, namely that "like objects placed in like circumstances, will always produce like effects." Hume says that this principle is inculcated in us by millions of "experiments" or experiences, and it is this fact which makes it possible, when we are confronted with a new causal connection which is similar to others we have experienced, to judge from a single instance that it *is* a causal relation. Ducasse, however, notes that if we accept this, any sequence whatsoever, even an accidental one, could be generalized as causally connected among its parts. Nor will it save Hume to reply that this in fact would not happen because we would have carefully removed all "foreign and superfluous" circumstances before making the judgment. For as Ducasse points out, such circumstances are clearly those which are not causally related to the effect, and removing such circumstances is in fact equivalent to discovering the cause. In short, Hume's "likeness" principle is not good for discovering causes by a single experiment, but only for generalizing the causal connection once we have already discovered it. Yet, Ducasse thinks that he has given an example in which causation *is* discovered by a single experiment. Hence, causation cannot consist in constant conjunction, for this is not what was discovered in his example.

Ducasse's View of Causation

Ducasse begins the statement of his own position with a specification of the data of the problem, that is, "the empirical facts the definition (of causation) must fit." These "consist of phrases that are actual instances of the employment of that term as predicate . . ." He gives several examples: that a particular hurricane caused a number of deaths, that it caused several boats to become caught on the top of a bridge, that his writing the words on his page did not cause the ringing of the doorbell which followed upon the writing. The problem then is to give a definition of "cause" such that when it is substituted for that word in descriptions similar to those just given, it does not change what is implied by the propositions expressed in those descriptions. It is also important to note that the question of truth and falsity does not arise here, because we are talking about what people *believe* to be a cause, and not about whether they were right or wrong in any particular case.

With this statement of the problem, Ducasse goes on to say that he does not, like Hume, believe that some statistical analysis contingent upon constant association is the appropriate analysis. Rather, he states his case in terms of what he calls an "experiment." Take a situation, S, in which two and only two changes occur. One of these changes, C, occurs in S at a time T_1 and the other, called E, "spontaneously" follows C at a time T_2. C may be introduced by any other natural means. In Ducasse's eyes, *if* we are aware that C was the only change introduced into S prior to E, then we will believe that C is the cause of E, and he thinks that "just this is what it means, to say that it 'caused' the latter (E)." This is not a "sign" that there is some hidden causal relation, it *is* the causal relation, and in describing it we have given the description of a causal relation. Now it will be evident that the means for discovering this relation is just Mill's Method of Difference as described earlier in this book, and Ducasse agrees.

It is essential to distinguish between causes, effects, conditions, and resultants in this analysis. A cause of an event, B, in the circumstances of the situation is another event, A, which is "sufficient to" B's occurrence, and the effect, B, is what was "necessitated by" A's occurrence. A condition of B is an event, A, which in the circumstances was "necessary to" B's occurrence, and a resultant of A was therefore an event, B, which in the circumstances was "contingent upon" A's occurrence. When speaking of "necessity," Ducasse makes it clear that he thinks there are logical, physical, and psychological necessity or sufficiency. He also makes it clear that in his view, causal relations are not two-termed or dyadic, but three-termed or triadic, the third term being some circumstance or state of affairs within which the causal connection occurs. For example, he thinks that although Charles I's head being cut off does not logically entail that he died, in the circumstances then prevailing, it was sufficient that he died for his head to be cut off. He believes that in these circumstances, the definition of "caused" in "Charles' beheading caused his death" ". . . fits the use the language does in fact make of those terms" (causal terms). If this is true, and if Ducasse's view of the task of philosophy is correct, then he has shown that the causal relation is perceivable, and if his analysis squares with what he has called the "data," then he is right.

Ducasse argues that Hume's analysis, in so far as it attempts to show that causal relations are unobservable, rests upon two propositions, one of which is true and the other false. The true proposition is that logical necessity is never observable among events, and the false one is that "necessitation" always means "logical necessitation." Ducasse suggests that it would have been merely perverse for the executioner to argue that the blow of the axe on Charles' neck "was not certainly but only probably what caused the head to come off."

DISCUSSION OF DUCASSE'S VIEW OF CAUSATION

Ducasse's analysis has many advantages over either Hume's or Kant's theory. For one, it certainly squares with our ordinary use of terms such as "cause" and "effect" better than either of the other two. Hume's view may have an initial plausibility on such a criterion, but it does not seem to stand up against Ducasse's objections, and especially against his counter-examples. Moreover, Hume himself seems to recognize these deficiencies in his theory. If we consider Kant's answer to the question "What does 'cause' mean?" at least we can say that his response is not "common sensical" in any normal meaning of those terms. Hence, if we take the task of philosophy to be the clarification or explanation of common-sense beliefs, then on this ground alone, Ducasse seems to have a better theory than either Kant or Hume.

But there is a very serious question as to whether or not this *is* the task of philosophy. Certainly, for example, the task of physics is not to explain our common-sense views of objects, at least as those objects are described in the sort of language which Ducasse has in mind. May it not be then that the correct analysis of causality is one which is not suggested to us by the ordinary uses of language, and the data provided therefrom?

Furthermore, though Ducasse is certainly right when he notes that we can often pinpoint the cause of an event on the basis of a single experience in which only one aspect of the total situation changes, there is still a moot point raised by the question "*How* is this possible?" Could we, without the many, many experiences we have all had in our pasts, in which like antecedents were followed by like consequents and the variation of a single factor turned out to be the indication of a cause, make such identifications? If the answer is yes, then both Ducasse and Hume are mistaken, for without previous experience they have no way to defend their analyses. If the answer is no, then which of them (if either) is right still remains an open question. It is an open question as to whether Ducasse is right because, although he may have given us an answer to the question "*What* do we in fact identify as a cause?" he has not answered the more basic complex question "How do we know that it is the cause and what is required in order for us to have this knowledge?" It will not do to reply that what we know tells us how we know, for this would beg the question.

It is an open question as to whether Hume is right because although he tried to answer both questions, he failed, as Ducasse has shown, to make his definition of causation accountable to the sort of counterexample raised by Ducasse.

In addition, although Ducasse has distinguished among logical, physical, and psychological necessity, he has not explained the latter two kinds in a manner that helps his case for a definition of causality. To say that something is "psychologically necessary" seems to mean nothing more than that it is somehow impossible for a person to think or conceive of something as other than it is. But this seems to have nothing to do with the question of whether it is in fact other than it is believed to be. And to say that something is "physically necessary" seems to mean nothing more than that it falls within the scope of physical laws. Now the importance of this rests upon what we conceive a physical law to be, and if the answer is that physical laws are descriptive of constant conjunctions in nature, as Hume would have it, then this does not help us a bit, for he denies that such laws are "logically" necessary and makes no provision for any other sort of necessity. And for Ducasse, a causal physical law is merely an empirical generalization which covers a large number, "usually 100 per cent," of causal cases which resemble one another in respect of being causes, given his definition of "cause." Hence, we cannot define "physical necessity" in his terms *via* the nature of law without begging the question of what sort of necessity exists in cases of causal connection.

The problem for causality in philosophy has not been solved. That is to say, no adequate analysis of the meaning of the word "cause" has been forthcoming. Such an adequate analysis would have to meet at least the following conditions:

1. It would have to account for the ordinary uses of the terms in our "causal vocabulary," for although the correct analysis may not be "common sensical," it could not contradict common sense unless the theory also showed why common sense was mistaken. The latter is of course a possibility.
2. It would have to incorporate the facts we know about the psychology and physiology of perception, and about how we learn to perceive, better than any of the three theories we have studied. Perhaps it is in this area that the answers to questions concerning *how* we can discriminate causes on the basis of a single test rest.

But as with many other problems in philosophy, mistaken theories can often be as valuable as correct ones dealing with less significant subject matter. The three men we have studied may be mistaken, but they are never uninteresting.

EXERCISES

1. Write a page defining the precise nature of the so-called "problem of causality." Is it a problem for anybody but philosophers? Why or why not?

2. Hume was an empiricist. What is that?

3. What did Hume mean when he spoke of the "experimental method"? What was the subject matter of this method?

4. What are the components which make up our knowledge of the real world, if Hume is right?

5. Does Hume think that any propositions are necessarily true? If any, which ones?

6. Do impressions exist independently of us for Hume? Do ideas? If they do not, then how do we know that our impressions and ideas resemble those of any other person? And if we cannot know that, then how can there be public objects of knowledge? Write a short essay on the problems involved in these questions.

7. What is a *synthetic a priori* proposition? An *analytic a priori* proposition? A *synthetic a posteriori* proposition? Which of the three did Hume reject? Why?

8. Why would the notion of an *analytic a posteriori* proposition make no sense for either Hume or Kant?

9. Discuss the role of the principle of the association of ideas in Hume's theory.

10. What kind of proposition is expressed by "All events have causes" if Kant is right? If Hume is right?

11. What is an object of knowledge for Hume? For Kant?

12. What are space and time for Kant?

13. Hume's analysis of the causal relation has been said to be primarily a psychological one, which some have said may deal with the problem of how we *know* causal relations, but not with the problem of what a causal relation *is*. Discuss this, and defend your position.

14. When Hume denies that causal relations are necessary, and Kant says that they are, do they mean the same thing by "necessary"? Why or why not?

15. What is the role of the categories of the understanding with regard to the causal connections among objects for Kant?

16. Compare Hume and Ducasse on the meaning of "necessity."

17. Compare the theories of Hume and Ducasse on the basis of the internal criteria, saying which is the better theory and why.

18. Compare the theories of Hume and Ducasse on the basis of the external criteria, saying which is the better theory and why.

19. Use the counter-example technique to argue against the Ducasse theory.

20. Some critics of Ducasse have argued that it is only because of our vast background of constant conjunctions of causes and effects that we can isolate the "single event which changed" which Ducasse claims as the meaning of "cause." What importance, if any, would the truth of this claim have for Ducasse's theory?

21. Kant's definition of "necessity" differs from Ducasse's. Discuss whether or not it is *inconsistent* with Ducasse's view of necessity in causality.

22. For Ducasse, the analysis of the meaning of "cause" is the analysis of what people *believe* they mean; in any particular case they may be mistaken, but this will not affect the accuracy of the analysis. How would Kant view this position? Defend your answer.

23. Kant was trying to show that science was possible in the face of the skepticism of David Hume. If Ducasse is right, is science possible or not? Would Kant agree with the answer you just gave? Why or why not?

24. In the light of the three theories we have just examined about causality, compose a description of the problem of causality, and then list the conditions which an adequate solution to the problem would have to meet.

25. Could science ever solve the *philosophical* problem of causality? Why or why not?

6

Epistemology

THE SCOPE OF EPISTEMOLOGY

At the beginning of Chapter 4 we noted that it is very difficult to define exactly what metaphysics is. As part of the justification for that claim, the overlapping of some areas of metaphysics and epistemology was mentioned. The same obstacles will obviously be encountered in any attempt to define "epistemology," but hopefully we can at least achieve a more detailed outline of some epistemological problems.

The Greek origin of the word "epistemology" suggests that it refers to the theory of knowledge, or to be slightly more precise, to that set of problems concerned with the ways in which we know or are said to know something, and to the supposed objects of that knowing. When one claims that he knows something (as opposed to believing it), it is normal to expect that one can offer some sort of defense for this claim. That is, we would normally expect the claimant to be able to give reasons which give more weight to his statement than it would have if it were "merely" a matter of opinion. This is not to say that statements of opinion, or belief, do not require supporting reasons, but it is to say that knowledge claims are somehow stronger, and somewhat different than, claims about beliefs or opinions. The difference between belief and knowledge is the oldest problem in epistemology. It was discussed in great detail by Plato and probably Socrates before him, and certainly by Aristotle. It has not yet been solved, and it still remains the topic of a vast amount of technical investigation in philosophical writing.

Similarly, the nature of the reasons offered for evidence of knowledge claims, or in support of them, and the nature of the states of mind which accompany the knowing situation are also ancient and still unsolved problems. Since it is impossible to discuss these issues without

177

discussing what is known, the analysis of the object of knowledge and belief is also an inseparable part of epistemology.

We shall be primarily concerned with the latter question—the analysis of the possible objects of knowledge and belief—and the central theme of all the problems discussed in the chapter will be the avoidance of skepticism, which is the position that knowledge of anything is impossible. An ancient maxim in philosophy states that *nihil est in intellectu quod non prius fuerit in sensu*—nothing is in the intellect that was not first in the senses. But even if this maxim is sound, and many philosophers have thought that it is not, the question now arises about the trustworthiness of the senses. If they are not trustworthy, if our sensations or perceptions are not veridical, or if we cannot know that they are, then how can we determine the accuracy of the concepts that we have of the things we perceive? We are in fact all familiar with situations in which we have drawn mistaken conclusions about what we perceive because we have misinterpreted what was given to our senses. An obvious example is the thirsty man in the desert who believes that he sees an oasis and sets his track toward it, only to find more sand. Clearly, he saw something; but his conclusions about what he saw, concerning its location in particular, and perhaps also its very nature, are mistaken. How are we to tell when something is an illusion, and when it is not? If there is no way to note the difference, then how can we make knowledge claims?

Moreover, it is a commonplace truth that you cannot see through my eyes, nor I through yours. How do we know that we are sensing or perceiving the same thing then? And there are some things which are in principle perceivable only by the individual who is the sufferer of them. Except in a metaphorical way, it makes no sense to say that you feel my pains and vice versa. Upon what grounds are my statements about my pains justifiable then, and what am I talking about when I make statements about someone else being in pain? Another way of expressing this problem is to ask whether the criteria for truth and meaningfulness are the same in first- as opposed to third-person statements about pain. This problem is a species of the general problem of the nature of and justification for statements about mental events as opposed to physical or perceivable ones. The general problem is often considered as a special branch of philosophy called philosophy of mind.

In the first part of this book, a considerable amount of time was spent discussing problems about truth and meaning, and the relation between the two. Both sorts of problems are obviously entangled in most epistemological issues. A particular group of philosophers called logical positivists who were prominent in the early part of this century thought that they had discovered a criterion which distinguished meaningful from meaningless sentences. This is of course very important, for no meaningless proposition could be either a knowledge claim or a statement of belief. But among the statements which are meaningless if we accept their criterion are most moral judgments, which would mean that there is no moral knowledge. This theory will be examined later in the text, but it is mentioned here to make the point that epistemological problems are to be found in ethics and meta-ethics. So far then, we know that epistemology deals with at least part of the subject matter of metaphysics, philosophy of mind, and ethics. Indeed, there is no branch of philosophy which does not involve such problems. Even the philosophy of mathematics presents us with the question of how and what we know when we know that mathematical propositions are true or false. If, as many thinkers believe, mathematical truths are tautologies, then we are presented with the difference between mathematical and physical truths, and the problem of how applied mathematics can be informative in any understandable way. In the philosophy of science, there is the question of how our belief that nature is uniform can be justified. Given the inductive base of our physical laws, there is an obvious relationship between this issue and many others in epistemology, metaphysics, and the philosophy of mathematics. And many areas of epistemology find their reflection in aesthetics as well. The nature of aesthetic perception, the status of value judgments about works of art, and the analysis of value-relevant properties are all intimately connected with the problems already mentioned.

In sum then, a very general and inadequate definition of epistemology might be this: epistemology is the study of knowers as they stand in relation to what it is that they claim to know. It follows from this definition and from the truth that knowers claim to know many truths in the other branches of philosophy, that there is an epistemology of ethics, of aesthetics, of mathematics, of the philosophy of science, and so on. Epistemology is therefore one of the two most inclusive fields in philosophy. If those philosophers who hold that the Real Being is identical with what is known to some knower or to all knowers were correct, then metaphysics and epistemology would be identical and equally inclusive. At the least, I think we are safe in claiming that these two fields are the broadest areas of the entire subject.

Let us proceed then to an examination of a theory about the sources of our knowledge, and some criticisms of it.

JOHN LOCKE AND THE THEORY OF IDEAS

John Locke is one of three philosophers commonly classified together as the British empiricists. They are called "empiricists" because in spite of their differences, they all have this much in common: they all hold it to be true that our knowledge of the physical world comes from one and only one source, our senses. Locke was born in 1632 in an era marked by the rejection of scholasticism on the grounds that it was arid, largely concerned with trivialities, and crippled by a sick reverence for the great thinkers of bygone times, principally Aristotle. Seventeenth-century thinkers, especially in the British Isles, were predominantly interested in discovery rather than in defending doctrines designed to support vested interests of various kinds, notably theological. They did not believe that traditional syllogistic reasoning was a possible method of discovery, and they were convinced that the assumptions of traditional philosophy were largely unverified and vague to the point of meaninglessness. Reason, rather than acceptance of authority or dogma, must become the touchstone of thinking men. Although Locke was by no means the first thinker to hold this conviction, the application of it in his *An Essay Concerning Human Understanding* became the most famous and debated work of his time. It is still considered today to be a sourcebook of intriguing and challenging ideas. The theories we shall consider here are taken from it. Perhaps the most famous of the critical attacks on Locke is that of George Berkeley. We shall consider many of these criticisms.

An Essay Concerning Human Understanding

There are a few major themes in Locke's *Essay* which may be clearly stated at the beginning. The first is his persistent denial of "innate ideas" in us. This doctrine of innate ideas is an old and recurring theme. Just what the ideas are which we are supposed to have naturally, that is, ideas we have which are not learned or garnered from experience, varies from theory to theory. Historically, it has been claimed that we are born with an innate idea or concept of God, of immortality, of basic moral principles, and of various relations such as causality. Locke denies the existence of any innate ideas at all. He claims that the mind is a *tabula rasa*, a blank tablet, and that everything which finds its way onto the tablet is written there through the senses, by abstraction from what is given to the senses, and by reflection. In the defense of his position here he has in mind primarily the great French philosopher René Descartes, some of whose views we will be studying in the chapter on the philosophy of science.

The second major theme in Locke's epistemological work is the *Representative Theory of Perception*, the major principle of which is that certain of our ideas are truly representative of their "originals" or properties of these originals. As we shall see, not all ideas are representative for Locke, but some very important ones are. This theory is one of the major positions which Berkeley attacked.

The third and last theme, for our purposes at least, is really a double one. It concerns, on the one hand, Locke's distinction between belief and knowledge, and on the other, his theory of truth. Both concern the nature of relations among ideas. Before we show how these themes are tied together in Locke's theory, we should think about the meaning of the term "idea."

Locke tells us that ideas are the only "immediate objects" of the mind. They are the "instruments or materials of our knowledge." They are "bare appearances, or perceptions in our own minds," neither true nor false when considered in and by themselves. They are of several sorts, which he discusses in the Second Book of the *Essay*. But Locke is also inconsistent in his use of the word, for at times he speaks of them as mental entities to be explained in terms of their parts and their causes, and at other times he speaks of them as propositional components which are either true or false. This would be perfectly alright if he did not confuse the two senses without explanation. But keeping this in mind, the reader of Locke can discover what he means by "idea" by examining the sorts of things which Locke believes to be the elements or materials of our knowledge.

Locke thinks that all our ideas are derived either in sensation or reflection. Together, sensation and reflection comprise all our experience, and are the "fountains of knowledge." Sensation itself gives us the ideas of sensible qualities, such as the ideas of (to use his examples) yellow, white, heat, cold, soft, hard, bitter, and sweet. Reflection is the perception of the operations of our minds, and from this source we derive our ideas of such mental activities as perception, thinking, doubting, believing, reasoning, knowing, and willing. These are the only two sources of our knowledge. Now the ideas of sensation and reflection are combined in various ways, and a survey of these will therefore complete the list of ideas. Those ideas which are not further analyzable into parts are called "simple" ideas, and all others are complex. The mind makes its complex ideas, but simple ideas are given to it in sensation. Hence, simple ideas are logically prior to complex ones. Some ideas come into the mind, as it were, by only one sense; others by more than one; there are some that are *only* ideas of reflection, and, according to Locke, there are others that are suggested to the mind by both sensation and reflection. Colors are an example of a kind of simple idea of sensation known only through one sense. Solidity is known only through touch. Space, extension, figure, rest, and motion are on the other hand known by more than one sense, usually sight and touch. Our ideas of perceiving and willing are derived solely in reflection, and these mental operations have several modes, such as remembering, judging, abstracting, compounding, and so on. For Locke therefore, unlike some later thinkers in the tradition such as David Hume, what we might call ideas of mental events (ideas of reflection) are as much empirical data as are ideas of sensation.

Some simple ideas "convey themselves into the mind" through any or all of the senses and also by reflection. Pleasure and pain, power, existence, and unity are examples. Complex ideas are constructs, made by the mind, out of simple ideas. The three major mental operations involved are combination, comparison, and abstraction. The latter function is the one which got Locke into the most trouble as far as Berkeley was concerned. No matter how they are made by the mind, complex ideas are one of three kinds: (1) modes, (2) substances, (3) relations. Modes are signified by such words as "triangle" and "murder." Their salient characteristic is that their objects do not subsist or exist by themselves but depend upon or are properties of substances. There are both simple and mixed modes. Simple modes are complex ideas composed of ideas of the same sort compounded together, as for example, the idea of a dozen. Mixed modes are complex ideas composed of different kinds of ideas, such as the idea of beauty. Substances are either single or collective. The set of ideas composing the complex idea of a particular man is a single substance, the idea of an army would be a complex idea of a collective substance. Finally, there are complex ideas of relations, which arise from the mental activity of comparing. Cause and effect, identity and diversity, are examples of ideas of relations.

Locke makes a very important distinction between what he calls "primary" and "secondary" qualities. Ideas, whether simple or complex, are in our minds. The cause of simple ideas is not in the mind: these causes are *qualities*, and Locke defines these as "the power (of a subject) to produce any idea in our mind." There are two kinds of these qualities, primary and secondary. Primary qualities are essential to the existence of a thing, and the ideas they cause in us are those of solidity, extension, figure, motion, or rest. For Locke, primary qualities comprise the real essence of body. Secondary qualities also produce ideas in us, but these qualities are not essential to the existence of a body. The ideas they produce in us are those of color, sound, taste, and the like. Both qualities produce these ideas in us by a physical impulse. Imperceptible particles make an impression upon our sense organs, and the impulse is carried to our brains by nerves. Locke believes that primary ideas truly resemble the qualities in the bodies, while secondary ideas do not resemble their causes.

Abstract General Ideas

There are, of course, general as well as particular ideas. Were there not, we should be unable to converse about men as opposed to an individual man. Locke attempted to describe how we come to have general ideas. He reasoned that they are the result of the mental operation called abstraction. The mind considers particular objects of the same kind, and takes out of the particular appearance those properties which are common to all, leaving out circumstances of particular times and places, colors, sizes, and so on. General ideas are therefore all *abstract* for Locke. The abstract general idea of triangularity is that which we abstract from our particular ideas of individual triangles, leaving out their particular size, kind, and so on. General *words* name these abstract general ideas.

One particularly important abstract general idea is that of *substance in general,* or *material substance.* Locke thought that all simple ideas carried with them the idea of a "substratum" in which they somehow inhere, and from which they result. It is the idea of subject in general, that which has qualities, and Locke admits that we have no clear idea of it: it is a substratum, a "support," "though we know not what it is." But how we get the idea is therefore a mystery, since it is derived neither from sensation nor reflection. Why then did Locke think that we have such an idea, and why did he think that is was necessary for the explanation of what we know? One suggestion is that he was influenced by his thinking about the traditional subject-predicate form of the sentence. Consider a sentence such as "The table is round, brown, fourlegged and three feet high." It is easy enough to explicate the ideas of secondary qualities named by such words as "brown" in terms of the primary qualities of the table. But what is it that "has" the *primary* qualities? What is the X that is extended, in motion, or at rest? Locke's answer is that it is a substance, not knowable directly, but by inference. Furthermore, since it follows from Locke's premises that the cause of our ideas is external to us, there must be real, efficient causality in the objective world. We are not directly familiar with any causal subject, except insofar as our ideas of primary qualities are truly representative. Our knowledge of causal subjects is therefore inferential, and is based upon the assumption that (1) the actual existence of sensations is sufficient reason for concluding that they have a cause, and (2) given that a sub'ect is not identical with its properties, then causal subjects are not perceived. The only other conclusion seems to be that there is an unperceivable substance which has the qualities of which we have ideas, and which causes them in us. The abstract general idea of substance in general is the idea of material substance.

It may be well to correct a possible misunderstanding over the use of the term "cause" in this discussion of Locke's philosophy. For Locke, cause or at least causality is a relation between ideas, and to that extent it is a function of the mind. What is exerted by substance is power, strictly speaking. But since Locke's major critic uses the word "cause" when arguing against the claim that substance, unperceived and unperceivable, can be the source of our ideas, it seems more appropriate to use that term here.

Locke makes a distinction between real and nominal essences which is based upon the theory of abstract general ideas. The nominal essence is the complex abstract general idea of the characteristics common to all the members of a class of things, and by which we decide that a given thing *is* that sort of thing. The real essence of anything is always of a particular given individual, and hence includes all the particular characteristics which are left out in the process of abstraction which gives rise to the abstract general idea. Among these characteristics are the insensible properties of the substance of the thing, and since we cannot know these but by inference, real essences are not known.

Kinds of Knowledge

Given this analysis of the components of reality, what does it mean to say that we know something? For Locke, this is a matter of the agreement or disagreement of ideas. The nature of this agreement and disagreement is difficult to explicate. What we might call intuition plays an important role in these concepts; for when we perceive for example, that the ideas named by the two sides of a mathematical equation are in agreement, we simply *see* this, and no further analysis is possible. In addition to perceiving the agreement or disagreement between ideas, there is also the question of agreement or disagreement between ideas and things which are *not* ideas. Hence, our knowledge that a substance is exerting power is coexistent with our knowing ideas of primary and secondary qualities which make up our complex idea of a thing. There is a third kind of knowing, that which he calls agreement or disagreement "of real existence," in which we presumably know that the idea we have of some being, for example God, corresponds or refers to an actually existing entity.

Knowledge, properly speaking, is restricted to: (1) intuitive knowing, which is exemplified by the intuitive recognition of the agreement of two or more ideas as in the perception of the truth of mathematical truths, and (2) demonstrative truths, in which a conclusion is not seen immediately to follow from a set of axioms or premises but is still known to follow certainly because each step before the conclusion (and finally the conclusion too) *is* seen intuitively to be implied by the preceding steps. In this use of the term "knowledge," Locke followed Descartes. All other "knowledge" is either probable, and hence opinion, or sensitive, which is more certain than opinion but not as certain as intuitive knowledge or demonstrative knowledge. Sensitive knowledge may be more precisely characterized as the knowledge *that* we are sensing rather than, say, dreaming. Truths about matters of fact are probable, and it follows that science is too. Given that it follows from Locke's premises that there are no necessary connections among the entities composing the natural world, the principle of uniformity in nature becomes suspect, as Hume was to see, and in Kant the magnificent attempt to combat the skepticism logically entailed by the empiricist's theory was to be made. The most important point here is that truth or falsity is a function of the agreement or disagreement of ideas. It is important because sentences containing signs to which there are *no* corresponding ideas are therefore either neither true nor false (meaningless), or Locke is wrong. Berkeley was to argue that the latter is the case.

Here then we have a theory about the nature of truth and falsity which rests upon another theory, the subject of which is the analysis of the components of everything that we can know. The former theory rests upon the latter, and if the one is unsound, so much for the justification of the other. John Locke's epistemological conclusions rest upon ontological or metaphysical premises, and the soundness of the argument will depend upon whether or not those premises are defensible. If an inconsistency in the theory could be shown, we know that it would be insufficient because from such a mistake, anything may be implied. If any of the premises are false, the argument is unsound. If the theory of truth depends upon the existence of ideas which do not in fact exist, then it is mistaken. If the Representative Theory of Perception leads to skepticism, then it is self-defeating. George Berkeley was convinced that Locke's theory was guilty of all of these errors, and we shall now consider his criticisms.

Berkeley's Criticisms of Locke

In order to understand Berkeley's criticisms of Locke, we must first know at least the major arguments of his own philosophy. By the time Berkeley was about to embark upon his career as a philosopher (his first work appeared in 1709), Locke already was the talk of the English learned world. Berkeley read Locke very carefully, and he was also intimately familiar with the science and mathematics of the time, especially with Newton's work. His reading convinced him that in an important way, philosophers and scientists were very often misled by words:

they took it for granted that for words to be meaningful (except for logical connectives), they had to name something. Thus, the Newtonians believed that words such as "force" and "gravity" named some sort of existing entity, and the disciples of Locke were convinced that "material substance" referred to something which was not even in principle perceivable. Yet in Berkeley's opinion, many such words do not name anything at all, and if that is what we mean when we say that they are meaningful, then they have no meaning. Careful examination of analysis will show that many terms of this nature in fact cannot name anything, or at least, cannot name what they are supposed to name, because the concepts of what they presumably name are self-contradictory. He thought this was true of "material substance," for example. This is not to say that Berkeley thought science to be composed of meaningless terms, for he did not. What he was questioning is the theory of meaning and truth according to which the *only* way in which such terms can mean anything is to name something. For Berkeley they have instrumental or pragmatic value, and hence are meaningful if they meet the criteria provided by the purpose for which they are used.

Berkeley began, as did Locke, with a study of the sources of our knowledge. These are the ideas imprinted upon our senses and the concepts we have of the operations of our own mind. That is all. Since it *is* all, we must be able to give an analysis of objects and their relations, plus our concepts, simply in terms of the ideas of the senses and the notions we have of our mental operations. Berkeley sets out to do this. Objects become clusters of ideas of sense which recur constantly in our perception. Their constant recurrence is the reason we give them names. We perceive no motion distinct from our ideas of sense, and consequently we have no grounds for asserting that there is efficient causation in the natural world. Instead, the relation between objects, and among kinds of ideas of sense, is that of sign-to-thing-signified. What I see suggests to me that if I do certain things, I will experience certain tangible sensations. Constant conjunction tells me that if I see fire and then put my hand in it, I will experience pain. The fire I see is therefore not the cause of my pain, but "the mark that forewarns me of it." Nature is a system of signs, a language. We *do* have knowledge of causation but not through our senses. Our immediate awareness of our mental activities—perceiving, willing, and so on—tells us that our minds are active causal agents. I can make changes in the world of perception by causing my body to move. So the world of perception, the world of visual ideas (lights and colors), tangible ideas (hardness, softness, pain, sense pleasure), and so on for the other senses, is an inactive world, although it is a world of signs. The only active, causal world is the world of minds.

Signs have no meaning for Berkeley unless they are interpreted by a mind. That is, all sign-relationships are three-termed: they require a sign, a significate, and a perceiver. To say that something is a sign is to say that it has significance to some mind. The existence of signs, then, as opposed to sign-vehicles (the idea considered merely as such, without its meaning, which is the significate) depends upon their perception by a mind. For Berkeley to say that a sign exists and hence to say that objects, which are complex signs or groups of ideas, exist, is to say that they are perceived. This is the *meaning* of "existence" when we are predicating it of entities in the world of perception. Human minds are naturally not perceiving all things at all times. Berkeley concludes from this that there must be a cosmic mind, God, who does perceive all things at all times; for if there were not, we should have to hold the absurd belief that things pop in and out of existence, as it were, when they are perceived at one time and not at another.

Minds are not possible objects of perception. Hence, when we say that minds exist, we cannot mean that they are perceived. What do we mean then? Berkeley argues that we mean that minds *perceive*. Whereas the existence of physical objects consists in *being* perceived, the existence of minds consists in their perceiv*ing*. There is no such thing then as an object which is not perceived, or a mind which does not perceive. Indeed, given the meaning of "exists," it is a contradiction of assert either of these propositions. And given that ideas and objects composed from them, and our mental activities, are the only *things* which we can know directly, then the only other existential claims which we are entitled to make must be validly inferable from these and only these types of data. It is this latter principle, plus the axiom that everything has a cause, that allows Berkeley to infer the existence of God as the cause (the perceiver) of the natural world. He also reaches the conclusion that God exists in another way, arguing that if nature is a language, which he believed on the grounds of similarities with artificial languages, then God stands to this language as we stand to our languages. This is an argument from analogy. For a fuller understanding of Berkeley's position and the grounds of his criticisms of Locke, read the first few pages of the section of chapter nine entitled "Berkeley's Unique Arguments About God."

Criticism of "Material Substance"

We now know enough about Berkeley's view to discuss his criticism of a major Lockean theory, the claim that material substance exists. There are two major facets to his attack. The first one rests upon the analysis of the meaning of "exists" which has just been given. By Locke's own admission, material substance is not perceivable. Thus, it cannot be known through sense. But neither is material substance a mind. Hence, it is not immediately known as are our mental activities. If it is neither a mind nor a possible object of perception, then, says Berkeley, it is nothing. Given Locke's own criterion of meaning then, it follows that they are meaningless words. Berkeley thinks that this is true. Those who deny this must say that something, not a mind, exists unperceived; but we have just seen that this is a contradiction, and contradictions are always false.

Some would say that although we do not know material substance directly, we may infer its existence, since without it we cannot explain the origin of our ideas. But if we infer anything we must do so either by analogy, or on grounds of resemblance. If we infer a cause of our sense ideas by analogy, the only justifiable conclusion is that the cause is a mind, since only minds are active, and hence causes. No inference on the grounds of resemblance would be acceptable, because ideas can only resemble other ideas (colors resemble colors, sounds resemble sounds, and so on) and material substance, not being perceivable, is neither an idea nor a set of them. Material substance is therefore not inferable as a cause of our ideas.

Even if we could infer the existence of material substance, it would be useless as an explanatory hypothesis. To explain the origin of our ideas, it would have to be active. But Locke tells us it is inert. It seems then that we do not know it by either sense or reason, that it is not inferable on any grounds, and that even if it were, it would be a useless entity. The very concept of it is contradictory, and the words "material substance" are meaningless.

As if this were not enough, Berkeley has still other weapons left. Locke says that material substance "supports" qualities in some way. It is a "substratum" in which qualities "inhere." It would seem that material substance must therefore be extended, since were it not, we could not conceive how it could support anything, nor be a substratum in any sense. But extension is itself a quality. It seems, then, that material substance must itself be supported by an extended body. And this leads to an infinite regress.

Criticism of Representative Perception

The attack on the theory of material substance is closely associated with Berkeley's criticisms of the theory of representative perception and of the doctrine of abstract general ideas. Let us consider the former first. You may recall that for Locke, our ideas of primary qualities truly resemble those properties of substance, its qualities which Locke defines as "the power (of a subject) to produce any idea in our mind," whereas our ideas of secondary qualities do not resemble their causes. Berkeley's criticism is simple: ideas of primary qualities therefore cannot resemble them. Furthermore, primary and secondary qualities, and their ideas, are not separable as Locke thought. How can we have an idea of color without an idea of extension? If this idea could even be conceived, Berkeley would be willing to abandon this theory. But it cannot be. Try to imagine a color that has no boundary, or on the other hand, try to imagine an extended area without color. Both are impossible. There is no boundary to the area of the image without color differentiation. Another reason that primary ideas could not resemble powers is that all ideas of whatever kind are inactive, while powers presumably are not.

Locke had claimed that our ideas of secondary qualities are subjective because they do not resemble their cause. Berkeley now thinks that he has shown this to be true of ideas of primary qualities as well: the same arguments apply in both cases. But these are the only sorts of ideas of qualities we have. If neither of them represents or resembles anything but other ideas, then the representative theory of perception is false. For Berkeley, this is certainly true, because things *are* what we perceive and nothing more: they are groups of bundles of ideas of sight, touch, taste, etc. There is nothing "behind" them which they can resemble or represent. There is only their cause, which is a mind or minds. If Berkeley is correct, then there is also simply no need for the material substance theory; because if things are simply what we perceive, there is no reason to assume that there is a support or substratum for them.

Criticism of Abstract General Ideas

Berkeley's refutation of material substance and representative perception as they are defended by Locke is generally sound. But his criticisms of the doctrine of abstract general ideas are not as good, because they are unfair to Locke, principally in their assignment of a meaning to "abstract general idea" which Locke certainly would have rejected. By that phrase, Berkeley means "abstract general image," and Locke does not mean this. This is not to say that all of his remarks on the subject are mistaken, for many of them are very important, and certainly of contemporary relevance. The central attack, however, is based upon this misinterpretation of Locke's writings, and this should be kept in mind in the brief description that follows.

Berkeley argues that all of the ideas which we have are particular in nature, that is, they are this color, or that sound, or this individual object. We do not have an idea (image) of a man who is both tall and short, fat and slim, black and white: he has one property or the other, but not both. There are no images of triangles which are isosceles, scalene, and equilateral all at once, or as Berkeley puts it, "all of these and none of these at once." Rather, when we have images of men and triangles, we have a mental picture of some one particular man, or some one particular triangle of a certain sort, and we use these images to *signify* generally. In other words, general abstract ideas are not required for general signification. The latter is a function of the *use* of the sign, and nothing prevents us from using a particular sign or a particular image to signify many things which resemble one another. As we said, it is clear that Berkeley is being unfair to Locke by interpreting abstract general ideas as abstract general images. They are much more closely akin to what we mean by a class concept; and no image is required to talk of such things, nor must we assume that they exist as particular things do. At the same time, however, Berkeley has a good point when he claims that it is not because general words name abstract general ideas that they are general; it is because they come to be *used* to name resembling things rather than simply one thing. Furthermore, some general terms do not seem to name or denote anything, the most obvious examples being general theoretical terms in science. Berkeley was surely correct in pointing this out and equally correct when he said that, if Locke is correct, sentences containing such terms must be meaningless. They are not, so Locke is wrong. Berkeley does not object to the notion of general terms; it is the "abstract" he does not like. The only sense of "abstraction" which Berkeley understands is that in which an observer pays particular attention to a given aspect or aspects of a thing and does not notice the other properties it has while so doing. Thus, we often consider a figure "merely as triangular, without attending to the particular qualities of the angles, or relations of the sides."

Not only does Berkeley argue that general terms do not denote abstract general ideas, but he also notices that some words do not signify any ideas at all; although such terms and the sentences in which they are used are certainly meaningful. Such assertions might be used to incite some passion or emotion, or to cause or inhibit action, without any ideas occurring to the hearer at all. But if the action is, in fact, caused or inhibited or the passion or emotion arises, why must we say that the utterance is meaningless? The more reasonable conclusion seems to be that there is more than one kind of meaning. The same is true of theories of truth. It cannot be the case that the truth-value of a sentence is simply a matter of the agreement or disagreement of ideas, for then sentences such as those just described would be neither true nor false. Instead of accepting this conclusion, Berkeley suggests, especially in the areas of mathematics and the sciences, that an instrumentalist or pragmatist theory of truth and meaning is a more acceptable alternative.

Few, if any, philosophers would want to say that Berkeley's own philosophical system is adequate. He did not accomplish the aims he set out to achieve, which were the refutation of skepticism, atheism, and determinism; and his views about such subjects as meaning and truth raised as many problems as they seemed to solve. His examination of Locke's theory of abstract general ideas has already been described as inaccurate. But the other criticisms seem to show that Locke was mistaken, if not in substance, then at least in his statement and defense of his views. Neither man solves any of the central problems of epistemology; but, as with many failures of genius, both of them enable us to understand these problems more fully and to criticize arguments dealing with this subject matter more accurately and adequately.

INNER PROCESSES AND PUBLIC KNOWLEDGE

The problem of other minds is another of the oldest problems in philosophy, and it is also marked by the innumerable aspects which it has. Strictly speaking, the problem is simply how we know whether or not there are other minds in addition to our own, it being assumed that the individual in the position of the observer does have a mind. But, of course, the very phrase "has a mind" is suspect, for it is clear that one does not have a mind in the way that he has apples in his pocket, nor is the behavior of minds to be characterized in the ways in which we characterize objects. Another part of the problem of minds, and hence of other minds, is therefore how one is to speak of mental "acts" in such a manner that one avoids reifying these "acts."

A third part of the problem is the analysis of the relations between mind and body; for, unless we are willing to defend a thoroughgoing materialism (which one might want to do of course), we will not want to argue that the relation between them is one of identity; and, if minds and bodies are in some way distinct, we must be able to explicate their individual existence. Unless one wishes to reify minds the explication of their relations will have to include specifications of their different ontological positions.

Finally, given that we have minds and that others have minds and that we know they do, then there is the problem of how an observer is to judge from the conduct of another whether that conduct is truly "representative" of his mental states. The word "representative" must be taken in a metaphorical sense here, of course, its force is to suggest that

if there is more to "mental" than behavior itself, there must be some
sort of correlation between the behavior and whatever else there is. It
is a part of this last problem to which we shall give our consideration
here.

We often hear philosophers discussing the "criteria" for certain states
of being, whether mental or physical. The state of being in pain is one
of these, and the central philosophical issues involved in the "pain-
criteria" problem are epistemological and logical in nature. There are a
great many such issues. Here we can only consider a few of them which
surround the situation in which one person, an observer, wants to say
of another person, an agent or actor, that he is in pain.

Wittgenstein's Analysis of Criteria for Pain

Norman Malcolm whote an article entitled "Wittgenstein's Philosophical Investigations" [1] some years ago in which he discussed Ludwig
Wittgenstein's analysis of criteria and, in particular, his analysis of what
criteria for saying that someone is in pain could be. In Malcolm's eyes,
Wittgenstein was trying to isolate and identify the "features" of a person's situation, his actions and environmental circumstances, which would
"settle" the problem of whether we would be justified in applying descriptions of mental states to him. For example, exactly what features
of someone's behavior and circumstances would justify us in applying
the description "He is calculating in his head" to him? What these
features are will be the criteria which settle the question of the applicability of the description, and of course, of the applicability of similar
descriptions to other similar situations. When the requisite features are
to be observed, we say that the agent does have the knowledge of the
given state which we wish to ascribe to him, and we are totally justified
in doing so simply on the basis of the presence of the criteria and nothing else.

One reason why this knowledge must be manifested by the agent
in behavior if we are to know that he has the requisite knowledge sufficient to apply the description to him, is that, in Wittgenstein's view,
private languages, and hence private ostensive definition, is impossible.
An ostensive definition provides us with immediate awareness of the
connection between a word or sign and what it signifies or names. But
words are *public* signs, or, to put it another way, private signs are not
knowledge-carriers and words are, and hence private ostensive definition
can never be the source of criteria from which we can conclude that
some agent is in a certain mental state.

---

[1] Norman Malcolm, "Wittgenstein's Philosophical Investigations," *Philosophical
Review*, 63 (1954), pp. 530–59.

Were there no behavioral and, hence, public manifestations of such states as pain and confidence, we would have nothing against which we could check a person's words in order to determine whether or not he understands them himself. If a man said that he was in pain but never exhibited the criteria for being in pain behaviorally, we would never know whether *we* were justified, when *he* said "I am in pain," in saying "He is in pain." This would be true in Wittgenstein's eyes even if we interpret feelings or mental states as "inner processes." Since the processes *are* inner, they cannot provide criteria for an observer who is trying to justify his claims about the agent's mental state or state of feeling.

Criteria are not the same as symptoms for Wittgenstein. A symptom of something is always, or almost always, found with that of which it is a symptom in our experience. But Wittgenstein claims that criteria are not like this. If something is a criterion for X, our knowledge that it is a criterion is ". . . a matter, not of experience, but 'of definition.'" When we establish that something is a criterion for something else, we thereby establish the existence of that something else "beyond question," and whenever the criteria apply or are satisfied by something (call it X), the occasion upon which they are satisfied is a repetition of "the kind of case in which we were taught to say" the word "X."

Suppose that we have an agent, S, such that the behavior and circumstances of S upon a given occasion satisfy the criteria, C, for being in pain. Wittgenstein wants to say that in such an event, S is in pain "beyond question," that C are not a matter of experience, but of definition, and that the situation in which S satisfies C is always going to be the sort of case in which we were taught to say that some agent is in pain. The certainty of our claim that the agent is in pain if he satisfies the criteria for being in pain is complete for Wittgenstein. The agent may even have certain brain processes going on which are not usually associated with pain, but, if he satisfies the criteria for being in pain, then he *"must"* be in pain, even though we can from time to time *change* our criteria for being in pain. Yet at the same time, what will constitute the criteria for any given state, such as being in pain, must meet rigorous conditions.

It is possible of course that a man may act as if he is in pain, or that he is in some hypnotic state and only believes that he is in pain, or something else of that sort. Expressions of pain, the behavioral manifestations, only count *as* manifestations and hence as criteria in "certain 'surroundings.'" Let us assume that we know what these certain surroundings are, as we presumably do in any case where the criteria are viable. Then, since a man *must* be in pain if he satisfies the criteria, we might expect that the description of the relevant pain behavior (the description of the criteria), when conjoined with the negation of all the descriptions of circumstances in which we would say that the subject is not in pain or in which a circumstance occurs which would falsify the claim that he is in pain, would *imply* that the subject is in pain. But, as it turns out, such an exhaustive enumeration of instances which would falsify the claim that the agent is in pain is impossible; so the entailment cannot be stated.

In spite of what seems to be a consequence of this, namely, that at least a logical skepticism about pain statements when the criteria are satisfied seems justified, Wittgenstein evidently still wanted to argue that someone *must* be in pain if the criteria are satisfied. He thinks that the degree of certainty here is as high as it can ever be for *any* factual claims. He does not want to say that this means it is impossible even to imagine or to conceive a situation in which we are deceived, but in fact we never accept such doubts. We "shut our eyes" in the face of them, as we do when we realize as philosophers that it is possible to doubt that some object we are presently perceiving exists, but nonetheless we believe that it does. The grounds for the possible doubt about the object of perception are that from descriptions of my sense impressions of the object no existential claim about it is entailed, unless one wants to accept a thoroughgoing phenomenalism which in this case would entail egocentrism. The lack of such an entailment does not cause us to doubt our perceptions, and Wittgenstein thinks that the case is parallel to the "He is in pain" example.

But we cannot avoid the issue that easily. The issue, of course, is the precise force of the "must" in Wittgenstein's claim that an agent must be in pain if he satisfies the criteria. What sort of certainty are we dealing with here? To say that it is merely belief or opinion will not do. The reason obviously is that they can be mistaken, in ways to which we cannot simply "shut our eyes." Our immediate problem, therefore, is to examine the nature of the necessity by virtue of which we must accept a man's being in pain if he satisfies the criteria for being in this state, given that the satisfaction of these criteria does not entail that his pain behavior must in fact be an expression of his pain.

Spectator and Actor Sentences

Call the sentence "He is in pain" a *third-person sensation sentence,* and the statement "I am in pain" a *first-person sensation expression.* The former may also be called a spectator sentence and the latter an actor sentence. Malcolm tells us that Wittgenstein characterizes all actor sensation sentences as first-person expressions. For such expressions, there is apparently no "paradigm," whereas for spectator sentences, there is a paradigm. This paradigm is the human body and its behavior. Whenever we predicate of a person such states as consciousness, pain, deliberation, and so forth, the statements of these are related to this paradigm. Because this is true, no questions about the possibility of other beings having these states or being in them normally arise, unless ". . . I forget that I use that paradigm in ordinary life."

In Malcolm's interpretation of Wittgenstein, such questions arise, together with the resultant use of arguments from analogy to justify them, when we attribute mental states to *non*human beings such as fish, animals, or reptiles. For humans, however, we have the criteria of their behavior, circumstances, and words. The criteria I use to judge that another person is in pain are not simply *identical* with the meaning of "He is in pain," because my own reactions, such as pity and sympathy for him, also enter into the meaning of this sentence. But one thing that does *not* enter into its meaning if Malcolm is right is the suggestion that the agent's words, behavior, etc., may have "behind" them some hidden inner process. The main point here seems to be that arguments from analogy in the analysis of behavioral situations are only used in those cases where human behavior is being used to characterize the behavior of nonhuman beings, metaphorically, in allegory, or in fable. In contexts involving purely human agents and spectators, arguments from analogy do not arise or ought not to arise because their very use assumes that the so-called "inner processes" are relevant to the meanings of third-person spectator sensation sentences. Given the truth of the claim that the paradigm for such sentences is that of human behavior and the obvious truth that inner processes are not a part of behavior, then it is clear that inner processes are not a part of the paradigm and hence not relevant to the determination of either the meaning or the truth of spectator sentences. This is what Wittgenstein seems to mean when he argues that what count as criteria for pain behavior are determined or are a matter of "definition" and not "experience."

Now it seems that there is a very good point here, which is verified at least in part when we consider the kinds of situations in which we *do* question the truth of spectator sentences. If someone says "He is in pain," and we question the speaker, when do we usually do this? And what is it we are questioning when we want to doubt the claim? Is it that we doubt that there is in fact the requisite "correspondence" between what we see and some inner process "behind" the behavior? Or is it rather that we are questioning whether the behavior which we do see ought to count as *pain* behavior, or some other kind, or not as criteria at all? Suppose the context is a play on a stage. Clearly, in such a case we would simply point out, should such a strange situation arise, that the circumstances are not those which the definition of criteria for pain require. We might also say, as Wittgenstein notes, that this is not the sort of situation in which we have been taught to say that someone is in pain. In short, we are questioning the classification of the behavior as that which meets pain criteria, and *not* the presence or absence of some inner process.

When we predicate consciousness of nonhuman beings, there is no question of their behavior's being confused with human behavior except in the case of animals which are remarkably similar to humans in *physical* ways. When the behavior is dissimilar, analogy comes into play, and with it, the puzzling over inner processes. In the case of animals such as chimpanzees, similar in physiognomy to ourselves, what we wonder is whether their behavior constitutes for them the criteria for pain. Malcolm is mistaken when he concludes that there is a use of analogy referring to inner processes in nonhuman animals if he means that *only* this kind of analogy is used; for, in the case of similar animals, the analogy is between our criteria and something very like them, and inner processes need not be relevant here. But this, of course, is confirming evidence for the thesis that inner processes are not relevant in contexts where there are behavioral criteria for spectator sentences. Furthermore, we only discover criteria in the way we learn words. When one learns basic or object-language words, he does so ultimately by ostensive definition. This is what the mother does when she says "Grandma" to her little one with a smile on her face whenever granny comes to visit, and until the child says "Grandma" or the childish equivalent whenever he sees that person. And this is just how we learn criteria for pain and other mental states. We do not need to *feel* pain ourselves, that is, experience it, to learn how to tell when another is in pain. We need merely to learn the definition, to learn the natural "words" for pain. We do indeed have to *experience* pain to know what pain is like ourselves; but that is quite different than knowing that another is in pain.

Related to this last point is Wittgenstein's argument that when you learn the language or criteria for pain, you learn the *concept* "pain." In his enigmatic way he asks: "Could someone understand the word 'pain,' who had never felt pain? Is experience to teach me whether this is so or not?" He is here trying to make us notice that my experience, which after all is *only* mine, could never allow me to know whether you or any other person had or had not *experienced* pain, though my observations of your behavior (which constitute a part of *my* experience) will allow me to know whether you meet the criteria for knowing how to use the word "pain." But this is compatible with the sense of "know" that was used in the penultimate line of the previous paragraph: you and I know things together, and each of us "knows" things the other cannot know, and "knows" them in a manner not communicable publicly. When we talk about criteria, we are talking about public knowledge. In Wittgenstein's eyes the question of the feeling of pain by an actor and what relevance that might have to that actor's understanding of the word "pain" can never be solved nor even illuminated through reference to elements in the *spectator's* experience. The truth conditions for first-person sensation *expressions* and third-person sensation *sentences* are unrelated except for this: the expression may be among the criteria which are satisfied if the sentence is true. Because analogies involving inner processes refer to something not a part of the behavior which provides the criteria, they are irrelevant so far as determining the truth of spectator sentences are concerned, and hence also to the determination of what will count as a criterion.

Re-examining the Criteria

The concept of just what a criterion is, is vague in all of this. Indeed, it is a central problem in the study of Wittgenstein's work, and we will not attempt to solve that here. Part of the problem in the case of pain criteria is that the criteria for *saying* "He is in pain" are not necessarily identical with those which establish the *fact* that he is in pain; because, if they were, then the satisfaction of the criteria for saying "He is in pain" would *imply* that he is in pain, and we have seen that this is not the case. But at the same time we have just seen how Wittgenstein insists that having the concept "pain" equals by definition knowing how to use the word "pain." So far as the spectator is concerned, the criteria for knowing at least when to use the word "pain" are the criteria for being in pain; and, we are told, if the behavior of the actor satisfies these criteria then for the spectator, he *must* be in pain. On the face of it, this seems very close to being an explicit contradiction, which becomes apparent when we state the various claims more carefully. Here is what has been said:

1. If he fulfills the criteria, then he must be in pain.
2. If he fulfills the criteria, then we are justified in saying "He must be in pain."
3. The criteria for saying "He must be in pain" are not necessarily identical with those establishing the fact of his being in pain.
4. "Having the concept 'pain' " means the same as "Knowing how to use the word pain.' "

The last statement in this list gives a necessary condition for understanding the first three. If we assume that we have the concept "pain," that is, we know how to use the word, then it seems to follow from sentence (1) that he must be in pain, and from sentence (2) that, given these assumptions, we are justified in saying "He is in pain." In reality there are two arguments packed into these four sentences. If we unpack them, we will get the following two arguments:

A

1. If he satisfies the criteria then he must be in pain.
2. He fulfills the criteria.
3. Therefore, he must be in pain.

B

1. If he fulfills the criteria, then we are justified in saying "He must be in pain."
2. He fulfills the criteria.
3. Therefore, we are justified in saying "He must be in pain."

Now what these two arguments seem to tell us is that one and the same set of criteria settles both the question of his being in pain and the issue of when we are justified in saying that he is in pain. Wittgenstein clearly would not want to hold that this is true, because he has already said that the criteria which would settle the two issues are *not* necessarily the same. We are therefore presented with a dilemma, and the solution to it appears to lie in a restatement of the questions involved.

The first question, or—since such matters are always complex—set of questions, is relevant to the first argument, called A. The issues concerned with settling a man's *being* in pain are not soluble for Wittgenstein. Indeed, they are not even statable for him, if a condition of stability is that the proposition stated in the sentence be a possible object of public knowledge. This is the set of problems associated with the explication of whatever it is that is "behind" the behavior, the "inner processes" to which we have been referring, in spite of the fact that Wittgenstein does not think we can refer to them. The inner processes are relevant, if at all, only to the meaning of the first-person sensation expressions. It appeared that Wittgenstein was well aware of this. It seems that this is why he raised the issue of doubt in the first place; for what other reason is there for pointing out that, although it is possible to doubt in the logical sense that when an agent meets the criteria for being in pain he actually is in pain, we shut our eyes to this possibility?

The only explanation would seem to be Wittgenstein's realization that even if we *want* to say that the criteria for the agent's being in pain and saying that the agent is in pain are identical, this cannot be said unless we either deny that there is anything "behind" the expression of pain or assume that the inner processes are a possible object of public knowledge; and Wittgenstein does not want to do either. Because of this, he denies that the two sets of criteria are identical; or, to put it another way, he holds that the denial of the identity of the sets does not entail that they are not identical. The reason is that the denial of identity rests upon the assumption that we cannot know that there *are* two sets of criteria, nor even what "criteria" would *be* for "inner processes." Wittgenstein would not say of the problem of the meaning of actor expressions that there is something wrong about assuming the existence of inner processes. He says that the mistake consists in assuming that inner processes are that which warrants our accepting these actor expressions as criteria for being in pain, when we are speaking from the spectator viewpoint. Making this latter assumption would be the gravest abuse of model and metaphor. The way out of the dilemma is, therefore, simply the realization that inner processes and their relations to the actor's behavior are *irrelevant* to the problem of spectator sentences and their relations to the criteria which warrant our acceptance of them. Having reached this solution, we can now return to the question of the force of the "must" in "He must be in pain," when his behavior meets the criteria for being in pain.

Remember that this is a third-person sentence, that is, it is uttered by an observer of an actor. In Wittgenstein's eyes, the question about the force of the "must" turns out to be a question about the relationships among the criteria involved, the circumstances involved, and the conviction of the spectator that the actor is in pain. One way of examining *this* set of problems involves a consideration of some of what Wittgenstein has to say about how we draw boundaries for various language games. He notes that the very concepts of "exact" and "inexact" are relative; because, in at least some contexts, to speak of something as inexact is to offer a reproach, and to say that something is exact is to praise, whereas this is not so in other uses of the word. The meanings of the terms will, therefore, vary with the end in mind and the extent to which we achieve it, just as, in playing various language games, we often "draw a boundary" for the game in the light of a "special purpose." It is the boundary which makes the concept usable for the particular purpose of the game, even though the boundaries themselves need not be precise or absolutely distinct; indeed, imprecise or inexact boundaries are in some games usable to the player's advantage.

The appropriate uses of words in the game of pain-language are indicated by the circumstances, which are the criteria for using the words. These same circumstances which are the criteria for using pain words are also the criteria for drawing the boundaries for this particular language game. Crying, groaning, writhing, saying "ouch," screaming, yelling "It hurts," grimacing and saying "I am in pain"—all of these are circumstances or criteria in the language game of pain words. They can take one another's place so far as their roles are concerned, in the way that, in Wittgenstein's view, the verbal expression of pain replaces crying. In addition to the uses to which we as spectators put our words, our reactions and our convictions are also based upon these criteria or circumstances. We would not feel pity for someone, for example, unless we were convinced that he was in pain, and what convinces us is the fact that he fulfills the criteria for being in pain. It is because the circumstances which provide the criteria for the boundary of the game may be indistinct that the convictions may be mistaken. So what is the relation of the criteria to the convictions? We know that it is not a logical relation, because even if all the criteria are fulfilled, nothing is entailed about the degree of conviction of a spectator. Yet the relation cannot be merely psychological, because the "must" in "He must be in pain" would then have no force at all. From my being convinced that someone is in pain, nothing at all follows about the object of that conviction.

There is one other possibility. It is that the "must" is a *pragmatically* necessary must; he must be in pain because of the necessity for going on, for playing the game, to use Wittgenstein's language. And why must we play the game? Wittgenstein says: "If I have exhausted the justifications, I have reached bedrock, and my spade is turned. Then I am inclined to say 'This is simply what I do.'" In short, the actor must be in pain because to persist in doubt is only possible if we deny that the circumstances or surroundings are the source of the significance of spectator sentences. But in this event, the only other source of their significance seems to be the positing of inner processes; and this is tantamount to skepticism.

The Argument Against Skepticism

A refutation of this skepticism is not achieved simply by pointing out how nice it would be to go on with the game rather than become a skeptic. Some skeptics appear to be quite happy. Nonetheless, it seems that Wittgenstein has indeed refuted this sort of skepticism and that he has done it in a manner which is quite similar to the method George Berkeley was trying to use when he argued against John Locke's theory of the material substratum.[2] Berkeley had set out to show that the skepticism which implied that the existence of the real world was logically problematic (and, indeed, perceptually problematic as well), was completely unfounded because the grounds of the skepticism itself were nonexistent. This is the purpose of his attack on the theory of material substance and its concomitant, the representative theory of perception. This theory of perception, as you can see from your consideration of it earlier in this chapter, could be thought to provide a foundation for the skeptical argument that, precisely because of the inaccessibility of the world of material substance, we can never really know that our perceptions are truly representative of reality, i.e., the cause of our perceptions.

[2] Paul Olscamp, "Wittgenstein's Refutation of Skepticism," *Philosophy and Phenomenological Research*, 26, no. 2 (1965), pp. 239–47. I wish to thank the editors of *Philosophy and Phenomenological Research* for permission to use arguments from this article.

This shadowy substance stands forever "behind" what we see, never to be known by us. But Berkeley saw that this skepticism rested upon an unproven assumption itself, which was that material substance is a necessary explanatory entity without which we can provide neither a test for accuracy nor an explanation of the origin of our knowledge of the real world. Berkeley was convinced, as you know, that this assumption was not only unproven but was in fact meaningless. If he was right, then there is no meaning to the phrase "material substance": even if we grant it meaning, the concept of material substance is useless as an explanatory entity; and even if it actually exists, we can never know that it does. If we cannot know that material substance exists, or, for that matter, that it does not exist, then any theory which assumes that we *do* know this, whether it states this explicitly or holds it implicitly, is unjustified. Indeed, insofar as it claims that we do know either when in fact we know neither, it is false. In Berkeley's eyes, the representative theory of perception makes just this assumption, and hence is false.

The point here is the analogy between Berkeley's arguments against Locke and the arguments which Wittgenstein seems to raise against a parallel sort of skepticism often found in arguments about the existence of mental states and other minds. For the parallel to hold, it is not necessary that both sides of it be correct.

The "Beetle in the Box" and Material Substance

Wittgenstein's point of attack is the "beetle in the box," the "inner processes," which is parallel to Locke's material substance. Like the latter, it is used to justify a skeptical attitude about a set of knowledge claims. In Wittgenstein's case this set is the class of third-person sensation sentences, at least those concerned with mental states, and perhaps many more kinds. And, like Berkeley, the basis of his attack upon the "inner processes" theory concerns the relevance which such processes have in the determination of the truth of these claims. Wittgenstein has demonstrated, or tried to demonstrate, that we do not know what criteria would be for inner processes. Since this is so, we have no grounds at all for holding that the criteria for inner processes *are* identical with those warranting the third-person sensation sentence "He is in pain." But, equally important for the argument against skepticism, we have no grounds for holding that the criteria for inner processes are *not* identical with those which warrant spectator sensation sentences. After all, if we *do not know* what criteria for inner processes are, nor even what they might be, we have no justification at all for saying *anything* about them. Because of this, it is impossible to establish that they have any relevance to the grounds for warranting third-person sensation sentences. The grounds which do warrant these sentences are the criteria provided by the behavior, circumstances, and surroundings of the actor. So even if there *are* inner processes (and it is compatible with Wittgenstein's position that they exist), we can never know, even in principle, what the criteria for them would be. Therefore, we cannot justify any skeptical theory which is based precisely upon the assumption that we *do* or *can* know the criteria or what they would be. All skeptical theories which question the veridical nature of spectator sensation sentences, even when all the necessary behavioral and circumstantial criteria have been fulfilled, assume the possibility of the absence of the inner processes which they believe to be the essential condition for the truth of such claims. They therefore assume the relevance of inner processes to the criteria for evaluating these sentences; and, if what Wittgenstein says is true, then this skeptical position is unjustified.

Summary of the Two Arguments

For pedagogical reasons, it might be a good idea to summarize both the skeptical arguments and the parallel refutations of them. In what follows, the capital letters name the skeptical claims against which George Berkeley argued and also his specific arguments, and the lower case letters name the skeptical positions which Wittgenstein attacked and his specific arguments.

- A. Since material substance is not sensible, it is only knowable *through* our sensations by inference from them.
- a. Since the inner processes of others are not sensible, not a part of the behavior and circumstances we observe, the only way they can be known is *through* public behavior, i.e., by criteria.
- B. Because our sensations can fail to be veridical in their representation of material substance, skepticism with regard to statements warranted by material substance is justifiable.
- b. Because criteria can fail veridically to testify to the presence of requisite inner processes, skepticism with regard to spectator sensation sentences is justifiable.

But:

- C. "Material substance" is either a meaningless term, or, if there is such a thing, we cannot know it. Therefore, any theory of knowledge (or in the case of skepticism, anti-knowledge) which rests upon the assumption that material substance is relevant to the determination of the truth of sentences about reality is at the least useless and at the most false, and skepticism is, therefore, unjustifiable.
- c. "Inner processes" are not the objects for which public behavior and circumstances constitute the criteria, and in fact we do not

even know what the criteria would be for such processes. Hence, any theory which is based upon the assumption that the criteria for pain are the criteria for inner processes, or which rests upon the assumption that inner processes are somehow relevant to the criteria for pain, is at the least useless and at the most false.

D. Skepticism concerning our knowledge claims about material objects is based upon the assumption that material substance exists. It is therefore unjustified.

d. Skepticism about our spectator sensation claims is founded upon the assumption that inner processes or the criteria for them are relevant to the third-person sensation claim that "He is in pain." Therefore, it is unjustified.

Wittgenstein's position here can, of course, be generalized to all cases involving mental states.

Knowledge "1" and Knowledge "2"

Is Wittgenstein correct? It would seem so. It has already been suggested that the analysis of the objects of our deliberations in situations where we wonder whether it is true that a man is in pain seem to confirm his view. We do not wonder about inner processes; we wonder whether what we see are in fact the criteria for being in pain. When we wonder whether chimpanzees are conscious, we do not wonder whether they have inner processes sufficient for warranting this claim; we wonder whether the behavior in the circumstances we observe constitute for them criteria for being in some conscious state. Furthermore, it seems to be true that there is no way whatsoever for me to know, directly or indirectly, your "inner processes," if you have any. The factors in terms of which I decide that you are in pain, that is, the factors which determine for me the truth of "He is in pain," are not factors which enable *you* to decide that *you* are in pain. Indeed, you do not "decide" that you are in pain at all—you either are or are not in pain, and no decision is required about it. You do not have evidence that you are in pain either.

What would it be like for you to wonder whether or not you are in pain? Would you examine your body in the hope of discovering the answer to this question? Suppose that you discovered a cut on your hand. Would your reaction be a sudden realization that you are in pain? Surely not. Hence there certainly seems to be a large difference between the status of first-person expressions and third-person statements about pain-states. From the third-person viewpoint this difference is expressible in just the way Wittgenstein suggests, namely, that the presence or absence of inner processes in the agent is logically and perceptually irrelevant to the determination of the truth values of spectator sensation sentences. Now if we make the distinction which has already been suggested between two senses of "know" and "knowledge," we can see that Wittgenstein's point clarifies the analysis of the knowing situation. All public knowledge, or at least all public knowledge concerned with sensation sentences, will be defined and circumscribed in terms of criteria which are a part of our behavior and circumstances. We might call this "knowledge 1." "Knowledge 2" will be comprised of the set of feelings, emotions, and mental states as they are immediately suffered by their subjects. Knowledge 2 cannot be characterized through the use of any language, for languages are in their very essence public tools requiring a basis of understanding accessible to all; and, hence, they cannot employ or include as foundational to the meanings and uses of signs any experience which does not have criteria. We are, of course, speaking here of a descriptive language of statements similar to the third-person sensation sentences we have been considering.

Such a classification is a useful one. It might be interesting, for example, to speculate about whether all of science concerned with sensation sentences is confined to knowledge 1 and about whether the province of poetry and music of the expressive variety is confined to knowledge 2.

THE FUTURE, THE PAST, AND THE UNIFORMITY OF NATURE

In Chapter 5 the fundamental issue which caused Kant's awakening from his self-confessed "dogmatic slumber" was his realization that if Hume was right, then science had no logical or ontological justification. Put in a nutshell, Hume's conclusion was simply that we have no proof that the future will resemble the past, which seems to entail that our faith in probable conclusions about the future course of the world is unfounded. His argument rests upon these claims: (1) you cannot support the conclusion that the future will resemble the past on the basis of evidence from experience, because by definition that evidence will be taken from present or past experience; (2) deductive reasoning cannot prove the conclusion without begging the question in the premises; and (3) there are no necessary connections in nature. Kant, of course, argued that the last claim was false, and tried to prove it.

Hume and Kant are not the only philosophers who have been concerned with this problem, and, in fact, it remains today a central topic in philosophy, especially in the philosophy of science. But, in addition to its interest for the philosophy of science, there is a large body of writing concerned with the epistemological aspects of the problem: how we can *know* that the future will resemble the past. We shall discuss here the views of two writers who think that we cannot know that the future will resemble the past and one writer who believes we can. The two philosophers who think that we cannot know are John Stuart Mill and Bertrand Russell, and the one who thinks that we can know is Frederick Will.

Mill's Argument

In *A System of Logic*, Mill argues that inductive argumentation is "generalization from experience." By this he means that we notice that a certain phenomenon or a certain property occurs in several individual instances, and from this we conclude that it will occur in all cases which are similar in the other respects in virtue of which the members of the class resemble one another. As Mill recognizes, such argumentation assumes that nature is uniform, and, strangely, he concludes that "if we consult the actual course of nature, we find that the assumption is warranted"—strangely, because we never consult the future, that is, observe it, and if the principle of uniformity is that the future will resemble the past, then we can never verify the principle by observation. What he probably means is that in all the cases we know, our *expectations* about the future were borne out. But to say this and to say that our expectations can be justified before the fact is to say two different things. The principle of the uniformity of nature is in Mill's eyes the fundamental axiom or principle of induction.

Mill also thinks that the principle of nature is *itself* a generalization, an inductive generalization, which is based upon still prior generalizations; and he thinks that what this means is that we must have made subsidiary laws or generalizations about many classes of phenomena before we concluded that uniformity was general across all classes. He then wonders how it is that the uniformity principle, which is a conclusion from several other generalizations, can be the justification for all other generalizations we make. It is a good question.

Mill notes that we do not expect nature to be uniform in all respects. We do not expect the periods of sun and rain to be uniform, nor the same days to be sunny every year. We are also mistaken about our generalizations in many cases. Prior to the advent of the white man in Africa, the natives no doubt thought that all men are black, and the Incas believed so implicitly that all men are dark-skinned that they believed the first white men who came among them to be gods. Swans had been known for 3,000 years before anyone saw a black one. In other words, we often believe that a general statement is true simply because we have no contrary instances, when our assumption would only really be justified if we had, in addition, evidence that if an exception were going to happen, it should already have happened; and for this we can have no evidence, or very little. The kind of induction Mill is speaking of here, which is the kind that the principle of the uniformity of nature is based upon, is induction by *enumeration*. In some cases it is possible to achieve certainty by this method, namely those cases in which the enumeration is exhaustive. But it is never certain in science, because it is not precise enough for the subject matter of science and does not apply to the future.

We also know that in science a generalization is sometimes not drawn from a large enumeration but from a single experimental instance, and Mill also wants to know why it is that we feel justified in making this kind of generalization in some cases but not in others. His answer is that, in cases of enumeration, there are no *other* generalizations upon which we can rest. The generalization that all crows are black depends not upon some other established uniformity but only upon our experience with crows. When we draw a general conclusion from a single critical experience in science, however, the entire spectrum of previous scientific laws in that area of science supports us. Mill concludes that inductions are the less fallible the more they rest upon previously established generalizations. Induction should relate new generalizations to broader, more established ones which have originally been established by enumeration. One kind of inductive reasoning consists in showing that one presumably well-founded generalization is, in fact, false, because it conflicts with one that rests upon a "broader foundation of experience"; and Mill concludes that the wider the foundation of experience, the better the generalization, that is, the more trustworthy it is. Among the broadest generalizations, based upon the broadest foundations, which he mentions are: (1) food nourishes, (2) fire burns, (3) water drowns, and (4) there is a law of causation.

Mill has not made his case. It certainly is true that *exhaustive* enumeration results in certain conclusions; but, if it *is* exhaustive, it is not inductive. If there are only 49 whooping cranes left in the world, and you determine by observing them all that they have the habit of standing on one leg while fishing, then you may certainly conclude that all known whooping cranes stand on one leg when fishing. But this does not enable you to draw the conclusion, with absolute certainly, that the next whooping crane born will have this property. And induction is about what will happen *next*, not about what has already happened. Furthermore, though the facts that fire warms and water drowns are well established, the law of causation is not of the same status as these. If it is true that all events have causes, then this, as Mill truly notes, is a generalization of generalizations—it is true, if true, of *all* classes of things, not of a limited class such as fire or water. It is established by an enumeration of *classes*, not by an enumeration of particulars. The question is, therefore, how an enumeration of classes is proven by an enumeration of instances, and Mill does not answer this.

Finally, the law of causation is but another name for the uniformity principle; and, if this principle is sound, then it holds good for the future as well as for the past. By definition all enumerations are of that which is past. No such enumeration can prove that what has not been enumerated ever can be enumerated; and this, coupled with the fact that what we need to know is whether what will be counted in the future will resemble what has been counted in the past, is the question Mill fails to face. No one is suggesting that we ought to ignore the uniformities of nature or the laws of science because we have not proven that nature is uniform. This would be the height of folly. But no one can say on the basis of Mill's claims that science is certain.

Russell's Argument

Lord Russell, in his marvelous little book, *The Problems of Philosophy*, also discusses the problem of induction. He later modified the views expressed there considerably, but we shall consider just this early work. In the sixth chapter, Russell divides the issues at stake into two kinds. First, there is the question of whether a great number of instances of the constant conjunction of two single things will allow us to infer that in each individual case of the occurrence of one of these things in the future, the other will follow. Secondly, there is the question of whether under the same circumstances a sufficient number of cases of the association of two things will justify us in concluding that the general law "A will always be followed by B" is true. Without grounds for believing in such general laws, we can never extend our knowledge beyond the particular things which we know here and now. If the laws of gravity and motion could not be expected to remain in force tomorrow as they did today, astronauts would most assuredly be taking a bigger chance. But, as Russell notes, the only reason we have for thinking that they will remain in force is that they have up until now. He does not question that past constant conjunction *causes* our expectations of future resemblances, and, indeed, no one disputes this. But the point is that these expectations are often disappointed. Russell notes that the chicken whose expectations concerning the farmer who feeds him every morning have been justified in the past is usually rudely disappointed when one morning the farmer wrings its neck. The problem is not with the cause of our expectations but with the justification for them.

Russell characterizes the belief in the uniformity of nature in these words:

The belief in the uniformity of nature is the belief that everything that has happened or will happen is an instance of some general law to which there are *no* exceptions.[3]

Science also assumes that there are subsidiary general laws to which there are no exceptions, the laws of motion and gravity being examples. But, as Russell notes, the constant conjunction of two things in the past, no matter how often the conjunction occurs, does not conclusively demonstrate that they will be found together in the future. That is, from descriptions of such uniformities it is not possible to deduce descriptions of other uniformities which have not yet happened. Even if we have a law which appears to have no exceptions, for example the law of gravity (as opposed to the chicken's expectations), we can never be sure that we *have* a law with no exceptions without begging the questions about the future resembling the past; and, indeed, our very belief in a law-governed universe is only a probable belief.

Probability, Russell notes, is always relative to some data; and because of this, it is not possible to *dis*prove the uniformity principle. For example, suppose that we have always found swans to be white in the past and, on this basis, we say that it is highly probable that swans will be white in the future. Along comes a black swan. It *still* remains the case that it is *more* probable that future swans will be white rather than black, because the probability is based upon the available data and there are vastly more white swans than black ones. In short, exceptions to the rule do not destroy induction as a form of argument. Even if black swans become more numerous than white ones, the *principle* of induction is not at stake; because it will then become more likely that the next swan you see will be black instead of white, and general laws change accordingly.

However, neither can the inductive principle be proved, at least not by an appeal to experience; because, again, all our evidence is by definition past evidence, and the uniformity-of-nature principle is about that which is as yet unexamined—the future. Whether what has yet to happen will have the properties of that which has happened can never be shown by looking at what has happened. Russell notes in the seventh chapter of *The Problems of Philosophy* that the principle of induction is not alone in finding itself in this "difficulty." When we make deductive inferences, for example, we assume the truth of the laws of logic, and we cannot prove that they are justified within the framework of a logic system without begging the question in just the way we do in the case of proving the uniformity principle by an appeal to the past. That is to say, all deductive proof presupposes the justification for the laws of

[3] Bertrand Russell, *The Problems of Philosophy* (London: Oxford University Press, 1912), chapter 6.

logic, or at least presupposes that they are justifiable, in just the same way that induction presupposes the justification for the uniformity principle. In fact, this truth seems a general one; in *no* area where we claim knowledge can we justify the *principles* of our knowledge in that area by reference to what we claim to be known.

Let us consider ethics. Assume that a principle in our moral system is that one ought not to cause unnecessary death, pain, or suffering. Suppose that we are presently examining a case in which the action to be analyzed is an instance of adultery. One might argue as follows:

> One ought not to commit adultery.
> Why not?
> Because its practice leads to the breakdown of marriage, which is a desirable social institution.
> Why is marriage desirable?
> Because it protects children until they can manage their own affairs.
> But why do that?
> Because they will suffer less.
> But what is wrong with that?
> One ought not to cause unnecessary death, pain, or suffering.
> But why?

The last "why" cannot be answered, if the *principle* in the system is the one we have suggested, and this holds true for any system, no matter what the principle is. In fact, as Aristotle noted, when you get to that stage all you can do is to ask for the *causes* of the principles, not the justification, if by "justification" you are looking for yet another law or rule from which the principle is deducible. "Principle" means "first," and a rule or law which is a principle does not follow from another one in the same system.

So in Russell's view, although we cannot disprove the uniformity-of-nature principle, we cannot prove it either. As has been mentioned, the nature of Russell's arguments changed afterward and came to involve a much more sophisticated view of causality than that which is evidenced in *The Problems of Philosophy*. This more detailed position may be found in the last four chapters of his book *Human Knowledge: Its Scope and Limits*.[4] But the fundamental idea that the primitive underlying uniformity of causality cannot be proven by appeal to experience is retained.

Will's Argument

Frederick Will's position was first outlined in an article entitled "Will the Future Be Like the Past?" in the journal *Mind* in 1947. He begins

[4] Bertrand Russell, *Human Knowledge: Its Scope and Limits* (London: Allen & Unwin, 1948).

that article summarizing the skeptical position as found in Hume's writings. Will disagrees with that position, the conclusion of which, as you know, is that attempting to prove the uniformity of nature by reference to past evidence is circular, that is, it begs the question. Will thinks that the skeptics have made a mistake; indeed, that there is a *contradiction* in their arguments. This would of course render their arguments unsound. The contradiction, he thinks, arises from a mistaken use of language which he sets out to expose and correct.

The method he chooses to argue against the skeptics' position is not that of choosing some scientific generalization and then showing that the procedure by which it was attained was not circular. He believes, rightly, that any such method would be criticized by saying that all such general laws assume the uniformity principle, which is what we must justify if induction is to be a good method of argumentation. Will chooses to state his position in terms of a claim made by J. M. Keynes in his famous work, *Treatise on Probability.*[5] Keynes enunciated his own principle of the uniformity of nature and argued that the content of the principle was this: that "mere position in time and space" are irrelevant to generalizations which have "no reference to particular positions in time and space." In short, if location in time and space make no difference or have no relevance to the determination of other similarities among events and objects, then whether an object or set of conjoined objects or events occurs at time T or at time T_1 does not matter so far as the question of determining whether, at another time T_2, they will resemble one another. If T is the past and T_1 is the future, the relevance of this point is clear: the assumption that arguments proving the uniformity of nature are circular and beg the question is based upon the premise that they move from claims about the past, T, to claims about the future, T_1. If location in time is not a factor, however, then the ground for the skeptics' claim is removed.

We ought, then, to be able to provide evidence for causal uniformity or sameness among events without reasoning in a circular manner. For purposes of simplicity, Will says that he is going to show only that it is true that temporal location is irrelevant to the proof of uniformity, because he thinks that the irrelevance of space can be shown in just the same way. The principle to be supported now becomes that "differences in time make no difference" to the possibility of giving empirical evidence for the uniformity of nature.

Now the problem becomes one of showing that time is irrelevant to inductive arguments. How can we show that resemblances between causally connected events will remain the same in the future *without*

[5] J. M. Keynes, *A Treatise on Probability* (London: Macmillan and Co., 1921).

bringing in their position in time? How can we show that maxims such as "Same cause, same effect" are well-founded and may be used as foundations for natural laws? Obviously, only by discovering uniformities in nature which are the same without regard to space or time. Unfortunately, Will fails to do this. Instead, he returns to a criticism of the skeptics' position concerning an analogy which he thinks makes their position plausible but which he thinks leads to a contradiction. The analogy is something like this: Suppose that there is an enclosure such that there are people living in it but they never get out of it; and, moreover, they never see, hear, smell, etc., anything which is outside or beyond the limits of the enclosure. Will says we will call the land outside of the enclosure the land of the Future, and that within it the land of the Present and Past. Since the larger part of the land of the Present and Past is past, he calls it simply the land of the Past. Some philosophers live in this enclosure; and, as is their wont no matter where they live, they speculate about that which they do not know, in this case, what is going on over the fence. In particular, one of these profound men is considering the proposition that on the other side, roosters do more fighting than hens. The discussion then turns to what evidence one can adduce in favor of this proposition. Since you cannot look over the fence, or in any other way know what is going on over there, you must get whatever evidence you can from what is within the enclosure. Thus, any evidence the philosopher can get for the support of "Roosters fight more than hens in the land of the Future," he must get from the land of the Past. Suppose that he notices that in the land of the Past, roosters do fight more than hens. If he now uses this as evidence that they do in the land of the Future as well, then he must assume that roosters here and roosters there are alike, at least in this way; and, of course, for *this* assumption he can gather no evidence at all from within the enclosure, which is *ex hypothesis* the only source of evidence at his disposal. Hence, to prove that roosters in the land of the Future fight about as much as they do in the land of the Past, the philosopher must beg the question.

Will thinks that the skeptics picture the relation between the past and the future in this way, and he thinks there is a lot wrong with the picture. The central mistake is that the analogy, or better, perhaps, the simile, represents the fence or border between the two lands as though it always stays in the same place, when in Will's eyes it does not. The area of the past always expands, and as it does, the fence moves outward. In so doing, what was once the future is revealed, the only difference in it now being that it is inside the fence rather than outside of it. Our natural laws (assuming that you and I are citizens of the land of the Past) have always been confirmed by what we saw inside the fence; but these same laws are *also* confirmed by whatever has just been revealed under the moving fence. And if what has appeared under the fence has *dis*confirmed a rule or law, the rule or law has accordingly been revised.

Now, asks Will, does this not show that we have evidence that the land of the Future resembles the land of the Past? Is not the continuously just-being-revealed land a source of evidence which our philosopher can use to support his claim that roosters fight more over there, just as they do here? The skeptic, as Will realizes, immediately wheels out his standard reply. "Look," he says, "you are only confusing the issue. What *you* say sounds plausible only because you overlook an important fact: once the land of the Future is under the fence, it isn't future any more; it's the land of the Past, and any roosters and hens you find there are not Future-chickens anymore but Past-chickens. And, as you know, you can't use them for evidence." But Will thinks that this reply conceals a logical mistake, a mistake similar to the following. Suppose that a prophet comes along (probably in California) who says that a utopia will come "next year." This year is 1970, so the utopia will come in 1971. But, lo and behold, when 1971 comes, the utopia has not arrived, so his followers ask the seer why it has not arrived. He replies, with suitable gravity, that he said it would come next year, so obviously since this year is 1971, they will have to wait until 1972. But when it gets here, 1972 will be this year, so they will have to wait until 1973, *ad infinitum*. Will says that the prophet is contradicting himself, for given his interpretation of the words "next year," next year can never get here, i.e., become this year. So in one and the same breath he is, in effect, asserting that something will come and that it cannot come, that is, will not come, which is a proposition of the form $(p.-p)$ and hence always false. In the same way, thinks Will, the skeptics have fooled us. They say that the future never gets here because, once it does, it is no longer the future but the past, and that this is the reason we can never tell that the future will resemble the past.

Will is trying to make the point that the skeptics claim time or temporal position *is* relevant to the solution for the problem of the uniformity of nature and, indeed, that the temporal factor is just what prevents the solution. But, Will thinks, their analysis of what time *is*, relative to the problem, is contradictory, so it is false. *His* analysis of it is not contradictory, and he thinks it is true because it more nearly fits the facts not only of the ways in which we gather and talk about our evidence but also the nature of time itself. So there are two parts to his argument: a negative one which is a criticism of the skeptical position, and a positive one, which is that time is irrelevant to the determination of the resemblances necessary to support the uniformity principle. Let us examine the argument against the skeptics first.

Summary and Critique of Will's Argument

This argument can be summarized as follows:

1. The skeptics (Hume, Russell, Mill, etc.) picture the relation between the past and the future according to a mistaken analogy.
2. Picturing the relation in this way forces them into a contradiction.
3. A theory that contains a contradiction is unsound.
4. Therefore their theory is a bad theory, and does not prove its point, which is that knowing that the future will resemble the past is impossible.

This does not seem to be a good argument, because the second premise is false and the first one may be too. Let us assume that the first premise is true. Does this force the skeptics into a contradiction? Will says that the contradictory claim is similar to this one: "X will occur in the future, but the future never comes," which is tantamount to saying "X will occur in the future, and X will not occur." But do any of the skeptics make such claims? They do not, and the question they are seeking to answer is not similar to "When will the utopia come?" which is the question to which the prophet's prediction is an answer. The question they seek to answer is "How can one show that the future will resemble the past?", given that we cannot assume that it will in the process of giving our answer. Their answer is that, for pragmatic purposes, we may expect the future to resemble the past, but we cannot *show* that it will, and therefore for *logical* reasons one *cannot predict* with certainty that it will be like the past *if* it comes. That is, they neither assert nor predict that the future will come, nor that, if it does, it will be like the past. In fact, they deny that such predictions are possible. But Will's prophet, on the contrary, must assume that such predictions *are* possible, for he makes one. The fact that he is mistaken in so believing because he contradicts himself proves only that he is mistaken and should not make the prediction. The skeptics do not make it; and by not doing so they avoid the contradiction, which only arises after all in the making of the prediction.

Secondly, even if we grant that the boundary between the land of the Past and the land of the Future is a moving one, does this harm the skeptics' position? Will seems to miss the *logical* point in Hume, Mill, and Russell. This point is the essence of simplicity. It is that if the definition of the past is "everything that is now or has been experienced," and that of the future is "everything that has not yet been experienced," then how are we to cross the boundary between the two, whether the boundary is moving or not? These definitions could be stipulative, and criticized as inadequate upon explanatory grounds; but, as a matter of fact, they seem to be reportive, because the words "future" and "past" *are* used this way in our language. As such, they seem to be true definitions. It does not matter to their truth that the past is increasing in content every moment. Moreover, Will is not justified, given the truth of these definitions, in assuming that what has just been revealed by moving into the land of the Past was, just before it was revealed, in the land of the Future. In making this assumption, moving border or not, he begs the question in just the way that Hume and Russell mentioned, namely, he assumes that what has been revealed—the future—is that which resembles the past. As Russell says, the question is then whether future futures will resemble past futures, which changes things not at all.

Finally, *is* it necessary for skeptical empiricists to picture the relationship between the past and the future in the way that Will suggests, that is, as an unmoving boundary? The proper reply seems to be that it is no more necessary for them to picture it this way than as a moving border, because, as we have just seen, it does not matter how it is pictured, as long as it is there. So if we interpret the first premise in this summary of Will's argument as asserting that the skeptics *must* picture the relation between the past and the future in the way that he suggests in order to make their case, and he would probably assert this, then it is a false claim, and the argument is doubly unsound.

If the skeptics' case holds no matter how they picture the boundary, then Will's own picture of it, the moving boundary, is of no help in the solution of the problem.

The Justifiability of Induction

What are we to make of all of this? One reply which has been given by Professor Karl Popper is, "nothing." [6] Popper thinks that philosophical induction has nothing to do with science. In the first place, in his view science is a process of making enlightened guesses called hypotheses, and then waiting for confirmation or disconfirmation. As such, it does not assume as an axiom that the future will resemble the past, and previous knowledge has nothing to do with the making of hypotheses except in so far as it provides us with a knowledge of the technical terminology with which to make them. Another reply is that the philosophical concept of a cause is in fact never used in modern science; and if we are to accept what is in textbooks in science, this is certainly true. But, on the other hand, it does seem to be true that science in some sense involves the expectation that the future will resemble the past; for, after all is said and done, future control over nature is the very end and

[6] Karl Popper, *The Logic of Scientific Discovery* (London: Hutchinson University Library, 1959).

raison d'être of science. And even if the ordinary language sense of "cause" is not used in the technical writings of modern science, it certainly *is* used in the public interpretations of the scientist's findings. They *are* saying that cigarette smoking *causes* cancer, are they not? When asked what "causes" means here, do they not give us an answer very similar to Hume's, though in quantified, mathematically expressed terms? Do they not give us the statistical correlations between the presence of such elements as tars and nicotine and the presence of cancer? Is this not very similar to constant conjunction?

It may be that what we need is a redefinition of "justified expectation," and a redefinition of what "induction" means in terms of this first new definition. Justified expectations are those that are (1) caused by past constant conjunctions, and (2) fulfilled. Inductions would then become inferences based upon justified expectations, such that we would not know whether *they* were justified unless and until subsequent expectations based upon them were, in their turn, shown to be justified, i.e., were fulfilled. What this approach does is *avoid* the issue of the uniformity of nature, by admitting that we cannot ever know that it *is* uniform, that is, by agreeing with the skeptics but at the same time with claims that induction does not require this uniformity as a premise in its own justification because the justification of induction is always in the past. That is, what it means to say that a generalization is a justified one is to say that expectations based upon it were fulfilled. This of course is a stipulative definition, but it is also fairly close to the ordinary language explanations offered in support of our belief in inductive generalizations. It is close to Popper's view, but it renders the making of hypotheses more than enlightened guesses, and it retains the relevancy of the ordinary notion of "cause." Such a theory would need a great deal of working out; and some modern approaches to probability theory are similar to this general outline, though much more detailed. At the least, then, we can say that the issue of the justifiability of induction is not closed, even if the skeptics are right, and it seems that they are.

THE PRINCIPLE OF VERIFIABILITY

In the second chapter, part of the discussion concerned theories of meaning and their consequences for certain other kinds of theories, especially in ethics. The issues we are going to discuss in this section are also concerned with meaning; indeed, the principle we are going to examine and the set of arguments against it are concerned with the very question "What are the necessary conditions for being meaningful?" We do not say, in this question, *what* the entity is which is or is not meaningful; for, as we shall see, that is part of the problem. In the second chapter, three main types of theories of meaning were examined, which were called the denotative, the ideational, and the behavioral theories. The denotative argued that, in essence, the meaning of a word was that to which it referred or that which it denoted. The paradigm for this theory of meaning was the proper name. Another version which more nearly met the requirements of an adequate theory argued that the meaning of a word is the relation between the word and what it names. Several difficulties with this view were examined, and it was concluded that some of them were fatal to it. The second theory, the ideational, had it that the meanings of words are the ideas associated with them, rather than some observable thing or a relation between the word and the thing. Many difficulties were also found with this theory, and again some of them seemed to be fatal. The behavioral theory of meaning, though able to overcome many if not most of the criticisms leveled against the other two views, was also found to be flawed. This theory argues that the meanings of words and of sentences or what is expressed in them consists in the responses that the utterance causes in one who hears it and in the behavior of the speaker when he utters the words, or in dispositions which the words have to cause such typical responses within the linguistic context, or in both of these. But again, for the reasons already given, this will not do.

Another view, not developed to the extent where it can really be called a theory, is the so-called "meaning is use" view made popular by the followers of Ludwig Wittgenstein. Related to this position, though not identical to it, is the current analysis of those who are students of J. L. Austin. The theory which we shall consider here was influenced by Wittgenstein. though it has many disagreements with him, and it would also have some affinities with Austin's views, though again not with all of them.

The Logical Positivists

"Logical positivism" is the name that has been given to the views of a set of thinkers who formed a group called the Vienna Circle in the 1920s. Many very prominent philosophers were either members of the group or at one time or another associated with it, among whom might be named A. J. Ayer, Rudolf Carnap, Herbert Feigl, Otto Neurath, Kurt Gödel, Moritz Schlick, and Ludwig Wittgenstein. Most of these men were familiar with mathematics and at least one other science. All of them were scientifically oriented and believed that most of the statements of metaphysics as traditionally done were nonsense. In this they agreed with Wittgenstein's book *Tractatus Logico–Philosophicus*.[7] With him

---

[7] Ludwig Wittgenstein, *Tractatus Logico–Philosophicus* (London: Routledge & Kegan Paul, Ltd., 1922).

they also believed that all logically true statements are tautologies which are non-ampliative, that the subject-matter of philosophy, if indeed it has one, is the analysis and clarification of language and that, in general, non-tautologous statements have to have some experiential content if they are to be meaningful. This is by no means a new idea of course. Hume and Mill, and many of the French positivists, held just the same view. But the logical positivists went further than any of these other thinkers had gone. For one thing, they asserted that all of metaphysics was senseless because none of the utterances of metaphysics was meaningful. Further, the "judgments" of ethics were in their view not judgments at all, that is, neither true nor false; and, hence, they too were technically meaningless, though many of the positivists thought that they had emotive meaning. The criterion of meaningfulness was for them that a proposition had to be either true or false. And it is important here to distinguish a *proposition* from a sentence, a statement, and an utterance. For our purposes, we can define a sentence as merely the string of words resulting from grammatical composition. A proposition, for the moment, we will consider as that which is asserted by a sentence. Clearly, the same proposition may be expressed by different sentences: for example, "It is raining" and "Il pleut" both express the same proposition.

This complete rejection of metaphysics has extremely widespread ramifications for philosophy, because it is difficult to separate many of the traditional issues in branches normally not called "metaphysics" in philosophy from issues and principles normally considered to be a part of this subject. If we were to restrict the rejection to claims such as "The Absolute is one," or, to use an example from A. J. Ayer, "The Absolute enters into, but is itself incapable of, evolution and progress" (which Ayer took from Bradley's *Appearance and Reality*), the consequences might be bearable. But the rejection is far more sweeping than this. Most epistemological theories, save for positivistic and behavioral ones of course, are also affected. Any assertions which posit the existence of universals as independently existing entities which are in principle unperceivable will be meaningless, as will all claims about anything which exists independently of our perception. Now it is a very commonly held view of many schools of philosophy that there is indeed an external world existing independently of our perceptions. All theories which argue for the existence of material substance, Locke's for example, hold this. If the positivists are correct, what such theories say is nonsense. This may seem sensible to you, but consider that the *denial* that material substance exists is *also* meaningless if they are right, and the theory becomes a bit more difficult to believe. Were both Berkeley and Locke talking nonsense? They must have been, if the positivists are correct.

If the logical positivists rejected metaphysics and ethics as disciplines containing meaningful judgments, then presumably they had some idea of what propositions *were* meaningful and some criterion or criteria for deciding whether some utterance was an expression of such a proposition. They claimed that all meaningful propositions were one of two sorts: either they were analytic, that is, tautologies, or they were synthetic, and a synthetic proposition was for them one which was verifiable empirically. That is, any meaningful sentence had to be such that we can show it to be either true or false by reference to the content of our experience. It was just because metaphysical statements could not meet such a requirement that they claimed they were nonsense, i.e., meaningless, and the same was true of ethical judgments.

Ayer's Definition of Verifiability

There was a wide diversity of opinion among the positivists themselves concerning the precise form that this principle of verifiability should take. Here, we shall be concerned primarily with the definition of the principle as put forward by A. J. Ayer in two editions of his book *Language, Truth and Logic.*[8] In the two editions, Ayer offers two different formulations of the principle, the second version being intended as a revision designed to account for certain criticisms which had been offered of the first version as well as to counter various other forms of the principle that had been given by other positivists. In the earlier versions, it was often assumed without question that the object of the test for meaningfulness was a proposition, but it was found that this was unsatisfactory, because the word "proposition" is a technical term in philosophy which refers to something which *is* either true or false. Since only meaningful utterances are either true or false for the positivists, applying the verifiability test to propositions would be redundant. Furthermore, many versions of the principle entailed that, to be meaningful, a proposition need only be such that it was logically *possible* to verify it. But clearly it is odd to speak of a verifiability principle applicable to propositions that need never be verified in fact. And we might ask how one could tell that a proposition was possibly verifiable unless and until it was actually verified. It was also asked how one could determine that a sentence expressed a meaningful proposition without determining exactly what the meaning of that proposition was, it being one thing to determine that a proposition p is meaningful and another to determine the precise meaning of this particular p. If the verifiability principle does not enable us

---

[8] A. J. Ayer, *Language, Truth and Logic* (London: Victor Gollancz, Ltd., 1936). The second edition was also published by Gollancz in 1947; see especially the introduction to the 2nd edition.

to determine the precise meaning of this proposition, then how *do* we determine this? And if we cannot, then how can the principle tell us that it has some meaning or other?   ,

In an attempt to answer this criticism, some positivists held that the particular meaning of individual propositions consisted in the set of experiences that would verify it. But this reply was found to be unsatisfactory for at least two reasons. One was that if the meaning of the propositions is *identical* with the set of experiences that would verify it, then we ought not to be able to say anything of the meanings of the propositions that we cannot also say of the experiences. It turns out that this is not the case. For example, I can say of the experiences that they are *mine*, but the meaning of the proposition is not; and, presumably, the proposition does not have temporal and sometimes spatial coordinates as do my experiences. The second objection was that although my experiences may be private, meanings, if they are identical with some of these experiences, are private too; and this view entails solipsism and relativism. Finally, it was asked whether the verifiability principle itself was meaningful, given that it had to be either analytic or verifiable. It cannot be analytic, for then it tells us nothing and *a fortiori* it does not tell us anything about meaningfulness. But if it is not analytic, then how do we verify *it?*

Ayer recognized many of these difficulties. In the second edition he first decides not to use the technical term "proposition" and instead introduces a new technical term "statement." A statement is what is expressed by "any form of words that is grammatically significant," and the latter "form of words" is what he means by the term "sentence." Now a statement is therefore what is expressed in any (indicative) sentence, whether the sentence is meaningful or not. The term "proposition" he now reserves for statements which are "literally meaningful," that is, either true or false. In short, for Ayer propositions now become "a subclass of the class of statements." A statement will be meaningful if it is analytic or if it is empirically verifiable. The question is, what does "empirically verifiable" mean? Ayer's answer is this:

. . . the principle is that a statement is verifiable, and consequently meaningful, if some observation-statement can be deducted from it in conjunction with certain other premises, without being deducible from those other premises alone.[9]

An "observation-statement" is one which "records an actual or possible observation." This version of the principle will not do for reasons which Ayer himself gives in the second edition. Let us call the observation-statement "O," and consider any other statement, even a meaningless

[9] *Ibid.* (2nd edition), p. 11.

one, which we shall call "S," after Ayer's usage. Let the "certain other premise" specified in the definition of the principle be "If S then O." "O" does not follow from "If S then O" by itself, but it *does* follow from "If S then O," and "S," by *modus ponens*. To use Ayer's example:

1. If the Absolute is lazy, this is white.
2. The Absolute is lazy.
3. This is white.

"O" here is "This is white," and "S" is "The Absolute is lazy," a statement which all positivists would clearly reject as meaningless. But, because "This is white" does not follow from either (1) or (2) taken by itself, both (1) and (2) meet the principle and hence must be meaningful. This is not acceptable to the positivists.

Part of the reason for the failure of this definition of the principle is also that a statement is defined purely in terms of its grammatical form, rather than as an entity that has a truth-value. Of course, Ayer had no other choice in this matter; for, if a statement is something that already has a truth-value, then, as has been mentioned, the verifiability principle is redundant. But just because of this, it is also possible to question the notion of logical validity which he accepts here. Normally, "valid" is a technical term in logic used to refer to a deductive argument whose form is such that it has no substitution instances where the premises are true but the conclusion false. This definition clearly assumes that the premises and the conclusion are capable of being *either* true or false; but, just as clearly, Ayer's "S" has been chosen because it is neither. He therefore seems to be forced into a dilemma: either his principle becomes redundant or he misuses the notion of validity.

Revision of the Definition

If we allow the criticism just given to pass for the moment, and if we accept *falsifiability* instead of verifiability as the criterion for meaningfulness, similar difficulties arise. This change of criterion was in fact suggested. But Ayer himself notes that, even in this case, any observation statement "O" will be incompatible with a conjunction composed of any statement (even a meaningless one) "S" and the conditional statement "If S then not O." So once again meaningless statements may be proved to be meaningful using the principle given in the first edition. To meet these objections, Ayer drastically changed the verifiability principle in the second edition of the book. The changed version is as follows:

. . . a statement is directly verifiable if it is either itself an observation-statement, or is such that in conjunction with one or more observation statements it entails at least one observation-statement which is not deducible from these other premises alone; and . . . a statement is indirectly verifiable if it satisfies the following conditions: first, that in conjunction with certain other premises it entails one or more directly verifiable statements which are not deducible from these other premises alone; and secondly, that these other premises do not include any statement that is not either analytic, or directly verifiable, or capable of being independently established as indirectly verifiable.[10]

Given these changes, a statement will now be meaningful if it is either directly or indirectly verifiable according to these definitions of "verifiable" in the two senses, direct and indirect.

Ayer thought that this revision ruled out the possibility that a meaningless statement could be proven meaningful if it was brought into the test as a part of a complex statement, the other part or parts of which were observation-statements. But, in fact, it does not accomplish its purpose. A clearcut proof of this was suggested by Professor Alonzo Church in a review of the second edition of Ayer's book.[11] He does it in the following way: let "O_1," "O_2," and "O_3" be any three observation statements, provided none of them entails any of the others. Then, let "S" be any statement whatsoever, even a meaningless one. Church shows that from these terms it is logically possible to make a complex statement which implies that either "S" or its denial is verifiable and hence meaningful, given Ayer's criteria. Again the argument hinges on the fact that it is logically permissible to include a redundant statement in any complex statement, and that this inclusion will be irrelevant to the confirmation of the complex statement itself. Consider then a complex statement of the form $(-O_1 \cdot -O_2) \vee (O_3 \cdot -S)$. If this statement implies "O_3," then according to Ayer's criteria, it is directly verifiable. That "O_3" is entailed can be shown as follows:

1.	$(-O_1 \cdot -O_2) \vee (O_3 \cdot -S)$	
2.	O_1 (the "other" observation statement)	
3.	$(-O_2 \cdot -O_1) \vee (O_3 \cdot -S)$	1, comm.
4.	$[(-O_2 \cdot -O_1) \vee O_3] \cdot [(-O_2 \cdot -O_1) \vee -S]$	dist. 3,
5.	$[(-O_2 \cdot -O_1) \vee O_3]$	simpl. 4,
6.	$(O_2 \vee O_1) \vee O_3$	5, D.M.
7.	$(O_3 \vee O_1) \supset O_3$	6, mat. imp.
8.	$O_1 \vee O_2$	2, add., comm.
9.	O_3	7, 8, M.P.

Therefore, (1) in this argument is directly verifiable, even though it contains the redundant "S."

Next, if we are given "S," and if we could show that with the complex statement $(-O_1 \cdot O_2) \vee (O_3 \cdot -S)$, it implied the observation state-

10 *Ibid.*, p. 13.

11 Alonzo Church, "Review of A. J. Ayer's *Language, Truth, and Logic*, 2nd edition," *Journal of Symbolic Logic*, 14, no. 4 (1949), p. 197.

ment "O_2," we could have shown that "S" meets the criteria for indirect verifiability This may be accomplished as follows:

1. $(-O_1 \cdot O_2) \text{ v } (O_3 \cdot -S)$
2. S (given)
3. $[(-O_1 \cdot O_2) \text{ v } O_3] \cdot [(O_1 \cdot O_2) \text{ v } -S]$ 1, dist.
4. $(-O_1 \cdot O_2) \text{ v } -S$ 3, simpl.
5. $- -S$ 2, double negation
6. $(O_1 \cdot O_2)$ 4, 5, Comm., D.S.
7. O_2 6. simpl.

"S" is therefore indirectly verifiable, and hence meaningful, which Ayer and the other positivists would not accept.

Finally, if we could show that from $(-O_1 \cdot O_2) \text{ v } (O_3 \cdot -S)$, the observation sentence "O_2" is implied or entailed, we would have shown that "$-S$" is directly verifiable according to the criteria, for then "$-S$" and "O_3" together also imply "O_2"

In all of these arguments it is again important to note that the inclusion of "S" is only permissible because of the distinction Ayer drew between a statement and a proposition and his willingness to allow statements as he defined them to be substitution instances in argument forms which are presumably either valid or invalid. If he were not willing to do this, then he would be caught in the dilemma which has already been discussed. Ayer no longer holds a positivistic position, because he is the sort of philosopher who abandons a position when it is shown to be mistaken. Various other attempts were made to revamp, redefine, and defend the verifiability principle, among them those of Rudolf Carnap, whose arguments are rather too complex for discussion here. It is almost misleading to characterize Carnap's theses as "revisions" of the principle, however, since they are in many ways totally new and should be evaluated on quite different grounds than those used here.

A Summing Up

We have now considered several different theories of meaning, including the denotative, the ideational, the behavioral, the emotive, the meaning-is-use theory, the Austinian analysis, and now the positivistic position. With the possible exception of the Austinian analysis and the meaning-is-use theories, all have been rejected. The reason that the other two have not been discarded is that they both leave open the possibility—indeed, they both appear to affirm—that there is no one theory of meaning. This is by no means as simple a claim to defend as it is to state. But if we are to account for the diversity of uses of language, in poetry and engineering, normal conversation and heated arguments, technical description and offhand impressions, expressions of emotion and logical discussion, *ad infinitum*, we must at least have a theory which is flexible enough to avoid the difficulties of the Procrustean bed, and at the same time avoid being so broad that it is uninformative. It must be tied to the kinds of uses of language that we actually perform, and it must account for the differences and the similarities between them. It therefore seems reasonable that we begin to formulate such a theory by investigating the various uses of language that there actually *are*, which of course includes the utterance of metaphysical, ethical, aesthetic, epistemological, mystical, and ordinary language as well as scientific and logical. There is no *prima facie* reason to argue that they must have anything more in common than the fact that they are utterances. Nor does there seem to be very good reason to claim that if they are to be true or false, they must all be true or false in the same way, that is, that there is but one set of meanings for "true" and "false." The specification of what truth and falsity signify will surely be contingent upon the theory of meaning we adopt; and if there are to be many kinds of meaning, then there will be many kinds of truth.

Even if it were possible to outline such a comprehensive theory or set of theories of meaning, it could not be done here. Suffice it to say then that those who seem to have come the closest to an adequate explanation of the problems are the pragmatists, Wittgenstein, and Austin. The pragmatists have recognized the fundamental truth that if "meaning" is taken in the broad sense of "significance," then it is foolhardy to exclude from the analysis of language the study of the practical effects of the uses of language upon our lives. Their mistake, as with so very many theories, was to believe that the *entire* solution could be found through an examination of these effects. This approach left out such obviously important elements as the nature of the speech act itself, the relevance of the mode of speech in varying contexts, the relation of the context to the beliefs of the user of the language, the relevance of these beliefs to what he says and how he says it, and so forth. Causes as well as effects are crucial elements in the analysis of meaning. It is not implied in this that the pragmatists completely ignored the causes, but for the most part they did concentrate upon the hearers' viewpoint and the effects of utterances rather than upon the utterances themselves.

Wittgenstein's *Investigations* is certainly among the first rank of thought-provoking works in theory of meaning. Especially through his concept of "language games" and the notion of "family resemblance" he brought philosophers to a realization of the incredibly complex nature of even the most simple languages, and he made us notice the simple but profound fact that actions as well as words can be and must be parts of languages. And a corollary of this fact is the awareness of the indefinitely large number of roles which circumstances play in determining the meanings of various uses of language. It is in the uses of language that we find its meanings, not in what given words point to or name and not in any correspondence between things and words or hidden ideas brought to mind by the hearing of noises.

Austin is in a sense more primitive than Wittgenstein. He performed seminal investigations concerning the nature of different sorts of utterings and speech acts, and it is here, it seems, that we must begin. What is it that we *do* when we speak, write, or otherwise use language? Only when we know the answers to this question, among many, many more, will we know the answer to the question, "What do we do when we mean?"

EXERCISES

1. Write a short essay in which you state in your own words the difficulties in drawing a precise distinction between metaphysics and epistemology.

2. What common position do philosophers called "empiricists" hold? Do you agree or disagree with this common position? Why or why not?

3. What is the representative theory of perception? What is an abstract general idea?

4. What types of ideas do we have according to Locke? What are their major characteristics?

5. What mental operations are involved in making complex ideas? What is the nature of the distinction between primary and secondary qualities? Are these qualities, either or both of them, in our minds?

6. Does Berkeley deny that there are general words? Does he deny that general words signify something? If they do signify, what is their significance?

7. What do general words name according to Locke? What does Berkeley say about this claim? Evaluate Berkeley's arguments.

8. Does Berkeley deny that the word "cause" has any significance when applied to events in the physical world? What is his analysis of the meaning of this word in that context?

9. Does the word "cause" have the same meaning in the mental world as it does in the physical world for Berkeley? What is the difference in their meanings, if there are any? Do we have ideas of causes for Berkeley? Do we have ideas of minds according to him?

10. Evaluate Berkeley's arguments against the representative theory of perception.

11. Write a short essay characterizing the differences between Ryle's approach to the analysis of human behavior and Wittgenstein's.

12. Write a short essay describing the consequences of the differences between first- and third-person sensation sentences for Wittgenstein.

13. What is the difference between criteria and symptoms for Wittgenstein?

14. Does Wittgenstein's assertion that there are no "private languages" mean that we cannot "talk to ourselves"? Defend your answer.

15. When he says that if the agent satisfies the criteria for being in pain, then he *must* be in pain, what is the force of this "must"?

16. Is the analogy that Wittgenstein draws between closing our eyes in the face of the logically possible doubt that the table we see is really there, and the logically possible doubt that someone is in pain when he fulfills the criteria for being in that state, a good analogy? Use the mechanisms for evaluating arguments from analogy given earlier in your answer.

17. What do you think Wittgenstein means by the word "concept"?

18. Are the two arguments given on page 198 valid? Why?

18. Does Wittgenstein's position seem to you to exclude the possibility of any kind of private *knowledge*? Why or why not?

20. Give a definition of skepticism which describes the position Wittgenstein is arguing against.

21. Write a page stating exactly what the problem of the uniformity of nature is.

22. What is wrong with Mill's answer to the problem?

23. If we could give an adequate account of why men *expect* the future to resemble the past, would we have given an adequate account of why it *does* resemble the past? Why or why not?

24. Why is the "law of causation" simply another name for the uniformity-of-nature principle?

25. Why does Russell divide the problem of the uniformity of nature into *two* problems? If there is a satisfactory answer to the first problem, does an adequate answer to the second follow from it? Why or why not?

26. Why, according to Russell, is it impossible to prove that nature is *not* uniform?

27. We cannot prove the uniformity principle if Russell is right, but neither can we prove the principles in *any* field, if we have a certain view of what "proof" is in mind. What is this certain view of proof? Can you think of any meanings for "proof"? What are they? Do any of them help to solve the problem at stake here? Why or why not?

28. Why is the irrelevance of location in time crucial to Will's arguments against Russell et al.?

29. If Will were correct in his picturing of the analogy which he thinks Russell and other skeptics use to characterize the relation between the future and the past, would his refutation of their position be sound? Why or why not?

30. What exactly is the contradiction implicit in the skeptical position according to Will? Are the two analogies which Will uses, the one about the prophet and the other about the fenced enclosure, both really illustrative of the same point? Why or why not?

31. Evaluate the arguments offered against Will's position.

32. What kinds of statements are there according to the logical positivists?

33. Upon what grounds would they deny that there are synthetic *a priori* sentences?

34. When the positivists claim that a sentence is meaningless, do they mean that it is what ordinary language would call "nonsense"? Why or why not?

35. What is the distinction between a proposition and a sentence? Why is this distinction important?

36. Are analytic propositions meaningful for the positivists? Are they verifiable? Why or why not? If they are verifiable, then how are they mean-

ingful? If they are verifiable, then how are they analytic? Is this a conflict which they cannot resolve? Why or why not?

37. What does it mean to say that it is *logically* possible to verify a proposition?

38. State Ayer's verifiability criterion in the first edition of *Language, Truth and Logic* in your own words. Compose an argument not used in the section which is consistent with this principle, but which makes at least one sentence meaningful which the positivists would not admit into the class of meaningful propositions.

39. Do the same exercise in connection with the second version of the verifiability principle offered by Ayer.

40. Compose a defense for the claim that a *single* comprehensive theory of meaning is not necessary, and in fact would be suspect on the face of it.

41. Give a positivistic analysis of the claim that man is immortal.

III

Moral and
Political Philosophy

7

Ethics and Meta-Ethics

RELATIVITY AND RELATIVISM

We are all very familiar with such proverbs as "One man's meat is another man's poison," "To each his own," and so forth. The essential element in the meaning of such sayings is the common conviction that the various properties, dispositions, and attributes which distinguish us from one another are of importance in our personal appraisal of values; and indeed this is quite true. It is very rare to find two humans with identical tastes in food, art, literature, or, for that matter, anything. Many discussions about the value of a particular painting end with one party saying to the other, "Well, let's face it, I just like it and you don't, so it's a good painting for me and a bad one for you." The remarkable fact is that such claims are normally thought to be quite acceptable. That is, it is not at all remarkable that one person likes a painting while another does not; but it *is* remarkable that this difference of *likes* is thought to provide justification for claiming that the painting is both good and bad at the same time!

Discussions of art are not the only place where convictions of this sort are often expressed. They are also to be found in ethical disputes and evaluations. We are all familiar with the view that what is right in one culture may be wrong in another, that a good man in Borneo may well be a bad one in Montreal. Indeed, we often make this sort of distinction within the confines of our own general culture, as when we assert that a certain action is morally permissible in view of the beliefs of some subculture though not permissible when viewed from the majority standpoint.

Such assertions and the arguments based upon them probably all rest in the end upon our knowledge of the widely differing value judgments made in the various cultures and countries of the world. There is no question that such differing judgments *are* made, nor is there any question that, within the individual cultures, accepted justifications may be offered in support of such evaluations. Not only is it true that evaluations vary with place and culture, but they also vary within a given culture over a period of time in which environmental conditions change.

Examples of variations in values are so manifold that the only problem is finding interesting ones. Prison conditions, even in debtor prisons, were unbelievably foul in England prior to the introduction of penal reforms by John Howard. Yet prior to the time of the reforms, the average citizen saw nothing immoral about the presence of filth, vermin, and conditions of starvation in prisons. In ancient times it was normal and morally acceptable for the victor in war to torture to death all the males of a subdued city, and sell the women into slavery. During the Spanish Inquisition one would have been considered mad if one questioned the practice of obtaining confessions by using the rack, and it was believed that the inquisitor did the heretic a great favor by burning him while he was in a state of grace after his recantation. Nor are we far removed from this now. In modern war we use absolutely ferocious engines of blight whose applications cannot be confined to enemy soldiers; and, indeed, it is now an accepted axiom of war that the enemy's cities and entire population are proper military targets. Only a minority of the populations of the modern powers questions the morality of this; yet not many years ago such an attitude was condemned by our religions and by international agreement, and we hanged war criminals for violating these customs. At one time in European history, brothels were founded and supported by city fathers, and no moral stigma was attached to the patronizing of them by prominent men in the town. Indeed, visiting dignitaries were often officially entertained there. Yet, in America, prostitution is the perennial target of reform by politicians and fervent moralists. In medieval Europe, it was the practice for courting couples to "bundle," which meant that they either visited one another in the girl's bedroom at night or, in addition, slept together in a state of semi-nudity, presumably without giving in to the obvious temptations.   Such behavior was socially approved, and certainly not morally condemned. It was the custom, not very long ago, to bind the feet of young girls in China. The effect was to cripple almost all female children of upper class families. Poorer Chinese had the quaint custom of selling their female children and occasionally killing them, for lack of ability to feed them. The Eskimos used to leave their old and sick out in the cold to die, whether they seemed to want this or not, and a similar custom is to be found among several African tribes.

Ethical Relativity

One could go on forever, but more than enough has been said to make the point, which is that great variations in value judgments among and within cultures is a fact. This is true of all sorts of value judgments, ethical ones included. It is therefore true that *ethical relativity* is a fact. Because this is so, any dispute about it could be settled in the same way that disputes about any factual question may be settled: one could look and see.

Cultural and ethical relativity being facts does not, however, enable us to claim of and by itself the truth of the quite different thesis that *both* of two conflicting value judgments are *correct, justified, or true.* If a man in culture A believes that the earth is flat, and a man in culture B believes that it is spherical, it certainly follows from this that some people believe the earth is flat and others that it is spherical (not flat). But it does not follow that the earth is both flat and spherical. This is not to say that evaluative judgments, and ethical evaluations in particular, are of the same sort of assertion as are claims about the shape of the earth: they probably are not, as we shall see later. It is simply to point out that, from the fact of cultural and ethical relativity, nothing at all follows about the truth of any claims concerning the justification or correctness of the competing judgments. It may be that competing judgments *are* both correct, though certainly this cannot be so in the case of contradictory sentences having truth-values definable within the same theory of truth. But if the competing judgments are both defensible, it is not because they originate in different places or at different times within a developing culture.

All of this seems fairly obvious. But if it is, then many students in elementary ethics courses miss the obvious; because it seems that the theory known as *ethical relativism* is far and away the most widely accepted moral philosophy. Our purpose here is to give a careful definition of ethical relativism, formulate its arguments precisely, and then refute it. To do this, it will be necessary to mention some problems which will be discussed at length later in this chapter. It might therefore be a wise idea to study our discussion of relativity and relativism in conjunction with our later discussion on the truth or falsity of moral judgments.

Ethical Relativism

Ethical relativism is the theory that holds that cultural and ethical relativity are true and that, in addition, the competing judgments made by members of the different groups and cultures are both correct. Consider a group, A, and a group, B, which are culturally different. Consider an individual, X, who lives in A, and an individual, Y, who lives in B. Ethical relativists hold that (1) due to the different cultures of A and B, X and Y may make differing moral judgments about one and the same thing. If J is a judgment and Q is an action, then X and Y may hold, respectively, that J is true of Q and that J is not true of Q. So far, we are speaking only of ethical and cultural relativity. But ethical relativists hold in addition that both J and not-J may be correct. Suppose that J in this case is "Killing is wrong." Not-J is therefore "Killing is not wrong"; and, if we assume that the possibility that killing is morally irrelevant is ruled out, then this is equivalent to the assertion "Killing is right." The ethical relativist is holding that (1) these two judgments may be made in different cultures, and (2) both of them may be correct in the respective cultures where they are made. Relativists are in effect arguing here that what is right and wrong, good or bad, is determined only in accordance with the standards in operation within a given culture. If the practice of killing serves the social needs of a particular culture, then it is right, and if not, it is wrong.

At this point two problems arise which must be settled before the evaluation of relativism can continue. The first is the nature of the object which is being evaluated, and the second is the question of whether moral judgments are *either* true or false.

Suppose that the object of the evaluation is an action. Two questions may be asked about it: (1) are there ever cases of the *same* action occurring in two *different* cultures? (2) Is it even possible to define what an action is without reference to such factors as motives and consequences and the opinions of these within a culture? The two questions may be closely related. If the answer to the second question is negative and if motives and consequences are evaluated differently in different cultures, then what counts as an action of the type A in culture X may be altogether a different action in culture Y. There is also the general question of whether actions can be defined independently of motives and consequences, no matter what cultures are involved. This general question is crucial because if the separation between actions on the one hand, and motives and consequences on the other hand, cannot be drawn, then it is difficult to see how we can have different criteria for evaluating agents as opposed to actions. If the criteria are not separate, then a man could not do an act with good intentions (motives) and bad consequences and still be a good man. But there are obvious cases where we do want to say just this sort of thing.

It is the contention here that actions, and motives and consequences can be separated, that the same action or type of action does occur in different cultures, and that ethical relativism is false, whether or not moral evaluations (or any other kind of evaluation) are true or false according to some theory of truth, such as the correspondence theory. The second problem—whether moral judgments are either true or false—is analyzed later in the chapter, and we will not attempt to give here a complete defense of any but the last claim. But something should be said to give you an idea of the dimensions of the first problem and the lines along which a solution to it might be pursued.

Characterizing the Action

At first sight it may seem simple to define, point out, or otherwise characterize some particular action or class of actions. It does not even seem notably difficult to do this with morally relevant actions, though they are more complex than normal acts. After all, it is not hard to say what murder, theft, lying, and fraud are. Or is it? What, for example, *is* murder? Do you ever see a murder? I should say that murder is wrongful or unjustifiable killing. If this is true, then killing and murder are not the same thing, since some killings may be justifiable, and perhaps even right and hence morally obligatory. Is there then some perceptual feature, that is, some sensible property of killings that are murders which allows us to distinguish them? Probably not. There are too many cases where, without knowing the motive of the agent, we cannot tell from the facts of the act alone whether it is an instance of murder or of killing alone. We *do* know quite a few things simply from a description of the form "X murdered Y." We know that Y is dead, that his death was the consequence of some act performed by X or by his agent or agents (which latter acts are still of course consequences of something X did), that X intended that Y should die, and that X's reasons for doing that which resulted in Y's death were unjustifiable.

It is informative to consider what we can deduce from a description just like this, if we use the verb "killed" instead of "murdered." Again we know that Y is dead, and that his death is an effect of some act which X or his agents performed. But we do *not* know either that X intended to kill Y, or that, if he did intend to kill him, his reasons were unjustifiable and his act wrong. In short, merely because we know that X killed Y, we do not thereby know whether X is responsible, and we do not have sufficient information to make any moral evaluation of his act. Why are we able to deduce the additional information from the first statement but not from the second? The answer is that the first judgment is redundant while the second is not. "Murder" *means* "wrongful killing." It does not mean this in *all* cases where the word occurs, but we shall consider only those cases where it does have such a meaning. Moreover, we must distinguish murders from such acts as assassinations and acts of negligence, willful or otherwise, which result in the death of another. Therefore, "murder" is really being used in the sense usually associated with "first-degree murder," plus the implication that the offense is moral as well as legal. With this meaning, "X murdered Y" enables us to make the foregoing deductions for the simple reason that it analytically contains them. If this is true, then "murder is wrong," if it is either true or false, is trivially true and its denial is a contradiction. Now trivial truths are not evaluations, because presumably the latter are informative and no trivial truth is informative except in the psychological sense. This same principle applies to the entire class of similar moral "judgments": "stealing is wrong," "murder is wrong," "rape is wrong"— none of these, strange as it may sound, is an evaluation, because the definition of all of the subjects of these sentences contains their predicates. This is, in fact, true of any sentence whose subject term names a *kind* of moral action.

The importance of this is simple: if what we need in order to make moral evaluations is something other than a tautology (given that moral judgments are either true or false, which we are assuming to be the case for the moment), then the subject term of such evaluations cannot be a generic name for a type of moral action. Hence, such subject terms must be such that, from a consideration of the judgment in which they occur, we cannot deduce any information whatsoever about the moral value of the act (what they name) without further information. In effect what this requirement does is reduce the possible scope-of-action terms which can be used in evaluations. This scope can be reduced in other ways as well. If we wish to speak of evaluations which are such that from them we can deduce the morality of the *agent* in addition to or apart from the moral value of the action, then, for the same sort of reasons as those just given, the terms used in the description must be such that from them alone we cannot deduce without any other information what the *motives* of the agent were.

The foregoing assumes, of course, a claim that is in many respects itself a matter for serious discussion, namely that agents are to be judged only or primarily in the light of their motives or intentions, while acts are to be judged upon other criteria, which seem always to involve their consequences. Let's take an example which illustrates the need to restrict our evaluations if we wish to judge agents as well as actions. "X maliciously pulled the trigger of the gun pointed at Y's head." The action here is pulling the trigger of the gun. We do not know whether a killing resulted nor whether the killing, if it occurred, was a murder. The gun might have been empty though X did not know it; his aim might have been bad; Y might have been wearing a bullet-proof hat, and so forth. But we do know (if we also know that X does things like this fairly frequently) that X is a bad man. We know it because malicious men are bad men, just as murders are wrongful killings. Hence, so far as agent morality is concerned, this example is redundant; or, more precisely, a sentence such as "If X maliciously pulled the trigger of the gun aimed at Y's head, then X is a bad man" is redundant, and hence not an evaluation of X.

There are, as was stated at the outset of these remarks, very many complex problems associated with these issues which cannot be resolved here. But enough has been said for our purposes in this discussion, because the point we wish to support here is that the same actions can occur in different cultures and at different times within the same cultures. These actions may or may not have the same consequences in the different cultures, and they may or may not have different motives. A killing or a pulling of a trigger may occur in Timbuktu or Paris or Mandalay, and the respective motives may have been to fulfill a vendetta, to protect one's mistress, or to steal a man's head. The consequences of the act of, say, pulling the trigger may be the agent's death on the scaffold, his choice as head of the tribe, or simply nothing aside from the death of the victim. The point is this: the same act can occur in these different cultures. The question is: is the act morally evaluable in opposite ways, and are these conflicting judgments both justifiable? And now we can see that this depends upon the occurrence of the same *consequences* in the different cultures, and, so far as agent morality is concerned, upon the agents having similar motives for the same act. If the consequence of moral significance is the death of a man in two cases of pulling a trigger, one in Guinea and the other in New York, then, other things being equal, it would seem that the act is wrong in both cases, though we cannot yet say that both agents are bad or, indeed, that either of them is bad. If it turns out that both of them have the same motive, and that this motive is simply to cause unnecessary human suffering to the victim's survivors, then we can say that both agents are bad men. On the other hand, knowing the motives of the two men does not *a fortiori* enable one to judge whether the act that they performed was right or wrong. Unless action and agent morality are separated, and unless there are different criteria for evaluating agents and acts, it proves impossible to separate teleological and deontological ethical theories. On a simpler plane, it makes the attempt to criticize theories such as ethical relativism much easier if we draw the distinction.

The Question of Truth or Falsity

The next problem which ought to be solved before proceeding to the actual arguments against ethical relativism concerns the question of whether ethical "judgments" are either true or false. As you will see later in this chapter, many philosophers believe that moral evaluations, indeed, all evaluations except those whose meaning is completely definable in terms of a standard which the evaluated object meets, are *neither* true nor false. Some philosophers have argued that expressions such as "That is wrong," "You ought not to do that," "He is a good man," and so on are commands, exclamations of approval or disapproval, imperatives of various kinds, disagreements in attitude or expressions of disagreements in attitude, multifunctional tools for persuasion, giving advice, threatening, exhorting, and so on, or special kinds of speech acts. All of these positions have one thing in common: no matter which of these things moral expressions are, such philosophers are agreed that they have no truth-value, that is, they are neither true nor false. If they are correct, then certainly X in culture A, and Y in culture B, are not contradicting one another when X says action Q is right, and Y says the same action Q is wrong. If they are not contradicting one another, then what is the ground of our objection that ethical relativism is false? Presumably the central thesis of that objection is that one and the same action cannot be both justifiable and not justifiable at the same time, that is, the opposite justifications cannot both be sound. It is difficult to see how such a thesis can be supported if we cannot claim that the conjunction of the opposite justifications and/or judgments is a contradiction, for how does one define the incompatibility of expressions?

The answer can be simply stated, though it is not a simple answer. It is that justification need have nothing to do with truth-values, since the criteria for justifying an action, or some moral evaluation of a man, can be stated within theories which do not presuppose that evaluations must be either true or false. What count as criteria for justification are not always the same thing in such theories. In some of them, an action is "justified" if the persuasive techniques used to get someone to do it are successful, while in other theories the issue of "success" in the sense of effecting one course of action rather than another has nothing to do with the question of which action or principle is correct. Clearly, such a theory will not do, but the reasons it will not do need not be *a priori* concerned with the question of whether or not evaluations are either true or false. Other theories argue that although evaluations are neither true nor false on a correspondence model, they might well be true or false given another theory of truth such as the instrumentalist or pragmatic theory. Also, such theories often argue that because evaluations are neither true nor false on a correspondence model is no reason to deny the possibility of logical reasoning in ethical arguments. It is possible, they say, to substitute evaluations into valid argument forms and hence have moral reasoning, the difference between this sort of reasoning and that in which the substitutions are either true or false being simply that, and nothing more.

Certainly there is something to this sort of argument. For example, no very good reason has ever been given in support of the thesis that the correspondence theory of truth is the only framework within which statements may be said to be true or false. And it is clear that the roles of language are much more complicated than the simple view which philosophers like John Locke held. On the other hand, most philosophers would still argue that the people who deny that ethical judgments are either true or false, the non-cognitivists, have not established a satisfactory explanation of what justification is; and this seems to be a valid criticism at this stage. Still, it is not certain that this deficiency is *because* of their denial that ethical utterances, expressions, or exhortations are neither true or false. Indeed, there is grave doubt whether *any* systematic ethic has ever provided an adequate schema for jusitfication. We seem warranted then in proceeding against ethical relativism in spite of this difficulty, provided *our* criticism of that view does not depend upon the further claim that ethical utterances must be either true or false on some particular model for a theory of truth, such as correspondence.

Nonetheless, the question of truth and falsity *does* have a bearing upon *some* questions associated with ethical relativism. Suppose, for example, that in culture A, the action of killing is said to be right on the grounds that every man must kill at least once in order to become a man, whereas in culture B killing is said to be wrong. If we assume for the moment that the judgment of culture B is correct, one way in which we could argue against the verdict of culture A is simply to point out that it is false that in order to become a man, one must kill. Even if some sort of test for manhood is required, there is no very clear reason why this must involve killing. Quite clearly, there are cases where not just one individual but whole cultures are simply mistaken in their beliefs that such action as ritual killing are essential for causing rain, for bringing warmth, or for some similar end. Nothing in our studies of the causal relations in the world gives us any reason at all to believe that there is any such relation between events like ritual killing and precipitation. It may well be, of course, that even after being told that there is no such causal connection, people in the culture continue to believe that there is. But that is not the point. It is the *justification* for their belief of which we are speaking, not the fact that they *have* the belief. Let us be very sure about this point: if some culture group believes that an action such as ritual killing is justified *because* it is essential for causing such an event as rain in a time of drought, then, if there is no causal connection between the one and the other, their justification is a bad one, i.e., it does not justify the claim that ritual killing is right.

Suppose that in culture B, ritual killing is said to be wrong because it causes unnecessary human death and suffering. Culture A, of course, says that although it causes death and suffering, it is not unnecessary, because water is essential to the life of the community as a whole. We know that rain is not caused in this way. The justification used in B is therefore better than that used in A. What we have here is a case of one and the same action, ritual killing, called right in A and wrong in B because of a difference in factual beliefs. In A, they believe that killing can cause rain, and in B they do not believe this. Both communities believe that water is essential to the life of the community, and, of course, this is true. But A is mistaken in its factual belief, and this may be proven. So although A holds this belief, it is not justified. From this it follows that a sufficient justification for a moral judgment never is constituted simply by the fact that the belief is held.

Criticism of Ethical Relativism

It may well be that ethical relativism begs the very question which is at issue. Let us demonstrate how this is so.

Let us state the thesis of cultural relativity in this way:

> (1) It is a fact that in two different cultures, A and B, some action Q, which is the same action in both A and B, is believed to be right in A but wrong in B.

[No one disputes the truth of (1).]
Ethical relativism may be stated in this way:

> (2) In culture A, the judgment "Q is right" is justifiable, and in culture B, the judgment "Q is wrong" is justifiable.

The predicates "right" and "wrong" might be replaced with one another of course, and if Q were a man or a consequence, rather than an action, "good" and "bad" might be used.

Now what ethical relativism asserts is that if (1) is true, then (2) is true. But we cannot move from (1) to (2) just by saying that (2) follows from (1). To make the inference, something else would have to be true, namely, that if any cultures are such that they contain conflicting moral evaluations, then all of the evaluations are justifiable. Stating it formally:

> (3) If different cultures contain conflicting moral evaluations, then the evaluations are equally justifiable.

If you order (3), (1), and (2) in just that sequence, you will find that you have a valid argument. But (3) is the statement of ethical relativism, and it therefore cannot be used to prove that we can pass from (1) to (2) without begging the question.

There is another possible criticism against ethical relativism, which holds only against some statements of it. If in statement (2) the word "justifiable" is taken as a normative term and not a descriptive one, that is, if it is taken as a term of recommendation, commendation, praise, blame, etc., then the ethical relativist would be asserting that the inference from the descriptive statement (1) to the normative claim (2) is valid.

In Part One, a fallacy called the factualistic fallacy was defined. It was noted there that some statements of this fallacy are suspect. However, it does seem to be the case that, from a statement or statements containing no normative terms, a statement or statements containing such terms is not deducible. The reason is a simple one: no conclusion of *any* deduction contains anything that is not already implicitly or explicitly in the premises. But if "justifiable" is a normative term, then the ethical relativist here is making just this sort of inference, and he would be guilty of the factualistic fallacy. Of course, this criticism would only apply against an ethical relativist who was also called a cognitivist, that is, who believed that normative statements and moral evaluations are either true or false; because, if he was a non-cognitivist, he would argue that (2) is neither true nor false. If that were true, then the concept of validity as we have defined it would be irrelevant, since it presupposes that the substitution instances of argument forms *are* either true or false.

What has been shown is this: the grounds for justification of a belief are not merely or even in part that the belief is *believed*. It is possible for the same action to occur in different cultures, and for there to be conflicting beliefs about the moral value of that action in those cultures. But from the fact that these different beliefs are held, nothing is entailed about their justification. Ethical relativism in effect holds that if the evaluations are believed, then they are justified. But to hold this and to prove it are two different things. We have seen that the inference cannot be justified without begging the question and that it may also be in some cases an instance of the factualistic fallacy. For these reasons, ethical relativism should be rejected.

THE NATURAL MORAL LAW THEORY

The need for scrupulous fairness is especially acute in this section, because the natural moral law theory has had and does have such colossal effects upon mankind. This theory, or perhaps more accurately, the successors of this theory, provide the philosophical foundation for the condemnation of artificial means of birth control. Current versions of the theory stem in large part from modifications in the arguments of Saint Thomas Aquinas. Accordingly, it is his view which we shall examine.

The position taken here is that the natural moral law theory is mistaken and that one set of criticisms which is effective against it was that raised by the English utilitarian, John Stuart Mill. For the most part the arguments brought against Aquinas here are Mill's.[1]

The fundamental assumption of the natural moral law theory is this: from what is the case, we may discover, or derive, or test, what ought to be the case. "What is" is "nature," the world of perception, and man's own makeup. From the properties of human nature, and man's relations with his fellow man and with the physical universe, it is thought that it is possible to derive rules of moral conduct and to justify such rules. These rules are thought to be universally true, and true for all time. They therefore presuppose, if they are to be derived from statements or descriptions of man's nature and his relations to other men and to the physical universe, that all of these are relatively fixed. Moreover, the theory presumes that man and the natural world is fundamentally teleological, that is, that events and creatures serve a purpose for which they are uniquely fitted. For example, a unique property of man is his relational faculty, his ability to make inferences, some of them quite complex. Man seems to be uniquely fitted for this sort of activity; it is "natural" for man to be rational, and since he seems unique in this respect, he is fulfilling a purpose uniquely human when he acts rationally. When man *realizes* this, that is, when he understands what the sorts of activities are for which he is uniquely equipped, he can choose a way of life which serves these ends or purposes. For everything in the universe, it is assumed that there is such a unique end which is best served by the creature best endowed with the properties to achieve it. Not every creature is capable of *choosing* to serve its end or not to serve it, because not all creatures are rational, and hence not all creatures have free will. This latter view was not always accepted; for example, at one time cattle and other animals were thought to be possible repositories of evil spirits.

The natural law theory claims that right or virtuous action is action in accordance with our nature. It is action intended to serve the purposes which a study of our nature indicates we are best fitted to serve. Wrong or vicious action is the opposite of virtuous action. Our knowl-

---

[1] John Stuart Mill, *Nature and Utility of Religion* (New York: The Bobbs-Merrill Co., 1958). Professor George Nakhnikian's introduction is very valuable.

edge of which actions are thus virtuous and which are vicious is practical moral knowledge. A good man is one who does virtuous actions
intentionally, and a bad one is one who does vicious actions intentionally.
Again, in all of this, the basic premise is the assumption that from what
is the case, we may discover what ought to be the case; and the conclusion is that, given our natures, action in accordance with them is
right.

It should not be thought that what has just been said is an absolutely
precise description of all natural law theories, for they are very diverse
and not all easily describable. Nonetheless, the basic premises are true
of most such theories and certainly true of the sort of theory Mill attacks, which is best exemplified by the views of Aquinas and Rousseau.

The latter two names raise another point: there are two very broad
kinds of natural moral law theory, the theologically oriented and the
purely naturalistic. Theologically oriented views ultimately base their
justifications for acting in accordance with nature upon the claim that
nature, and hence natural laws, are derivative from God, whom we
ought to obey. Purely naturalistic theories leave this part out. Aquinas
is a theologically oriented natural moral law theorist, and Rousseau is
a purely naturalistic theorist.

Saint Thomas Aquinas

Since the writings of Saint Thomas Aquinas are the chief foundation
for the opposition to artificial birth control, it will be informative to
consider a few of his remarks about natural moral law which illustrate
the description given of the views of this theory. He says:

. . . law is something pertaining to reason . . . a rule and measure of acts,
whereby man is induced to act or is restrained from acting . . . the rule and
measure of human acts is the reason . . . it belongs to the reason to direct
to the end . . . The natural law is promulgated by the very fact that God has
instilled it into man's mind so as to be known by him naturally . . . the rational creature . . . has a share of the eternal reason, whereby it has a natural
inclination to its proper act and end; and this participation of the eternal law
in the rational creature is called the natural law.

The precepts of the natural law . . . are self-evident in two ways: first, in
itself; secondly, in relation to us. Any proposition is said to be self-evident in
itself, if its predicate is contained in the notion of its subject . . .

We should note here that when Aquinas says that a precept is self-
evident "in relation to us," he is speaking of the psychological and
biological issues of our ability to perceive its self-evidence in the first
sense. Clearly, some people are not mentally or physically capable of
understanding the notion of analytical self-evidence, nor is it always clear
that a proposition is of this kind at first glance. To continue:

The first principle in the practical reason is . . . that good is that which all things seek after. Hence this is the first precept of law, that good is to be done and promoted, and evil is to be avoided. All other precepts of the natural law are based upon this.

Hence it is that all those things to which man has a natural inclination are naturally apprehended by reason as being good, and . . . their contraries as evil . . . every substance seeks the preservation of its own being, according to its nature; and by reason of this inclination, whatever is a means of preserving human life, and of warding off its obstacles, belongs to the natural law.

As regards the common principles whether of speculative or of practical reason, truth or rectitude is the same for all, and is equally known by all . . . as to certain more particular aspects, which are conclusions, as it were, of those common principles, it is the same for all in the majority of cases, both as to rectitude and as to knowledge; and yet in some few cases it may fail . . .[2]

Interpreting Saint Thomas here, he appears to be saying that the principles, or causes, of moral action are the same in all men and equally known to all men. But the more particular applications and implications of these principles are not equally known, whether for cultural, environmental, mental, or physical reasons. To take the largest possible example, "Do good and avoid evil" is presumably known to all and in all, but that theft is evil rather than good might not be equally known.

From these excerpts, which are the essence of the "natural" part of Aquinas's natural moral law theory apart from its theological connections, we may begin to formulate and simplify the theory more precisely. The following statements are key points:

1. Reason is the "rule of measure" of acts.
2. The nature law is instilled by God into every man's mind.
3. We have "natural inclinations" to our "proper acts and ends."
4. Precepts of natural law are self-evident (i.e., their predicates are contained in the notion of their subjects).
5. All those things for which we have "natural inclinations" are "naturally apprehended by reason as being good."
6. The common principles of natural law are equally true for everyone.
7. The common principles of natural law are equally known by all.

In addition to these seven specific statements, at least the sense of which is clearly present in the quotations, an argument concerning the fundamental principle of all and any natural moral law theory is implicitly present in the second quotation.

We might organize it as follows:

1. Good is that which all thinks seek after.
2. Evil is that which all things avoid.

2 Thomas Aquinas, *Summa Theologica* (London: Burnes & Oates, 1916–1937), question 94, articles 2–4.

3. Men have natural inclinations for some ends.
4. Hence, men seek after these ends.
5. Hence, these ends are good.
6. Good is to be done and promoted.
7. Hence, men ought to seek after that which they do seek after.

By the same token of course, one can conclude from these same premises that men ought not to seek after that which they do not seek after, i.e., have a natural antipathy towards. These arguments directly concern the assumption that what ought to be is derivable from, or based upon, or is testable by, what is, which is the basic principle of all natural moral law theories.

We now have at least one and perhaps two specific arguments to examine, plus seven other statements which must be examined as to their truth or falsity. To accomplish these things, we shall now turn to Mill's arguments, and then offer another critical viewpoint.

Mill's Criticisms

Mill's first attack is simplicity itself. What, he asks, do we mean by "nature"? He suggests two possibilities. When we speak of the nature of a thing, we may be speaking of its entire capacity for exhibiting phenomena, and a "natural law" concerning that thing will therefore be a series of descriptions, and perhaps predictions based upon them, of the thing's behavior, reactions, and so on in all the circumstances in which we find it. If we are speaking of nature in this way, then the sum total of nature is the object of the descriptions of all natural laws, that is, the "aggregation of the powers and properties of all things." This may be taken as a reportive definition of one way we use the word "nature."

A second sense of the word "nature," or a sense of the word "natural," is that in which it is opposed to "artificial," or "man-made." Hence, given this meaning, nature is comprised of all those events and objects which occur without the interference of man.

Although these are in the worlds of science and ordinary discourse perhaps the most common meanings of "nature," they are not the only ones. When we speak of a "child of nature," we often mean a child without affectations. In some contexts, "natural" simply means "frequent."

But we ought to be clear at the outset that one thing "natural" *cannot* mean, if the natural moral law theory is to be sensible at all, is "good," nor can it mean "right." If it did mean either of these things, then the theory would be trivial. We shall return to this point shortly, for it is vital.

Consider then the meanings, the reportive definitions, which Mill has suggested, beginning with the last two mentioned. A moment's reflection will tell you that if "natural" meant "frequent," it would be irrelevant in moral contexts. What does the frequency or rarity of an event have to do with its goodness or badness? If the only instance of murder were the famous Cain and Abel case, and hence if murder were an extremely rare event, would that be the *reason* murder is wrong? On the other hand, given that murder is a much too frequent event in reality, does this make it right? Of course not. So we can dismiss this sense of "nature" and "natural" so far as moral issues are concerned.

The second last sense of "nature" mentioned above concerned the absence of affectations. It may or may not be an attractive quality of most persons to be natural in this sense; and, in certain circumstances, it may be even morally relevant: for example, if pretension really upset some friend of yours, it would be perverse and perhaps even immoral of you to act this way in his presence. For this reason, a rule such as "act naturally" may perhaps be a moral rule. But the point is, if it *is* a moral rule, it is a subsidiary one, not a principle, and only covers a small segment of relevant moral conduct. Moreover, as Mill points out, what is often natural in the sense of what would happen without affectation, is worse than the affectation itself. We shall leave it to your imaginations to conjure up examples.

So we come to the first two senses of "nature." Before examining them directly, let us return to the earlier point about the impossibility of "nature" or "natural" meaning "good" or "right." This is part of a broader claim which may be made about these words as they stand in relation to moral principles, which is that whatever the basic moral principle of any moral theory might be, it cannot be a definition, whether stipulative or reportive. The reason is simple: moral rules are injunctions, guides to action, prescriptions; definitions are not any of these, with the possible exception of the case where we might construe a reportive definition as an instruction for the use of language. More force is added to this stand if we consider how we can "break" a definition, for any moral rule is capable of being broken. To "break" a definition, you have to misuse language in the case of true reportive definitions, or simply contradict yourself in the case of stipulative definitions. But this it not how moral rules are broken. Swearing is a breach of the moral rule prohibiting blasphemy; it is not a violation of a definition. Stipulative definitions and, according to some philosophers, reportive definitions are tautologies. But moral rules cannot be tautologies; for, if they were, they would be completely uninformative, again with the possible exception that we construe them as instructions for the use of a word as with reportive definitions. But certainly the supporters of the natural moral law theory would not want to hold this, or, if they do, they are holding a ridiculous position. They would not want to hold it, because surely they want to say that natural moral laws tell us what to do and what not to do, which these laws could not do if they were tautologies. Hence, if they *do* insist upon retaining this belief, or one related to it, such as the one announced in statement (4) on page 242, we may dismiss the theory as trivial and irrelevant—trivial because that is what all tautologies are, and irrelevant because that is what a "moral" theory is which cannot provide any guidance for anyone.

This topic is related to another important preamble to the discussion of Mill's criticisms, which is the distinction between natural laws and prescriptive laws. Mill does raise this issue in the essay called *Nature,* from which the criticisms here are taken, but he does not examine it at length. Prescriptions tell or advise us what to *do,* and we have a choice as to whether or not we shall obey such laws. Natural laws on the other hand are simply the result of inductive correlations between and among constant conjunctions of events which we find in the natural world. Clearly we have no choice about obeying natural laws such as the laws of gravity: one cannot *choose* to fall up instead of down! Flying machines do not violate Newton's laws—they confirm them.

Finally, before actually criticizing the theory from Mill's position, there is one more point to be raised, which he also raises. It might be argued for the natural moral law theory that although the basic principle of the theory, whatever it might be, cannot be a definition and must be a prescription, it is possible to construe it as enjoining us to look to nature as a *test* for rightness or wrongness. Now if this were so, it would be tremendously important. But given the meanings of "nature" and "natural" it cannot be so, and the reasons why finally lead us directly into Mill's major remarks.

Remember the two meanings of "nature" which we still have to consider: the first is "the totality of everything that is," and the second is the sense of "natural" which is opposed to "artificial" or "man-made." Take the first sense, and ask yourself in what way the totality of everything that is can be used as a test for rightness or wrongness. A moral principle which attempted to assert this claim might be something such as "Whatever is in accordance with anything that is, is right," or in imperative form, "Follow, imitate, obey whatever is the way it is." There are two fatal objections to this. The first is that if we are to take it at all seriously, then we must admit that it is useless; since anything you can possibly do is in accordance with the totality of whatever exists, and hence the rule permits anything and everything. If you do not take the principle in this absurd sense, then you might interpret it as an injunction to make full use of your knowledge of nature in deciding to do anything. This is sensible, but morally irrelevant, since you can use such knowledge to do good, evil, or actions which are morally irrelevant.

It would then be a maxim of prudence, not ethics. And if, in desperation, you interpret the principle as an injunction to obey natural laws, then it is again useless because you have no choice in the matter, as we have seen.

Perhaps the second sense of "nature" and "natural," that in which it is opposed to "artificial" and "man-made," will offer more promise. What then would it mean to enjoin upon ourselves the duty to imitate or obey nature in some way in this sense? Seemingly, it could only amount to urging ourselves not to interfere in the doings and workings of the natural world. This, of course, would be absurd. It would, among other things, imply that only those actions and consequences flowing from some sort of "natural instinct" rather than from any planning or deliberation involving the control of physical forces and so on was justified. Yet the very theorists who hold the natural moral law theory enjoin upon us the life of reason, not instinct. Nor will it do to say that interference with natural processes is permissible only when it serves our necessary interests. What justification could be brought for this as opposed to, say, changes which are for aesthetic or pleasurable motives?

Finally, we are faced with the undeniable fact that the natural world as unchanged by man is not a very pleasant place. It is, to use Mill's words "such as no Being whose attributes are justice and benevolence would have made with the intention that his rational creatures should follow it as an example." Nature kills and tortures, or at least, events which would be called murder and torture if performed by human beings, occur every day in the natural world. The good suffer and the evil prosper in many cases, and the innocent perish. "She" causes every human to die at least once, and millions of others are deprived of the means even to live. Of course, we are not implying that the natural world is some sort of causal, conscious agent with malevolent intentions. Nonetheless, seemingly unmerited suffering and death does take place; and if man did not interfere, there would be much more of it. The fact that man himself causes much the same type of evil does not alter these facts.

Re-examining "Natural Law"

In the light of these criticisms, let us now return to the statements and the argument which we have culled from Saint Thomas Aquinas, and see what relevance the criticisms have to them.

The fourth statement, that the precepts of natural law are self-evident, if it is true, renders the theory uninformative and trivial, because it has been shown that the maxims corresponding to natural laws cannot be definitions whether stipulative or reportive. Hence the theory is either trivial and uninformative, or it is based upon an assumption which is false.

The fifth statement, that those things for which we have natural inclinations are apprehended by reason as being good, seems to be false. There are surely some inclinations which we have, such as the propensity to murder, which are not known to be good. Furthermore, the word "natural" in "natural inclinations" seems to be redundant and perhaps even without any significance at all, given Mill's examination of the possible meanings of the term.

The sixth statement is certainly true if by "natural law" we are speaking about such laws as those governing gravity, provided we mean that these laws *hold* for everyone. But such laws are descriptive, not prescriptive, and are hence morally irrelevant. If we are speaking about some prescriptive law, some injunction or command, then all the problems with the meaning of "natural law" and "nature" which Mill raises come into force. Therefore, the sixth statement seems either irrelevant to moral philosophy (at least in the way our antagonists would have it) or vague as to be for all intents and purposes meaningless.

If by "principle" we mean "cause" rather than some first statement, rule, law, or description, and hence interpret statements (6) and (7) to mean that we all have the same inclinations and capacities and that we are all equally aware of these, then both (6) and (7) are simply false for obvious reasons.

When these criticisms are applied to the *argument,* we can claim the following things about it: the argument is valid, but only if the first two premises are definitions which are tautologies. This renders the argument, which is the foundation of the whole theory, morally irrelevant for the reasons already given. Then, if the first two sentences can be interpreted as guides or tests about what is good and evil, then either they are useless and uninformative, for the reasons given, or they are prudential and not moral maxims, also for the reasons given.

Finally, there are two other criticisms which have not been discussed before now, because they are tentative. The first criticism applies if we consider the first, second, fifth, sixth and seventh statements in the argument as rules, injunctions, or commands. If they are so construed, then there is a serious question as to whether they can be parts of an argument at all. In what sense is "Do not commit adultery" true or false? Certainly commands are not the same sorts of utterances as declarative sentences, and certainly they do not seem to be either true or false on the correspondence model, though they may be according to some pragmatic or instrumentalist theory of truth. This problem has apparently never been worked out by the natural law theorists.

The second criticism assumes that the argument in question *is* an argument, that is, that its component statements may be either true or false, and that its form is such that some of the statements, the premises, are intended to prove others, the conclusions. This second criticism concerns that philosophical fallacy which is called the naturalistic or factualistic fallacy. In the second chapter that fallacy was defined as the mistaken deduction of statements containing normative words such as "ought" or "should" from statements of fact, which do not contain such terms. As the argument is presently stated, it is not, strictly speaking, guilty of this mistake, because statements (1) and (6) provide the normative basis for the deduction of (7) or could be expanded to do so. But G. E. Moore, the inventor of this fallacy, also tendered an argument called the "open question" argument against theories which identify goodness with some natural property or thing.[3] If, for example, one claims that goodness and pleasure are identical, that is, if one defines goodness as pleasure, Moore maintained that it was always possible to ask "Yes, but is pleasure good?" even in the face of this definition. If goodness and pleasure *were* really identical, this question would be senseless, because it would be tantamount to asking "Is pleasure pleasure?" or "Is good good?" But the question does not seem to be senseless, and hence, Moore concludes, goodness and pleasure are not identical. Now in the theory we are considering, goodness is deemed to be identical with that which all things seek after. By logical analogy, if the open question argument holds in the case of goodness and pleasure, it also holds in this case.

This last criticism is put forward tentatively because the open question argument is not always held to be sound criticism. It would not hold, for example, if the definition of goodness were stipulative. If the definition were reportive, then, surely, it is true that at least one of the ordinary meanings of "goodness" *is* "pleasure," and of "good," "pleasurable." But if the natural moral law theory intends that the *only* definition of "good" is what is stated in the argument we are considering, then the open question argument seems a sound criticism, and all the other remarks about the unacceptability of definition in the premises of the argument also come to the fore.

It has been mentioned also that the theory presuppose that a teleological view of at least man's role in the universe is correct and that perhaps it also presupposes that the proper analysis of *all* entities and events in the universe is teleological in character. If it assumes the latter, then all the evidence brought to bear in support of evolution is opposed to the natural moral law theory, provided that we are speaking of that

[3] G. E. Moore, *Principia Ethica* (Cambridge: The University Press, 1903).

sort of natural moral law theory which is non-theological, i.e., purely naturalistic in import. If we are speaking to the theological natural moral law theorists, then the additional question of whether or not God exists is relevant; and, if God does exist, the questions of whether God is personally involved in our welfare, whether he is a good God, how his commands are manifested in nature, and so forth, are also issues to be solved. The question of God's existence will be examined in a later chapter. The conflict between the evolutionary hypothesis and the teleological view of nature is examined in the chapter on the philosophy of science.

These criticisms taken together seem to prove, as much as anything can be proven in philosophy, that the natural moral law theory does not meet the criteria which have been suggested for the evaluation of arguments. If these criteria are justified, then it would seem that those who hold the theory must either reformulate it to meet or at least to avoid the criticisms which have been raised, or they should reject it. This is all the more important because of the critical effects adherence to this theory has upon the population growth of the world.

ARE MORAL JUDGMENTS TRUE OR FALSE?

Perhaps no other topic in ethics and meta-ethics has occupied the attention of moral philosophers in this century more than has the question of the truth or falsity of moral judgments. For that reason alone, it is impossible in the space we have here to discuss fully the issues involved, and we must adopt a compromise procedure. First, a brief outline of the major tenets of non-cognitivism as it was supported primarily by A. J. Ayer and C. L. Stevenson will be given. As the premises of the theory are stated, criticisms will follow. Following this, the problem of "good reasons" as it pertains to some arguments by R. M. Hare will be examined.[4] Hare's theory is a contemporary one, while Ayer's theory came out in its original version in the 1930s, and Stevenson's theory appeared in his *Ethics and Language,* first published in 1941. Thus, we will cover a large part of the arguments about this topic over the last 35 years or so, though by no means all of them.

The Non-Cognitivist View

All non-cognitivists believe that moral judgments are neither true nor false, and hence that objective moral knowledge is impossible. Since cognitivists affirm precisely the opposite in both cases, they cannot both

---

[4] R. M. Hare, *The Language of Morals* (Oxford: The Clarendon Press, 1952); also see Hare's *Freedom and Reason* (Oxford: The Clarendon Press, 1963).

be correct. The non-cognitivists, or the emotivists as Ayer and Stevenson and their adherents are often called, are very sensitive to the wide variations in the use of language. They often express this by arguing that there is more than one kind of *meaning* involved in ethical judgments, and they usually include at least descriptive meaning, plus "emotive," "commendatory," or some other sort. This is by no means a novel idea, though it did not become popular until our time. The peculiar relationship between normative ethical judgments and actions had been noticed by Aristotle, who argued that the proper conclusion of a practical syllogism (a syllogism concluding that some act ought to be done or not be done) was not really a proposition but an action. Hume, Hutcheson, and Berkeley all noticed the close connection between ethical judgments and emotions, and Berkeley argued that the raising of some emotion or the causing or inhibiting of some action, without any intervening idea occurring to the agent, was precisely the function of many such judgments.

A. J. Ayer thought that ethical judgments were ejaculations or commands rather than factual statements. When one says "His taking that money was wrong," one is not making the same sort of statement as one would be if one said something like "His house is red." We are not, as the cognitivist thinks, ascribing a property to an action when we say that it is right or wrong, which is of course exactly what we are doing when we predicate redness of houses or height of a man. What we are doing is expressing our disapproval of the act and/or urging others not to do the same thing. Stevenson was sure that descriptive and emotive meaning were very closely related, and in fact he thought that they were not even completely separable. Rather, for analytic purposes, we pay more attention to one sort or the other depending upon the intent of our theory. Stevenson felt that the very names "descriptive" and "emotive" meaning were misleading because emotive meaning is defined by him as the disposition of a term or phrase to evoke a *range* of emotional responses. Thus, there are really very many different kinds of emotive meaning. There are other sorts of meaning too, definable in terms of the disposition which the term or phrase has. For example, "pictorial" meaning is what a sign has if it has a tendency to evoke images. A sentence or indeed a single sign may therefore have many different kinds of meaning.

A persistent difficulty with the Stevensonian version of non-cognitivism is precisely this proliferation of kinds of meanings. It is compatible with his theory that a given sign or expression has an indefinitely large range of meanings because any one term might have an indefinitely large number of associated psychological reactions. Because of this, any analysis of meanings offered by the emotivist is going to be extremely vague and probably quite inaccurate and incomplete in cases of moral judgments, given that the emotive responses to them are widely divergent and very complex. It may be, however, that this is merely a comment upon the state of our knowledge about ourselves.

Stevenson thinks that moral judgments are also expressions of attitudes of different kinds. In cases of disagreement involving such expressions, he distinguishes two sorts: disagreement in belief and disagreements in attitude. The former are differences about matters of fact, but since there are no ethical "facts" according to him and to Ayer, the latter are disagreements about what ought to be the case, not about what is. Our expressions of attitudes in ethical disputes are attempts to get others to share those attitudes. Although there is no necessary or logical connection between the two sorts of attitudes, it is clear to Stevenson that attitudes may often be altered by correcting a mistaken belief.

For Stevenson, even descriptive meaning is analyzed to the dispositional model. The descriptive meaning of a term, phrase or sentence is its disposition to produce "cognitive" mental processes such as thinking (making inferences), believing, supposing, and presuming. So the differences between descriptive and emotive meaning are to be specified in terms of the different psychological reactions which they have a tendency to evoke.

In addition to the vagueness mentioned above, which Stevenson admits, there is certainly reasonable doubt as to the adequacy of this theory of meaning, especially as it pertains to individual words. The question "Does a word have a meaning because of its disposition, or a disposition because of its meaning?" is at least sensible. Yet if Stevenson is correct, the disposition and the meaning are identical. If he is right, then the sentence "A sentence has a meaning because of its disposition," and its partner "A sentence has a disposition because of its meaning," should either both be tautologies or both be senseless. But they seem to be neither. Furthermore, terms which are stipulatively defined surely have no dispositions of the sort which Stevenson discusses. Yet, just as surely, they have meanings; for otherwise, of course, they would be senseless.

Furthermore, what are we to make of various sounds which spark some reaction or other but which have no specific disposition to do so? In a dark room at night, *any* unsuspected sound has a disposition to arouse fear, or to frighten, and so forth. Are we to say that this is a part of the meaning of all words and sounds?

The Dispositional Theory of Meaning

With these doubts in mind, we come to the theory of moral reasoning suggested by Stevenson, which had a considerable influence upon Hare, whom we have yet to consider. Stevenson certainly accepts the prin-

ciple that reasons may be given in support of an injunction to perform
an action; but, at the same time, he continues to argue that ethical disagreements are primarily disagreements in attitude. The reasons given
in support may be simply statements of belief, whereas the conclusions
will always be expressions of attitudes. Now the question is, what is
the relation between the reasons and the conclusion? It is not a relation
of entailment, for such a relation cannot obtain unless both the reasons
and the conclusion are either true or false. Moreover, it seems to follow
from Stevenson's claims, that, in a case where the reasons are statements
of belief and the conclusion or conclusions disagreements in attitude,
there is not only a problem with truth-values but also a difference in
meaning, the reasons and the conclusion having different kinds of meaning. The relation seems to be nothing more than a causal one: that is,
the reasons, which are statements of belief, *cause* a change in the expression of the attitude. As we shall see, this causes some very serious
problems with respect to the analysis of what *justification* is. Surely no
one, even the most convinced cognitivist, wishes to argue that emotion
plays no role at all in moral situations, even if, as the cognitivist would
wish to maintain, that role is subsidiary to that of reason. But even
though all of us would admit that we feel more deeply about moral
issues than about our normal everyday concerns, that does not seem to
be a compelling reason to conclude that we must rest the entire case for
morality and moral reasoning upon the ground that many moral terms
cause some emotion among a range of emotions in their interpreters.
The fact that the speaker or writer of the term, phrase, or sentence, and
the hearer or reader of it, are or are not in some emotional state as a
consequence of the use of the sign seems not to be *necessarily* connected
with the *meaning* of what is said or written, though it may be of great
importance to the question of the *effectiveness* of the use of the signs.
But for the emotivist, the meaning of an ethical term (where "term" includes both phrases, individual words and sentences) is its disposition to
evoke one or more among a range of emotions in the person to whom it
is directed. This seems to depend upon an overly narrow conception of
what is involved in the use of signs, even in ethical contexts. Do we
not, as a matter of fact, use moral terms in ways other than in order
to cause emotions or emotive responses whether in ourselves or anybody
else? Is not the evoking of emotion an incidental by-product of many
uses of ethical terms, if it is a by-product at all? Certainly this seems to
be the case in many of our discussions about the justification for some
particular act, or when, for example, we are talking about the goodness
or badness of some person whom we do not know particularly well.

There are also problems with the dispositional theory of meaning in
ethics which I shall call "directional" problems. They are especially

acute in cases of signs with vague meanings, or multiple ones. For example, suppose that it is characteristic of some person that in certain contexts, he uses certain terms to refer to some situation, person or object. Another person, hearing him, might well take the terms as meaning a state of the user of them, while at the same time, it might well be the case that the user's intention is to refer to some object, or cause some reaction in the hearer other than the one given here. The point is that with the dispositional theory of meaning, it is difficult, perhaps impossible, to separate the intentional component of meaning, that due to the intention of the user, from the "reactive" component, i.e., that which actually is constituted by the reaction of the hearer or reader. Now the emotion associated dispositionally with some term may have little or nothing at all to do with the intention of the user. For example, if I swear, the emotive response evoked may well be directed at me, whereas if the emotive theory were correct, it ought to be directed at the subject of which the ethical term is predicated. And in fact, we are never very sure of the emotional reactions of people in moral situations, because this depends to such a great extent upon the behavior patterns and habitual associations of the individual. It is true that the use of terms may help in itself to establish such behavior patterns, but even if this is the case, the evoking of an emotion is not then the meaning of the ethical term, but rather the result of stimulating action according to the specific behavior pattern. Hence the "emotive meaning" of the sign is at most a "disposition of a disposition," a "second-order" disposition as it were.

Although commands, entreaties, and exhortations can be used to control behavior, the control of behavior is not identical to the control of emotion. Because of this, there is no systematic way for the emotivists to analyze the direction of emotion in the use of moral terms, and this seems to be a necessity for any theory which purports to describe systematic uses of moral terms and which holds that the meaning of moral terms depends upon their emotive effects.

The emotivists, indeed all non-cognitivists, believe that the persuasive function of words and sentences is most important in moral contexts. The emotivists believed that this function cannot be performed without the evoking of emotions. Although persuasion is surely a central factor in the use of moral terms, it seems doubtful that the emotions are always the fundamental factor in this process. Rather often, it seems that the claim that the emotions are the fundamental factor in persuasion is to confuse the jobs for which we use moral signs with what one author calls our "ulterior purposes" in using them. We can, of course, influence and persuade others without using words, and in many contexts, the persuasive effects are greater the less words are used. Humans can be conditioned to respond in any number of desired ways and by any number of methods; so any analysis of persuasion ought to include much more than simply the analysis of the use of words for persuasion. Stevenson restricts his analysis to *verbal* meaning, and offers no justification for doing so, although words are but one kind of sign. Suppose that we are using a species of sign language rather than known words and that the interpreter whom we are trying to persuade is not familiar with the language. To understand what we mean, he must concentrate very intently, watching our gestures, expressions of the face, and so on. In many such situations, it is quite likely that no emotional response would be forthcoming from the interpreter, because such responses are almost always immediate, almost reflexive, and the necessity for careful concentration makes immediate responses difficult. Yet surely we could in at least some instances persuade someone to do something with moral import in just this way. Now the question is, if we can do it with sign language, then why not with verbal language? If emotive response is not essential for persuasion in the one case, then why is it in the other?

The Non-Cognitivist Theory of Truth

So far the topic of criticism has been largely the theory of meaning of the non-cognitivists. Theories of meaning and theories of truth are closely related, as we know. It is now time to move closer to a critique of their theory of truth. Early emotivists, such as A. J. Ayer, held that moral sentences are expressions of feelings rather than assertions that we have those feelings. Such expressions are not for Ayer, nor for Stevenson, significant in the way that the statements of science, or normal observations sentences, are. To put it the way Ayer did, "The presence of an ethical symbol in a proposition adds nothing to its factual content." If I say "You acted wrongly in stealing that money," I have said nothing more than "You stole that money" so far as the factual content of the propositions is concerned. The only other addition is that I have expressed my moral disapproval of stealing. There are no referents for the ethical symbols in such a statement. In fact, the only ethically relevant propositions which are either true or false are those which give definitions of moral terms or judgments about the justification for the use of certain terms in certain contexts, in short, meta-ethical propositions. Exhortations or expressions of emotion are really not propositions at all; they are technical nonsense, given the thesis that, to be meaningful, a proposition must be either true or false.

Now Ayer's case only works if all meaningful statements are either tautologies or scientific claims. The latter category is taken to include ordinary observation statements. If it could be shown that this disjunction of all meaningful statements into either tautologies or scientific statements did not exhaust the class of meaningful statements, then Ayer would be wrong. Professor A. P. Brogan is among those who have pointed out that it is not exhaustive.[5] If Ayer were correct, then, to be meaningful, all moral statements would either have to give descriptions of the features of the particular case at hand or be merely meaningless (technically) expressions. But he does not account for the possibility that moral statements might involve reference to rules or principles of ethical systems, in accordance with which particular judgments would be justified.

Furthermore, the criterion for meaningfulness in Ayer's system depends upon our accepting only one meaning or definition for the terms "true" and "false," namely, that postulated by the correspondence theory of truth. We are speaking, of course, of descriptive meaning—that sort which would be explicated by Stevenson through the disposition which a descriptive term has to evoke cognitive responses and by Ayer through the mechanism of the referential theory of meaning. But there are other theories of truth, and hence of meaningfulness, which are quite amenable to ethical judgments. One such system is the coherence theory of truth, according to which a statement is given a truth-value on the grounds of its consistency or inconsistency with the other propositions in that system. The concepts of truth and falsity in any system cannot be defined within it, as a study of Euclid's geometry will demonstrate. Such postulates are not said to be either true or false within the system, but are said to be warranted, validated, or vindicated. Brogan points out that there is no reason given by Ayer for thinking that ethical systems differ in this respect from any other sort of system. But we do not claim that the postulates of other systems are meaningless, so why ought we to do this in the case of the axioms of ethics? And upon what grounds could either Ayer or Stevenson deny a truth-value posited according to the coherence theory to ethical judgments? There seems to be no defense against this criticism in the works of either Ayer or Stevenson. Nor, by the way, is there a defense against it in Hare, though the coherence theory of truth would certainly provide Hare with a means for predicating truth-values of ethical judgments.

Some philosophers, including John Dewey, have even disputed the basic claim of the emotivists that there are no referents for ethical terms.[6] As Dewey notes, it is curious that Stevenson claims that interjections are signs of emotions and that he even names many of the particular emotions of which they are signs. Dewey does not understand

[5] A. P. Brogan, "A Criticism of Mr. A. J. Ayer's Revised Account of Moral Judgments," *Journal of Philosophy*, 56 (March, 1959), pp. 270–80.

[6] John Dewey, "Ethical Subject Matter and Language," *Journal of Philosophy*, 42 (December, 1945), pp. 701–12.

what this sign relationship is if it is not denotation or designation, and that means that such expressions refer. If Dewey is correct, then of course ethical statements are either true or false, and the emotivists are wrong.

There are other criticisms of non-cognitivism's theory of truth, but it is often difficult to claim that they concern *just* the question of truth and falsity and nothing else. Indeed, this has been evident in what has just been discussed. Broadly, however, we can divide the types of criticisms into those which are primarily directed against a theory of meaning, those opposed to a theory of truth, and those which concern the problem of justification. Let us now move on to the third category, keeping in mind that the criticisms here will almost always have some relevance in the other two categories as well.

The Problem of Justification

First, let us consider the theory of justification of the emotivists taken as a group. They hold, as we already know, that the aim of moral discussion is to change attitudes by persuasion; and, unless they can provide us with a sound method for differentiating between good and bad reasons for being persuaded, they will not be able to separate ethical justification from simple propaganda. It may be that there *is* no distinction, but this is a conclusion that most non-cognitivists have not been willing to admit. In propaganda, *what* is said does not matter so long as the desired end is attained, that is, one reason is as good as another provided that they both work. Certainly there is some truth in this for moral purposes too, since most of us would admit that, if we have two equally good reasons for a course of action, it does not matter which of them we use for persuading someone to do something if they are both effective and relevant. Because the situation in moral discussions is practically oriented, however, there is a difference between telling someone something and persuading him to do something. The question is, does *what* the person is told make a difference, and if so, how does the emotivist account for this fact? Surely what is said ought not to make any difference, if the expression is sufficient to cause the appropriate response in the agent. The emotivist would reply that, in cases where disagreements in attitude are rooted in disagreements in belief, what is said matters a very great deal; and this presupposes that beliefs and attitudes are two different sorts of mental states or phenomena. Stevenson holds that the cognitive elements in an ethical argument are accounted for in the reasons for the judgment, which do not contain any ethical terms and which are true or false. Differences in belief, unlike disagreements in attitude, are logical in nature and can be settled by discovering which of the competing beliefs is true. This dichotomy between supporting reasons for a judgment and the (hopefully) consequent agreement in attitude seems to be founded upon two assumptions. First, beliefs and attitudes are logically distinct, and, secondly, agreement in matters of fact or belief does not depend upon agreement in attitude. Neither of these assumptions is defended in Stevenson's work, and both of them seem to be questionable.

Consider the second assumption first. Attitudes are directed towards objects. This fact, and the fact that some attitudes are directed toward certain sorts of things rather than others, plus the truth that some attitudes, to use P. H. Nowell-Smith's terms, are "pro" while others are "con," is the basis of the claim that attitudes may be redirected or intensified. It is also the basis of Stevenson's broad classification of attitudes into those of approval and those of disapproval. But if the difference among attitudes rests upon the fact that they are interested or directed in various ways and to various objects, is this not also true of beliefs? They are interested and directed too, and the focus of their interest and direction happens to concern matters of truth and falsity, while other attitudes are not so directed. The correlation between believing that something is true and having a favorable attitude toward the object of the truth (and vice versa in the case of false propositions) is in many cases quite clear. Beliefs and attitudes are both affective-ideational processes which differ not in kind, but in the objects towards which they are directed. If this is true, then beliefs and attitudes are not logically distinct (if this means generically distinct). So the first assumption is false; and if beliefs are a kind of attitude, then the second point is false too.

We might also consider the truth of the general claim that persuasion is involved in all ethical judgments, as it must be if the emotivist is correct. In both statements of fact and ethical judgments, I am telling something to someone, or, at the very least, in *some* ethical judgments and in all factual claims I am telling something to someone. In the moral judgment, I am telling someone what to do. In the factual, I am telling him what is the case. Certainly the interpreter of what I say can and might disagree with me in both instances; and, if he does, then I can and might try to convince him. The point is that persuasion can be used not only in the case of moral injunctions but also in statements of fact. To hold that persuasion is only used in the case of ethical statements, or at least to hold that the ethically relevant parts of moral utterances are purely persuasive, is to ignore the fact that many ethical situations involve asking for, and giving, an answer to the question "What shall I do?" and in such cases, persuasion would not seem to be needed in every case. Therefore, in addition to being a key component of non-moral judgments, it turns out that persuasion is *not* a key component of all moral judgments. If this is correct, then it cannot be the case that effectiveness is the result solely of persuasion in moral situations, which is just what the emotivists must hold.

Professor Richard Brandt accused Stevenson of holding what he calls the "blind emotive meaning" theory.[7] This theory concerns the mechanism of the directive influence which ethical utterances have on the emotions and attitudes of the persons to whom they are addressed. Principally, the blind emotive theory argues that the hearing of a verbal expression usually causes substantial emotional and attitudinal changes in the interpreters of signs and that it does this *independently* of what the sign is taken to mean and independently of any changes that the hearing of the sign might produce in the cognitive field. This is the reason it is called the "blind" emotive theory. This thesis is particularly important for Stevenson's arguments, because for him the very essence of persuasive definition is the case where the emotive effectiveness of a term remains fixed, while there is a *change* in the cognitive meaning.

By the terms "cognitive field" Brandt means what is perceived, believed, and expected by a person, and this is taken to include the meaning of what is said to him as well as the interpreter's apprehension of the feelings and attitudes of the user of the sign, i.e., the person who is speaking to him. In opposition to the blind emotive theory Brandt places another view, which he calls the "cognitive field theory." This theory holds that the emotive and attitudinal effects of the use of signs are not independent of changes in cognitive field but that, on the contrary, such changes arise *only* in conjunction with changes in perception, belief, understanding, etc. If the blind emotive thesis is tenable, it should be possible to produce terms which have the same meaning but different emotive effects. Stevenson has not produced such a pair of terms. Furthermore, if we are to say that there is such a thing as blind emotive meaning, then there should be tests for distinguishing between the blind emotive effects of the use of a term and those which are dependent upon changes in the cognitive field. Stevenson, apart from merely saying that there are such differences, does not provide the tests. It would seem therefore that he is not justified in claiming that there is such a thing as blind emotive meaning.

In very many ethical situations, what is uttered is not appropriately interpreted as a statement intended to be either true or false, but rather as a *rule*. For example, if someone says, "Thou shalt not steal," he is not uttering anything which is supposedly true or false, and it is therefore no criticism of him to say what he says is technically meaningless

---

[7] R. B. Brandt, "The Emotive Theory of Ethics," *Philosophical Review*, 59 (1950), pp. 305–18; 535–40.

because it is neither of these. The appropriate questions to be asked of rules are not pertinent to the question of truth-values. They are such questions as "Does this rule hold?" and "When is the rule applicable?" Furthermore, we can and do ask of some particular action whether it falls under some rule. If we say in an ethical context "That is stealing," we may be doing nothing more than identifying the act as a member of the class of thefts. For the use of such procedures as identification and applying a rule there are established procedures and meta-rules in any language. But the emotivist never considers such meaningful but non-truth-functional linguistic devices in his consideration of ethical language. At the least then, his analysis is incomplete.

Choices made on the basis of comparison and evaluation are characteristic of reasoning when justifications for one course of action rather than another are involved. Comparison and evaluation are cognitive functions of activities of the mind which involve the making of inferences. If the emotivists are right, the reasons offered in support of an ethical choice are descriptive statements having a persuasive force, while the conclusion is the expression or evoking of an emotion among a possible range of responses. An expression of emotion does not imply anything at all; and, since it has no truth-value, it is not implied *by* anything. No ethical choice can ever be the conclusion of deliberative processes involving comparison and evaluation on the basis of reasons if this is true. Yet surely our everyday experience flies in the face of this. If it does, then the emotivists must either defend a theory which does not seem to square with the experience of normal moral agents, or they must defend a theory of moral reasoning which permits inferences while at the same time denying that moral utterances are either true or false. This is indeed what other non-cognitivists, such as R. M. Hare, choose to do.

This question of the nature of moral reasoning raises a closely related one: what is the meaning of "moral" in "moral reasoning"? We often try to isolate properties which distinguish sorts of things from one another, and we say that an entity or sort of event belongs to one sort rather than another in virtue of having the differentiating property. What is it then that makes terms moral terms? For Ayer at least, and perhaps for Stevenson, it is the emotive function of the term. But there is some question as to whether this differentiates the terms used in moral reasoning from any other sort of terms. Dewey pointed out that a skillful criminal lawyer defending his client makes use of a great many non-cognitive devices for the purpose of influencing a jury, perhaps even against its will. But he asks, with some justification, whether or not we consider these devices part of the legal procedure of the trial *qua* legal, and I am inclined to agree with Dewey when he concludes that emotive responses no more make terms peculiarly "ethical" than the non-cognitive moves of the lawyer are made "legal" just because they are used in a trial. The point is not only that there is some question whether emotive meanings separate moral terms from other sorts, but also whether there are special emotive meanings which we *only* find in moral contexts. How, for example, do we separate the emotive responses which are found in ethical contexts from those which occur in love situations, and countless others? It seems that Ayer and Stevenson are forced to hold that there are no particularly ethical uses of language, but only linguistic devices for exciting emotional responses which are not "ethical" on that account.

In all of what has been said of the emotivists, two points keep recurring again and again. They are that, without truth-values, there is some question about the very possibility of moral reasoning and argumentation at all; and, secondly, what counts as a *good* reason seems for the emotivists to depend simply upon effectiveness. Both of these factors will arise again in our examination now of some problems associated with the meta-ethics of R. M. Hare.

The Problem of Good Reasons

There are many aspects to the problem of "good reasons." Two of them will be analyzed here. The first is how to define a good reason, and the second is how to reconcile a basic conflict in what Hare calls "ways of life." In his major philosophical writings, Hare is trying to set up a logical framework (in which the major tenets are what he calls "universalizability" and "prescriptivity") in order to relate the essential descriptive reference and commendatory force which he sees as the basic components of moral judgments. Historically, such attempts have fallen upon the fate of all efforts to derive normative conclusions from factual premises. This mistake is expressed in what we know as the factualistic fallacy, which has also been called "Hume's Hurdle" and "Kant's Conundrum," because both of those philosophers also realized its importance. Hare, however, thinks he has avoided it. It seems doubtful that he has, and it also seems that he has failed to provide a sound definition for what a good reason is. If he fails to do this, then basic conflicts in ways of life also become insoluble.

Let us use Hare's own examples in setting out the problem. Suppose that a particular strawberry is a good strawberry, and that it is called a good strawberry. Two questions might now be asked: why is the strawberry good, and why do you call it good? If one said that the strawberry was large, red, and juicy, then that would be taken as a reason (and presumably a very good reason) for saying that the strawberry is a good one. Nonetheless, it is important to notice that "This strawberry is large, red, and juicy" does not *entail* "This is a good strawberry." In spite of the lack of entailment, Hare argues that if you know what the properties of the strawberry are and if you know the meaning of the word "good," then the only additional information you need in order to tell whether the strawberry is good is "the criteria in virtue of which a strawberry is to be called a good one, or . . . the characteristics that make a strawberry a good one, or . . . the standard of goodness in strawberries." Sentences which simply describe the properties of strawberries have what Hare calls "descriptive" meaning. There are also terms, phrases, or sentences which merely commend, and these have "prescriptive" meaning. If you did not know what makes a strawberry a good one, you would still know that I was commending this strawberry if I called it good. Terms which have both descriptive and prescriptive meaning at the same time are said to have "evaluative" meaning. Hare says that evaluative meaning remains constant no matter what the term is nor the object of which we are speaking. But he seems to have made a mistake here, given what he himself says, because valuative meaning is composed of prescriptive and descriptive meaning, and only the prescriptive component is the same for all objects, since we say that different things are good for different reasons. He ought to say that it is prescriptive meaning which remains constant and not evaluative meaning. Descriptive meaning varies because objects have different properties in virtue of which we say they are good, which is why the reasons for saying they are good are different. There are very important and close relations between descriptive and prescriptive meaning, because the evaluative force of a word can actually change the descriptive meaning for any class of objects; that is, we can alter the standard for saying that something is good through the evaluative force of a term. Indeed, evaluative meaning is always used, either directly or indirectly in order to influence choices.

Descriptive and Prescriptive Meaning

The question of the nature of the relation between descriptive and commendatory or prescriptive meaning is crucial, for upon its satisfactory analysis depends the solution to the problem of good reasons for Hare. It is not a logical relation, as we already know, since the description of the strawberry and its properties does not entail that the strawberry is good. It cannot be a causal one, because in that event the remarks we have considered about propaganda and justification would come into effect here. It may be, of course, that they *will* again be important, because Hare may not be able to escape the problem which Ayer and

Stevenson had. But we have not considered the additional mechanisms of Hare's theory as yet.

Hare says that "to universalize is to give the reason," and he believes that both descriptive and moral judgments are universalizable. By this he means that if something is red, then anything like it in the "relevant respects" must also be red. The reason is that if "This is red" is true of a particular object but not of other objects like it in these relevant respects, then the assertion that these other resembling objects are not red involves a "misuse of the word 'red'." It is a misuse because when we say something is red, we mean that it is a member of a class of things, namely, those things with the property redness. Descriptive meaning and descriptive universalizability, therefore, rest upon the concept of resemblance.

In the case of moral judgments, the difficulty is in deciding just what a relevant similarity is, for if that cannot be decided we cannot universalize our judgments in the way we can with descriptive judgments. Other than that, Hare thinks that the problem of formulating rules for prescriptive and descriptive meaning is the same logical sort in both cases, because universalizability depends in both cases on descriptive meaning. We already know that moral judgments are evaluative; that is, they have both prescriptive and descriptive meaning. He is saying that it is in virtue of their descriptive meaning that they are universalizable. Since giving good reasons presupposes universalizability, it must depend upon descriptive meaning in some central way. Hare says that, in the making of a moral judgment about something, we make the judgment because of *non*-moral properties which the object of our judgment has. The reason for our moral judgment, our decision to act, etc., is a statement about these non-moral properties, or some of them. Reasons are of course always reasons *for* something, and there are rules for the making of reasons. An ethical naturalist who believed, for example, that goodness was identical with pleasure, would hold that a sufficient reason for saying that an act was right or a person good is that pleasure was involved, other things being equal. In Hare's view, this alone would not be sufficient, because it fails to take account of the commendatory force of moral terms, which is not explicated in the simple identification of goodness with a natural property or properties. "Pleasurable" does not have the commending force that "good" has.

But even if what he claims here is correct, have we learned anything about the relation *between* descriptive and prescriptive meaning? If I say that it is "because" of non-moral properties that I morally commend something or someone, have I given any information about the force and meaning of this "because"? We know it is not a logical "because," since we know that the statement of the reasons does not entail the commendation. We know that it cannot be simply causal, because of the "propaganda fallacy" and because such a theory would permit gross injustices provides the reasons offered were effective in causing them to happen. Hence, to say that moral judgments are universalizable because of their descriptive function is uninformative, since descriptive universalizability does not imply prescriptive universalizability, or at least Hare does not show that it does. It will not help to call the meanings of terms which have both types of meaning by a third name ("evaluative" meaning) for this does not explain how the types of meaning are related, which is what we need to know. But there must be *some* relation between them, for if there is not, descriptive meaning cannot provide a foundation for good reasons offered in support of a moral judgment. In fact, if there is no relation between them, and moral judgments have as their central function the commendatory role which Hare sees as their essence, then how can we even say what a *good* reason is? If we operate from his premises, there is some question about our ability to do this; and the explanation of why this is so also illuminates the explanation of why conflicts in any case of opposed principles or ideals are irreconcilable if Hare's theory is correct.

Evaluating a Good Reason

Let us first examine the concept of a "good reason" more closely. If Hare is right, then to ask "Good what?" is to ask ". . . for the class within which evaluative comparisons are being made." To ask for what makes something good is to ask for its "virtues" or "good-making characteristics." The class of good reasons is certainly a class within which evaluative comparisons can be made and are made. Were this not so, the concept of a *good* reason would be empty. A reason is good with respect to other reasons which are bad, or better, and so forth, and as an empirical matter we certainly do make such evaluations in our ordinary lives. If we do make such evaluations or comparisons of good reasons, then they must have certain "virtues" or "good-making characteristics," and these properities will presumably be non-moral ones, even in the case where the good reason is a reason for a moral judgment. Such properties as truth, relevance, practicality, and so on would be candidates for such properties, virtues, or good-making characteristics. Therefore when I ask you what is "good" about a reason, or why you call it good, I am asking you for these characteristics. Hare agrees. He says that when I ask you what is good about something, I am asking "What features of it are you commending?"

Suppose that R is a good reason, and that I say it is. From this it immediately follows, if Hare is correct, that (1) I am commending R;

(2) I am commending R because R has certain properties such as truth, relevance, and so forth which are either good (commended) or good-making (properties which cause me to commend); and (3) the properties which R has are what Hare calls "relevant particulars," that is, they are the features of R which I am commending. Hare then must hold that a sufficient condition for R's being a good reason is that I commend it, or someone does, provided that there is at least one instance of the application of the rule under which R falls as a reason.

It evidently follows from this that if R has a, b, and c as its properties, then a, b, c are only properties on the basis of which R is commended (is a good reason) if a, b, c are themselves commended, or cause me to commend because of properties which *they* have which are commended, *ad infinitum.* We are seemingly committed not only to an infinite regress, but to one which, in some contexts, will involve an infinite proliferation of properties of properties.

Another and perhaps clearer way to state the same criticism would be to begin with the fact that, for Hare, the meaning of "This is a good R" is its use to commend R, conjoined with its informative function. To ask "Why is R good?" is to ask for R's good-making characteristics. But of course, merely to give these properties would not explain why R was a good reason, because (1) "good" is a term of commendation and so cannot be defined in terms of a non-evaluative nature, (2) the good-making characteristics of R are properties denoted by non-evaluative words, and (3) giving the properties alone therefore does not allow me to commend R. So, if R is to be a good reason, then the definition of R must include evaluative words, that is, it must commend R, or the properties of R, on the basis of other reasons which are commended, and so on.

It might be helpful to consider the criticisms in yet another way. Here are two sentences:

(1) R is good.
(2) R is true, relevant, and practical.

We can certainly understand (1) without understanding (2), and vice versa. If we understand both of them, we see that (1) is not entailed by (2), nor (2) by (1). They have different meanings, and conjoining them does not alter this fact:

(2A) [R is good] and [R is true, relevant, and practical.]

This last statement is still equivalent, by simplification, to two sentences whose truth-values need not be equivalent, and whose meanings are different, because their uses are different according to Hare. The use of (1) is to commend, of (2) to refer, among other things.

Let us say that there is some action (call it A) of which some evaluator asserts "A is good." Call this last sentence (3). We ask the judge why A is good, and he replies, "Because R, and R is good." Now this will not do, because the meaning of "R is good" (1) is to commend R, or if you prefer, its meaning consists in commending R, and the relation between your commending A and why you commend it is not explicated by the statement that you commend it because you commend something else. But neither will it do to say that you commend A because of (2). The reason is that if I then ask why (2) is a good, you, as evaluator, must either commend R again, which solves nothing, or give another reason, which puts us back at the beginning again, or repeat yourself. If the evaluator gives the conjunction of (1) and (2), (2A), as his reason for commending A, then the appropriate rejoinder is a conjunction of the criticisms here given of both (1) and (2).

Hare speaks of the "inverted-commas" use of "good," which includes many uses of the word in which one is not commending anything, as when we are speaking *about* the word or using it in contexts where the clear implication is sarcastic. But this will not do as an escape here, because one *is* commending when he calls a reason a good one, and by definition this is not the case with the inverted-commas use. And once again, it will not do to say that a good reason is simply one which causes me to commend, because in that event the notion of a *good* reason is superfluous and empty.

Hare's Bases for Moral Justification

All of the criticisms just given have force because of the gap between descriptive and prescriptive meaning which Hare seems to have failed to cross. The same problem leads us into the second part of the discussion here, which is the irreconcilable conflict between what he calls "ways of life" and what we should call ultimate principles. The issue is couched in terms of justification. A complete justification of some decision to act would include the principles or rules according to which we judge the decision, an account of the act's presumed consequences (or, if the judgment is *post hoc,* an account of the effects we know to have happened, plus an account of those we believe will follow), and a summation of the normal effects of following the principles according to which we act in this case, the latter being in fact a specification of the content of the principles. In the end, as Hare says, we must give a fairly complete description of the way of life which is consistent with the specific decision in this case, for presumably we will always act according to these same principles if we think them justified, or we will act immorally. In fact, we never do give such complete justifications—life is too short. But attempts to do so have been made, and Hare claims that the great religions are such systems of justification, or attempted justification. If we assume that in some case the complete justification *has* been made, however, what would happen if the person asking for the justification still insisted "But why *should* I live like that?" In Hare's opinion, what would happen is simply that we could not answer the question, because we would already have said all that *can* be said. All we could do is say that he had to make up his own mind because this would be a decision of first choices, a choice of principle. But, Hare thinks, this does not make it an arbitrary choice; for, given the hypothesis proposed, the chooser would have at his disposal all the possible information supporting and opposing the possible choices, and if he could not make a decision then, there would be simply nothing more to do.

In a book called *Freedom and Reason*, which appeared after *The Language of Morals* from which most of the facts presented so far have been taken, Hare adds "inclinations" to the list of things needed for a moral justification. The things required for a complete analysis of justification are now what Hare calls the "facts of the case," which include what has just been given, prescriptivity and universalizability, and inclinations. Inclinations come in this second work of Hare's to play a central role in the attempt to relate descriptive to prescriptive meaning, and therefore universalizability to prescriptivity. You will recall that universalizability hinges upon descriptive meaning. It is also the case for Hare that if a moral judgment is not universalizable, then we cannot consistently recommend or commend the course of action which is prescribed by that judgment. It is because of my inclinations that I cannot sincerely assent to particular singular prescriptions, and hence to the universal prescriptions which follow from them when they are conjoined with certain factual statements. To take an example, I am not inclined to be slaughtered, and hence I cannot sincerely assent to the singular prescription "Let me be slaughtered." Now this singular prescription could be implied by any number of factual statements when these were conjoined with any number of universal prescriptions. If Hare is correct the universal prescription "Let the children of Jewish parents be slaughtered," conjoined with the factual statement "I am the child of Jewish parents," implies the singular prescription "Let me be slaughtered." As it happens, I am not the child of Jewish parents, yet I reject both the universal and the singular prescriptions. In order to do this, says Hare, I must put myself in the position of one who does have Jewish parents by being prepared to give equal weight to my own inclinations and those of others, and this is what turns prudential into moral reasoning.

Yet it is clear that in some cases I am *not* prepared to give equal weight to your inclinations when they are in opposition to mine, and

Hare, recognizing this possibility, says that this is possible because we disagree about the facts, or because one of us lacks "imagination," or simply because "their different inclinations make one reject some singular prescription which the other can accept." We are apparently to be spared the disagreeable consequences of such confrontations by a fortunate co-incidence, namely that in most of the "important" matters of life, our inclinations tend to be the same. This is certainly a moot point, and one which seems to beg the question about what is or is not "important." The central issue is the role and importance of inclinations or interests. They are so essential to Hare that if you consider your interests and those of other people secondary to the unholding of an ideal, that is, if you adhere to principles for ideal and non-utilitarian reasons, the "universalized self-interest" at the foundation of his argument will not work. Hare calls such a person a "fanatic."

It is obvious that the concept of "having an ideal" is very important here. To have an ideal for Hare is to "think of some kind of thing as pre-eminently good within some larger class." To have a moral ideal is to believe that a certain man or sort of man is a pre-eminently good sort of man. It might also be to think that some sort of society is a pre-eminently good sort of society. Furthermore, he seems to believe, though he occasionally speaks in ways that indicate the contrary, that to have ideals implies that one has interests. The reason is that if we have ideals, we automatically have an interest in achieving the accomplishment of what the ideals posit. In all of this, we can see that the ultimate golden rule is toleration and the readiness to respect the ideals of others as we do our own.

Without raising the question of whether there are cases of fundamental conflicts of principle in which neither party need be a fanatic, it is possible to criticize Hare at this point by questioning his assertion that prescriptions conjoined with factual statements *entail* other prescriptions. An example of this was given a short time ago:

(1) Let the children of Jewish parents be slaughtered.
(2) I am the child of Jewish parents.
(3) Therefore, let me be slaughtered.

We can note immediately that, for Hare, it is somehow permissible to grant the truth of the second premise, yet reject both prescriptions. The concepts of "rejection" and of "assent" are not clearly related, except in a psychological way, to the concepts of truth and falsity. They therefore have nothing to do with the concept of validity as we understand that concept and as it is described in Part One. But it is informative here to consider the grounds upon which the three statements which compose this "argument" might be rejected. Hare claims that (1) and (3) might be, and normally would be rejected upon the grounds of my inclinations. Two would not be rejectable upon such grounds. My parentage is not a matter which will be altered one whit by my rejection or acceptance of it, and I cannot understand what it means to accept or reject heredity unless it simply means that you like what you are, or do not like it. And, of course, whether you like it or not will also have no effect upon the fact.

Another way to put the point is to say that (2) is to be rejected or accepted upon the grounds of its truth or falsity, while truth or falsity are irrelevant to the acceptance or rejection of the other two statements. Truth and falsity are *very* relevant to the question of validity however. Indeed, as you will recall, an invalid argument by definition is one whose form is such that there is at least one substitution instance of it such that the premises of the substitution instance are true while the conclusion is false. Whether or not these three "statements" even constitute an argument is therefore debatable. If (1) and (3) can be neither true nor false, then certainly, to make the weakest claim possible, they do not constitute an argument of the same *type* as those we have considered thus far. And if they are a different sort of argument, then the concepts of validity, rules of inference, methods of proof and invalidity, and so on, would have to be defined and stipulated in advance before we could say this. Hare certainly does not satisfy these requirements. Just what moral "reasoning" is without the concepts of validity and invalidity is not clear, nor is reasoning without arguments and without criteria for distinguishing good ones from bad ones. We have two such sets of criteria: validity and soundness. Hare, and the other non-cognitivists, seem to have neither. Until they do, it seems very difficult to credit them with having discovered the correct analysis of moral disagreement, proof, and justification. That moral disagreement attempts to prove a position as the correct one and that efforts to justify actions and decisions *do* take place in daily life are both obvious.

Conflicts in "Ways of Life"

Now let us return to the question of conflicts of principle. That there are such conflicts seems unquestioned. And that the participants may be other than fanatical, even though their disagreements be theoretically insoluble, also seems to be at least possible. Assume that we do have a case of two opposed "ways of life" or ideas, that the two opponents do not lack "imagination," and that they agree over the facts but have different inclinations. Further, assume that both ideals cannot be fulfilled but that one of them can be. The problem is now to justify one ideal rather than the other, and it seems that this cannot be done using Hare's theory; because, if he is right, the ultimate ideal is the last good reason we can offer in either position. Let us note that Hare is not alone in this situation. There seems to be no moral theory that can solve this problem. But not all of them fail for the reasons Hare does.

There are two ways we can look at the argument. One is to interpret it as pertaining to the relation between the ideal and saying that something, a new way of life, is good. Here the ideal will be a good reason for saying that the way of life is good, and all the problems we have just discussed will come to bear upon it. On the other hand, we might interpret the argument as pertaining to the relation between properties characterized in the ideal or ultimate good reason, and something's *being* good. But for Hare, to say that something is good cannot be merely to say that it possesses certain properties, for them moral judgments become a sort of descriptive judgment. Intuitionism and naturalism are both this sort of theory, which Hare calls descriptivism, and he rejects both, primarily because they do not account for the commendatory force of moral terms.

We are then in the position that if you ask "Why is that way of life good?" I shall be forced into describing, giving the properties of, the way of life to which I have committed myself. But this will not do, since giving the way of life or its properties and commending them are two quite different things, seemingly unrelated. For the way of life to be commended, for it to be a good reason, it or its properties must be commended *ad infinitum*. The fact that we reach a point in practice where we cannot continue this justificatory procedure has nothing to do with it. The regress is a *logical* result of the theory proposed by Hare.

It can be replied, as Hare would wish, that the question "Why is that way of life good?" (or as Hare puts it, "But why *should* I live like that?") cannot be answered when it is asked in the context of an ultimate ideal. This is so, according to Hare, because *ex hypothesis* everything has been said which could have been said, and he further adds that to refuse to accept this is like refusing to accept a complete description of the universe because no further facts about it can be given. However, if this is the reply, then we must assume that we *know* there is nothing else to be said. The issue now is what the relation is between *this* knowledge (the knowledge that nothing further can be said), and the fact that a way of life is or is not good. "S knows P is true" implies that P is true, and P in this case is "No further reasons can be given in support of this way of life." Suppose S does know P. Just what is it that he knows? Surely it is purely and simply that, for a given way of life, L, once you have said a, b, and c in favor of it, you cannot say any more. The force of the "cannot" here might be logical in the sense that the ideal is not derivable from anything whereas the reasons are derivable from the ideal plus factual assertions, or it might be psychological. If it is a "logical cannot," then our criticisms of Hare's theory and the place of validity in it come into play. But, whether it is a logical or a psychological "cannot," we may still ask one very pertinent question: "What has the fact that no more reasons can be given for L to do with the *goodness* of L?" There seems to be no connection between the two questions.

The initial plausibility of the comparison between our inability to give further reasons for the ideal and our inability to give further facts about the universe once a complete description of it has been given is misleading and depends upon a concealed mistake. In the case of the universe, we assume that we are talking about true descriptions. But in the case of moral justifications we are not talking about factual truths, but about (at least) commendations. In order to justify the comparison between the two, the essential relation between descriptive and prescriptive meaning would have to be explained and defended, and this has not been done.

Even if we assume that one of the ideals does prescribe a truly good way of life, there is still a dilemma; for then the way of life in question must be good whether it is commended or not, since in such a case whichever way of life we choose will be one which is commended by one party and not by the other. Hence, to know that the way of life is good will *not* be to know that it is commended, but to know something else about it, presumably that it has certain properties, or that it meets certain criteria. But this is descriptivism, which Hare rejects.

Yet what happens if we do *not* know which of the two lives is better? In this case, if there is a difference between saying something is good and its being good, as Hare maintains, we seem to be forced into complete ethical skepticism. It might be replied that we are confusing the question of how we *know* that something is good with the question of what it means to say that it *is* good and the reasons for that claim. But that would be true only if the distinction between the reasons for something's being good and the reasons for saying that it is good did not already presuppose that we can and do know that some things are good and others not. It seems clear that the distinction does make this presupposition and that Hare and other moral philosophers accept it. We are forced into ethical skepticism in the case where we do not know which ideal is good for these reasons. Whether we know the properties of an act, person, or thing, or whether we know that the act, person, or thing is condemned, or whether we know both, will not allow us to conclude that the act, person, or thing is good or right, bad or wrong, unless we can explicate the relation between descriptive and prescriptive meaning; and this has not been done. Even if we know the conditions which warrant our *saying* that something is good, this does not, if Hare is right, entitle us to claim that we *know* that the thing *is* good, that is, to claim that the commendation is justified. His attempt to explicate the relation between the grounds for being good (the thing's properties, which are either natural or non-natural) and commending the thing has resulted in an infinite regress, as we have seen. This regress is a logical result of the theory; and, therefore, even if in practice we come to a point where we can in fact no longer continue our justifications, the criticism is not vitiated. An ideal or "way of life" turns out to be nothing more than the last "good" reason which we find we can in practice give. Knowing that some reason, call it L, is the last one we can give does not imply anything about the goodness of the way of life expressed in L. Hence, knowing that L is the last reason we can give does not enable us to decide which of the two ways of life in conflict is good, or even which is the better. If the theory does not enable us to make this decision, it does not enable us to know right from wrong or good from bad, and this is ethical skepticism.

Meaning and Truth as Central Issues

Throughout our discussion of non-cognitivism, it has become evident that Ayer, Stevenson, and Hare all believe that at least two—and in Stevenson's case many more—kinds of meaning are involved in the process of moral "reasoning." They may be called "descriptive" and "prescriptive" meaning in the cases of all three philosophers, though the analysis of the two types varies among them. Stevenson, as you will recall, analyzes meaning in terms of disposition to evoke one or more among a range of emotions, and the meaning of a cognitive term being its disposition to evoke one or more among a range of cognitive responses. Hare thinks that meaning and use are identical. Hence, the meaning "good" is its use to commend. Both the "meaning is use" theory and the dispositional theory of meaning can be criticized. But here the major point about meaning has been the seeming inability of any of the non-cognitivists we have considered to relate these two different *kinds* of meaning, and the penalty for this inability has been a failure in their attempts to base moral *justifications* for the most part upon descriptive meaning while relegating moral judgments themselves to prescriptive or emotive meaning.

This inability to relate descriptive and prescriptive meaning is of course but one facet of the problem of moral reasoning, albeit a crucial one. A related aspect is the question of the truth and falsity of moral judgments. Certainly in the case of the early Ayer, there was a failure to take account of more than one possible theory of truth, and this may also be true of Stevenson and Hare. The problem with the latter philosophers is that their respective theories of meaning make it difficult to provide any theory of truth for moral judgments and their reasons other than one which would center around the criterion of effectiveness. But even so, neither of these men makes any serious attempt to formulate or defend even such a primitive pragmatic theory, even though they deny that moral judgments are either true or false on a correspondence theory. Such sophisticated issues require sophisticated solutions, which have not been completely explicated and defended even now, though attempts have been made. There is some reason to believe that here, as with so many areas of philosophy, a separate science will be needed before the final solution is found. The separate science is linguistics. In any event, it seems fairly clear that the central meta-ethical problems associated with this set of issues are the discovery of adequate theories of meaning and truth.

The Many Views of Moral Judgments

As with political confrontations, in most cases there are no easy answers to our moral disagreements with others, and we cannot presume to be able to solve the central areas of contention here. We have characterized the central issues as those of meaning and truth. There are other problems which may, in fact, be but different ways of stating the meaning–truth issues. We might well say that the bones of contention are half epistemological and half ontological. What do we mean when we say that we *know* an act is right, an action is good, and so forth? Any attempt at an answer usually brings in ontologically relevant factors. Some say that part of all of the answer consists in specifying the *object* of knowledge and that what this is in the case of a moral judgment is a set of natural properties, such as being pleasurable and the like. For others, the properties are non-natural, uniquely moral attributes, perceivable through a special moral sense, or, in the eyes of some philosophers, through the intellect. Mill, Moore, Shaftesbury and Ross have held these or related views. For still others, the question is wrongheaded in the first place, a conceptual confusion, because moral judgments are emotive or at least, neither true nor false, and knowledge claims presuppose truth and falsity.

Hare seems to be on firm ground in his belief that intuitionism, with its fatal privacy, is false, and the same appears to be the case with other forms of descriptivism for the simple but profound reason which G. E. Moore gives: moral judgments and descriptions do not seem to have the same kinds of meanings. Nonetheless, the modern non-cognitivists have been near the mark in their insistence that the problem of deciding what a "relevant similarity" is among moral entities finds its analogue in the problem of descriptive resemblance. That is, there certainly seems to be an analogy between the ways in which we reason about similarities among possible objects of sense perception and the ways in which we justify the application of our moral judgments to numerically different moral acts and persons. In both cases, the respective judgments seem to rest upon our perception of *resemblance* among the relevant entities and their characteristics. To notice this fact and to explain it are two quite different things. The relation between descriptive and prescriptive meaning is not explained by calling terms which have both by a third name, as Hare does with his concept of "evaluative" meaning. *Two* kinds of meaning, not one, are still involved.

If intuitionism is wrong, if Ayer, Stevenson, and Hare are wrong, and if many other forms of descriptivism are wrong, then what *is* the correct analysis? We do not know. But I think we *can* say what this analysis will have to do to be acceptable and what it cannot be at pain of being false. It cannot rest upon an authoritarian basis. That is, ultimate justifications cannot rest simply upon the command of some being to do some act or other, even if this being is God. From claims that some being or other said something, whatever it is, nothing at all follows about whether we ought to do what that being prescribes. Many men, and, if we are to believe antiquity, gods, prescribed courses of action for other men (and gods) which were wrong. Secondly, if ethics is to be anything other than opinion, the final analysis will have to provide some *ontological* grounding for moral justification. If redness were not a fact, independent of the perception of it by some perceiver, then two things could not be red. Similarly, if two acts were not right, or wrong, as the case may be, independently of the perceivers of them, then rightness and wrongness, goodness and badness, at least in the moral sense of the latter terms, would remain a matter of opinion—a conclusion which, though in no way impossible, seems unacceptable at the present time. We say that it is in no way impossible because it is not a logical contradiction to assert it; and, if an analysis of moral judgments were given which met the tests with which we are familiar for adequate theories, we should have to accept it. A. J. Ayer, for one, thought at one time that his theory had met these tests and that ethics as an independent discipline did not exist. But the criticisms of Ayer, Stevenson, and Hare seem sufficient to show that the game is not yet up.

Aside from rejecting authoritarian theories, and assuming some ontological ground for moral judgments if ethics is more than opinion, there must also be in any adequate meta-ethical theory a mechanism for relating factual and evaluative claims. All the men we have studied have realized this fact. There seem to be only two alternatives open to the solution of the problem. Either there are publicly knowable "value facts" which have some qualitative distinction differentiating them from normal facts (and hence differentiating their descriptions from normal descriptions), or a new deontic or value logic enabling us to leap Hume's Hurdle is required. Both alternatives have been extensively investigated, the former much more so than the latter. The "value facts" hypothesis seems doubtful for obvious empirical reasons. If we cannot relate descriptive and prescriptive meaning, then the reconciliation of opposing evaluations seems impossible, Austinian analysis notwithstanding. It therefore seems that either ethics is impossible, or there is a value-logic which will cross the gap. In the light of such recent work as that of Hintikka, Castenada, and Von Wright,[8] there seems reason to hope that such a logic will be forthcoming.[9]

EXERCISES

1. Distinguish between the thesis of ethical relativity and the thesis of ethical relativism.

2. Think of three proverbs which express the common conviction that ethical relativism is true.

3. Why is the question of whether the same action occurs in different cultures important for the evaluation of ethical relativism? Why is the question of whether it is possible to define an action independently of reference to motives and consequences important for the evaluation of this theory?

4. Suppose that moral judgments are either true or false. What logical kind of judgment is "Murder is wrong"? Why? Is it an evaluation? Why or why not?

5. Are the ten commandments moral judgments? Why or why not? Are they either true or false? Defend your answer in the light of theories of truth discussed in this book.

6. Formulate and evaluate the arguments in favor of ethical relativism.

7. Formulate and evaluate the arguments against ethical relativism.

8. How might the factualistic fallacy be used against the ethical relativist?

9. Compose an argument analogous to the kind used by the ethical relativist, but which does not concern ethics, and evaluate it. Of what evaluative technique is the result an instance?

10. Do you agree that ethical relativism has been disproven in the text? Defend your answer.

11. What does it mean to say that an action is "unnatural"?

12. If an action is unnatural, does it follow that it is wrong? Why or why not?

---

[8] The following are of interest in connection with deontic logic, though they are difficult: H. N. Castaneda, "Imperatives, Oughts and Moral Oughts," *The Australasian Journal of Philosophy*, 44 (1960), pp. 277–300 and G. H. von Wright, *Norm and Action* (London: Routledge & Kegan Paul, Ltd., 1963).

[9] I wish to thank Professor Gilbert Ryle for permission to use in this chapter segments of my article "Hare's Failure to Define Good Reasons," *Mind*, vol. LXXXIX, n. s. no. 314 (April, 1970).

13. Discuss Mill's analysis of what "natural" or "nature" can mean.

14. Why would Aquinas say that a law of nature is a tautology? That is, given that laws of nature are self-evident, why does he choose this sense of "self-evident" rather than the other which he mentions? He also thinks that these ethical principles are instilled in the mind of man by God. Is this a possible meaning of "self-evident"? Why or why not?

15. Does the fact that men have natural inclinations to do some things and not others have any logical bearing upon whether these inclinations are right or wrong? Why or why not?

16. How is the factualistic fallacy possibly related to the natural moral law theory?

17. Why is it true that moral rules cannot be definitions?

18. Why is it true that moral rules cannot be descriptions?

19. If we interpret the natural law theory as enjoining us to obey natural laws, why is this not a help to us in guiding our moral conduct?

20. How does the "open-question" argument apply to the theory? Do you think that this is a good criticism? Why or why not?

21. What is the central belief of all non-cognitivists?

22. Why is the proliferation of kinds of meanings for moral judgments a difficulty for Stevenson's theory?

23. Can a moral judgment have both cognitive and emotive meaning for Stevenson? *Must* it have both, if he is right? Why or why not?

24. Need the intention of the user of a sign and the dispositional reaction of the hearer of it have any connection if the dispositional theory of meaning is correct? Why or why not?

25. Is the criticism of Ayer and Stevenson which says that they have concentrated without justification on a single theory of truth justified? Why or why not?

26. Discuss the problem of justification in ethics from the non-cognitivistic view-point, attempting to defend them. Your answer should be about three pages long.

27. Discuss the problem of justification from the viewpoint of the critic of the non-cognitivist. Your answer should be about three pages long.

28. What is "blind emotive meaning" if Brandt is right?

29. Discuss Hare's analysis of moral reasoning. In your answer be sure to define universalizability and descriptive meaning and specify whatever relations there are between them. Evaluate his arguments using the criteria developed in this book. Evaluate the arguments used against Hare in the same way.

30. Compare Stevenson and Hare on the subject of the relations between descriptive and emotive (or commendatory) meaning. Who has the better case? Why?

8

Political Philosophy

MORAL AND LEGAL JUSTICE

Among the burning issues of our time is a very ancient and much debated problem which becomes prominent again and again in times of reformation, revolution, and important social change. This issue, though simply stated, is extremely complex and has never been solved. It is this: What is the relation between the juridical law of a society and the moral law? Is legal justice also moral justice? Is an infraction of the legal law also a moral infraction? And conversely, are all moral infractions also legal ones, or ought they to be? Is it possible to disobey a law justly? Both sides of the question have been vigorously supported by various philosophers, statesmen, politicians, and legal authorities in modern times, and they were debated with equal intensity by Plato, Socrates, and Aristotle. Throughout this chapter disagreements over this subject will become evident again and again. No actual solutions to the questions involved will be found here, but a definite position will be taken for one side of the question over the other. The position that seems correct is that legality and morality are *not* coextensive and that, hence, the morally correct disobedience of legal laws is possible and, indeed, morally obligatory in certain contexts. Yet we do not want to argue that the distinction is clear cut for in some cases legal laws and moral laws seem to overlap in content, though the sanctions attached to them and their forms differ.

The first thing to realize is the genuine complexity of the problem, and one way to become aware of it is to learn a little about just what law is, and about the justifications which have been offered in support of various kinds of law and specific statutes. This is not as simple to discover as it might sound. For one thing, since each of the 50 states in the union has its own statutes and common law, there are 50 different

276

legal jurisdictions in the country and significant differences among the various states. Of course, the federal government also has a system of law, and the area of applicability of those laws is defined by the Constitution, though the scope of the area increases and decreases both as the Supreme Court interprets the articles of the Constitution and by Congressional action. Each of the 50 states has two kinds of law, common and statute. The federal government has only statute law. Statute law is the body of laws which are enacted by a legislature. Common law consists in the history or precedents of decisions in particular cases. The basic classification of common law rests not upon the decisions *per se,* but upon the kinds of cases that have been considered. In England until fairly recently all law was common law, even criminal law. In America, criminal law is statutory, whereas contract law and tort law are usually a part of the common law.

The fact that statute law is all "on the books," so to speak, might make one believe that it is easier to understand, or at least easier to define, then common law. But this is not always the case. If one counts the Constitution itself as statute law, then at least some such law is notoriously obscure and difficult. Contradictory rulings about the interpretation of given articles in it are frequent in the history of the country, and with the passage of time and the advent of a new technology there are constant attempts to extend the meaning of its provisions to cover situations which its authors could not possibly have envisioned. By the Constitution, Congress is empowered to regulate interstate commerce, but the Constitution does not define interstate commerce. Nor does it define freedom of speech, nor guarantee justice to anyone, let alone define what justice is. It presumably prohibits involuntary servitude, but does not say whether the military draft constitutes such servitude; and, since it does not define what a human being is, venal men have argued that it does not prohibit the owning of black slaves. It is obvious that we ought not to blame the men who wrote the document for this state of affairs, for no group of men can foresee the future with sufficient accuracy to predict all the peculiar situations which will arise requiring novel applications of old laws and the judicious ignoring of others. It is still against the law to cross water on Sunday in at least one state in the union, but the builders of roads and railways were happily not impeded in their progress because of this. Who could have foreseen, when the law forbidding the transportation of a stolen vehicle across state lines was passed, the invention of the airplane? The invention of this infernal machine required a decision about whether airplanes were in the class of vehicles. The decision? They are not!

Because of the need for constant interpretations of the law, which interpretations constitute a body of precedents in any given jurisdiction, it is not possible to distinguish between statute and common law upon the grounds that one of them is comprised of the body of precedents while the other is not. The difference lies solely in their origin, given that by making decisions, courts make law. The origin of statute law is an act of a legislative body, whereas common law arises by the act of courts dealing with similar cases about the same issues through the course of time.

Most American law was explicitly adopted from the common law of England, and it has been said that the exportation of English common law is the greatest contribution to civilization which that wondrous island and its people have made. Common law obviously began at some point in time, and it follows that there are thousands of decisions for which there were at the time no precedents. In such cases, one often finds as a justification for the decision given the phrase "the memory of man runneth not to the contrary." This is a way of saying that the decision is in accordance with the customs and habits of the people, as these can be remembered. The dilemma involved in distinguishing between moral and legal justification is forced upon us at once here. The fact that some course of action or some deed is inconsistent with the customs of a country does not *a fortiori* make it wrong as we know from our examination of ethical relativism and from our considerations of natural moral law. Yet here again this problem confronts us. If one argues that from a characterization of the customs of a people and a statement asserting that an action is inconsistent with such customs, it follows that the action is wrong, one is guilty of the factualistic fallacy. Even if the makers of common law believed that the law and morality were the same, or that one was derivative from the other, or that morality was derivative from the customs of a people alone, we can safely say that this is a mistake without further specification. That is, we may safely say that such a justification of the claim that ethics is the foundation of the law, or the law the foundation of ethics, is insufficient.

Roman and Greek Law

These last few remarks concern only very old law. A more systematic attempt to relate law and morality develops when we come to the time of the Romans and the famous *Jus Gentium,* or the law of the people. The *Jus Gentium* was exactly what the name implies. It included the customs common to all of the diverse realms and races which were a part of the Roman Empire, no matter what their particular differences. At the same time, the concept of the *Jus Naturale* or the natural law was known and accepted, especially in the time of Imperial Rome. It is even to be found in the writings of Cicero about Greek jurisprudence. The ties between the two systems, the one primarily concerned with legality, the other with moral right, came with the realization that universality was the property common to both. That is, the *Jus Gentium* was discovered by noticing that it was common to all peoples, and the natural law was defined in terms of its application in virtue of that universal characteristic of human beings, rationality. The natural law comprised the set of principles of conduct affirmed by right reason. In the second century after Christ the great Roman jurist Gaius identified the two laws. It was the perfect melding of Greek conceptualization and Roman practicality, and it has served as the foundation of western law almost until the present day. What we now know as law is the offspring of this twin concept, the union of Greek natural law and the Roman *Jus Gentium*. It should also be noted that many common law decisions stem from times when legal and ecclesiastical law were either identical or overlapping. Indeed, in later eras such as the so-called "Dark Ages," a theologically based natural-law justification for the temporal power of the Church in the making and execution of the law was offered. But because of the difficulties in distinguishing ecclesiastical law from moral law in many cases, we shall concentrate here upon the latter rather than the former.

The law in practice is what is applied in individual cases to resolve conflict. Its validation is found in the natural law, which is discovered by man through the exercise of his reason. If the natural law is an ethical law, as in the Greek mind it was, then the validation of legality is the moral law. Morality or the moral life, for the Greeks, was the life of the rational man; that is what they *meant* by being moral. That law discovered through the exercise of reason as the essence of rationality is hence the code for living a moral life. If to act legally is to act according to the natural law, it is *a fortiori* to act morally, and if this is true, then morality and legality are identical.

The Greeks were not all monotheistic, and even the ones who were did not often argue that the natural law itself was justified in virtue of the wishes, properties, or commands of a god. In fact, the problem of justifying natural law itself was no more a problem for the Greeks than was the problem of justifying axioms a problem for Euclid. Axioms, whether geometrical or ethical, are discovered; they are what they are and that is that. To ask why what is *is* simply confuses a perfectly clear issue, unless we are asking for the causes of what is. And, of course, to discover the cause of something is not to justify it but to explain it. Justification and explanation, as Socrates teaches, are not the same thing.

With the rise of Christianity, especially in the Middle Ages, a new dimension was added to the Greco-Roman concept of legal-natural law. The law was deemed to come from God, not man, and this fact alone was taken to be a self-evident justification of it. Morality became the prerogative of the divine being in the sense that it was constituted by what he willed. When men discovered what the right rules of conduct were, they were discovering the will of God as it is expressed in the laws of nature and of rationality, which are not two sets of laws but different modes of the same expression. The contribution of Christianity, in the eyes of the medieval theologian-philosophers, was the discovery *that* law was the expression of God's will. Disobedience to civil law became for a time almost tantamount to disobedience of God's law. This doctrine was to have long-lasting and pernicious effects, causing much suffering to millions.

In practice, however, there was little effect from the philosophical and theological debate in the arena of the practicing lawyers until the times of the Inquisition and James I of England. What transpired in the Inquisition had little effect upon our own systems, but the English confrontation did. When the Roman Church began to be surpressed in England, the source of justification for the law did become a serious social and political issue. James I argued in favor of the theory that came to be known as the "Divine Right of Kings." This held that kings were subject to no one but God and their own consciences, which implies that the sovereign is not subject in his person to the law of the land since, as God's appointed agent, he is the source of this law and may change it by *fiat*. Thomas Hobbes offered formidable support for this view in his *Leviathan*, in which he argued, among other things, that a commonwealth originates through the willing surrender of individual rights to a sovereign in return for the protection of certain basic safeties. Hobbes's theory is discussed in detail in the latter part of this chapter.

English Common Law

There was great opposition to James's theory. Part of the basis for the opposition was the doctrine of natural law itself. If that theory is correct, given the additions to it in the Middle Ages, then law emanates directly from God and applies to all his subjects without exception, including kings. Sir Edward Coke argued against James I that just *because* the law, which includes the common law, has its source and its justification in God, James was subject to God, his conscience, *and the law*. Astonishingly, Coke won the fight, and the Divine Right of Kings theory died in England, though kings still remained very powerful. The natural law theory used to overcome James in effect identified the common law of England as a part of the natural law. The words "part of" are important, because no pretext is being made that all matters of relevance to the natural law are also such that judicial decisions have been made about them. The relation between common law and natural law is therefore that of part to whole, and not one of identity.

We observed before that the common law of England has often been claimed as that country's most important contribution to our civilization. It was in fact literally exported from England by traveling Englishmen in the belief that they carried with them as their birthright their heritage of law.

English common law was carried to the United States by early settlers as their birthright. Not only the common law itself, but its justification in terms of the natural law of which it was presumed to be a part, was brought in with the settling of the New World.

Natural and Judicial Law

Yet there was even then an important difference in the formulation of natural and judicial law. This difference consisted in the fact that the sanction, the penalty for violating the law, was formulated in the legal version of the law but not in the natural law itself. We discover that we ought to act in certain ways if we act rationally, but we do not discover that we shall be punished if we do not act in these ways, or so it was thought. We might state the formulation of a legal rule according to the philosophical natural law theory as follows: If a man violates the natural law L, then sanctions X, Y, Z will be imposed. The sanctions are not a part of the law L; they are imposed by *man* upon other men who do not act in accordance with L. And a knowledge of L is presupposed by the formulation of the legal rule containing it. Nonetheless, given the presupposition that L is justified by its source, God, then the legal rule rests upon a moral foundation. This is also true even if it is thought that L requires no justification beyond its rationality, as was the case with the Greeks and the Romans.

What does a judge do with such a rule? Obviously, he applies it. To do this, he must know two things: (1) what L is, and (2) whether the act under examination falls into the class of acts which are a violation of L. Suppose that L is the prohibition against wrongful killing of another human. The law cannot be enforced unless the judge knows this, and also knows that there is reason to believe that the act now being considered is an instance of the wrongful killing of a human. The purpose of trials is just that: to determine whether or not the act *is* such an instance. It is because of these reasons that the primary role of an American judge under the system of natural legal law was the *discovery* of just what the natural law is, and the primary role of the jury was to decide whether or not the individual cases were instances of violations.

A very neat distinction between natural and artificial legal laws was also drawn. It is perfectly illustrated by the role of duress as an excuse in the cases of treason and murder. For most crimes, including treason, duress is an excusing defense. It is not usually a defense against the murder of an innocent person, however. The reason is that the killing of an innocent person is deemed to be an offense against a natural law of God, whereas the law against treason is artificial, invented by the state for its own protection, and hence is not a universal law. You may recall that a necessary condition for anything's being a natural law is universality. The eminent jurist, Blackstone, who believed in the natural law theory of legal law, summarizes this when he says:

Duress is a defense to positive crimes so created by the laws of society, and which therefore society may excuse; but not as to natural offenses so declared by the law of God, wherein human magistrates are only the executioners of divine punishment.[1]

Notice in the quotation how it is presupposed that the magistrate knows what natural offenses have been declared by God. Notice also the first crack in the wall of the natural legal law theory: it is the distinction between artificial laws, defined here as offenses "so created by the laws of society, and which therefore society may excuse," and the natural moral laws of God. The vast majority of our statute offenses are precisely laws which have been created by society for its own protection and which, according to Blackstone, we may therefore excuse. If the natural law and the moral law are identical, and if the ethical justification for juridical law is its identity with the natural law, then it follows that most of our law is in fact not justifiable on this ethical basis. From being a part of the natural law, much of our codified law has now passed outside that class and stands on its own as the creation of society and nothing else.

The Dred Scott Case

It has been noted that under the natural legal law theory, the central role of the judge was to *discover* the law of nature. How does one go about this? Natural law, as you should remember, is rational; that is its very essence. Hence, the judge should be able to discover it through the use of his reason, given that what is discovered through reason is what is rational. Clearly all but the most abhorrent egotists have doubts about their own rationality upon occasion. The obvious course of action in such an event is to ask other rational agents what their opinion is. If they all agree with him, he can be as certain as we can possibly be that

[1] Sir William Blackstone, *Commentaries* (Philadelphia: W. Y. Birch & Abraham Small, 1803), Book IV, chapter 2.

his decision is correct. This sounds all very well, but it ignores an important fact about men—they can all be wrong at the same time. An inglorious and terrible example of exactly this is to be found in the records of the still infamous Dred Scott slavery case of *antebellum* days. Scott was a slave who escaped from his "owner," and came to roost in the north. His master brought suit to have the wretched man returned to him, since, under the law, slaves were property. Roger B. Taney was the Chief Justice of the United States at that time, and the natural legal law theory, with the already mentioned belief about the role of the judge, was current. Here is what Taney said in explanation and in attempted justification of his decision:

Negroes had for more than a century before been regarded as beings of an inferior order, and altogether unfit to associate with the white race, either in social or political relations; and so far inferior that they had no rights which the white man was bound to respect; and that the negro might justly and lawfully be reduced to slavery for the white man's benefit. He was bought and sold, and treated as an ordinary article of merchandise and traffic, whenever a profit could be made by it. It was regarded as an axiom of morals as well as politics which no one thought of disputing or supposed to be open to dispute; and men in every grade and position in society daily and habitually acted upon it in their private pursuits, and as well in matters of public concern without doubting for a moment the correctness of this opinion. The opinion thus entertained was naturally impressed upon the colonies. And accordingly a negro of the African race was regarded by them as an article of property, and held and bought and sold as such, in every one of the thirteen colonies which united in the Declaration of Independence and afterwards formed the Constitution of the United States.

In this series of remarks, we might note (1) the appeal to custom and historical opinion, (2) the fact that Taney is supporting his own interpretation of the natural law by reference to this custom, (3) the reference to the fact that the opinion was held not only to be a natural law but a natural moral law, and (4) the unstated implication that the men who held these opinions were reasonable.

The question immediately arises as to how one could argue against such an interpretation of the natural law. There are several ways. The most obvious is to argue that the judge in the case was mistaken when he thought he had discovered a natural law. In this case, for example, we could argue that the inferiority of negroes could not be some sort of natural law by showing that the traits commonly exhibited by them at this time were not due to heredity but to environmental circumstances such as the very slavery in which they were being held. After all, nothing in the natural moral law nor its legal counterpart guarantees that a legal judge or a moral judge cannot make a mistake in his findings. Furthermore, in the Scott case, it might have been argued that the judge's appeal to all reasonable men was in fact not such an appeal, because it did not take into account the large and growing number of abolitionists who denied exactly what Taney affirmed. Third, one could disprove the law by finding many counter-examples in the form of educated, literate, intelligent blacks who were clearly superior to many whites. Fourth, though it would not have held much water at the time, one could have shown that from the fact that certain opinions were held and had been held about white superiority, nothing at all is logically implied about the justification for slavery, and, in general, that from purely factual premises, normative judgments do not follow. The latter move is a modern one of course, and constitutes an attack on the theory itself and not just particular decisions rendered under it, as do the first three objections.

Decline of The Natural Law Theory

The natural moral and legal law theory came to be the last bastion of those who defended slavery. It remains their last bastion, for there are people who still advocate both the theory and slavery of one sort or another. In England, it was Coke *versus* James I that was the beginning of the end; here it was the Dred Scott case. Our jurists came to realize that the natural law theory provided a convenient cover to those judges who wished to justify the enshrinement of their personal prejudices under the guise of having "discovered" a natural law. It enabled them to do this because the natural law, in spite of all that was claimed for it, provided no standards for making legal decisions; rather, it left particular decisions to particular judges and their individual tastes, convictions, and allegiances. But although the Scott case opened the crack in the dike here, the first *major* defeat for the theory came in England with the rise of the utilitarian reform movement there.

It is difficult for us now to realize the cruel and oppressive use of the law in the eighteenth century and before. This was especially true of the criminal law in England. Most of us are familiar with the fact that children were publicly hanged for minor offenses such as picking pockets; and, prior to the implementation of Howard's prison reforms, starvation, incredible filth, bribery, and corruption were all the rule rather than the exception in English prisons. If we knew nothing more, this would certainly be enough to raise the hackles on any man of minimal sensitivity. Finally, things became so obviously pernicious that a movement for change arose, illustrated by the refusal of public juries to convict defendants. The novelist Charles Dickens and the philosopher Jeremy Bentham were perhaps more responsible than any others for reforming the criminal law in England. Dickens's novels, as any schoolboy knows, are full of the social misery of the lower classes in England, and are contemptuous of the law and the hypocritical snobbery at the bottom of the establishment's acceptance of the "natural order" which resulted in the execution and torture of innocents. But, for our purposes, Bentham is the more important of the two men, because he attacked natural law theory at the very foundation of the attitudes of which we are speaking.

Bentham and Utilitarianism

Bentham said "Natural right is simple nonsense: natural and imprescriptible rights, rhetorical nonsense . . . nonsense upon stilts." In place of the natural law theory, Bentham offered utilitarianism. An act is right if it produces more pleasure than pain. If an act, or a kind of act, meets this criterion of rightness, then it should not be outlawed. If it produces more pain than pleasure, then it should be outlawed. It is not quite as simple as this, of course, for various utilitarians concentrate upon the individual act itself, others upon the general practice, and still others on the rules governing practices. Problems about what exactly will count as pleasure and what as pain, how consequences are foreseeable in the long run, and how to measure the pleasure or pain resulting from an act also arise; and most philosophers would be convinced that at least Bentham's version of utilitarianism is not sound. That, however, is not the point here. The point is that Bentham introduced a theory which allowed for both natural and social change and, at the same time, presumed to furnish an ethical basis for the law which was not (at least directly) founded upon the divine dictum. Other theories were to argue, and had already argued, that utilitarianism was itself dependent upon a version of natural law, but if this is true, then it certainly is a different sort of natural law than that assumed prior to Bentham.

If the principle of utility, the pleasure–pain principle in Bentham's version of utilitarianism, is the touchstone against which we may decide and ought to decide what actions the law should prohibit and encourage, it is also the criterion for deciding what means ought to be used to enforce the law. The theory of punishment espoused by the utilitarians is widespread even today. For violation of a law, painful consequences or sanctions ought to be imposed, since the criminal is the man who causes more pain than pleasure to society. Punishment has two purposes: to deter the criminal from committing further acts of crime by making it more painful than pleasurable to do so, and, by making him an example to deter others from committing crimes in the first place. This is the deterrence theory of punishment current here now. An adequate refutation of this theory would be constituted by showing that sanctions did not deter agents, or certain sorts of agents, from committing the same acts again, and that punishment to one agent did not deter others from committing the same crime. This is the form taken by present attacks on this view. It is also interesting to note that if there are acts which are immoral but not deterrable by punishment, then they could not be prohibited in a utilitarian theory of law because that theory requires the inclusion of deterring sanctions for breaking the law. Moreover, we ought to note that in the utilitarian theory, if that which causes pleasure in one society is different from that which causes it in another society, then ethical and legal values become relative to those societies, and this view has been shown to be mistaken in the section discussing ethical relativism.

On the other hand, the question of whether or not the law can punish an act is a non-ethical question. It is a matter for factual investigation. Can the law in practice be enforced? To this extent, the utilitarian legal theory is non-ethical. That is, the utilitarian theory can be looked upon as being applicable to rules rather than to individual cases. When applied to individual cases in the realm of ethics, the theory enables us to decide whether or not a given act is right or wrong in terms of its productivity of pleasure or pain. This alone does not involve the positing of sanctions in the light of the moral value of the action. When we speak of the utilitarian evaluation of *rules,* at least legal rules, we are talking about a different matter; we are trying to judge the effectiveness of a law, and the utilitarian conclusion about this is a function of the enforcement possibilities for the law. It is in this way that only those duties to which enforceable sanctions can in practice be attached are expressible in a utilitarian system for legal rules, and the deterrence theory of punishment is to this extent non-ethical. And, it still follows that the utilitarian will have to permit immoral acts under his legal system if he cannot enforce the rules which prohibit such acts.

This inadequacy in utilitarian theories of punishment is recognized in fact as well as in speculative writing about the topic. And it is important to note that this very recognition is an implicit admission that moral and legal right differ. An outstanding case is Regina *versus* Dudley and Stevens. Messrs. Dudley and Stevens were sailors who were shipwrecked on a raft with the cabin boy from their ship. They had little food, and as time went by and it ran out altogether, starvation seemed imminent. In this situation, the sailors killed the cabin boy, and ate him. After their rescue, the facts came out and they were brought to trial for murder. The verdict was guilty and they were sentenced to death. But it was recognized that what they did was certainly not deterrable by any legal sanctions, because in effect, as one wit noted, the law in such a case would be arguing that a man must die now in order not to die a little later. As a result, the sentence was commuted to six months in jail.

Another example, which was later enshrined in a motion picture, concerned the case of the United States *versus* Holmes. Again it was a case of shipwreck, although this time nobody was eaten. There were too many people in the lifeboat, and it was in danger of capsizing. The first mate told Holmes, a sailor on the ship, to start throwing people overboard, beginning with single men, and proceeding as necessary to married men, women, and children. The survivors were reluctant to agree to this idea, and struggles ensued; apparently two women were thrown overboard. It was implied that this occurred because they were causing trouble, not because the space was needed at that point. The jury refused to indict Holmes for murder but tried him on the lesser charge of manslaughter and gave him six months imprisonment together with a fine. The fine was later remitted.

The same recognition of the limitations of sanctions for deterrence is recognized in the statutes of many states concerning homicide. Although duress is not *usually* a defense against murder, it *is* in New York, for the same reasons given in the shipwreck–cannibalism case. The same sentiments are expressed in the so-called "back to the wall" theory, which says that killing is only permissible if the agent has no choice other than to kill or be killed.

The criticism of the utilitarian view has reached a fever pitch in our times. One of the favorite targets is New York's M'Naughton rule, which states that insanity is a defense against murder only if the agent did not know at the time of his crime the difference between right and wrong. This in itself is vague enough, and it is surprising that no defense has been based upon the claim that the law is ambiguous over the definitions of "right" and "wrong." Even allowing this, however, psychology tells us that a man may know the difference between right and wrong and still be unable to prevent himself from committing the crime. That is, psychology tells us that responsibility does not hinge upon a knowledge of legal or moral values. If this is true, then knowledge of right and wrong does not deter and the M'Naughton rule is irrelevant in such cases because it rests upon a false assumption. Exactly the same criticism is used against capital punishment, namely that it does not in fact deter, and that knowledge of its application will not prevent other agents from murdering. There are other criticisms of this institution, of course, of which one of the most prominent is that it is only applied in practice to the poor and underprivileged.

It appears then that the first great setback for the natural law theory came with utilitarianism, and in particular with the deterrence theory of punishment. This involved the separation of legal and moral justification, because the justification for a legal rule became its enforceability and practicality, which are non-ethical criteria. The application of utilitarianism in morally relevant contexts does not require the specification of sanctions and conditions for their viability, whereas in legal contexts it seems to do just this.

Further Decline of the Natural Law Theory

The second great attack against the natural law theory came in the United States and was based in economic issues rather than in political or ethical ones, though in any such claim one must recognize that in some areas it is impossible to separate the three sorts of cause.

The American ideal as conceived by the forefathers of the country was firmly based upon the "natural rights" view of man and his governments. Jefferson thought and said that government was justified only to the extent that it enabled the citizens of a country to act in accordance with their natural rights. Just what these "natural rights" were was not quite clear, though it was generally agreed that life, liberty, and the pursuit of happiness, freedom of speech and worship, and other similar rights, were among them. But hand in hand with this view went the fatalistic acceptance of poverty, disease, and suffering, which rapidly developed into the complacent idea that one always has the poor with one and that there are classes of people who are "naturally" less well off than other classes because of characteristics usually thought to be related to their race, creed, or national origin, though occasionally extended to properties such as one's voting preferences. For very many decades, the peoples of this country continued in these convictions without undue agitation resulting from the personal tragedies which often resulted.

Personal tragedy and national calamity, however, differ only in numbers, and the Great Depression of 1929 translated the one into the other. The depression was of course first and foremost an economic occurrence, though its roots lay in political and psychological soil. As an economic phenomenon, the most obvious effect it had upon the law in this country concerned the concept of the contract. It would be difficult to think of a more sacrosanct institution in the history of the United States political-legal-economic culture than the contract and the laws and traditions which surround it. Here was one case such that the legal and moral obligations *surely* were identical, for in becoming a party to a contract, one was clearly making a witnessed promise verified under the law. If it was wrong to lie or to break a promise, then it was wrong to break a contract, for it is merely a species of promise. Now the depression immediately effected changes in the laws governing contracts which cannot be justified if the natural law theory is correct. An outstanding example was the Minnesota Mortgage Moratorium Act, which was passed into law by the legislature of Minnesota during this time. Under the terms of this statute, courts were empowered to permit mortgagees to take more time to pay the mortgage than was allowed in the contract as originally drawn. The purpose, of course, was to prevent banks from foreclosing upon mortgages which were not being kept up in the general financial pinch of the times. The justification offered was that the contractual obligation was left intact, while the enforcement of it was changed to allow more time for fulfilling the obligation. It certainly was a popular decision, since most of the farmers in the state held contracts with their banks, and very few of them had enough money to continue their payments. Since the cost of producting farm goods was higher than the prices the farmer could get for his produce, it was inevitable that foreclosures would ruin the farmer throughout the land.

The Supreme Court of the United States upheld the constitutionality of the Minnesota Mortgage Moratorium Act—by a vote of 5 to 4! The four votes in opposition argued that the natural right of contract, since it *was* a natural right, could not be altered by man, given that it was derived from the very nature of man himself, which is an expression of the will of God. The majority, however, apparently felt that mortgage laws are created by man for his financial benefit.

The same view prevailed when the United States left the gold standard. At that time, there were about 100 billions of currency which could legally be exchanged for gold from the Treasure, and there were only about 4 billions of bullion in the Treasury to cover these obligations. The expedient was the passage of a law enabling the fulfillment of the obligation by payment in the normal currency of the country, and the suspension of gold payments. The Supreme Court again voted 5 to 4 to uphold the decision, the dissenters again holding the sanctity of contractual obligations.

As with contractual obligations, the right to hold and protect private property has always been deemed sacred in the United States, and again it was justified upon the grounds of natural right. With the rise of organized labor in this country, the right to protect private property became a defense for strikebreaking and the issuing of injunctions against strikes. Temporary injunctions were usually followed by permanent ones, in some cases so generally worded that they could be applied to almost any anti-management activity. But in these cases the problem of enforceability became acute. No one could force the hundreds of thousands of John L. Lewis's men to work when they did not want to do so, and the same was true of the strikes in the railroad industry. Eventually, unenforceability won over the natural law theory.

The really big mistake of the natural law theorists was not so much in the basic principles of the theory itself—though for strictly philosophical purposes these are suspect as well—but in their insistence that these

principles were absolutely fixed and unchangeable. They thought that
the natural right to hold and protect private property, given that it was a
natural right in 1300, was still a right in 1920 and had not changed. If
particular circumstances seemed to make exceptions to the rule incumbent,
that was just too bad. "This too will pass away" was the prevailing reply.
The ultimate answer of judges and legislators sensitive to the problem of
enforceability as well as to the opinions of their constituents was simply
a refusal to enforce natural rights. Often the law was revised to account
for changes in social conditions. "Yellow dog" contracts required as a
condition of employment that the employee agree not to join a union,
and labor union organizers often found themselves subject to injunctions
that forbade their activities on the grounds that they were inducing another to break his contractual obligation. The Supreme Court argued
that such injunctions were an impediment to the freedom to make contracts, and the Norris-LaGuardia Act ultimately solved the problem by
depriving courts of the power of injunction for enforcing yellow dog contracts while reaffirming the right to freedom of contract. As a result of
such decisions, themselves arising from changing social and economic
conditions involving the majority of the populace, the natural law theory
as a legal theory slowly died. In ethics and theology it survives in some
circles.

Recent Trends

In its place is the view called "legal realism," which in its theoretical
applications is not much better, but is at least flexible. Another name for
this theory is "legal positivism," and its major tenet is that the power of
the law derives immediately from the sovereign power and its ability to
enforce the law. Ethical considerations are not relevant in such a
schema, or to put it another way, "right" in its legal context simply means
what is enforceable under the law and nothing else. This is understandable from the viewpoint of a rejection of and reaction against the natural
legal law theory, but it clearly has serious defects as a theory. If it were
correct, then Mr. Justice Holmes would have been correct when he
argued that a law is justified if and only if it conforms to the customs
and beliefs of society, which he believed to be a matter, not of ethics,
but of anthropology and sociology. Motivation for adherence to the rule
of law becomes reduced to egotistic self-interest, that is, it becomes a
matter of whether the individual wants to break a law badly enough to
put up with the penalty for doing so. The view is found in the current
willingness to break contracts, and other laws, given that the penalties
are bearable. "Ought" becomes a redundant term in the formulation of
the law if this theory is correct, because, in effect, all that the law states

is a prediction devoid of normative content. It becomes a statement of the form "If events *a, b, c* occur, then official action *X, Y, Z* will follow." No question of *meriting* sanctions in virtue of the nature of the deed is raised, no moral suasion is exercised. The only pertinent questions are whether or not the agent wants to do *a* enough to put up with *X*, and whether the state has the power necessary to impose *X*, given *a*. This is the position of Thrasymachus in Plato's *Republic*. If it is a sound position, then either there is no morality, or morality and legality are identical, or they are *completely* separate. This confusing statement will be clarified in a moment.

Today, the Supreme Court of the United States seems to be changing the course from this theory to a new approach. It is a course characterized by moral sensitivity rather than by strict constitutional interpretation. To this extent, the critics of the court are correct when they argue that the justices have done more than they are constitutionally required, and perhaps empowered, to do. The Warren Court tended to treat arguments before them according to the "rule of the case" method, which is really no rule at all, meaning in practice that if it can be shown that a lower court has rendered a verdict resulting in an injustice, they will agree to rule upon it. And the ultimate ruling will usually be in favor of what the justices believe to be justice even if precedent is opposed to their decision. The rub, of course, comes when we are asked what justice is. The court does not operate according to some standard moral theory; rather, each of these men has his private views of what constitutes right and wrong action, and they act according to their individual convictions. Some of these convictions must seem atrocious to adherents of the natural law theory of legality and morality. Mr. Justice Black, for example, has argued that since corporations are not persons, discriminatory legislation may be passed against them; and, as we all know, matters of race, creed, or national origin have been destroyed as viable criteria for most legal distinctions. But at the same time, if we are to accept as a sound basis for legal decisions the individual *moral* conscience of given men, then we must be prepared to accept this justification in those cases where a judge's conscience sees the matter quite differently than our own.

Thus far in this chapter we have presented a short history of the law from ancient times to the present. What questions of philosophical importance can we derive from it about the relation between law and morality? At least the following seem to be pertinent to all the theories suggested:

1. Is there an ethical foundation for the law?
2. Is there a difference between moral and legal right and wrong?
3. Are the concepts of moral and legal justice the same?

4. Are the logical structures of legal and moral systems the same?

5. Do legal and moral "judgments" have the same sort of truth-values?

6. If legal and moral rules and judgments are different, that is, if moral and legal right are different, then which takes precedence over the other, if there is a relation of precedence between them?

7. If the answer to (6) is that there is such a relation of precedence, what is the justification for claiming that one rather than the other sort of right is basic or takes precedence?

8. What is the role of moral versus legal sanctions, if they are different?

9. What is the form of a legal rule, and is it different from the form of a moral rule?

A Theory from Plato's *Republic*

There are very many more questions which might be asked about this topic, questions which would take us into very many different disciplines aside from philosophy, such as sociology, anthropology, theology, and so on. Clearly, we cannot answer even a few of those questions here. At most, there is room to consider two views of the relation between moral and legal right. Both of these positions are taken from the writings of the great Plato, and they are theories which he criticizes. The first theory is that of Thrasymachus in the third chapter of the first book of the *Republic*.

Thrasymachus, very angry at what he considers the sophistic perform-ance of Socrates, has become involved in a conversation concerning the nature of justice, and now proposes to define "just" and "right." He is quite specific about it at first. He says that the word "just," or "right" (he does not distinguish between the two) means only "what is to the interest of the stronger party." No social contract is implied in this. What the weaker party wants or says is immaterial. Nor do the words "right" and "wrong" have any other meanings than "that which is in the interests of the stronger" and "that which is not in the interests of the stronger." The nature of the ruling stronger party is also irrelevant. It may be a despot, a democracy, or an aristocracy, but the principle is the same: when the ruler makes the laws, he thereby defines the meaning of "right" for his subjects, as well as "wrong," "wrongdoer," "unjust," and so forth. It follows that no matter what sort of state we are considering, terms such as "right" and "just" have the same meaning, even though the particular interests of the stronger ruling party might differ from state to state. In all of them, it is nonetheless the interest of that stronger party which constitutes right. Perhaps more accurately we can say that action in accordance with laws that serve that interest is right action; action that does not serve that interest, i.e., which is a violation of the law, is wrong.

Socrates (Plato always speaks under this name) does not totally disagree with the idea that, whatever justice or right conduct is, it is at least related to interest. But he does question whether it is always the interest of the stronger. He begins his attack by asking whether or not a ruler, in any sort of state, can be mistaken in the matter of what is in his own interest. Thrasymachus agrees that they can indeed be mistaken. Now since rulers make laws in their own interests, then if they are mistaken about those interests, they may well formulate laws which they *believe* to serve that interest, but which in fact do not. Even if this is so, says Thrasymachus, subjects act rightly when they act in accordance with the laws of the ruler, and wrongly when they do not, because as he has said, "right" *means* acting in accordance with the laws which the ruler has laid down. Now Socrates immediately points out that this implies a contradiction. The contradiction is this: "It is right to act in accordance with what is in the interest of the stronger, and it is right to act in accordance with what is not in the interest of the stronger." The reason is obvious. Suppose that a ruler makes a law which he believes to be in his own interest but which is not. If Thrasymachus is correct, the subject is acting rightly when he acts according to the law, and, in effect, he will also be acting *against* the ruler's interests because the ruler has made a mistake. Now if it is really true that the subject acts rightly when he acts for the interests of the ruler, here is a case where he must have an obligation *not* to obey the laws of his ruler (assuming he knows that they are not in the ruler's interests).

This is a very important point, and one which, all by itself, seems an adequate refutation of the view that what is right and what is legal are always the same. It needs only the premise that men may make mistakes about what their own true interests are. Given that, and the fact that men are rulers, whether one or many, it follows that it is possible for there to be laws contrary to the interests of the ruler. If what is just is associated in some way with what our own true interests are, then it is possible for there to be unjust laws. Naturally, this requires further elaboration, for the thesis that justice and true interest are related must be defended. Also, it is clear that to account for all cases and types of law, we must be able to extend the argument to laws which do not originate with the "stronger party" or at least, which may not originate there. Finally, if we are to make our investigation of the meaning of "right" and "justice" broader than merely the topic of the legal significance of these words, we will sooner or later have to discuss what they mean in terms of the individual's own personal interests, and how these relate to the interests of the state. This is indeed just what Socrates tries to do in the rest of the *Republic*. But now let us return to Thrasymachus.

Thrasymachus now redefines what he means by "ruler" in an attempt to avoid Socrates' criticisms. He says that when we speak in the "strict" sense, a ruler does not make mistakes about his own interest when he is ruling. When we speak of a physician, it is not the man who makes mistakes of whom we are speaking, but the man in the correct practice of his art. The correct practice of an art requires knowledge and skill. If a man knows, he does not make mistakes which are due to ignorance. Hence, the ruler *qua* ruler does not make mistakes when he makes laws governing his own interests. When he does make mistakes, it follows that he is not acting as a ruler.

Though he need not have done so, Socrates accepts this revision of the definition, because it has led into the subject of ruling as an art. To pursue this, he asks Thrasymachus to tell him what the interest of the practitioner of an art is. For example, what is the business of a physician? To treat his patients. Of a ship's captain? To exercise skill and authority over the crew. Hence it seems that every craft has no interest other than its own "greatest possible perfection." Socrates illustrates what he means by referring to medicine again. It is because the human body has its weaknesses that medicine was invented, and medicine is the science of helping to overcome the weaknesses and defects of the body. The science of medicine has no weaknesses or defects itself except in the sense that it may lack the technology needed to solve some difficulty with the body; that is, something is a weakness of medicine only in the light of what the interests of its subject, the body, are. An art does not look after its own interests; it looks after the interests of that which it serves— in the case of medicine, the body's interests. To put it another way, an art only exists for the sake of something else, not for its own sake. Since this is so, the practitioner of the art demonstrates his skill by serving the interests of the subjects of the art. When a groom practices his skill, he serves the needs of horses, not the needs of grooming. It follows that every art "serves the interests of the subject on which it is exercised," and every *artist* serves those interests when he practices the art.

If ruling is an art, as Thrasymachus has claimed, then the ruler, who is the man who practices the art of ruling, serves not his own interests but those of the subjects whom he rules, provided he rules correctly. If the ruler is the stronger, it follows from this that if action in accordance with the law is what is right and if the law concerns the interests of the ruled and not the ruler, then "right" cannot be simply what is in accordance with the interest of the stronger unless the interests of the strong and those of the weak are the same.

Again however, the major point is that a set of arguments purporting to show that the legal and the right are identical have failed. Further, the suggestion has been made that justice is related to the interests of the ruled, not the ruler, provided that ruling is an art. And if ruling is an art, then it requires knowledge to practice it, which implies that a man may be mistaken and hence rule badly. An *unjust* law becomes possible now. It will be a law which in fact does not serve the interests of the ruled, even if the ruler believes it to do so, whether the ruler be a single person, a group of people, or the majority. This theory has the ring of truth about it, incomplete though it is. Consider repressive legislation concerning the rights of minority groups. Assume that such legislation is the expression of a will of the majority of the people, which in the example is the ruler. We may now ask the meaningful question, "Are the majority correct in believing that this set of laws is in their true interest in the long run?" I am introducing the concept of the "long run" here intentionally. So long as this is a *meaningful* question, so long as it is *possible* that the answer be "No, they are wrong," then legal and moral justice are not identical. If one has an obligation which is moral aside from his legal obligations, then it is possible, given that moral obligations take precedence over legal ones, that one might have a moral duty to disobey a legal law. People in a position of power had this sort of obligation in Germany prior to and during World War II. This is what was meant by saying that this theory has the ring of truth to it.

A Theory from the *Gorgias*

A second theory, this time taken from Plato's dialogue *Gorgias*, concerns the relation between convention or public custom, and "natural" law, so far as the meaning of "justice," "right," and so on are concerned. The supposition of this theory, which is stated by Callicles, (the Socratic devil's advocate in this case), is that legal and moral right are *not* identical, provided we agree to the assumption that what is natural is what is moral. For the moment, let us accept this assumption for purposes of argumention. Callicles begins his argument by stating that nature and convention are normally in opposition. Callicles is accusing Socrates of confusing the two in his criticisms of a position stated earlier by Polus, another opponent. In that discussion, the central question was whether or not it was worse and uglier to do wrong than to suffer it. Socrates has argued that doing wrong was uglier and worse. Callicles now wishes to argue that, even if this is true according to convention, it is not true by "nature" and Socrates has therefore misled them by speaking as though the doing of wrong was worse and uglier by both standards.

Callicles has no difficulty imagining that the makers of conventional laws, who are the "weak" majority, makes these laws in accordance with their own interests. Their interests include keeping superior and stronger men in a state of fear and enforcing the majority will upon them. Among the devices used to ensure this result is the creation of the convention which teaches that it is worse and uglier to do wrong than to suffer it, that injustice consists in seeking to be superior over one's fellow man, and that equality ought to be the aim of society. But in Callicles' eyes, this is certainly not the case in the natural world, and all one need do to verify this is to look around him. In nature, the stronger rules and establishes his ascendancy over the weaker by any means he sees fit to adopt. If there is a principle of justice in the natural world, it is precisely that the state of justice *consists* in the rule of the strong. If men act according to the principle of natural justice, it follows that they will act in this manner, and such action is action which follows the "law of nature." The clear consequence of this view is that either legality and morality are different, the one being a function of convention, the other of nature, or there are two distinct moral codes, the one invented, the other existing in the natural world. It is clear that, no matter which of these interpretations we might choose, Callicles believes that the natural code ought to take precedence over the conventional; for he says that, as opposed to the "equality is morality" view of convention, a man of "sufficient capacity" to escape from conventional restrictions will live according to the "light of natural justice."

Socrates begins his attack on Callicles' view by asking for a clarification of his terms, which is a standard opening move in the method of the Socratic dialogue. He asks Callicles if by "natural justice" he means that the words "stronger" and "more powerfully," and "better" and "stronger," mean the same thing. Callicles says that this is what he does mean. Socrates points out that the many who make the laws are stronger than the few who hold Callicles position. Hence, the laws of the many are the laws of the stronger. If Callicles is correct, it follows that they are also the laws of the better. Callicles has also pointed out that according to these laws, the laws of convention, justice is related to equality and it is uglier to do wrong than to have it done to you. Now if the principle of natural justice is that the stronger is the better, then it is *not,* as Callicles seems to think, true that convention and the natural law stand in opposition to each other. Indeed, since the multitude are stronger and hence better than the few, *their* laws are just according to the principle of natural justice rather than the views of minorities. To be consistent, Callicles ought therefore to advocate that we obey these laws.

It is clear that Socrates himself—that is, Plato—does not accept the principle that the laws of the state are just without further qualifications. We know that from the first theory we considered, and Plato's arguments against it. Socrates here is pointing out that from Callicles' principles and premises themselves the logical opposite of what he has affirmed in fact follows.

Callicles is well aware that this is true. He therefore redefines what he means by "stronger." Now he means "better" by it, and by "better" he in turn means "worthier," by which he means "more intelligent." He still holds, however, that the better, now the more intelligent, deserve more than the worse, and that the more intelligent ought to rule and the lesser ought to be ruled. That this too will not do is shown very quickly by Socrates. He asks us to imagine a situation in which there is a supply of food available for a group and in which the group consists of all sorts of people: weak, strong, young, old, and so forth. But there is only one physician among the group, and it is presumed that the physician, because of his training, knows most about matters of diet and is therefore the best equipped to care for and distribute the food. This physician is stronger than some members of the group and weaker than the others. The question is now asked, ought the physician, because of his knowledge about matters of diet, receive more of the food than the other members of the group? Or, on the contrary, should he be restrained from taking more of the food, and ought he not distribute the food according to the needs of each person, having himself more than some but less than others, according to the needs of each individual? This course of action, indeed, seems to be the one most consistent with the knowledge that the physician possesses, for it is clear that he might endanger the health of all by giving them more than they need, or less, or by giving them the wrong diet. It seems to follow from this that from the fact that a man knows more than others, it is not implied that he deserves more himself. Socrates has in mind here the conclusions drawn in the criticisms of the earlier theory, namely that even if he who knows most about ruling ought to rule (and Plato believed this to be true), it does not follow that the knowing ruler ought to have more than his subjects, nor that he ought to serve his own interests through his ruling rather than the interests of the ruled. Indeed, he ought to serve their interests and not his own, unless the two coincide.

Morality and Legality: Further Questions

What conclusions can be drawn from the criticisms of these two theories about the questions asked earlier concerning the relation between legality and morality? To some of those questions, what we have studied in the last few pages gives us no answer. To others, we can answer only that we know what Plato's opinions were. But to a few, we can give fairly complete replies, providing we grant certain assumptions. We can say that legal and moral right *need not* be the same, though they *may* in part coincide. If we deny this, then we must either say that they are wholly different, or that they are identical, or that there are relations of implication, though not mutual implication, between them. If we say that legality and morality are wholly different, then it cannot be the case that a legal rule can prohibit a moral offense. This is false, as the cases of murder, rape, theft, and so on clearly prove. If we say that they are identical, then we must say that the concept of an unjust law is contradictory; and we must rule out the possibility that laws can be improved. Yet it seems quite evident that unjust laws have, in fact, existed in the history of man; and even if that were not the case, we should have no difficulty in conceiving laws that, were they enacted, would certainly *be* unjust. It also seems evident that laws can and should be improved and that justice is better served if efforts for such improvements take place.

If we say that legality and morality are different but that logical relations hold between them, though not relations of mutual entailment, then we are saying that some moral law implies that the moral offense is also a legal one, or vice versa. Given that the existence of juridical law is contingent either upon decisions of precedent or upon enactment by a legislature, then the existence of some moral law does not seem to imply that either of these events must take place. Secondly, there are many formal laws that seem to be morally irrelevant, other things being equal. For example, in normal circumstances, we could say that laws prohibiting overparking do not prohibit a moral offense. There are circumstances under which overparking might be a moral offense, to be sure, as when a man knowingly does not move his auto when another man with a demonstrable need taking precedence over his asks him to do so. Nonetheless, not all legal offenses are moral ones; so some laws at least imply nothing about morality.

We also know that, at least in Plato's opinion, morality takes precedence over legality, and this is an opinion that should not be difficult for most of us to share. Certainly it is a fact that, in general, we feel more deeply about moral matters than about legal ones, except in those cases, predominantly in the field of criminal law, where the two coincide. There is an artificiality about the law, where this is not a pejorative term, which is not a property of our moral codes. The law is invented in our society by a vote in most cases. Morality is not. Furthermore, it seems that changes in our moral codes *causally* effect changes in our legal systems and that the converse, though not impossible, occurs much less frequently. There comes to mind no case wherein the fact of legality was used to *justify* a *change* in morality, though moral convictions are commonly used to justify arguments for a change in the law. Even in those cases where the law has, in fact, effected moral changes, the usual arguments imply that in these cases the law *truly* reflects what is right, whereas the existing moral code does not, thereby insinuating both that the law and morality are different and that morality takes precedence over legality.

The very concept of "precedence" is difficult to analyze here, because if we grant that morality and legality are different, then, in saying that one takes precedence over the other, we seem to be saying that it is possible to evaluate apples and autos by the same criteria. It is not difficult to explain the claim that one *moral* rule takes precedence over another *moral* rule: who does not understand what we mean when we say that, if you have to choose between telling an otherwise harmless lie and permitting a murder, you ought to tell the lie? Nor is it hard to understand the notion of legal precedence within a legal system. Right of access takes precedence over ownership in cases where one man's property surrounds the property of another, for example. But when we apply the concept of precedence to both systems rather than within them, matters become less clear. What we seem to mean when we say that morality takes precedence over legality is simply this: if we can show that some law forces people to commit immoral actions in order to obey it, or that it prohibits persons from attaining some status to which they have a moral right, or that the sanctions attached to the law are such that their implementation causes immorality, then this constitutes a justification for rejecting or changing the law and for refusing to obey it. But the converse is not the case: the proscribing of certain actions or persons by the legal code is not of itself sufficient justification for declaring a practice or a set of actions immoral. To know that a legal offense is wrong, or that a person who has broken the law is bad, you have to know *something else* as well.

Generally, this view of moral precedence seems to be accepted, though *what* is moral rather than immoral is often a matter of controversy even on the local level. Whether the position is *justified*, even if it is accepted, is another matter, and one which we cannot investigate here.

To some of the other questions that were asked, factual answers are possible. For example, there is in fact an ethical foundation for some laws, since history tells us that they were enacted as laws because of moral convictions. We can also say that moral and legal sanctions are different in fact, because no one is imprisoned, for example, for a violation of a moral law that is not also a legal one. And finally, it is a clearly factual matter that moral and legal justice are not the same, given that legal justice is constituted in the application of the sanctions required under the law. It may be legally just that a man be executed for the murder of someone, while at the same time this may be morally unjust. Further, if justice consists in the application of sanctions, at least in part, and if moral and legal sanctions are different, then the two types of justice differ at least to that extent.

Our discussion does no more than begin to resolve the issues with which we began; but, in this area at least, we perhaps ought to be content with a clarification of the issues and a new awareness of their complexity.

KARL MARX AND THE COMMUNIST MANIFESTO

It is very difficult to interpret the *Manifesto* without encountering vehement disagreement from others with a quite different view of it. Karl Marx has had a simply enormous influence upon vast numbers of people, and many of those who call themselves his followers cannot agree even among themselves about the exact meaning of what he wrote. Most philosophers agree in general with the view to be presented here.

Marx would be classified as a naturalist, a philosopher who believes that everything which exists is a part of the natural world and that whatever may be known about reality, about nature, either is or can be known by science. He was also a materialist, a person who believes that mind has no distinct existence apart from matter, and a determinist, for he thought that all events have causes which necessitate their effects. He was greatly influenced, perhaps decisively so far as his writing is concerned, by two factors. One was the philosophy of Georg Wilhelm Friedrich Hegel, and the other was the conditions of the working class in England near the middle of the nineteenth century. Marx's theory is called *dialectical materialism,* and the "dialectical" part owes a great deal to Hegel. The materialism in his theory must be studied within the context of economics and sociology. It is necessary then to say something about Hegel in order to understand Marx.

Marx and The Hegelian Dialectic

Hegel is most famous for a method of explication which he thought to be reflected or expressed in the actual real world of fact. This method is called the "dialectic." It explains all historical change as a result of the conflict between two opposing forces which Hegel calls the thesis and the antithesis. From the clash there results a third force, a synthesis, which has unique characteristics of its own, though it also has properties traceable to the opposing forces from which it arises. The original conflict arose between being and nothingness, and the synthesis was becoming. Becoming resembles both being and nothingness, because it is the process of passing from nothingness to being, but it is identical to neither of these opposites, nor to their sum total. Syntheses in their turn become theses in conflict with antitheses, giving rise to still further syntheses, and so on.

This process is not infinite. Ultimately, in Hegel's view, there will be a final synthesis, one which does not become a thesis. This final reconciliation will be between matter and spirit, and Hegel calls the final synthesis the "Absolute Idea."

Marx was not particularly interested in the abstract Hegelian metaphysics, but he was struck by the manner in which the method of the dialectic seemed to explain the evolution of history, particularly economic history, in terms of the conflict of opposites resulting in new situations which themselves became elements in still other conflicts. Marx became interested more and more in only one aspect of the dialectical theory of history, namely social struggle, and the play of material forces within this struggle. He began to apply the theory of dialectic to the conflict of material forces within society, and he concluded that the advent of the socialistic or communistic state would be the inevitable outcome of the clash between these forces.

Marx was not the first to believe that socialism or communism was the wave of the future. There were people who were socialists and communists and who called themselves by these names long before Marx wrote about it. But for the most part, these socialists thought that their systems would triumph for idealistic reasons. They believed that socialism was the system of moral right and that when men came to realize this they would act accordingly. Because of this, they were known as utopian socialists. But Marx was not this breed of socialist. Because of his conviction that the Hegelian view of historical evolution was correct, he wrote that the coming of socialism was inevitable; it must occur because of the inexorable march of dialectical development in history. Marx was a determinist. Man's ideas, social ideals and otherwise, are determined by his environment and in particular by his economic environment. The laboring and capitalist classes are natural enemies, and given that nature is all there is and that the economic forces operative within out societies are what they are, nothing can prevent this. What *ought* to be has nothing to do with it; what ought to be and what is are identical and both alike are determined by the same necessary historical laws.

History offers, in Marx's view, ample confirmation of this theory. One example is that of the English and the American colonists—thesis and antithesis—resulting in a new nation with some of the characteristics of both opposites but also with its own unique character. From the predominantly agrarian feudal society there arose the class of skilled artisans, who, when they had formed themselves into guilds and come to control the means of skilled production, formed the first capitalists. Between the capitalists and the leaders of the feudal agrarian society a thesis and an antithesis developed again, and a clash of interests and methods arose, resulting in the new industrial state. In this state the new capitalist class manages capital, while the other members of the society manipulate the means of production without owning it, in return for some monetary compensation. The new working class is called the proletariat; it has interests quite opposed to the capitalist class. The interests of the proletarian and the capitalist in their own survival lead to a clash between the two groups. That clash is manifested in strikes, lockouts, labor violence, supression of union shops, price and wage ceilings, and so on. Out of this clash, Marx believed, a new kind of society, a synthesis, will arise. It will be class*less*, because the ownership of capital and the means of production will be in the hands of all rather than in those of a few as in the state of capitalism. The economic role of the capitalist will no longer be needed, because the proletariat becomes educated in the use of capital during the course of the clash. Not much else can be said about what this new synthesis will be like, because it will have, as with all other syntheses, characteristics which are unique as well as those which it will share with the opposites it replaces. But one thing Marx was sure of: this synthesis will inevitably come to pass, because its causes, the thesis and antithesis of capitalists and proletarians, are already operative. If history happens according to the necessary laws of the dialectic, then socialism or communism is as good as here.

A Critique of Marx's Theory

It is advisable to formulate the basic presuppositions of Marx's theory individually before undertaking to criticize it:

1. The history of societies is the history of class struggles. One such struggle occurred between the feudal class and the forerunners of modern capitalism. The capitalists, in changed form, survived, and created the worker class.
2. The capitalists and the workers, or proletariat, form the present thesis and antithesis. The antagonism between them is due to: (a) unequal distribution of wealth; (b) contrary interests; (c) the fact that the capitalists own the means for producing wealth, whereas labor is what really is the measure of worth.
3. The state, as presently structured, exists to protect the interests of the dominant class. This state will be destroyed by the class conflict, and there will be no dominant class afterwards.
4. Since such struggles are determined by inexorable laws whose operation is reflected in history, the coming of the communist state is inevitable; that is, the coming of a classless society with public ownership of everything is inevitable.

These four precepts, which together constitute an argument, are only supportable if: (a) determinism is true; (b) the economic interpretation of history is the only viable interpretation; (c) dialectical materialism is a sound theory; (d) the class struggle, since it depends upon (b) and (c), is not limitable, that is, it must proceed to its "logical" conclusion, the synthesis. The most effective criticisms of Marx's political philosophy which can be made involve the refutation of (a), (b), (c), and (d).

Determinism says that: for everything which exists there are antecedent causes or conditions such that whatever exists cannot happen without them and cannot but happen once they occur. Everything is therefore caused, and nothing could have been other than it is. This is why Marx thought that the advent of the communist state was necessary or inevitable.

Determinism as a theory is difficult to refute in any simple way, because the suppositions underlying the theory are complex. Two oversimplified points may nonetheless be raised. First of all, the type of determinism espoused by Hegel seems to confuse, indeed identify, two different sorts of necessity. A sentence is logically necessary if its denial is a contradiction. But what does it mean to say that something is causally necessary? Is it a contradiction to say that, although winter is coming, it will not be cold this year in northern Canada? Is it a contradiction to say that all of the relevant antecedents for some event have happened, but the events does not happen? It would be supremely surprising if effects that followed upon known causes in the past did not happen in the future, but that is not the point. The point is, is it a logical contradiction to assert that causes happen or have happened but that the effects do or did not take place? It seems not. If it is not a logical contradiction, then what is a "causal contradiction" if it is not simply the assertion that expected effects did not take place? It seems that, although the causes of an effect may be said to "necessitate" that effect in some way or other, this is certainly not to say that the effects are *logically* necessary. Historical necessity is not logical necessity, whatever else it might be. If it *were* logical necessity and if thesis and antithesis are logical opposites, anything whatsoever would be implied by their clash, since from a contradiction, as you know, anything follows. Hegel himself was aware of this for he said that the opposites in the dialectic quarrel were contraries, not contradictories. But if historical necessity is not logical necessity, then it is not a logical contradiction to assert that all the antecedent circumstances for the advent of the classless state are present but that this state will not come to pass. It is now incumbent upon the "inevitability" thesis of Marxism to tell us what is meant when it is said that communism is "necessitated," "inevitable," or "determined."

The second presupposition of Marxism is that the economic interpretation of social history is sound. This claim is related to determinism in that it posits the *kind* of cause which determines the coming of communism. It tells us that the ideas we have are determined by our position in the economic structure of the capitalist society and that massive historical phenomena such as the Russian and American revolutions are only truly interpreted in terms of economic interests and motives. If this theory is sound, then we have no free will (which is implied by determinism) because there are no spontaneous mental acts or choices. Secondly, the theory implies that there are no other relevant factors determining our ideas, besides economic ones.

Beyond the foregoing remarks in opposition to determinism, the arguments against the thesis that there is no free will are given in Chapter 4 under the heading "Determinism and Free Will." For that reason, we shall not go into them again here.

Of the claim that only economic factors are relevant in determining our ideas, it may be said that either this is an incomplete categorization of the causes of our motives and ideas, or it is a generalization so broad and vague that it is uninformative and certainly insufficient as the foundation for a theory of history. It is incomplete if we restrict the meaning of the word "economic" to its normal meanings. When we do this, such common motives and drives for dominance as vanity, rivalry, ego-satisfaction, simple aggressiveness, the love of power *per se,* and simple love and hatred of others are not to be included in the connotation of "economic" motives. And this does not even mention the possibility that there are purely altruistic motives from which man acts, a subject which is partially discussed later in this chapter. Moreover, if we consider the effects of some of these motives in history, the view of Marx that man is politically concerned only to the extent of his own desires for self-enrichment, seems not only simplistic, but false. History is full of examples of men who have given up wealth and power for glory. Nations often give up their riches in war with other nations when they could have enriched themselves by abstaining from war or joining the other nation. Anyone who believes that Churchill and England fought against Hitler's Germany for *purely* economic reasons simply has not read the history of World War II.

The economic theory of history also conveniently overlooks the role of religion and nationalism is the history of the world. The analysis of religion as the "opiate of the people" often given by Marxists ignores the fact that, opiate or not, religious convictions very often have an immense effect upon political convictions. Consider presidential elections in the United States before John Kennedy, or the Thirty Years' War ended by the Treaty of Westphalia in 1648, or the Crusades. It is no doubt true that economic factors entered into some of these conflicts and that whole wars and policies of imperial expansion have been followed for partly or even predominantly economic motives; but that these events were *wholly* due to these causes seems false.

On the other hand, if we wish to broaden the connotation of "economic" to include all of the motives which have been mentioned, then the Marxian thesis becomes uninformative; for it makes it impossible to conceive even a *possible* counter-example to this interpretation of history.

Finally, is it true that all our ideas, or at least those that are politically relevant, derive from our economic position within society? A sufficient riposte seems to me to rest upon the points already mentioned: if we use "economic" in its normal sense, then the answer is "no." If we broaden the meaning of this word to include any possible cause of a politically relevant idea, then the thesis is uninformative.

The third presupposition of the *Manifesto* is that dialectical materialism is a sound theory. If determinism and the economic interpretation of history are unsound, then so is dialectical materialism, because it is a fusion of both. But there is a third criticism to be brought against this theory, and it concerns the *nature* of the social transformations which it predicts. Such changes, if Marx is right, take place by revolution. Mere transformation or partial changing of the presently existing structures is not allowed. The conflict is between the old and the new, and what replaces them is unique, though there is some resemblance to the two "dead" opposites which have passed. The third criticism is simply this: is it accurate to characterize social changes as "revolutions" or to predict that this is the form they must take? Are they not, in many if not all cases, *evolutionary* in nature? Technological changes resulting from advances in science have wrought immense social changes. In the fields of medicine and communications alone, the effects of research have placed before us the need to restructure many of our laws and institutions. Great numbers of people oppose these changes on the grounds that they necessitate more federal control over the lives of the citizenry. Yet the alternative to such increased federal involvement seems equally unacceptable to even larger numbers. The alternative in the case of medicine seems to be the inevitable limitation of the accessibility of modern curative techniques to a privileged few, and in communications the alternative seems to be the possibility of a monopoly with almost unlimited power to influence the choices of the people. The passage of medical aid legislation and the creation of the Federal Communications Commission are in part explicable in terms of the opposition to these alternatives. But a revolution was not required before their advent. Why then ought we to expect a revolution in all future cases of massive social change?

This criticism brings up the fourth presupposition: that social conflict resulting in the classless state is inevitable, and that the conflict is not limitable. We can now see how this supposition is really a conclusion from the first three claims. The criticisms of these claims, if sound, reflect accordingly on the fourth. If evolution, not revolution, characterizes many social changes, then the conflict is limitable. Furthermore, if determinism, the economic interpretation of history, and dialectical materialism are unsound, then social struggles are not "necessary" and hence not "inevitable." Marx himself asks us to give him any examples of a class surrendering its power "without a bloody class struggle." Such examples are not difficult to find at all. Some frequently mentioned ones are the start of the Jacksonian era, when the aristocracy of the original eastern colonies allowed themselves to be outvoted by rural citizens and dropped church and property qualifications for political office; the peaceful acceptance of the Reform Bill of 1832 by the English Establishment—Marx himself realized how this seemed to fly in the face of his theory; the freeing of the Russian serfs by Alexander II in March of 1861; the limitation of privileges accepted by the French of Canada in 1867; the voluntary granting of independence to most of her former colonies by England; the acceptance of the income tax by the capitalists of the United States, not to mention the capital gains tax.

It is now time to return to the original argument in the light of the criticisms of its foundations. The first premise is false, as a plethora of counter-examples shows. *Some* history is doubtless the history of class struggles, but by no means all.

The second premise is also false. There are doubtless many quarrels between the capitalists and the working class; but it is false that the capitalist class alone rules the country, as the income tax, the influence of the farmers, the unions, and the non-laboring middle class show. In addition, the capitalists do not own all of the means for producing wealth, as a perusal of the shareholders of any large corporation will prove; and, hence, the interests of the capitalist and the worker do not always totally diverge. Finally, it seems to be doubtful that the amount of labor is the measure of worth: supply and demand, whim, and innumerable other factors enter into it. The third premise may be questioned upon the same grounds. The conclusion is false because determinism of the type Marx espoused seems to be false. The argument of the *Manifesto* therefore seems to be unsound.

Further Criticisms

There are yet other criticisms which may be offered of Marxism, and at least three of them seem important enough to mention here. The first of these concerns a major principle of the Marxist explanation of the present class struggle, and it is stated as part of the second premise in the argument—that the antagonism between the capitalists and the proletariat is due in large part to the unequal distribution of wealth. Only if the distribution of wealth is equalized, says Marx, will this antagonism be overcome, and only in the inevitable revolution will it be equalized.

But surely this is false. It is not simply a matter of the distribution of wealth *per se,* but the *manner* of its distribution. Would it matter if everyone had the *same* amount of wealth, provided that everyone had enough to satisfy his wants and needs? And can we not, within the capitalistic system, ensure that all men have enough, though not that all men have the same? It is not, then, the fact that some men have more than others that causes antagonisms but that some men have almost nothing while others have more than they can possibly use. The distribution need not be equal, but it must leave no one in need. And surely that is what we are trying to do within the framework of capitalism today.

Secondly, Marx holds that, where goods are held in common, as he thinks will necessarily be the case in the classless society, there will be perfect liberty as well as equal distribution of wealth. But the Marxist analysis of the human animal seems to contradict the very possibility of this state. In any state, classless or not, administrative personnel, people in charge of distribution, those responsible for internal order, and so on will be required. They will, in fact, hold power—if not absolute, then relatively more power than those not in these positions. And if Marx is correct about the motives from which people act, these officials could not ignore the opportunity to enrich themselves in every possible way. By so doing they would reintroduce once again the inequalities in the distribution of wealth which the coming of the classless state was supposed to obliterate. Does this not make Marxism a self-refuting theory?

Finally, there is a criticism which might be called the "moral argument" against Marxism. In effect, Marx removes the grounds for condemning any of the means to an end which have happened in the past or will happen in the future. This is an effect of his version of determinism. The struggle between the Democracies, Russia, and the Axis Powers is not a subject in which there is a place for moral praise and blame, for all men and all nations are determined in their action. If the overthrow of the law, genocide, torture, and the killing of millions not even politically involved are necessitated in the process of revolution, then that is simply the way it will be, and nothing can be done to stop it. If this is true, then the attempt to be moral is fruitless, for there is no such thing. That adherence to such a theory might well lead to absolute barbarism should be obvious. There is therefore all the more reason to understand why adherence to it is not justified, which is what we have tried to show.

HOBBES AND THE COMMONWEALTH

Few theories about the structure, origins, and rights and duties of the citizens in a government have ever had the influence that Thomas Hobbes' famous *Leviathan or the Matter, Form and Power of a Com-*

monwealth, Ecclesiastical have had.[2] It was written in 1651, and Hobbes, an Englishman, was born in 1588. Personally a man of common sense, prudence, loyalty, and learning, Hobbes lived to be 91 years of age and to see himself reviled, slandered, and hated. This intense dislike of him was due to the prevailing conviction of the times that he was a rigid monarchist and an atheist to boot. In the times after the beheading of Charles I and during the stark Puritan days of Cromwell's England, one could not have a much worse reputation. At times he even thought it prudent to flee his homeland and take refuge in France because of fear for his safety due to his royalist sentiments. He and Baruch de Spinoza are probably the most reviled philosophers of all time; and, in both cases, the attitudes towards them were largely unjustified. Hobbes's theory of government, for example, does not force him to accept only the monarchist form of state. In fact, one of the things that is wrong with the theory is that *any* government which is actually in power is justified by it. Moreover, he was no atheist.

Hobbes is in the tradition of British empiricism also exemplified by Locke, Berkeley, and Hume. The sources of our knowledge are sense impressions and memory of them. From these sources, by reasoning about the materials of our knowledge and the propositions we form about them, we come to a knowledge of consequences and causes. The subjects of science and philosophy are causal explanations, and these concern only those things which can come into being and are subject to "composition or resolution." This does not mean that philosophy is concerned solely with the causal relations between what we normally call bodies. Hobbes thinks that there are two types of bodies, one "natural" in the sense that it occurs independently of the acts of men in the natural world, and the other artificial, which he calls the "commonwealth," and which is made by the acts and decisions of men. It is this second sort of body, and its causes and structure, with which we will be concerned here. But precisely because the commonwealth is a creation of man, we cannot understand its causes unless we understand man. The study of man Hobbes calls *ethics*, and it includes an examination of man's dispositions, behavior, and what affects him. The social and political behavior of man, which includes an analysis of his duties to the state, is treated separately by Hobbes, and he calls this subject *civil philosophy*. Strictly speaking, both ethics and civil philosophy, (insofar as the latter deals with the individual behavior of individual men), belong in the subject of natural philosophy; since this is the part of philosophy which deals with natural bodies, and man is a natural

2 Thomas Hobbes, *Leviathan*, Herbert W. Schneider, ed. (New York: The Bobbs-Merrill Co., 1958).

body. When man is considered as a participant in the state however, we come to the study of the commonwealth.

Hobbes's Concept of Cause

The notion of a cause is difficult to understand in the writing of Hobbes. For our purposes, we may accept a simplified version of this complex view. Consider two things or events, X and Y, and say that X is the cause and Y the effect or consequence. Furthermore, realize that not only must X have certain properties in order to be a cause but Y must also have certain properties in order to be an effect. For example, if I am X, and the effect Y is the hearing of what I say in a perceiver P, then not only must I have the properties of being able to speak a language that P speaks, being able to pitch my voice at a level which normal perceivers can hear, and so on, but P must have the properties of being able to hear what I say, being capable of discriminating the sound of my voice from other sounds that he may hear at the same time, and so on. By "cause," Hobbes means all those properties which both the cause in the narrow sense (X in the example) and the effect in the narrow sense (Y) must have in order for the event specified to come about—in this case, the hearing of what it is that I say. Clearly then, Hobbes means by "cause" something much broader than the normal meaning of the term would lead one to believe. In fact, not only the properties of the entities X and Y are included in the connotation of "cause" according to him but also any other conditions which, though not strictly speaking properties of these entities, are nonetheless necessary for the existence of the state of affairs under examination. When he says that he is going to examine the "cause" of something such as a commonwealth, we would therefore be well advised to interpret him as meaning the total set of conditions necessary for the existence of the commonwealth.

Within the total set of conditions necessary for the existence of an event, person or state, Hobbes also distinguishes particular kinds of causes, more closely akin to the notions with which we are familiar. In fact, we may with a fair degree of accuracy claim that the relevant notion or concept of cause which he uses to explain the origin of the commonwealth is the concept of an efficient cause. An efficient cause is for him the set of properties in the agent which is required for the existence of an effect which is actually produced. Now it is evident from this that Hobbes is espousing the theory of hard determinism if we are speaking about a context in which the sole members are bodies. He is saying that, given an existing effect, there are a set of sufficient conditions in an agent which must be present, given the existence of the

effect. Given the rest of Hobbes's theory, this version of hard determinism is certainly consistent with and, considered alone, perhaps
identical to, the sort of fatalism espoused by Richard Taylor, which was
considered and rejected earlier. We might also note at this point that
his theory is inconsistent with the thesis that man has a free will, if
what the latter means is that there are decisions which we make which
have no sufficient antecedent conditions. And this is just what Hobbes
does mean. In fact, Hobbes is a mechanist of the Cartesian variety,
with the additional belief that so-called "mental phenomena" are no
exception to the rule.

Desires and Aversions

Precisely because Hobbes does hold a Cartesian version of physical
determinism, he is concerned with motion, which he construes as local
motion of the parts of bodies. All change is explained in terms of this
kind of motion, but there are two sorts of motion which are peculiar to
living bodies. First, there is vital motion, which includes all non-
volitional movements in the body, such as blood circulation, digestion,
and so forth. The second sort of motion peculiar to living bodies is
voluntarily action. Voluntary motions always begin with the imagination's conception of the object of the motion. When we have what
Nowell-Smith might call a "pro-attitude" toward the object, this is called
appetite or desire; and when our attitude is negative, it is called aversion. These two kinds of endeavor, both forms of local voluntary motion,
are the basic foundations of human conduct and indeed of all animal
conduct. For purposes of discussion Hobbes also draws a distinction
between desire and aversion, which are the names for our attitudes or
endeavors when the objects of them are absent, and love and hate, which
are the names for these attitudes when the objects of them are present.

Hobbes believes that the words "good" and "evil" are used by men
respectively to name the objects of their desires, and the objects of their
aversions, or, when the objects are present, the objects of their loves
and hates.

Just as appetite or desire and aversion are forms of voluntary motion, so the passions are forms of appetite and aversion. Since the
former are motions, so are the latter. Conception takes place in the
brain with the appropriate external stimulus, and the passions are functions of the heart. The names which these passions have in our languages
arise from their ends and from the convictions we have about the
desirability of obtaining them. Some of the names also result from
considering many passions together rather than each singly, but a more
detailed discussion of this subject need not concern us here. What *is*

important about his theory of the passions for our purposes is that good and evil are for Hobbes relative to the desires and aversions of particular men prior to the formation of a commonwealth; and also in that state, which he calls a "state of nature," all action is selfish in the technical sense which he has just given. If he is correct, altruistic action always has an egoistic foundation explicable in terms of desire or aversion in a particular person. Before proceeding to the structure of the commonwealth itself, we might also note that voluntary action when this means deliberate action is explained by Hobbes as the sum total of the desires, aversions, and passions which take place in a man until the achievement of the end at which he aims, or until he abandons the seeking of it. Will and acts of will become in his eyes merely the last act of desire or aversion or passion immediately prior to the achievement of the end or the abandoning of it. Since this is all that will is, it would seem to follow that animals other than men are deliberate, willful creatures, and Hobbes thought that this was so. Very odd conclusions follow from this, as one might expect. For one thing, if there is such a thing as moral responsibility, then beasts are morally responsible and therefore presumably merit award and punishment, praise and blame, just as we do. There would be nothing logically odd about a commonwealth of animals if Hobbes is correct, given that the same environmental conditions, or similar ones, pertain to them as to us. But Hobbes seems not to have considered these consequences of his theory.

From his definition of will follows his definition of liberty. Liberty is simply the power to do what one wills, that is, to attain that which one desires and to avoid that to which one has an aversion. It is the desire for this power to attain what one wills that is the basic cause of our mental abilities and hence what gives us superiority over the beasts. Had Hobbes been familiar with the work of Darwin, he would surely have agreed with the claim that it is merely a happy accident of evolution that we are the rulers of the earth rather than some other species. But clearly, he has all the problems of the theories known as determinism, fatalism, and ethical relativism; although he would disagree with the latter claim for reasons we shall now consider.

The "State of Nature"

In a state of nature, all of us seek our own conservation. Hobbes thought that, in the state of nature, we all begin on about an equal footing, since physical and mental deficiencies may be overcome by developing prowess in another area. That is, the mentally weak person can presumably make up for this deficiency in strength, in cunning, or in other ways. Our search after self-conservation involves our various desires, aversions, and passions. (We ought to construe the meaning of "self-conservation" when studying Hobbes in the broadest possible sense, namely, as the attempt to get whatever we desire and avoid whatever we dislike.) Clearly, we cannot all satisfy all our desires and aversions. Some of us want the same things as others do; yet it is only possible for some and not all of those desiring a particular thing to have it. In addition, we form opinions of one another, and all of us want the other fellow to think of us as we think of ourselves.

In a state of nature, then, we find distrust of our fellow man, competition, sometimes vicious, among men, and a desire for a very high opinion in the eyes of our fellows. These three things, which Hobbes names competition, diffidence, and glory, are the wellsprings of actions in a non-organized society, that is, in a state of nature. In this state, where each person would be dependent upon his own strength and wits to gain his goals, all our lots would be extremely precarious. There would be no protection against assault, piracy, murder, and all the other possible modes of attack upon a person or his possessions. Possession itself would consist merely in the personal power of preventing others from taking what one had. There would be no motive for cooperation, and the rules of life would be "catch as catch can, and the devil take the hindmost." There would be no laws, for these presuppose an organized society with a mechanism for enforcement, and no morality, for "good" and "evil" refer in such a state merely to what individuals desire and to that which they dislike, and there is no guarantee that different individuals will like and dislike the same things. One and the same thing will be both good and evil if one man desires it and another has an aversion to it. Where there is no law and no objective foundation for the meanings of terms such as "good" and "evil," there is neither legal nor moral justice and injustice. In fact, in such a state the tendency would be to distrust one's neighbor, guard one's possessions and take any means to obtain them, and, in general, to have a disposition to war with other men upon any occasion of threat, insult, or intended or actual assault. This is the nature of man. He cannot help the way he is; and, without a commonwealth, he is legally and morally free to do whatever he wants to do and whatever he can do for his own well-being, simply because there is no legality and no morality (which for Hobbes were identical anyway).

Hobbes calls this state of nature a state of war, even if actual fighting is not taking place. It is sufficient that there be a constant disposition for it to take place. That there would be this disposition is evident to Hobbes from the cursory observation of men living in *organized* society. They arm themselves, lock their doors, think ill of their neighbors, and look with a jaundiced eye upon protestations of brotherly love. And in some areas of the world, where the commonwealth is not well established, such a state, or one close to it, actually does obtain. Government arises only when man realizes his precarious existence can be overcome by prudential cooperation. The commonwealth is the result of such mutual self-interest, and we shall now examine its structure.

Hobbes's Doctrine of Sovereignty

Not all of men's passions incline them to a state of war. We also have desires for peace, and when our reason tells us that this state of peace would better enable us to achieve our ends than its opposite, we desire it. Reason tells us how it is possible to achieve a state of peace. *What* we discover through the use of right reason is what Hobbes calls a "law of nature." Hobbes believed that we, in fact, live according to such rules, the evidence being that we do have governments based upon them. There are three basic laws. The first is that "every man ought to endeavour peace, as far as he has hope of obtaining it; and when he cannot obtain it, that he may seek, and use, all helps and advantages of war." The second law is "that a man be willing, when others are so too, as far forth, as for peace and defense of himself he shall think it necessary, to lay down this right to all things; and be contented with so much liberty against other men, as he would allow other men against himself." The third law is "that men perform their covenant made." A covenant or contract is the transference of natural rights (those which we have in a state of nature) to another person, called a sovereign, in which the fulfilling of the sovereign's part of the contract may be left to another time, that is, in which the sovereign may be trusted. Although most rights are transferable to a sovereign, some are not. The right to defend one's life cannot be transferred or given up, because one cannot do good to oneself by not defending his life when it is threatened. It is, of course, possible that the sovereign may threaten the subject's life. But even here the subject does not lose his right to defend himself, because the original ground of transference was self-interest; and even within a society or commonwealth this remains true on the personal level.

The transference of rights to a sovereign is a covenant, and it does not hold until the commonwealth is in being. What it is for a commonwealth to exist is simply that an enforcing power which will compel man to abode by his covenants has been created and is in operation. The commonwealth, or Leviathan, is a body, and its causes are the properties discovered in individual men which we have already discussed: their desires, aversions, and passions. The immediate causes of the commonwealth are the transference of rights, and this takes place either by saying so explicitly or by accepting the transfer implicitly. The person or persons who receive the rights are called the sovereign, and upon the transference the individuals who have given up their rights become the subjects of the sovereign. It is very important to notice that the sovereign himself is *not* subject to the laws thereby created, because he is not a contracting party in the covenant. Men have contracted with other men to surrender their rights to a third person, the sovereign; the sovereign has not contracted to transfer any of his rights to anybody. His part of the contract consists in protecting the rights of the other parties; but, since he is not included, he still has the *natural* right to do whatever he can to get whatever he desires and hold it however he may be able. If he chooses to do this by abusing his power over his subjects, there is nothing unjust or illegal about this; for to be either legal or moral the commonwealth must first exist and the actions in question be subject to evaluation by its laws, but the sovereign's actions are not subject to evaluation because he has not transferred his rights.

Men covenant to transfer their rights to a sovereign in the first place because they are afraid of each other. What keeps the commonwealth in being after the transfer is also fear—fear of the sovereign's power over them. This is perfectly consistent with Hobbes's analysis of human nature, and ought not to be taken as a pejorative judgment on Hobbes's part about the commonwealth. Whether the sovereign is one person, a few, or many depends upon the nature of the original contractual transfer of rights. But clearly Hobbes's doctrine of sovereignty is not affected by what particular form of government is chosen; or, at least, the doctrine of transferring rights is not affected. The entire theory is *logically* affected, as we shall see, because it has the consequence that, in a democracy, where the sovereign is the majority of the people, such people are not subject to the law if Hobbes is right.

Hobbes does not think that sovereignty can be given to a person or persons conditionally, because the sovereign himself, not having transferred any of his rights, is not a party to the convenant and has none to give up *legally*. Conditional sovereignty would imply that the sovereign contracted to surrender his ruling power under certain circumstances, and this would necessarily involve the transfer of some of his rights. Since the sovereign has only natural rights, he may of course choose simply not to exercise his power, or to abandon it, and in that way reliquish his position. He may also be overthrown, though only when he cannot protect the subjects of the commonwealth any longer (because this is the sole reason for having a sovereign and a commonwealth in the first place). If and when this happens, we are in a state of nature again and the formation of a new commonwealth may or may not occur. The obligation to obey a sovereign also becomes void if he is defeated in war and surrenders or if the commonwealth falls because of civil war. Here again, the obligation exists only so long as the ruler can, in fact, protect the interests of the ruled, and the obligation is therefore one of prudential self-interest and nothing else. And, as has already been mentioned, any individual man may resist the sovereign if he requires that man to kill or wound himself, to testify against himself, or to submit to assault or torture, even if this is in the interest of all of the rest of the members of the commonwealth.

Evaluating Hobbes's Theory

What are we to make of freedom in such a commonwealth? In the state of nature, men are free to the extent that they can get and hold anything which they can in fact obtain and defend, and no means to possession and defense are barred because there are no laws. With the advent of the commonwealth, certain of these means are barred, as are certain of the goals; and the means of defense are taken away and placed in the hands of the sovereign. Of course, no state, no matter how rigid, has laws governing all human activity; so, to the extent that our actions are not legally relevant, they are free. The scope of this class of free actions changes as the class of laws is added to and revised. As we have just seen, some actions are under no circumstances proscribable by the law because the right to do them is not transferable. But if freedom means the right to act contrary to the laws of the commonwealth, then there is no such thing in Hobbes's eyes.

Finally, we ought to note that no refutations of Hobbes's theory can be based upon the contention that in *fact* societies with laws did not originate in the way in which Hobbes seems to think they did on occasion. His theory will be sufficiently justified if he can defend the claim that a state of nature is *logically* prior to the commonwealth, given the truth of this theory of the nature of man.

Hobbes has argued for a number of very important points. The crucial ones might be summarized as follows:

1. Human nature is such that, in a state of nature, man would always act only for his own personal interests, using any means to seek and defend his ends. Altruistic action is impossible, given this nature.
2. The explanation of why men form commonwealths is to be found in this theory about his nature, when conjoined with the realization that on his own, no man can seek, obtain, and defend all that he wants, and often not even what he needs.
3. Outside the commonwealth, terms such as "justice," "right," "wrong," "ought," and so forth have no meaning; or, if they have meaning, they refer only to actions relevant to individuals and

their personal needs. Hence, in the latter event, a "right" action for X might be a "wrong" action for Y if they have contrasting desires.

4. Given the commonwealth, the terms mentioned in (3) have the same meaning for all, and what their meanings are is defined in the laws made by the sovereign. Hence, the law and morality are identical.

5. In giving our rights and the power to enforce the law to a sovereign, we create an obligation to obey him and his laws because of the covenant we make with him.

6. The sovereign is not bound by the laws he makes.

Hobbes's theory of the commonwealth was and is extraordinarily influential. Most people in our society, in fact, *do* believe that man is basically a selfish and egoistic animal who makes laws to protect him from himself as well as from outside forces. Many think that the law and morality *are* coextensive, and that we have not only a legal but a moral responsibility to do whatever the sovereign requires. Most national figures speak in terms of the realities of power politics and argue that the value of a society is only as high as the power to enforce its laws is strong. Many would argue that Hobbes might well have claimed historical accuracy for his theory, though he does not, because many of our commonwealths did arise in the way he describes. These beliefs are reflected in many common sayings of our language, such as "might makes right," "to the victor go the spoils," "only losers are nice guys," and so forth. In our business communities, despite pious proclamations to the contrary, legality rather than ethics is often what matters most; and even so-called "business ethics" is usually based upon prudential considerations about public relations rather than upon convictions about the foundations of moral principle. In the face of all of this, how are we to criticize Hobbes? In the first place, his theory as a whole is only as strong as the theory of human nature upon which it is based. So let us examine that theory first, the best known critic of which was Joseph Butler, who was a bishop in eighteenth century England.[3]

Criticisms of Psychological Egoism

The view of human nature which Hobbes holds is called psychological egoism. It purports to be a factual theory, that is, an accurate description or characterization of the ways in which man as a matter of fact does act and will act, given the chance. For Hobbes, the soundness of this theory is not called into question once the commonwealth is established. After all, the theory of human nature he espouses is the *raison*

---

[3] Joseph Butler, *Fifteen Sermons upon Human Nature* (London: G. Bell & Sons, Ltd., 1958). See especially the eleventh sermon.

d'être of the commonwealth, and only the restrictions of the state prevent a reversion to his normal conduct. Another theory which is a form of psychological egoism is called psychological *hedonism*. This view argues that men are so constituted that they always act for their own pleasure. It is not necessary to interpret Hobbes as a hedonist; but, the theory is defined here because, if we substitute "satisfaction" for "pleasure," it is fairly close to Hobbes's view, certainly close enough so that Butler's arguments may be applied to him. Butler specifically had Hobbes in mind in his writings.

Butler argues that it is factually false that we are so constituted physically and psychologically that we perform all of our acts because we will receive pleasure, satisfaction, or happiness from them. We must, in his view, perform the acts before we achieve satisfaction from the goals we obtain. As he says, ". . . all particular appetites are toward external things themselves, distinct from the pleasure arising from them . . . there could not be this pleasure were it not for that prior suitableness between the object and the passion."

In addition, Butler thinks that there is a distinction between what he calls "self-love" and our several particular and individual appetites, passions, and "affections," and he also thinks that many thinkers, including Hobbes, have confused them. As a result of this confusion, thinks Butler, Hobbes was led to believe that altruistic actions were impossible.

Our particular appetites and passions are those such as hunger, love, benevolence, and self-interest. All of these have as their objects something other than the self. When you are hungry, you are hungry for food. If one covets something, it is a specific object such as money or another man's wife. If you are benevolent, you are benevolent to a particular person. All of these desires, then, are for *particular* objects. But self-love, which is Butler's term for self-interest, is ambiguous. In its normal use, the term is general and not particular: that is, when we speak of a person acting from self-love, we are speaking of him as one who acts for his interests or happiness in general, and he might choose several different means to achieve this end by satisfying several different passions or appetites. Self-love is different in kind than the particular appetites. It functions as a principle of reflection through which we determine which of our particular appetites and passions are in fact in our true interests. Suppose, for example, that some individual has an appetite for sugar. Now this is clearly a particular appetite, that is, its object is sugar and not any other thing. Equally evident is the fact that massive amounts of sugar are not good for one's health and hence are not in our true interests. Self-love as a principle through which we determine what is in our interest would therefore dictate that we not indulge this appetite. But self-love is therefore not directed toward any particular object, because the same sort of reasoning applies to almost any passion or appetite one might think about. Too much exercise is not good for your health either.

Because self-love is general, and particular appetites, passions, and effections are not, self-love does not *prima facie* exclude any particular appetite except those whose satisfaction would be harmful to our true interests. Another way to say this might be to point out that the appetite for revenge and the one for benevolence cannot be directed toward the same person at the same time; yet one may act benevolently, or perhaps even vengefully, and still act from self-love if the act is in his own interests. Now if Butler is right, benevolence is a particular appetite. If Hobbes is right, men act only for their own interests. Hobbes's conclusion was that one cannot act altruistically, that is, benevolently. But this is a mistaken inference which rests upon the failure to see the distinction between general self-love and the particular appetite for benevolence. Butler draws the right conclusion, which is that benevolence may be in our true interest and that, therefore, not only is altruistic action possible, but, even from a pragmatic viewpoint, we often ought to act that way.

It is important here not to confuse self-love with selfishness. Butler draws a distinction between what he calls "reasonable or cool self-love" and "immoderate self-love" or "supposed interest." He is here contrasting the desire for those ends the attainment of which *actually do* confer happiness with the desire for those ends which are *mistakenly thought to* confer happiness. People often think that the particular enjoyments which make up the sum total of happiness are those which arise from "riches, honors, and the gratification of sensual appetites"; but surely this is a mistake of serious import. Too much of this sort of gratification would clearly not be in anyone's interest, and people who do hold such opinions are in reality confusing immoderate self-love and cool or reasonable self-love. What we call selfishness might be in conflict with cool self-love, because selfishness occurs in a clash between opposing particular desires such as that for riches and that for benevolence.

So far, then, Butler has made two points against Hobbes: (1) benevolent or altruistic action is possible; and (2) when one desires something, he does not directly desire the pleasure or happiness resulting from the thing, but the thing itself. It will help if we go over the arguments in support of these two points again, for they are the center of the attack upon psychological egoism in general and psychological hedonism in particular. Consider the particular case first. If we assume that psychological hedonism is correct, then it is true that we always act so as to promote our own pleasure. Hence, we could receive no pleasure from an act or object unless we first had some interest in an object external to us. But, in this event we must act to obtain the object and not merely the pleasure, and it follows that psychological hedonism is false.

The counter-example technique works very well against this theory as well. It is difficult to see how we could explain the action of an atheist who sacrifices his life for another who may be a total stranger by saying that he did it for his own pleasure. Nor does it seem to be true that, when we say things we do not really mean in a state of anger, we are doing something for our own pleasure. The so-called "hedonistic paradox" also arises here. You may test it for yourself by trying to do something in order to give yourself pleasure. Often it turns out that the effort is self-defeating; and, in the calculation of the means to get the pleasure and happiness of life is in the living of it, not in some end to be gained by it.

The criticisms of the general theory of psychological egoism, of which psychological hedonism is a species, rest on the distinction between particular appetites such as hunger, hate, benevolence, etc., and the general principle of self-love. This distinction makes altruistic action possible. Now when we add to the distinction the fact that, in order to discover what is in our own interests, we must first have interests and affections toward external objects, we see that it is psychologically false that we always act only for our own interests, whatever they may be.

Criticisms of Ethical Egoism

We now know, then, that the theory of human nature proposed by Hobbes, upon which his explanation of the origin and form of the commonwealth is based, is not sound. But another theory is also accepted by Hobbes, which is closely akin in its factual basis to psychological egoism. This theory is *ethical* egoism, which asserts that men *ought* to do that, and only that, which is in their own interests. It is one thing to say that men do in fact always act only for their own interests and another to say that they ought to do so. If psychological egoism as a theory is false, is does not follow, however, that ethical egoism is. If anything, the *truth* of psychological egoism would seem to imply, if not the falsity, at least the irrelevance of ethical egoism. After all, if men *always* act for their own interests, they presumably cannot act in any other way; and, if they *cannot* act in any other way, what sense does it make to say that they *ought* to act in the way that they do act, since they will in any event? There is another reason that ethical egoism would not follow from psychological egoism, which is that the latter is a factual theory and the former a normative one, and any inference either way would be deductively invalid because of the factualistic fallacy. We must therefore criticize ethical egoism on its own grounds.

First, what does Hobbes say that makes it incumbent upon him to hold this view? The major claim concerns the meanings of "good" and "bad" and other normative terms both in a state of nature and in the commonwealth. We know that these words in a state of nature are used merely to name that to which we have attractions and repulsions respectively. In the commonwealth, to say that an action is right is to say that it is in accordance with the law of the sovereign and nothing else. And to say that a man ought to do an act in the commonwealth is to say that he should act in accordance with the law. But, of course, the laws of the commonwealth are calculated to serve the mutual interests of men in the belief that they will accomplish more in this state than in a state of Nature. It follows that men ought to do what is in their own interests. Even the exclusion of the right to life from among those rights transferred to the sovereign in the covenant is based upon the principle that a man cannot be obligated to act contrary to his own interests. It would therefore seem that Hobbes holds the theory of ethical egoism, which in his case is coextensive with the morality of the commonwealth and also with the legality of it (since moral and legal laws are the same for him). If we can show that ethical egoism is a false or unsound theory, we will have cast serious doubts upon Hobbes's thesis that morality and legality are identical as well as upon his views of the meanings of normative terms.

There are two ways in which ethical egoism is usually supported. One way is through the use of what we might call a logical argument, and the other is *via* a psychological one. The logical argument for ethical egoism states that it is true by definition, since the very *meaning* of ethical terms is defined in terms of self-interest. Hence, they would argue that by "x is right" people mean "x makes us happy," or "x is in our personal interest." The theory is giving us a reportive definition of these moral terms. If one ought to do right actions, it would seem to follow that one ought to act for his own interests or happiness. Indeed, according to this view of the theory, it would be a contradiction to assert than an action was right but contrary to one's own interests.

But any such definitional view of ethical egoism has incumbent upon it the onus to explain why it is that most people who use normative terms must, if they are right, use them incorrectly. After all, we are speaking about an ethical theory and one which must account for illegitimate as well as appropriate uses of moral language if it is to enable us to make moral decisions. In our normal moral discourse, we want to say that one has an obligation under certain circumstances to protect one's family even at the cost of one's life. We want to say that sometimes a soldier does the right thing when he gives up his life for his country. We do not want to say that men who apparently valued the welfare of others, such as Jesus and Socrates, were doing what was wrong because they were not acting in their own interests. Rather, we want to praise the rightness of their actions and the goodness of their characters. None of these things is possible if the ethical egoists are correct. But it is the job of the theory to explain normal phenomena, not the other way around. It has not given us the *true* reportive definitions of our moral words.

The psychological argument for ethical egoism is something like this: given the normal psychological causal laws, every person always acts in a manner calculated to serve his own interests. If this is true, then it is impossible to ask anyone to act against his own interests, (as he would be if he were to give up his life for a cause, for example), because it is senseless to ask a man to do that which he cannot do. It would be as silly to ask a man to act against his own interests as it would be to ask him to defy the laws of gravity.

The trouble with this argument—apart from the fact that it assumes the truth of psychological egoism which we now know to be false—is that it is a two-edged sword. It is indeed ludicrous to require that a man do that which he *cannot* do. But it also follows from the same premises that it cannot ever by anybody's duty to do anything which he in fact *does not* do, since everything he does is in his own interest, given the requisite psychological laws. Hence, discussion of what we ought or ought not to do is senseless in the first place, and ethical egoism is not an ethical theory at all; for, if it is correct, it is impossible for there ever to be any wrong action and it will always be the case that everything which ought to be done will be, is being, and has been done. Clearly, this is absurd.

There is also a conflict in ethical egoism between my willing that I ought to do what is in my own interests and what I must also will to be consistent, namely that everyone else do likewise. In such a situation, conflicts are inevitable, and I will find myself willing that you do what is in your interest when in order to do it you would have to frustrate my interests. This will result because of the variations in interest which we all seem to have in the short run at least.

Another difficulty for ethical egoists arises from the same source, and it is that the theory does not provide us with adequate criteria for giving advice in moral situations. Suppose that I am in business competition with a man named Smith and that it would be to my advantage if Smith went bankrupt. You owe a large sum of money to Smith, without which he will fail in his business, and you come to me to ask for advice about whether you ought to pay him or not. Because I am an ethical egoist, I say you ought not to pay him. Now a couple of weeks later, you owe *me* money, and again you come to me to ask whether you ought to pay it. I now say, most assuredly yes, and I still say this even if we both know that you can get away with not paying me without penalty. Clearly, my own interests will not provide sufficient criteria for consistent moral advice.

A Critique of Hobbes's Philosophy

Now we know that the foundation for Hobbes's political philosophy, insofar as it rests upon this theory about the psychological nature of man, is inadequate. We also know that the moral theory which he accepts, ethical egoism, is incorrect. He also claims, as we know, that what is moral and what is legal are identical. If his moral theory is inadequate and if some of the criticisms of it do not rest upon the assumption that morality and legality are *not* identical and are otherwise adequate, his legal theory will be incorrect too. Certainly at least one of the criticisms offered against his moral theory seems to meet this test. It is that criticism which showed that, given the truth of psychological egoism, morality becomes senseless if ethical egoism is true. Remember that if a man cannot act but in the way he does, then it makes no sense to ask him to act otherwise, for whatever reasons—legal, moral, or prudential. The same will be true of his legally relevant actions.

There are other criticisms which one may give of Hobbes's identification of legal and moral law, but many of these were examined earlier in this chapter. The conclusion reached there, which is that it is false that legality and morality are coextensive, seems wholly justified. If that is right, then we now know that Hobbes's first, fourth, and fifth claims, given above, are false.

Let us now examine quite briefly the sixth claim, which is that the sovereign in a state or commonwealth is not bound by the laws he makes. It will be well to remind ourselves of three facts here: (1) the sovereign surrenders none of his rights in the covenant which originates the commonwealth, and that is why he is not a party to the covenant in such a way that he is bound by its laws; (2) sovereigns, like other beings, have normal desires and wants and, if Hobbes is right, must act in accordance with them; (3) the sovereign may be one, a few, or many, depending upon the form of the state or commonwealth considered.

The first and the third points are related through one of the criticisms that may be brought against the theory. Suppose that the sovereign in the state we are considering is the majority of the people, as it is in a democracy. Nothing in Hobbes's view prevents the sovereign from being this majority, as we know from point (3). But now a very strange paradox follows, which you have no doubt noticed already. It is that the majority of the people do not need to obey the laws of the commonwealth in which they are the sovereign, because no sovereign transfers his natural rights in the covenant which gives birth to the commonwealth. Furthermore, the enforcement power which the sovereign possesses in a democracy now may be legitimately used only against the minority. We may draw one of two conclusions from this: either (a) democracy is not a possible form of commonwealth or (b) Hobbes's theory is paradoxical, because it is supposed to provide and explain a system within which most men may achieve most of their wants and needs but, in the case under discussion, must exclude most men from the state. The proof that democracies are a possible form of commonwealth is that there are democracies. Hobbes's theory is therefore paradoxical.

Point (2) relates to the earlier criticisms of ethical egoism. You will recall that the Hobbesian version of this view rests upon his acceptance of psychological egoism, which we know to be false. But assume for the moment that it is not and that Hobbes is right. Now psychological egoism is a form of determinism. It posits that, given the laws of their nature, men will in fact act only to serve their own interests. If this is true, then sovereigns, being men, are also subject to these laws. Suppose a case wherein the interests of the sovereign are not compatible with those of the subjects. Recall also that the sovereign is not subject to the laws he makes. Now consider the case of democracy again, and assume that in this democracy, the interests of the sovereign and the subjects are diametrically opposed. Here then we have a case in which (a) the subjects are obliged to obey the sovereign, (b) the sovereign majority will act contrary to the interests of the subjects, (c) both the sovereign and the subjects will act only in their own interests, and therefore, (d) the subjects will act contrary to the interests of the sovereign. It follows that the subjects will always act illegally and immorally and that permanent strife will exist between subject and sovereign unless and until their interests coincide. But the very purpose of the commonwealth is to avoid precisely this situation. Furthermore, given that determinism does not provide for the sort of freedom which would be compatible with a meaningful morality, the very concept of morality seems irrelevant not only to the sovereign (it is irrelevant to him because he is not subject to the law) but also to the subjects. The reason, again, is that it makes no sense to demand that a man act other than he does if in fact he cannot act other than he does.

For a final criticism, we might return to the claim, implicit in the third and fourth claims, that the sovereign, through his laws, *makes* right and wrong. We might ask the question "Does the law make the right, or does the right make the law?" The point here is that a concept of rightness and wrongness must exist before it is enshrined in anything, including a law. If the sovereign has no notion of rightness and wrongness, then how can he express it in a law? It will not help to reply that "right" and "wrong" simply refer to actions in accordance with or in opposition to the laws of the sovereign, because this is just to say that the right is simply the legal, and we already know that this is a mistake. It would seem, then, that the law cannot make the right, as it no doubt sometimes does; the right, or a concept of it, must exist first. If it exists first, then it exists before the law and hence before the commonwealth. Right, therefore, does not seem to originate in the manner Hobbes believes.

It will have been clear to you that many of these criticisms are related and that many of them concern ethics as well as politics. This is not a criticism of the criticisms—it merely points out the truth Aristotle noticed centuries before Hobbes, which is that ethics and politics are integrally related. In Aristotle's eyes, politics is, or ought to be, the highest arena for the exercise of ethics. If Aristotle is right, then not only morality but also politics is impossible in a strictly deterministic world.

EXERCISES

1. In a recent widely publicized speech, a national political figure criticized those who dared to put their personal moral opinions above the common convictions of the majority as expressed in the law. Evaluate his criticism.

2. Why does the natural legal law theory hinge, historically speaking, upon the properties of the universality and discoverability of the law? From what two older theories does it spring?

3. The Greeks did not think that a justification for acting rationally (naturally) was required. The thinkers of the Middle Ages did think a justification was required. What justification did they provide? Was this an adequate justification? Why or why not?

4. Formulate Coke's position against James I in argument form. Is it a good argument? Why or why not?

5. How does the logical form of a moral law differ from that of a legal law?

6. Discuss the distinction Blackstone draws between natural and artificial or man-made law. Is it a defensible distinction? Why or why not?

7. What is the function of the judge according to the natural law theory of legal law? Is it a defensible function? Why or why not?

8. What is the utilitarian criticism of the natural law theory of legal law? Do the criticisms Mill raised (which were discussed in the last chapter) have a bearing upon the topic of this section? Why or why not?

9. Why is the deterrence theory of punishment crucial for the utilitarian view of the law? If the theory fails in the cases of certain crimes, what effect does this have on the utilitarian position?

10. After the discussion of the history of the law there is a list of nine philosophical questions raised by the discussion. Show how the arguments taken from Plato in the last part of the section relate to the issues raised in these questions.

11. Why is Marx's theory called "dialectical materialism"?

12. Suppose that in fact, history did proceed as Marx thought it did; that is, suppose that all social change resulted in fact from a clash between two or more opposing forces. Would this prove that the dialectic movement of history was logically necessary? Why or why not?

13. Discuss the meaning of "necessary" in connection with Marx's analysis of historical development.

14. What are the differences between utopian socialists and Marxists? Was Marx the first communist?

15. By showing that many social changes do not conform to Marx's analysis, what critical technique are we using?

16. Analyze the argument which the basic presuppositions of Marx's theory form, and evaluate it according to our criteria.

17. If Marx were correct, what would be the consequences for moral philosophy? Why?

18. Suppose that determinism is true. Does this alone make Marx right in his analysis of history and social change? Why or why not?

19. Why does the significance of the term "economic motive" become vague to the point of uselessness if we accept Marx's analysis of the reasons for which men act?

20. Write a short essay which argues that a perfectly classless society is causally impossible, given the present psychological nature of man.

21. What doe Hobbes mean by "cause"?

22. What are the causes of the commonwealth for Hobbes?

23. Hobbes is a mechanist. What are three consequences which he must hold because he is a mechanist? Why must he hold them? Is mechanism true? Why or why not?

24. What do the words "good" and "evil" mean in a state of nature for Hobbes? What do they mean within the commonwealth?

25. Hobbes believes that all so-called altruistic action is at bottom selfish. Examine his position here, and agree or disagree with it in the light of our criteria.

26. Does Hobbes think that morality and legality within the commonwealth are the same or different? What bearing, if any, does his exclusion of the natural right to defend one's life from the class of rights given to the sovereign have upon his position on the issue of the relation between morality and legality within the state?

27. Why is a sovereign not subject to the laws of the commonwealth? Trace out some of the consequences of this view.

28. Is it true to say that ethical relativism is the theory which Hobbes espouses in a state of nature? What about in the commonwealth? Defend your answers.

29. Evaluate all of Butler's criticisms of Hobbes's theory of human nature, using our criteria.

30. How, if at all, are psychological and ethical egoism related?

IV

Philosophy
of Religion
and Aesthetics

9

Three Arguments for the Existence of God

THE TELEOLOGICAL ARGUMENT

Of all the arguments for the existence of God, the teleological argument, or, as it is often called, the argument from design, is probably the best known. Certainly among non-philosophers it is the most popular, because on the face of things it seems to have a lot of evidence on its side. What seems to be is not always what is however, and we shall see that this argument is a weak argument from analogy. Before outlining the argument, it is well to note one fact: if all of the known arguments for the existence of God were shown to be invalid, weak, or unsound, this would not prove that God does not exist. It would prove that no one has shown that he exists. The two are very different conclusions. It might in fact be the case that it is technically impossible, even in theory, to prove that God exists. If this is the case, it still does not show that God does not exist. It shows exactly what it says it shows, and nothing more. Conversely, if all the arguments purporting to prove that God does *not* exist were shown to be invalid, weak, or unsound, this would not prove that he *does* exist.

What then is the importance of discussing arguments for the existence of God? The importance is that apart from the intrinsic interest in the question, arguments purporting to show that God exists often are used as a foundation for *other* arguments and theories. Many of these other theories concern, for example, the ways in which we ought to conduct ourselves with regard to our neighbors, the sorts of actions we ought to perform, even the kinds of thoughts which we ought to attempt to suppress. They have also been used as part of an attempt to explain the origin of the universe and to predict the eternal role of man in the general scheme of things. It has been argued that man's free will depends upon God's existence and that, without a divine being, there is no *rationale* for the theory that human beings are immortal. Now if the arguments upon which these other views are based are themselves weak or unsound, then so are the theories which are thought to follow from them, at least to the extent that their soundness of strength rests upon that of the theistic arguments. These theories might of course follow from *other* premises or be supportable on grounds not connected with arguments for the existence of God, but these are not relevant to the present topic.

What then is the teleological argument for the existence of God? In essence, it is very simple. Its conclusion is that, after considering the structure of the world, it is no more reasonable to conclude that God does not exist than it would be to conclude that a watch you might find in the desert had no designer. The precision reflected in a human contrivance such as a watch is evidence for the conclusion that watches and things like them have human designers. An incomparably greater degree of precision, power, and intelligence is reflected in the natural world. The seasons follow upon one another inexorably; there seems to be a precise relation between cause and effect, means and ends. So precise is this order that we can make with considerable accuracy a very large number of accurate predictions about the future. Human beings are astonishingly well adapted to handle the tasks which they perform. Hence, there is a very great similitude between the universe at large and the contrivances of human beings. If our contrivances reflect the fact that we caused and designed them, if they provide evidence for the existence of human designers, then surely the universe may be truly said to provide evidence for a cosmic designer, God. The argument, then, is an analogy: As human contrivances stand to humans in respect of their origin and design, so the universe stands to God in respect of its origin and design.

This is one of the two most popular arguments for the existence of God, and it is easy to see why it is. Anyone who has followed the course of the stars, the path of the tides, the motion of the planets, the gestation of animals, would surely find the view that all this is an accident singularly unlikely and perhaps even downright foolish. But it is, we shall see, a giant step from the claim that it is no accident to the conclusion that God is the designer of the universe.

It might be well to recall the basic form of analogical arguments, and the factors bearing upon their strength, before we criticize the teleological argument. Analogical arguments have this form:

> A, B, C, . . . n have properties a and b;
> A, B have property c;
> Therefore, C has property c.

In our present case then:

> Human contrivances (watches, cars, houses, and so on) exhibit regularity, constant relations between causes and effects, fitness between means and ends, and design. So does the universe.
>
> Human contrivances having these properties have designers.
>
> Hence, the universe also has a designer.

To test the aptness and strength of the analogy, we must consider the number of resembling instances in the two cases, the number of dissimilarities between them, and the strength of the conclusion relative to the premises. We must also determine whether any of the philosophical mistakes have been committed and, if called for in our discussion, compare the theory with alternative views of the external criteria.

Criticisms of the Teleological Argument

This argument has been examined hundreds of times, but the best and most thorough criticism of it was made by David Hume in his *Dialogues Concerning Natural Religion*.[1] Many of the criticisms used here, though not all, came from this source, and it is recommended for further and more intensive reading.

Analogical arguments are, of course, intended only to be probable. Thus, even if the teleological argument was strong, it would not conclusively prove that Got exists. To be strong, analogical arguments require many relevant similarities between what is compared. If there are many *dissimilarities*, the argument is weak. Consider the following dissimilarities between human products and the universe.

1. There are very many human products; there is but one universe. Hence, there are no repeatable instances which can support the divine designer theory.
2. We can and do observe human designers at work. We cannot observe the divine designer. At least part of our conviction that

---

[1] David Hume, *Dialogues Concerning Natural Religion*, Norman Kemp-Smith, ed. (New York: Social Sciences Publishers, Inc., 1962).

human products have human designers is based upon the association we have between the observation of them working and what
they produce. There is no such evidence in the case of the
divine designer.

3. Human designers work with tools—their hands, mechanical exten-
sions of them, fire, lubricants, and so on. With what does the
divine designer work?

4. Many human products are designed for a purpose which is their
raison d'être and of which we may have knowledge. Even many
works of art have such an explanation. What is the purpose, the
raison d'être of the universe? (Remember that this question would
have to be answered without begging the question of God's existence.)

5. One and the same human product may have *many* human designers. We would not be justified upon finding a watch in the desert
to assume that only one man worked on it. Why then does the
design in the universe indicate the existence of only one God, if
it does this?

6. When human designers produce something, they do not create the
materials with which they work; they rearrange what they already
have. Should the divine designer be therefore co-existent with
the materials with which he works?

7. It is consistent with what is claimed about human designers in the
analogy that they *did* exist but no longer do. Nothing about the
watch in the desert entitles us to claim that its maker is still alive.
May we therefore claim that the divine designer is now dead?

8. When we conclude that something has been designed by a human
being, we normally are aware of the entire structure of that thing.
If we were not, our conclusion would not be as well-founded as
when we are. If, for example, we notice a machine which has a
pointer on a dial such that the pointer moves back and forth at a
regular rate, we might conclude that the machine is designed;
but it might well turn out that, upon examining the rest of the
machine, we discover that most of its parts have been removed
and that those which remain are in almost total disarray. It was
our originally limited perspective which caused us to attribute
order to the whole machine, when in fact we were mistaken. May
this not be true of our view of the universe?

There are two other criticisms which are not dissimilarities but which
we should still consider. One of these rests upon a category mistake,
and the other questions either the goodness, the power, or the omniscience of God.

You may recall that a category mistake consists of using within one
framework language which is more appropriate to another framework
and then forgetting that you have done this by coming to believe that the

terms have the same meaning in both settings. Now the argument from design uses the term "designer" and the term "design" with reference to both human designers and designs and to God and his work. There is some question whether there is merely a difference in degree of some sort involved here or whether the terms have completely different connotations. Certainly, they have completely different denotations, unless we include all human products within the class of divine works, in which case the teleological argument begs the question for obvious reasons.

The criticism which questions either the goodness, power, or omniscience of God is often called the argument from natural evil. It rests upon the principle that from the works of human beings we often can and do infer something about the designer with regard to his personal characteristics. Some of these inferences are normative in nature: a pornographer is not a good man. Let us for purposes of discussion assume that the teleological argument is strong. What kind of place is the universe or that part of it with which we are familiar? May we conclude from it that its designer is all-good, all-powerful, and all-knowing? Are these the attributes of a designer who permits or designs unwarranted suffering through disease or natural disaster? If God designed the universe in which these events occur, then either he cannot or he will not prevent them. If he cannot, then he is not all-powerful; if he will not, then he is not all-good. If he does not know about them, then he is not omniscient.

It seems, then, that the argument from design, the teleological argument, is a weak argument; and even if it were not, would certainly not prove, even probably, the existence of a being resembling the concept of the traditional Judeo-Christian God. Further, this much seems decidable without even raising the issues of whether propositions about a spiritual being are capable of being either true or false, and if so, how they may be known to be so. Our conclusions also seem to have been established without the necessity of comparing the theory of explanation suggested by the argument from design to any other theory. If we did this, of course, questions about the possibility that statements in the argument are neither true nor false would be raised, together with questions about the scope, fruitfulness, predictive value, and testability of the argument as a theory. What the conclusions of such investigations would be may be left to your consideration.

BERKELEY'S UNIQUE ARGUMENTS ABOUT GOD

The argument to be discussed here is unique. Actually, it consists of *two* arguments, one called the "necessary argument," the other called the "probable argument." Both are to be found in the writings of George Berkeley, an Irish philosopher who lived from 1685 to 1753.[2]

The following principles are presupposed by both of Berkeley's arguments:

1. Like effects have like causes.
2. Resemblance in proportion is a sufficient ground for arguments from analogy.
3. From a difference in degree, magnitude, etc., in an effect, we may infer a like difference in a cause.
4. Nothing is that is not caused.

The Necessary Argument

The necessary argument is easily statable, although it rests upon a complex analysis of the world of perception. This analysis concludes that if we examine what we perceive, we will see that our sensations are inactive, that is, that motion is not a datum of perception. Motion consists in a series of changes of position through time and is not something in itself. There are no necessary connections among the entities we perceive; that is, although we perceive white smoke when green wood is thrown upon a fire, there is nothing which *necessitates* this sequence; it may not happen that way in the future. Moreover, although our various sensations may only resemble other sensations, resemblance itself is not an idea of sense. No efficient causes are perceived in the natural world, though events which we name "causes" certainly are perceived. We do not, however, perceive any *action* by these causes. When you see a billiard ball move across a table and strike another, what you see is something like a motion picture: a series of images of one ball at different positions through time, followed by a series of images of the second ball at different positions in time.

A different sort of experience, which is non-sensory, informs us that we have minds and thay they are active, have no extension, and can cause changes in the world of perception. To verify this, Berkeley thought, you have merely to decide to raise your arm and then watch it go up. Berkeley was therefore a dualist, because he thought that reality was composed of two different sorts of entities: active, unextended minds, and inactive, perceivable sensations, or as he calls them, "ideas of sense." This bifurcation of reality is the result of his careful analysis

[2] A. A. Luce and T. E. Jessop, eds., *The Works of George Berkeley, Bishop of Cloyne*, 9 vols. (London: Thomas Nelson and Sons, Ltd., 1948–1957). The primary references for the arguments are: *Dialogues Between Hylas and Philonous*: pp. 202, 238; *New Theory of Vision*: 109, 127–30, 140, 143, 147; *Alciphron IV*: 5, 7; *Alciphron VII*: 12; *Theory of Vision Vindicated and Explained*: 39, 40, 42; *Draft Version of the Introduction to The Principles of Human Knowledge*: pp. 137–39; *Principles of Human Knowledge*: 65; *Philosophical Commentaries*: no. 221.

of two sorts of our experience which are in his view the *only* kinds of experience, namely, sense experience and the immediate awareness of our minds.

Now if, as Berkeley believed, there is nothing that does not have a cause, and if causes are active, then the only causes are minds, for they are the only active things. It follows that all ideas of sense or sensations have causes (because everything does) and that their causes are the acts of minds. Berkeley's name for the relation between minds and bodies is "perception." The cause of all ideas of sense is therefore their perception by some mind. This is the import of Berkeley's dictum *"esse est percipi"*—to be is to be perceived. Whatever is perceived *must* be perceived, for if it were not, it would not exist. To say that any object exists is to say that it is perceived.

Now, rather obviously, there are many possible objects of human perception which, as a matter of fact, are not being perceived at some given moment in time. The top of Mount Everest might be an example. Yet, if Berkeley is correct and if the top of the highest mountain in the world is not being perceived at some time, then at that time it does not exist. But this is ludicrous. The top of Mount Everest does not, as it were, pop in and out of existence whenever some human climbs it. It follows that there must be some other mind, a non-human mind (since by hypothesis we are speaking of times when no human mind is perceiving it), that continually perceives all things, even when human minds are not. On the basis of just three claims, his version of the principle of sufficient reason (the fourth principle given on page 334), the nature of the real world as revealed by his analysis of our two sorts of experience, and the nature of causes in particular, Berkeley formulated an argument that he believed to be a demonstration of the existence of God requiring no scientific inquiry or lengthy dialectic. Briefly, the argument might be formulated this way:

1. The existence of ideas of sense (and hence of the objects composed from them) consists in their being perceived by some mind.
2. Some objects are not perceived by human minds at all times.
3. Some changes in the world of ideas are not instituted by human minds.
4. Therefore, there is a cosmic mind which perceives all things at all times.

The Probable Argument

The necessary argument is related to the probable argument, which is the argument from analogy. If God is the cause of changes in the natural world which occur independently of human minds, and if minds, including God, operate for reasons, that is, purposively, then a study of nature should give us some idea of the purposes for which God acts and, hence, some idea of God's attributes. The reason that the inference from the regularity of natural effects to the existence and nature of God is probable and not necessary is that the observed regularities of nature are contingent on God's will, and we cannot know that he will continue to will them in the same way in the future.

The central premise in the probable argument is the astonishing claim that nature is a language. Although there is some scholarly difference over the matter, Berkeley seems really to have meant this; that is, he did not mean that nature was *like* a language, but that it really is one. To establish this claim, Berkeley undertook a careful examination of the properties of languages. He concluded that they all have at least the following properties:

1. Words may suggest absent or present things.
2. As sounds suggest things, so in the same way characters (letters) suggest sounds.
3. The relation between a heard or a written word and what it signifies is not necessary, but is founded simply upon constant conjunction.
4. Words have no meaning until we know what it is that they signify.
5. Since words are arbitrary, it is not them or anything about them, but their scope, variety etc., that is, their uses, which constitute a language.
6. Mistakes about language are due to errors of the understanding, for sense never errs; you see what you see, whether words or anything else, so if you misinterpret language it is because of mistaken inferences drawn from what you see.
7. Inferences about the future meanings of language can only be probable, because language is arbitrary.
8. Although what signs we use for what purposes is an arbitrary matter, we must use our signs consistently once we have accepted them, or they will have no public meaning.
9. Because signs or words are arbitrary, some of them must be defined by ostensive definition.
10. The same word can have different meanings in different contexts.
11. Because we are normally more interested in the meaning than in the word, we often overlook the sign and concentrate on what is signified.
12. Not every word need name or denote something. For example, some are used primarily to cause or inhibit emotion or action of various kinds without having to cause ideas or images to do so.

Berkeley was convinced that the ideas which make up the natural world have all of these properties. His book *An Essay Towards a New Theory of Vision* is an attempt to explain the relations between the sensations of sight and touch in terms of just these properties of language. In other works he extends the explanation to cover all the data of all the senses. He said that nature is composed, as is language, of

> . . . arbitrary, outward, sensible signs, having no resemblance or necessary connexion with the things they stand for and suggest . . .[3]

and that these natural signs teach us an "endless variety" of things, such as "what to shun and what to pursue," "how to regulate our motions, and how to act with regard to things different from us, as well in time as in place." The relation between natural signs, our ideas of sense, is not one of cause to effect (minds are the only causes) but of "sign to thing signified." Fire, as unusual as it may seem, is not the cause of my pain but "the mark that forewarns me of it." When I hear the coach coming, the sounds, my auditory ideas of sense, are the signs for the visual data I shall have when it comes around the corner. When I feel the chill on the air early in autumn, this is a sign that I had better harvest my tomatoes soon. An enormous number of such connections in the natural world teaches us an astonishing range of things—when to sow and when to reap, the fact that sleep refreshes, and how to act in our best interests. In short:

> . . . the articulation, combination, variety, copiousness, extensive and general use and easy application of signs . . . that constitute the true nature of language . . .[4]

are to be found in nature, and therefore it really is a language. He says that this is "really and in truth (my) opinion . . . you have as much reason to think that the Universal Agent or God speaks to your eyes, as you have for thinking any particular person speaks to your ears."

As we conclude from our observation of the behavior and speech of another person that he has certain attributes, so, if Berkeley is correct, we may draw certain conclusions about the attributes of God. He believes then, that the following analogy is strong:

> "Man : artificial languages :: God : the language of nature"

It is important to notice that this is a slightly different sort of analogy than that which we have thus far considered. It is an analogy of *proportion*, very much like that you are acquainted with in numbers, as when we say that 2:6::3:9. Although it is a new kind of analogy for our purposes, it is historically the oldest kind of analogy. Moreover, in this particular case, it rests upon an analogy of the type we considered when discussing the teleological argument, namely, the analogy between artificial languages and the natural world. That analogy might be schematized as follows:

[3] *Ibid., Alciphron IV,* 7.
[4] *Ibid., Alciphron IV,* 12.

Artificial systems of signs and the natural world have properties (1) through (12).
Artificial systems of signs are languages.
Hence, the natural world is a language.

Since the analogy of proportion rests upon this more primitive analogy, if the more primitive one is weak, then so will the analogy of proportion be at fault.

So far we have two analogies which are involved in Berkeley's probable argument. But there are actually *three* of them, for the proportional analogy does not work unless it is true that other minds stand in a relation to their ideas similar to that in which I stand to mine. This third analogy may be expressed in this way:

Other minds : their ideas :: my mind : my ideas.

This, too, is an analogy of proportion. In order for this analogy to be strong, it must be the case that ideas produced by my mind have certain characteristics in which they differ from ideas which I do not produce, and it must also be the case that in some respects my ideas are similar to ideas which I perceive but do not cause. This analogy therefore depends upon the relation of resemblance. Given that like effects have like causes and that I know the relations between my mind and the ideas I produce, then, if I perceive a similarity between my ideas and others, I am justified in inferring that the cause of these other ideas is a mind similar to my own, that is, that the cause of these other ideas is active, unextended, perceives, understands, wills, and so on. Given the additional maxim that from a difference in degree, magnitude, etc., in an effect I may infer a like difference in its cause, I may also conclude from the nature of some ideas I perceive that their cause is either more or less intelligent, moral, etc., than I am.

From my point of view, the set of visual and auditory signs which another mind produces when he speaks or writes is, of course, a set of ideas which I do not cause, but which I perceive. From the perception of such ideas, I infer not only the existence of another mind, but certain properties about it, such as the intelligence, the motives, the goodness, and so on of the speaker. Now if the natural world is a language, caused by a mind, I ought to be able to make similar inferences about that mind. If, as Berkeley assumed, we may from a difference in degree, magnitude, etc., in effect infer a like difference in a cause and if the natural world is a more magnificent, informative, beautiful language than our artificial languages, then we may draw appropriate conclusions about its author.

The probable argument is therefore really at least three arguments. First, other minds must stand to their ideas as mine does to mine.

Secondly, nature must be a language. Third, the author of nature must stand to it as do men to artificial languages. With the added premise that differences in effects are grounds for inferring differences in causes, this completes this theory. For our purposes it will be sufficient to summarize the conclusions of his argument by saying that Berkeley concludes that God exists and has the traditional attributes of the Judeo-Christian God.

Criticisms of Berkeley's Arguments

Though the two arguments just outlined are intimately related, they are also obviously different. The one is deductive, the other a complex of three analogical arguments of two different kinds. They must therefore be evaluated upon different grounds and according to different criteria. Although they differ, they have a common defect which renders the deductive argument invalid and, at the same time, destroys the ground for two of the analogies in the probable argument.

This defect concerns the nature of the relation in which God stands to the world of sensation or ideas of sense. This relation is, according to the necessary argument, that of perception. But the nature of God's "perception" is a conundrum indeed. For example, Berkeley says that although God knows pain, he does not suffer it. Indeed, God apparently has no ideas of sense at all; for this implies that he may be affected by some other being, and Berkeley denies this. What God's "perception" is also bears upon the question of what his "ideas" are. They are clearly not sensations, that is, ideas of sense. Furthermore, if the existence of mind consists in the activities it performs, such as perceiving, and if God's perception, willing, understanding, and so on are not like ours, there is some question over the meaning of the term "existence" when used in connection with God.

In the first chapter a short version of Berkeley's necessary argument was used to illustrate the fallacy of equivocation. If all of the terms in an argument do not mean the same thing whenever and wherever they are used, then this fallacy is committed. By Berkeley's own admission, "perceives" does not mean the same thing when speaking of God as it does when used to name an activity of human minds. If you look again at the necessary argument, you will see that this fact renders it invalid. The conclusion does not follow from the premises unless "perceives" *does* mean the same thing in all the statements in the argument.

The reasons for the invalidity of the necessary argument lead directly to the first of the criticisms of the probable argument. You will recall that there are three analogies in this argument. This first criticism concerns the relation of two of them. In order to argue with any plausibility that man stands to artificial languages as God stands to the natural language, we must first establish not only that nature is a language but also that other minds stand to their ideas as my mind stands to its ideas. In short, "other minds : their ideas :: my mind : my ideas" is the basic or most primitive of the three analogies. The "other" mind which is important here is, of course, God. But the criticism of the necessary argument has just shown that in fact God does *not* stand to his ideas, whatever they might be, as my mind stands to mine. Hence, the basic analogy fails. If it fails, then so does the analogy "man : artificial languages :: God : the language of nature." This is the case *even if* the third analogy, the one establishing the similarities between nature and artificial languages, is quite strong. *This* third analogy was predicated upon the possession of common properties by nature and artificial languages which had nothing to do with the nature of the relation between minds, nature, and language. But of course, "Man : artificial languages :: God : the language of nature" *is* based upon the similarity of the relation or relations between our minds and artificial languages on the one hand, and God and nature on the other hand. Artificial languages are composed of sounds, gestures, visual data such as letters and words, etc. We stand to them as perceivers and interpreters of them. But God cannot stand in the same sort of relation to nature, for reasons which we have already considered. Therefore, the analogy fails, and it cannot be offered as strong evidence for the thesis that God has certain attributes.

The non-proportional analogy concerning the claim that the natural world does constitute a language is questionable on other grounds, statable in the same form as we stated the arguments against the teleological argument. You ought to be able to think of many ways in which nature and artificial languages *differ*—many more ways, in fact, than those respects in which they are similar. Berkeley himself points out two dissimilarities: the natural language was *created*, and it is the same in all nations and climes. Artificial languages are neither.

Some authors have noted that Berkeley often seems to speak of God's ideas as "archetypes" or forms of our ideas rather than as sensations. Our ideas of sense would then have to resemble these archetypes in some way or other in order for the arguments to work. We shall not discuss this theory which, in the end, faces the same difficulties just considered.

THE ONTOLOGICAL ARGUMENT

Saint Anselm was a monk who was born about 1033 and who died in 1109. He is the inventor of the ontological argument for the existence of God. If the teleological argument is the most popular theological argument for non-philosophers, then, just as surely, the ontological argument is the most intriguing for philosophers. Controversy over most of the other arguments, including the argument from design, is now fairly minimal. But interest in and writing about the ontological argument remains at a high level. Its critics are among the most eminent men, but so are those who have argued that it is valid. Descartes put forth his own version of it, which is in itself the subject of much controversy; Leibniz believed that, with some clarification and addition, it would stand; Kant thought that it was fallacious; Aquinas did not like it; Hegel supported it; Collingwood believed in it; Gilbert Ryle argued against it; it was reformulated by Hartshorne and Malcolm; and it carries on still. In this section we shall consider the argument in four of its guises. First the original argument as stated by Anselm will be given; then René Descartes's argument will be stated, followed by Leibniz's addition to Anselm's version. Finally, the formalized version of the argument as stated by Charles Hartshorne will be given. Then, in the order in which the arguments have been presented, criticisms will be considered, and we shall try to decide whether, in fact, this is a valid argument, and if valid, whether it is sound.

Saint Anselm

One of the attractive features of the ontological argument is the apparent ease with which it can be stated. Its essential parts can be found in chapters two through four of Anselm's *Proslogion* and in his *Responsio* (reply) to one of his critics. The argument hinges upon Anselm's definition of God—that God is a being "something than which nothing greater can be conceived." He argues that we do have this concept, that is, the thought of a being greater than which nothing can be conceived. It follows that the idea of God exists in our minds. Now the question is, does it also exist independently of our minds in reality?

At this point, two implicit assumptions are required. The first is that of two things, given that we have ideas of both and that both otherwise have exactly the same properties, the more perfect of the two is the one that exists in reality. For Anselm, "greater" in his definition of God means "more perfect"; and, if what has just been said is true, existence is a perfection. To be a perfection, it must also be a property. The second assumption is that different kinds of existence are different kinds of perfecting properties. A being such that it has existence in the sense that we have an idea of it is not as perfect as a being such that it has this sort of existence plus existence in reality as well.

Realizing these things, Anselm's argument can now be completed. God, he thinks, is a being of whom we have an idea, and that idea is of a being greater than which no other can be conceived. Since the idea *is* of such a being, then the being must exist in reality and not just in our idea of it; for if it did not, it would be something other than the being greater than which no other can be conceived. Why? Because it is possible to conceive of a being who exists not just in our ideas, but in reality as well, and this being would be more perfect than one which had all its qualities except that it existed only in our minds. So if our idea of God is an idea of the *greatest* being, that being must exist in reality. In fact, Anselm thinks that the being greater than which nothing else can be conceived cannot be conceived *not* to exist and that the conception of this being is therefore greater than any conception of any being which can be conceived not to exist. If it is not possible to conceive of God as not existing, then God must be eternal, that is, there must be no time at which he came into existence (for then he would not have existed before that time), nor a time when he ceases to exist (for then he would not exist after that time). In fact, the notion of an eternal being with either a beginning or an end is contradictory. Let us, then, state the argument in its entirety in a formal way, using Anselm's words:

1. Thou art a being than which nothing greater can be conceived.
2. This . . . fool, when he hears of this being—a being than which nothing greater can be conceived—understands what he hears.
3. What (the fool) understands is in his understanding.
4. It is one thing for an object to be in the understanding, and another to understand that the object exists.
5. Whatever is understood, exists in the understanding.
6. That than which nothing greater can be conceived cannot exist in the understanding alone.
7. Suppose it exists in the understanding alone: then it can be conceived to exist in reality.
8. (If it exists in reality then this being) is greater.
9. Therefore, if that, than which nothing greater can be conceived, exists in the understanding alone, the very being, than which nothing greater can be conceived, is one, than which a greater can be conceived.
10. This (9) is impossible.
11. Hence, . . . there exists a being, than which nothing greater can be conceived, and it exists both in the understanding and in reality.
12. It is possible to conceive of a being which cannot be conceived not to exist.
13. This (being) is greater than one which can be conceived not to exist.
14. If that than which nothing greater can be conceived can be conceived not to exist, it is not that than which nothing greater can be conceived.

15. This (14) is an irreconcilable contradiction.
16. (Axiom of logic): Contradictions are always false, and hence their denials are always true.
17. There is . . . so truly a being than which nothing greater can be conceived to exist, that it cannot even be conceived not to exist; and this being thou art, O Lord, our God.

The Cartesian Version

René Descartes thought that the ontological argument was substantially correct, though he believed that it needed some support and restatement. The Cartesian version is more complex than Anselm's, because it really can be broken down into two proofs; though they are not entirely discontinuous. Furthermore, he states his version in more than one place, and the versions are not exactly identical. How the versions' *loci* of discussions of God and his roles are related in Cartesian writings is the subject of debate, and much depends upon whether one takes the view that his work is to be viewed as a unified whole. Certainly he thought it should be viewed that way. He argues that what is said in the latter part of his work, *Meditations of First Philosophy*, is logically implied by what comes before in the same work; and the rules for thought which he lays down in his *Rules for the Direction of the Mind* are certainly those which he follows in his *Discourse on Method* and in the works on science to which it is an introduction. It seems right that we should indeed view his work primarily as a unified theory with different applications in different areas. The main discussions with which we shall be here concerned are in the third and fifth of the *Meditations*.

The fundamentals of the Cartesian method are discussed in a later chapter, but it seems more appropriate to examine his method of "methodological doubt" here. It is the method of the *Meditations;* and, although its use is implicit in his other works, it has more relevance to metaphysics than to science. Most importantly for our purposes, it ultimately depends, like his other procedures, upon the viability of two criteria which serve as marks for the truth of any proposition: clarity and distinctness. Any proposition with these two marks is known intuitively to be true, and intuition is for Descartes a faculty of the mind. An intuition is therefore a case of grasping, "seeing," comprehending, or knowing a truth clearly and distinctly. There is only one other operation of the mind for Descartes—deduction, and, at every step in deduction, intuition is involved. To know that God exists is therefore *a fortiori* to know intuitively, that is, clearly and distinctly, that the proposition expressed in "God exists" is true. Furthermore, Descartes held a theory of innate ideas, and knowledge of clear and distinct ideas is knowledge of *innate* clear and distinct ideas. The journey to knowledge is therefore a process of removing the obstacles to an awareness of these ideas. In the *Meditations* this process takes the form of rejecting any proposition which it is possible to doubt. Eventually, a proposition which it is *not* possible to doubt is discovered, namely, "I think, therefore I am." The grounds for claiming that it is not possible to doubt this proposition are: even if I doubt, I must exist; and, since doubting is a form of thinking, then if I think, I must exist. It is even possible to doubt the truth of mathematical propositions in this "hyperbolical" manner, for it is logically possible that there is an "evil genius" who constantly deceives us. But even to be deceived, one must exist; and, for Descartes, existing for human minds consists in thinking. The only thing about the proposition "I think, therefore I am" which assures us of its truth is that we apprehend it clearly and distinctly. This, however, does not, after all, turn out to be all that is required for certainty. In addition, God must exist. And, most importantly, God must exist as the guarantor of the criteria, which leads to the version of the ontological argument that Descartes presents in the fifth mediation.

Descartes's First Argument

The first proof is designed to prove that, whenever we clearly and distinctly apprehend that some property or properties belong to the essence of a thing, then that is true. Only if clarity and distinctness have an objective ground for validity will this be substantiated. Only an all-powerful God who is not a possible deceiver can remove the hyperbological doubt which the hypothesis of the evil genius makes possible. We might still have the *idea* of a perfect God, but we need to know that, in reality as well as in idea, the essence of God contains his existence. In Descartes's eyes, one of the things wrong with Anselm's argument was that it lacked just such a guaranty. He thought that Anselm went from the true statement "The word 'God' has a signification" to the invalidly drawn conclusion, "God exists." Descartes wants to avoid the same difficulty in his own argument; he does not want to argue that because we have a clear and distinct idea of God, it follows that God exists outside of our idea.

He begins moving toward the proof presented in the fifth meditation by stating in the third meditation that, when we speak of having an idea, we may be speaking of two different things or be considering the idea in two different ways. We may be considering the idea as an image or as a mode of thought or way of thinking. Considered as modes of thought, all ideas are the same. But considered as images, one idea differs from another according to what it is that the idea presumably represents. One idea will be more perfect than another if what it presumably represents is more perfect than what the other presumably represents. Here, Descartes introduces a principle which he takes as axiomatic and self-evident, i.e., as clear and distinct. It is that for any effect there must be at least as much reality in the efficient and total cause as there is in its effect. The notion of "total" cause is important here. Its point is simple: if our idea of a thing which exists objectively had some property that the object did not have, then that property would of necessity have come from nothing. That something should come from nothing was for Descartes an absurdity. It follows, then, that for any representative idea, for any image, all of its properties must have their cause in the object they represent (if, indeed, they do represent). We do not yet know that any of these ideas do represent, of course; we are merely speaking of (1) ideas themselves, which exist and have properties *qua* ideas, and (2) the necessary conditions for the existence of the properties of the idea, *if* it is a representative idea.

In Descartes's view, we ourselves can logically be the cause of all of the ideas which we have, save for one. That one idea is the idea of God. In the case of all other ideas, there is nothing in them, no property of them, which forces us to conclude that there must be something outside ourselves which is the cause of them. Descartes can make this assumption only in the light of his theory of innate ideas, of course; and, clearly, the argument is only as good as that theory is. If it is a false theory, as it certainly appears to be, then the argument does not work. But for our purposes here, this can be ignored for the moment. Certainly Descartes thinks that there is "very little" that is perceived clearly and distinctly in our ideas of corporeal bodies, other men, and other minds, and that nothing rules out the possibility that the source of these ideas is in Descartes himself.

The idea of God however, is different, and it could not have proceeded from within ourselves. First, consider what "God" means: "a substance that is infinite, eternal, immutable, independent, all-knowing, all-powerful, and by which I myself and everything else, if anything else does exist, have been created." The idea of God contains all of these properties. It has objective reality as an idea in its own right, and, because it does, we can ask for its cause. This cause cannot be Descartes himself because there is nothing infinite, immutable, and so forth about Descartes; no source from within him is such that it could be the origin of his idea of God, given that the cause of an idea must have at least as much reality as the idea itself. It follows that the cause of the idea of God is outside of me, exists objectively in reality, and is at least as perfect as the idea of God. Descartes also thought that the idea of God was in fact less perfect than its cause; because, of the two forms of existence (ideational and objective), the latter is a more perfect property.

This assumption is essential for his version of the ontological argument. Before moving to that argument, let us formulate the first argument more carefully:

1. I have an idea of a being that is immutable, perfect, all-knowing, infinite, etc.
2. Nothing comes from nothing.
3. There must be at least as much reality in the total cause of a thing as in the thing itself.
4. I am not myself the cause of my idea of God, nor is any other object, event, or human.
5. Hence, there must be a being which is the cause of this idea, and which therefore has the properties of the idea.
6. Objective existence is a greater perfection than ideational existence.
7. Hence, the cause of my idea of God, which is God, is more perfect than my idea of God.

Descartes's Ontological Argument

Now it is time to consider Descartes's version of the ontological argument. From the first argument, it is clear and explicit in the Cartesian version that existence is both a property or predicate and a perfecting property or predicate. It is an attribute which beings may be meaningfully said to have or not to have. We are here speaking of objective existence in particular. Given this hypothesis, or rather, truth, Descartes now proceeds to examine the idea of God. His intention is to try to discover what those properties are which belong to the idea of God in its very essence; that is, he wants to discover what the properties are which I clearly and distinctly see to belong to the essence of my idea of God. By analogy, he examines my idea of a triangle. We notice there that the properties of having three angles whose sum is equal to two right angles, of being such that the greatest side of a triangle is subtended by its greatest angle, and so forth, are essential to the idea of a triangle. Without having these properties, the idea I have, whatever else it might be, is not the idea of a triangle. My defense for this claim is that I see clearly and distinctly that it is so.

Now, in the case of my idea of a triangle, one of the properties which is *not* essential for the ideational existence of a triangle is that there be triangles objectively existing in reality. Hence, it is not legitimate to argue from the truth that there is an idea of a triangle to the conclusion that there is at least one objectively existing triangle. But suppose that we had an idea such that its existence was *not* separable from its essence. In that case, the inference from the existence of the idea to the objective existence of the cause of the idea would be legitimate. And, of course, Descartes does think that we have such an idea, namely the idea of God. An idea of God without objective existence as an essential property is an inconceivable to Descartes as is the idea of a rectilinear triangle whose three angles do not equal the sum of two right angles. Moreover, says Descartes, our idea of God is the *only* idea we have such that its essence includes the objective existence of its cause, and it is not possible to formulate the idea of two such beings. God therefore exists in objective reality. Here is a more formal statement of his argument:

1. All things have properties which are such that without them, the thing could not be what it is. These are essential properties.
2. If we clearly and distinctly perceive that certain properties belong to the true and immutable nature of something (the thing's essence or form) then those properties may be truly predicated of that thing.
3. An examination of our idea of God discloses distinctly and clearly that objective existence in reality truly belongs to his essence.
4. Therefore, God truly exists in objective reality.

Leibniz's Argument

Gottfried Wilhelm Leibniz also thought that Anselm's argument was substantially correct but that it needed one addition to make it both sound and valid. He began with the assumption, as did Descartes, that existence is a predicate and a perfection. Further, he thought that it would be silly to think of God as a merely possible being, for given the fundamental soundness of Anselm's argument, if God has the property or predicate of objective existence, then he does not possibly exist, he actually does. But Leibniz did not think that either Anselm or Descartes had shown that God was a *possible* being, which, of course, he must be if he is to be an *actual* being. Leibniz therefore undertook to show that God was a possible being. He began by stating that anything at all is to be considered as possible until it is shown that it is not possible. The problem is therefore to show that it cannot be shown that God is not a possible being. What then could show that God was not a possible being? His answer was that no being such that the concept of it contains a contradiction is possible. To discover that God is possible is therefore to discover that the idea or concept of God which we have does not contain contradictory parts. The attempt to do this is simple. All being is either necessary or contingent. If there were no idea of necessary being, then there would be no idea of contingent or dependent being. There is an idea of contingent being; therefore there is an idea of a necessary being. The idea of contingent being is possible, so it follows that the idea of a necessary being is also possible.

Leibniz was also concerned to show that a necessary being, who would be the being possessed of all possible perfections, was not impossible from the viewpoint of having incompatible perfections. He accomplishes this by defining a perfection as a simple quality. Simple qualities are indefinable because they are not reducible to any other qualities or parts. In this sense, the properties of God are simple. But, according to Leibniz, simple qualities can never be shown to be incompatible with other simple qualities, since to do so would require showing that the terms which denote the qualities could be further defined, i.e., reduced, which by hypothesis is impossible. A demonstration of such incompatibility is therefore impossible.

Finally, Leibniz argues that in the simple consideration of the concept of God as the subject of all possible perfections, we do not find any obvious incompatibility. That is, it is not evident that such incompatibilities are present. He concludes that the idea of God is not self-contradictory and that hence God is a possible being. With this addition, he thinks that the ontological argument is sound and valid.

Hartshorne's Argument

The final argument we shall consider is more complex than the others, partly because it involves the use of modern symbolization and partly because it includes premises from both Anselm's first argument and from some later remarks he makes concerning the definition of God as a being who cannot be conceived not to exist. Norman Malcolm and Charles Hartshorne have defended this form of the argument, and what follows is an explication of Hartshorne's position.[5] The heart of this argument concerns the logical status of the question of God's existence, given Anselm's definition of God. In short, it assumes that if God exists, he does so necessarily, and hence, that his non-existence is impossible; or, if God does *not* exist, then he does not exist necessarily and his existence is impossible. Then the argument asserts that the existence of God has not been proven to be logically impossible, so we can assume that it is logically necessary. We shall first consider a rendering in English of the symbolically expressed argument; then, for those who have studied quantified symbolic logic, the formal version will be given.

1. There is at least one perfect being if, and only if, it is analytically true that there is a perfect being. (This is Anselm's principle, which Hartshorne and Malcolm understand to be that perfection does not exist contingently or dependently but necessarily or independently.)

---

[5] In the *Encyclopedia of Philosophy* under "Onthological Argument for The Existence of God."

2. Either it is analytically (necessarily) true that there is at least one perfect being, or it is not analytically true that there is at least one perfect being. (This is simply an instance of the law of excluded middle.)

3. It is not analytically true that there is at least one perfect being if, and only if, it is analytically true that it is not analytically true that there is at least one perfect being. (This is an instance of Becker's postulate, which is an axiom of modal logic asserting that if anything has modal status, then it is always necessary. As we shall see, there is some doubt about both the postulate and its application here.)

4. Either it is analytically true that there is at least one perfect being, or it is analytically true that it is not analytically true that there is at least one perfect being. (Given that Becker's postulate is sound, plus the law of excluded middle, this follows from 2 and 3.)

5. It is analytically true that it is not analytically true that there is at least one perfect being if, and only if, it is analytically true that there is not at least one perfect thing. (This follows from the first premise in this way: The consequent of the first premise is "It is analytically true that there is at least one perfect being." If this is false, then it is necessarily false. If it is necessarily false, then since the relation between the antecedent and the consequent in that premise is one of strict implication, the antecedent must also be necessarily false. The fifth premise asserts this.)

6. It is analytically true that there is at least one perfect being, or it is analytically true that there is not at least one perfect being, (This follows from 4 and 5).

7. It is not analytically true that there is not at least one perfect being. (This is a statement of Leibniz's claim that perfection is not impossible. Hartshorne also accepts it as an "intuitive" truth, or at least as a claim that is not intuitively false and has not been shown to be false.)

8. It is analytically true that there is at least one perfect being. (This follows from 6 and 7 by disjunctive syllogism.)

9. It is analytically true that there is at least one perfect being if, and only if, there is at least one perfect being. (This is an axiom of modal logic, which asserts that a proposition is analytically true if and only if the proposition is true.)

10. Therefore, there is at least one perfect being. (This follows from 8 and 9 by modus ponens.)

Wherever "analytically true" occurs in the argument, the words "necessarily true" may be substituted for them, and "necessarily true" means "true by the necessity of the meanings of the terms employed." Now let us look at Hartshorne's symbolic version. In this argument, N means analytically or necessarily true, the arrow signifies strict implication, and $(\exists x)\,(Px)$ means "There is at least one perfect being."

1. $(\exists x)\ Px \rightarrow N\ (\exists x)\ Px$	Anselm's principle
2. $N\ (\exists x)\ Px\ v - N(\exists x)\ Px$	Excluded middle
3. $-N\ (\exists x)\ Px \rightarrow N - N\ (\exists x)\ Px$	Becker's postulate
4. $N\ (\exists x)\ Px\ v\ N - N\ (\exists x)\ Px$	From (2) and (3)
5. $N - N\ (\exists x)\ Px \rightarrow N - (\exists x)\ Px$	From (1)
6. $N\ (\exists x)\ Px\ v\ N - (\exists x)\ Px$	From (4) and (5)
7. $-N - (\exists x)\ Px$	"Possible perfect being" principle
8. $N\ (\exists x)\ Px$	From (6) and (7)
9. $N\ (\exists x)\ Px \rightarrow (\exists x)\ Px$	Modal logic axiom
10. $(\exists x)\ Px$	From (8) and (9)

Criticisms of the Ontological Argument

There have been many criticisms of the ontological argument in its various forms. We shall begin with an examination of the original argument, and then proceed through the others. Some of the critcisms are applicable to only one of the versions, while others apply to all of them. Criticisms that apply to all of the versions are marked with an asterisk.

From the beginning, the criticisms of the argument, have largely concerned two moves in it. One is the move from the existence of a concept or idea to the claim that something that corresponds to the concept or idea exists. In addition, as we have seen, this move is presumed in at least some of the versions of the argument to be a "necesary" one, so that a necessary connection between the idea or some of its properties is being asserted. Another way of saying this is to argue that from the fact that any X may be conceived in such and such a way it does not follow that what is so conceived exists independently of that conception.

The second focal point of criticism is not exactly a "move" but an assumption which must be true if the argument is to be sound. This assumption is that existence is a property. To this second criticism we can add a third, which is that even if existence is a property, this does not imply that it is a perfection. Of course, if it is not a property, then it is also not a perfection.

Let us consider these two criticisms in order, as they apply to the original argument, and then study the rest of the remarks we can make about it.

First Criticism

* From the fact that a concept has certain properties, nothing follows about the object or cause of the concept.

We all have a concept of a triangle. We know that if it is a concept of a triangle, then its interior angles add up to 180 degrees, and we know that it must have three sides. We can conclude from the study of the triangle-concept that *if* anything is a triangle, then it must have these properties. Now, having drawn this conclusion, have we shown that there are triangles? Concepts of triangles and triangles are two different sorts of things, and it seems that we have only drawn conclusions about the *concept* of a triangle but not about any triangle. Similarly, the argument of Anselm seems to move from an apparent conflict between two concepts or ideas to the conclusion that one of the concepts must have a corresponding object. The two concepts are of two beings perfectly alike except that one of them exists in reality as well as in idea. But the most Anselm seems entitled to infer is that *if* there is a perfect being, then he would have to exist in reality as well as in concept; and this conclusion does not assert that there is in fact such a being.

Second Criticism

 * *Existence is not a predicate.*
Immanuel Kant was the first philosopher to argue that the argument was wrong-headed and proved nothing, because it hinges upon a mistaken assumption, namely that existence is a property. Kant, as we know, distinguished among three kinds of propositions. The three kinds are analytic truths, synthetic *a posteriori* truths, and synthetic *a priori* truths. Kant is willing to grant that, if existence is a predicate and God exists, then the sentence "God exists" is analytically true. But in Kant's view, sentences which assert existence are not analytically, but synthetically true, and, moreover, they do not assert that existence is a property. To determine that something exists, we must test our experience. For example, suppose you want to know whether the quarter that I say I have in my pocket exists. If I could not show it to you, if I could not spend it because I did not have it, or if it had no specific color that could be perceived by anyone, then it would be nonsense to say that it exists. And it would not be contradictory, but simply false, to say that it did exist in such circumstances. That is, I would be saying in effect that I had something which was round, spendable, of a specific color, and so forth, when in fact I did not. When we say that something of which we have an idea exists we are doing no more than saying that there is something *not* an idea which corresponds to the idea. We are not saying that the something which corresponds to the idea has, in addition to the correspondence between it and my idea of it, another property, namely existence.

John Hick points out in his article about the ontological argument in the *Encyclopedia of Philosophy* [6] that this same point about existence not being a predicate is a feature of Bertrand Russell's theory of descriptions.

[6] *Loc. cit.*

We cannot go into that theory here, but, roughly, the point is that an analysis of descriptions discloses that when we assert existence, we are asserting that there is a corresponding object to some given description; and when we deny existence, we are simply asserting that there is no such corresponding object. What the existential quantifier says in symbolic logic is that there is an instantiation of the proposition qualified by this symbol; and when the symbol is negated, it says simply that there is no such instantiation. "Exists" is therefore not a predicate symbol; rather, it qualifies an entire proposition. Predicate symbols, on the other hand, modify individuals when the propositions in which they occur are instantiated. We ought, therefore, to determine not whether God has a property called "existence," but whether or not there is an instantiation for descriptions of God, such as "The all-powerful being," etc. To say simply that "God exists" tells us nothing about his properties. And the final point here is that we cannot determine whether descriptions of God have an instance unless we *do* something—the descriptions are not self-evident because they are, in Kant's terms, synthetic.

The same sort of point was made by G. E. Moore when he noted that if existence was a predicate, then it should add to our knowledge of the subject which has it. But although the predicate "growl" in "Tame tigers growl" amplifies our knowledge of tame tigers, our knowledge of such beasts is not amplified by the sentence, "Tame tigers exist." [7]

Third Criticism

* *If existence is a property, it is not clear that it is a perfecting property.*

Both of the first two criticisms appear to be substantially correct, though we have yet to consider the other versions. If this position is correct, then, of course, existence is also not a perfection, since to be so it would have to be a property. But even if we grant the opposite of the criticism and agree that existence is a property, it does not seem evident that it is a *perfecting* property. The concept of perfection is very difficult to analyze. In some cases, of course, it is not all that difficult, namely those in which perfection is expressed comparatively. One racer is *better* than another if he can run faster, or with more endurance, and so forth. But it is not clear that the concept of perfection is exhausted by an enumeration of all known standards, and a listing of those entities which most nearly meet them. Furthermore, the standards with which we are familiar are all either invented by us, found in nature and categorized by us, or attributed anthropomorphically by us to things we do not ob-

---

[7] G. E. Moore, "Is Existence a Predicate?" *Proceedings of the Aristotelian Society,* Supplementary vol. 15 (1936), pp. 175–88.

serve. One thing, however, is clear: in no case of normal perfection or standards related to it do we count existence as a property which perfects anything. And the case is complicated if we talk about different *kinds* of existential perfection. Why, of two things, one of which exists conceptually and the other in fact, is the latter more perfect? Why not the former? And if something exists in both modes, why is it more important for that? We cannot here push this beginning to its conclusion, and it remains in spite of all that has been written about existence as a predicate or property, a little explored question. It surely *is* justifiable to say, however, that it is not self-evident that if something exists factually as well as conceptually, it is more perfect than something which exists only conceptually. And if this is true, if there is nothing *a priori* about the assumption of Anselm, Descartes, Leibniz, and Hartshorne to this effect, then the thesis needs to be defended. So we can add this third criticism to our list of remarks applicable to all the arguments.

Fourth Criticism

* *It is false that we have, all of us, a clear and distinct idea of a being greater than which no other can be conceived.*

This fourth criticism, which is applicable to all arguments similar to Anselm's, is related to the third, though much more general. Anselm, of course, does not use the criteria of clarity and distinctness. But he does claim that even the fool *understands* the claim. What is it that he understands? Presumably that a being which is the greatest that can be conceived is one that is infinite, all-powerful, all-merciful, pure actuality, all-knowing, and so forth. What does "infinite" mean? "Eternal?" How about "all-powerful?" What is power? A powerful man is one who can, for example, lift very heavy things, perform many tasks requiring great physical exertion without exhaustion, think in depth for a very long time, rear many healthy children, withstand brainwashing, etc. Is God merely the *most* powerful man? Of course not, or at least, of course not for the authors of the arguments we have considered. But what *is* he then? The point is that no one can answer this question easily. And we have in the briefest way mentioned but one of the properties which make God, if he exists, that being greater than which no other can be conceived. We have one advantage here: this is a question that can be settled by an appeal to experience, if we can all believe that we are giving truthful responses. I promise you that my answer is the truth, and I find upon careful examination that I do *not* have a clear and distinct idea of a being, greater than which no other can be conceived. Answer the same question yourselves. I wager that your answer, carefully considered, will be the same as mine.

Fifth Criticism

* The concept of "necessity" does not help to prove that an entity, God, corresponds to the idea we have of a necessary being.

The fifth criticism concerns the concept of "necessity." We already know what it means to say that a proposition is necessarily true: its denial is a contradiction if it is. If we are talking about logical necessity, then only sentences have this property—or, if you prefer for technical reasons, propositions. God is not a proposition nor a sentence. He is therefore not logically necessary. Well, then, what other sorts of necessity are there? Some say that there is factual necessity, or, if you prefer, causal necessity. This thesis is discussed in connection with determinism, where it seems that determinism is mistaken. But even if this is wrong, causal necessity is not really relevant here, because God is not a causal agent nor an event of the sort belonging in the empirical world. If he is neither logically nor causally necessary, then what is left? We could, of course, stipulate that God is a being who must exist, but the arguments would all beg the question if this were done; and, in any event, with the question about the necessity involved, the force of the "must," would remain.

It seems that we can truly say that the sort of necessity assumed in the arguments is factual necessity; furthermore, by "necessary," both Anselm and Descartes seem to mean nothing more than "eternal." This will not help them however, because we now must return to the fact that from the existence of a concept of an eternal being, it does not follow that there is one. And this does not take into account the possibility that we have no such concept to begin with. If this is true, then the necessity attributed to God by these thinkers is not proven because the existence of God is not proven; and the latter seems to be a condition for proving the former. In Hartshorne's case, there is a special wrinkle which we shall examine shortly; but, in general, the criticism applies to his argument too.

Criticisms of Descartes

All of these criticisms seem to apply to all of the versions of the argument. There may be more of them, but these are sufficient for our purposes. There are, in addition, some interesting criticisms of the particular arguments, especially of Descartes's version. The first of these concerns the criteria of clarity and distinctness which Descartes requires as marks of the truth of a proposition so far as our knowing this truth is concerned. You may recall that in the third meditation, God is required to guarantee the criteria. If he did not exist, or if we did not know that he exists, then we would have no protection against the hyperbolical doubt made possible by the "evil genius" hypothesis. At the same time, when we come to the fifth meditation, the ground for claiming that existence is an *essential* property of God is that one clearly and distinctly sees this to be the case. Without this intuitive knowledge, the Cartesian version of the ontological argument will not work. It seems fairly obvious that, if one is to take Descartes's own words literally here—and, surely, if any philosopher ever intended that his readers do that, Descartes did—he begs the question. God must exist if clarity and distinctness are to be adequate criteria for knowledge; clarity and distinctness must be adequate criteria if we are to see that existence is essential (i.e., a necessary part of God's essence); we clearly and distinctly see that this is so; therefore, God exists. This is what he says, though with many more steps in the argument and with a distinction we have not discussed. That distinction is between what we know and the order in which we come to know it and between what there is and the order of dependency upon it. But the latter distinction does not matter for our purposes, because we are here concerned with a proof of knowledge. Descartes thought this to be a demonstration, a proof from premises known to be true, and the first five criticisms themselves cast doubt upon this belief. But the proof is still required, even if we assume as he did that we already know that God exists and merely need to show how it is that we know this. The point is, of course, that this is inadequately shown. So the first criticism of the Cartesian version of the argument is: Descartes begs the question of God's existence in his justification of the criteria of clarity and distinctness.

The second criticism of Descartes concerns his third premise, which is the axiom that there must be at least as much reality in the total cause of anything as in the effect. The issue is again one of meaning. In scholastic terminology, phrases such as "as much reality" presumably had a meaning, and that is the terminology Descartes is using when he offers his version of the argument. As we have seen, Descartes is thinking of the "total cause" of our idea of God when he argues that it must have as much reality as its effect, the idea. At least part of what this means is that there is something about the idea of God which forces me to conclude that there is something outside of myself which is the cause of this idea and that, if this is so, then that cause must be at least as perfect and have all of the properties which my idea has. Two immediate points come up here: First, the phrase "at least as" does not force us to conclude that the cause of the idea, God, is any *more* perfect than the idea of him, which Descartes admits is inadequate. Second, nothing that Descartes says implies that God has no *other* properties than those represented in our idea of him, nor is it implied that the properties of God, other than perfection itself, are perfecting properties. Hence, the same criticism of the concept of perfecting properties that was raised earlier comes into force here.

The idea of a cause having at least as much objective reality as its effect is misleading when applied to God because there is a difference in ontological status between God and our idea of him. Gilbert Ryle has called this a category-mistake. When the notion of causality is applied in a context other than its normal one, no mistake is made. But when we *forget* that we are using the word in this unusual way, then we have made an error. The same appears to be true of the notion of "reality." I understand it also if I am speaking about the world of mental events, such as my decisions, willings, desires, and so forth, though this does not mean that these things are events in the way that a train accident is an event. But I am not at all sure that I understand the concept of reality when it is applied to a divine being, and this becomes the more confusing when the reality of god is defined in terms of yet another category-mistake namely, his causal relations to an idea which I presumably have. Moreover, this is not to mention the criticism already given of Anselm, namely that it seems doubtful that we have the idea in the first place.

We have already discussed Kant's criticism that existence is not a property and, hence, not a perfecting property. If that is so, then existence cannot be a necessary part of the essence of God, as Descartes would have it. But furthermore, even if existence is a property, we only know that it is a necessary part of the essence of God by intuition, the analogy being that we see this in the way that we see that geometrical figures have certain essential attributes. This is an inadequate analogy. Mathematical definitions are stipulative. There are no triangles lying around, and the discovery that the interior angles of a right-angled triangle add up to 180 degrees is not like the discovery that the orbit of Mars is elliptical. When we discover the facts about the concept of a triangle, we are learning something about the meanings of words; but this is not what we are discovering when we learn about planetary orbits or the paths of stars. If Descartes is right, we must be learning something about the concept of God when we learn that existence and essence are inseparable in that concept. But it is still a discovery about a concept and not about something not a concept. When one discovers that having 180 degrees and three interior angles are inseparable properties of the concept of rectilinear triangles, he does not discover that there are rectilinear triangles; when one discovers that properties X and Y are inseparable from the concept of God, he does not discover that there is a God. And what X and Y are is irrelevant. If X happens to be called "existence," then whatever that name is, it names a property of the concept, not of something else.

Intuition itself is a suspicious concept, aside from the fact that Descartes certainly seems to beg the question of the existence of God by requiring that God exist in order to guarantee the viability of the criteria of clarity and distinctness (which, in turn, are the marks of an intuition). The trouble with intuition is its fatal privacy. It requires, on the one hand, that to be viable and valuable in proofs, we must all have similar intuitions, and, on the other hand, that knowledge be an individual thing not accessible to others. Clarity and distinctness cannot be properties of propositions; for, if they were, all of us would find the same propositions clear and distinct, given equal mental capacity. Or, if we did not, then we would require *two* sets of criteria: clarity and distinctness in propositions and clarity and distinctness of states of mind. If we have only the latter set of criteria, then nothing whatsoever follows about the truth or falsity of a proposition from the fact that the state of mind or perception with which or in which we apprehend it has certain properties. That is, if I am in a concentrating state of mind, for example, it does not follow that what I perceive in the way of propositions will have one truth-value rather than another. If clarity and distinctness are states of mind, then the same is true in that case. The most that Descartes can claim is psychological certainty about the truth of the proposition "God exists." But we are all familiar with people who are psychologically certain that something is true when, in fact, that of which they are so certain is false.

Criticisms of Leibniz and Hartshorne

A similar criticism can be made of Leibniz and his attempt to save the argument. He realized himself that the fact that we cannot see that something is impossible does not of itself show that it is possible. When he argues that the being God is a possible being because the concept of God is not a contradictory concept, he is saying that we do not *perceive* a contradiction in this concept. But this does not show that there is no contradiction, and it begs the question about whether we have a clear and distinct idea of God (which, of course, would be an idea of God that was not contradictory). If it was not such an idea, then for Leibniz God would not be possible. And if it is such an idea, then there is no need to show that God is a possible being. So no matter which way Leibniz turns, he either begs the question by positing a clear and distinct idea which entails that God is possible and hence actual, or he must assert that we do not have such a clear and distinct idea and, hence, becomes subject to the criticism that our not perceiving a contradiction in the idea does not entail that there is no contradiction. Either way, the proof is inadequate.

The argument as put forward by Hartshorne is more complex in form, and correspondingly difficult to criticize, though not from all aspects. A very difficult criticism, which we shall not investigate here, concerns the adequacy of Becker's postulate. Intuitively, it is not obvious. Unfortunately, however, it is not sufficient to refute this argument to say that Becker's postulate is not intuitively obvious. Fortunately, more may be said about it, not all on the sophisticated level of the modal logicians. But none of it is simple. What Becker's postulate says in Hartshorne's version of the ontological argument is this:

(1) If it is not analytically (necessarily) true that there is a perfect being, then (strict implication) it is necessarily true that it is not analytically (necessarily) true that there is a perfect being.   This is equivalent to the following:

(2) If it is possible that there is not a perfect being, then it is analytically (necessarily) true that it is possible that there is no perfect being. In turn, both of these statements are equivalent to:

(3) It is necessarily (analytically) the case that if it is not necessarily (analytically) true that there is a perfect being, then it is necessarily (analytically) true that it is not necessarily (analytically) true that there is a perfect being.

Now the whole problem would be clearer if we could think of examples that were not concerned with the existence or non-existence of a perfect being. Let us first use an example which seems to illustrate the sense of "necessary" which is used by Anselm himself:

(4) If it can be true (is possible that it be true) that a proposition p is true by definition (whether explicit or implicit) then p is true by definition.

What we must do then, if this illustration of what Anselm meant by "necessary" is accepted, (the word "necessary" need not be mentioned in the illustration of its meaning) is to find an example involving this use which is also a form of Becker's postulate, and then show in particular how this form has an instance which is false. Consider:

(5) If it is conceivable that not-p is inconceivable, then not-p is inconceivable. The word "inconceivable" here incorporates Anselm's meaning of "necessary." Example (5) is a bit tricky, because, in fact, there are substitution instances of it which make Becker's postulate doubtful *if* we accept this interpretation of Anselm's sense of "necessary." Let us then be perfectly fair and give two examples or interpretations of the postulate which are in fact satisfactory for Becker:

(6) If it is possible that a proposition p has nothing but true substitution instances on a truth-table, then p has a true substitution instance on a truth-table.

(7) If it can be shown whatever it is like for a proposition p to have all true substitution instances on a truth-table, then p has all true substitution instances on its truth-table.

It seems that (6) and (7) are acceptable, given Becker's postulate. But what of this example, which seems to be an instance of (5):

(8) If it is conceivable that "Some copper is not malleable" is inconceivable, then "Some copper is not malleable" is not conceivable?

Consider the case where at some time, it is conceivable that people will discover (as they have not at this time) that all copper is malleable. Two scientists, or if you like, alchemists, are discussing the matter. One says, "But you know, we haven't run across any specimens of this metal yet which are not malleable." The second replies, "Yes, I know. It is conceivable that some day we will all say that it is inconceivable that some piece of metal could be copper and not malleable." Here, the second man is clearly saying that the definition of copper will come to include the property of malleability. But the point is that is does not yet include that property at the hypothetical time and in the hypothetical circumstances of which we are speaking. That is, it is *possible* at this time that it will be necessarily (analytically) true that at some other time it will be necessarily (analytically) true that all copper is malleable. But it is not yet the case, though it is possible that it will be. Now the purpose of these examples is to show that Becker's postulate fails when *tense* operators are introduced into the argument. When they are, the postulate becomes something like this:

(9) If for any proposition it is conceivable that it (the proposition) will become analytic, then it is inconceivable that it is not analytic.

Now (9) is clearly false. The question is then, is the introduction of tense operators into the postulate justified? It seems to be, provided we are speaking about the context of the ontological argument. This is apparently because Anselm, Descartes, Leibniz, and Hartshorne must hold that the concept of God at any given time t is the same as that at any other given time t. This, of course, is amenable to treatment by Becker's postulate. But it is an assumption which seems false on the basis of the evidence which we have concerning the historical definition of God. Indeed, the concept of God is being redefined even today. They may reply, of course, that the original concept, as defined by Anselm, is the only possible concept. But *that* claim, that is, the claim that his is the only possible concept of God, is not proven by Anselm, nor by any of the other arguments offered. Moreover, Becker's postulate rests on the true claim that if a proposition p is analytically true, then the denial of p is a contradiction. But it then seems to say that if "not necessarily not p" is a contradiction, then p is analytic; and this is *not* true. "Necessarily not *p*" means that the proposition "not *p*" does not have a truth-table that has nothing but "F's" under "not *p*"—but this does not imply that it has nothing but "*T*'s" under "not *p*." "Not *p*" may be a *contingent* statement, in which case it does not imply that *p* is analytic.

We can conclude, then, that this claim that is essential if Hartshorne's version is to work is not proven. There are other criticisms of the Hartshorne position. One which is fairly common is that put forward by Professor John Hick in his article on the argument in the *Encyclopedia*. According to that argument, Hartshorne uses two different concepts of "necessity" in his presentation. The two different concepts are onto-logical, or factual necessity, and logical necessity. As we know, logical necessity is a property of propositions and nothing else. A proposition is logically necessary if its denial is a contradiction. The question is whether propositions which assert that a given entity or sort of entity exists are logically necessary in this sense. Basically, the issue is whether or not existence is a matter of empirical verification, or at least possible experiential verification in the broad sense. Logically necessary propo-sitions do not require such verification, because they are true by virtue of the meanings of their terms and nothing else. One does not need evidence to confirm the truth that all bachelors are unmarried.

What does Anselm intend the proposition "God exists" to be? Is it a logically necessary truth or not? Seemingly, he does not intend it to be a tautology, for these are uninformative and require no proof at all. If these two sorts of necessity are the only two sorts, then the proposition must be factually and ontologically necessary rather than logically necessary. There are other reasons, which we need not con-sider here, for believing that Anselm held this view of the nature of the necessity of the proposition. What we do need to consider is whether in Hartshorne's argument the statements assert one or the other sort of necessity; and it seems that they assert logical necessity. That this is the case you can determine by a reconsideration of the argument. But in the other statements or premises, he is asserting the other sort of necessity, because he begins, after all, with what he believes to be a restatement of Anselm's principle, which we have decided asserts on-tological necessity rather than logical. The most that the argument can establish is what it does in the first six premises, which is what Anselm achieved centuries before. What he proved was that *if* a perfect being exists, then his existence is ontologically necessary; that is, he is without beginning and without end, independent and timeless. But "if," though a small word, is a very important one. If there were men with two heads on Mars, then many other things might follow. But they do not, and there are no men with two heads on Mars.

Faith and Rationality

It is important for many reasons to remark at this point that, even if all of the arguments for the existence of God which have been outlined and all of those which have not been given are unsound, this does not prove that God does not exist. This is scant comfort for the convinced theist; for what it boils down to is the claim that what he believes is not proven, though the best minds in history have tried to prove it. Yet it is an important technical point, for it remains logically possible that God exists, and, in some sense, it leaves room for that nebulous thing called faith. We will not discuss what faith is, let alone what justified faith is. Certainly, it is a misused concept. It has been used to justify the existence of ghosts, the execution of the innocent and the guilty, and the belief in God and in gods, in goblins and in witches. But it has also been used to characterize the belief of a man and a woman in the love and fidelity of one another, belief of a man in the future of his children, our trust that the future will in salient features resemble the past, our belief in science and in modern religions (some fairly devoid of superstition of the old variety), and our abiding hope that somehow mankind will muddle through. Sadly, in all these matters we may be wrong. This is at once the dilemma and the strength of faith. It cannot admit a pessimism that is at least possible and at worst justified, while at the same time it is one of our few bulwarks against the despair that is incumbent upon accepting this pessimism. Faith is an attitude. It is not self-justifying, unless one is willing to accept the pragmatic justification offered by Rousseau, William James, and others. But pleasing effects do not require truth as a condition. Such an argument for the existence of God requires only simplicity of mind and a willingness to hide one's head in the sand, and this is the antithesis of the attribute which has brought man whatever progress he has achieved— rationality. Our emotional and psychological lives are crucial, for without them we would not be *human* beings. The same is true of rationality, the ability to draw inferences validly.

EXERCISES

1. If it is true that all of the arguments for the existence of God which are known are not good arguments, why does this not prove that God does not exist? If all of the arguments designed to prove that God does not exist are not good arguments, why does this not prove that God does exist?
2. In addition to the intrinsic interest the question has, what other reasons have caused men to try to prove that God exists?
3. State the teleological argument in precise analogical form.

4. Invent another analogical argument, not concerned with theological matters, which is weak in the way that the teleological argument is weak.

5. In addition to the dissimilarities listed, name five others which work against the argument.

6. Discuss the role of the category-mistake in the criticisms of the teleological argument.

7. Why would the teleological argument not prove the existence of the Judeo-Christian God, even if it were a strong argument from analogy?

8. Discuss the argument from natural evil. Do you think it is a good argument? Why or why not?

9. If someone concluded from the fact (assuming that it is a fact) that all of the parts of the universe are designed, that therefore the universe as a whole was designed, what fallacy would he be committing?

10. Does it follow from the claim that the universe is not an accidental happening that it was created and designed by a supreme being? Why or why not?

11. Examine the principles which Berkeley's arguments assume to be true. Are they well-founded principles? Why or why not?

12. What are the objects for Berkeley? What are causes? Are objects causes? Why or why not?

13. How are the necessary argument and the probable argument related?

14. How many different arguments from analogy are present in the probable argument? How many different *kinds* of argument from analogy are used? What is their order of dependence upon one another?

15. Give five properties of languages which are *not* properties of nature.

16. What equivocation does Berkeley's necessary argument commit? Is this also a category-mistake? Why or why not?

17. If one of the analogical arguments fails, does the entire probable argument fail? Why or why not?

18. Argue against the possibility of knowing that the analogy "Other minds : their ideas :: my mind : my ideas" is a strong analogy.

19. Assume for the moment that Berkeley is right when he says that nature is a language. Now argue that even if this is true, the analogy "Man : artificial languages :: God : the language of nature" is not a strong analogy.

20. The teleological argument does not prove the existence of the Judeo-Christian God, even if it is a strong argument. Assuming that Berkeley's arguments are sound and valid and strong, does he come any closer to proving the existence of this particular God? Why or why not?

21. Shorten the argument composed from Anselm's words to those claims which are absolutely essential to the ontological argument.

22. Why does Anselm say that the ninth statement in his argument is "impossible"?

23. Why does Descartes require the criteria of clarity and distinctness to be justified before he can support his version of the argument?

24. How does Descartes beg the question in his attempt to justify the criteria of clarity and distinctness?

25. Why does Descartes think that it is not possible that I am the source of the idea of God which I have?

26. Criticize the Cartesian version of the ontological argument on the basis of his use of the term "perfection."

27. What addition did Leibniz think the argument needed to make it sound and valid?

28. Discuss the claim that existence is not a property. Do you think that this is a true claim? Why or why not?

29. Discuss the role of the concept of "necessity" in the ontological argument. Do you think that the arguments about this concept which are given in the section are well-founded? Why or why not?

30. Why does faith in the existence of God not prove that God exists? Or, if you think that it *does* prove that God exists, then defend your position.

10

Some Theories in

Aesthetics

THE AESTHETIC ATTITUDE

We will discuss the aesthetic attitude here in two ways. First, we will examine some aspects of the theory of the third Earl of Shaftesbury in an effort to discover something about that strange property often attributed to this attitude which is known as "disinterestedness." Second, we are going to study the possibilities for an empirical analysis of aesthetic perception in an effort to isolate properties which might be sufficient to distinguish this attitude from any other. In order to discuss Shaftesbury's theory, we must first analyze the theory of human nature and ethics which he held, since for him the aesthetic attitude is closely bound up with the moral attitude.

Shaftesbury's Reaction to Hobbes

Shaftesbury is supposedly the originator of the concept of disinterested pleasure. To understand the sources of this concept in his writing, it must first be understood that he was concerned to support a view of human nature in opposition to that put forth by Thomas Hobbes. Hobbes, you will recall, had argued that man is an essentially egoistic creature who creates systems of civil moral enforcement to protect himself from himself. For Hobbes, the impulse toward self-preservation is the driving force in man and is directed toward the preservation of the individual, not society. The norm for the conduct of man in his "natural" state, was according to Hobbes simply that of personal profit or harm. Pleasure and pain arouse appetite, desire, or aversion in us; appetite is endeavor toward something and aversion is appetite away from it. We have certain innate appetites and aversions, such as the appetite for food, while other appetites and aversions are learned from experience. All delight or pleasure has its source in the satisfaction of appetite, and the only source of continued contentment is therefore in the continual satisfaction of appetite. The process of satisfaction thus involved is called "felicity" by Hobbes. Because of the subjective nature of all appetite, there is no objective distinction between good and evil for the individual, and such concepts only arise within society where the good of the whole is at stake, that is, the common rather than the individual interest. Since the common interest depends, in Hobbes's view, upon the principle of egotism, so does all practical philosophy, i.e. ethics. The only reason for the existence of the state is that it is the most ingenious and best of the devices which men have discovered to guarantee as much as possible of their selfish interests, given that the alternative is the state of nature or war.

The reaction to Hobbes was instantaneous and vicious in many cases. This was particularly true in the first half of the eighteenth century, and among the thinkers who wrote against him was Shaftesbury. Hobbes's opponents insisted for the most part upon the innately social nature of man, and many of them also insisted that man was possessed of a unique moral sense by which he discerns moral values of himself and apart from the arbitrary will of the state or God. Shaftesbury was one of those who held these views.

Shaftesbury tried to use the methods of empirical psychology to examine man first as he is in himself, then as he relates to society, the whole of mankind, and finally to the universe as a whole. He sees that there is an egoistic bent in man, but he also thinks that man has an altruistic side to his nature. The secret of morality is not self-preservation alone, since we are parts of larger systems such as society and the universe at large. We need no metaphysics to arrive at these conclusions, merely a consideration of man and his world. In nature there are parts, mental and physical, which cannot be understood without reference to entities outside of themselves. Hence, before we can decide on the goodness or badness of any being, we must know something about its relations to other beings, because it is by the passions and affections of men that we decide their worth, not merely by a study of the structure of the individual thing. The study of the relations of men to things other than themselves shows that we are a part of a greater whole, and reveals that we were made for that whole as a means for an end. Our good or evil is to be measured in proportion to our striving after unity with the whole, or to the degree that we achieve harmony with it. Since for Hobbes morality arises only in the relations among men, this concept of looking outside the nature of man for the answer to questions concerning his moral nature, as well as into the structure of man himself, may not seem inconsistent with what Hobbes said. But there are already two ways in which Shaftesbury disagrees with him. For Hobbes we can understand the motivating principle behind organized societies simply from the analysis of man's selfish nature, and secondly, for Hobbes, the whole of society is for the sake of the individual. Neither of these is true for Shaftesbury. The first of these disagreements will now concern us.

Shaftesbury's View of Man's Moral Nature

If Shaftesbury is right, man is a social animal and society has its origins in the union of the family. Man has innate instincts toward his fellow creatures and no ulterior motives in his socializing. Because of this, his happiness is necessarily tied to that of his kind. To discover what this happiness is we must understand the original elements in our moral nature, which are self-regarding affections, benevolent affections, and the "moral sense." Hobbes of course referred to only the first of these things. Shaftesbury wants to explain three things in terms of these elements. First, that to have benevolent affections which are directed to the good of the public is the chief means of self-enjoyment, and to lack these affections leads to misery. Second, that to have self-regarding affections which are too strong in regard to the others leads to misery also. Third, that to have "unnatural" affections which tend neither to the good of the public nor to that of the private individual is the highest degree of misery of all. The moral sense is not mentioned in any of these goals; instead, it is that through which we know that our affections and passions are in the proper harmony with society and the universe. In individual men, when our passions and affections are in the proper balance, a state of *virtue* is the result. The emphasis is on the character of men rather than on action or any ulterior end to be achieved by it. The essence of the mature man is the resolution of the altruistic and egotistical impulses within him.

But Shaftesbury also speaks of our affections as directed toward the good, and he calls the good "*interest*." How do we reconcile the ethical ideal of the mature man as a personal harmony, which seems to refer to character rather than to any extrinsic end, with this claim? The answer lies in the meaning of "interest." The resolution is accomplished when we learn that, in fact, a man will contribute to his own interest or good or happiness and also to that of the public to the degree that he is virtuous. Virtue and interest are handmaidens of harmony.

The principle or harmony is a central one, perhaps *the* central one, in Shaftesbury's ethics, and it is based not upon reason but upon feeling. The ethical judgments by which we approve or disapprove of our impulses rest on our ability to make our own functions the object of study or reflection. But this reflection is not merey a knowledge of one's own inner states: it is an *emotion* of reflection, which is formed by the moral sense. By the principle of harmony Shaftesbury tries to prove that benevolence is indispensible for the conception of a moral man. Because benevolence is extra-regarding, and because the good of the whole and the individual are coextensive, altruistic affections are essential for moral goodness.

Because Shaftesbury thinks that the moral sense is a faculty of feeling rather than of reason or rationality, he assimilates the moral to the aesthetic. Let us then take a closer look at the moral sense itself, paying special attention to the meaning of "interest" in connection with our examination of this sense. Shaftesbury tells us that the moral sense becomes rationalized through education and practice. At the beginning of our moral lives, we do not apprehend the moral as such. Rather, though the moral sense is innate in us, it is more similar to a dispositional faculty than to a receptacle for pre-knowledge in the platonic sense. He tells us that he would prefer "instincts" or "preconceptions" or "presentations" as the name for that which is given by moral sense and the sense of beauty—something which "nature teaches exclusive of art, culture, or discipline." Such preconceptions are not only a guide for particular actions, but a source of principles, an example being the idea of order.

The moral sense can therefore be trained. It possesses a property or characteristic which Shaftesbury sees as providing the criterion for a good or a bad character. Because of this, it gives at the same time a test of right and wrong. This characteristic is the property of a character, disposition, feeling, or action to promote the general good, or as he usually calls it, "the good of the species." To this end, he says that it is not enough that an action contribute to the good of the species merely by accident. If the agent does not have the intention or affection of benevolence in his actions, if he acts from self-good alone, he is not good. The ruling affection from which he acts must be a natural affection for his kind. Benevolence is therefore the most important of the moral virtues.

The moral sense is also spontaneous. It feels the agreeable and the disagreeable in our natures immediately. It apprehends the harmonious and the dissonant in our natures as a part of the whole. It cannot help but admire or scorn. This immediate apprehension does not seem to refer to "interest" in Hobbes's sense. Surely Shaftesbury is not speaking of the pleasures of the senses which provide us with fleeting satisfaction only to be replaced by nagging desire afterwards. He says that when will and pleasure are called synonymous and when everything which pleases us is called pleasure, then it becomes meaningless to say that pleasure is good. In the same vein, if we hold that the pleasures of the mind and the enjoyments of reason are the same as the pleasures of the senses, surely we are not using the word "pleasure" in its normal sense. In fact, the two types of pleasure are opposites of each other. Yet at the same time, as we have seen, he wants to argue that reason is subsidiary to the feelings in the sphere of moral and aesthetic perception. There are two senses of "feelings" and emotion here. He admits that, in the process preceding action, the end is always at first suggested by some passion, appetite, desire, or affection, which cause has its source in the emotional part of our nature. But these actions as such are not moral. It is only when the immediate approval of the moral sense, that approval which he is constantly comparing to "taste" in art, pronounces upon the morality of an action, quality, or character that we can distinguish between what is moral and immoral, right and wrong, lovely and ugly. Whereas the self-regarding passions and affections are egotistic, the moral sense operates on the principle of benevolence and the principle of harmony. Since the benevolent affections take precedence over the self-regarding, the "interest" of man in doing good cannot be egotistical. Even though we act in the first place on the instigation of self-regarding interests, Shaftesbury tells us that:

Never did the soul do good, if it came readier to do the same again with more enjoyment. Never was love, or gratitude, or bounty practised but with increasing joy, which made the practicer still more in love with the fair act.[1]

It would seem that we come to recognize that acts are intrinsically good or evil in themselves and that the moral sense is the medium through which we come to apprehend these qualities. Virtue, indeed, becomes something in itself, in the nature of things, not dependent upon anything outside of itself, not a custom, not fancy, not will. From this it would seem to follow that virtue is deserving of our attention *per se*, aside from any personal reward or satisfaction of interests which might follow upon attaining it. Virtue, it is true, does satisfy our interests better than anything else; but that this is the *reason* we should be virtuous is questioned by Shaftesbury.

[1] Anthony Ashley Cooper, Third Earl of Shaftesbury, *Characteristics of Men, Manners, Opinions, Times*, J. M. Robertson, ed. (London: G. Richards, 1900), vol. 2, p. 36.

The Concept of Disinterestedness

This theme becomes especially evident in his philosophy of religion. He tells us that supreme goodness is only understandable to those who know what goodness itself is, that is, that "supreme" is an adjective, and that virtue cannot be known to deserve reward unless we first know that virtue is valuable itself. This is the beginning of the concept of *dis*interestedness in Shaftesbury's philosophy. It becomes a part of the concept of moral and aesthetic ends as desirable in and for themselves. Professor Ernst Cassirer notes that the distinction rests upon the difference between feeling and mere sensation. It is the difference betwen an object produced in us, and the apprehension of whatever it is that makes an object valuable for its own sake.

The concept of disinterestedness is developed in connection with Shaftesbury's idea of God, and the nature of the worship of God. He accepted a version of the teleological argument. He believed that of all the entities of the universe, the mind of God had to be the most amiable, the most engaging, and of the highest satisfaction and enjoyment. We need not search the cosmos for God; the order in nature is reflected in both the macrocosmic and the microcosmic, and we may recognize God by direct intuition through the moral sense and by inference from such intuition. He sees the relation of God to the world as analogous to that between the soul and the body. Nature is the vesture of God; he the soul of nature. God can have no conflicts in interests as we find in man. There is no malice in God, and as general mind he can have no *particular* interests. To God, the good of the whole and of the individual are the same. It therefore follows from the wisdom and goodness of the deity that if nature be regarded as a whole, everything with regard to that whole must be for the best. Our actions therefore ought to be directed toward the good of the whole and God is worthy of our worship for his own sake. The divine love is pure, simple, unmixed, and its object is its own excellence. In it there is no other thought of happiness than its own perfect fruition. God, then, is a disinterested being. His attitude as such is aesthetic; it has no other object than his own perfection, his own objective perfectness as completely harmonious with the universe. Two facts bear special notice here. First, though disinterestedness is attributed to God as the defining characteristic of his attitude, it is as yet merely a concept, not an attitude, for us. Our idea of God is abstracted from the order and harmony we perceive in the universe, and the quality of disinterestedness is an attribute which we believe such a being must have to be perfect. Second, the disinterested attitude as an attribute of God is never a self-regarding affection but always benevolent. This may be seen by considering the intimate connection between Shaftesbury's concept of this attitude and his notion of divine love.

How may we worship God? We surely adopt the wrong attitude if we do so from the hope of reward and the fear of punishment. This is an attitude of self-interest, not in accordance with the principle of acting for the good of the whole. The true, the best way to worship God is to adopt the attitude "which proceeds from an esteem or love of the person served, a sense of duty or gratitude, and a love of the dutiful and grateful part, as good and amiable in itself . . ." The "excellence of the object, not reward or punishment," should be our motive. We should strive to contribute to the good of the whole by forsaking that attitude which refers all things to ourselves and subverts the interest of the whole to the good and interest of we who play a small part in it. Man must *willfully suspend* his personal selfish desires for the appreciation of the order in things as it manifests the good and the beautiful. God is the summit of values, to be desired for his own sake and not for ours. The moral attitude thus becomes benevolent and disinterested in the sense that it involves the dormant state of desire and will, the removal of all practical considerations from the sphere of moral consideration, and the harmonious union of sense and mind in the appreciation of that which is an end in itself.

We noted previously that, for Shaftesbury, virtue consists in the resolution of the self-regarding and benevolent affections in man and that the principle of reconciliation is harmony. Virtue was said to be valuable because it contributes to the good of the whole. Virtue is a state of order, and the order in virtue is the same as that in the universal order of things. It is therefore not only valuable because it contributes to the harmony of the universe, but also because it is valuable for its own sake, as is the worship of God. The love of virtue, as the love of God, should be disinterested, and the object of moral education ought to be the establishing of such a disinterested love of virtue. Only when a man learns this can he be said to be truly moral. The disinterestedness which was a part of Shaftesbury's concept of God now becomes an *attitude* for him which men ought to adopt toward moral and religious matters.

The Moral and the Aesthetic

The question now becomes whether or not this attitude is carried over into the aesthetic area. Professor Fowler points out that, for Shaftesbury, who has a concept of a moral and social system whose parts are in constant proportion to each other and so perfectly adjusted that the smallest deviation will affect the unity of the whole, a close connection between morality and art is necessarily suggested.[2] In fact, the connection between the external beauty of objects and the internal beauty of actions and characters is a cornerstone of Shaftesbury's entire system. "No sooner the eye opens upon figures, the ear to sounds, than straight the beautiful results and grace and harmony are known and acknowledged." The word "straight" indicates that the apprehension of beauty, as with moral rightness, is *immediate*. Further, "harmony" is a defining characteristic of the beautiful, as it is for the moral. The value of virtue, you may recall, insofar as it is an object of disinterested pleasure, is due to the harmony it achieves with the whole of the universe. Harmony with the whole and good are the same thing for Shaftesbury. If we can also establish that harmony with the whole is what makes beauty worthy of attention and if we can establish that this attention and recognition of the beautiful takes places through the moral sense, then, assuming the two sorts of perception to be the same, we may conclude that for Shaftesbury one and the same attitude is involved in the appreciation of both the moral and the beautiful, and we will know his theory of aesthetic perception.

The ideas of harmony, proportion, and unity as valuable in themselves came into currency in ancient Greek times, and Shaftesbury is open in acknowledging his debt to them. In Plato, their use reached its height. For him it is the form Beauty which is the beautiful, not particular things. Eros, or love, produces aspiration toward Beauty, and Plato tends to identity the self-beautiful with the concepts of the true and the good. The common elements in objects which exemplify Beauty are proportion, harmony, and unity of parts. This is for Plato a harmony of forms rather than matter, for in his eyes matter is disruptive of unity and harmony. He identified the forms of Absolute Beauty and Absolute Goodness, and in the *Eudemian Ethics* his pupil Aristotle says that he identified the Good with the One. There is also some evidence for claiming that Plato identified the ideal or form of the Good with God. The secret of the good life for Plato is a life which illustrates harmony and proportion, and when in this state it also exhibits the beautiful. There are degrees of beauty, and materially beautiful things have a relatively low degree because Beauty is itself immaterial, a form. Material things appeal to and are known through the senses while the form Beauty is an object of contemplation for the intellect and for the rational will. Because of the preponderance of the passions over reason, there are degrees of goodness in man.

---

[2] Thomas Fowler, *Shaftesbury and Rutcheson* (New York: G. P. Putnam's Sons, 1883), p. 67.

The parallel with Shaftesbury's theory is not difficult to see. Man is moral for him if there is a balance between his self-regarding and benevolent affections. Fowler notes that Shaftesbury identifies Goodness, Beauty, and Truth, and this is true. The beautiful has harmony and proportion and what has these properties is also true. Whatever is both beautiful and true is good. The moral sense is the same sense which apprehends Beauty. As this sense is applied to external objects in the apprehension of their harmony and proportion, it is a sense of beauty. As it is applied to human action, characters, and dispositions, it is the moral sense. When it is applied to the whole universal order of things and to the moral government of the world, it becomes a religious sense, through which we apprehend the supreme Beauty, Goodness, and Truth, God. In this ascending scale of beauty which rises through the simplest objects in nature through man as a moral being to the order of the universe and God, there is all of value that there is. The analogy with Plato's views is clear, and it holds with regard to both beauty and goodness. Since these are identified along with the moral sense and the aesthetic sense or taste, it follows that the appreciation of Beauty is centered in or characterized by disinterested pleasure, as is the appreciation of virtue.

The Apprehension of Beauty

The aesthetic object, which is apprehended by the moral sense or the aesthetic sense, is not material, nor is it art as such. To be art, something must exemplify Beauty, and it is the latter which is apprehended. Nor is the beautiful the useful. The material world is not the cause of Beauty, for mind alone can regulate or form Beauty. Mind is what gives form to matter, and without it matter is ugly, or as Shaftesbury puts it, matter is then "dead form." Mind inculcates design into the universe, and harmonious design or order is the heart of Beauty. Man and God are the only two designers in the universe, and man is the less perfect because he is both former and formed. God, the former even of that which forms, is the principle source and fountain of Beauty in this world. Architecture, sculpture, and painting are all forms given to matter by man, and, as such, they are first in the order of beauty above dead forms. Next come human ". . . sentiments, resolutions, principles, determinations, and actions; . . . whatever flows from your good understanding, sense, knowledge, and will . . ." Included in these principles are the notions of justice, honesty, fairness, and so forth. The presence of these concepts in us, or as products of our minds, is due to nature, not art, by which Shaftesbury means that they are the result of our natural moral sense and not fabricated from our experience. Man acknowledges that he has a sense of justice, pride, and worthiness by the very fact that he exhibits anger, gratitude, pride, and shame.

To support his idea of form as the defining feature of Beauty Shaftesbury uses the example of "mere figure" in natural beauty. He notes that there are certain figures which are immediately pleasing to even the very young child, such as a round ball, a cube, and a die. The reason we appreciate these immediately is that "there is in certain figures a natural beauty, which the eye finds as soon as the object is presented to it." It is simply there. This immediate and disinterested pleasure in the form or figure is once again due to the harmony in the order of the universe, as is the case with the immediate apprehension of virtue and the disinterested pleasure in it. There is then but one more thing to show about the nature of the objects of aesthetic apprehension before we draw our conclusions about Shaftsbury's theory, which is to prove that he does not think that aesthetic pleasures satisfy our self-regarding desires.

Body enjoys by sense. But Shaftesbury thinks that no matter how beautiful we may find a particular dish, we disdain to apply the name of "Beauty" to it. We do not refer to gourmet delights as beautiful because in them form is only an "accidental note or token of what appeases provoked sense and satisfies the brutish part." We enjoy Beauty "in a nobler way and by the help of what is noblest, (our) mind and reason." As he says,

. . . the riotous mind, captive to sense, can never enter in competition, or contend for beauty with the virtuous mind or reason's culture; so neither can the objects which allure the former compare with those which attract and charm the latter, . . . for whatever is void of mind, is void and darkness to the mind's eye . . .[3]

Since sense is not satisfied in the apprehension of Beauty, desire and will are dormant in aesthetic perception. Its only interest is in the contemplation of the object for its own sake. These are the characteristics of the attitude of disinterestedness, and the pleasure which this attitude involves is disinterested pleasure. The apprehension of Beauty gives rise to this sort of pleasure. It is not objects as such that are the objects of this apprehension, but rather the form and harmony of them. All the other elements, such as color in a painting for example, or its shape and texture, are subordinate to the composition as an harmonious unity. This is because color and *qualia* are such that they satisfy our sense appetites, whereas aesthetic perception strictly speaking does not involve this in Shaftesbury's eyes. In this sense, the objects of aesthetic appreciation are limited in his theory by the definition of the attitude. Nothing which pleases the senses and serves the purpose of satisfying appetite in art can

[3] Cooper, *op. cit.*, p. 143.

ever be the object of aesthetic pleasure. In reality in fact, Shaftesbury can be forced into saying that the vehicle in which Beauty is expressed is never the object of the aesthetic attitude—Beauty itself is.

Whether or not aesthetic objects must necessarily be limited in order to define the concept of aesthetic disinterestedness is another question with which we shall deal at greater length later in this chapter. Its essential characteristic seems to be that it is not associated with any practical purpose or desire. In Shaftesbury's case, the limits on what will count as an aesthetic object seem to arise not because of the aesthetic attitude's definition but because of the definition of Beauty and of the moral sense. But if *personal* disinterestedness is a necessary condition for aesthetic disinterestedness, then there seems to be no reason to limit the objects of possible aesthetic appreciation because of its definition.

There is also another possibility, which is that Shaftesbury is more interested in the creative artist when he speaks about disinterestedness than in either the observer or the created thing. He often seems to be concerned with the operative forces constituting the inner coherence of the universe; and, if this view is correct, then true aesthetic enjoyment is to be found in the process of forming and creating rather than just in analysis, introspection or dissection. Man, as artist, is a creator; the emphasis is on the act of creation, the process of becoming, rather than merely the appearance of the beautiful. For Shaftesbury then, if this interpretation is correct, Beauty is not a concept nor an idea but a dynamic energy or "function of the spirit." What the artist does is discover and confirm the form manifested in nature.

It seems doubtful that Shaftesbury is, in fact, primarily concerned with this aspect of the subject of aesthetics in his writing. In his major work, *Characteristics of Men, Manners, Morals and Times,* there are only two pages where he deals with this subject. In the rest of the book, he is preoccupied with harmony, form, God, and mind in its attitude of moral and aesthetic perception. It would still seem to be true that the artist, to be a true knower of the beautiful, must be an acute aesthetic perceiver, as well as a creator.

In sum then, we can say this much of this theory about aesthetic perception and its objects:

1. The aesthetic attitude is disinterested.
2. It arises first in ethics through the moral sense, and later in the concept of God in religion.
3. The appreciation of virtue for its own sake is completely disinterested, or ought to be.
4. Goodness, Truth, and Beauty are one and the same.
5. Form in its harmony is the object of aesthetic perception, and everything has some form.

6. The definition of the aesthetic attitude does not directly limit what can be an aesthetic object, but such limits arise, for Shaftesbury, as a result of his psychological and epistemological theories, which we have not discussed in detail.

A Contemporary Empirical Approach

Now we move to a more modern view. It is, much more than the one we have just examined, an empirical rather than a metaphysical approach. It begins with the awareness that the very word "aesthetic" comes from Greek "aisthetikos," which means perceptive or having to do with the senses. Aesthetic perception is, therefore, a species of perception having to do with the senses in some way or other. The problem is to find out what it is that differentiates it from some other kind of perception. In order to discover this, we shall examine two very broad categories of experience, the *instrumental* and the *non-instrumental*.[4] It seems clear that aesthetic experience belongs to one of these two categories. A central difference between them is a matter of reference. Instrumental experience essentially involves aiming at an end or goal, and the explanation of the experience always includes reference to that goal. Non-instrumental experience does not seem to be goal-directed, or at the least the phrase "goal-directed" has a different connotation in its case than in the former. In an instrumental experience the response to the present object of perception is determind by the agent's interest in some other person, object, event, or situation to which the perceived object directs his attention. Here the perceiver is not interested in the immediate object of perception but rather in that object to which his attention is directed. As opposed to instrumental experience, the *non*-instrumental perceiver is *dis*interested with regard to all objects other than the one he is immediately perceiving. Aesthetic perception and appreciation is disinterested in this way.

At this point we have no reason to confine the attribute of disinterestedness to the aesthetic attitude, because the non-instrumental category of experience includes many species which are not aesthetic. By itself disinterestedness is not sufficient to distinguish between aesthetic and non-aesthetic experiences. It may, however, be necessary to isolate

[4] Some of the terminology in the following discussion may be found in: Herbert Hahn, "A Contextualist Theory of Perception," *California Publications in Philosophy*, 22 (Berkeley and Los Angeles: The University of California Press, 1942); and in Bertram Morris, *The Aesthetic Process* (Evanston, Ill.: Northwestern University Press, 1943). The uses of these terms here differ, however; for further study of them, see Paul Olscamp, "Some Remarks about the Nature of Aesthetic Perception and Appreciation," *Journal of Aesthetics and Art Criticism*, 24, no. 2 (December, 1965), pp. 251–58. I am grateful to the editor of this journal for permission to use some material from this article.

a group of other attributes such that, when they are added to disinterestedness, they together are sufficient to define the aesthetic attitude. At the least, it seems that we can isolate *some* aesthetic experience in this way from all other sorts of similar events.

It is a mistake to take "disinterestedness" as the antonym of "interest," if we are talking of the former in the context of the aesthetic experience and the latter in the context of instrumental experience. Disinterestedness is rather a special *kind* of interest, in which the attention of the perceiver is entirely focused upon the present object of perception and nothing beyond it. Since this sort of interest is involved in many cases where what is apprehended does not seem to be an aesthetic object, it is not a sufficient defining predicate of the aesthetic attitude; or, to look at the other side of the coin, if we say that it *is* sufficient, then the class of aesthetic objects is indefinitely large. But in spite of this, disinterestedness *does* seem to enable us to distinguish between the instrumental and non-instrumental kinds of experience, because none of the former sorts are, by definition, disinterested. We must therefore make distinctions *within* the class of non-instrumental experiences to separate those that are aesthetic from those that are not.

A second property usually predicated of the aesthetic attitude is "immediacy" which is a term somewhat lacking in clarity. It is, for example, true of all and any experience that it is immediate in the sense that it involves an apprehension of what is given without interference to the senses or the mind. We also often speak of immediate concerns, as opposed to secondary or less important ones or events that are immediate relative to others because they occur prior in time to those others. Clearly, none of these senses of the term will help us. But there are other meanings closer to what we need. We often mean something closely akin to "uninterrupted absorption" by "immediate" when we are talking about our perception of an object or its quality and form. This is one sense which is certainly relevant to an analysis of the aesthetic attitude. Again, however, it is not by itself nor in conjunction with disinterestedness sufficient to define that attitude, because we are often uninterruptedly absorbed in the perception of things that are not aesthetic objects. "Immediate" is also taken to signify "non-associative," and this sense too is relevant to the definition of the aesthetic attitude, provided we distinguish it carefully from disinterestedness itself. Finally, when we say that our perception is immediate, we often mean to indicate the absence of essential discursive processes. But this cannot be true of all kinds of aesthetic perception. If it were, we would have to say that a mathematician who is absorbed in his work is not dealing with an aesthetic object; and, at least in the case of pure mathematics, we *would* want to claim the status of aesthetic object for some formal proofs. So this much is clear: whenever a restricting condition arises for the pre-

dication of disinterestedness or immediacy of an attitude which we want
to call "aesthetic," it seems to concern the relation between the aesthetic
perceiver and his object. Either we do not want to count the object as
an *aesthetic* object, or we want to say that attitudes with this or that
property which is also a property of the aesthetic attitude are not themselves instances of the aesthetic attitude. A more profound investigation
in the nature of the experience itself, and into the nature of an aesthetic
object, is therefore required.

Instrumental and Aesthetic Experience

In an instrumental experience, there is little consciousness of the object
of present perception. There is attention to and consciousness of the
reference of this object of present perception to some other object which
is the end or object of the present object or of the perception of the
present object. The consciousness involved in the perception of the
original object is a realization of the *meaning* of what is perceived,
because its meaning is in part its reference to another object or datum
which is its end. This consciousness of the reference of the present perceived object to another object is not the same sort of consciousness as
that of the present object itself. The focus of attention is not on the
presently perceived object as object, but rather as a *sign or signal* of that
for the sake of which it is perceived. In this state of *identification* the
signed or signaled object must be involved, as must be the recognition
of the relation between the two objects as one of "means to end." The
central area of concentration in instrumental experience is just relationship.

Because of all of this, the awareness of the object of present perception and its qualities is cursory. There is little or no contemplation of it.
There is instead an adjustment to a future situation. The predominant
attitude or characteristic of the attitude is therefore one of anticipation,
which is an attitude such that when one knows what to expect in the
future from past experience, it is determined by those past experiences.
In instrumental perception, anticipation has a characteristic which it does
not have in aesthetic perception: there is a discarding or rejection of the
object to which it is a response. The means is treated as if it were of
less value or worth than the end which is anticipated. It is, so to speak,
a "one-way" referential attitude. This is not true, as we shall see, in
aesthetic perception.

Nonetheless, there is some sort of anticipation in aesthetic perception;
because, if there were not, we could not explain normal phenomena such
as the expectation of future developments of a theme in a symphony, the
development of a plot in a drama, and so on. In aesthetic experience,
however, the qualitative appreciation of the object perceived is not re-

jected, discarded, or minimized as it is in instrumental perception. The very concept of the means–end relation as found in instrumental experience is foreign to the aesthetic experience. The relation of part-to-whole *is* essential in aesthetic experience, of course, as exemplified in the play-within-a-play in *Hamlet,* the various movements which together make up a symphony, and so forth. But the earlier movements of a symphony are not *means* to the latter ones, nor are they any less worthy nor "for the sake of" the latter movements. We can make a very good case for the claim that the early movements would be without point without the later ones, and vice versa. Moreover, we do not examine the earlier movements in the cursory way in which we examine the present object of perception in instrumental experience. Instead, we are involved in a complete qualitative appreciation for the whole work, and this is essential for its full appreciation.

The factor of external sign signification also seems to be missing from aesthetic perception. The meaning of the antecedent perceptions in such experience is in some sense carried over into the subsequent ones. Although this is difficult to state with precision, illustrative examples are not hard to find. The continuing relevance and appreciation of themes in Bach and jazz fugues is one instance. The perceptive process in instrumental experience seems to be characterized by its adjustmental meaning, whereas the contemplation quality is more characteristic of aesthetic perception. We mentioned that the reference in instrumental experience is "one-way," but in aesthetic experience there is an essential interrelatedness between the earlier and later parts. It makes perfectly good sense to speak of the object of present perception as less important than its end in instrumental experience, but it makes little if any sense at all to speak about one segment of a tapestry as of less value than another. The means is subordinate to the end in instrumental experience; but in aesthetic perception, although one aspect of it contributes to and supports another, there is no relation of subordination. The diffusion of color in a painting may and does help to focus our attention upon some point in it, but the light is not a *means* to the point of focus, nor is it somehow "subordinate" to it. True, in the technical analysis of some painting we may speak of the artist's use of light as a means for focusing our attention, but such analysis is not a part of aesthetic appreciation. We do not value the quality of light in a Titian for the sake of the subject it illuminates, even though we may realize upon study that just that quality of light and no other is exactly what is required for the full appreciation of the subject of the work.

It might seem that by claiming the aesthetic object to be characterized by both contemplation and anticipation, we are denying another of its traditional attributes, immediacy. This attitude is often said to be immediate in the sense that it involves neither memory nor anticipation. But it seems to me that in this reply the term "anticipation" is not being used in the way it has been used above to characterize the attitude. Anticipation as found in instrumental experience *is* incompatible with the contemplative aesthetic attitude. But the difference between that kind of anticipation and the sort which is a quality of aesthetic perception has been given. In the latter sort, the anticipation involved presupposes an in-depth or intensive qualitative appreciation of the antecedent and consequent processes in the aesthetic object, whose existence through time is an essential part of the work, as in a symphony or a play. The most interesting part of this possible reply, however, is that which concerns memory. Some have claimed that memory is not involved in aesthetic appreciation because of its non-discursive character. That is, given that it is contemplative, it is claimed that because the calling up of images and information through memory is usually involved in discursive thought, then memory cannot be involved in aesthetic appreciation. But this is an invalid argument. It does not follow from the premises here that there are no non-discursive uses of memory. Further, it is clear that empirical analysis of the aesthetic experience shows that memory must be involved in some ways. How could one appreciate any play, novel, symphony, indeed any work of art which essentially involves the passage of time, unless one could be aware of the earlier parts while moving through the later ones? This is not to say, however, that the appreciation of the object involves the use of remembered or recalled information for the purpose of making judgments about it, and this sort of use of memory *is* ruled out by the contemplative character of the experience. In addition, the role of memory here, in the aesthetic context, differs in other ways from its normal use. A play or a novel often covers a specific time span which is not a *real* time span. It was an axiom of some kinds of drama that the period covered ought to be no longer than 24 hours. Other plays cover the lifespan of a man, a dynasty, or the like. Yet the play or the novel do not "take" 24 hours, or a lifetime, or epochs. They take as long as it takes to perform them, or to read them. In one sense then, we are using our memories *fictitiously*, because we are "remembering" events which did not actually happen, and relating them to others that do not actually happen, at temporal intervals which are not what they are said to be, because there were no real events between which they were intervals. But these special uses of memory are obviously involved in aesthetic experience, and to that extent the claim to the contrary is false.

Another difference between instrumental and the aesthetic experience concerns what can be called the "control factor." In instrumental experience one must be able to control the means leading to the end. In control relations, there must be a subject–object relation between the controller and what is controlled, and in this relation the controller is active and the controlled is passive. In the aesthetic experience this does not seem to be so. The full realization of the value inherent in aesthetic appreciation is only achieved when the perceiver as well as the perceived contributes to the experience. The object participates as the cause of the reactions of the appreciator; and, in turn, his realization of the felt quality and formal properties of the object contributes to still greater realization of value. This is not a controller-controlled relationship, because the mutual contribution needs, as it were, an "entering-into" the object by the perceiver in which the consciousness of subject *versus* object is not present, or at the least is blurred. What is perceived controls the perceiver as much as the converse.

Analyzing the Aesthetic Attitude

Many of these differences are relevant to certain properties of the objects of perception as well as to the modes of perception in the two kinds of experience. Here, we cannot undertake a detailed analysis of the nature of aesthetic objects, but we should try to understand at least those facets of the topic which are directly related to our discussion of aesthetic perception. Part of the argument against the claim that disinterestedness is a sufficient defining condition of the aesthetic attitude is the difficulty of defining the class of aesthetic *objects* in the light of the fact that disinterestedness is a characteristic of many attitudes whose objects do not seem to be aesthetic ones. It seems possible to exclude some disinterested attitudes from the "aesthetic" category by noting certain other characteristics of those attitudes which aesthetic perception does not have, and by noting some properties of the aesthetic attitude which those other attitudes do not possess. That is, disinterestedness by itself does not seem sufficient to define the aesthetic attitude; yet, it appears possible to limit the membership in the class of aesthetic objects by reference in some cases to the attitudes towards those objects. It seems to be true, for example, that the judge, the playing child, and the scholar pursuing knowledge all have a disinterested attitude but not always an aesthetic one. It would not seem to be the case that the object which the child contemplates is *a fortiori* never an aesthetic object, but there seems to be nothing strange about claiming that it is not when the attitude of the child at play is the mode in which it is apprehended. It might be possible, therefore, to limit the class of aesthetic objects by reference to the attitudes held toward them, provided it were also possible to specify those properties sufficient for defining the asthetic attitude and provided it were possible to specify those properties which would disqualify an attitude from the aesthetic category. For at least some attitudes, it would seem that we could do the former. Here, we shall not attempt to do the latter.

It should also be possible by empirical investigation to isolate some features or properties of kinds of objects which are constantly associated with aesthetic perception. Moreover, it should be possible by the same method to discover some properties of objects which are almost never found in objects which are aesthetically appreciated. This would provide added criteria for defining the class of aesthetic objects. Some of these have been mentioned indirectly already. It has been noted that the *qualitative* aspects of the object seem to be foremost in the aesthetic apprehension of it, so any object whose qualitative aspects are unimportant will probably not be an object of aesthetic perception, and will probably not be an aesthetic object at all. It also means, especially in the visual arts, that the appearance rather than the matter of the object is of direct concern. It is the *arrangement* of the material which seems to occasion the aesthetic experience in painting, and the visual and tactile appreciation of sculpture. The formal arrangement and the quality of a work of art are not necessarily the same, because qualitative perception is usually sensory whereas the analysis of formal properties seems to disclose non-sensory elements.

The issue of belief and disbelief is also important in the analysis of the aesthetic attitude. We do not believe when we see a play that the action depicted, for example, murder, is really happening. It may therefore be that in some cases those objects which compel our belief are not aesthetic objects. This is not to say that we are never aware that real events sometimes correspond to the work of art, as in *Guernica*. But in purely aesthetic contemplation, there is a willful suspension of belief, or perhaps better, an ignoring of the factual representative function of the work and a concentration on its other qualities. In still other cases, there is a willful suspension of *dis*belief. *Oedipus Rex* does not portray a series of real events, and Furies do not really turn into Humanities; and either a belief that they did or a belief that they did not would inhibit appreciation of the plays, because it would prevent the attitude from being disinterested.

The aesthetic attitude is often scrutinized by saying what it is *not* rather than what it is. It has been called involuntary, because it cannot be attained by an effort of will; and it has been called non-rational, though not irrational, because it is non-discursive. Mary McCloskey says that we must distinguish it from some emotions with which it is often confused, among which is the "thrill of feeling which is a response to something vividly perceived. . . ." The latter often arises from the quality of our perceptions just as the aesthetic attitude does. On the other hand, many aestheticians have argued that the aesthetic attitude is precisely an emotion, or that it at least embodies one, and that this expression is the intention of the artist. But this seems to be misleading. Emotions are clearly present in some aesthetic experiences, but surely it is also true that *intense* emotion often hinders aesthetic appreciation. Roger Fry and Clive Bell want to say that aesthetic "emotion" is like an "intellectual emotion," an intense appreciation of the formal properties of the object. But this is an old emotion indeed, for it seems to have no organic sensation as a component, at least in the apprehension of purely formal objects such as elegant proofs. Further, if organic sensation is involved in emotion, but not in aesthetic perception, then what justification is there for calling the latter "emotional" in any usual sense? It would seem on the contrary that the mode of apprehension peculiar to aesthetic apprehension is just that—peculiar to aesthetic perception. Professor Harold Osborne is another scholar who argues that aesthetic apprehension is emotional. He also mentions that in such perception the "normal impulse to action is recessive," and this latter point seems to be important and true.[5] It is not, however, *exclusively* a property of the aesthetic attitude.

There is a final negative property, as it were, which is characteristic of the aesthetic attitude, which may be called its non-consumptive character. This property is best defined by illustration. Compare your enjoyment of a fine Mozart symphony, or the later Beethoven quartets, with your enjoyment of a fine wine, a delicious meal, and a good cigar. It is difficult to tire of a fine work of art; but appetites are easily satisfied, though with more pleasure in some cases than others. The enjoyment of aesthetic value contributes to the creation of more of that value; but, no matter how good the dinner, you are full in a short time.

Summarizing Aesthetic Experience

At this point it might be well to summarize the characteristics which have been predicated of aesthetic perception and appreciation and then see what we can conclude from the list:

1. There is no consciousness of a distinction between a perceiver and a perceived, a controller and a controlled, or a means and an end in this sort of perception.
2. There are no discursive processes necessarily associated with it.
3. No act of will is involved in its instigation, though the voluntary suspension of belief or disbelief is a necessary condition for aesthetic enjoyment in some cases.
4. Normal impulses to action are recessive in aesthetic perception.
5. Aesthetic perception is not identical with any known emotion,

---

[5] For a more detailed discussion, see: Mary McCloskey, "Some suggestions in Aesthetics," *Philosophical Quarterly*, 12, no. 46 (January, 1962); and Harold Osborne, *Aesthetics and Criticism* (London: Routledge & Kegan Paul, Ltd., 1952).

and is not properly described as an emotion if the term is to retain its normal meanings.

6. It is disinterested.
7. It is contemplative.
8. It is non-consumptive.
9. The enjoyment of the felt quality of the aesthetic object is continually augmented in aesthetic perception.
10. It is immediate, that is, there is uninterupted absorption in the object, and it may also be immediate in the sense that it is non-associative.
11. It is constantly conjoined with heightened perceptual alertness and always involves a high degree of consciousness.

It would be difficult, if not impossible, to discover any instance of a non-aesthetic experience which has all of these qualities, though there are some non-aesthetic experiences which have some of them. On the other hand, it seems that it is fairly simple to discover instances of experiences which we count as aesthetic and which do have all of these marks. So it seems safe to say that whenever all of these characteristics are properties of an experience, that is sufficient to define the experience reportively as an aesthetic one. This does not imply that aesthetic experience has no other qualities in addition, nor that an experience is not properly called aesthetic if it lacks some of the qualities named. And the thesis could be disproven if one could describe a non-aesthetic experience which had all the properties. Now, of course, this makes the notion of "sufficiency" rather strange. How can it be "sufficient" for an experience to be aesthetic if it meets these conditions, while it is possible to disprove the claim that it is aesthetic even if it has all the properties? The reply is that we are not speaking of strict logical necessity here but rather of a working reportive definition of an aesthetic experience which in the light of new discoveries might be profitably revised or expanded. This is all that an empirical investigation of the nature of this mode of perception, or any other for that matter, can accomplish.

In the last analysis the aesthetic experience cannot be known by description. It must be known by acquaintance if it is really to be understood. It follows that the role of the philosopher or the critic in this area is normative; he can tell you what to look for, lead you to it, clarify the conceptual confusions, or some of them, which you might have about the work of art or the nature of your perception of it (perhaps at the cost of supplanting your confusions with different ones), but he cannot appreciate the painting for you. A man with no eyes cannot see colors, and a man with eyes, even if led to the spectrum, ultimately must see for himself. This is, in fact, how all of us finally come to an understanding of color words, by the method of ostensive definition. When one ostensively defines something for somebody, he does not thereby guarantee that the second person will understand the definition. But that is all that any teacher can do after all.

In the case of Shaftesbury, we studied a view of aesthetic perception and appreciation that was based upon a complex metaphysical system, and many of the principles of that system are subject to grave doubt—in some cases, as you can discover for yourself, to the fatal detriment of the theory. What evidence is there that we have a "moral sense"? Is his argument for the existence of God adequate? Does the value of a work of art indeed reside in some sort of "harmony," some set of formal properties? What does it *mean* to say that Goodness and Beauty are the same thing? And what does it mean to say that both of these are identical with Truth? These are but the beginning of a long series of questions that can be asked of Shaftesbury's theory, and to some of them he has no acceptable answer.

The contemporary approach that we have just discussed uses a quite different method. Rather than a deductive method, it is inductive; rather than *a priori*, it is *a posteriori;* rather than metaphysical, it is empirical. It proceeds to an examination of a set of data given in a special sort of experience, which we call "aesthetic," and seeks to determine what the perceivable or knowable, i.e., experiential properties of that kind of experience, are. Having isolated some of these properties, it seeks to decide whether other kinds of experience also have them; and the answer is, so far as we know, not *all* of them, though they may have some. Using these findings, it proposes a tentative definition, sufficient for working purposes, of the aesthetic attitude. The definition is the conjunction of the set of properties. So this is a minimal claim, having as part of its virtues its heuristic role, and as another part its ability to avoid criticisms based upon unverifiable metaphysical claims. At least some metaphysical statements are meaningful. And, as you have seen in the discussion of meaning and verifiability, it also seems that on some theories of truth, they are either true or false. But it is also the case that in very few instances do they succeed in explaining phenomenal experiences better than empirical investigation when what is required is not an explanation of a problem such as resemblance, but rather a reportive definition or a stipulative one founded in the analysis of experience.

EXPRESSION AND ART

Works of art are often said to be "expressive." In fact, the so-called "expression theory of art" is one of the most prominent aesthetic theories. According to this view, works of art are in some sense a language or a set of languages which express feeling, emotion, or intentions. The theory has its origins in the Renaissance period, and in the eyes of some scholars, such as Harold Osborne, it probably has its genesis in the obsession of the thinkers of that period with the concept of the artist as genius. The creative process within the artist became the subject of much fascinated speculation, and it was thought that the product of the artist, the work of art, was the medium through which he communicated with the aesthetic observer. As such, the work of art came to be construed as a language through which the artist-genius enabled us to share his discoveries. In Osborne's words:

The underlying theory is, in its baldest form, that the artist first lives through a certain experience; he then makes an artefact which in some way embodies that experience; and through appreciative contemplation of this artefact other men are enabled to duplicate in their own minds the experience of the artist. What is conveyed to them is not abstract knowledge *that* the artist had such and such an experience, but an experience of their own as similar as possible to the artist's experience in all its aspects, including its affective and emotional content.[6]

Depending upon the particular theory then, not just feelings and emotions may be communicated or evoked, but also thoughts, concepts, the artist's perceptions of things, and the like.

It is important to note at the beginning that the expressionist theory of art is a complex of theories and not just a single one. It is a theory about the artist, for presumably it asserts that the artist intends to evoke or cause or communicate something (presumably also he knows what it is that he wishes to communicate); it is a theory about the work of art, for it is a language through which the artist's intentions are made manifest; it is a theory about the aesthetic perceiver, for if the work of art is a good one, that is, a successful one, then the perceiver of it will have certain experiences which will be similar to the artist's. These theories are related, of course. But the set of arguments which make up the theory as a whole may be evaluated separately, and that is what we shall try to do here. If any of the individual arguments does not meet our criteria, then of course the theory taken as a whole will fail. But in order to do this, it would first be better to consider a more careful version of the position. Let us consider Robin G. Collingwood's version, as expressed in his fine book *The Principles of Art.*[7] Then we shall consider some of the problems raised by his views. Finally, we shall try to assess the significance of the theory from the viewpoint of the aesthetic observer.

Collingwood's Theory of Expression

Collingwood begins with what he takes to be a commonplace truth, namely that the artist expresses emotions when he creates a work of art.

[6] Osborne, *op. cit.*, p. 143.
[7] Robin G. Collingwood, *The Principles of Art* (Oxford: The Clarendon Press, 1938).

The problem is then to say what it is that he does when he does this. One thing he does is to "speak" to us through a "language," his medium. He tells us of, or communicates to us, a feeling or an emotion of which he is aware or conscious. If he were not conscious of it, of course, he could not communicate it to us. When anyone speaks in any language, he speaks to someone, though he may or may not intend to "arouse" in that listener the emotions he is characterizing, if that is what he is talking about. Actually, "characterizing" is the wrong word to describe what the artist does. He is not *trying* to arouse in us the same emotion that he has. To do that he must approach us in a certain way by a certain means known to produce the kind of emotional response he wishes to cause, and he cannot do that until he already knows what his own emotional state is. In order to know what his own emotional state is, he must *express* his emotions, and Collingwood thinks that this act of expressing his emotion is "an exploration of his own emotions." A work of art is just this exploration of the artist's emotions. It is *not* a description of them, because whenever we describe anything, we "generalize" it, that is, we "bring it under a conception, to classify it. Expression, on the contrary, individualizes." It is, indeed, the expression that individualizes which makes the work of art unique. One can, of course, set out to evoke or cause an emotion in another, and when he does he is setting out to evoke a particular *sort* of emotion by using a particular *sort* of means which one knows to be effective in producing that kind of emotion. When one does this, one is not seeking to produce *this* particular emotion, or that one, but this *kind* or that *kind*. But this is not artistry; it is craftsmanship. Craftsmanship is the use of standard procedures to produce standard ends. There is good craftsmanship and bad craftsmanship, but there is no unique craftsmanship; because "unique," in the context of works of art in any event, is for the expressionist (at least for Collingwood) the exploration of *this* emotion by *this* particular man in *this* particular work.

In the expressing of his emotions, the artist comes to be clear about them; that is, he comes to know and understand what these emotions are, whereas before the process of expressing them, he did not have this awareness. In this sense, art is prior to the craft, for the craft presupposes a knowledge of the means to evoke emotion. What the aesthetic perceiver does is to *witness* this discovery of the artist about himself, and this witnessing "enable(s) them (the observers) to make a similar discovery about themselves." Collingwood thinks that this is true of all the kinds of art, whether music, painting, sculpture, or literature. So what the theory tells us is this:

1. What the artist does when he makes a work of art is to express his emotion or emotions.

2. In the very expression of these emotions, the artist becomes aware of them, comes to know and understand them.

3. It is the *individuality* of this effort that distinguishes art from craft.

4. The aesthetic audience (a) witnesses the artist discovering his own emotions, and (b) is thereby enabled to make a similar discovery about himself.

5. The work of art is therefore a language through which discoveries of the artist about himself are revealed or made known.

6. This analysis is good for any form of artistic endeavor and for any work of art.

Criticisms of Expressionist Theory

There are very many difficulties with this theory, and most of them center upon the precise meaning of "expression" as it concerns (a) what the artist intends, (b) the work of art itself and its relation to the perceiver, and (c) the role which expression plays in the critical evaluation of a work of art. Many criticisms based upon these three points have been raised in the last fifteen years because of two very influential articles, one by John Hospers and the other by O. K. Bouwsma. Not all of the criticisms which follow emanate from these sources, but some of them do and, in any case, the student of this subject should read these papers.[8]

One hallmark of Collingwood's theory, and many other expressionists, is that the process of expression begins in the artist in a state of unclarity and ends up in the work with at least more clarity. It seems to follow from this that the artist cannot plan his work of art carefully ahead of time and then execute it. Indeed it would seem that if he tries to do this, he will end up being a craftsman and not an artist; for to be a work of art the product must *be* the expression of the process of clarification, not the *result* of an already clarified emotion. Now this is at least in part an empirical claim; that is, it makes an assertion about what goes on in the mind of an artist when he is making a work of art. Presumably then, we could check this by finding a truthful artist and asking him about it. However, a random questioning of a number of artists has brought the response that Mr. Collingwood does not know what he is talking about. Three of them said that they had spent *months* in the deliberate planning of their works of art, and two of these set out to execute a concept given them by foundations or others for a commission. Only when the planning was complete did they execute the work itself. The planning included all sorts of things that were absolutely irrelevant

---

[8] O. K. Bouwsma, "The Expression Theory of Art," in Max Black, ed., *Philosophical Analysis* (Englewood Cliffs, N.J.: Prentice-Hall, Inc., 1963); John Hospers, "The Concept of Artistic Expression," *Proceedings of the Aristotelian Society*, vol. 55 (1954–55), pp. 313–44.

to the artists' clarification of their own emotions. For example, one of the works was a sculpture of a Christ-figure, and among the planning factors were the size of the nave in which it would be hung, the sort of stone out of which the church was made, the angle of vision of the worshippers given the location of the pews, and the nature of the lighting in the church. But in spite of all of this, the end produce was a work of art. It was a *good* Christ-figure, though it was not representational; and, so far as the artist could see, it clarified none of his emotions and enabled none of the observers to make discoveries about their own emotions. What does all of this prove? Surely at least this much: if the expressionist theory of art is making a general claim about the processes "in" the artist when he makes a work of art, and if that claim excludes the possibility of the artist already having clarified whatever he does clarify before he makes the work, then the expressionist theory of art is false. This is so because the process is not always (though it may be sometimes) as the theory would have it; planning presupposing clarification of emotion and everything else does take place, yet the result is still a work of art.

We might also ask just exactly *what* it is that the artist expresses in his work of art, when in fact he is expressing anything. (If the first criticism is sound, then he may be doing this sometimes but not always.) And the corollary of this is to ask what the nature of the relation is between whatever is expressed and the expression of it, i.e., the work of art. The analogy upon which the expressionists are depending here is, of course, that of normal languages. They are asserting that as language stands to expression, so the work of art does as well. We have already had numerous encounters with the difficulties of explicating how language expresses a cognitive meaning, an emotive meaning, or anything else. If we say that the work of art is expressive as emotive utterances are, then these same difficulties will arise again here. (See Chapter 7, pages 250–57). And we might ask why it is that the meaning of the work of art has to be purely *emotive*, rather than cognitive. Indeed, if we are to take the side of empirical evidence again and ask the artist and the perceiver what their intentions and reactions are respectivly, we will discover that cognitive as well as emotional responses are to be included. In fact, if we are to take the expressionist view that Collingwood espouses, the meaning of the work ought to be always more cognitive than emotive. This is so because the result of the work is the realization *that* something is the case, a *recognition* or discovery that one's emotions are of such and such a nature rather than a having of those emotions; and this is a cognitive rather than an emotive response.

To express emotion is not to evoke or produce, as Collingwood himself notes. But in fact, is this what we do when we perceive a work of art? Do we make a discovery about our emotions, and do we think that we are witnessing the discovery of the artist's emotion? Certainly it is true that when I read a novel or hear certain kinds of music, I *feel* emotions. I might, for example, feel sad. (For some reason, feeling sad when one hears music is an example that occurs again and again in Bouwsma, Hospers, et al.) But is my *feeling* sad a discovery *about my* emotions? There might be a discovery about the music, namely, that this kind of music makes me feel sad, and, if there is in any sense a discovery about me, the discovery is that I have a propensity to feel sad when I hear this kind of music. But the feeling itself is not the discovery. It is just a feeling. Nor does there seem to be much evidence that whatever feeling I have (if I have feelings under such circumstances) is similar in any way to the feeling or emotion which the artist is presumably clarifying when he makes his work of art. Even if we did discover that we had such and such a feeling upon listening to such and such a musical composition and the artist as a matter of fact did not have this feeling and was not engaged in clarifying this particular emotion, would that affect our evaluation of the work of art itself? Would we, upon discovering that whatever discovery we had made about our emotions was not similar to the emotion the artist was trying to clarify, then reject the work of art as a bad or inferior work? It doesn't seem so; rather, it seems that we would be inclined to reject the expressionist theory of art.

But this may appear to be a simplistic view of what it means to say that a piece of music or some other sort of work expresses an emotion. After all, is it not true that we say that a composition is sad, or gay, or otherwise, whether or not we happen to feel sad or gay when we hear it this particular day? We may, as Hospers points out, be tired, or in a sour mood, or have heard the piece many times this week, or have indigestion, or the gout. But that will not deter us from saying that the piece is sad or gay. Perhaps we mean that we have a *disposition* to respond gayly or sadly to the piece, which would not require us to have this actual response each and every time we hear it. But no, says Hospers, this will not do because it ignores the factor of aesthetic "distance," aesthetic distance being a composite of those features of the aesthetic attitude which earlier in this chapter, were called disinterestedness, non-consumptiveness, and the property of being contemplative. After all, we do not say that someone really appreciates a tragedy if he begins to cry in the middle of it. And if we actually had to *be* sad, or to *be* gay in order to appreciate the work, we would have to say just the opposite.

Art as Communication of Emotion

There is an epistemological side to one of the problems mentioned in the list above which should be explored a little further. It was noted that if whatever discovery about our own emotions we happened to make while perceiving a work of art did not coincide with the emotion which the artist was trying to clarify in it, we would not change our evaluation of the work of art. One version of the expressionist theory of art, though not Collingwood's, holds that it is the function of the work of art to *communicate* the artist's emotion to the perceiver. To quote Harold Osborne's description of this version of the theory, ". . . when we appreciate correctly there is formed in our own minds through the medium of the work of art . . . a state of mind as like as possible to the state of mind of the artist." And suppose for the moment that this is true. Now, how shall we ever *know* that this communication has been achieved? One way is to describe or report our own emotional state of mind and then ask the artist what he thinks of it. If he says "That's it, that's it right on the nose! That's what I was trying to say," then we presumably can get as close as possible to the ideal state of communication between artist and observer. But what if the artist is dead, and has left no diary or record of what he was trying to "say" in his work. Or what if he did leave a record but, like the artists questioned earlier, says he wasn't trying to communicate any particular emotion at all? Then surely we have no way of telling whether he was successful, if this is what he was trying to do; or, if he was *not* trying to communicate emotion and we hold this theory, then we have no gauge against which we can test the work at all. We can of course say, *ad hoc*, that he was doing this whether he knew it or not. But *ad hoc* explanations are suspect, and the more so when the artist is not here to defend himself against them. And even if we admit the type of explanation and if he left no diary or record, we can never say that he met the test of successful communication; we can never say that yes, our state of mind is very like that of that artist when he created his magnificent work. If the criterion of the *worth* of the painting is related to the success or failure to communicate emotion, then we cannot judge whether the *vast* majority of art is good or bad; for, in the vast majority of cases, the artists have died, and have left no records of things of this sort. But of course we *do* make such judgments, and therefore at a minimum, we can safely claim that success or failure at communication of emotion is certainly not the only criterion for evaluating art, and in most cases is not at all a criterion for evaluating art.

Osborne mentions another interpretation of the theory, which is also discussed metaphorically by Bouwsma. According to this version the artist is expressing his feelings, emotions, or character through his work. Presumably then the artist would have succeeded in his attempt if he did, truly, express his feelings, his emotions, or his character in his work. But again, the question is how we are to *tell* that this is so, even if it is one of the things that is accomplished in a work of art. That there is a possible correlation between types of art and types of character is not something one should deny off hand. For example, artwork of talented inmates in insane asylums shows certain definite characteristics involving shades of color and the placing of certain forms. These are, of course, statistical correlations, that is, certain similarities in the paintings, for example, of schizophrenics, which are not found in those of any other variety of mental patient, recur again and again, and a foundation for the probability of their occurrence in the future is thus established. The question nonetheless may still be asked, are these paintings an expression of the characters of these patients? Or are their distinctive features due to the aberrations caused by the illness? One's character is after all the set of dispositions which one has to act in various ways given certain stimuli. And when one is ill, mental illness included, one does *not* act in character, for that is why we put people in asylums. Nor will it do to reply that these odd and striking paintings are expressive of the characters of schizophrenics, or of a particular schizophrenic, but not of normal people. The most we are entitled to claim in either case is that this sort of behavior is found together with this kind of art. After all, smoke is found with most fires, but it is not *expressive* of fire; even in a play where smoke is used to signify fire, it *signifies* it, it does not express it. Even if we accept a theory of causation in which statistical correlation is sufficient to justify causal claims, enabling us to say that this particular sort of effect in painting is caused by the schizophrenic, we are still not entitled to say that the painting is an instance of *self*-expression; for self-expression is intentional, and the schizophrenic does not *intend* to paint the way he does. At the very best, then, we have a theory about the origins of art, a causal theory. This of course would be valuable in itself, were it possible to verify it, to discover criteria which would enable us to evaluate the work, and so forth. It will enable us to do none of these. We already know, from past chapters, the category-mistake involved in predicating causal properties of hidden or occult processes; we also know of the difficulties involved in making knowledge claims about that which is not in principle a public object of knowledge, which emotions and feelings as here construed are not. These two factors alone prevent any progress. The claim is an empirical one if anything, but it cannot be verified; and it is so broad that it is uninformative.

In both the case of art as intended self-expression and the case of art as communication of a kind of emotion, it is well to remember that, if Collingwood's version of the theory is correct, neither of the products of these endeavors can be art in the first place. Character is composed of *kinds* of action and emotion, and the self which is expressed is a *sort* of self, and hence the product exhibiting or expressing either is not unique. This criticism is more difficult to support in the latter case than in the former, but it can be supported in both.

Hospers notes that, even if it is true that the artist does have a range of emotions and feelings when he creates his art, it is silly to say that the audience or the observer should have the same feelings or emotions in all cases. Suppose we say that the myth is true, and that the artist agonizes and suffers when he does work. Should the observer suffer and agonize too? Does the observer *need* to do this in order to appreciate the work of art? Furthermore, we know that some emotions which we feel *could* not have been in the mind of the artist when he composed his work. Hospers uses the example of an observer suffering from the Oedipal conflict which motivates Hamlet's inaction. But as Hospers truly notes, this conflict is a result of Freudian psychology and subsequent investigations, and it certainly could not have been in Shakespeares' mind when he wrote the play.

Santayana's Theory

There are two other versions of the theory to be considered. The first is George Santayana's. This great aesthetician argued that the emotion was to be found in the very work of art itself, rather than in the reaction of the audience or the mind of the artist. In music the joy or sadness is perceived in the notes of the composition itself as heard, in writing ". . . in the very words I hear." O. K. Bouwsma, in his inimitable style, suggests that this is a very curious theory, indeed. Suppose that Cassie is reading her book and what she reads arouses Cassie's emotions. Given the situation, we would not be surprised to find out that Cassie sobs, cries, and otherwise carries on. Then Bouwsma says:

But this isn't all. Cassie is confused. Actually she is crying but she thinks the words are crying. She wipes her tears off those words. She sighs but the words heave. The sentence of Santayana suggests that she sees the sentence she reads through her tears and now her tears misserve her much as blue moods or dark glasses do. So Cassie looks through sadness and the sentence is tearful. What a pathetic fallacy! . . . Imagine what this would be like where sentences aroused not emotions but a toothache. And now you confused the toothache with the sentence, and before someone prevented you, you sent the sentence to the dentist.[9]

The point of course is that if joy and sadness are to be in the words or the notes, then the joy and sadness cannot be the kind that Cassie has but the kind that *can be* in notes and words. To discover what this could mean, Bouwsma suggests what he says is a "foolish theory" about what understanding a sentence is like. The theory is that "Understanding a sentence is speaking the sentence in a certain way. . . . the meaning of the sentence consists in a certain reading of the sentence." He notes that if this were true and if someone spoke a sentence and did not under-

---

[9] Bouwsma, *op. cit.*, p. 89.

stand it, the only thing to do would be to speak it again and again. This of course will not do as a theory of meaning, for there are other ways to clarify what we mean, even though, in order to grasp the meaning of a sentence in some circumstances, it may be true that all that is required is to read it or speak it again.

But Bouwsma argues that what was a foolish theory with regard to the meaning of the sentences is *not* foolish when we come to poetry and music. (Poetry, of course, was the paradigm case for the expressionists, especially the romantic poets.) He says:

Do you get the poem? Do you get the music? If you do not, pointing, gestures, translations will not help. (Understanding the words is presupposed.) There will be only one thing to do, namely, read the verses again, play the music once more. And what will the joy and sweetness and the sadness be like? They will be like the life in the living thing, not to be distinguished as some one part of the poem or music and not another part, or as some shadow that follows the sounded words or tones. 'In the very words you hear', like the squirrel in fur! [10]

He notes that, whereas the meaning of sentences is translatable, this is not true with the significance of music and poetry. This is one reason that it makes sense to ask for what the sentence expresses (it can be given in other *words*) but not for what the poem or composition does. The analogy with language used in the expressionist theory of art is misleading. It leads us to believe that what is expressed in art stands to the art as what is expressed in language (the meaning) stands to the language. But what is really the case is that expressiveness is a *characteristic* of the music and the words in art, not something that is denoted or connoted by it. As Bouwsma puts it, ". . . . the sadness is to the music rather like the redness to the apple, than it is like the burp to the cider." Once we realize this we will not, he thinks, be tempted to ask *what* it is that the music expresses, any more than we would be tempted, when told that the apple was red, to ask what was expressed by the apple in its redness. We may still ask why the music is sad where this question is not tantamount to asking what it is that the music expresses but is rather similar to asking for information about the characteristic sadness. And Bouwsma suggests that among the possible answers are that the music has properties which resemble those of people who are sad: ". . . It will be slow, not tripping; it will be low, not tinkling. People who are sad move more slowly, and when they speak, they speak softly and low."

But of course, music or poetry *need* not be sad, nor joyous, nor anything else; and, when this is so, we are not justified as many expressionists have thought we are in positing some other, uniquely aesthetic emotions

[10] *Ibid.*, p. 91.

just to defend the theory. Nor does the fact that music is sad or joyous somehow make it a better piece of music, because bad music and bad poetry can have these characteristics too. So Bouwsma is saying that *some* music and poetry may have the characteristics of expressiveness (given his analysis of this), but that other examples may not, and that whether they do or they do not will not bear upon the evaluation of the work of art.

Hospers notes of Santayana's theory that if its import is that an element of a work of art (call the element A) and an emotion (call it B) are "so indissolubly fused together in my mind that I do not think of them as separate entities" when I perceive the work as expressive, then it is difficult to know what to make of this. On the one hand, this cannot mean that A merely reminds me of B, for then A and B are not fused. On the other hand, if I am confounding or confusing A with B, than talking about expression at all is simply deluding because it involves a false identification of A and B, which are after all two distinct things. And when I take A to express B, I do *not* usually confound them. So a question remains about what it is that I am doing when I "fuse" A and B, because elements of works of art, such as musical notes, and emotions, are so different that it is difficult to see how they can be fused in any of the normal meanings of the term.

Expression as a Property of Art

After making these comments about this version of the theory, Hospers turns to a view much more similar to Bouwsma's, which involves the analysis of expression as a property or characteristic of a work of art. He notes that it is possible to say that music is expressive even though the artist, when he wrote the piece, may have had no emotions or different ones than those we associate with the piece, or even though we do not know whether the artist had any emotions in the creating of it. An analysis of what it means to say that some work of art is expressive in this way will involve the isolating of certain features of the work, call them A, B, C, D. Sad music, for example, will have these features. Now to defend the claim, Hospers thinks that we would have to point out certain resemblances between A, B, C, D and, for example, the facial features and other behavior of people when they are sad. It is possible, of course, that people will have these features and not be sad, but *usually* when they are sad they have the features and *usually* when they have the features they are truly sad. Since the composer need not have any of the features the music has, this relieves us of the burden that many of the other versions of the theory have, such as the "expression as communication" view, or Collingwood's position.

This Hospers–Bouwsma version of the theory has its advantages and its disadvantages. One of the advantages is that the theory is susceptible to the kind of analysis of metaphors suggested later in this chapter. There it is argued that epiphoric metaphors are logically reducible to similes but that the assertion of resemblance in the simile is one holding among properties rather than among the entities having the properties. That there are difficulties with this view is not questioned, but it seems to be a more adequate theory than others which attempt to account for the problems discussed there. If that theory is applied here, then to say that, for example, a given piece of music is expressive, is to state a *metaphor* rather than a straightforward description. Furthermore, the metaphor, as Bouwsma and Hospers point out, is to be analyzed in terms of a relation or relations of resemblance between characteristics which the music has and characteristics or properties which sad people have. This kind of statement of resemblance would be stated as indicated later in the text. It would appear that this can be done and that the analysis is the best one that the expressionist theory of art can offer.

The theory is certainly not without its limitations. As Hospers notes, many of the properties by virtue of which we call people sad are in fact not those by virtue of which we call music sad, and vice versa; and when we examine the question of just what properties humans and music have in common, it is difficult to find very many that actually do resemble one another. Bouwsma's example of the music being, like sad people, sad and slow, may be one, but there are not many. And there will always be the added difficulty of defending our own views of what constitutes a property of sadness in music and people against those of others. Yet it seems that whatever few properties there may be which meet the requirements of resemblance will suffice for justifying the claim that this version of the expressionist theory of art will explicate a portion of what we mean when we say that are is "expressive."

However, it must also be said that the theory with which we have ended bears little or no resemblance to the one with which we began. You may recall that there were six claims made by *that* theory. The first was that what the artist does when he makes a work of art is to express his emotion or emotions. We know that this is certainly not necessarily true, for empirical investigation disconfirms it as a general truth. It may be true in some cases, but it is false in others. The second claim—that, in the expression of his emotions, the artist becomes aware of them and comes to know and understand them—is likewise limited, if true at all, to those apparently few cases in which this in fact happens. Nor does it seem to be true that this is what distinguishes an art from a craft, as Collingwood would indicate. There are obviously many cases of fine art in which the clarification of the artist's emotions does not take place and which are therefore not individuated because of this. This was the third claim. The fourth claim is false as a general truth for the reasons given against the first three—if the work of art and the process of making it is not in all cases as the fourth statement would indicate. The fifth assertion—that the work of art is a language through which discoveries of the artist about himself are revealed or made known—will follow from the first four statements only for the class of cases of which they are true. Even then this theory for these limited cases will have to contend with all the criticisms raised about what "communication" of emotions means, how one can know that the artist's emotions are the same as the spectator's, what this has to do with evaluation, and so forth. And the sixth claim—that the expressionist theory is good for any form of artistic endeavor or work—is false as that theory is there given. Moreover, even with the revamping that the theory has been given here, it will only hold for a limited number of cases, namely those which in fact do have properties resembling those which humans have when they are said to be in given states. So the old theory did not work very well.

The new theory makes the following limited claims:

1. There are some works of art which are said to be "sad," "joyful," etc. Such works of art are often said to *express* sadness, joy, and so forth. The task of the expressionist theory of art is to give an appropriate analysis of this claim.
2. When it is said that a musical composition is sad, for example, the appropriate analysis is as follows:
   (a) The piece has certain properties, say A, B, C, such that these properties resemble certain other properties a, b, c, when a, b, c are properties of humans in a state of sadness.
   (b) If the assertions of resemblance made in (a) are true, then we may say that the musical work is expressive of sadness as the human with the requisite properties may be said to express sadness.
   (c) It is understood that when such claims are made, no claim is being made about some *other* thing, such that it is manifested or signified or symbolized by A, B, C, or a, b, c.
3. What the emotions of the artist actually are or were, or what the emotions of the perceiver actually are or were, is irrelevant to this version of the expressionist theory of art.
4. The properties described are irrelevant so far as the normal determination of the worth of a work of art for aesthetic purposes are concerned. They may be relevant in other respects, of course, such as evaluating the work for propaganda purposes.

It should be clear that we would be quite justified in dropping the word "expressionist" from the description of this theory altogether, and perhaps that might be a good idea.

METAPHORS AND SIMILES

In Part One of this book we did not investigate the mechanisms of symbolic logic completely for obvious reasons of space. The problems to be discussed here take us beyond the level of symbolization which was reached there, though not so far beyond that you will not be able to comprehend what is said. The additional logical mechanisms used here are multiple quantification (in which, as one might expect, more than one quantifier is used in the translation of a single sentence), and the symbolization of relations, at two different levels. At the first level of relations, a statement of relation holding between two *entities* is symbolized; whereas, at the second level, the relation is said to hold between the *properties* of the entities. Although the concepts involved in such a distinction and their implications are very complex, the logical point is not, and the role of the symbols should become clear by referring to the English translations which are provided in each case.

The Truth or Falsity of Metaphors

The problem we are going to consider will be set within the context of contemporary disagreement about an ancient question: are metaphors either true or false, and if either, how? [11] In the dictionary, we find that a metaphor is a 'short similitude," or a "word expressing similitude without the signs of comparison." The "signs of comparison" mentioned here are words such as "like" or "as," and when these words occur in the comparison, the result is normally thought to be a simile, not a metaphor. Aristotle agreed with this view, for he thought that the difference between metaphors and similes was to be found very largely in the fact that the explicit comparison (the use of "like" or "as") is not used in metaphors. He thought that in all cases of metaphor, a name belonging to one thing is given to another thing. The name might be of a genus, a species, or a particular thing, and so the kinds of metaphor might be given by listing the combination of sorts of name together with what they are used to name. The name of a genus might be given to another genus, or to a species; the name of a species to another species, or to a genus. Aristotle thought that the relation of genus to species was different from that involved in things related by analogy, and he also thought that there were metaphors which rested upon the ground of analogy. In all of these kinds of metaphors, if they are apt, we are indicating by their use "an intuitive perception of the similarity in dissimilars."

[11] I am grateful to the editor of the *Journal of Aesthetics and Art Criticism* for permission to use portions of a forthcoming article of mine entitled "How Some Metaphors May Be Either True or False."

Yet modern scholars seem to think that the grammatical distinction between metaphors and similes is unimportant for philosophical purposes, and the essence of metaphor consists, to use Philip Wheelwright's words, in "the quality of semantic transformation that is brought about." Certainly Wheelwright thinks, as do many other aestheticians, that metaphors are much more than elliptical similes, which is what Aristotle seems to have believed. Another present-day thinker, Paul Henle, thinks that the nature of metaphor is explained by the fact that signs become metaphorical when they are used to refer to objects which are not the ones they literally denote but which have some of the properties of the ones they normally name. This position seems to be close to Aristotle's, and the simple difference which the latter man sees between simile and metaphor is certainly consistent with Henle's view.

Wheelwright argues that the similarities between the compared entities in cases of metaphor need not be obvious and, indeed, cannot be such if the metaphor is to be a good one. The comparison must "come as a shock . . . of recognition," due to the "adroit" choice of dissimilars. He also thinks that "textbook logic" cannot handle such comparisons because many of the differences between metaphorical and non-metaphorical speech are non-logical. We shall have occasion to consider some of these later on.

It is only fair to note that the great Aristotle was not as unaware of some of the more subtle aspects of metaphor as his critics seem to think. He knew that surprise is essential to a good metaphor and that it is based upon just the comparison of unexpected things that Wheelwright mentions. Obvious comparisons are not the foundation of good metaphors for Aristotle. The words used in metaphor cannot be strange, for then we would be merely puzzled; they cannot be ordinary either, for then there would be no surprise; what must be involved is a new *use* of ordinary words to convey something fresh and unexpected. The beauty of the words used themselves and the "proportion" of the asserted relation between the compared entities were also important to Aristotle, for they have a bearing upon the fittingness or aptness of the metaphor. A metaphor might be ruined simply because the sound of the words in it fails to be beautiful.

Now clearly, the problem of the appropriate spheres of logical and what might be called aesthetic analysis in the field of metaphor involves questions about metaphorical *meaning* as well as the problems of fitness or aptness. Some philosophers have argued that ordinary, literal, or if you will, empirical language, and metaphorical language, have at least two quite different sorts of meaning, which are not reducible to one another. Professor Monroe Beardsley has characterized metaphorical meaning as resulting from a "shift" in extension and intension which comes about from the ways in which a metaphorical modifier modifies its subject. We may notice this shift when we consider sentences in which the modifier and subject terms are used non-metaphorically. The trouble with a purely logical approach, such as that which seems to be inherent in the attempt to reduce metaphors to elliptical similes, is that it seems unable to account for this shift which results in the special meaning of metaphors. It certainly does seem to be the case that metaphors have a special kind of meaning, because they are not often safely usable in arguments (equivocation usually results) and because there seem to be *degrees* of metaphorical meaning. In addition, some thinkers such as Beardsley have claimed that truth and falsity are related to metaphors in strange ways, since in many cases it seems to be the obvious *literal falsity* of a metaphor which enables us to know that it *is* a metaphor. His example is "That (building) is a dump." If it actually *were* a real dump, we would not take the sentence as a metaphor. Hence, the literal interpretation of it must be false if it is to be a metaphor.

Yet it seems that in all of this discussion there is only a seeming conflict rather than a real one. It is not clear why metaphors or at least some kinds of metaphors cannot be *either* true or false. Depending upon the context, their truth or falsity may be one of the criteria for judging whether they are fit or apt; and whether they are true or false need not have anything to do with their special meanings. It is this set of claims which will be explicated and defended in what follows, though only in conjunction with one kind of metaphor.

Diaphoric and Epiphoric Metaphors

Professor Wheelwright distinguishes between "diaphoric" and "epiphoric" metaphor.[12] Diaphoric metaphor is such that new meaning arises from the sheer and simple juxtaposition of elements which need involve no comparison at all. In such a metaphor, there are no imitative or mimetic factors involved, because no relations of similarity are expressed. Dissimilar elements are juxtaposed and synthesized, involving, in Wheelwright's words, "the sheer presentation of diverse particulars in a newly designed arrangement." The use of such metaphor presupposes "the broad ontological fact that new qualities and new meaning can emerge, simply come into being, out of some hitherto ungrouped combination of elements." Examples of diaphoric metaphor are non-imitative music and the most abstract sort of painting.

In all types of metaphor there is what Wheelwright calls "semantic motion," which he characterizes as "the double imaginative act of out-

[12] Philip Wheelwright, *Metaphor and Reality* (Bloomington: Indiana University Press, 1962), p. 72.

reaching and combining that essentially marks the metaphoric process." It is the *means* by which this is accomplished that distinguishes epiphoric and diaphoric metaphor. In the former, comparison and some sort of similarity between what is compared are absolutely essential, while in the latter, as we now know, they are completely absent. The word "epiphor" means "transference" and Aristotle used it to refer to the transference of a name from that which it usually names to something else. If Wheelwright is correct, the semantic motion in epiphoric metaphors is from that which is usually named to that which is "vaguer, more problematic, or more strange" by comparison. An illustrative example is, "Life is a dream." Epiphoric metaphor therefore begins from a "literal base of operations," a "standard usage," and a literal meaning understood by the users of the language, and these serve as the basis of the comparison to be made. As has been mentioned, this comparison is the very heart of epiphoric metaphor. *Only* epiphoric metaphor will be considered here.

A Theory of Epiphoric Metaphor

The metaphor which we shall use is "Man is a wolf," and its singular form "Some men are wolves." It is a metaphor with some history in philosophy, its most notable occurrence perhaps being in Hobbes. To prove the theses which will be defended here, it is necessary to use a symbolic language. Using the symbolism developed in Part One, and interpreting "Man is a wolf" as equivalent to "All men are wolves," and "Some men are wolves" as equivalent to "There is at least one thing such that it is a man and it is a wolf," these two sentences might appear to be translatable as

1. $(x) \ (Mx \supset Wx)$
2. $(\exists x) \ (Mx \cdot Wx)$

But these formulations will not do, unless we are to accept the thesis that metaphors are always false; because there is nothing which is both a man and a wolf, and it is false that all men are wolves. It is in fact the *obvious* falsity of both metaphors when stated in this way that might lead one to believe that this is a clue to the criterion or criteria for some phrase or sentence's *being* a metaphor. But the problem here is that the literal interpretation of the two sentences does not capture what we really want to say. "Man is a wolf" surely is not intended to say that man has thick fur, four legs, a long tail, howls at the moon, and eats raw meat, even though men do these things upon occasion. Rather we want to assert that men or some men resemble wolves *in certain respects*. If we interpret metaphors in the simple literal way given above, we miss the point. How then might we assert the latter claim? Resemblance is resemblance in respect of common properties, or at least, in respect of resembling properties. One might therefore argue that what we are really saying in "Men are wolves" is something such as "Man is vicious, and wolves are vicious, and men resemble wolves." Where "Mx" means "x is a man," "Wx" means "x is a wolf," "Vx" means "x is vicious," and "Rxy" means "x resembles y," this sentence and its singular equivalent might be rendered symbolically as follows:

3. $(x)\ (y)\ \{(Mx \supset Vx) \supset [(Wy \supset Vy) \cdot Rxy]\}$
4. $(\exists x)\ (\exists y)\ \{(Mx \cdot Vx) \cdot [(Wy \cdot Vy) \cdot Rxy]\}$

Exact English equivalents of these two sentences would be:
"For any x and for any y, if x is a man then x is vicious; then if y is a wolf then y is vicious, and x resembles y."
"There is at least one x and there is at least one y such that x is a man and x is vicious, and y is a wolf and y is vicious, and x resembles y."

These renderings have the advantage that neither of them *is always* false. But at least the singular version is inadequate, because it asserts the existence of both resembling individuals. Yet, clearly there is an infinite number of possible metaphors of the epiphoric type which are such that we would not want to assert the existence of one or the other of the resembling entities, even though we would still want to compare them.

This fact might suggest that the problem posed by the use of the existential quantifier could be overcome if we reinterpreted the sentences this way, where the symbols all have the same meaning as in (3) and (4):

3'. $(x)\ \{Mx \supset [Vx \cdot (y)\ (Wy \supset \{Vy) \cdot Rxy\}]$
4'. $(\exists x)\ \{(Mx \cdot Vx) \cdot (y)\ [Wy \supset (Vy \cdot Rxy]\}$

These sentences are not always false when instantiated, and the singular sentence does avoid the difficulty of having to assert the existence of both the resembling entities. But they still seem to be inadequate renderings, because what they tell us is that men and wolves are both vicious and that they resemble one another; whereas what we really want to say is that man's viciousness resembles wolves' viciousness and that it is in this respect that all men or some men resemble wolves. After all, we do not want to say that when a man is vicious he is vicious in just the same way that a wolf is; so it cannot be the case that when men and wolves are vicious they have the same property in common. The following will serve quite well in asserting this; and, when rendered in completely general form rather than with the particular symbols we are using here, it will do as a general statement form for any simple epiphoric metaphor:

5. $(x) [Mx \supset (\exists F) (\exists G) (MF \cdot WG \cdot FRG)]$

The singular partner would be:

6. $(\exists x) [Mx \cdot (\exists F) (\exists G) (MF \cdot WG \cdot FRG)]$

In these two sentences, "F" and "G" are properties (F might be the viciousness of man, G the viciousness of wolves) and the letters in heavy type, **M**, **W**, **R**, are second-order predicates, that is, predicates or properties of predicates or properties. The English translation of (5) is: "For any man there is a property F and a property G, such that F is a manish property and G is a wolfish property, and F resembles G." The translation of (6) is: "There is at least one x such that x is a man, and there is at least one property F and at least one property G, such that F is a manish property and G is a wolfish property, and F resembles G."

This formulation has several very important advantages. Both of them may be either true or false. (5) is false if (a) men do not have F, (b) F does not resemble G, (c) G is not a property of wolves, or (d) any combination of these. (6) is false if there are no men or if there are, if any of (a) through (d) are true of the man or property or properties in question. Note that the actual existence of wolves is not a condition of the truth of either (5) or (6). This would be important in cases such as the Churchillian epiphoric metaphor about the "iron curtain." Or to take another example, if we say that someone has a "Jovian countenance," we do not want to have to assert that there is a face of Jove such that the countenance we are considering has properties which resemble Jove's actual face. To state the point in the language of logic, no quantification over individuals corresponding to the metaphorical modifier is required in this rendering.

In addition, the rendering leaves open the possibility that there are resembling properties other than those just mentioned which might be added in a more complex metaphor, and it leaves the issue of whether or not there are non-resemblant properties untouched. The latter is important for purposes of deciding whether or not the metaphor is apt. Furthermore, this version leaves open the possibility that all the properties of men might resemble those of wolves without forcing us to say that in this event men become wolves. The reason is that what is asserted here is resemblance, not identity, and resemblance implies different resembling entities, be they properties or individuals.

There is another important problem solved by this method of translation. In the cases of statements (1) and (2), and (3) and (4), we would want to say that somehow (1) meant at least (3), and (2) meant at least (4). If we consider (5) and (6), we will see that provided that there are men or a man, then the statement of resemblance between the properties of men and wolves is entailed, in the case of (5) by modus ponens, and in the case of (6) by simplification. But, in the original mistaken formulation (1 and 2) we would *not* want to say that (3) and (4) entail (1) and (2), or at least, we would certainly not want to say this in the cases of all epiphoric metaphors of the type we want to be able to handle. For example, we do not want to say that the existence of political detentes entails that they resemble iron curtains. (5) and (6) satisfy these requirements, for by itself the statement of resemblance between the relevant properties does not entail that there are men or a man.

Finally, the lack of mutual entailment relations between the parts of each of the two symbolic statements renders vacuous an important criticism of theories of metaphor which have claimed that their essential feature is a comparison of objects. The criticism is that, according to such theories, if A is metaphorically a B, then the converse is also true. This, however, is obviously false in such cases as "That man is a lion" and "That lion is a man," which are Beardsley's examples, because the resemblant properties attributed in the two statements are not the same. However, since (5) and (6) do not imply "Wolves are men" and "That wolf is a man" respectively, there is no difficulty here.

Meaning and Use in Metaphor

What has been said so far seems to show that metaphors of the sort we are considering may be either true or false and that they are logically reducible to similes, for the symbolic rendering of the corresponding similes will turn out upon examination to be exactly the same as that we have already examined. It should be emphasized again that this is true only for the type of metaphor being considered here—epiphoric metaphors. But this claim is not incompatible with the claim that metaphors of all sorts have special kinds of meaning, not reducible to what Wheelwright calls "literal meaning." It is now time to discuss this problem.

It is clear that meaning is related to use. It is equally clear that there is no obvious relationship between the meaning of a sentence and its logical structure. By this nothing very complicated is meant. In the sentence "The man is honest," the sentence may change its meaning several times over by emphasizing different words in it, by stating words in a skeptical or sarcastic tone of voice, and by various other means. None of these changes in meaning is dependent upon the logical structure of the sentence. It may be a necessary condition for a sentence's having meaning at all that it have a certain *syntactical* structure, but that is not logical structure. "River down by he the is" is probably senseless, while "He is down by the river" is not. The point is that it is not a necessary condition for a change in meaning that a logical change in the structure of the sentence take place, because the logical structure of sentences with quite different meanings is the same. What has been said about epiphoric metaphors thus far has to do with their logical structure; and if, as seems to be the case, these metaphors are reducible to similes by virtue of a common logical structure, it does not follow that any changes in their meanings are thereby necessitated. Even if, as seems clear, the logical reduction involves the exposure of an implicit relation (that of resemblance between properties) which is normally "hidden," any change in meaning which results will vary with the *particular* properties among which the relation is claimed. It *may* be the case that in some instances, changes in logical structure *are* related to changes in meaning, even in special meanings. Metaphors whose point is that entities resemble one another by virtue of logical properties might be one class which would be affected in this way. But admitting this is still compatible with the claim that logical changes do not *a priori* imply changes in meaning.

The explanations of special metaphorical meaning are usually non-logical in nature. They concern such factors as emotive association, literary and artistic context, the intention of the user of the metaphor, poetic license, the willful suspension of disbelief, and so forth. Professor Wheelwright has examined the differences between the ordinary and the expressive uses of language at length; but for our purposes, his discussion of the properties of characteristics which expressive language has as opposed to or in addition to those of ordinary language is most important. Among the differences are the following characteristics which expressive language has, but which ordinary language does not have:

1. *Iconic signification*—the symbols used in certain arts have themselves an intrinsic value as well as a referential function.
2. *Plurisignification*—terms used in metaphors and other forms of artistic expression often have more than one "legitimate reference, in such a way that its proper meaning is a tension between two or more directions of semantic stress."
3. *Soft focus*—such terms often do not have "definite outlines" and therefore cannot be "adequately represented by terms that are strictly defined."
4. *Contextualism*—some symbol, though it might have a definite range of meaning, and even the same meaning throughout a work of art if analyzed according to some standard criterion, nonetheless "shifts about within moderate limits" because of both its iconic and plurisignificative nature.
5. *Paralogical dimensionality*—the property of having a dimension of

meaning wider than the mere universality and particularity which terms have when considered strictly from the viewpoint of their logical uses.

6. *Assertorial tone*—these terms have degrees of denial or affirmation or both rather than the simple "either true or false" values which all sentences have in the eyes of logicians.

7. *Paradox*—arises when two statements whose conjunction is a logical contradiction are still metaphorically acceptable because of the aesthetic role of the "contradiction."

8. *Significant mystery*—Wheelwright's name for the property ascribed to poetic utterance when we realize that its truth is more than the total of the weight of the deductive and inductive evidence which can be adduced for it. Or, to put this point another way, the meaning of metaphor is never exhausted by answers to questions asked about them, because intuition is always involved.

Some of these points, in particular (6) and (7), seem to apply more to diaphoric than to epiphoric metaphor, or to metaphors which are a combination of both types. Others seem to be characteristics of epiphoric metaphor, and not incompatible with what has been claimed so far about this kind of utterance. Theories of truth and meaning are not the same thing, though often the distinction between the two becomes blurred, as point (8) above indicates. There are, of course, many relations between meaning and truth; for it seems that to be true or false a sentence must be meaningful, though the converse does not seem to be the case. There seems to be no oddness in speaking of a sentence as having more than one kind of meaning, but there is at least a *prima facie* suspicion when we claim that a sentence has more than one kind of truth. In the case of epiphoric metaphor, there seems to be more than one sort of meaning involved but only one kind of truth. The truth of a metaphor of this kind is discovered by determining whether there is a real correspondence among the properties compared. But this is only one factor among many involved in determining the meanings, and more than likely it concerns what we should call the normal rather than the special meaning of the metaphor. The truth or falsity of the metaphor is relevant for artistic purposes insofar as it may provide a criterion for judging the aptness of the metaphor within given contexts.

Aptness in Metaphor

It is hard, if not impossible to find anything which constitutes solid evidence against this view. Why might it not be true that factors such as aesthetic perception and emotion, willful suspension of disbelief, and the others mentioned earlier, enter into the determination of the special meaning of metaphors, while at the same time they have truth-values by virtue of the presence or absence of the asserted relation of resemblance which has been discussed? It has been noted that the property of having truth-values does not seem to be a necessary condition for meaningfulness. But on the other hand, nothing prevents a meaningful metaphor from being either true or false. In fact, in the case of the kind of metaphor we are considering here, is it not the case that they would not have the meaning *that they do have* (though they might have some meaning or other) if they were not either true or false? This does not rule out some special meanings which they might have; but, after all, the total meaning of a metaphor is composed of both its normal and its special meanings. By analyzing the meaning of an epiphoric metaphor in terms of the relation of resemblance asserted in it between two properties or sets of properties and by claiming a truth-value for it according to whether the relation is present or not, we do not thereby rule out its having other special sorts of significance. Even if it is the case, as most thinkers about the problem claim, that in metaphorical contexts a metaphorical modifier takes on a new intention which it might have in no other context, this does not entail that the metaphor loses its old extension, or that it becomes irrelevant. Whether the old extension becomes irrelevant or not seems a matter for empirical investigation. It might well, of course, do just that; but, in the case of epiphoric metaphor, it would seem to have to remain relevant in order that the new metaphor even take on its new intention. What would a metaphor such as the "spiteful sun" (another of Beardsley's examples) mean at all if spitefulness were not a possible property of some person and if the sun could not have a property or properties such that it or they resembled spitefulness? This does not imply, as Professor Beardsley seems to think, that some entity *actually* has the property. It is quite enough if it is believed to have the property, even if the belief turns out to be false.

Even if it is true that epiphoric metaphors are either true or false, there is no requirement that they be true *rather* than false. It is certainly conceivable that there are contexts in which a metaphor would be better were it false rather than true. But it is also the case that the truth of a metaphor may be a test of its aptness. It would be difficult to understand what Churchill meant when he called Lord Atlee a "sheep in wolf's clothing" unless he at least believed that Atlee had properties resembling those of sheep, for example, meekness, while pretending to be the opposite. But even if Churchill did believe this, one might argue that the metaphor was not apt on the grounds that it is false; that is, one might claim that Atlee was not sheepish in any way. Obviously, this is not the only reason that might be given for rejecting the metaphor, but it is one reason. It is true that the requirement that the old extension remain relevant therefore leaves open the question of what is or is not an "appropriate" metaphor, but there seems to be nothing wrong with this if one believes that some metaphors are appropriate and others not and that one reason for inappropriateness in some contexts at least is their falsity. "Sheepish Churchill" seems inappropriate precisely because the sentence "Churchill is sheepish" is false. Since "sheepish" means "like a sheep," this is a simile. But the metaphor "Churchill is a sheep" would be logically reducible to the simile and would be rejected on the same grounds. "Churchill the lion" or "Churchill the bulldog," on the other hand, both seem quite appropriate, other things being equal, precisely because the implicit statement of resemblance between some of the properties of the man and some of the properties of lions and bulldogs is true in each case.

It might be argued that the claims made here are true but irrelevant to the topic of metaphor on the grounds that they consider metaphor not *qua* metaphor, but *qua* literal statements which are either true or false. Such a criticism might further argue that the case can be made only if it could be shown that there is some *necessary* connection between truth-values and normal meaning and metaphorical special meaning. This can be accomplished in the case of epiphoric metaphor, provided only that we speak about necessary and sufficient conditions rather than logical necessity. We shall hold that a necessary condition of an epiphoric metaphor's having special meaning is that it meet these requirements:

1. It must have a normal meaning, where this means that the metaphorical modifier must refer to possible properties which are possibly resemblant.
2. The normal meaning must remain constant "on some level of analysis" throughout the context in which the metaphor is used.
3. Given that normal meaning involves a comparison which is an assertion or a resemblance, the metaphor is either true or false.

If (1) does not hold, the epiphoric metaphor will turn out upon examination to be either senseless or diaphoric. (2) must hold if (1) does, because if it did not then by hypothesis the meaning is not then normal as one can see from Wheelwright's remarks about special expressive meaning. The only other alternative is that more than metaphor is involved. If (1) holds, (3) must; because, if we have two properties, F and G, which are possibly resemblant, then they are possibly not, and which they are is a matter of confirmation or judgment. It would therefore seem that the three requirements are necessary though not sufficient conditions for any assertion's being an epiphoric metaphor.

None of what has been said contradicts the positions of Wheelwright and Beardsley, and it is perfectly compatible with both Henle and

Aristotle. It would appear that the theory presented here exposes the artificiality of the apparent disagreements among them. It is instructive to see whether the theory also escapes some of the other pitfalls which some of these men find in other theories of metaphor.

Professor Monroe Beardsley calls his own theory of metaphor the "Revised Verbal-Opposition" theory.[13] In it he argues that metaphorical attribution involves two major ingredients, which are a "semantical distinction between two levels of meaning, and a logical opposition at one level." What this means is clarified when he notes that, if we use the word "spiteful" in a metaphorical context, we preclude the possibility in that context of using the word to denote spiteful people and of comparing them in the metaphor. It is not the denoted but the connoted characteristics which are signified in metaphorical contexts. Were this not so, that is, if the metaphorical modifier merely performed its denotative function, we would not have the "special" meanings of metaphors which distinguish them from other modes of speech.

The theory defended here earlier is certainly compatible with this argument. Properties, not individuals, are compared in metaphors, and there is no objection to the thesis that a shift from denotation to connotation occurs in at least some epiphoric metaphorical contexts.

Beardsley also analyzes the purpose for which we refer to properties in metaphorical contexts. It is to enable us to view these properties as having a "new status as elements of verbal meaning." Moreover, he argues generally that any adequate theory of metaphor must account for or at least provide for the "novelty," the "unpredictablility" of metaphor, arising from the changes of meaning, even quite radical ones, which are so commonplace in the astute use of this mode of expression. It would seem that he is quite right here and that there is no reason why the theory which has been suggested for epiphoric metaphor cannot meet these tests. Wheelwright's arguments also meet them, with but slight modification. But in the theory presented here, some other facts have been discovered, at least about epiphoric metaphor. If what has been said is correct, then the special meanings of metaphors have little to do with their logical structure. First, since the reduction of epiphoric metaphors to similes is a logical matter, such reduction ought not to bear directly upon the question of special meaning. Secondly, at least one criterion for judging the aptness or fitness of metaphors is acceptable according to this theory, and accepting such a criterion does not involve the consequence that the converse of a comparison must follow from that comparison. You may recall that Beardsley argued against theories of metaphor in which the central premise is that they are comparisons

[13] Monroe Beardsley, "The Metaphorical Twist," *Philosophy and Phenomenological Research*, 22, no. 3 (1962), pp. 293–307.

between objects on the ground that a metaphor such as "That man is a lion" would, according to such a view, have to imply its converse, "That lion is a man." That the theory presented here does not involve this pitfall was shown above. The criterion provided in the theory given here is that of truth and falsity, which is certainly related to aptness, appropriateness or fittingness in at least some contexts. And finally, this view seems to avoid the necessity for taking some metaphors as literally false in order to claim that they are metaphors.

At the same time, it must be admitted that serious difficulties do arise. Let us consider but two of these. Both of them were suggested by Professor Bernard Harrison of the University of Sussex.

One Criticism of the Theory

The first difficulty and probably the most important one is focused upon the very concept of resembling properties, which is the heart of our analysis. Suppose that we have two properties which we shall call P and P'. These properties will either be complex or dispositional, or they will be simple in the analytic sense, that is, unanalyzable into smaller parts. Let us assume that they are complex or dispositional properties. If they are, then any sentence which asserts that P resembles P' will be replaceable by a more explicit sentence which asserts that there is a *third* property P'' such that any entity which has P' will share P'' in common with all entities which have P. Professor Harrison suggested the rather graphic example "Lust resembles hunger." He thinks that this metaphor, if taken to assert a resemblance between the properties or some of the properties involved, is replaceable by a a longer sentence such as "Anyone who lusts has at least in common with the one who hungers that he is kept in a ceaseless uneasiness by the lack of what would satisfy his desire." Obviously the complete exfoliation of the meaning of the metaphor might well require more explanation than this one sentence.

Now consider a case in which the resembling properties are simple rather than complex. Again, consider Professor Harrison's example, "John's redness resembles Arnold's redness." This example confronts us in a more obvious way than does the first one (though both involve the issue) with the problems of resemblance and difference. What the example before us asserts is that John is red, and Arnold is red and that their respective rednesses are different but also the same because they resemble one another. In the first complex example the sameness among the properties was analyzed in terms of the positing of a third property in which both the resembling properties shared. Is this what we must do in the second case as well?

We know that the two colors of the two men are different colors. Let us therefore for the sake of clarity specify the example somewhat by saying that Arnold is rather more pink than red, and revise our sentence to read "John's redness resembles Arnold's pinkness." Now Professor Harrison pointed out that the exact meaning of this latter sentence is really a puzzle. We might want to claim when we say this that John's redness and Arnold's pinkness are the same *sort* of color, meaning thereby that redness is more like pinkness than it is like some other sort of color. But if that is what we mean, then many philosophers would want to say that "John's redness resembles Arnold's pinkness" is a synthetic *a priori* proposition; and, therefore, if it is true, it must be necessarily true. The problem then is to explicate the notion of "truth" and "necessity" which is involved here; and, as we know, this is a notoriously difficult matter. Any theory which moves from one problem to another problem which is even harder ought to be suspect on the face of it. Hence, Professor Harrison thought that this is not what could have been meant in the theory.

The comments, so far as they constitute a criticism, can be summarized in one claim, which is that, if the view given here is correct, then some epiphoric metaphors and perhaps all of them are necessarily true because they are synthetic *a priori* truths. It is quite possible to agree with the analysis proposed by Harrison for statements of resemblance between complex or dispositional properties and even to agree with his analysis of how one would explicate statements of resemblance between simple properties; but it is quite another thing to agree that these sentences are synthetic *a priori* assertions. Consider our primary example, the claim that the viciousness of men resembles the viciousness of wolves. This seems to mean that they are of the same *sort* of viciousness, and this, in turn, seems to imply that part of what this means is that the viciousness of man is more like that of wolves than it is like that of, say, boa constrictors. Now the question is this: is the sentence "The viciousness of man is more like that of wolves than it is like that of boa constrictors" a synthetic *a priori* sentence? It seems that it is not. Certainly it is difficult to explain just what sort of sentence this is, but one very important factor mitigates against the view that it is synthetic *a priori*. This fact is that the truth of this sentence seems confirmable or discomfirmable by an appeal to experience. There is nothing that is conceptually odd about the notion that, by some weird evolutionary changes, men might become vicious more in the manner of boa constrictors than in the manner of wolves. Surely a visitor from another planet would be doing nothing very strange and certainly nothing absurd if he set out to determine the truth or falsity of such claims by observing the behavior of men, wolves, and boa constrictors. It seems, too, that it *would* be odd for some earthling to tell him that he need perform no such check on the grounds that he could discover the truth or falsity of the claim simply from an examination of the terms in the sentences. The same thing seems to be true of an assertion such as "John's redness resembles Arnold's pinkness." Part of the meaning of this sentence may indeed be the claim that the redness and the pinkness are of the same sort of color, that is, that there is a class of colors to which they both belong, or that there is a "single" color of which they are both shades. But if it is true, as has been suggested, that one can decide the truth of such sentences by an empirical investigation, then whatever the correct analysis of the sentences may be, they cannot be synthetic *a priori* claims. If their truth can be so decided, then they must simply be synthetic sentences.

The foregoing also seems to be the case with epiphoric metaphors. We do not normally, in the examination of the metaphorical mode of expression, ask whether a metaphor is true or false. We ask whether it is fitting or not, apt or inappropriate. But the grounds for its aptness, or one possible ground, has been shown to be its truth-value. And certainly we decide whether epiphoric metaphors are true or not on the basis of our perception, not on the basis of something about the terms of the expression. That this may not be wholly satisfactory in reply to criticisms such as the one raised by Professor Harrison is evident. But further investigation would demand lengthy studies in the areas of metaphysics, epistemology, and logic, which are inappropriate here. It is sufficient to rest the arguments offered here upon the easily understood claim that epiphoric metaphors are confirmable by experience; for, if that is true, then the onus is on the proponents of the "synthetic *a priori*" view to show that there are other compelling reasons for adopting their claim.

A Second Criticism

The second objection which Professor Harrison raised is more general in nature than the first but of almost equal importance. The objection centers on the belief that there is an implicit assumption about the function of metaphors which is in fact not justified. The assumption is that the role of metaphors such as "Man is a wolf" is to "say something about the properties of men and wolves." Professor Harrison suggested that this was false or misleading and true, if at all, only in what he called a "Pickwickian" sense. In his eyes, the function of metaphors is to show that some conceptual scheme which is adequate for the explanation of the behavior of one type of entity is also adequate for explaining the actions of another sort of entity. This is why a behavioral psychologist of the strict determinist variety might say that men are rats or why a Cartesian might argue that animals are machines. In order to understand metaphors such as these in Professor Harrison's eyes, we must have an explanation of the "purport" of the metaphor. He believes that, in the case of "Man is a wolf," made famous by Thomas Hobbes, such an explanation was given in Hobbes's theory of the passions. If this view is correct, then the author or user of a metaphor intends to assert the applicability of the conceptual scheme which is the explanation of the purport of the metaphor to the two sorts of entity involved. The theory of metaphor which has been offered here then becomes "Pickwickian" because it follows in Professor Harrison's view that all that has been noted is that the property which the entities have in common if the metaphor is a good one is simply that they are explicable in terms of the same conceptual scheme. This is not very informative if this is the very purpose of metaphor.

In reply, it might be noted first that the criticism, if it is to be directed against the theory given here, must be restricted to epiphoric metaphor. Secondly, nowhere in the theory is it implied that the *only* function of metaphors of the "Man is a wolf" sort is to say something about the properties of men and wolves. It would seem that this particular metaphor does in fact say something about these properties, namely that they resemble each other; but it does more than this, as the discussion of special meaning and the agreement in essentials with Wheelwright's classification of the properties of metaphors should demonstrate. Even on the level of normal meaning, it is possible for a metaphor to do more than assert a resemblance between properties. Together with other statements, metaphors might well imply imperatives such as "Beware of man," or at least they might well do this if we were to accept a non-cognitivistic view of the nature of validity and inference. It is not even necessary that the assertion of resemblance among properties be the most important function of metaphor. It is merely a necessary condition for a metaphor's being epiphoric that it makes such an assertion.

It also does not seem to be accurate to characterize the assertion of resemblance as "Pickwickian." To defend the theory against this claim, let us consider what conditions two things or sets of things must meet if they are to be explicable in terms of a single conceptual scheme. As an example, we might consider stimulus–response psychology, which we shall call "S–R," and consider rats and men as the entities to be explained. In order to know that rats and men are explicable in terms of S–R so far as their actions are concerned, we must first know that *either* men or rats are so explicable. Even if one of the species is to be subject to S–R analysis, certain conditions must be met. Consider the property which rats have of reacting positively to non-toxic substances containing sugar. Such substances, other things being equal, do quite well as reinforcers for certain types of responses in rats. Of course, there are simply thousands of such possible reinforcers, but the point is that there must be *some* or we could not explicate the behavior of rats in terms of S–R. If having the property of reacting to some reinforcers is a necessary condition for explicability in terms of S–R for rat behavior and if man is also explicable in terms of S–R, then man must also have to have such a property or properties or some other properties which resemble these. Men and rats must therefore resemble one another in respect of having this resembling property, whereas rats and stones need not. If, as seems to be the case, properties themselves can and do resemble one another, then any conceptual scheme such that the existence of resemblant properties is a necessary condition for its applicabilty will by the same logic imply that the two classes of entities which are explicable by this scheme must have relevant resembling properties. Now this is surely to say more than merely that the two kinds of entities are explicable by the same conceptual scheme, and if so, then the theory of epiphoric metaphor being defended is not Pickwickian.

The Range of Metaphor

A complete philosophical analysis of all kinds of metaphor would include at least the following:

1. An explanation of the differences among kinds of metaphor.
2. An explanation of the concept of "normal meaning" in metaphors.
3. An explanation of the concept of "special meaning" or meanings in the use of metaphor.
4. An examination of the logical structure of metaphors.

In what has been presented here, some remarks have been made about one sort of metaphor, and these remarks concerned primarily the logical structure of this kind of metaphor, plus a defense of the theory against criticisms directed against some of its possible implications. Metaphors are part and parcel of our ordinary discourse as well as of our art, our literature, our religions, and our science. The study given here is overly brief even for its limited scope, and it is hoped that some realization of the immensity of the area will suggest it as a field of interest to those who might become future philosophers.

EXERCISES

1. One of the theories in this section has been called predominantly an "empirical" view, and the other was said to be based upon a "complex metaphysical system." Discuss the theories from the viewpoint of this difference.

2. The empirical theory results in eleven claims which are presumably empirical claims. Do you agree that they are empirical claims? Why or why not?

3. No doubt at one time or another you have experienced some emotion or other while attending a play or a concert, or while listening to music, etc. How does this square with the claim that emotion is not an essential ingredient of the aesthetic experience?

4. Shaftesbury claims that we have a "moral sense," which is also an aesthetic sense. How would you argue against this claim?

5. The empirical theory purports to offer a definition of the aesthetic attitude. What kind of definition is it? Is it a good definition? Why or why not?

6. The terms "a priori" and 'a posteriori" are used to characterize the two theories. Which one is a priori? Why is it a priori? Which one is a posteriori? Why is it a posteriori? What is the difference between calling a theory "a priori" and "metaphysical"? Between calling it "a posteriori" and "empirical"?

7. It has been argued by some philosophers that there are no necessary and sufficient conditions for defining the aesthetic attitude. Does the empirical theory escape this objection? Do you think the objection is well-founded? Why or why not?

8. What is "disinterestedness"? Why is it not a sufficient condition for defining the aesthetic attitude?

9. If the aesthetic attitude is disinterested, does this limit the class of objects which can be aesthetic objects? Why or why not?

10. Formulate the two theories as deductive arguments, and criticize them, using our criteria.

11. What does Collingwood mean when he calls a work of art "expressive"?

12. Aside from Collingwood's view, how many other versions of the expressionist theory of art are discussed in the chapter? Give a definition of what is meant by "expressive" for each one.

13. Are any of the expressionist theories presented "empirical" theories? Why or why not? Are any of them clearly not empirical theories? Why or why not?

14. Why does Collingwood think that the artist in his work cannot be trying to express a kind of emotion?

15. Why is the view of art as a "language" misleading? In addition to being misleading, is it a false view? Why or why not?

16. Discuss the claims of the expressionist theory of art from the viewpoint of the analysis presented in the section on theories of meaning.

17. If we grant that emotions are somehow expressed in works of art and that the emotions so expressed are the artist's, do we merely by granting this commit a category mistake? Why or why not?

18. Bouwsma speaks of Cassie's "pathetic fallacy." What is this fallacy, and how does Cassie commit it, if she does?

19. Bouwsma says his "foolish" theory about understanding sentences is not foolish when applied to poetry and music. Is it? Why or why not?

20. The last sentence of the section says that if the criticisms given have been adequate and the suggested revamping of the theory sound, then we might just dispense with the word "expressionist" in the name of the theory. Is this true? Why or why not?

21. What is the difference between an epiphoric metaphor and a diaphoric metaphor? Would you characterize this difference in terms of a difference in definition? Why or why not? If it is a difference in definitions, are both the definitions of the same sort? What sort are they?

22. Suppose someone told you that all epiphoric metaphors are false when

taken literally. How might you set out to disprove this claim? Assume that Beardsley is talking about epiphoric metaphors when he says that all metaphors are false when taken literally and that you have disproved his claim. Assume also that the claim that he has made is a part of the definition of epiphoric metaphors. What are the consequences of your refutation for his definition? Does it become false? A bad definition or inadequate? Why or why not?

23. It is argued in the section that the truth or falsity of an epiphoric metaphor may be among the criteria used to judge its fitness or aptness. Analyze this concept of "fitness" or "aptness" in connection with this sort of metaphor. That is, say what you think should be included among the criteria, and why.

24. Why is it important that we do not have to assert the existence of both or all of the resembling entities in an epiphoric metaphor?

25. Why, if the analysis given is correct, may we not be content with asserting a resemblance among individuals rather than among properties of individuals in epiphoric metaphors? Use examples in your answer.

26. Why do we not want to say that statements (3) and (4) on pages 400–401 entail statements (1) and (2)? Use examples in your answer.

27. Of the properties of the expressive uses of language which Professor Wheelwright gives, which are empirical properties and why are they "empirical"?

28. Why does Professor Harrison think that the sentence "John's redness resembles Arnold's pinkness" is a synthetic *a priori* truth?

29. Do you agree with Professor Harrison that the function of metaphors is to show that some conceptual scheme which is adequate for the explanation of the behavior of one type of entity is also adequate for explaining the actions of another? Why or why not?

30. Formulate the replies to Professor Harrison's criticisms as arguments in deductive form and evaluate those arguments, using the criteria developed in Part One.

V

Philosophy of Science and Types of Philosophy

11

Philosophy of Science

A VIEW OF METHOD IN SCIENCE

Science is now so much a part of our lives that some of its technical aspects are common knowledge, even among those with little formal education in its various disciplines. It may seem strange, but, at one point not very many hundreds of years ago, people were preoccupied with the attempt to describe what scientific method is and whether or not there are differences in its method as compared to those of other disciplines. In this section, we shall begin with a discussion of scientific method couched in terms of its relations to philosophy, and in particular we shall consider what René Descartes thought about the subject. Among other things, Descartes is famous for the invention of a particular *philosophical* method known as the method of methodological doubt. But he was also a mathematician and a scientist of note, and he had a lot to say about the kinds of procedures followed.

Descartes and Science

Descartes invented analytic geometry, and he also wrote two treatises on optics and meteorology. The geometry, optics, and meteorology—that is, the three essays in which these subjects are discussed—were appended to Descartes's *Discourse on Method,* and the Discourse was the preface to these three works.[1] He said that the three essays constituted an actual illustration of his scientific method; so we ought to be able to discover what it was from a study of all four pieces. He also spoke of his method frequently in his correspondence, some times with other

[1] René Descartes, *Discourse on Method, Optics, Geometry and Meteorology,* Paul Olscamp, ed. and trans. (New York: The Bobbs-Merrill Co., Library of Liberal Arts, 1965), p. xv. My thanks to the Bobbs-Merrill Company for their permission to use material from this book.

scientists of note; and in his philosophical works he often wrote of how philosophy and science are related. Naturally, there has been a lot of writing about the Cartesian view, and most though not all of it takes a fairly uniform view of what he said. We shall refer to this standard view of the Cartesian method as the "traditional" view. It is exemplified very well in Professor Leon Roth's *Descartes's Discourse on Method*,[2] although this does not imply that Roth holds all of the positions attributed to the traditional view.

Here, we shall be trying to solve three basic questions:

1. How are the Cartesian metaphysics and the principles of the particular sciences related?
2. The theory of innate ideas, his metaphysics, and his view of the role of intuition all confirm the fact that Descartes was a rationalist rather than an empiricist. What then is his method of doing science, and how does it differ from the empiricists' scientific method?
3. Are synthesis and experimentation parts of analysis in the Cartesian method of doing science?

We shall discover in our investigation of the first question that Descartes tried to derive the principles of science in two ways. First, he tried to show that they could be deduced from the self-evident principles of his metaphysics. The metaphysical principles were themselves reached through the sort of analysis which he uses in his *Meditations on First Philosophy*. Secondly, he thought that he could discover these same principles of science by deriving generalizations from experience and the experiments performed within the particular sciences, which experiments are used to confirm or disconfirm either the principles or the subsidiary laws derived from them or both. In this procedure, the principles and subsidiary laws are considered as hypotheses. If it is true that the principles of science can be derived by both of these methods, then this would provide us with a metaphysical justification for the empirical method and empirical confirmation for the metaphysical findings; and for Descartes this would have been a perfectly normal assumption. He explicitly claimed that the foundations of his physics are demonstrable, and that the demonstration is a part of his metaphysics. In a letter to Huygens in 1645 he complained that he was being unjustly accused of not confirming his scientific findings by experiment. On the contrary, he affirmed that not only did he experiment incessantly, but that the results he thereby obtained could be taken as confirmation of the principles of his physics, even though these are also deducible from his metaphysics.

---

[2] Leon Roth, *Descartes's Discourse on Method* (Oxford: The Clarendon Press, 1937).

If this is not true of all of the subsidiary laws of the Cartesian physics, it is certainly true of its principles.

Actually, there seem to be no significant differences in the ways in which empiricists and rationalists actually *do* science. Certainly the work of an eminent empiricist in science such as Newton illustrates significant and sometimes striking similarities of method when compared to the work of Descartes. Since both wrote works about optics, the opportunity for comparison is excellent. It discloses that for all intents and purposes the methods are identical, from which we might well conclude that the differences between rationalists and empiricists rest in their metaphysical presuppositions and not in their science.

The answer to the third question is not so simply given and cannot be summarized briefly. But it turns out to be the most important question, and we shall therefore now proceed to an investigation of analysis and synthesis in Descartes.

Analysis and Synthesis in Descartes

It was Descartes's belief that the search for knowledge in any field at all had to proceed according to the same basic method, with additions as required by the particular subject matter. Searching for knowledge and "proving" one's conclusion after one knows the principles of the field under examination are not the same thing. The search is more important than the *ad hoc* proof. So to understand his method in the actual doing of science we must understand the different processes of discovering, and demonstrating or proving, first. The heart of the process consists in the use of a set of rules for using the natural capacities and operations of the mind correctly. There are only two of these faculties, which he calls "intuition" and "deduction." Deduction differs from intuition only because it involves a "certain movement or succession" and because it "does not require an immediately presented evidence such as intuition possesses; its certitude is rather conferred upon it in some way by memory." Only the first principles of knowledge are known by intuiton, and the conclusions from these are known by deduction. The method for using these two faculties of the mind has two parts, called "analysis" and "synthesis." It was the method used by the Greeks and the parts are used both to discover truth and to demonstrate it. Analysis is the way we discover truth and synthesis the way we demonstrate it. Analysis is often called the inductive method; and, according to Aristotle, Socrates invented it, (though Aristotle was probably mistaken here). Through it we derive general principles from particular sets of facts. One of the uses of synthesis or the axiomatic method is to present in deductive form that which has already been discovered analytically. Descartes wrote that his *Medi-*

tations illustrate what analysis is, and that much of the *Principles of Philosophy* is in synthetic or axiomatic form. One of the clearest statements about the differences between analysis and synthesis which we can find in the writings of Descartes is this:

> . . . there are two things that I distinguish in the geometrical mode of writing, viz., the *order* and the *method* of proof. The order consists merely in putting forward those things first that should be known without the aid of what comes subsequently, and arranging all other matters so that their proof depends solely on what preceeds them. . . . Further, the *method* of proof is two-fold, one being analytic, the other synthetic.
>
> *Analysis* shows the true way by which a thing was methodically *discovered* and *derived*, as it were from *effect to cause* . . .
>
> *Synthesis* contrariwise employs an opposite procedure, one in which the *search* goes as it were from effect to cause (though often here the *search* itself is from cause to effect to a greater extent than in the former case). It does indeed clearly demonstrate its conclusion, and it employs a long series of definitions, postulates, axioms, theorems and problems, so that if one of the conclusions that follow is denied, it may be at once shown to be contained in what has gone before . . . Yet this method . . . does not show the way in which the matter taught was discovered.
>
> It was this synthesis alone that the ancient Geometers employed in their writings, not because they were wholly ignorant of the analytic method, but, in my opinion, because they set so high a value on it that they wished to keep it to themselves as an important secret.[3]

The italicized portions are particularly important because a careful examination of them reveals the following:

1. The method of proof contains *both* analysis and synthesis.
2. In using analysis, we discover and derive the explanation of something by discovering that it is an effect of one cause or set of causes *rather than* another, and to discover this, plus discovering how the causes and effects are related, is to discover the explanation.
3. The "search," but not the proof, proceeds from effect to cause in synthesis, and thus the search in analysis proceeds from cause to effect.
4. When we exhibit what we have discovered "in synthetic style," we are showing how conclusions about the effects are related to their principles or causes logically, but to show this is not to depict how the causes and their relations to their effects were discovered.
5. In any adequate demonstration, each statement depends upon the truth of the statements preceding it.

The most important points in the passage for our purposes are: (1) that synthesis is used in the search for principles, not just in their subsequent demonstrations; and (2) that, if analysis is the process of discovery, the causes with which it *begins* cannot be *known*, that is, they are hypotheses.

---

[3] Descartes, *op. cit.*, p. xxvi.

If we are going to claim truth for what follows from principles, then we must know that the principles are true, and the results of analysis for Descartes is the certain knowledge that they are. Plato said that in analysis the starting assumptions are treated as "hypotheses" until they are intuitively known. Descartes referred to these assumptions as "involved and obscure propositions" (rule 5, *Rules for the Direction of the Mind*) and they are probably identical with what he elsewhere called "suppositions," "assumptions," and "hypotheses." The metaphor which Plato used to characterize the whole process of analysis–intuition–synthesis was a stepped arch in which the coping stone of intuition held together the two sides—analysis and synthesis. Aristotle also used a metaphor to illustrate this method, and his example was a racetrack in which the principles or *archai* were apprehended at the half-way mark. Plato, Aristotle, and the ancient geometers therefore believed that, without prior analysis, synthesis was unjustified and that the ultimate justification of both was intuitive apprehension of the principles. So for them, if scientific knowledge was to be demonstrative, it must depend upon analysis and intuition. The traditional view of Descartes has it that this was his position too, but it seems that this is not correct when extended to his work in science.

The best (clearest) sources for information about Descartes's views about the method for using intuition and deduction are the fifth, sixth, and twelfth of the *Rules for the Direction of the Mind* and the second and sixth sections of the *Discourse on Method*. It is quite clear from these that he thought that analysis was more important than synthesis, because it is the process in which deduction and intuition are used to discover the principles used in synthesis. This is very important for our purposes, because the traditional view does not seem to realize that deduction (synthesis) and intuition are both used extensively in *analysis,* that is, that deduction has more importance than its use in simple demonstration after principles have been discovered; indeed, it is used in the process of discovery as well. But the traditional view sees the role of analysis as justifying the principles of physics (physics is the basic science for Descartes) in two ways, neither of which presumably need involve deduction. It shows systematically how we derive these principles and justifies them by the clarity and distinctness of intuitive awareness.

The famous method of methodological doubt in the *Meditations* is the first instance of the consistent use of analysis for purposes of discovery. Here the analytic technique consists in the systematic rejection of every proposition which it is logically possible to doubt in an effort to discover one which does not seem subject to this failing. The one not possible to doubt which is eventually discovered is of course "Cogito, ergo sum"—I think, therefore I am. But the process of discovery does not stop here; because, given that this proposition is true and known to be so, Descartes tried to find others, using the first one as a justification for them. In the *Rules* this process might be characterized by saying that after beginning with complex and obscure propositions and doubting them wherever possible, we reduce them to simple natures or universals. These are intuited in the light of "an unclouded and attentive mind" and, once so known, are expressed in propositions formulating the universals or simple natures as principles, laws, and causes, which are the explanations for the complex and obscure propositions with which we began. Analysis is complete at this point, and we can then proceed to exhibit what we have discovered in the synthetic manner. This same method is attributed to Descartes in both the spheres of metaphysics and science by the traditional view. In order to discover why it is inadequate we must now consider the Cartesian view from a wider perspective.

The Scope of Philosophy for Descartes

Descartes used the word "philosophy" with a much broader scope than is given to it now. It was almost equivalent to our word "wisdom," and included metaphysics, physics, and all other sciences relatable to physics in certain ways. Nothing is a science in his eyes unless it stands to physics in these certain ways, and we must also be able to reason in all the sciences in a uniform way. The method of reasoning is applied to the study of order and measurement, which are the essential ingredients for the study of anything. What the *units* of measurement are does not matter for purposes of the method, though it does matter for the particular sciences, for the units are their subject matter. Mathematics studies order and measure among numbers, astronomy among stars, physics among particles, and so forth. But the method, considered most generally, may be called "Universal Mathematics" because it deals with universal order and measurement, not restricted to a special subject matter. Analysis is in fact this universal mathematics.

Just as the ancient geometers could only claim that their theories were true if the principles from which they followed were known to be true, so from the metaphysical viewpoint the same was true of Descartes's physics. In metaphysics, the principles of physics are derived. All the other sciences are only included in human wisdom if their principles are derivable from the principles of physics, and are therefore indirectly related to metaphysics.

Descartes knew that a purely *a priori* metaphysical derivation of the principles of physics would not show that physics was applicable to this particular world. He thought that such a derivation would provide us with the laws applicable to any possible world, because any world we might discover would be composed of extended bodies governed by the laws of motion and he thought that through analysis we could discover the simple natures of these bodies, and therefore the principles explaining them. But to know that some of these laws apply to the particular bodies of this world we would have to know that these bodies exist; and, in order to know this, we have to know that our perceptions are veridical. This he tried to show by proving the existence of a God who was good and who therefore could not deceive us. But he also gave a prominent place to experimentation in this context; and, perhaps significantly, not once in his actual works in science is the divine guarantee of our perceptions mentioned. It may indeed be confined to his metaphysics rather than his physics. This does not mean that the metaphysical derivation of physics is unimportant. Indeed, in a letter to Mersenne in 1638 he claimed that the demonstration of the principles of physics is not possible without their prior metaphysical justification, and to the same man in 1641 he wrote that his six meditations "contain the entire foundations of my physics." But he also claimed that he had reduced the laws of physics to the laws of solid geometry, which he saw as the laws defining extended bodies, the subject matter of physics. Hence, Descartes seems to have thought that the metaphysical analysis of the *Meditations* justified the principles of physics dealing with extended bodies. Since these principles are the laws of solid geometry, plus the laws of motion (mechanics), he must have believed that he had discovered and successfully used the secret of the ancient geometers. If, in addition, God exists and does not deceive us, then our perceptions can be trusted and what we perceive are the three-dimensional extended objects of solid geometry. Hence, we can now perform experiments to confirm which of the laws that we have derived metaphysically do actually apply to what we perceive.

The Roles of Experimentation

Descartes did not carefully distinguish among the various roles of synthesis, and some of the resulting problems raise important logical and philosophical difficulties for us. He was equally careless in discussing the roles of experimentation. Normally it is argued that there are three basic functions which experiment serves. The first role is related to his theory of innate ideas. According to this theory, the principles or causes of anything in the real world can be discovered from "certain germs of truth which are naturally in our souls." God is the source of these germs of truth, or innate ideas or dispositions as they are more normally called. So he thought that all our knowledge is either the result of the development of innate ideas or dispositions, or an inference from them. The impetus for the formulation or development of these ideas is provided by some experience, and this is the first role of experimentation, i.e., designed experiences. This is not sufficient for knowledge, however, since all experience is of the particular, whereas laws are general. What experimentation does, then, is to provide the impetus which causes us to formulate the concepts of laws and principles already dispositionally in our minds.

Secondly, experience or experimentation is a means by which we confirm that there are objects which correspond to our concepts of ideas.

The third function of experimentation concerns the fact that there are an indefinite number of particular effects which can be derived from the general laws which we discover through analysis. In order to decide which of these effects are actually operable in this world, we design experiments. The first move in this procedure is the specification of the problem to be solved, and then we must decide how the specified effects depend upon their causes, that is, which among a number of possible explanations is the correct one. The third function is obviously related to the second, but there are also differences between them. Descartes used experiments properly speaking to confirm explanations of effects, and not just to confirm that there are effects. Experiment, in short, provides us with data for analysis on the basis of which we first formulate the problem, and then derive the general laws and principles innate in our minds. Following this, we must be able to decide which among a multitude of effects derivable from these principles actually occur, and, finally we must satisfy ourselves that our explanation of these effects is the correct one.

Descartes often said that he considered knowledge of the world without physical experimentation impossible. He performed many experiments in optics, meteorology, and anatomy; but, at the same time, he said on at least one occasion that "my physics is nothing else but geometry," which seems to contradict his claim that experimentation is necessary. In the light of this, then, a still closer examination is warranted. We will therefore proceed to an examination of his actual procedures in the doing of science itself.

Cartesian Scientific Method

In several places Descartes summarizes this procedure. The clearest comment is to be found in the eighth *Discourse on Method*. He tells us there that he first attempted to discover the first causes or general principles of everything that is or can be in this world. To do this, he makes only metaphysical assumptions, such as the existence of God.

Then, given that he has the principles, he tries to see what effects he can infer from them. Given that the principles are the laws of solid geometry and mechanics, he thinks that from them he can infer the natures of macroscopic phenomena such as the heavenly bodies, the nature of objects and elements composing the earth, and so on. He then proceeds to a more detailed consideration of smaller phenomena, studying them by attempting to ascertain their particular causes, treating the phenomena themselves as effects for this purpose. "Many particular experiments" are used at this stage in the procedure. One of the things he discovered in this process was that many different general laws can explain many different particular effects in many different ways. So he had to discover just *how* the given particular effect depended upon its particular cause. In order to discover that, experimentation of a particular sort is required, namely those of such a nature that "their result is not the same when we explain (the effect) by one hypothesis, as it is when we explain it by another." In other words, to decide which cause, principle, or law explains a particular class of effects, we must perform experiments such that they enable us to discover which among a number of possible hypotheses is the true explanation; and, to do this, we must perform critical experiments. This is what he actually does in the scientific works.

An examination of the *Discourse* alone might lead one to believe that what Descartes intended to do in the scientific works was to perform an analysis of the complex and obscure propositions which we find at the beginning of our investigations, and then, only *after* arriving at the principles or laws involved by intuition and deduction, deduce conclusions from them. This reading might then lead one to believe that, after the synthesis, experiments would be performed for the sole purpose of deciding which of the derived conclusions actually applied to this empirical world, while other experiments would provide the occasion for formulating the laws and principles in the first place. This is not the procedure he followed. He discovered, as has been pointed out, that the universal mathematics would not enable him to know *a priori* that some laws were applicable to this world; and, partly because of this, he used synthesis as a *part of* analysis. This means in effect that, because we can only arrive at an intuitive knowledge of principles through analysis and because any laws or propositions about effects deduced from these principles can only be known to be true if the principles are so known, then principles not known to be true must be treated as hypotheses and the laws deduced from them cannot be known to be true. If synthesis is used as a part of analysis, which is the method of discovery, then the principles of these syntheses must be hypotheses. From what follows it will be clear that this is the way

Descartes treated them in the actual doing of science. He posited hypothetical explanations of given effects and then decided which was the correct one by performing critical experiments designed to confirm one hypothesis as the law and disconfirm the others. This is the hypothetico-deductive method, and it is the method whereby we test our hypotheses either directly or indirectly through inductive examination. It is the method of modern science.

This was no accidental discovery. Descartes actually intended to use it. What has been said not only truly describes what he did in the *Optics* and the *Meteorology* (experimentation is not important in the geometry), but it reconciles the apparent contradiction mentioned a little while ago. When he spoke of his physics as "nothing but geometry," he was clearly speaking of pure or unapplied physics on the metaphysical level. He referred to applied mathematics as "mixed mathematics," and he recognized that the complete mathematization of physics and hence of all other sciences is impossible. The reason is that, although mathematics is used to interpret the given in experience, it does not thereby justify its own application. For this metaphysics is needed. He referred to both "abstract geometry" and to "another kind of geometry," whose purpose is to explain natural events. In the same year that he made that distinction and in a letter to the same man, Mersenne, in correspondence with whom he had made the first distinction, he notes a difference between "demonstration" as it applies in abstract geometry and "demonstration" as it describes physics, mechanics, optics, and astronomy. In these sciences no pure deduction is possible because of the empirical element involved, and it is because of this empirical element that we must treat possible explanations as hypotheses until confirmed by experiment. He says "I shall put forward all that I am going to write just as an hypothesis. Even if this be thought false, I shall think my achievement worthwhile if all the inferences from it agree with experience." (*Principles* III) In this case the hypothesis is that the universe is composed of tiny particles of the same shape which revolve around their own centers.

In the *Discourse,* writing of his theories in the appended *Optics* and *Meteorology* to which the *Discourse* is the preface, Descartes calls them hypotheses and then describes how they are to be confirmed. He notes that in the scientific works, the last conclusions are proven by the first principles, and the first principles are proven by the effects derived in accordance with them. He claims that this is not a circular argument, because experimentation gives a high degree of certainty to the derived effects and the first principles or causes of these effects "do not serve so much to prove these effects as to explain them; but, on the contrary, the hypothetical principles or causes are proven by their effects." Consider this in the light of the comments he makes about experimentation elsewhere in the *Discourse* which have been discussed above. He is telling us that, in order to discover the causes of effects, we must examine the effects and use experiments in this study. The primary role of experiment here is to ascertain which among a number of different possible ways in which the effect *could* depend upon the cause is actually the way in which it *does* depend upon it. It is still not clear, however, how these experiments are used to achieve this knowledge, nor is the structure of an experiment according to Descartes yet obvious. The best way to gain this understanding is to consider a number of examples which he actually uses. The first of these is his use of the concept of an "hypothetical world" in the *Discourse*. He resolves to:

. . . speak only of what would happen in a new world, if God were now to create somewhere, in imaginary space, enough matter to compose it, and if he agitated the parts of this matter diversely and without order, so that he made of it a chaos as confused as the poets can imagine, and that afterwards he did nothing else except lend his support to nature, and left it to act according to the laws which he established.[4]

In short, he is offering the hypothesis of a model world. Having verified that given these assumptions, he can explain any event in this model world, he proceeds to show that the effects discovered in the actual world are the same as those which would occur in the model and that the same causes will explain them.

This procedure of using a model in the design of experiments used for the purpose of explaining something other than the model is one of the most common modern scientific techniques, although it is not new. In the fourth section of the *Meteorology* Descartes is explaining the nature of winds. Noting that the winds of the earth are usually caused by the expansion of gases, he notes in addition that there is an invention which will help us to understand this principle. It is a hollow copper ball called an Aeolipile, and since it illustrates the causes of winds well, he proceeds to explain it. In effect, he is proceeding here as he did in the case of the hypothetical world: given a model, the copper ball, which works according to the same causes as the winds on earth do but is subject to fewer variables, he explains the principle by using the model and then verifies his findings (the effects) by using this same explanation to account for appropriate phenomena in the actual world.

This same method is used in his discussion of the body of man. He speaks of the body of a man "entirely similar to ours," except that instead of a rational soul, it has "one of those fires without heat" ignited

[4] *Ibid.*, p. 67.

within it. Given this hypothesis, he thinks that he can explain all the bodily motions in the model as effects of this "fire." As part of the attempt he performs an experiment with the heart of a large animal, because "it it in everything sufficiently similar to the heart of a man," the purpose of the experiment being to confirm his hypothesis about how the blood is sent by the heart to the rest of the body. Having done these things, he compares the human body to a "machine which, having been made by the hands of God, is incomparably better designed and has in itself more admirable movements than any of those (bodies) which can be invented by man." Having completed his explanation of the movements of the heart and its arteries, he states his belief that, given the correct principles and the disposition of the parts of the body in specifiable ways, we can completely explain the motions which follow, just as we can safely predict the motion of the hands of a clock given a knowledge of the "force, situation and the shape of its counterweights and wheels."

Examples of Cartesian Method

Descartes's procedures bear a remarkable similarity to those of the modern era. Analogies can be clearly seen in such cases as Einstein's prediction that light waves would be seen to bend because of the gravitational attraction of the sun, and the discovery of the planet Neptune by Galle and Leverrier in 1846. The similarities with the latter case are especially intriguing. Given the truth of Kepler's laws and the soundness of Bouvard's calculations of the motions of the planets, these men concluded that there was only one explanation for the variance in the orbit of Uranus, which was that there must be another planetary body at a location X in the heavens. An experiment was performed, Neptune discovered, and the hypothesis confirmed. In Descartes's case, if we assume that a given motion or motions follow upon a given configuration of parts, then there is only one explanation of how the supply of blood remains constant throughout the body, and that is his theory of the circulation of the blood, which was similar to Harvey's. Further, if this theory is true, then there must be some connection between the veins and the arteries. It is possible to design such experiments; and, upon performing them, we indeed verify this connection. Hence, the hypothesis of the circulation of the blood is sound, which in turn verifies the hypotheses about the relation between motions and the configuration of the parts of a body. Both hypotheses are therefore sound.

This explanation of the Cartesian method corresponds to his own descriptions of it. His third rule in the *Rules for the Direction of the Mind* notes that for explanatory purposes he has often assumed an order "among those (objects) which do not naturally precede one another." Here he is positing an hypothesis about an assumed but unknown order of causal dependency in those instances where such a dependency is not readily apparent. To discover whether the hypothesis is justified we must test it experimentally. For this purpose, it is often fruitful to use metaphor and analogy, and an example of such a metaphor occurs in the twelfth of the *Rules* where he is explaining the nature of sense perception. This is the famous comparison of the way wax receives an impression from a seal vis à vis the ways in which the senses receive their impressions. He there argues that he means to assert more than a mere analogy, and, indeed, that the relation asserted in the two resembling instances *is the same*. It is clear that he means the same principle is operative in the two cases.

Another example of the positing of an hypothetical causal order is to be found in his explanation of magnets, also in the twelfth rule of the *Rules for the Direction of the Mind*. Seeking to answer the question "What is the nature of the magnet?" we should proceed in this way:

1. We should gather together all the observations of magnets which we can get.
2. We should "try to deduce the character of that intermixture of simple natures which is necessary to produce all those effects" which we have noticed as typical of the behavior of magnets; that is, from the observations, we must formulate hypotheses expressing the principles of magnetic phenomena.
3. We attempt to explain the behavior of particular magnets using these principles, in an experimental context.

If we succeed, the hypotheses are confirmed. To formulate the hypotheses, we must discover the relations among the components and elements of a thing which will explain its effects, and to do this we must know the order of causal dependency among those elements. How we go about making this discovery, or, more accurately, what it is that we should watch for in trying to make it, is discussed in the sixth of the *Rules*:

. . . we ought, in the case of every series in which we have deduced certain facts the one from the other, to notice which fact is simple, and to mark the interval, greater, less, or equal, which separates all the others from this.

The simplest element of an object or event which is the one not dependent upon the others and upon which all the others depend, is called the "absolute." This word refers to "whatever is considered as being independent, or a cause, or simple, universal, one, equal, like, straight, and so forth." On the other hand, whatever is "dependent, or an effect, composite, particular, many, unequal, unlike, oblique, etc." is said to be "relative." The first or least dependent in a causal series will therefore be the absolute to that series, and all else will be relative to some degree, the degree depending upon its position in the series.

Near the beginning of his *Optics* Descartes informs us that two or three "comparisons" will be used to help explain the nature of light. They will be used in a certain way, namely that which seems to Descartes "the most convenient to explain all those of its properties that experience acquaints us with, and in order to deduce afterwards all the others which cannot be so easily observed." This procedure, thinks Descartes, is similar to that of the ancient astronomers, who made many assumptions or hypotheses, some of them false, but nonetheless, because these hypotheses referred to *observations*, they led to "very true and well assured conclusions." In the same spirit, he proposes an hypothesis about the nature of light:

> . . . a certain movement or action, very rapid and very lively, which passes towards our eyes through the medium of the air and other transparent bodies, in the same manner that the movement or resistance of the bodies that (a) blind man encounters is transmitted to his hand through the medium of his stick.[5]

With this hypothesis, he proceeds to explain what happens when we see. He uses other hypotheses in the effort, one of which is the assumption that rays of light are refracted and reflected much as is a ball striking surfaces of various consistencies at different angles. He then tests these hypotheses empirically and is satisfied that the results confirm them. The most important experiment in the *Optics* involves the use of the eye of an ox, by which he confirms his explanation of the causes of the image on the retina of the eye of the animal. Having completed this experiment, he argues that, given the similarities between the ox eye and the eye of a man, the explanation is the same in the latter case.

Descartes knew that hypotheses based upon analogies or models, such as that involved in the experiment with the ox eye, must be based upon *closely* resembling pairs. At the same time, he knew the importance of relevant dissimilarities. As with the comparison between the cane through which the blind man "sees" and the nature of the medium through which light is transmitted to our eyes, he introduces yet another comparison to clarify the manner of transmission in the light of the dissimilarities in the first comparison. He asks us to consider a vat full of grapes and wine such that there are holes in the bottom of the vat. Descartes accepted the contemporary maxim that nature abhors a vacuum, and he also thought that all substances were porous. It follows that all these pores or openings had to be filled with something and that,

[5] *Ibid.,* p. 67.

in the case of a transparent body such as the fluid through which light passes, it had to be a very "subtle and fluid material." Considering the wine as the subtle fluid and the grapes as the solid bodies between the pores, we can see how light tends in straight lines, namely, in the same way that the wine tends in a straight line toward the holes at the bottom, even though it might not always succeed in getting there via the shortest route. He is, again, *assuming* that light moves in this manner, and on the basis of this assumption he then tries to explain refraction and reflection.

Not only did Descartes use the explanatory power of hypotheses as a criteria for evaluating them, but he also used difficulties discovered by the pioneers in his fields as guides in formulating his own theories. For example, when he is discussing the structure of the nerves, he divides them into three parts: the membranes which enclose them, their interior substance, and finally "the animal spirits, which are like a very subtle wind or air which, coming from the chambers or concavities in the brain, flow away by these same tubes throughout the muscles." He notes that the anatomists of his time made these three distinctions but failed to distinguish their uses accurately, for they thought there were two kinds of nerves, one sort used for sensation and the other for motion. This led to several difficulties for them; and, to avoid these, Descartes argues that motion must be explicable according to the same principles as sensation.

His explanation of movements and the nervous structure of the body is not correct, but that is not the point here; rather we are interested in the method he uses. Here he rejects an hypothesis on the grounds that it fails to account for the fact that the same set of nerves are clearly used for both sensing and moving, something he thought he had discovered through observation. He therefore substitutes another hypothesis on the grounds that it does agree with what is observed. In all these cases the power of the hypothesis to explain the observable phenomenon is taken as confirmation of it.

Methodology and Evaluation

At the start of the *Meteorology* he claims that he will follow the same procedure that he used in the *Optics,* which entails that "I must make use of certain hypotheses at the outset, as I did in the *Optics.*" In the *Meteorology* these include the assumptions that all bodies are made of small variously shaped particles which have small spaces between them no matter how accurately they are put together. The spaces are filled with a "fine material" which moves at great speeds varying under different conditions. When these hypotheses are added to those already discovered in the *Optics* which there concerned the nature of light, we can explain the sensations of heat and cold and most meteorological phenomena. His explanation of heat and cold, or the sensation of them, consists in showing that when we sense heat, the frequency of the vibrations of the small particles of a body is very high, causing a corresponding high vibration in our nerve fibers, whereas on the contrary, both frequencies are very low when we experience cold. A simple experiment which he takes to verify this consists in blowing against your clasped hands. If you blow just over the clasped fingers, "swiftly and with even force," causing "hardly any agitation," you will sense cold, but in the smaller spaces between your fingers where your breath passes "more evenly and slowly, it will agitate their small particles more, and you will have a sensation of greater warmth."

As a final confirmation of his meteorological theories, he describes a series of observations he made from February 4 to February 7, 1635. He observed the shapes and sizes of snow and ice crystals, the types of clouds from which they came, and the wind and temperature conditions which caused them. He had previously explained what the necessary conditions would be for the formation of such crystals, and on the basis of his observations, he claims that "I confirmed my belief in all that I had imagined concerning this matter." He pursues exactly the same course later in the *Meteorology*, when he attempts to explain the causes of the rainbow. First, noting that the arc of the rainbow appears not only in the sky but also in drops of water of uniform shape which are illuminated by the sun, he resolves to make a "large drop" in order to examine the arc better. For this purpose he fills a round and transparent flask with water and studies the arc formed therein when the flask is illuminated. After describing his observations of the arc in the flask and then in a prism, he offers an explanation of his findings and then applies this explanation to the rainbow seen in the heavens. Later, using the comparison between rolling, rotating balls and the movement of light which he had used earlier in the *Optics* to explain the action of different light rays in the rainbow, he claims that this explanation "enabled me to solve the most important of all the difficulties that I had in this matter." The most important difficulty here was the explanation of the relations between the colors of the rainbow. He explains them by the speed of the rotation of the particles "of the fine substance which transmits the action of the light." He concludes:

And in all of this, the explanation accords so perfectly with experience, that I do not believe possible, after having carefully studied both, to doubt that the matter is such as I have just explained.

The purpose of the model or "comparison" is especially clear in this experiment. The rainbow in the sky is a much more complex phenomenon than the glass flask, but the *relevant* factors in both are the same in the experiment, namely, the relations between the colors. The model thus offers a simplified situation in which the factors causing the rainbow can be studied apart from complicating and irrelevant events which are always present in the natural occurrence of the rainbow. Once we have discovered the cause and effect relationships in the similar cases, we can extrapolate from them and apply our findings in the natural world.

Descartes explicitly claims that there are only two ways to disprove what he says. The first is to prove by experimentation that what he has assumed is false, and the second is, given the soundness of his hypotheses, to show that what he deduces from them cannot in fact be so deduced. That is, we would either have to demonstrate experimentally that the effects did not depend upon the causes in the way which seemed to be indicated by Descartes's experiments or show that the causes were not the ones he assumed, or we would have to show that, although he had posited the correct hypotheses, he had made some mistake or mistakes in his deductions from them. This is very similar to the way in which theories are disconfirmed in modern science.

Finally, there are the criteria of simplicity and elegance which are used today, and which were used by Descartes, in evaluating an explanation in science. Descartes gives a statement of these criteria which could be used today by our scientists: ". . . it seems to me that my explanations ought to be approved all the more because I shall make them depend on fewer things." This was not a particularly novel approach even in Descartes's time, for Ockham had enunciated the principle before him; but it is nonetheless a clear way of stating it. It implies that, of two explanations for the same phenomenon, the one with the fewer premises, the fewer dependencies, ought to be accepted. It is not always the case that this will be the correct explanation, of course, and that is why the criteria of consistency, compatibility with observation, susceptibility to confirming or disconfirming critical experimentation, fruitfulness, etc., all have to be met as well.

A Modern Comment on Descartes

It was mentioned at the beginning of this chapter that Professor Leon Roth's book, *Descartes's Discourse on Method*, would be taken as an exemplification of the traditional view of the Cartesian method; and a different view in opposition to this normal understanding of what Descartes did has been given. But there are other, modern writings, which are more in the trend which the discussion here exemplifies. At least two of these should be mentioned, and the salient points of difference between what has been presented here and what is claimed in these works should be noted. The first more modern comment is that of Professor Alan Gewirth.[6] This is an excellent article, aware of the subtleties of Descartes's procedures but nonetheless often misleading in its treatment of the place of synthesis and experiment in the method. This is not to say that the treatment is wholly mistaken, for it is not. For example, Gewirth understands, as most other commentators have not, that the analytic method uses both analysis (as the method of "breaking down" or "reducing" complex propositions and phenomena into their simplest parts or natures) *and* deduction. But it does not seem that Gewirth clearly sees the significance of this discovery. That the discussion here is at least more complete becomes important when we consider the emphasis that Gewirth places upon the "guiding" and "controlling" roles of experimentation, which are effects of the use of experiments in setting up the problem to be explained and analyzed. Good examples of these roles of experimentation and the place experiment has in determining the relations between its parts have been considered here, as in the case of the magnet and Descartes's explanation of the nature of light in the *Optics* prior to his attempts in the same work to explain how it is that we see. Here, Descartes is outlining the problem to be examined, and in Gewirth's words, ". . . determining the deduction's direction and testing its truth." But this does not place the emphasis where it *should* be, which is on the point that deduction and experiment are also *both* parts of analysis or the process of discovery.

What we have examined here includes a much more thorough examination of the experimental techniques used in the *Optics* and the *Meteorology* than is to be found almost anywhere else. This provides us with more than the mere advantage of a wider data base. One claim which has been repeated here is that both synthesis and experimentation are involved in analysis, and a second one is that there are more roles for experimentation in Descartes's philosophy than either that of determining which of two or more plausible explanations is the one that actually does apply in this world or of verifying the existence of the objects to be explained. Both of these conclusions depend to a large extent for their support upon an examination of what he actually does with the various experiments which he performs, and the best *loci* for these experiments are the *Optics* and the *Meteorology*. They are, after all, the two major works of Cartesian science. Gewirth argues that "experience," (and, hence, given his use of the work, experiment), is ruled out by Descartes as an "aid in the accomplishment of the reduction" from "complex and obscure" to the "simple and absolute." But surely any proposition about vision or about meteorological phenomena prior to the analysis Descartes applies to them meets his definition of

---

[6] Alan Gewirth, "The Role of Experience in the Cartesian Method," *The Journal of the History of Ideas*, 11, no. 2 (April, 1941), *passim*.

a complex and obscure proposition. And, just as surely, if the examination here is accurate, he uses both experimentation and synthesis as parts of the process of analysis by which he reduces the explanations of these propositions to the simple natures or universal laws by which we can explain them. If this is true, then Gewirth is wrong in his interpretation.

Gewirth admits that he does not concentrate upon Descartes's actual scientific procedures, but upon the "official rules" of the method as given in the *Rules for the Direction of the Mind* and the second part of the *Discourse*. The emphasis in these works is on *knowing* the simple natures intuited at the end of the reductive process, and it is clearly true that *certain* knowledge, being the result of an operation of the mind or understanding for Descartes, plus the properties of clarity and distinctness possessed by propositions expressing simple natures, is not a function of sense and therefore not a function of either experiment or experience. Yet this does not rule out either of these as central factors in the process by which we arrive at the simple natures and simple propositions expressing them. And science itself is not concerned so much with the moment of knowing, as it were, as it is with the practical procedures of discovery and explanation, which are in the original concerned with the world of sensibility. *That* part of the Cartesian method ought surely to be studied by what he *did* in science, and an examination of what he did discloses that part of the process of discovery, that is, analysis or reduction is the discarding of competing hypotheses made on the basis of critical experiments. This is not adequately described by characterizing the role of experiments as one of "guiding or controlling" subsequent deductions, nor as one of merely setting up the problem to be analyzed. Experimentation is a necessary though not sufficient part of analysis because it is essential for drawing the distinctions Descartes demands between what is absolute and what is relative, etc., and this is required *before* we can attain a knowledge of the principles which explain the events in question.

Further, Professor Gewirth does not pay adequate attention to the Cartesian use of models, though he does make some brief reference to "comparisons." Yet models play a central role in modern science and in the works of Descartes, and the understanding of the experiments in the works we have examined is not possible unless we see this. The use of the Aeolipile ball to characterize the origin of winds and the flasks filled with water which Descartes uses to model the rainbow in the *Meteorology* are every bit as much models as is the model of the molecular structure of some atom which we use in the chemistry lab.

Finally, in connection with Professor Gewirth's analysis, it should be mentioned that he does not discuss at all the view that for Descartes the empirical discovery and confirmation of principles which could also be reached by metaphysical derivation would serve as confirmation for the findings of both disciplines. Certainly, a complete study of this issue is necessary, and it cannot be undertaken here. But the point does bear upon the different types of "necessity" of which Descartes often speaks. He mentions logical or deductive necessity, causal necessity, and metaphysical necessity, the latter of which seems to be identical with neither of the other two types. Descartes is often accused of confusing logical and causal necessity and of importing the former into the world of the latter. But this may not be justified as an accusation, and the relationship between science and metaphysics is, it would seem, the point of departure for any serious discussion of these problems.

Another Modern Study

Professor L. J. Beck's book, *The Method of Descartes*, is a fine example of distinguished scholarship, but there are two points concerning the nature of the Cartesian scientific method which should be examined critically, even if only briefly. These are, again, the place of synthesis in the method of analysis or discovery and the place of experiment in the overall method. It should be noted first that insofar as these issues are related to the ultimate question of the relation between the principles of physics and metaphysics and the meaning of "knowledge" for Descartes, a detailed study of metaphysics would be involved. Beck says that he cannot do this in a book about methodology, and we obviously cannot undertake it now. But at least this point should be kept in mind: there is a traditional difference in philosophy between knowledge and true belief; and, for Descartes, Beck believes that the latter is the best we can achieve in physics or applied philosophy. Yet it is clear that in some cases at least, Descartes thinks the principles of physics can be derived metaphysically.

Beck calls the sort of Cartesian analysis which we have been studying a moving "from the unknown to the known on the hypothesis that the unknown is the known." Since many examples of this procedure (the process of offering hypotheses and then testing them), have already been given, let us consider some of Beck's remarks which clearly point to differences and then try to support the interpretation presented here. One argument depends upon a confusion between "synthesis" and "deduction." Deduction is an operation of the mind for Descartes, whereas synthesis is a process involving, in addition to deduction, intuition and "enumeration." Synthesis is also sometimes understood to refer to the process of demonstrating what is already known by exhibiting it in the form of a logical deduction. Yet Beck says such things as "analysis is sometimes described as a special form of deduction," ". . . analysis does not always take the form of a deduction . . ." and "synthesis, which is in essence a deductive reconstruction . . ." all of which are misleading without further clarification. For example, what are we to understand by "The analytic method . . . needs synthesis, once the resolution of the problem has been completed . . ." without knowing whether he is speaking of the process, the mental operation, or the exhibition? And by exhibition does he means the synthetic approach, as decribed above, or the intellectual operation, when he claims that Descartes held a method ". . . which laid all the emphasis on the deductive approach and set as its ideal mathematical demonstration from self-evident principles"? For given one of the meanings of either deduction or synthesis, these remarks are either uninformative or false. The interesting place of synthesis, the process, is as a part of analysis, and in this role synthesis does not come in only after the problem has been resolved but much before that. It is, in fact, impossible to resolve the problem at all unless we first enumerate and then serially deduce the laws and principles which explain the causal relationships, which in turn explain the events under investigation. Unless we enumerate and assume various hypothetical causal orders, and then deduce in conjunction with experimentation, how could we ever decide between two explanations on the grounds that the "result is not the same, when we explain it by one hypothesis, as it is when we explain it by another"? That this enumeration occurs either prior to analysis or as part of its first moves is demonstrated again by the fact that it would be impossible to "assume . . . an order among those objects which do not naturally precede one another" for purposes of discovering the correct explanation if enumeration was not part of the "resolutions" of the problem, for then we would not know the number of the objects to be ordered.

This whole issue is raised again when Professor Beck is discussing acts of "mixed" knowing, that is, ". . . not a pure act of the *vis cognoscens* but an act, partially at least, dependent on the mind as linked to the body and its organs." He notes that such "mixed knowledge" is an essential prerequisite of "all reasoning" and then qualifies this to read "all deductive reasoning." He truly notes that this fact about the Cartesian method implies a "striking qualification of doctrine" and that the sixth part of the *Discourse* assumes it to be understood. Further, he mentions that many commentators have not noticed this important change in procedures. Once again, however, Beck is misleading and seems not to have fully appreciated the import of his discovery. For what it amounts to is evidence to support the thesis given here that "mixed knowing," in any problem about physics, is the necessary starting point for *analysis;* and, insofar as experience or experiment (the latter being a designed experience) are involved in the resolution of the data known and their relevance to the total problem, then experiment is also a part of analysis. Moreover, the quotation is also misleading in its reference to "deductive reasoning." Not all analysis is deductive in form, and, even when it is, the hypotheses posited as tentative explanation for the events in question are not known (intuited) in the strict sense to be true and hence do not cease to be hypotheses until the final intuitive steps of the analytic process—that is, until they are seen to be ultimately identical with principles derived metaphysically. It is the latter step which seems to be the coping stone of the Cartesian method seen as a whole. Without it, all our true knowledge remains theoretical and all our practical knowledge remains hypothetical. But in order to reach that final step in which derived metaphysical principles and physical principles discovered analytically are identified through intuition, we must, if we are dealing with a problem in physics, begin with "mixed knowledge" of the empirical world. We must use experiments to choose between alternative hypotheses and to resolve the problem, and we must use synthesis as part of the method of discovering the true explanatory principles. Only under this interpretation does it seem possible to support Descartes's own claim that his theory and his practice are consistent and that the latter is in fact an illustration of the former in action.

The Question of Experimentation

This brings us more particularly to the question of experimentation. Beck gives a famous quotation from Descartes about Galileo in a letter to Mersenne in 1638, the gist of which is that Descartes accuses Galileo of "merely look(ing) for the causes of certain particular facts" without having examined the "order" of the points in the problem. The problem is the law of falling bodies. Beck uses this quotation as support for the traditional claim that, since the *existence* of extended moving bodies can only be "deduced" as *possible*, "to say that extension and its modes exist requires a justification over and beyond the analytical deduction itself. In other words, the physical sciences need a metaphysical justification in order, so to speak, to set themselves up in complete independence." But this seems to place the cart before the horse and to misjudge the place of experiment and the point of the quotation. It seems to make Descartes's metaphysics *ad hoc*. However, the *Meditations* is prior both chronologically and logically to the *Discourse* and its essays. Metaphysics is the ground for trusting experimentation and experience, and experimentation is in its turn part of the analysis by which we discover the metaphysical-physical principles at the foundation of all particular events. We do not do the experiments and *then* provide the metaphysical justification for them. The point of Descartes's criticisms against Galileo is not that experimentation is not worthy of serious consideration but rather that it should always be conducted with a view to discovering the explanation of the particular *class* of events and not just some particular event; that we should then relate the explanation of the particular class to the general *principles* explaining *all* natural phenomena; and that experimentation should be conducted in conjunction with a careful study and use of the principles of causal and logical dependency—admonitions which no serious scientist can ignore.

Both Beck and Gewirth emphasize that role of experimentation which consists in setting out the problem for analysis at the expense of one of its other equally important functions, namely, *confirming* explanations which are discovered for the subject of investigation. Beck says:

It is through the classification of data derived from sense-perception that the problem is 'set out' in such a manner that the particular field of knowledge to be covered can be summed up in a few contrasting alternatives. In a sense, then, experience may be said to set the deductive process going.

And:

In the physical sciences, then, we are dependent on sense experience for the 'determination' of the problem and the possibility of making our initial hypothesis.[7]

This is true. But it is by no means the end of the matter; nor, for purposes of analysis, is it the most important function of experience and experimentation. The sixth part of the *Discourse* makes this quite clear: we must discover which of the various ways that an effect *can* depend upon a cause is the way that it does, *in fact*, depend upon it—that is, we must choose among different hypotheses. That choice obviously cannot be made until after the hypotheses have been formulated and the process of their formulation involves first role of experience. But, then, how do we now choose among them? Descartes says:

. . . to do that I know no other expedient than *again* to search for certain experiments, which are such that their result is not the same, when we explain it by one hypothesis, as it is when we explain it by another.[8]

That is, we need experiments which are *different* than the ones used to set up the problem in the form of alternative hypotheses, which will enable us to choose between them, i.e., confirm one and disconfirm the other. Given that this experimental procedure is part of the method of

[7] L. J. Beck, *The Method of Descartes* (Oxford: The Clarendon Press, 1952).
[8] Descartes, *op. cit.*, p. 52.

discovering the principles at the foundation of the events to be explained, it is a part of analysis. And given that, in order to test the connections between the hypotheses and the particular events, we must discover that the laws governing the subsidiary events are deducible from the principles, then deduction is a part of this analysis. This is seldom clearly stated by either Beck or Gewirth. Beck notes that the laws derived from experiments in the Cartesian method are "merely hypotheses," which cannot constitute ". . . real knowledge, that is, the knowledge by which we apprehend the fundamental principles of scientific explanation, the premises of scientific deduction." He concludes:

His method, on the basis of his own claims, is essentially a method of 'discovery' of the simple and easy principles. The synthetic exposition follows upon the actual discovery of these principles. Deduction is both analytic and synthetic. The 'gap' is recognized by Descartes and is bridged by a view . . . which takes the discussion beyond the level of methodology to that of metaphysics.[9]

Yet shortly after making this true summary, he goes on to claim that Descartes was much more interested in the explanation itself than in facts and experiments; and as evidence he notes Descartes's remark that Harvey's theory might be confirmed by an experiment performed on a dog's heart, but that ". . . this only goes to show that experiments themselves can often furnish the occasion for our being deceived, when we do not sufficiently examine all the causes which they may have." He then notes Descartes's claim that we can only decide the issue between Harvey and him on the basis of "other experiments which cannot agree both with the one and the other." It seems quite clear that here we are not to choose between experiments on the basis of explanations but rather just the opposite, which certainly indicates the importance Descartes attached to experimentation as a part of the analytic method.

In summary, then, the aim of analysis is to discover the principles which will explain the causes of an event, and to do this we must discover the causal order of the elements involved. After this discovery we exhibit the discovered order in deductive form through synthesis, and then we use experiments in order to decide which of the possible explanations actually applies to the events in this world. All this is known and surely true of Descartes's theory. But with the investigation given herein, it becomes clear that, in addition, Descartes uses hypotheses in the process of discovering the causal order, and that he uses experimentation as a part of the method of *discovery*. Experiment is therefore not confined in his system to setting up the problem, to providing the occasion for formulating innate ideas in propositional form, or to choosing between various explanations *after* we have discovered the relevant

[9] Beck, *op. cit.*, pp. 248–49.

principles; it plays a central role in the discovery of the principles themselves. Moreover, insofar as deductively arranged explanations used as hypotheses are also a part of the effort to discover principles, formal deduction too must be used as a part of analysis, since that is what he calls his method of discovery. Thus, even though synthesis is also used to present the explanation formally after it is known, this is not its only nor its most important role. These findings describe what Descartes actually does, and the examples which have been given are representative of his procedure in every effort he made in the scientific field. The descriptions of his procedures do not appear to differ at all from the typical methods used by empiricists. Thus, it seems that there is no difference between Descartes and the Rationalist method and, for example, the method followed by Newton, Harvey, Boyle, and Priestly. Descartes is a Rationalist not because of his scientific procedure but because of his metaphysics and the relations he believes to be necessary between the principles of physics and metaphysics. In this area, he proceeds by purely *a priori* reasoning, and experiment plays no important role. But when it comes to the attempt to show the relevance of the scientific principles derived from his metaphysics to the world in which we live, Descartes is no more of a Rationalist than is Newton.

ANCIENT TELEOLOGY AND THE PHYSICAL WORLD

No conflict between two different kinds of explanation in science is of greater antiquity, nor still as rigorous, as is that between teleological and non-teleological explanations. The current discussions concern those sciences which deal with living organisms such as biology, and sciences such as physics and mechanics. In older days, before the distinction between living and inanimate matter was as precisely drawn as it is now, teleological explanations were thought to be good for physics itself, even though the distinction between explanation in terms of intention and purpose, as opposed to purely causal explanations, is at least as old as Socrates.

The issues involved, and the attempts at solving them, can become extraordinarily complex. Therefore it would seem appropriate to "ease into it," as it were, and discuss the simpler problems before tackling the more difficult ones. We will therefore discuss first the teleological Aristotelian explanation which was given to motion and falling bodies, with special attention to inertial motion, and we will see how and why this kind of explanation fell as a result of attacks emanating from the new science, particularly from the findings of Galileo, Kepler, Descartes, and Newton. Why the newer theories are better than the older will be explained.

After this opening discussion we will continue our investigation, this time concentrating upon an argument of some complexity tendered by Professor Ernest Nagel in an article "Teleological Explanation and Teleological Systems." This article concerns the still current dispute over whether biology requires distinctively teleological explanations as opposed to physics and chemistry.[10] At the end of that section a summation of our findings will be given.

Aristotle's Four Causes

Aristotle was an intellect of prodigious dimensions. He was the founder of several sciences, a logician whose codifications and discoveries ruled the subject until the late nineteenth century, a metaphysician whose writings and arguments are still being defended and criticized, an ethicist and aesthetician of almost unequaled talent, and a physicist whose arguments and theories virtually controlled man's view of his world and its place in the universe for almost a thousand years. He died about 348 B.C., in an age when the technical side of science was virtually non-existent; yet his influence is still being felt today. If anyone ever required evidence for the claim that philosophy has practical application or for the truism that the pen is mightier than the sword, this man and his teacher for more than twenty years, Plato, should certainly satisfy him. The hold he had over the minds of other thinkers for many centuries is illustrated by the fact that in the Middle Ages nobody thought it necessary to name him in order to be understood by others when speaking about his work. He was called simply, The Philosopher.

Like all Greeks at the time, Aristotle was interested in the nature of physical change. Given that there is evidently order of sequence in the world, what is the explanation of that order? With Aristotle a completely systematic explanation was for the first time forthcoming. His explanation rested upon a four-fold cornerstone which we shall call the "four-causes" schema. The four causes which he thought operative in any change were the efficient, formal, material, and the final causes. The four-cause schema arose from Aristotle's analysis of why a thing is what it is. He intended the explanation to be good for anything whatsoever. Take, for example, a house. We may begin by asking what it is that the house is made from, what are its materials. The answer gives you the *material* cause. Now we can ask for the explanation of the form or shape of the house, that is, its plan, and this gives us the *formal* cause of the house. The structure or form of the

---

[10] For good background material for this discussion see Herbert Butterfield, *The Origins of Modern Science* (London: G. Bell & Sons, Ltd., 1957).

house is its *essence*, that by virtue of which the thing is what it is. This notion will become much more important in a little while, for the form or essence of a thing is that by virtue of which the thing belongs to a class of entities, a type of being. Third, we can ask for the immediate cause of the house, the agent or force which makes it, brings it into being, and that is the carpenter of course. He is called the *efficient* cause of the house. But carpenters, like all other human agents, act for reasons; so let us say that in this case the carpenter's reason for building the house was to shelter himself and his family. This is the *final* cause of the house. As we shall see, acting "purposively" is not restricted to humans for Aristotle.

At this point, we should consider a definition of what a teleological explanation is in Aristotelian terms: such explanations always involve the positing of an efficient cause that always acts for the same final cause. In a sense then, things change for Aristotle because they want to, strange though that may sound in the case of inanimate objects such as planets, falling objects, and so forth. Naturally, the force of the words "want," "desire," and so on are not the same when applied to men as to other beings; for those other beings do not have rational wants and desires, and rationality is what distinguishes men from all other species. Take a traditional example, the acorn, and Aristotle's analysis of how and why it becomes an oak tree. In his eyes the acorn has within itself the energy for its own change into the tree. It is by virtue of the "nature" of the acorn that it grows into an oak, and not something else. The nature of something is analyzed in terms of the typical or characteristic changes manifested by the thing. Now this entails that the formal cause of a thing be contained in it if we are not talking about artificial or man-made products. In the latter cases—for example the case of the house—the formal cause, the blueprint for the house, and the efficient cause, the energy of the carpenter, originate outside of the house. The essence or the nature of houses does not include carpenters and blueprints. But in the case of something like an acorn, which does not require any outside stimulus nor any imposed organization, the fact that acorns always become oaks and not something else is explained by placing the formal cause within the nature of the acorn as well as by making the acorn its own efficient cause. Acorns, of course, are not conscious beings; but they do have a tendency to "behave" in certain ways, and they are in a sense, according to Aristotle, willing beings. What the acorn "seeks" is becoming an oak tree, which is the final cause of the acorn. So the acorn contains within its own nature all the principles or causes of its change into an oak tree. It contains the potential for becoming organized into an oak tree, the willing, tendency, or aim for the goal of becoming an oak, and the energy necessary to make the change. It even contains, potentially, all the wood of the future oak tree; for, after all, the wood does not come from someplace outside the oak tree, or so Aristotle thought.

To us, such an analysis seems just silly when it is used to explain how natural objects which are not animate behave, but it is not difficult to understand how such a view could attract intelligent men. The universe is an ordered place, and to the Greek mind especially, order implied an ordering intelligence. Intelligence acts for ends, that is the property which distinguishes between intelligent action and random or unintelligent behavior. So to explain order, we require both intelligence and the end for which the intelligence acts. In addition, we require a description of the *mode* in which the intelligence acts (the plan or formal cause) and the materials with which it works. Aristotle was primarily interested, as a natural philosopher or scientist, in the subjects of biology and zoology, especially in the classification of animals according to genus and species. You will recall that there is a kind of definition called *per genus et differentiam*, which is one of the inventions of Aristotle. It proceeds by discovering those properties which make a thing a member of a class and then those properties which make the thing unique. Among the properties which biological entities have for Aristotle is a principle of change within themselves. This is most obvious, of course, in the case of ourselves. We offer explanations of our behavior in terms of what we want to achieve, want to do, that which we have not yet in fact accomplished. These are our *purposes,* and purposive explanation is teleological explanation. Aristotle sees *all* of nature in this sense and widens the notion of final causation to include willings and tendencies in addition to conscious intentions. In effect, he holds a panpsychist view of the universe; that is, he sees everything as having a soul, or at least a principle of change acting for a final cause within it.

Different things have different natures, that is, they act for different ends and in different ways. When we know the nature of something, we have the explanation of why it acts the way it does: it acts the way it does because it is the sort of thing it is. The Aristotelian form of scientific explanation is therefore one of classification. If one discovers a thing and wishes to know why it behaves the way it does, then one *identifies* it as belonging to a class of things with a known nature, i.e., things that behave in the way this thing does. This particular hairless biped which is risible, can speak, and so forth does these things because he is a member of the species *homo sapiens,* and the essence of the members of that species is that they are rational, risible, and so forth. Once the entity is identified as a member of the class whose nature is known, the job of explanation is finished. This is not, of course, always as simple as it sounds, and the circularity is not always as evident as it is in the case of "This entity acts the way it does because it is a man, and all men act that way."

The Aristotelian Theory of Motion

The essentially anthropomorphic view which Aristotle takes of the physical universe leads him to explain even the behavior of things like stones and rocks in terms of purposes. Rocks, indeed all heavy objects, have a natural tendency to fall toward the center of the earth. In the Aristotelian view, places are qualities of bodies, and when a body changes its place, that is, its location, it changes a quality of itself. Bodies such as falling bodies, therefore, will to change their place or location. If a body changes in this way, and changes itself, then that is natural motion. So unimpeded falling bodies are the exemplar of natural motion. All other kinds of motion, which means all motion other than that of unimpeded falling, is violent or unnatural motion, because when left alone, bodies only move toward the center of the earth. In short, for any but falling motion, there must be a force outside the falling body, not a part of its nature, which accounts for the unnatural motion.

This theory of unnatural or impelled motion was to prove the downfall of Aristotelian physics. The first thing it necessitated was the addition of the theoretical requirement that if a body was moving in any direction but toward the center of the earth, there must be another body constantly in contact with it which was moving it. One conclusion was that as soon as this second moving body ceased to push the first body, it would immediately stop moving, and fall straight down. Furthermore, it was thought that so long as the medium through which the bodies were moving remained unaltered (we would say of the same density and so forth), then even if the force exerted upon the body was constant there would be no acceleration, that is, the moved body would retain the same velocity throughout the period of its movement. But if the medium did vary, then the speed would increase or decrease, becoming less as the density of the medium increased, and more as it decreased. Theoretically then, if the body was moving in a vacuum, the velocity would be infinite, and this is one reason why the Aristotelian physicists thought the existence of a vacuum was impossible.

Though the theory seemed to account for the ordinary facts of unaided observation, there were certain events which it did *not* explain. Among these were the facts that the planets do not fall toward the center of the earth, nor anywhere else, that falling bodies accelerate, and that projectiles, for example an arrow shot from a bow, or a thrown stone, continue in flight though nothing seems to be in contact with them and imparting motion to them. The first fact was explained by claiming that the planets' natures were such that they willed to travel in circular paths (Kepler was not to come along for some time yet) as opposed to the natural motion of falling bodies on earth. This in effect meant the positing of two different kinds of natural motion, one natural to the planets and the other to falling bodies on earth, and the two are not the same. Given the external criteria for evaluating theories which we have studied, a theory would be better than this one if it could explain both kinds of motion by the same set of laws, which is what Newton and Kepler managed to do.

The second fact, that falling bodies accelerate on earth, was explained in terms of the motion of the medium around the falling body. Given that a vacuum is impossible and that air or some other medium is displaced by a falling body, then the space left by the displaced air must be immediately filled with something; and it was argued that the air which was displaced in front of the body immediately moved to fill the space at the rear of it, hence imparting greater speed to it. Furthermore, as the body fell closer to the earth it was thought that the higher column of air above it exerted a greater pressure upon it, coupled with increasingly lighter resistance beneath it as the distance between the body and the earth diminished. And finally, as Butterfield notes, there was a clearly teleological and voluntaristic addition, namely that bodies moved more "jubilantly" as they neared their natural resting place.[11]

Criticism of Aristotelian Physics

Projectile motion, as exemplified in the case of the arrow, was explained by the "air-replacing-displaced-air" theory. Now something very important happens in both the cases of the arrow and of the accelerating falling body. It is this: the reason that the air moves to fill the space left by the displaced air is that there *is* space left by the moving projectile to *fill*, that is, the projectile leaves a vacuum behind it. But Aristotelian physics requires that a vacuum be impossible—not physically impossible, but *logically* impossible. The reasons are simple: a vacuum is nothing. Nothing is just that; it cannot exist, for by hypothesis, anything that exists is something. Hence, when we say that a vacuum exists, we are saying that something which cannot exist, exists, which is a logical contradiction. Furthermore, as has been mentioned, if there was a moving body in a vacuum then its velocity would be infinite. A consequence would be that it could be in an infinitely large number of places simultaneously. But this too is a contradiction, given that place is a quality of the thing for Aristotle. A thing cannot have the quality of both being at a place and not being at a place at the same time. But the cost of these arguments is very high indeed; it is that the Aristotelian theory itself implies still another contradiction, namely that there is not a

---

[11] Butterfield, *op. cit.*, p. 6.

vacuum even though one is necessary in order to explain both natural accelerating motion and unnatural projectile motion. Any theory which implies a contradiction is unsound, and Aristotelian physics is therefore unsound.

In the seventeenth century the criticisms of the Aristotelian physics began to gather force, and the nature of motion was the focal point of these attacks. They culminated in the experiments and arguments surrounding the law of inertia. After the acceptance of this law, teleological explanation in physics was dead, and the universe was no longer a place characterized by volitions in inanimate bodies but rather a machine. Science after this time also does not draw a distinction for physical purposes between qualitative and quantitative change. All change becomes quantitative. The point of attack was again the nature of the motion of projectiles and the explanation of the fact that falling bodies accelerate. The beginning of the end of course was Copernicus, but we shall not discuss his findings here. Rather, we shall be primarily concerned with Galileo, Kepler, and Descartes.

The Law of Inertia

The inertial law received its perfect formulation in the writings of Descartes. The law states that a body in motion continues that motion in a straight line unless something acts upon it to change that fact. The law rests upon the assumption that bodies do not move themselves, which is in fundamental opposition to the teleological Aristotelian view of things. Furthermore, place is no longer a property or quality of a body —it is a measurement. And velocity changes so that it is no longer just speed but a composite of speed and direction. The law itself is of course an ideal; conditions in actual physical space only approach the perfect conditions it states, but they never actually reach it. Yet there are several immediate advantages. It meets the observed conditions much better than the old theory did. For example, if Aristotle were correct, a thread tied to a ball ought to stream out *ahead* of it rather than behind, given that projectile motion is due to the pushing of the air replacing the vacuum behind the projectile. And the new law does not require us to posit volitions in inanimate objects nor purposes in terms of which they act, nor does it require the explanations we give to be quite so obviously circular as the "it acts that way because that is its nature" kind of theory. Moreover, although the original proponents of the new view (Galileo for instance) did not realize it, it could account for the fact that it is false that projectiles travel in straight lines and also false that they immediately fall in a straight line when their momentum is exhausted. Finally, the new physics did not require a different theory for the motion of the planets, for the fact that they did not fall down was accounted for by the fact that they did not encounter the resistance of the atmosphere. This latter explanation was false, of course, but the point is that the actual explanation is nonetheless consistent with the law. Considering the external criteria again, the new theory requires the positing of fewer explanatory entities than the old, and hence meets the test of simplicity better. It does not require separate laws to explain the motion of the planetary bodies, and so it is more fruitful than the old one. It contains no contradictions, and, hence, it meets the internal criteria better than Aristotle's view. And it accounts for the observed facts better than the old view does.

Two other important features of the science which gave birth to the inertial law should be noted, though they took some time to develop. The first is that mathematics came to play a more important role than it ever had before, because it was the language most amenable to stating quantitative relations. As Professor Butterfield notes, without the analytic geometry which Descartes invented and the differential calculus invented by Newton and Leibniz, Newton's physics would not have been possible. The second feature is the increased use of experimentation both in the discovery and the confirmation of hypotheses. This, too, was not something that happened overnight. Copernicus published his *De Revolutionibus Orbium* in 1543, but it was left to Tycho Brahe, the indefatigable Kepler, and to Galileo and Descartes really to turn the corner to modern experimental science.

Both of these trends can be illustrated in Galileo's famous experiments with the balls rolling down the inclined plane. The balls are of different weights and sizes. When they roll down the plane, they accelerate, and the rate of acceleration can be measured. The first experimental conclusion is that they accelerate at the *same* rate, contrary to the Aristotelian theory. No matter how steep the angle of the board is, this fact is still the case. If Galileo's instruments had been sensitive enough and his board long enough, he would have noticed a slight difference in their speeds, which would be due to the size of the balls and the resistance they encountered. This is accounted for in the Cartesian version of the law in any event. Furthermore, although Galileo's board was of a finite length, he noted that what stops the balls from rolling is the end of the inclined plane, and he guessed correctly—the genius is the man who sees the obvious!—that otherwise they would just have kept on rolling forever. Here then we have the two salient claims of the inertial law: that bodies accelerate at the same rate, and that unless something impedes their motion, they will continue at a uniform rate of velocity. It was only a slight leap of the imagination to the hypothesis that what was true of rolling bodies would be true of freely falling ones. And given the mathematization of the law, it was only another step, though a much larger one, to its generalization for any body, celestial or terrestial. Galileo did not make the last leap, though his successors did. There is one final leap, which Galileo barely saw, from the generalization of the law to its ideal application in a vacuum, which removes the factor of resistance. We have here, then, the use of an experiment which leads to the formulation of an hypothesis.

Now how is the hypothesis confirmed or tested? By making *predictions* based upon it and then either observing phenomena, or, at a later stage exemplified in the science of Descartes we have studied, actually inventing critical experiments and seeing if the prediction comes true. Thus, the new science also invents the concept of *evidence*, a concept which was foreign to the teleological view of the ancients, in which explanation was identification and further confirmation was unnecessary.

The Triumph of the New Science

Johann Kepler was a mystic, a fanatic, and one of the greatest mathematical geniuses of all time. His teacher was Tycho Brahe, and what Kepler did was to organize all of Brahe's findings to discover the principles of order underlying them, especially Brahe's planetary observations. He then expressed these principles in mathematical terms, that is, he quantified them; and all this enabled him to make his own greatest discovery, his planetary laws. These included the nature of the orbits of the planets and the formulae which enabled him to gauge the velocity of the planets in their orbits. Instead of a series of discrete entities endowed with volitions, the universe had now become a machine.

The division which the Aristotelians had drawn between natural and unnatural motions falls along with the distinction between planetary and earthly motion, given the universal applicability of the law of inertia and the new science of dynamics to which it gave birth in Descartes and Newton. Unnatural motion now becomes nothing but another species of motion, or at least, it does with the advent of Newton and the laws of gravity. It was not entirely discarded by Galileo, for one question that Galileo never answered was what caused bodies to move when there was *no* obvious external body acting upon them. He saw that what Aristotle called unnatural motion required an outside agent; he did not see that even natural motion does, namely, the gravitational attraction of the earth. But once this step *was* made, the destruction of the teleological volitional theory was complete, at least in the cases of inanimate bodies. In any event, Galileo did see, for both natural and unnatural motion, that no ghosts in machines were needed.

Here then we have the case of two competing theories which are attempting to explain precisely the same set of events. The events are the nature of terrestial and celestial motion and, in particular, the behavior of projectiles. The two explanations are the Aristotelian teleology, and the new experimental science. The latter theory is the better theory because it meets all the internal criteria, of consistency, truth, and validity, and it also meets the external criteria better than Aristotle's theory. That is, it is simpler, more fruitful, wider in scope, and enables us to make accurate predictions. The Aristotelian thtory, on the other hand, meets neither set of criteria as well as the new science does. It is inconsistent, requires the proliferation of explanatory entities (volitional agents), contains false statements which do not square with observational data, and has a smaller scope than the new science because it must posit different explanatory principles for the motion in the heavens than for that on earth. Also, it enables us to make fewer predictions, it is circular, and it does not have an adequate notion of evidence. But it was not sufficient to refute merely one part of the Aristotelian system, because each of the parts was tightly connected to the rest of them. And so, for example, his biological classifications and his systematization of the natural sciences continued to dominate western thought long after his physics had been rejected, and his laws of logic were thought to be impeccable. Somehow it was thought that he had just made some *factual* errors instead of conceptual ones as well. These are among the reasons that it was suspected that teleological explanation, though inadequate perhaps for physics, was essential for the explanation of the behavior of living organisms, the paradigm again being human behavior. These are not the only reasons, but they are among the most powerful for this belief. New ways of stating the defense for the necessity for teleological theories have of course been invented, some of them using the very technology which now rules the sciences.

We must now turn to the modern issues between biology and physics concerning teleological explanations.

TELEOLOGY IN CONTEMPORARY PHYSICS AND BIOLOGY

The Nature of Biological Laws

It is generally agreed that modern methods used in the physical sciences are adequate for the study and analysis of inanimate phenomena, and certainly they have been astonishingly fruitful. The same methods have often been used, with great success once more, in the study of living organisms; and many scientists have concluded in the light of these successes that no other methods are needed and, indeed, that sooner or later such subjects as biology will become an actual part of physics and chemistry. On the other hand, there is a body of opinion that denies that this is possible. Some of those opposed to the position argue that unique methods of explanation are required in biology and that there are logical bars which prevent biology from becoming a part of physics and chemistry. That is, they argue that the laws of biology are not logically equivalent to any of the laws of physics and chemistry and that it is impossible to derive biological laws from the laws of these other subjects. There are several reasons why they hold this position, some of them more important than others. One of the less important arguments is that terms occur in biology which do not occur in physics or chemistry and are used in the statements of the laws of biology. Since they do not occur in the physical sciences, the laws of biology are not derivable from the laws of the physical sciences. This objection is invalid. It is true that terms are used in the laws of biology that are not used in physics; but this does not imply that revisions cannot in principle be made in the statement of the laws of both fields such that the appropriate derivations could be made, even if they cannot at present be performed.

The more important objection rests upon the claim that biology studies a subject matter which is fundamentally different from that of the physical sciences, *so* different in fact that the sorts of explanations used in physics and chemistry cannot account for these phenomena. A quite different mode of explanation is required. The reason is that animate bodies seem to be *purposive,* and the evidence for this is that such organisms are *self*-regulated, *self*-maintained, and *self*-reproducing. Many of them, perhaps all, seem to act in the light of future, as yet unactualized goals, which fact is expressed in biology by speaking about the distinctive *functions* of the structures composing such bodies. This goal-directed characteristic of biological entities is not manifested by the subject matter of physics; or, perhaps more accurately, physics does not study anything with the aim of explaining such behavior. As Nagel notes, a stone and a cat are all of a piece for physics—they both obey the laws of gravity. The biologists go on to argue that because animate organisms are goal-directed and because their parts work upon one another in such a manner that the whole serves a given goal, their structures cannot be conceived simply as sums of their parts. Even the parts can therefore not be understood unless the explanation uses the notion of teleological explanation—that is, unless the functions of the parts are explained in terms of the goal or goals which the organism serves. And teleological explanation, they argue, involves the use of explanatory devices and techniques which are *only* appropriate within a science that explaines this kind of behavior. Hence, the type of explanation used in biology is not derivable from physics.

Nagel's Argument

We have just been discussing teleology in Aristotelian physics. We discovered that the distinction between animate and inanimate objects which is presupposed in this chapter was not found in earlier days, and this is one reason that physics and biology are not clearly separate disciplines in ancient science. Final causes had about the same place in both subjects. Not only is this not the case in modern science, but the concept of a final cause has also been drastically changed. No one, for example, now argues that "purposeful" behavior is to be analyzed in terms of volitions, and the goal-oriented actions of other organisms are not anthropomorphically characterized. To specify an explanation as "teleological" means now, even in biology, no more than that the laws explaining the behavior of the class of entities under investigation is *functionally* oriented. When stated in English these explanations typically include such phrases as "in order to," "the function of x is to," "for the purpose of," and so forth. Hence, a teleological explanation of the biological role of the alimentary canal in vertebrates (to use Nagel's [12] example), might be given as follows: ". . . the function of the alimentary canal in vertebrates is to prepare ingested materials for absorption into the blood stream." The problem then is to see whether or not it is possible, for every teleological explanation, to give a non-teleological one such that there is no difference in content between the two, that is, to give two explanations such that they both assert the same thing. Nagel argues, for example, that the teleological explanation "The function of chlorophyll in plants is to enable plants to perform photosynthesis" does not differ insofar as the asserted content is concerned from the non-teleological explanation "Plants perform photosynthesis only if they contain chlorophyll." The difference in the two is that the first concentrates upon the *consequences* toward which the system is "aiming," while the non-teleological version centers upon a statement of some or all of the necessary and/or sufficient conditions for the system's continued orderly operation. As Nagel states it:

The difference between teleological and non-teleological explanations is thus comparable to the difference between saying that B is an effect of A, and saying that A is a cause or condition of B . . . . the difference is one of selective attention, rather than of asserted content.[13]

Furthermore, if the two kinds of explanations *were* different in content, then the investigatory procedures and the nature of the evidence for the

[12] Ernest Nagel, "Teleological Explanation and Teleological Systems," in *Readings in the Philosophy of Science*, Herbert Feigl and May Brodbeck, eds. (New York: Appleton-Century-Crofts, Inc., 1953), pp. 537–58.
[13] *Ibid.*, p. 541.

content of the one ought to be different than for the other. But we do not seem to have such a difference. Nagel even made the stronger claim that the "conceivable" evidence for the one sort of explanation is the same as for the other.

To opine such claims and to prove them are two different things however. Many biologists argue that, although teleological explanations imply non-teleological ones, the converse implication, from non-teleological explanations to teleological ones, does not hold. They argue that if such a mutual implication were justified, then just as the teleological explanation is presumably replaceable by the non-teleological one, so the converse ought to be the case. But, they say, it is not the case. Ask the physicist whether he thinks that his laws can be stated teleologically, or do it yourself, and you will see the absurdity of it. How could the law of inertia and the laws of gravity be stated teleologically, without returning to the Aristotelian days, or effecting the mechanisms of quantification used in physics?

This objection is not entirely well-founded, for in fact some of the physical sciences do use so-called "variational" or "isoperimetric" explanations which at least resemble teleological ones, and the principles of mechanics can be given this kind of statement. Moreover, one possible reason why the physicists and chemists do not use this sort of explanation may be found in the fact that physics, unlike biology, is not very much concerned with special classes of organized bodies, and so they do not generally, says Nagel, ". . . investigate the conditions making for the persistence of some selected physical system rather than of others." Nonetheless, it is certainly true that there are important differences between the subject matters of the physical and the natural sciences.

The Case of Homeostasis

The single most striking difference can be illustrated by studying the complex process in human bodies known as homeostasis. It is this process which enables the body to maintain a fairly uniform internal temperature in the face of wide changes in its environment which would otherwise cause temperature changes fatal to us. It is clear that in some sense or other, the physiological processes of our bodies are functionally capable of maintaining this temperature range, and it is equally clear that this achievement necessitates that many distinct systems in our bodies interact with one another. What biology does is to study these interacting processes *in the light of the consequence* they achieve together, namely a fairly uniform temperature in spite of environmental changes. Normally the subjects which physics studies do not exhibit this regulative ability, the ability to persist when persistence requires adaptive changes in the light of varying environmental conditions. So, given the empirical foundation which this difference rests upon, the problem we have to face is this two-fold one: (1) Is it possible to describe the "distinguishing structure of 'goal-oriented' systems in such a way that the analysis is neutral with respect to assumptions concerning the existence of purposes or the dynamic operation of goals as instruments in their own realization?" (2) If it is true that teleological explanations are normally employed in the explanations of these so-called goal-oriented systems, does this have a significant bearing upon the question of whether the two sorts of explanatory systems are equivalent? Nagel thinks that the answer to the first question is yes, and to the second, no.

Take the case of homeostasis as a paradigm for a biological system. The typical property of such systems is that they persist in maintaining some particular state in the face of changes in their environments, or, at least, they persist in moving toward this state. Call the state "G." The system which maintains G will be called "S," and the environment of the system S will be "E." For Nagel's purposes, he assumes that E remains constant—that is, that there are no changes in it. We also assume that S has several parts and that the activities of at least some of these parts are causally connected to the occurrence or non-occurrence of G. Assume that there are three such parts, and we shall call their states at any given time "A," "B," and "C," with subscripts which will indicate the precise values of the three states. Thus, the description of S so far as it is causally relevant to the occurrence or non-occurrence of G at some specific time will have this logical form: $(A_x B_y C_z)$ where "x," "y," and "z" are the determinating subscripts.

The next assumption is this: there are limits to the parameters of the states A, B, C, because clearly, to use Nagel's example again, if we are talking about the state of a blood vessel which is a part of a system S, the human body, it is not the case that one of the parameters within which the vessel can vary in size is, say, five feet. A diameter of this magnitude would not be a possible state of the vessel and hence not a possible value for a state, say A. So the set of values for any of the state variables will be a member of a class whose dimensions are the maximum and minimum parameters permissable for the part of S of which it is a state. Call these classes K_A, K_B, and K_C, respectively for the three states A, B, C. So anything can be a value of $(A_x B_y C_z)$ only if the values of the variables belong to one of the other three classes. At the same time, this means that the values of A_x, B_y, and C_z may vary independently of one another, because the parameters of K_A, K_B, and K_C vary with the nature of the part of the system we are talking about. Although a blood vessel cannot be five feet in diameter, the colon can be more than five feet long.

Finally, we are to assume that S is a *deterministic* system insofar as the occurrence or non-occurrence of G is concerned. That is, given the values of A_x, B_y, and C_z, within the parameters of the K-classes, their occurrence is sufficient for the occurrence of G, and given the occurrence of G it is necessary that A_x, B_y, and C_z have such values.

Now suppose that S at a particular time is in the state $(A_oB_oC_o)$, and that if it is in this state then it either has G or changes will take place in S, expressible in (A_x, B_y, C_z) such that G will occur at a later time. This state of S Nagel calls a "G-state," by which he means a state such that it is potential for G; and, indeed, given the assumption of determinism, G is as good as here. It should be noted, however, that not all possible states of S are G-states, for one of the states A, B, or C may have such a value that, for example, the maintenance of homeostasis in the system of the human body is not possible and death occurs. And by the same token, and for the same mathematical reasons, more than one G-state for S is possible, because a higher value for one of A, B, C, may be compensated for by a lower value in one of them. At any given time, however, it is evident that S can have only one G-state.

The interesting case for the argument Nagel presents concerns a situation in which there is more than one possible G-state for S. At a particular time t_o, let us say again that S is in the G-state $(A_oB_oC_o)$, and the environment of S, E, is constant. Suppose that a change occurs in S such that the value of A_x changes. At a later time t_1 then, what constant is substituted in the variable A_x will depend upon what the change in S has been. Now since there is more than one possible G-state for S, then if these possible changes to those G-states are dependent upon the values which A_x may have, there is a range of values K'_A which is a subclass of K_A. Let us assume that the members of the subclass K'_A are the values A_1 and A_2. Now we also know that not all states of S are G-states, that is, states which will cause the occurrence of G, so assume that *neither* of $(A_1B_oC_o)$ or $(A_2B_oC_o)$ are G-states of S. If this is the case, we have shown that at least these changes in the value of A will turn the state of S from a G-state into a non-G-state. If these were the only changes in S, and S would no longer be causative of G at the time t_1 when the changes happened.

But now let us assume that this is *not* the case, because when the value of A_x at t_1 changes so that the new value falls in the subclass K'_A this change is accompanied by *other* changes in the values of B_y and C_z. The changes in B_y and C_z with relation to the changes in A_x which fall in K'_A, will constitute the members of the class K'_{BC}, and for each value of A_x which falls in K'_A, there will be corresponding changes in K'_{BC} which compensate for the changes in K'_A so that at the time t_1 when all these changes take place, S remains in a G-state instead of ceasing to be in one. This works conversely as well, that is, if the changes in the states of S which are values in the class K'_{BC} are not accompanied by a corresponding change in the value of the class K'_A, then S is also not in a G-state.

On the basis of this formal schema, Nagel introduces some definitions. S will be a system which is analyzable into a "structure of parts," some of which will be causally connected to the occurrence of a state or feature or characteristic of S called G. This set of parts which is causally connected to G will be describable in terms of a set of state-variables, these values at particular times being independent of each other though none of them may vary outside of the parameters of some class of values whose parameters depend upon the properties of the parts of S. Secondly, Nagel defines what he calls a "primary variation" for any system S. A primary variation is one such that if during a period of time T, a change occurs in one of the values for the states of S at some time t_o within T, which is of such a magnitude that this change alone would be sufficient for S's ceasing to be in its G-state, then at a later time t_1 which is still in T, all the possible values of (say) A, the state which changed, would make up the class K'_A. Third, if A has a primary variation, then the other states (say B and C) also change in a manner sufficient to remove S from its G-state at t_o, and at a later time t_1, but still within T the values of these other states comprise sets of the complex class K'_{BC}. Finally, Nagel defines what he calls "adaptive variations." Such a variation occurs when the changes in the values for K'_A and K'_{BC} "correspond to each other in a uniquely reciprocal fashion." When this relationship is established, that is, when any change in the values for K'_A relative to a state A of S are accompanied by reciprocal changes in the values for K'_{BC} relative to the states B and C of S, at a given specific time t_1, then S is in a G-state at that time. The changes in S which are members of K'_{BC} are the adaptive variations relative to those in K'_A, that is, they compensate for the changes in K'_A.

When the conditions given by these definitions hold for a system S, then Nagel says that the parts of S (A, B, C) which are causally connected to G may be said to be "directly organized during the period T with respect to G." In short, the definitions provide *in toto* and under the requisite conditions a schema within which goal-oriented entities may be explained. He believes that the definitions together can be generalized to include an indefinitely large number of state-variables ($A_x B_y C_z$ ... N_n) and that there can be primary variations for more than one of these. Moreover, we may now introduce variations in the environmental factor E, for this merely complicates the explanation, without changing its structure in principle.

It is the compensating factor built into the related variables (within the ranges of the classes K'_A and K'_{BC}) which provides the seeming property of freedom which goal-oriented entities have. That is, the state of G of a system S which is goal-oriented is in some part "independent" of the variations in A, or in B, or in C, provided these variations are within the parameters of the classes just named. Although G does depend upon the states of S, a change in any *one* of the three-state system S we have been considering is not sufficient for the non-occurrence of G, given the compensatory changes in the other two, and the number of states of which this was true would presumably increase as the total number of parts or states of S increased. The period throughout which G persists is also specifiable in terms of the association between the primary changes which take place in A, in the range of K'_A, and the compensatory changes in B and C, in the range of K'_{BC}. As Nagel says, "The more inclusive the range K'_A that is associated with such compensatory changes (in the range K'_{BC}) the more is the persistence of G independent of variations in the state of S." In Nagel's belief, this is a sufficient account for theoretical purposes of teleological explanations.

Equating Teleological and Non-Teleological Explanations

If the account is accurate, then Nagel thinks that it is not necessary to include "purposes and goals" in an explanation in order to account for all of the salient features of biological entities. He admits, however, that the schema may have the fault of being *too* inclusive, and his defense of it in the face of this criticism is that the very distinction between systems which are goal-directed or goal-oriented and those which are not is very vague. In any event, he believes that he has shown that "the defining characteristics of (teleological) systems can be formulated entirely in non-teleological language; and in consequence, every teleological explanation . . . must be translatable into an equivalent statement (or set of statements) which is non-teleological." The only reason that it seems odd to formulate physical laws in teleological terms is that the former explanations concentrate upon the initial conditions under which systems called "goal-directed" initiate their various processes and persist in them while teleological explanations concentrate upon the "culmination and products of specific processes, and upon the contributions of parts of a system to its maintenance." The difference, in Nagel's eyes, is reducible to one of emphasis and perspective.

Nagel has one other important point to make, perhaps the most illuminating of the entire paper. He notes that many biologists draw a distinction between structure and function, and argue that whereas biology is predominantly concerned with function, physics is more concerned with structure. Consider the study of the eye. Physiology normally studies the structure of the eye, that is, the spatial relations of its various parts. Biology studies its activities or functions and the ways in which the various parts contribute to these activities. Now functional studies are primarily oriented to the study of the states of the eye through *time* rather than to their spatial organization. Biology seeks to discover and explain "sequential and simultaneous orders of change in the spatially ordered and linked parts of organic bodies." It is clear from this that the two kinds of studies cannot be dissociated, for there could be no incompatibility in the two kinds of explanations. But on the other hand, it is also clear that from a description of the spatial organization of the eye we cannot deduce the future temporal changes in it, unless we are predicting upon the basis of past found conjunctions, which would be inductive and not deductive reasoning. As Nagel notes, you do not know how a clock works when you know the spatial organization of its parts; you must also have the laws of mechanics. So *if* we are to interpret the demand for an explanation of why a particular biological structure is associated with certain specific functions or activities and not others as a demand for a *deduction* of the latter from the former, then we cannot answer the question. But in Nagel's view, that is because the question is at fault: it demands what is not logically possible. The point here rests upon one we considered some time ago, namely the uniformity of nature principle. Any description of the spatial structure of the eye will be good for a specific time if it is sufficiently detailed. The causal functions of the parts of the eye are temporally as well as spatially organized events. Hence, to ask for a deduction of the functions of the eyes from its spatial characterization would be to beg the question of the association between the two by assuming that future functions would be coordinated with past spatial organization in known ways, when in fact that is just the question being asked.

Criticisms of Nagel's Thesis

Nagel's thesis is very difficult to criticize from the viewpoint of its technical structure; but it is possible to offer certain criticisms, some specific and others general, which at least render the argument suspect. Many of these criticisms hinge on a central assumption of the theory, which is that the human organism is a member of the class of organic entities which is explicable in the terms he suggests. The point of these criticsms will be this: is Nagel correct in the unstated assumption that human behavior is completely explicable within the sort of schema he suggests, even if all other biological entities are?

First, some weaker points. Nagel argues that one piece of evidence against the thesis that teleological and non-teleological explanations are not equivalent in content is that all the "conceivable empirical evidence" for the one sort is also evidence for the other. But we are not interested in *conceivable* evidence, only actual evidence. From the fact that you can or cannot conceive that something is the case, nothing follows about whether it is or not. Moreover, there is some question about the truth of this claim, at least in the case of human beings. It depends, of course, upon what we shall accept as evidence. But clearly one sort of evidence which we accept as relevant to the behavior of human beings is that kind in which *reasons* for present action are given which refer to future goals. Reasons are not the same as causes. We do not have to argue that the as-yet-actualized goals are causal factors in the agent's action in order to say that they are relevant to the explanation of his present actions. Now Nagel's theory does not account for reasons as well as causes. But surely the reports of motives are to be considered as *some* kind of evidence, and there seems to be no reason not to accept them as "empirical" evidence, provided we realize that another man's intentions are not a possible object of public knowledge. To deny that we accept this sort of evidence is to fly in the face of empirical common sense; for it is impossible to go through a single day in the presence of others without encountering reports of intentions.

Nagel claims that the physical sciences "in general" are dealing with a much wider class of entities and with a much wider sphere of application for their functions and consequences than the biologists are. He thinks that this is one reason the physicist is reluctant to speak in terms of the functions of things, preferring instead to concentrate on the conditions for their existence and development. Now again we must decide what we shall count as "physics" and "biology" but certainly it is true that this is a dubious claim if it purports to describe the activities and interests of a great number of men called "physicists." A large number of physicists seem to be working upon subjects of a carefully defined and limited scope, and in their discussions of their work they very often use phrases such as "the behavior of this sort of particle under these conditions" to describe the field of their interest and study.

The most important criticism concerns our old friend, the fallacy of begging the question. Nagel assumes that for any given G-state which is "realized at a given time" there is another actual state of the system S such that S or the state of S at that time *determines* the G-state. He generalizes this by saying that he assumes that "S is a deterministic system with respect to the occurrence of G-states." Once again, the case of that strange animal the human being comes to the forefront. Certainly we would want to accept, at least provisionally, the claim that at least the involuntary motions of human beings are determined, and some of these involuntary motions, such as those of the alimentary canal, are systems of the sort Nagel wishes to discuss. However, not only is there evidence that startling changes can be wrought in the so-called "involuntary" movements of humans by concentration of thought, but there is also an entire area of their "behavior" which is called "voluntary" for the precise reason that it does *not* seem to be determined. Recent studies indicate that the rate of the heart, for example, can be changed in either direction to surprising magnitudes by *willing* such changes. We must certainly include among the subjects which biology studies not just the actual physical change in such phenomena, but their causes as well, though, of course, there are many other disciplines which study them, such as psychology. In Chapter 4 the issue of determinism was discussed at length, and the conclusion was that it is false. The point here is that Nagel's theory assumes that it is *true*. An assumption of this kind is acceptable for purposes of discussion providing that it is either proven afterward or that the truth of the assumption is not a necessary condition for the soundness of the theory. At least the latter provision is violated by Nagel; for if S is not deterministic with respect to G-states, then his thesis fails. He then cannot account for the compensatory variations in the other states of S which enable him in turn to include functional analysis in his system.

The notion of "independence" which Nagel uses in his theory is misleading. It depends upon the ratios between the number of primary variations in a given state and the compensatory changes in other states of a system. But these ratios, in turn, depend upon the relationship between the range of values within the parameters of the K'_A class and those within the $K'_{BC} \ldots {}_N$ classes. The more of the values of K'_A that are associated with the values in the other classes, the more independent the "persistence of G" is of the changes in any *one* of the parts of S that are causally related to it. Modern biologists, unlike their ancient predecessors, do not want to claim *complete* independence of even some changes in their subject matter of the changes in the states of that subject matter. But this is *exactly* what some versions of anti-determinism, including libertarianism, claim; and, in those cases of theories which deny determinism on the ground that a cause is not *sufficient* for its effect, the degree of causal independence is not of the statistical variety suggested by Nagel. In order to support his argument Nagel would have to show that libertarianism is false and that the sort of independence he defines is sufficient for explaining such facts as the process of human decision-making. He admits at one point, as has been mentioned, that the distinction between goal-directed systems and those which are not goal-directed is very vague. He does not mention that one way the distinction is often drawn, at least for human beings, is by denying that his assumption of determinism is true.

In spite of these criticisms however, (which are not all of the possible arguments against his position), it seems that Nagel has accomplished something very important. He seems to have shown that, at least for non-human organic systems, and perhaps for those human organic systems which are involuntary, teleological and non-teleological explanations do not differ in content. Furthermore, he has argued persuasively that the demand for a *deduction* of the function of an organic body, given only its physiology description in a spatial context, is logically wrong-headed—it asks for the impossible, and hence it is a meaningless demand. He has not, however, explained how the explanation of intentional action can be given in a non-teleological framework if we are to include reasons as well as causes in that explanation.

EXERCISES

1. If Descartes is right, what are the relations between metaphysics and physics? Is metaphysics necessary to explain the foundations of physics for him, or can he do without it? Why or why not?

2. What is the relation between physics, solid geometry, and mechanics for Descartes?

3. Deduction, it has been argued, is a part of analysis for Descartes, which is the process of discovery. Discuss the role of deduction in this process for him. Is *demonstration* a part of analysis for Descartes? Why or why not?

4. Is demonstration a part of the Cartesian metaphysics? What does Descartes mean when he says that the foundations of his physics are demonstrable? Are they demonstrable *within* physics?

5. What are the two operations of the mind for Descartes, and what roles do they play in his philosophy?

6. Discuss the meanings of the terms "absolute" and "relative" with regard to the "causal order" which Descartes seeks to discover in material things.

7. State a proposition which Descartes would consider as "complex and obscure" and then, using the analysis he suggests, break it down into his "simple parts." Then, order these parts according to whether they are absolute or relative, dependent or relatively independent, etc., in the way you think he would have done.

8. Why is a good God who will not deceive us essential for the Cartesian metaphysics?

9. Discuss the different roles of experimentation in analysis according to Descartes.

10. Do you agree that the scientific method Descartes proposes is in essential respects similar to that of present day science with regard to the process of discovery? Why or why not?

11. Outline the argument which the Aristotelians would offer as an explanation of the motion of projectiles. Your premises will have to include the specification of the kinds of motion they accepted.

12. Evaluate your answer to (1) using the internal and external criteria developed in Part One.

13. Outline the argument which the Galileans and Cartesians would offer as an explanation of the motion of projectiles. Why is this a better explanation

than the Aristotelian explanation? Use the criteria developed in Part One in your answer.

14. Discuss the four-fold causal analysis Aristotle invented with regard to its usefulness in explaining the artificial products of man, such as the house, though using other examples. Do you think it provides an adequate explanation? Why or why not?

15. Aristotle takes an essentially anthropomorphic view of the universe. What does this mean? Why do you think he took this view?

16. The law of inertial motion is an idealization. Why is this not a criticism of it?

17. In the teleological Aristotelian view of the universe, is there a possibility that category-mistakes may be committed? Why or why not?

18. It has been said that the ancient view of natural explanation is circular. Why is this? Is it true? Use examples in your answer.

19. Why is the concept of "evidence" unnecessary in Aristotle's teleological explanation?

20. In the modern science, the universe is like a machine. *Is* it actually a machine? Why or why not? If you say that it is, will you be committing a category-mistake? Why or why not?

21. What is the difference between the meaning of "teleological explanation" in the discussion of Nagel, the same words in the discussion of Aristotle?

22. What is the argument, formulated in deductive form, which some biologists use to defend the thesis that teleological explanation as defined here is essential in biology? Assuming that Nagel uses the terminology and method given in Part One for the evaluation of arguments, what would he say about the biologist's arguments?

23. Why is determinism an essential premise of Nagel's argument? Is it hard or soft determinism?

24. Suppose that determinism of the variety he espouses is true. Is his theory then correct? Why or why not?

25. Is the difference between teleological and non-teleological explanations as defined here *merely* one of concentration upon the functions and consequences of the organism or its parts, on the one hand, and upon the necessary antecedent conditions for the existence of the organism or state on the other? Why or why not?

26. The conceivable evidence for the one kind of explanation is the same as that for the other if Nagel is right. What is the difference between "conceivable" and "actual" evidence?

27. Consider the counter-example techniques of Part One. Are any of these techniques applicable to the arguments in modern theology? Why or why not?

28. Nagel offers a set of definitions based upon his explanatory schema for S, for "primary variations," and for "adaptive variations." Examine these definitions. What kind are they? Defend your answer.

29. Why is it not possible to deduce the functional description of a biological organism from a description of its physiology?

30. Formulate a set of arguments *against* the thesis that reasons (as opposed to causes) should be construed as "empirical" evidence in the explanation of human behavior in some cases. If reasons are not empirical evidence, then are they evidence at all? Are they *a posteriori* truths? *A priori*? Neither true nor false? Defend your answers.

12

Types of Philosophy

REALISM AND NOMINALISM

Many texts in philosophy are organized either according to the "types of philosophy" or the "problems" schema. Thus, some texts approach the discipline by outlining certain common positions held by several philosophers, while others deal with what they hold their common positions *about*, namely, the problem which they were trying to solve. This text has adopted neither stance, because here the focus of attention has been upon a common method for analyzing *both* problems and schools of thought. In this last chapter, however, it may be of value to discuss some of the best known views about certain issues in philosophy under their common names. The categorization of these views has been left until now because by this time the student ought to have a more adequate basis upon which to consider them knowledgeably and because he will recognize in what follows some of the views of thinkers whom we have already discussed. Several times in the body of the text the problem of "universals" and the problem of "resemblance" have been mentioned but no detailed discussion of them has been given. Now the problem of universals will be examined, and the relation of this set of problems to the issue of resemblance will be described.

The Problem of Universals

In the third century a philosopher named Porphyry noted the following in the introduction he wrote to one of Aristotle's works:

For the present I shall not discuss whether genera and species really exist or are bare notions only; and if they exist whether they are corporeal things, or incorporeal and rather separated, or whether they exist in things perceived by

the senses and in relation to them. For these questions are profound and demand other and more acute examination.[1]

At first sight this may seem to be a strange assertion. "Animal" is a
genus and "man" is a species of the genus animal. What might it mean
to question whether or not they exist as corporeal or incorporeal things?
After all it is obvious that there are animals and that there are men,
though it may not be exactly as obvious that men are animals. What is
"profound" about this question? The answer is indicated by Porphyry's
second sentence wherein he asks after the *manner* of their existence.
There are indeed men—this man, and that one, and so forth. The same
is true of animals—there is this animal and that one, and this cat, which is
a kind of animal, and that dog, another kind of animal. What is clear
then, what is obvious to the perceiving mind, is that there are *individuals*
who are men and animals and maybe both. But it is *not at all* obvious
that men and animals and cats and dogs exist if what is meant is that
not only do individual men, animals, cats, and dogs exist, but also that
animality, manhood, cathood, doghood, etc., exist. These are not individuals (after all, there is no dog whose name is Fat Albert who is an
animality) but something else. Why on earth should anyone think that
there are such "things" anyway? The answer lies in the reply to questions such as "Why are Fat Albert, Bertie, Gordie, and Frodo Baggins
all *dogs*?", "Why are they all *animals*?", and "Why are Paul, Bernie, Dick,
Alan, and Wally all *men*?" The answer is not exceedingly difficut in the
case of asking why x and y and z are all men or animals. We can reply
(though it would not do for long), by saying that "animal" is a name
not just of this man or that man, that is, it is not a proper name, but a
name of many things, among which are x, y, and z. But what about a
word such as "red" which is not the name of a thing, or of many things,
at all? It is a name of a *quality* or a property of things, and now the
question is, does the property exist independently of the things, or only
"in" the things, or, in some strange way, in both? Furthermore, we can
now see that the first tentative answer to the question (that "animals"
and "men" are merely words that name many things instead of one),
will not do because after all there is a *reason* why they name many rather
than one, which is that the many particular things which they name have
something in *common* in addition to their name: they have one or more
qualities or properties in common. So the question of the existential
status of the qualities in virtue of which we say that something is a man
or a dog or an animal, or red or soft or hard still remains. In addition,
what are we to make of words and complexes of words which do not

[1] R. I. Aaron, *The Theory of Universals* (Oxford: The Clarendon Press, 1952),
chapter 1.

name things, but relations between things—phrases such as "to the north of," "greater than," "included in," and so forth? If qualities are that in virtue of which we say that one thing and another thing are the same, then the question about the existential or ontological status of animality, manhood, and so forth is reducible to a set of questions of the same kind about the qualities which place individuals in these classes.

This is exactly the way Aristotle saw the problem. For him, a universal, that in virtue of which many are said to be one, is that which the objects in question have in common. That which many have in common may be predicated of them all, so a universal is what may be predicated of many. In addition, we may say things about the universal, because it is possible to talk about the quality redness, or the set of properties which compose manhood or animality, and so forth. But since a universal is that which many things *share*, it is not itself an individual thing such as the many particular things which have it. Redness is not a thing as a red hat is a thing. Now our question is, what is a universal?

Whether one is a realist of several possible varieties or a nominalist depends upon how one answers this question. The first theory we shall consider, a realist theory, is that of Aristotle's famous teacher, Plato.

Plato's Theory of Universals

Plato arrived at the conclusion that universals must exist through his theory of knowledge. For him as for most of the Greek philosophers, an object of knowledge could not be identical with any object of sense. The reasons were complex, but in essence the major ones were that sense perception is of the world of appearance (which is changing and therefore always in a state of becoming), whereas knowledge is always of the real, of what is, not of what is coming to be, or ceasing to be. Even if objects of perception were objects of knowledge, that would not exhaust the objects of knowledge; some of them are clearly not even *possible* objects of perception. Some things are known by intellection alone. Nor is knowledge analyzable as true belief for beliefs are something which may be either true or false, while knowledge is by definition always true. Even if we analyze what is believed into its parts so that we are minutely familiar with them we still do not necessarily have knowledge; for the parts themselves must be known, and they are not further analyzable. In other words, analysis will not be equivalent to the process of knowing. The object of true knowledge must therefore be unchanging, existent, and not known to the senses. Plato thinks that true knowledge aims at definitions, and that the unchanging element of a definition is a universal concept. There are different "degrees" of universals; that is, there is a hierarchy of values in the class of universals. The concept of Goodness is of greater value than the concept of redness. But for Plato, though particular good things change and particular red things change, Goodness and redness do not. There is an objective reference which these unchanging concepts have, for otherwise they would be nothing, and in some sense or other they are more "real" than the objects of sense-perception.

Plato thinks that particular individual things such as dogs, are "imitations" of the ideal or universal Dog. The universal is what is named by the predicate in sentences such as "Albert is a dog," and when we know, we discover these universals. The concepts we have of doghood, goodness, redness, and so forth refer to what Plato calls "Forms," which Aristotle also calls "Ideas." Plato thought of them as objective, independently existing entities, which are self-subsistent, and are somehow manifested in particular things. It is in virtue of this participation in the forms that particular things resemble each other. The supreme form is the Good, which Plato also identifies with Truth and Beauty. The forms never change, and hence they never cease to be or begin to be as particulars do. They do not exist as objects do, in space, and hence an entire range of questions, such as where they are, how large they are, what they are made from, and so forth cannot even be asked sensibly of them. To ask these questions seriously would be to commit a category-mistake. When we affirm a common property of a particular, we are affirming that the entity shares in some form, which is to say that it belongs to a species or class, the defining feature of which is the participation in that form.

Plato nowhere explains the exact nature of the relations between forms and particulars in a satisfactory way, nor does he provide any mechanism for limiting membership in the class of forms. These two major problems led to many criticisms of the theory, most of which Plato had thought of himself though he did not solve them. Aristotle, for example, gave a famous criticism that has come to be known as the "third man" argument. Suppose that S is a man. As such, he participates in the form Man. But if this is true, does it follow that the form is wholly or entirely in S, or only partly? It would seem that it can only be partly in S, for other entities participate in the form at the same time that S does, and to say that the form Man is entirely in S when S is a man would mean that there are at least as many forms of Man as there are individual men, which seems to be an unjustified proliferation of forms. Aristotle asked furthermore how we could explain the relation between S and Man. Is it that the particular man S and the form Man resemble each other? If so, how are we to account for this resemblance? If Plato is right, surely there must be a *third* entity, a form, in which both S and the form Man participate, and this leads to an infinite regress. Plato was aware of this problem. He realized that if he said that the form was entirely or wholly in many particulars, then either he would have to deny that the many participate in *one* form, or, if he said that the form could be only partly in many particulars at once, then he would have to say that the single form was divisible into many parts. The first alternative was unacceptable for the reasons already given, and the second was too; for to say that the form is one or unitary, but is indefinitely divisible, i.e., has an indefinite number of parts, is contradictory. At the bottom of such criticisms is the conviction that Plato never managed to bridge the gap between the forms and particulars, and that there is no reason for this gap in the first place.

Aristotle thought that forms are knowable only *in* objects, and that hence there is no reason, at least epistemologically, to posit their separate existence or subsistence. His doctrine is known as the *universalis in re* theory. The Real is indeed the unchanging or the universal, but it is only *qua* component of the world of change and becoming that the unchanging is knowable. If this were not the case, then there would be no way for us to jump from our knowledge of the sensible world to a knowledge of the world of forms or ideas. We must know the forms in things before we know the forms themselves.

The implied value-hierarchy in the world of forms is also not defensible. If there is a form for every predicate which is predicable of many, then there are forms for mud, hair, and whatever mundane thing one can conceive in addition to the forms of Truth, Beauty, and Goodness. To say that some of these are of intrinsically greater value than others implies that some of them share to a greater degree than others in a form, Value, which leads to just the earlier sort of criticism Aristotle stated.

Ockham and Nominalism

Plato's theory is vastly more complex and detailed than this sketch, but at least the main principle of Realism of one variety is given here. A theory which is opposed to Realism is Nominalism. As one might expect, nominalists deny that universals have any existence separate from particulars, and indeed they deny that there are universals *in* particulars as well. The originator of Nominalism was William of Ockham. Like many other modern thinkers, he saw many philosophical problems as composites of logical and linguistic issues and confusions. His rejection of universals is based upon a logical analysis of the terms which compose propositions. Ockham was much less familiar with the Platonic version of realism than he was with the neo-Aristotelian views defended by the church philosophers of the ninth through the middle of the fourteenth centuries. There were a number of unique characteristics of these theories. One was the grounding of universals, or "archetypes" as they were often called, in the mind of God. Another was the positing of a "chain of being," an ordered and increasingly valuable series of beings, reflecting in themselves the archetypes in the mind of God. At the same time, however, a reaction against the strict realist position (the one asserting the independent existence of universals) was current prior to Ockham. What Ockham did was to ground this reaction, justify it, through his logical analysis of the functions of terms in propositions.

Ockham argued that universals cannot be things and that only particulars or individuals exist. Universals, of course, are not particulars; and if it is true that only individuals exist, then to say that a universal exists is to utter not just a falsehood but a contradiction. In short, he thought that part of the *meaning* of "exists" is the concept of *individual* existence. If we grant that this is true, then the problem is to give an adequate analysis of terms which purport to refer to, connote, and (according to some theories) denote universals, without having to posit that universals exist. He begins this by distinguishing among several kinds of terms. The first distinction is between categorematic terms and syncategorematic terms. The former are those which have a meaning that may be understood even when they do not occur within a proposition. For example, all proper names and even generic words such as "table," "chair," and so forth are categorematic terms. But there are other terms which, when uttered outside of any context, are meaningless. Logical connectives such as "and" and "or," quantifiers such as "some" and "all" are examples.

There are also terms which are called "first intention," and those which are of "second intention." To understand this distinction it is necessary to understand the difference between a conventional and a natural sign according to Ockham. All words which refer to things are conventional signs, since it is only in virtue of a custom known by a mind which has the concept associated with the thing and the word that they have meaning. A natural sign is not a word or a term. Rather, it is a *concept*, and in Ockham's view concepts are not conventional, nor is their existence contingent upon that of conventional signs. With this distinction we can now return to the problem of universals.

Terms of first intention are those which signify things. In the sentence "Dogs are four-footed," the word "dogs" refers to things, is a term of first intention, and is a conventional sign. But some words do not refer directly to things and among these are terms which refer to other terms. Some of these terms are syncategorematic or logical terms; they refer to a term or terms with certain functions. The word "universal" is also one of these terms, which are called second-intention terms. This word refers to a class of words used to signify many things; it does *not* itself refer to things or a thing, such as redness or goodness, but to other terms. Terms are particulars, and therefore the second-intention word "universal" refers to particulars. The mistake that the realists made was to confuse first- and second-intention terms; or perhaps more accurately, they did not see that there are second-intention terms at all, except in the case of syncategorematic terms. This is not true of all realists, for Aristotle and several others saw the distinction. But they evidently did not realize that the appropriate analysis of "universal" is that it is a second-intention term. Since the word "universal" refers to a class of terms or words, it follows that particular universal words such as "redness" are used to signify many things.

There is perhaps another sense of "universal" in Ockham, and that is the sense in which it refers to a concept, or natural sign. Concepts are the meanings of terms of first-intention, though they do not presuppose the existence of these terms. "Chien" and "dog" are different words, but the concept of both is the same. When we think, we think concepts, not terms. But the natural sign or concept also stands for things, as first-intention terms do. In that sense, as first-intention terms are universals standing for many things, so concepts are too. This does not mean that there is some general "thing" corresponding to the concept; it merely means that like first-intention terms, concepts can be signs for many things. Nor does this view necessarily imply that concepts are subsistent entities, or "abstract general ideas" in Locke's sense, because Ockham calls the concept an "act of the understanding."

Ockham may seem to have done the realists in, as it were, but it is not quite so simple as that. Ockham has not solved the problem of resemblance. It is a fact that existing particulars resemble each other and that we perceive this resemblance. We notice that x is red, and that y is red, and they resemble each other in virtue of this common property. The common property is not the red in x, for that is, so to speak, x's red; and for the same reason, the common property is not y's red. To put it another way, the resemblance between x and y cannot be explained in terms of either of the *particular* reds, because it is just the particular reds which resemble each other. Resemblance is a relation between and among things; it is not a property *of* things as the resembling properties themselves are. We can say "x is red" intelligibly, but not "x is resemblant." It is tempting to say that the relation of resemblance is primitive, not further analyzable, and simply given in experience as the experience of particulars or particular qualities are given. But even if resemblance is given it is not given as are particulars or particular qualities. Unlike the apprehension of particulars it presupposes something for its existence, namely, the particulars between which it as a relation holds. Given the nominalist's position, it is still a sensible question to ask "But *why* does 'dog' signify this, and that, and the other thing?" It is not an answer to this question to say that the *word* "dog" is a universal, for it is not in virtue of the *word* that the convention governing its use arises: it is because of the objective resemblance of *things* which have four legs, bark, eat meat, and so forth, that the word becomes a universal term. So, the realists would say, call the word "dog" a universal if you will; the fact remains that it *is* universal because of something, an objective relation, resemblance, which holds among things, and to explain *that*, they would say, you have to have objective universals, not just universal words.

The problem is not solved, and some philosophers have argued that it is not soluble in principle. No pretense about a solution can be made here, but that is not our primary purpose. The intention here is to give you an idea of the difference between realism and nominalism. There are of course several different kinds of nominalists, just as there are many different kinds of realists. There are extreme realists who hold that *only* universals exist, and argue that all perception of particular existents is an illusion, and there are extreme nominalists who say that there need be no similarity among things, and even that in fact there *is* not. Such extreme positions, as with all extreme positions, fly in the face of common sense. Whatever the correct theory therefore, it probably lies between the extremes.

IDEALISM AND MATERIALISM

There are many meanings for the philosophical term "idealism." There is the absolute idealism of the metaphysican Hegel, the transcendental idealism of the synthesist Kant, and the empirical idealism of the phenomenalist. The latter view stems from the philosophy of our old friend George Berkeley, who called his theory "immaterialism," and it is his view which we shall examine here. Berkeley's views have been mentioned several times in this book, in the criticisms of Locke, the arguments for the existence of God, and in connection with theories of meaning and truth. This is a measure of the scope of his interests and influence, for in truth no book in philosophy can discuss these issues without saying something about Berkeley. In fact, he is very often credited with being the *inventor* of idealism as we now understand it, and certainly he was a primary influence upon many other idealists, such as Josiah Royce and Immanuel Kant.

Berkeley's Idealism

There are certain basic principles which may be said to define idealism as a theory. First, mind neither originates in nor is it reducible to matter.

Secondly, if matter exists (and some, perhaps most idealists deny that it does), then its existence depends in some sense upon mind. In short, either matter does not exist, or if it does, mind is ontologically more primitive than matter, because the existence of the latter is dependent upon the former. How these principles are articulated and defended is what distinguishes one idealist from another.

At first sight the assertion that matter does not exist and that the fundamental stuff of reality is mind seems absurd. When Boswell's friend, Dr. Johnson learned a version of Berkeley's theory (an incorrect version), he attempted to refute him by kicking a stone. His intention, of course, was to show the absurdity of denying that there are real things. But as we shall see, the idealist certainly does not deny that objects exist and Johnson was wrong. The word "idealism" had been used not only to characterize such theories as Berkeley's and Kant's, but also other realist theories, such as Plato's and the Neo-Platonists'. But when used in connection with these views, it indicates that reality consists in the world of ideas or forms, and does not have the same connotation as it does for Berkeley. Berkeley's position is essentially an epistemological one first, and an ontological one second. That is, he begins with a theory of knowledge, and it is only on the basis of that theory that he claims a certain status in reality for objects, minds, and their relations. He begins, as we know from earlier chapters, with an analysis of the components of our knowledge. They are few, and quite simple: the "ideas" of the various senses, our immediate knowledge of our own minds (we have "notions" of our mental operations, not ideas of them), and relations. The ideas of our senses are light and colors (sight), tangible sensations (touch), sounds (hearing), odors (smell), and sensations of taste. Our notions of our mental operations are of our willing, understanding, loving, hating, and so forth. Since mind is not a possible object of sense perception, we cannot have idea of it. Ideas can only resemble other ideas. Colors are only like other colors, smells like other smells, etc. Now Berkeley moves from this analysis to a series of *prima facie* simple claims, but they have tremendous consequences. Our sense perceptions only exist "in our minds," which is his way of saying that your perceptions are yours, mine are mine, and that is that. When you perceive a color, say red, that idea of red, that perception of red, is in no other mind but yours. This seems simple and straightforward enough, and it also seems true. When you are *not* perceiving that red, then that perception of red does not exist, which also seems simple enough, and true. Exactly the same point may be made for any perception of any idea for any of your senses. The general conclusion is therefore that for any of your perceptions, they only exist when you are, so to speak, "having" them. This is true not just for you but for all perceiving minds. When they are not perceiving, their perceptions do not exist; that is, their ideas of lights, colors, smells, tastes, and sounds do not exist. Through our senses, these are the *only* things we know. There are not lights, colors, etc., and *something else*. In short, when we give a complete description of what it is that we know sensibly, the list is exhaustive when we have gone through the ideas already named. This is true for all minds. Our knowledge of the physical world is our knowledge of our ideas.

Berkeley then moves to a consideration not of individual ideas and kinds of ideas, but of objects. Given that we know *only* the ideas given to our particular senses through those senses, then if objects are known sensibly they too must be analyzable in terms of ideas. They are, according to Berkeley, *sets* of ideas. This apple is red, and has this tangible quality, this taste, this odor, and nothing else. When you have said this about the apple, there is nothing else that you can add to the description which is a possible component of the apple and a possible object of knowledge for you. There are apples because the same set of perceptions, ideas, or at least similar sets of these ideas recur again and again in our experience, and to make discourse about them possible, we use the same word "apple" to refer to the similar sets of ideas. But as the existence of our individual ideas of sense is contingent upon our sensing them, so the existence of the set of ideas is also; after all, it is a difference between a single idea and a group of them, not a difference between one kind of entity and another kind. It follows that the existence of objects is contingent upon their being perceived. What this means is clear: what we know as physical, material things or objects do not exist unless some mind is perceiving them. This reflects one of the central tenets of idealism: the existence of material entities is dependent upon minds, and mind is ontologically prior to matter.

It is clear that human minds do not perceive all things at all times, and in the earlier study of Berkeley's argument for the existence of God it is shown how he uses this fact as a premise from which he infers that there is an all-and-always-perceiving mind, God, whose existence accounts for the continuity of the physical world.

Berkeley is not denying that there are material things. He is not saying that there are no tables, no chairs, no apples, and so forth. He *is* denying that these objects exist independently of the knowing mind; he *is* denying that even if they did, we could know it; he *is* denying that there is some unknown and unknowable "material substance or substratum" underlying or "supporting" ideas, which enables them to exist when they are not perceived. He thinks that the word "matter" is misleading, given the philosophical connotations that it has. But if people insist upon calling tables material objects, that is just fine with him, says Berkeley. He is concerned to say what they *mean* by "material object," and he insists that any adequate account be consistent with common sense. When we ask the normal man what he means when he says that the coach exists, he replies that he sees it, hears it, and so forth. And what is it that he sees and hears? Lights and colors and sounds. And do these exist independently of him? No, they do not. The tree falling in the forest makes sound *waves* when no one is around, but it only makes *sounds* when someone hears it fall.

Because of the misleading nature of the concept of matter, Berkeley called his theory "*immaterialism*"; he was denying that material substance, the unknown "behind" what we perceive, is a possible object of knowledge. His arguments against Locke on this topic have been given in the discussion of Locke and the theory of ideas. His views caused a great stir, and were held in contempt by those who, like Dr. Johnson, misinterpreted them as a denial that physical things exist. But when understood accurately, it is an exceedingly difficult theory to refute, especially when it is taken in conjunction with Berkeley's criticisms of the material substance theory and the doctrine of abstract general ideas.

Some Criticisms of Idealism

Some criticisms of Berkeley have been given in other parts of this book. Here one or two more might be mentioned briefly. First, Berkeley makes a leap from the claim "Objects of knowledge only exist when they are known" to the claim "Objects themselves only exist when they are known." He defines the object of knowledge in terms of our immediate familiarity with ideas, as we have seen. Bertrand Russell pointed out that Berkeley had failed to notice at least two different senses of "know." There is knowledge by *acquaintance*, and knowledge by *description*. The latter includes inferential knowledge and knowledge of truths, while the former is direct and immediate. It is true that the objects of knowledge by acquaintance only exist when they are known, but this is not true of knowledge by description. When I know that the Empress of China once existed I do know something, but I do not know the Empress of China directly. Nor need I know her directly. But this is still knowledge. There is of course knowledge by description of presently existing entities too, and such knowledge does not imply that the object of knowledge is being or must be perceived since it is not contingent upon contemporaneous knowledge by acquaintance. Hence, Russell argues, Berkeley has not shown that "to exist" means "to be perceived" in the case of objects.

Secondly, Berkeley realized that he had not solved the problem of resemblance, and also that he had not solved the problem of equivocation involved when he posits God's "perception" as the guarantee of the continuity of the real world. God's perception, as has been mentioned, is not like that of man. In correspondence with the American Dr. Samuel Johnson Berkeley seems to accept a theory of archetypes in which things exist ideally in the mind of God, while they exist perceptually when known by human minds. The fact remains, however, that if objects as known by God do not have the same status as when they are known by men, then an object not perceived by some human mind at some time at least changes its ontological status, and Berkeley never overcomes this criticism. Similar objections apply to any other idealistic theory which posits God as the being who maintains the universe. Royce is a good example.

Two other classic criticisms of idealism ought to be mentioned. One concerns what is called the problem of *solipsism*. A solipsist is a person who believes that there are no grounds for affirming that any being other than himself exists. If Berkeley cannot defend the assertion that his perceptions are similar to yours, but that yours are at the same time different than his, and if he cannot support the analogy which he wishes to draw between his mind and his ideas, and your mind and your ideas, then he is caught in this position. We have no ideas of other minds so we cannot know them directly through our senses. And we can only have direct acquaintance of our own minds, though Berkeley does say that we can have notions of relations, God, and other minds. The question is: how is it possible to have such notions? The sound of your voice is to me *my* idea of sense, even if what you are telling me is that you have a mind, will, understanding, and so forth. It is not possible for me to see through your eyes, nor to experience your willings. Upon what grounds then may I draw the analogy between your mind and ideas, and mine? It seems that there is no way for Berkeley to "get outside" the circle of his own perceptions and notions. Given the *esse est percipi* doctrine of ideas and objects and the *esse est percipere* theory of minds, the only justified existential claims I may make are those which concern the objects of my immediate knowledge, a class within which your mental activities and your perceptions do not fall.

The second criticism was raised by George Edward Moore in a famous article called "The Refutation of Idealism." There he argues, principally against Berkeley, that the good bishop failed to see the difference between asserting "Blue exists," "Consciousness exists," and "Consciousness and blue exist." If it is true that the existence of blue *consists* in being perceived, then to say that blue exists, and to say that the consciousness of blue exists, is to say the same thing; for blue cannot exist without the consciousness (perception) of it, and if the perception of it exists, then blue does too. Berkeley has failed to see, in Moore's eyes, the difference between consciousness and the object of consciousness. The existence of the one does not imply the existence of the other; but if Berkeley is right they must imply one another. For Berkeley to say that blue exists but the consciousness of blue does not is a *contradiction*. Now, says Moore, you can see just from an examination of the sentences "Blue exists" and "The consciousness of blue exists" that they do *not* mean the same thing, and do *not* entail each other, so Berkeley must be mistaken, and *esse est percipi* must be not only false, but contradictory. Moore's argument may not hold against Berkeley, though it does hold against idealists who do not have the theological grounding for the continuity of the physical world that Berkeley had. This is a pyrrhic victory for Berkeley, because as we know his explanation of how God's perception supports the world of objects when humans are not perceiving it fails. Nonetheless, he does avoid Moore's criticism because all things are present to the consciousness of God at all times for Berkeley and given this, to say that blue exists but the consciousness of it does not *is* a contradiction.

Materialism

Whereas idealism argues that the essential nature of the real world is mental, or at least that the world is mind-dependent, *materialism* denies this. Materialists argue that matter and nothing else exists. Because of this they also argue that there is no teleological manifestation in the universe, that is, that no mind directs the causal occurrences in the natural world. All causes are material causes, and there are no supernatural phenomena. Furthermore, modern materialists argue that all kinds of experience, and all kinds of properties, are reducible to physical properties. Qualitative analysis is therefore reducible to quantitative analysis, and the mental behavior of minds is explicable in terms of matter and motion, as are minds themselves. So there are two basic claims to be exfoliated: (1) the principle that nothing but matter exists, and (2) the principle that all experiences and properties normally called "mental" or "qualitative" are reducible to interactions among matter.

The first question the materialists must answer is, just exactly what *is* this matter which is supposed to be the only thing that exists? Is it the "material substance" of Aristotle and Locke? We have already considered arguments against that position which indicate that either there is no such thing, or that if there is we cannot know it, or both. Is the materialist speaking of the matter of the physicists? Small particles interacting according to law? And if he is speaking about this sort of matter, is it true that all of the phenomena with which we are familiar are explicable in terms of this framework? Are, for example, our moral concepts, willings, understandings, lovings, desires, emotions, aesthetic experiences, qualitative judgments (this painting is good, that one bad), fictional characters—are all of these simply a matter of the interaction of particles? And what are these particles themselves? It is notoriously difficult even for the physicists themselves to say just what the basic entities of physics are. Witness the continuing discussion over the wave versus the particle theories of light, the nature of points, the question of exactly what space and time are, and so forth. We know that even if we are capable of giving a precise definition of matter, the idealist would argue that it must be given in terms of what we perceive, directly or indirectly, and that from this analysis it follows that matter is not possibly the basic or fundamental "stuff," let alone the only stuff, for it is dependent for its existence upon mind. We also know that the realist, the man who believes that universals must exist (whether independently or only in things), would argue that even if matter exists it cannot be the only thing that exists; for matter alone will not provide us with the explanation of relations among objects. C. D. Broad tells us in *Scientific Thought* that the common-sense notion of a particle of matter traditionally includes at least the following properties:

1. It must not be dependent upon the perceiving mind for its existence and it must be perceivable by many minds. It is, as Russell says, public, and this presumably differentiates it from mental events and consciousness which are private.
2. The qualities of matter are in some way correspondent to the senses with which we perceive them, but the qualities reside in the matter and not in our senses. Even when we are not looking at the red ball, it is still red.
3. Matter persists relatively unchanged whether observed or not.
4. Matter has a position in space, that is, individual pieces of matter do, and they move from place to place, retaining some shape, size, and position at all times independently of our observation.[2]

As Broad notes, however, these properties are not as simple to explain as they sound, because when we attempt to define them more precisely we have to make the very distinctions between appearance and reality, between what we perceive and what we think exists independently of the variations inherent in different perceptions, which are the fount of the difficulties noted by realists on the one hand and idealists and nominalists on the other. Philosophy as a whole gives us good reason to think that matter meeting these requirements does not exist as an object of knowledge. The chief difficulty in Broad's eyes is to reconcile the requirements of relative stability and permanence independently of any perceiver, with the fact that our perceptions of objects vary widely from

[2] C. D. Broad, *Scientific Thought* (London: Routledge & Kegan Paul, Ltd., 1923), pp. 299–33.

perceiver to perceiver at any given moment, and from moment to moment, while the object is not supposed to have undergone any physical changes. Modern quantum physics adds to the problem with such arguments as that suggested by the Heisenberg principle, which purports to show that the act of measuring microcosmic physical phenomena itself influences the outcome of the measurement, at least when we are trying to measure position and momentum. The moral, of course, is that the characteristics of matter are not totally independent of mind, since their very definition must include the effects of mind upon matter.

Naturalism

The hardest test for the materialists, however, comes with the attempt to explain everything in terms of the interactions of particles. Strictly speaking, the addition of this claim about explanation to the basic principles that only matter exists and that all causes are material causes turns materialism into the thesis known as "naturalism." Naturalism therefore holds that matter is the basic stuff of the world, that qualitative phenomena are explicable quantitatively, and that anything that is knowable is knowable by science. The hurdles in the path of proving the latter claim are indeed formidable. If correct, naturalism must be able to take any body of knowledge-claims, such as those from the realm of morals, and must then explicate these claims in terms of science. Moreover, if "materialism" is taken in the strict sense then ultimately the science in terms of which the concepts of morality are explicable is physics, or, at best, chemistry and physics. Moral concepts are to be defined in terms of the imagined satisfaction of human desires and needs, and moral rules are really axioms or directions for the achievement of such satisfaction, subject to empirical confirmation or disconfirmation. Human desires and needs arise from the peculiar structure of the human organism; descriptions of needs are descriptions of states of this organism, and at bottom such descriptions are not normative at all. They contain no terms such as "ought" or "should," "right" or "wrong." These moral terms arise only in the context of the expression of our needs in ordinary English, and they refer to no objective non-scientific and non-material reality. Moral problems, moral dilemmas, come about as a result of the clash of human desires and needs, and are therefore only resoluble in terms of the management of human capabilities for achieving the satisfaction of such wants. Naturalists are therefore claiming that moral systems, bodies of propositions about moral concepts, actions, consequences, motives, and so forth, are ultimately explicable in terms of the physico-chemical interactions characteristic of the human organism. The same is true of theology. It is clear that materialism and naturalism reject the belief that there is a non-material, non-natural God, and argue that the belief in such a being is explicable in terms of anthropology, sociology, etc., which are in turn reducible to explanations in terms of physics and chemistry.

Some naturalists would probably reject the assertion that natural sciences must be reducible to physics and chemistry if their thesis is to be supportable. At the least, however, they would have to admit that explanation in natural science must be *consistent* with explanation in physics and chemistry, that is, that no law of the natural sciences contradicts any law of the physical sciences; and to make *this* assertion is sufficient, when it is conjoined with the principles of materialism, to make it incumbent upon them to explain why reducibility is *not* a requirement of naturalism. It seems that to hold the naturalistic thesis is to hold the reducibility thesis for all sciences.

The Problem of Reducibility

What then is a precise statement of the problem of reducibility? To discover this, let us turn again to Ernest Nagel. In an article entitled "Emergence vs Reductionism"[3] Nagel attempted to state the conditions which would have to be satisfied if biology is to be reduced to physics and chemistry. His outline is related to the thesis, which we have studied earlier, that teleological explanation is not essential in biology. The absence of design or conscious plan in the universe is, of course, a naturalistic claim. Here, however, we are not so much interested in the connection between the two sets or arguments, nor in whether biology specifically is reducible to physics and chemistry. We are interested in the more general claim that if naturalism is true, then the explanations of all phenomena are statable in physico-chemical terms. Nagel's schema will enable us to understand the problem more clearly with the stipulation that whatever explanation of whatever subject we are considering be formulated as a theory.

Let S_1 and S_2 be two sciences, such that S_2 is supposedly reducible to S_1. We want to know what conditions would have to be met in order that this be accomplished. The first condition is this: all terms which occur in the laws and the statements of S_2 must be either explicitly definable with the help of the vocabulary used in S_1, or we must have well-established empirical (scientific) laws available, such that they enable us to state the sufficient conditions for applying the laws and statements of S_2 exclusively in terms of expressions found in the explanatory

---

[3] Ernest Nagel, "Emergence versus Reductionism," in *Philosophic Problems*, Maurice Mandelbaum, Francis W. Gramlick and Alan Ross Anderson, eds. (New York: The Macmillan Co., 1957), pp. 249–61.

principles of S_1. Nagel calls this first condition the condition of "definability." The second condition is the condition of "derivability." As you might expect, this condition requires that the statements of S_2 must be such that they may be logically inferred from some set of statements of S_1.

As Nagel notes, the fulfillment of the first does not imply that of the second. Even for biology, physics, and chemistry, no one yet has been able to fulfill the two conditions. This, of course, does not show that it is not possible to do so, and no theoretical objection, no logical hurdle, has been discovered which would indicate that it is impossible to perform the reduction in principle. It has proven possible to fulfill the condition of definability now and then, but often the second condition proves to be the stumbling block. In the case of biological organisms, one of the reasons the second condition is not fulfilled is, in the view of some biologists, the fact that the behavior of an organism is not simply a function of the sum of its parts, that we cannot treat living things as merely sums of parts, as we can often do in the case of inanimate objects. We saw this same sort of objection in the case of teleological versus non-teleological explanation. But here we can expand the objection to include all those actions and beliefs of humans comprised by moral philosophy, politics, and so forth. Now Nagel thinks that at least a part of the difficulty rests with the concept of a "sum." He thinks that as the biologist uses it, it means that the behavior of the organism is not the sum of the behavior of its parts. He wants to show that if this is what they mean by "sum," then we cannot answer the question of whether or not the behavior of the whole is a sum of that of the parts unless we relate the body to some body of theory in terms of which it is purportedly explained. Exactly how Nagel sets out to prove this claim is not of central importance to us now, but what is important is his conclusion. It is that although some given whole may not be a sum of its parts relative to one body of theory, it may be relative to another. Hence, we cannot claim that some body's behavior is or is not analyzable simply as the sum of the behavior of its parts unless and until we can specify the body of theory relative to which the body, and others like it, is to be considered. If, therefore, a biologist denies that some organic body's behavior is explicable according to the "sum" concept, this may mean nothing more than that the body of theory relative to which its behavior would be so explicable is not yet known. But it would not mean that the behavior of the body was *in principle* not explicable according to the "sum" concept.

Generalizing, the same will be true, if Nagel is correct, of human behavior, including in "behavior" the expression of man's ideals, his social intercourse, and so forth.

Now the materialist-naturalists have not made a very strong case for themselves here. They have not yet defined the very concepts with which they work, such as "matter" itself, with sufficient precision; they have not solved the problems involving the distinction between appearance and reality; and the best they can say about the reducibility thesis is that no objection in principle has been found against it. But although this is all true, it is not quite fair to the materialists when we consider the welfare of the theories against which it competes. Those who would argue that God exists have not been able to support their claims with adequate proofs, and those who wish to argue the non-reducibility of mental experience to physical terms have had to depend upon the individual's unique experience of his own immediate acquaintance with his willings, understandings, and so forth, because by definition these cannot be the objects of public, and hence not of scientific investigation. Furthermore, of all man's endeavors science has been more fruitful, and therefore given us more reason to expect future results, than any other area. Some efforts at the quantitative explanation of qualitative phenomena have been successful, while others have not. The question remains whether the reason for the lack of success in some cases is simply complexity which our scientific conceptual schemas have not yet mastered, or something else.

Three Objections to Naturalism

Let us consider for a moment three objections to naturalism which assume that much more than mere complexity prevents reductionism from being true. The first of these argues that naturalists and materialists beg the question in their own favor. They do this, the objection goes, by ruling out any concept of evidence that does not meet the criteria for *scientific* evidence. This means that all personal experiences are forbidden as evidence unless they are publicly knowable, for example. In short, the naturalists do not show that, for instance, a theory which purports to prove that God exists is mistaken, and *then* reject it; they reject it because even prior to examining the theory, they claim to know that it is not acceptable because it does not use acceptable methods and evidence of proof, the latter being naturalistic methods and evidence. To this accusation the naturalist replies that he is first of all only interested in theories which purport to give us information and explanations about the natural world. Thus, any theory which purports to do this must have some connection with nature, that is, with the empirically observable. Otherwise the theory would be irrelevant to what it purports to explain. *Some* empirical statements must be implied by the theory, or it will explain nothing about the natural world. But what empirical statements

are implied by any argument for the existence of God? Even the cosmo-
logical argument, the argument from the necessity for a first cause, posits
God as a radically different *sort* of cause than those found in the natural
world, and even if God does exist, that alone allows us to make no predictions and to explain no events in the natural world. It is not, therefore, that the naturalist argues that claims about the spiritual or the
supernatural are false, but rather that they are *irrelevant* for the purposes
of natural explanation.

To this it is sometimes replied that the naturalist himself accepts
principles that are not empirically provable, such as the uniformity of
nature principle, the claim that all knowledge comes from experience,
and so forth. But the naturalist replies that these principles are not
merely knowledge claims, but are rules or statements of procedure which
define what science is. The naturalist does not deny that there are many
kinds of experience which do not result in what he calls knowledge, and
he makes no pretext that such experiences are a part of science. But if
you *do* wish to make scientific knowledge claims, then you must "play
the game," as it were, and playing the game involves accepting the definitions of evidence and knowledge which the naturalist accepts.

The next objection is that in fact, it *can* be shown that there is an
objection in principle to the reductive thesis, contrary to what the naturalists would have us believe. If the naturalist is right, then presumably
such events as the expression of our emotions are explicable in terms of
physico-chemical events, without remainder. If, for example, an agent
is happy, then his happiness is explicable in terms of certain brain states,
nerve reactions, and chemical changes. Call the agent "S." If the naturalist is correct, then statements about S in a state of happiness, such as
"S is happy," should be logically equivalent to statements about S's brain
states, nervous reactions, and chemical changes taking place within him,
or to these statements plus a set of descriptions of his behavior. If this
is true, then it cannot be the case that the statement "S is happy" is true,
while the set of other statements is false, or vice versa. Moreover, not
only must there be this logical equivalence, but there must also be no
difference in *meaning* in the two statements or sets of statements. The
naturalist would probably not want to hold the position that certain
behavior statements must always be true if "S is happy" is to be true,
because S might carefully conceal his happiness, or perhaps even act
as though he were angry rather than happy, for whatever reasons. But
the naturalist *would* have to hold that S's happiness was identical to the
physical and chemical changes going on within S if he is to be consistent.
Notice that he cannot rest with the assertion that the physico-chemical
changes are simply necessary conditions for S's happiness; they must be
both necessary and *sufficient*, and the descriptions of these changes must

be identical logically and in meaning with "S is happy." The opponents of the naturalist now say that in fact a simple examination of the two sets of statements will suffice to show that at least they are not equivalent in meaning, and at most are not logically equivalent either. Ask S whether, when he says "I am happy," he means that a given amount of adrenalin is present in his system, that certain changes take place in his nerve synapses, and so forth. He will deny that this is what he means. These may be in part the *causes* of his happiness, but causes and effects are not identical. Now if this is true, then it is not the case that statements about S's happiness imply statements about brain states, etc. But, if the two sets of statements *were* equivalent logically and in meaning, then this could not be, for a relation of mutual entailment would hold between them. Hence, the critics argue, there *is* an objection in principle to the reductionist thesis, and this restriction may prevent fulfillment of the condition of definability, let alone the condition of derivability.

This objection is related to a final one which has been mentioned before in other connections. It is that our private immediate awareness of our mental states is such that we know those states without having to consult any of the evidence which the naturalist requires as verification for our being in them. We may know nothing about the physiological procesess which accompany our states of happiness, but we can still know that we are happy. Yet, if the naturalist is right, we should know the one when we know the other. Since we need not, the naturalist is wrong.

For the analysis of publicly observable behavior, naturalism or at least behaviorism may indeed be adequate. But if it is true, as has been consistently urged throughout this book, that the world of our non-public, private experiences provides us with a kind of knowledge which is not verifiable even in principle, and does not stand in need of verification, then naturalism does not account for all possible kinds of knowledge. This does not mean that there is some kind of substance in addition to matter; it does not entail the positing of occult causes or ghosts in machines. But it does mean that we have at least two different kinds of knowledge, one not reducible to the other, and that a complete explanation of the human experience and the human being must include both.

PRAGMATISM

Pragmatism and some of its theses about meaning and truth have been mentioned before in this book. But the theory has not been discussed in detail, and since it is the most influential native American philosophy it seems appropriate to investigate it at greater length. For the most part, we shall examine the view of pragmatism which William James espoused, rather than the theory of Charles Peirce, the original founder of the school.

Solving Disputes Pragmatically

There are a number of different ways to consider pragmatism, and one of the most basic is to study it as a *method* for resolving disputes. James in fact characterized this method by a story involving a dispute. Several friends of James were on a hunting party in the mountains, and were sitting around the fire in the evening after supper. James was out taking a walk. A discussion began about a man standing facing a tree, with a squirrel on the opposite side of the tree. The man tries to catch sight of the squirrel by running around the tree, but he never succeeds because the squirrel always keeps the tree exactly between himself and the man. The question is, does the man go around the squirrel or not? When James came in from his walk, he was called upon to settle the issue. He said that if by "going around" is meant that the man passes from the north of the squirrel to the east, then to the south, the west, and finally to the north again, then the man does go around the squirrel. But if "going around" means that the man is first of all in front of the squirrel, then on his left side, then behind his back, then on the right side and finally comes to face him again, then the man does not go around the squirrel because they are always belly to belly, so to speak. James records that his solution was not very well received by the group as a whole, but he thought that it illustrated the method of pragmatism by illustrating each of the concepts involved in the problem by tracing out their consequences, or, more precisely, their *practical* consequences. If the solution to some problem does not make any difference which would not be present if some other solution to it were adopted, then any dispute over which of the solutions we adopt is silly. Practically speaking, that is, so far as their effects are concerned, the solutions mean exactly the same thing. The other side of the coin, of course, is that if a dispute is serious, then we ought to be able to show that whichever of the possible solutions we adopt does make a practical difference. This is a statement of the first and most important principle of pragmatism when viewed as a method, or a theory about method: the meaning or significance of anything consists in the practical effects or results which it produces. If there are none, then it is meaningless and not worthy of dispute. If we are talking about statements, then two statements with the same effect have the same meaning, and if they have no effect, that is, if accepting them makes no practical difference in our lives, then they have no meaning. This is true of single statements as well, that is, if any given statement is such that whether we accept it or reject it, the effect is the same, then the statement and its denial have the same meaning, and if both of these have *no* effect, then both are meaningless. The theory does not apply merely to statements. The same results hold of actions and other events as well. Our concept of the thing, be it statement, action, person, or event, is precisely our concept of its effects upon us, and will therefore include our reactions to it, our expectations about it, and so forth. Charles Peirce, not William James, was the originator of this concept. But James and John Dewey became the leading advocates of the principle and carried it into many spheres outside the realm of philosophy. It is an exceedingly important principle. According to pragmatism, if the practical effect in your life of believing in God is no different from what your life would be if you did not believe in God, then both theism and atheism are meaningless for you. If materialism and idealism have no practical effects in the ways we reason about the world, then they are meaningless too, and so on for any theory.

Pragmatism as an Empirical Theory

By nature pragmatism is an empirical theory. Abstract claims, trivial truths, purely verbal or semantic solutions to problems, absolutely fixed and unchanging "truths"—all of these are abhorrent to it. James is opposed to dogmatism of all varieties because he believes that truth and meaning are functions of effects, which constantly change. He believes that there is more than one way to view the universe and its components, and perhaps because of this the pragmatists do not really argue for the truth of any special theory about reality. They merely advocate a certain method for investigating the significance of things, by examining their practical effects in the empirical world.

If we adopt the pragmatic method of searching for truth, some other more traditional methods become closed to us. History teaches us that man has searched for a central principle or truth which would of itself suffice to reveal the mysteries of the universe to him. There have been many different names for this principle, among them "god," "matter," "reason," the "Absolute," "energy," and so on. When Descartes and Newton discovered matter, motion, and the relations between the two, they thought they had at last solved the riddles of the physical universe; and Aristotle was convinced before them that he had found the truth in his Prime Mover. Bertrand Russell breathed more easily when he convinced himself and many others that guilt based upon the fear of a non-existent hereafter is not worth the candle. The theologian sleeps soundly and piously when he believes he has shown that the existence of evil is justified in an all-wise but inscrutable God. But by themselves none of these beliefs will stand alone, without tracing out their practical effects. When we do this, we find that none of these answers are sufficient to solve even one problem permanently, because problems are always changing, new ones arising, old ones recurring again. That old time religion is *not* good enough for us, because grandfather did not have to cope with the atomic age, germ warfare, the neutron ray, and the laser. Witch doctors will *not* do, because cancer is more sophisticated than that. Telescopes and Ptolemy do not mix, even though Ptolemy did very well for quite some time. Theories must be revised in the light of our increasing awareness of new data, and the penalty for not doing so is failure to get along in a world of new knowledge. Theories are merely *instruments* for the discovery and formulation of *particular* truths and as new truths come into being, old ones must be revamped or discarded. There is no single principle which explains everything and the universe is pluralistic.

Not only does pragmatism talk about a method for discerning truth, but also about the nature of truth itself. If method is an instrument for discovering truth, and if the theories we use according to the method constantly change as the facts and our awareness of them do, then truth cannot be a stable, absolute concept. It must be *relative*—to the theories we impose upon fact, to other truths we already accept, to our expectations about the future, to ourselves. When men first discovered the concept of a law-governed universe, they were stunned with the magnificence of their new truth. They thought they now had "the" secret, they believed they had seen the blueprint of the Real, the eternal truths in the mind of God as exemplified in our world. But as we have progressed, as we have to modify our older theories in the light of new discoveries, men have come to see that their natural laws are but approximations, seeing the world from special points of view. It will not do to say that there really is a divine plan, but that we haven't yet found it all, for the unknown can have no practical bearing upon our lives, and is hence meaningless. The truth of our ideas is their power to "work," to bridge the old and the new, to satisfy our thirst for continuity and regularity, yet enable us to reach new knowledge. It is that property of an idea which allows us to fit it in with older ideas that we accept, but at the same time gives us new abilities to get around in our world better than we did before. It thereby increases our satisfaction, and truth is indeed a normative concept for the pragmatist rather than a descriptive one. Truth which is purely objective, having no relations to our beliefs about the past and future, giving no satisfaction and having no practical effects for us, now, is nonsense.

At this point then we may say three things about pragmatism:

1. It is a method which looks for the meaning of any object of knowledge in its practical effects here and now upon the knower.

2. It finds the practical effects in the empirical world and not in abstractions, self-evident principles, and dogmatism.
3. It holds that truth is relative to our past beliefs, the satisfaction we derive from it, and our increased ability to deal with our surroundings.

Truth is not a relation of correspondence between ideas and the world, but a relation between our minds and the empirical world in which our particular thoughts play their parts just like any other factor in the universe.

It is perhaps important to note that although pragmatism is opposed to abstractions and dogmatism, this does not necessarily make it incompatible with religion, nor biased in favor of materialism. It is indeed opposed to those religions whose concept of God is of a being totally removed from the possibility of practical effects in our lives, and it is opposed to dogmatic religions which argue that truth cannot change, and that they have the truth. But if the beliefs of some religion make a practical difference in our lives, if they enable us to get along with our world better, then to that extent they will be true. And if they cohere with bodies of other acknowledged truths, then they will be even more true.

Pragmatic Truth

It is obvious from all of this that for the pragmatists, truth is a matter of *degree*, and this means that a proposition is not either true or false but not both for the pragmatist, but true at one time, false at another, and at any time more or less true than at other times. Does this mean that there are no statements which are fundamentally opposed, such that one of them must be false? No, because even if truth is a matter of degree, there are occasions on which one statement, even if only partially true, or true to a certain degree, may still stand in opposition to one which is wholly false, and we can decide which of them is false by once again examining their practical effects, as well as by seeing whether the statement in question contradicts other statements which are accepted as true.

In fact, even very abstract statements give comfort to people, enable some of us to get along better than we otherwise might, and to this extent James admits that they have a truth-value too. The major point is that truth is a normative concept for the pragmatists; insofar as the statement or belief has a beneficial effect upon our lives, a "pro" value (as P. H. Nowell-Smith might say), then it is true, and insofar as the opposite is the case, then it is false. A statement is true when it is profitable to our lives, false when not, and which it is, is a matter for empirical investigation. Truth is a species or category of good, not something totally distinct from it. It is goodness as practical value of the positive rather than negative sort. Truth-judgments are therefore in the last analysis value judgments, and to say that X is better than Y is to say that it is truer, where X and Y here are statements. To our original list of three truths about pragmatism, we may therefore now add two more:

4. Truth is a matter of degree.
5. Judgments of truth are judgments of value, where "value" of the positive sort is something that profits our lives.

And since these five principles imply, when taken with the pragmatic analysis of the empirical world, the obvious fact that value and hence judgments of truth change, we may add a sixth pragmatic claim:

6. Since values change, and judgments of truth are judgments of value, then what is false may *become* true, and conversely.

A remark about the pragmatist's use of definition, James's in particular, is pertinent here. As Berkeley held that "to be" means "to be perceived," and as the naturalist holds that to be a fact is to be a possible object of scientific investigation, so James is holding that to be meaningful *is* to have practical effects. Nothing is true that is not meaningful, so to be true means to have some among a range of possible practical effects.

Some short remarks also ought to be made about the pragmatic conception of verification, because this is closely tied to the concepts of truth and meaning for them. Verification for James is a process, a process by which we are led from truths which we already accept to new ones. Truth, as you know, is in pragmatic eyes closely related to the concept of an instrument for action; that is, it is something which is sought for practical reasons or effects, and which in its turn is valuable just because of those practical effects. This is the explanation of James's assertion that "It is useful because it is true" and "It is true because it is useful" have the same meaning. To be useful, in the sense of having practical effects, is to be true, and conversely. To discover that something is useful is at once to verify it, because its usefulness is its truth.

Pragmatism was in its heyday an immensely attractive theory because it seemed to account for a great deal of historical fact, especially in science, and because it had a great influence in other areas, especially the law. Moreover, it obviously fit, in its more popular versions, into the "rule of thumb" experimental attitude of an America in which almost everything had yet to be tried. The wave theory of light was true, (useful) until the Wilson Cloud Chamber experiments, at which time it became false, (less useful) because the particle theory was now more fruitful, that is, it enabled us to make predictions which had greater practical effects upon our lives. When Einstein predicted that light waves would be attracted by the gravitational field of the moon, the general theory of relativity was not true; it *became* true, truth happened to it, when the light waves were observed to bend, when the practical effects of the theory were made manifest in our lives. This does not deny our older ways of thinking; indeed, James called pragmatism a "new name for some old ways of thinking." The influence of pragmatism was felt in the law as well as in science. Oliver Wendell Holmes, a close friend of James, was a member of the Supreme Court during the days of the Great Depression. The principal test which he applied in deciding whether a law was true to the constitution was the pragmatic test of whether it would lead to a good life for the people in the society which it affected. While other judges were arguing about the natural legal law theory and about absolute principles, Holmes was trying to find out whether a law would have practical effects such that men would be happier. It is worth noting that most of the majority opinions against which Holmes dissented have since been overturned, and most of his dissents have now become law. Of most influence was his conviction, again purely pragmatic, that what makes men happy at one period may not be the same as it is at another period. Law becomes pragmatically true or false according to the changes in what enables men to deal with their environment most effectively.

Criticisms of Pragmatism

As with all of the theories which we have considered, there are defects with pragmatism too. The first of these concerns the relation between truth and usefulness. To be consistent with the rest of his theory, James ought to say that "true" and "useful" are synonyms. But if he does this, then to say that something is true because it is useful, or vice versa, is to say something completely trivial, namely that something is true because it is true, and useful because it is useful. The pragmatists surely wish to say much more than this. They want to teach us more than the use of a new word. Moreover, if they are right, how can we distinguish between the true and the false? To be true *or* false a statement must have practical effects. But there are not true effects and false effects, and even if there were, this would not of itself tell us how to distinguish between them. How then are we to tell which effects make a proposition or statement true, and which ones make it false? James tells us that to be true, the effects must have value for our lives, but obviously we must know which effects have this kind of positive value *before* we know that the statement is true, if we are to know that it is true. This, however, is impossible for him, because to say that the sentence is true and to say that it has beneficial effects (is useful) are one and the same, and it makes no sense to say that in order to know that the statement is true, we must know it is true before we know it is true! He offers a second criterion for true statements, namely that they cohere with other statements accepted as true. But this does not help his case because just the same problem arises with the earlier statements and beliefs. Moreover, it is logically possible for everyone in the world to hold contradictory beliefs and still be quite satisfied. Yet surely it is strange to say that contradictory beliefs are true. The penalty for saying this is quite severe. Ultimately it results in the destruction of the laws of logic, which in turn destroys the possibility of communicating with each other. In terms of pragmatic "practical effect" language, we might state the problem this way: If you hold p to be true, and I hold it to be false, one of us is presumably wrong, and one of us right, assuming that we are not both wrong. But if James is correct, we may be both right at the same time, or both wrong, even if we mean exactly the same thing by p. If this is true, then given James's own criteria the distinction between truth and falsity itself becomes meaningless, because it has no practical effect. And if the distinction has no practical effect, then the laws of logic become meaningless and unimportant because they depend in part upon the concepts of truth and falsity.

James realized part of this difficulty, and he sometimes spoke of the concept of truth as not just being concerned with the concept of how one moment of experience may lead into another, but also, perhaps even primarily, with the concept of that other moment's *worth*. But this will not help, for it merely transfers the difficulties just mentioned to the concept of "worth." Now, instead of asking how we distinguish between truth and falsity, we ask how one distinguishes between the worthwhile and the not worthwhile. If the pragmatist's answer is that what is worthwhile is what enables me to get along and so forth, then since what enables me to get along is perhaps different from what enables you to do so, we are back where we started.

There is also a moral dilemma for pragmatism. What is true becomes what is successful for them, and the successful is defined in terms of individual satisfactions. But we often want to say that action which serves some peoples' desires and therefore satisfactions is wrong. And successful propaganda is not necessarily the truth.

There *is* a way to save much of what is good in pragmatism. If we take the "practical effects" of two propositions as a *test* or a *criterion* for distinguishing which of them is true and add coherence with other beliefs which have survived the test, then we have a beginning. We shall also have to drop the requirement that truth is *identified* with the practical effects, and claim instead that truth is something that is progressively *discovered*. Our beliefs in the truth of given propositions at any given time may be wholly mistaken, wholly correct, or partially correct or mistaken. Which of these states our beliefs are in will again be determined by the "practical effects" test, which at the very least will enable us to reject some of them as wholly false, if they also do not meet the coherence test. "Practical effects" now come to include, as you can see from a moment's consideration, all of the external criteria, and "coherence" may now include all of the formal criteria discussed in Part One of this book.   Many of the other modes of evaluation which we have examined will be included in the "practical effects" when they are used to evaluate single statements. We shall also have to make certain metaphysical assumptions, such as the uniformity-of-nature principle (kinds of practical effects must be expectable if theories are to be constructed). What we shall be able to retain is the reasonable pragmatic admission that at any given time, beliefs differ widely, and even false beliefs have worthwhile effects upon occasion, at least until supplanted with more effective ones. But in addition, we can now explain this without having to assume that contradictory beliefs are both true or both false, because now truth is independent of the stage of discovery in which minds happen to stand at given moments in time. Furthermore, we retain the pragmatic insight that the discovery of truth proceeds through an evaluation of the effects that our beliefs have upon our lives in their relations to their environment, being modified as those relations change, and in the light of new factual information which we did not have before.

Finally, we must separate the theories of meaning and the theories of truth which are implicit in pragmatism. Statements may be meaningful, but false. They may also be meaningful, false, and have practical effects in our lives. The practical effects are not of themselves sufficient to determine the truth or falsity of a belief, but the pragmatists were on the right track when they argued that these effects *are* sufficient for determining whether or not a proposition is meaningful. It may even be that they were largely correct when they argued that not only *whether* the proposition was meaningful could be determined, but also its fairly precise *particular* meaning. Take the case of the squirrel on the tree with the man on the opposite side. To the mariner vitally interested in the gyroscope which enables him to navigate his ship, which of the senses of "go around" we use is of the utmost importance, precisely because of the practical effects of his beliefs about this instrument. And the meaning of the statement he believes about the instrument is readily apparent in his actions based upon them. On the other hand, the two statements "The Absolute is blue" and "The Absolute is not blue" have no practical effects in the lives of anyone, and are meaningless.

We cannot here go into a full-blown defense and exposition of this neo-pragmatic theory. Let it suffice to say that with other modifications similar to these, pragmatism enables us to explain the varying truth-claims which men make in the sciences, their moral philosophies, indeed in their daily lives, while many other theories do not. It provides us with a basis for a methodology in science, and a means for determining meaningfulness. It does not solve the problem of the nature of truth, but we have seen that this complex set of issues has not been solved by any other theory as yet either. It enables us to reject dogmatism while retaining sufficient flexibility to allow divergent religious beliefs a place in the schemes of man. It does not force us into the paradoxes of determinism and materialism, but in the end, it will have to face the issue between nominalism and realism because it must assume, if it is to be modified successfully, that nature is uniform. On balance, it is one of the more satisfactory theories we have examined.

EXERCISES

1. Define Realism.
2. Formulate the argument for the thesis that universals must have an independent existence or subsistence.
3. Why, for Aristotle, is a universal not an individual?
4. Why does Aristotle think that universals must exist only in particular things?
5. Apply the "third man" argument to a particular case of an exhibited universal, other than the case of man.
6. State the nominalistic argument against the existence of universals in deductive form, and test your argument for validity.
7. If Ockham is correct, then sign relationships between things and conventional signs must all be three-termed relations. Why is this so?
8. Do you think that Ockham is correct when he says that universals do not exist? Why or why not?
9. Why has the nominalist not solved the problem of resemblance, even if he is correct about the non-existence of universals?
10. What sort of solution would you propose to the problem of resemblance? Defend your theory.
11. Define "idealism."
12. Do idealists deny that physical objects exist? Why or why not?
13. What are the components of knowledge according to Berkeley? Is he correct? If not, what are the other components of our knowledge which he does not give?
14. Why does Berkeley call his theory "immaterialism"? Reread the part of Chapter 6 entitled "John Locke and the Theory of Ideas," and then relate Berkeley's arguments against the existence of material substance to his idealism or immaterialism.

15. State Berkeley's argument for idealism clearly and carefully, in such a way that you can apply Russell's criticism about the two meanings of "knowledge" to it. What kind of fallacy has Berkeley committed here?

16. Is Berkeley a solipsist? Why or why not?

17. What are the theses of materialism? Of naturalism?

18. Explain and evaluate the reductionistic thesis.

19. Discuss the conditions of definability and derivability in the context of the reductionalistic thesis, and relate this discussion to Nagel's discussion of teleological and non-teleological explanation in Chapter 10.

20. Evaluate two of the criticisms of naturalism which are offered in the text, using the criteria established throughout the book. When the naturalists argue that our moral experience is explicable in terms of physical science, do they run the risk of committing the factualistic fallacy? Why or why not?

21. What are the six principles of pragmatism? Which ones are affected by the suggested revisions of the theory at the end of the chapter? How are they affected?

22. Discuss the relationships existing among the pragmatic conceptions of meaning, truth, and value, and evaluate them.

23. Give an example not used in the text which illustrates (a) two different statements whose practical effects do not differ, (b) two different statements whose practical effects do differ, (c) two different statements with no practical effects. What are the differences in the truth-values of (a), (b), and (c)?

24. Are there any statements which are meaningful but false for James? What kind of value is "false" for the pragmatists?

25. Why is pragmatism an empirical theory, whether considered as a method, or a theory about meaning and truth?

26. Why is pragmatism anti-dogmatic? Consider a set of statements or a theory accepted by some group as dogma, and criticize it using the methods of pragmatism.

27. What does James mean when he says that in addition to practical effects, the coherence of statements with those already accepted as true is important? Does he mean by "coherence" what the coherence theory of truth means? Why or why not?

28. Evaluate two of the criticisms offered of pragmatism, using the evaluative mechanisms you now know.

29. Compare the pragmatic theory of truth with one other theory of truth, and evaluate the theories using the external criteria.

30. With the suggested revisions of the theory, the external criteria come to be included in the "practical effects" of the pragmatic method. How may we interpret the external criteria as "practical effects"?

Conclusion

It is not customary for textbooks to have conclusions, because, for the most part, they do not approach their content with a systematic method nor do they have consistent themes. In this book, an attempt has been made to do these things. It is the purpose of these brief concluding remarks to mention some of these common themes and relate them to the method which has been used.

The first of the consistent themes is that, insofar as philosophy is a discipline, its claims must be formulable as arguments and theories. In every case we have examined, an attempt has been made to emphasize the formal structure of the arguments, implicitly or explicitly; and in the exercises the student has been encouraged to concentrate upon this aspect of the subject matter. There are schools of thought which are called "philosophy" which are not amenable to this sort of treatment. When the man in the street is asked what his philosophy is, and replies that the fewer things a man depends upon the easier life is, he is approaching the stage of justification by argument. He is not yet a philosopher, but what he has said contains within it the premises and conclusions that training would make explicit. He believes that freedom from desire is good, that dependence upon superfluous things impinges upon this, and that therefore the less of the latter the more of the former. He probably could not, without extensive training, defend this view, though there are exceptions to every rule. Until he reaches this latter stage, what he says can no more be called "philosophy" than can the grandmother's exhortations to use mustard plasters for colds, though she does not know why, be called "medicine."

Philosophy is therefore the formulation and criticism of theories, concerning, among other things, the subject matters we have discussed. The defense requires particular tools, many of which were examined in the first part of the book. Doing philosophy well presupposes a mastery of the tools, just as a man is a good mechanic only when he knows how to use his tools for repair and construction. He is not a good mechanic if he simply knows the parts of the car, nor is a man a good philosopher if he simply knows the arguments in various theories. Much of the work of philosophy is destructive, because many of the arguments have used the tools of the trade incorrectly or made mistakes which the correct use of the tools makes clear. But knowing that an argument is not a good one is just as much an advance in knowledge as knowing that it is. Many thinkers who criticize some theory are in turn castigated because they have nothing with which to replace it. This is a bad argument, because knowing that something is false does not imply that you know some replacement that is true. Even though most of the arguments and theories we have analyzed have not stood the tests given them perfectly, we may still count *this* knowledge as an advance in learning.

Some arguments however have come out fairly undamaged. One of these is the thesis that there are at least two kinds of knowledge, private and public, and that the one is not reducible to the other. Certain other arguments have been founded upon this basic one, and one of these was the theory that private events and the knowledge of them are irrelevant to the determination of the truth of knowledge claims made about public events. Partly because of the viability of this distinction, but also for other reasons, it was argued that determinism is a theory about the world of public knowledge that is not true when applied to the world of mental events as well. For similar reasons, it was argued that teleological explanations do have a place in our sciences, at least insofar as they are concerned with the explanation of human behavior of certain kinds, and it was suggested that reports of feelings and other mental events should be accepted as evidence, in a wider concept of what is empirical. Once again on the same basis, materialism and naturalism were rejected as insufficient for the explanation of human experience.

The arguments against mental determinism and in favor of the "two kinds of knowledge" view were also brought to bear against Marx's theory of economic and political determinism as well as against Hobbes's version of the commonwealth and its explanation. Related though different premises were used in sections of the discussion of moral and legal law in the attempt to show that the expressionist theory of art is unsound and in the arguments against the natural moral law theory. The distinction between the two worlds and the modes in which they are known was also evident in the discussion entitled "Mental Causation and the Category-Mistake," and one of the most famous attempts to relate mind and the physical world of knowledge was discussed in our examination of Kant's Copernican revolution. The latter was of course influenced by Berkeley as well as Hume. Berkeley's philosophy, still another attempt to relate mind and body and at the same time, distinguish between them, was discussed and the reasons for its failure analyzed.

These facts are mentioned for two reasons. The first is to make obvious the multiple relevance of given themes in philosophy throughout the various branches of the subject. In metaphysics, philosophy of science, moral and political philosophy, aesthetics and the philosophy of religion, and many more areas, this single problem of the relation between mind and body and the explanation of the two different entities comes to bear. It is still not solved. The second reason this should be noticed is that in spite of all the analysis to the contrary, the basic human conviction that there *is* some kind of distinction between the mental and the physical persists, not just in ordinary life, but in philosophy. The central job of philosophers is to render common sense facts and ordinary beliefs coherent, to provide explanations for them and to reject false analyses of them. This should teach us that simple convictions are exceedingly difficult to understand when examined closely. Our beliefs in the uniformity of nature, our power to cause changes in the physical world, our freedom of will—all are commonplace examples. But we *have* made progress, because we have discovered that some explanations will *not* do. We know now, in at least some cases, what they did not know in ancient days, namely, what criteria the theories which explain these beliefs must meet. The purpose of this book is to help the student to know when a theory meets some of these criteria and when it does not.

One other factor is required in addition to the kind of technical evaluation we have been studying. It is intellectual objectivity and honesty. Mastery of the tools of evaluation will do little good if you permit your feelings to interfere with your application of them. It is difficult to give up beliefs with which you have been reared, but sometimes it is necessary if one is to be rational and honest. In the last analysis, this is a moral commitment which only the individual can make, for it cannot be forced upon anybody.

Selected Bibliography

Chapter 1

Any good introductory logic text will serve as supportive reading for this first chapter. Two especially good ones are:

COPI, IRVING. *Introduction to Logic.* New York: Macmillan, 1961.

SEARLES, H. L. *Logic and Scientific Methods.* New York: The Ronald Press Co., 1968.

The section on "Logic" in *Encyclopedia of Philosophy,* volume 4, pp. 504–71, is also excellent, though quite advanced. In addition:

BECK, L. W. "Remarks on the Distinction Between Analytic and Synthetic." *Philosophy and Phenomenological Research* 9, no. 4 (1949): 720–26.

BLACK, MAX. *Critical Thinking.* Englewood Cliffs, N.J.: Prentice-Hall, Inc., 1952.

HAMLYN, D. W. "Analytic Truths." *Mind* 65 (1956): 359–67.

KANT, IMMANUEL. *Immanuel Kant's Critique of Pure Reason.* Translated by N. K. Smith. London: Macmillan, 1953.

PUTNAM, HILLARY. "The Analytic and the Synthetic." *Minnesota Studies in the Philosophy of Science* 3, no. 5 (1962): 358–97.

SALMON, WESLEY. *Logic.* Englewood Cliffs, N.J.: Prentice-Hall, Inc., 1963.

Chapter 2

The sections dealing with meaning and truth in the *Encyclopedia of Philosophy* are recommended, as well as the treatment of the informal fallacies in the logic texts selected for readings in the first chapter. In addition, the following might be consulted:

ALSTON, W. P. *Philosophy of Language.* Englewood Cliffs, N.J.: Prentice-Hall, Inc., 1964.

AUSTIN, JOHN. *How to Do Things with Words.* Cambridge, Mass.: Harvard University Press, 1962.

AUSTIN, JOHN, and STRAWSON, PETER. "Truth." *Proceedings of the Aristotelian Society,* supplementary vol. 24, no. 3 (1950): 111–28 & 129–56.

BERKELEY, GEORGE. *Alciphron or the Minute Philosopher.* London: Thomas Nelson & Sons, Ltd., 1948.

BUCHLER, JUSTIS, ed. *The Philosophy of Peirce.* New York: Harcourt Brace Jovanovich, 1940.

CHAPPELL, V. C., ed. *Ordinary Language: Essays in Philosophical Method.* Englewood Cliffs, N.J.: Prentice-Hall, Inc., 1964.

FEIGLE, HERBERT, and SELLARS, WILFRID, eds. *Readings in Philosophical Analysis.* New York: Appleton-Century-Crofts, Inc., 1949.

FRANKENA, W. K. "The Naturalistic Fallacy." *Mind* 48, no. 4 (1939): 464–77.

HINSHAW, V. G. "The Pragmatic Theory of Truth." *Philosophy of Science* 2, no. 2 (1944): 82–92.

JAMES, WILLIAM. *Pragmatism: A New Name for Some Old Ways of Thinking.* London: Longmans, Green and Co., 1907.
————. *The Meaning of Truth.* London: Longmans, Green and Co., 1914.
KINCADE, JAMES. "On the Performatory Theory of Truth." *Mind* 67, no. 3 (1958): 394–98.
LOCKE, JOHN. *An Essay Concerning Human Understanding,* Book III. Edited by J. W. Yolton. London: J. M. Dent, 1961; New York: R. P. Dutton, 1961.
MACDONALD, MARGARET, ed. *Philosophy and Analysis.* New York: Philosophical Library, 1954.
MOORE, G. E. *Some Main Problems of Philosophy.* London: Allen & Unwin, 1953.
MORRIS, CHARLES. *Signs, Language and Behavior.* Englewood Cliffs, N.J.: Prentice-Hall, Inc., 1946.
OGDEN, C. K., and RICHARDS, I. A. *The Meaning of Meaning.* New York: Harcourt Brace Jovanovich, Inc., 1938.
PLATO. *Thaetetus.* Notes by Lewis Campbell. Oxford: The University Press, 1861.
————. ————. Notes by Francis Cornford. New York: Harcourt Brace Jovanovich, 1935.
RUSSELL, BERTRAND. *An Inquiry Into Meaning and Truth.* New York: W. W. Norton and Co., 1940. *Problems of Philosophy.* London, New York, Oxford: The University Press, 1964.
RYLE, GILBERT. *The Concept of Mind.* London: Hutchison University Library, 1963.
————. "Systematically Misleading Expressions." *Proceedings of the Aristotelian Society* 32, no. 4 (1931–32): 139–70.
SKINNER, B. F. *Verbal Behavior.* New York: Appleton-Century-Crofts, Inc., 1957.
STRAWSON, P. F. "On Referring." *Mind* 59 (1950): 320–44.
URMSON, JAMES. *Philosophical Analysis: Its Development Between the Two World Wars.* Oxford: Clarendon Press, 1965.
WITTGENSTEIN, LUDWIG. *Philosophical Investigations.* Oxford, B. H. Blackwell, Ltd., 1958.

Chapter 3

An excellent summary of several positions in both mathematical and philosophical induction, plus a bibliography of recent work in the field, can be found in:

KYBURG, HENRY. "Recent Work In Inductive Logic." *American Philosophical Quarterly* 1, no. 4 (1964): 249–87.

The following works are especially recommended:

BARKER, STEPHEN. *Induction and Hypothesis.* Ithaca, N.Y.: Cornell University Press, 1957.
BECK, L. W. "The Principle of Parsimony in Empirical Science." *Journal of Philosophy* 40 (1943): 617–33.
BLACK, MAX. *Problems of Analysis.* Ithaca, N.Y.: Cornell University Press, 1954.
HUME, DAVID. *An Enquiry Concerning the Human Understanding.* Edited by L. A. Selby-Bigge. Oxford: Clarendon Press, 1936.
KEYNES, J. M. *A Treatise on Probability.* London: Macmillan & Co., 1921.
KNEALE, WILLIAM. *Probability and Induction.* Oxford: Clarendon Press, 1949.
MILL, J. S. *A System of Logic.* London: Longmans, Green, Reader & Dyer, 1875. (Especially Book III.)
NAGEL, ERNEST, ed. *John Stuart Mill's Philosophy of Scientific Method.* New York: Harcourt Brace Jovanovich, 1950.
NAGEL, ERNEST. *The Structure of Science.* New York: Harcourt Brace Jovanovich, 1961.

POPPER, SIR KARL. *The Logic of Scientific Discovery*. London: Hutchinson & Co., 1959.

REICHENBACH, HANS. *The Theory of Probability*. Berkeley: University of California Press, 1949.

RUSSELL, BERTRAND. *The Problems of Philosophy*. London: Oxford University Press, 1912. (Chapter VI.)

Chapter 4

ANSCOMBE, G. E. M. "Aristotle and the Sea Battle." *Mind* 65, no. 3 (1956): 1–15.

———. *An Introduction to Wittgenstein's Tractatus*. London: Hutchinson & Co., 1967.

AUSTIN, JOHN. *Philosophical Papers*. Oxford: Clarendon Press, 1961.

BROAD, C. D. *The Mind and Its Place in Nature*. London: K. Paul, Trench, Trufner & Co., 1925.

CAMPBELL, C. A. "Is 'Freewill' a Pseudo-Problem?" *Mind*, 60, no. 3 (1951): 441–65.

———. "In Defense of Free Will." In *Value and Obligation*, edited by R. B. Brandt. New York: Harcourt Brace Jovanovich, 1961.

DESCARTES, RENE. *Discourse on Method*. Translated by P. J. Olscamp. Indianapolis: Bobbs-Merrill Co., Inc., 1965.

———. *Meditations*. Translated by John Veitch. La Salle, Ill.: Open Court Publishing Co., 1945.

———. *Principia Philosophiae. oeuvres de Descartes*, part IV, vol. VIII–1. Edited by Charles Adams and Paul Tannery. Paris: J. Vrin, 1964.

FLEW, ANTHONY. *Body, Mind and Death*. New York: Macmillan, 1964.

———. *Essays in Conceptual Analysis*. London: Macmillan & Co., 1956.

GINET, CARL. "Can the Will Be Caused?" *Philosophical Review* 71 (1962): 49–55.

GRAUNBAUM, ADOLF. *Modern Science and Zeno's Paradoxes*. Middletown, Conn.: Wesleyan University Press, 1967.

LEHRER, KEITH. "Can We Know that We Have Free Will by Introspection?" *Journal of Philosophy* 57 (1960): 145–57.

NOWELL-SMITH, P. H. *Ethics*. London: Penguin Books, 1954.

QUINTON, A. M. "Pluralism and Monism." *Encyclopaedia Britannica* vol. 18 (1960): 88–90.

RUSSELL, BERTRAND. *Principles of Mathematics*. 2nd ed. London: Allen & Unwin, 1937.

———. *A History of Western Philosophy*. New York: Simon and Schuster, Inc., 1946.

RYLE, GILBERT. "Achilles and the Tortoise," in *Dilemmas*. London: Cambridge University Press, 1960.

———. *The Concept of Mind*. London: Hutchinson University Library, 1963.

SCHLICK, MORITZ. *Problems of Ethics*. Englewood Cliffs, N.J.: Prentice-Hall, Inc., 1929.

STRAWSON, PETER. *Individuals*. London: Methuen & Co., Inc., 1959.

TAYLOR, RICHARD. "Fatalism." *Philosophical Review* 71 (1962): 56–66; 72, 497–99.

———. *Metaphysics*. Englewood Cliffs, N.J.: Prentice-Hall, Inc., 1963.

———. "I Can." *Philosophical Review* 69, no. 3 (1960): 78–89.

WISDOM, JOHN. *Other Minds*. Oxford: B. H. Blackwell, Ltd., 1952.

Chapter 5

BURNET, JOHN. *Early Greek Philosophy*. 2nd ed. London: A. & C. Black, 1930.

BUNGE, MARIO AUGUSTO. *Causality—The Place of the Causal Principle in Modern Science*. Cambridge, Mass.: Harvard University Press, 1959.

DUCASSE, C. J. *Nature, Mind and Death.* La Salle, Ill.: Open Court Publishing Co., 1951.

———. *Truth, Knowledge and Causation.* London: Routledge and Kegan Paul, 1968.

HUME, DAVID. *Treatise of Human Nature.* London: Oxford University Press, 1941.

———. *Enquiry Concerning Human Understanding.* Oxford: Clarendon Press, 1936.

KANT, IMMANUEL. *Critique of Pure Reason.* Translated by N. Kemp Smith. New York: St. Martin's Press, 1961.

KÖRNER, STEPHEN. *Kant.* Harmondsworth, England: Penguin Books, 1955.

PAP, ARTHUR. *An Introduction to the Philosophy of Science.* New York: The Free Press of Glencoe, Inc., 1962. (Especially Part Four.)

RUSSELL, BERTRAND. "On the Notion of Cause, with Applications to the Free Will Problem." *Mysticism and Logic.* London: Allen & Unwin, 1954.

———. *The Problems of Philosophy.* London: Oxford University Press, 1912.

SCHLICK, MORITZ. "Causality in Everyday Life and in Recent Science." In *Readings in Philosophical Analysis,* edited by Feigl and Sellars. New York: Appleton-Century-Crofts, Inc., 1949.

SMITH, N. K. *The Philosophy of David Hume.* London: Macmillan & Co., 1941.

WARNOCK, G. J. "Every Event Has a Cause." *Logic and Language.* 2nd series. Oxford: B. H. Blackwell, Ltd., 1953.

Chapter 6

AARON, R. I. *John Locke.* 2nd ed. London, New York: Oxford University Press, 1937.

ALBRITTON, ROGERS. "On Wittgenstein's Use of the Term 'Criterion.'" *Journal of Philosophy* 56, no. 22 (1959): 845–67.

AUSTIN, J. L. *Philosophical Papers.* Oxford: Clarendon Press, 1961.

AYER, A. J. *Language, Truth and Logic.* London: Victor Gollancz, Ltd., 1947.

———. *Logical Positivism.* New York: The Free Press of Glencoe, Inc., 1959.

———. "The Principle of Verifiability." *Mind* 45 (1936): 199–203.

———. *The Problem of Knowledge.* London: Macmillan & Co., 1956.

BARNES, W. H. F. "Meaning and Verifiability." *Philosophy* 14 (1939): 410–21.

BROAD, C. D. "Berkeley's Denial of Material Substance." *Philosophical Review* 63 (1954): 155–81.

CHISHOLM, R. M. *Perceiving: A Philosophical Study.* Ithaca, N.Y.: Cornell University Press, 1957.

———. *Theory of Knowledge.* Englewood Cliffs, N.J.: Prentice-Hall, Inc., 1965.

CHURCH, ALONZO. "Review of A. J. Ayer's Language, Truth and Logic," 2nd ed. *Journal of Symbolic Logic* 14, no. 4 (1949): 197.

CORNMAN, J. W. "Private Languages and Private Entities." *Australasian Journal of Philosophy* 46 (1968): 117–26.

FEIGL, HERBERT, and SELLERS, WILFRID, eds. *Readings in Philosophical Analysis.* New York: Appleton-Century-Crofts, 1949.

FLEW, ANTHONY, ed. *Essays in Conceptual Analysis.* London: Macmillan & Co., 1956.

GRICE, H. P. "Meaning." *Philosophical Review* 66 (1957): 377–88.

HEMPEL, C. G. "Problems and Changes in the Empiricist Criterion of Meaning." *Revue Internationale de Philosophie* 4, no. 11 (1950): 41–64.

KNEALE, W. C. "Verifiability." *Proceedings of the Aristotelian Society* 19 (1945): 151–64.

LUCE, A. A., and JESSOP, T. E. *The Works of George Berkeley, Bishop of Cloyne.* 9 vols. London: Thomas Nelson & Sons, Ltd., 1948–57.

MALCOLM, NORMAN. "Wittgenstein's Philosophical Investigations." *Philosophical Review* 63 (1954): 530–59.

Moore, G. E. *Some Main Problems of Philosophy.* New York: Macmillan, 1952.
Nell, E. J. "The Hardness of the Logical 'Must.'" *Analysis* 21 (1961): 68–72.
Nelson, E. J. "The Verification Theory of Meaning." *Philosophical Review* 63 (1954): 182–92.
Olscamp, P. J. "Wittgenstein's Refutation of Skepticism." *Philosophy and Phenomenological Research* 26, no. 2 (1965): 239–47.
Passmore, John. *A Hundred Years of Philosophy.* London: Gerald Duckworth & Co., Ltd., 1957.
Popkin, Richard. "The Skeptical Crisis and the Rise of Modern Philosophy." *Review of Metaphysics* 7 (1953–54): 132–51.
———. "Berkeley and Pyrrhonism." *Review of Metaphysics* 5 (1951–52): 233–46.
Price, H. H. *Perception.* London: Methuen & Co., Ltd., 1932.
Schlick, Moritz. "Meaning and Verification." *Philosophical Review* 45 (1936): 339–69.
Strawson, Peter. "Philosophical Investigations." *Mind* 63 (1954): 70–99. *Review*, Volume 63 (1954): pp. 216.
Turbayne, C. M. *The Myth of Metaphor.* New Haven: Yale University Press, 1962.
Warnock, G. J. *Berkeley.* Baltimore: Penguin Books, 1953.
Wellman, Carl. "Wittgenstein's Conception of a Criterion." *Philosophical Review* 71 (1962): 433–47.
Will, F. L. "Will the Future Be Like the Past?" *Mind* 56 (1947): 332–47.
———. "Is There a Problem of Induction?" *Journal of Philosophy* 39 (1942): 505–13.
Yolton, J. W. *John Locke and the Way of Ideas.* London: Oxford University Press, 1956.

Chapter 7

Aquinas, Thomas. *Summa Theologica*, Part II. New York: Benziger Brothers, 1947.
Ayer, A. J. "On the Analysis of Moral Judgments." In his *Philosophical Essays.* New York: St. Martin's Press, 1954.
Brandt, Richard. "The Emotive Theory of Ethics." *Philosophical Review* 59 (1959): 305–18; 535–40.
———. *Ethical Theory.* Englewood Cliffs, N.J.: Prentice-Hall, Inc., 1959.
Broad, C. D. *Five Types of Ethical Theory.* New York: Harcourt Brace Jovanovich, 1934.
———. "Some of the Main Problems of Ethics." *Philosophy* 21 (1946): 99–117.
Calderon, H. N. C., Castaneda, H. N., and Nakhnikian, George, eds. *Morality and the Language of Conduct.* Detroit: Wayne State University Press, 1963.
Copleston, F. C. *Aquinas.* Harmondsworth, England: Penguin Books, 1955.
Ewing, A. C. *Ethics.* London: English University Press, 1953.
———. *The Definition of Good.* New York: Humanities Press, 1947.
Falk, W. D. "Action-Guiding Reasons." *Journal of Philosophy* 60 (1963): 702–18.
Frankena, William. *Ethics.* Englewood Cliffs, N.J.: Prentice-Hall, Inc., 1963.
Hare, R. M. "Universalizability." *Proceedings of the Aristotelian Society* 55 (1954): 295–312.
Hospers, John, and Sellars, Wilfred, eds. *Readings in Ethical Theory.* New York: Appleton-Century-Crofts, Inc., 1952.
Kant, Immanuel. *The Moral Law, or Kant's Groundwork of the Metaphysics of Morals.* Translated by H. J. Paton. London: Hutchinson's University Library, 1948.
Kluckhorn, Clyde. "Ethical Relativity." *Journal of Philosophy* 52 (1955): 663–77.
Moore, G. E. *Principia Ethica.* Cambridge: The University Press, 1903.

NEWELL-SMITH, P. H. *Ethics.* Baltimore: Penguin Books, 1954.

OLSCAMP, P. J. "The Many Meanings and Uses of 'Good.'" *Dialogue* 3, no. 1 (1964): 72–80.

PRICHARD, H. A. *Moral Obligation.* Oxford: Clarendon Press, 1949.

ROSS, W. D. *The Right and the Good.* Oxford: Clarendon Press, 1930.

SELBY-BIGGE, L. A., ed. *The British Moralist.* Oxford: Clarendon Press, 1897.

SINGER, M. G. *Generalization in Ethics.* New York: Alfred A. Knopf, Inc., 1961.

STEVENSON, C. L. *Ethics and Languages.* New Haven: Yale University Press, 1944.

———. *Facts and Values.* New Haven: Yale University Press, 1963.

SUMNER, W. G. *Folkways.* Boston: Ginn and Co., 1906.

TAYLOR, P. W. "Four Types of Ethical Relativism." *Philosophical Review* 63 (1954): 500–516.

WESTERMARK, E. A. *Ethical Relativity.* New York: Harcourt Brace Jovanovich, 1932.

VON WRIGHT, GEORGE. *Norm and Action.* London: Routledge & Keegan Paul, 1963.

Chapter 8

AQUINAS, THOMAS. *Summa Theologica.* New York: Benziger Brothers, 1947. Part II.

AUSTIN, JOHN. *The Province of Jurisprudence Determined.* London: J. Murray, 1832.

BENTHAM, JEREMY. *The Limits of Jurisprudence Defined.* New York: Columbia University Press, 1945.

BERLIN, SIR ISAIAH. *Karl Marx.* London: Oxford University Press, 1939.

COHEN, M. R. *Law and the Social Order.* New York: Harcourt Brace Jovanovich, 1933.

FINDLAY, J. N. *Hegel.* London: Allen & Unwin, 1958.

FRANK, JEROME. *Law and the Modern Mind.* New York: Brentano's, 1930.

HART, H. L. A. *The Concept of Law.* Oxford: Clarendon Press, 1961.

HOBBES, THOMAS. *Leviathan.* Edited by Michael Oakeshott. Oxford: B. H. Blackwell, Ltd., 1946.

HOOK, SIDNEY. *From Hegel to Marx.* London: Victor Gollancz, Ltd., 1936.

LAIRD, JOHN. *Hobbes.* London: Ernest Benn, Ltd., 1954.

LOCKE, JOHN. *Essays on the Law of Nature.* Edited by Wolfgang von Leyden. Oxford: Clarendon Press, 1954.

MacINTYRE, A. C. *Marxism, An Interpretation.* London: Student Christian Movement Press, 1953.

MARX, KARL. *Economic and Philosophical Manuscripts.* Translated by M. Milligan. London: Universal Distributors, 1959.

MARX, KARL. *Capital.* Chicago: C. H. Kerr & Co., 1912.

MARX, KARL, and ENGELS, FRIEDRICH. *The Communist Manifesto.* New York: Monthly Review Press, 1964.

MILL, J. S. *Nature, in Nature and Utility of Religion.* Edited by George Nakhnikian. New York: Library of Liberal Arts, 1958.

ROSS, ALFRED. *On Law and Justice.* Berkeley: University of California Press, 1958.

STEPHEN, SIR LESLIE. *Hobbes.* Ann Arbor: University of Michigan Press, 1961.

SUMNER, W. G. *Folkways.* Boston: Ginn and Co., 1906.

WARRENDER, HOWARD. *The Political Philosophy of Thomas Hobbes.* Oxford: Clarendon Press, 1957.

Chapter 9

AQUINAS, THOMAS. *Summa Theologica* (Part a, Question 2, Article 4). New York: Benziger Brothers, 1947.

ARMSTRONG, D. C. *Berkeley's Theory of Vision*. Parksville: Melbourne University Press, 1960.

COLLINGWOOD, R. G. *An Essay on Philosophical Method*. Oxford: Clarendon Press, 1933.

DEANE, S. N., ed. and trans. *St. Anselm: Basic Writings*. La Salle, Ill.: Open Court Publishing Co., 1962.

DESCARTES, RENÉ. *Meditations*, III and V. Translated by John Vistch. La Salle, Ill.: Open Court Publishing Co., 1945.

FLEW, ANTHONY, and MACINTYRE, ALASDAIR, eds. *New Essays in Philosophical Theology*. New York: Macmillan, 1955.

HARTSHORNE, CHARLES. *The Logic of Perfection*. La Salle, Ill.: Open Court Publishing Co., 1962.

HICK, JOHN. *Classical and Contemporary Readings in the Philosophy of Religion*. Englewood Cliffs, N.J.: Prentice-Hall, Inc., 1963.

HICK, JOHN, and MCGILL, A. C., eds. *The Many-Faced Argument*. New York: Macmillan, 1966.

HUME, DAVID. *Dialogues Concerning Natural Religion*. Edited by N. K. Smith. New York: Social Sciences Publishers, 1962.

KANT, IMMANUEL. *Critique of Pure Reason*, Book II, Chapter 3. Translated by N. K. Smith. New York: St. Martin's Press, 1933.

KNEALE, WILLIAM. "Is Existence a Predicate?" *Proceedings of the Aristotelian Society*, supplementary vol. 15 (1936): 154–88.

LEIBNIZ, GOTTFRIED. *New Essays Concerning Human Understanding*, Book IV, Chapter 10. Translated by Alfred Gideon Langley. New York: Macmillan, 1896.

LUCE, A. A., and JESSOP, T. E., eds. *The Works of George Berkeley, Bishop of Cloyne*. 9 vols. London: Thomas Nelson & Sons, Ltd., 1948–57.

MALCOLM, NORMAN. "Anselm's Ontological Arguments." *Philosophical Review* 69 (1969): 41–62.

MOORE, G. E. "Is Existence a Predicate?" *Proceedings of the Aristotelian Society*, supplementary vol. 15 (1936): 175–88.

MYERSCHOUGH, A. "Berkeley and the Proofs for the Existence of God." *Philosophy and the History of Philosophy*, Volume 1. Edited by J. K. Ryan. Washington, D.C.: Catholic University of America Press, 1961.

OLSCAMP, P. J. "Some Suggestions About the Moral Philosophy of George Berkeley." *Journal of the History of Philosophy* 6 (1968): 147–56.

————. "The Philosophical Importance of C. M. Turbayne's 'The Myth of Metaphor'." *International Philosophical Quarterly* 6 (1966): 110–31.

PALEY, WILLIAM. *Natural Theology: Or, Evidences of the Existence and Attributes of the Deity. Collected from the Appearances of Nature*. Indianapolis: Bobbs-Merrill, Inc., 1964.

PIKE, NELSON, ed. *God and Evil*. Englewood Cliffs, N.J.: Prentice-Hall, Inc., 1964.

SILLEM, E. A. *George Berkeley and the Proofs for the Existence of God*. London: Longmans, Green & Co., 1957.

Chapter 10

ABRAMS, MEYER H. *The Mirror and the Lamp: Romantic Theory and the Critical Tradition*. New York: Oxford University Press, 1953.

ARNETT, WILLARD. *Santayana and the Sense of Beauty*. Bloomington: Indiana University Press, 1955.

BEARDSLEY, M. C. *Aesthetics from Ancient Greece to the Present*. New York: Macmillan, 1965.

————. *Aesthetics: Problems in the Philosophy of Criticism*. New York: Harcourt Brace Jovanovich, 1958.

————. "The Metaphorical Twist." *Philosophy and Phenomenological Research* 22 (1962): 293–307.

————. "Metaphor." *Encyclopedia of Philosophy* 5 (1967): 284–89.

BLACK, MAX. *Models and Metaphors.* Ithaca, N.Y.: Cornell University Press, 1962.

BOSANQUET, BERNARD. *A History of Aesthetic.* New York: Macmillan, 1957.

BOUWSMA, O. K. "The Expression Theory of Art." In *Philosophical Analysis,* edited by Max Black. Englewood Cliffs, N.J.: Prentice-Hall, Inc., 1950.

BRETT, RAYMOND. *The Third Earl of Shaftesbury.* London: Hutchinson's University Library, 1951.

BUTCHER, SAMUEL. *Aristotle's Theory of Poetry and Fine Art.* London: Macmillan & Co., 1923.

CARRITT, E. F. *What Is Beauty?* Oxford: Clarendon Press, 1932.

CASSIRER, ERNST. *The Philosophy of the Enlightenment.* Princeton: Princeton University Press, 1951.

———. *The Platonic Renaissance in England.* Austin: University of Texas Press, 1953.

COLLINGWOOD, R. G. *The Principles of Art.* Oxford: Clarendon Press, 1938.

DONEGAN, ALAN. "The Croce–Collingwood Theory of Art." *Philosophy* 33, no. 125 (1958): 162–67.

DUCASSE, C. J. *The Philosophy of Art.* New York: L. MacVeagh, The Dial Press, 1929.

FOWLER, THOMAS. *Shaftesbury and Hutcheson.* New York: G. P. Putnam's Sons, 1883.

HARTSHORNE, CHARLES. *The Philosophy and Psychology of Sensation.* Chicago: University of Chicago Press, 1934.

HENLE, PAUL. *Language, Thought, and Culture.* Ann Arbor: University of Michigan Press, 1958. (Chapter VII.)

HOSPERS, JOHN. "The Concept of Artistic Expression." *Proceedings of the Aristotelian Society* 55 (1954–55): 313–44.

———. "The Croce–Collingwood Theory of Art." *Philosophy* 31, no. 119 (1956): 291–308.

———. *Meaning and Truth in the Arts.* Chapel Hill: University of North Carolina Press, 1946.

KENNICK, W. A. *Art and Philosophy: Readings in Aesthetics.* New York: St. Martin's Press, 1964.

OLSCAMP, P. J. "Some Remarks About the Nature of Aesthetic Perception and Appreciation." *Journal of Aesthetics and Art Criticism* 24, no. 2 (1965): 251–58.

———. "How Some Metaphors May be True or False." *Journal of Aesthetics and Art Criticism* 29, no. 1 (1970): 77–86.

OSBORNE, HAROLD. *Aesthetics and Criticism.* New York: Philosophical Library, 1955. (Chapter 7.)

RAPHAEL, DAVID. *The Moral Sense.* London: Oxford University Press, 1947.

SANTAYANA, GEORGE. *The Sense of Beauty.* New York: Scribner's, 1896.

SHAFTESBURY, THIRD EARL OF (ANTHONY ASHLEY COOPER). *Characteristics of Men, Manners, Opinions, Times.* Volume 2. Edited by J. M. Robertson. London: G. Richards, 1900.

STOLNITZ, M. J. "On the Significance of Lord Shaftesbury in Modern Aesthetic Theory." *Philosophical Quarterly* 11, no. 43 (1961): 97–113.

———. " 'Beauty': Some Stages in the History of an Idea." *Journal of the History of Ideas* 2, no. 2 (1961): 185–204.

TURBAYNE, C. M. *The Myth of Metaphor.* New Haven: Yale University Press, 1962.

WHEELWRIGHT, PHILLIP. *Metaphor and Reality.* Bloomington: Indiana University Press, 1962.

———. *The Burning Fountain.* Bloomington: Indiana University Press, 1954.

Chapter 11

ARISTOTLE. *Physics.* 2nd ed. Translated by Richard Hope. Lincoln: University of Nebraska Press, 1961.

ARMSTRONG, D. M. "Is Introspective Knowledge Incorrigible?" *Philosophical Review* 72 (1963): 417–32.

BECK, L. J. *The Method of Descartes.* Oxford: Clarendon Press, 1952.

BLAKE, R. M.; DUCASSE, C. J.; and MADDEN, E. H., eds. *Theories of Scientific Method: The Renaissance Through the Nineteenth Century.* Seattle: University of Washington Press, 1960.

BRAITHWAITE, R. B. "Teleological Explanations." *Proceedings of the Aristotelian Society* 47 (1947): 1–20.

——. *Scientific Explanation.* Cambridge: Cambridge University Press, 1953.

BURTT, E. A. *The Metaphysical Foundations of Modern Physical Science.* New York: Doubleday & Co., 1954.

COHEN, M. R., and NAGEL, ERNEST. *An Introduction of Logic and Scientific Method.* New York: Harcourt Brace Jovanovich, 1934.

DANTO, ARTHUR, and MORGENBESSER, SIDNEY, eds. *Philosophy of Science.* New York: Meridian Books, 1950.

DESCARTES, RENÉ. *Discourse on Method, Optics, Geometry and Meteorology.* Edited and translated with Introduction by P. J. Olscamp. New York: Bobbs-Merrill Co., The Library of Liberal Arts, 1965.

——. *Rules for the Direction of the Mind, in Philosophical Works of Descartes.* Translated by E. S. Haldane and G. R. T. Ross. Volume 1. Cambridge: Cambridge University Press, 1931.

FEIGL, HERBERT, and BRODBECK, MAY, eds. *Readings in the Philosophy of Science.* New York: Appleton-Century-Crofts, Inc., 1953.

HANSON, NORWOOD. *Patterns of Discovery.* Cambridge: Cambridge University Press, 1958.

HESSE, MARY. *Models and Analogies in Science.* New York: Sheed & Ward, 1963.

NEEDHAM, JOSEPH. *Order and Life.* London: Cambridge University Press, 1936.

POPPER, SIR KARL. *The Logic of Scientific Discovery.* New York: Basic Books, 1959.

RANDALL, J. H. *Aristotle.* New York: Columbia University Press, 1960.

ROTH, LEON. *Descartes' Discourse on Method.* Oxford: Clarendon Press, 1937.

RUSSELL, E. S. *The Directiveness of Organic Activities.* Cambridge: Cambridge University Press, 1945.

SOLMSEN, FRIEDRICK. *Aristotle's System of the Physical World.* Ithaca, N.Y.: Cornell University Press, 1960.

THOMPSON, D. W. "Aristotle the Naturalist." *The Legacy of Greece,* edited by R. W. Livingstone. Oxford: Clarendon Press, 1922.

TOULMIN, STEPHEN. *Philosophy of Science.* London: Hutchison & Co., Ltd., 1953.

WHITEHEAD, A. N. *Science and the Modern World.* New York: Macmillan, 1926.

WOODGER, J. H. *Biological Principles.* London: Routledge and Kegan Paul, 1929.

Chapter 12

ARRON, R. I. *The Theory of Universals.* Oxford: Clarendon Press, 1952.

ALLEN, D. J. *The Philosophy of Aristotle.* London: Oxford University Press, 1952.

BERKELEY, GEORGE. *Aleiphron.* London: Thomas Nelson & Sons Co., Ltd., 1948. VII, IV.

BRACKEN, H. M. "Berkeley's Realisms." *Philosophical Quarterly* 8 (1958): 41–53.

BUCHLER, JUSTUS. *Charles Peirce's Empiricism.* New York: Harcourt Brace Jovanovich, 1939.

CARRE, M. H. *Realists & Nominalists.* London: Oxford University Press, 1946.

CHERNIS, HAROLD. *Aristotle's Criticism of Plato and the Academy.* Baltimore: The Johns Hopkins Press, 1944.

DARWIN, CHARLES. *The Origin of Species.* London: C. A. Watts & Co., Ltd., 1959.

DEWEY, JOHN. *Democracy and Education.* New York: Macmillan, 1916.

——. *Essays in Experimental Logic.* Chicago: University of Chicago Press, 1916.

——. *Reconstruction in Philosophy.* New York: H. Holt & Co., 1920.

——. *Human Nature and Conduct.* New York: H. Holt & Co., 1922.

——. *The Quest for Certainty.* New York: Minton, Balch & Co., 1929.

——. "The Development of American Pragmatism." In *Philosophy and Civilization.* New York: Minton, Balch & Co., 1931.

——. *Logic: The Theory of Inquiry.* New York: H. Holt & Co., 1938.

——. *Theory of Valuation.* Chicago: University of Chicago Press, 1939.

EWING, A. C. *Idealism.* London: Methuen & Co., Ltd., 1934.

JAMES, WILLIAM. *The Will to Believe.* London: Longmans, Green & Co., 1897.

——. *Pragmatism: A New Name for Some Old Ways of Thinking.* London: Longmans, Green & Co., 1907.

——. *The Meaning of Truth.* London: Longmans, Green & Co., 1909.

——. *Collected Essays and Reviews.* London: Longmans, Green & Co., 1920.

LANGE, F. A. *The History of Materialism.* Translated by E. C. Thomas. New York: Humanities Press, 1925.

MOORE, G. E. "The Refutation of Idealism." In *Philosophical Studies.* Paterson, N.J.: Littlefield, Adams & Co., 1959.

NAGEL, ERNST. "Are Naturalists Materialists?" *Logic Without Metaphysics.* New York: The Free Press of Glencoe, Inc., 1957.

OCKHAM, WILLIAM. *Philosophical Writings,* edited by P. F. Boehner. Edinburgh: Nelson, 1957.

PERRY, R. B. *The Thought and Character of William James,* Volume II. Boston: Little, Brown & Co., 1935.

PLATO. *Phaedo.* Translated by R. Hackforth. Cambridge: Cambridge University Press, 1952.

——. *Republic,* edited and translated by Francis Cornford. Oxford: Clarendon Press, 1941.

PRICE, H. H. *Thinking and Experience.* Cambridge, Mass.: Harvard University Press, 1953.

SKINNER, B. F. *Science and Human Behavior.* New York: The Free Press of Glencoe, Inc., 1953.

SMART, J. J. C. *Philosophy and Scientific Realism.* New York: Humanities Press, 1963.

STACE, W. T. "The Refutation of Realism." *Mind* 43, no. 170 (1934): 145–55.

TAYLOR, ALFRED EDWARD. *Plato, The Man and His Work.* London: Methuen & Co., Ltd., 1908.

——. *Aristotle.* London & Edinburgh: T. C. & E. C. Jack, Ltd., 1919.

VIGNAUX, PAUL. *Le Nominalisme au XIVe Siècle.* Montreal: Institute d'études médievales, 1948.

Index

Ruling, as an art, 294
Ruskin, 69
Russell, Bertrand, 58–59, 205, 207–9, 475, 486
Ryle, Gilbert, 49–50, 69, 96 ff.

Santayana, George, 392–95
Schlick, Moritz, 121, 124–25, 127–28, 133, 216
Scientific method, 420
Scope, 85
Scott, Dred, 282–84
Searles, John, 69
Secondary qualities, 182
and ideas of, 182
Self-interest, 312
Sentence-constants, 13
Shaftesbury, Third Earl of, 272, 364–65, 366 ff.
Shorter truth-table technique, 16–17
Signs, 186–87
Simple sentences, kinds of, 7
Simplicity, 85
Singular sentences, 25–29
Skepticism
and other minds, 200–203
and science, 147, 163–64
and Wittgenstein, 205 ff.
Skinner, B. F., 48
Socialism
and communism, 301
utopian, 301
Socrates, 321
Soft determinism, 121
Solipsism, 476
Solubility as a dispositional property, 107
Soundness, 4–6
Sovereignty, and Hobbes, 313–14, 321–24
Speculative metaphysics, 151–52, 155
Speech acts, 52
Spinoza, Baruch de, 308
State of nature, 311–12
Statements, 22
Statute law, 277
Stevenson, C. L., 49, 63, 249 ff.
Stipulative definition, 44
Strawson, Peter, 60–63
Substance, in Locke, 182–83, 187–88
Substitution instance, 17
Supreme Court of the United States, 288–91

Syllogism, 17–18
Syncategorematic terms, 46–47
Synthesis
in Cartesian science, 421 ff.
in Kant, 149, 158
in Marx, 301–2
thesis and antithesis, 301
of understanding, 167
Synthetic
a posteriori, 151
a priori, 35, 151, 154
Synthetic propositions, 143

Taney, Roger B., 283
Tautologies, 34
Taylor, Richard, 114 ff.
Teleological argument, 79, 329–30
Teleological explanation, 444 ff.
Testability, 85
Theories, definition of, 82–85
Thrasymachus, 291–95
Transcendental, and transcendent, 156
Truth, 54
theories of, 55 ff.
Truth-functionality, 7
Truth-tables, 8–9
Truth-values, 7

Uniformity of nature, 204 ff.
United States vs. Holmes, 287
"Universal mathematics," 424
Universals, 467–69
Utilitarianism, 285

Validity, 4, 5, 6, 17, 19, 30–31
Variables, 13
Verifiability, 55
principle of, 215–16, 218 ff.
Vitalism, 104

Warren Court, 291
Wealth, distribution of, 306
Wheelwright, Phillip, 398–99, 405, 407–8
Will, Frederick L., 205, 209–13
Wittgenstein, Ludwig, 51, 53, 63, 193 ff., 216, 223

"Yellow-dog" contracts, 290–91

Zeno of Elea, 95 ff.